Koren Talmud Bavli

THE NOÉ EDITION

SHEKALIM

Steinsaltz Center

KOREN

תלמוד בבלי

KOREN TALMUD BAVLI

THE NOÉ EDITION

שקלים

SHEKALIM

Daf 13a through Daf 22b

COMMENTARY BY

Rabbi Adin Even-Israel Steinsaltz

EDITOR-IN-CHIEF

Rabbi Dr Tzvi Hersh Weinreb

SENIOR CONTENT EDITOR

Rabbi Dr Shalom Z Berger

EXECUTIVE EDITOR

Rabbi Joshua Schreier

STEINSALTZ CENTER

KOREN PUBLISHERS JERUSALEM

Supported by the Matanel Foundation

Koren Talmud Bavli, The Noe Edition
Vol. 5b: Tractate Shekalim, Daf 13a through Daf 22b
Paperback, ISBN, 978-965-7765-44-9

First Hebrew/English paperback edition, 2020

Koren Publishers Jerusalem Ltd.
PO Box 4044, Jerusalem 91040, ISRAEL
PO Box 8531, New Milford, CT 06776, USA
www.korenpub.com

Steinsaltz Center

Steinsaltz Center is the parent organization of institutions established by Rabbi Adin Even-Israel Steinsaltz

PO Box 45187, Jerusalem 91450 ISRAEL
Telephone: +972 2 646 0900, Fax +972 2 624 9454
www.steinsaltz-center.org

הִנֵּה יָמִים בָּאִים, נְאֻם אֲדֹנָי יֱהוִֹה, וְהִשְׁלַחְתִּי רָעָב בָּאָרֶץ,
לֹא־רָעָב לַלֶּחֶם וְלֹא־צָמָא לַמַּיִם, כִּי אִם־לִשְׁמֹעַ אֵת דִּבְרֵי יהוה.

Behold, days are coming – says the Lord God – I will send a hunger to the land, not a hunger for bread nor a thirst for water, but to hear the words of the Lord. (AMOS 8:11)

The Noé edition of the Koren Talmud Bavli
with the commentary of Rabbi Adin Even-Israel Steinsaltz
is dedicated to all those who open its covers
to quench their thirst for Jewish Knowledge,
in our generation of Torah renaissance.

This beautiful edition is for the young, the aged,
the novice and the savant alike,
as it unites the depth of Torah knowledge
with the best of academic scholarship.

Within its exquisite and vibrant pages,
words become worlds.

It will claim its place in the library of classics,
in the bookcases of the Beit Midrash,
the classrooms of our schools,
and in the offices of professionals and business people
who carve out precious time to grapple with its timeless wisdom.

For the Student and the Scholar

DEDICATED BY LEO AND SUE NOÉ

Steinsaltz Center

Executive Director, Steinsaltz Center

Rabbi Meni Even-Israel

Managing Editor

Rabbi Jason Rappoport

Senior Content Editor

Rabbi Dr. Shalom Z. Berger

Editors

Rabbi Joshua Amaru, *Coordinating Editor*
Rabbi David Jay Derovan
Betzalel Philip Edwards
Rabbi Dov Karoll
Rabbi Adin Krohn
Sally Mayer
Rabbi Avishai Magence, *Content Curator*
Rabbi Jonathan Mishkin
Jay Shapiro
Shira Shmidman
Rabbi Michael Siev
Avi Steinhart
Rabbi David Strauss
Amiel Vick
Rabbi Abe Y. Weschler

Copy Editors

Aliza Israel, *Coordinator*
Bracha Hermon
Ita Olesker
Debbie Ismailoff
Shira Finson
Ilana Sobel
Deena Nataf

Language Consultants

Dr. Stephanie E. Binder, *Greek & Latin*
Rabbi Yaakov Hoffman, *Arabic*
Dr. Shai Secunda, *Persian*
Shira Shmidman, *Aramaic*

KOREN

Design & Typesetting

Raphaël Freeman, *Design & Typography*
Dena Landowne Bailey, *Typesetting*
Tani Bayer, *Jacket Design*

Images

Eliahu Misgav, *Illustration*
Yehudit Cohen, *Image Acquisition*

Digital Edition

Raphaël Freeman, *Team Leader*
Eliyahu Skoczylas, *Senior Architect*
Tani Bayer, *User Interface Design*
Dena Landowne Bailey, *Concept*
Rabbi Hanan Benayahu, *Concept*
Laura Messinger, *Commercial Liaison*

Introduction by the Publisher

The Talmud has sustained and inspired Jews for thousands of years. Throughout Jewish history, an elite cadre of scholars has absorbed its learning and passed it on to succeeding generations. The Talmud has been the fundamental text of our people.

Beginning in the 1960s, Rabbi Adin Even-Israel Steinsaltz שליט״א created a revolution in the history of Talmud study. His translation of the Talmud, first into modern Hebrew and then into other languages, as well the practical learning aids he added to the text, have enabled millions of people around the world to access and master the complexity and context of the world of Talmud.

It is thus a privilege to present the *Koren Talmud Bavli*, an English translation of the talmudic text with the brilliant elucidation of Rabbi Steinsaltz. The depth and breadth of his knowledge are unique in our time. His rootedness in the tradition and his reach into the world beyond it are inspirational.

Working with Rabbi Steinsaltz on this remarkable project has been not only an honor, but a great pleasure. Never shy to express an opinion, with wisdom and humor, Rabbi Steinsaltz sparkles in conversation, demonstrating his knowledge (both sacred and worldly), sharing his wide-ranging interests, and, above all, radiating his passion. I am grateful for the unique opportunity to work closely with him, and I wish him many more years of writing and teaching.

Our intentions in publishing this new edition of the Talmud are threefold. First, we seek to fully clarify the talmudic page to the reader – textually, intellectually, and graphically. Second, we seek to utilize today's most sophisticated technologies, both in print and electronic formats, to provide the reader with a comprehensive set of study tools. And third, we seek to help readers advance in their process of Talmud study.

To achieve these goals, the *Koren Talmud Bavli* is unique in a number of ways:

- The classic *tzurat hadaf* of Vilna, used by scholars since the 1800s, has been reset for great clarity, and opens from the Hebrew "front" of the book. Full *nikkud* has been added to both the talmudic text and Rashi's commentary, allowing for a more fluent reading with the correct pronunciation; the commentaries of *Tosafot* have been punctuated. Upon the advice of many English-speaking teachers of Talmud, we have separated these core pages from the translation, thereby enabling the advanced student to approach the text without the distraction of the translation. This also reduces the number of volumes in the set. At the bottom of each *daf*, there is a reference to the corresponding English pages. In addition, the Vilna edition was read against other manuscripts and older print editions, so that texts which had been removed by non-Jewish censors have been restored to their rightful place.

- The English translation, which starts on the English "front" of the book, reproduces the *menukad* Talmud text alongside the English translation (in bold) and commentary and explanation (in a lighter font). The Hebrew and Aramaic text is presented in logical paragraphs. This allows for a fluent reading of the text for the non-Hebrew or non-Aramaic reader. It also allows for the Hebrew reader to refer easily to the text alongside. Where the original text features dialogue or poetry, the English text is laid out in a manner appropriate to the genre. Each page refers to the relevant *daf*.

- Critical contextual tools surround the text and translation: personality notes, providing short biographies of the Sages; language notes, explaining foreign terms borrowed from Greek, Latin, Persian, or Arabic; and background notes, giving information essential to the understanding of the text, including history, geography, botany, archaeology, zoology, astronomy, and aspects of daily life in the talmudic era.
- Halakhic summaries provide references to the authoritative legal decisions made over the centuries by the rabbis. They explain the reasons behind each halakhic decision as well as the ruling's close connection to the Talmud and its various interpreters.
- Photographs, drawings, and other illustrations have been added throughout the text – in full color in the Standard and Electronic editions, and in black and white in the Daf Yomi edition – to visually elucidate the text.

This is not an exhaustive list of features of this edition, it merely presents an overview for the English-speaking reader who may not be familiar with the "total approach" to Talmud pioneered by Rabbi Steinsaltz.

Several professionals have helped bring this vast collaborative project to fruition. My many colleagues are noted on the Acknowledgments page, and the leadership of this project has been exceptional.

RABBI MENACHEM EVEN-ISRAEL, DIRECTOR OF THE STEINSALTZ CENTER, was the driving force behind this enterprise. With enthusiasm and energy, he formed the happy alliance with Koren and established close relationships among all involved in the work.

RABBI DR. TZVI HERSH WEINREB שליט״א, EDITOR-IN-CHIEF, brought to this project his profound knowledge of Torah, intellectual literacy of Talmud, and erudition of Western literature. It is to him that the text owes its very high standard, both in form and content, and the logical manner in which the beauty of the Talmud is presented.

RABBI JOSHUA SCHREIER, EXECUTIVE EDITOR, assembled an outstanding group of scholars, translators, editors, and proofreaders, whose standards and discipline enabled this project to proceed in a timely and highly professional manner.

RABBI MEIR HANEGBI, EDITOR OF THE HEBREW EDITION OF THE STEINSALTZ TALMUD, lent his invaluable assistance throughout the work process, supervising the reproduction of the Vilna pages.

RAPHAËL FREEMAN, EXECUTIVE EDITOR OF KOREN, created this Talmud's unique typographic design which, true to the Koren approach, is both elegant and user friendly.

It has been an enriching experience for all of us at Koren Publishers Jerusalem to work with the Steinsaltz Center to develop and produce the *Koren Talmud Bavli*. We pray that this publication will be a source of great learning and, ultimately, greater *avodat Hashem* for all Jews.

Matthew Miller, Publisher
Koren Publishers Jerusalem
Jerusalem 5772

Contents

For the vocalized Vilna Shas layout, please open as a Hebrew book.

Introduction to **Perek V**

The main topic of this chapter is the various officials who served in the Temple. Apart from the regular sacrifice of communal offerings, thousands of people would visit the Temple to pray and bring their private offerings. The performance of the Temple service thus required a large number of priests, as well as thorough planning and organization.

The Temple officials also dealt with issues such as improvements to the city, access roads to the capital, and projects for the public good. It was therefore necessary to appoint people who could deal with complex economic and organizational matters. In many cases, it is likely that there was not only an officer, but an entire department appointed to perform and supervise the tasks at hand.

Certain functions required many participants, for example, the preparation of the shewbread or the incense. Likewise, the sewing and mending of the priestly garments were performed by tailors employed by the Temple, and a special doctor was appointed to care for the priests' medical needs. This chapter provides a list of these officials, as well as a partial description of their work.

In addition to these officials, there were several functionaries of various levels of importance in charge of Temple finances. This included administering a system by which, in exchange for payment, the Temple would supply private individuals with the animals they require for their offerings, as not all people were able or willing to bring animals from their own flock. The smooth running of these operations necessitated a permanent bookkeeping system for receiving the money and supplying the variety of requisite services.

Finally, the chapter discusses the Temple chamber where donations for charity money were collected.

הלכה א מתני׳ אֵלּוּ הֵן הַמְּמוּנִּים שֶׁהָיוּ בַּמִּקְדָּשׁ: יוֹחָנָן בֶּן פִּנְחָס עַל הַחוֹתָמוֹת, אֲחִיָּה עַל הַנְּסָכִים, מַתְיָה בֶּן שְׁמוּאֵל עַל הַפְּיָיסוֹת,

HALAKHA 1 · MISHNA These are the officials[HN] **who served** in specific positions **in the Temple: Yoḥanan ben Pineḥas** was responsible **for the seals.**[B] One who paid for a specific type of sacrificial item received a seal, which he presented to the Temple official in exchange for that item. **Aḥiyya** was responsible **for the libations,** i.e., the wine, oil, and flour prepared with the level of ritual purity necessary for the libation offerings and the meal-offerings, which accompanied many animal offerings. Aḥiyya supplied the libations to those who presented the appropriate seal. **Matya ben Shmuel** was responsible **for the lotteries,** which were used to select priests for the various Temple services each day.

פְּתַחְיָה עַל הַקִּינִּין,

Petaḥya was responsible **for the pairs**[N] of birds,[BN] i.e., the turtledoves or pigeons, brought by a *zav*, a *zava*, a woman after childbirth, and a leper. They placed the appropriate sum of money into the horn designated for this purpose, and each day Petaḥya oversaw the purchase of birds from that money and their sacrifice in the proper manner.

פְּתַחְיָה זֶהוּ מָרְדְּכַי וְלָמָּה נִקְרָא שְׁמוֹ פְּתַחְיָה – שֶׁהָיָה פּוֹתֵחַ דְּבָרִים וְדוֹרְשָׁן, וְיוֹדֵעַ בְּשִׁבְעִים לָשׁוֹן.

Incidentally, the Gemara mentions: **Petaḥya is Mordecai** from the book of Esther. **And why was he named called Petaḥya,** which resembles the word for opening [*petaḥ*]? The reason is **that he would open,** i.e., elucidate, difficult **topics and interpret them**[N] to the people, **and** because **he knew all seventy languages**[N] known at the time.[N]

HALAKHA

These are the officials – אֵלּוּ הֵן הַמְּמוּנִּים: There was a permanent need for special Temple officials responsible for the following fifteen areas: (1) The timetable of Temple duties, (2) locking the gates, (3) guarding, (4) Levite singers, (5) the cymbal and other musical instruments, (6) lotteries, (7) pairs of birds, (8) seals, (9) libations, (10) healing the priests suffering from intestinal disease, (11) the water supply, (12) preparation of the shewbread, (13) preparation of the incense, (14) preparation of the Temple curtains, (15) and the preparation of the priestly garments. This is the opinion of the Rambam. The Ra'avad questions his omission of an official responsible for the garment shreds used for wicks (Rambam *Sefer Avoda, Hilkhot Kelei HaMikdash* 7:1, and the comment of the *Kesef Mishne*).

BACKGROUND

The seals – הַחוֹתָמוֹת: Although each individual was permitted to supply his own animal and flour for his offering, in practice this was difficult for those who visited the Temple from far away. They would purchase the necessary items either in the markets of Jerusalem or through the appropriate Temple official. Buying the offering in the Temple ensured that their offering would not be defective in any way. When the petitioner paid the official for the sacrificial item, he received a receipt in the form of a seal. He presented this seal to another official, who supplied him with the appropriate item. At the end of each day, both the receipts and the amount of money actually collected were tallied and the amounts compared. In the event of a deficit, the official who received the payments was required to make up the difference from his own pocket. Each day's seals were stored in a place called the chamber of seals.

The pairs of birds – הַקִּינִּין: The two types of birds that can be brought as offerings are pigeons [*benei yona*] and turtledoves [*torim*] (Leviticus 1:14). The *tor* is identified as *Streptopelia turtur*, while the *yona* is identified as *Columba livia domestica*.

NOTES

These are the officials – אֵלּוּ הֵן הַמְּמוּנִּים: According to one opinion, all the officials who served in the various positions during the entire Temple period were called by the name of the first person who served in that role. Some authorities mention that this was also the practice of the Egyptian kings, who were all called Pharaoh after the first one, and the dynasties of Abimelech and Melchizedek (Vilna Gaon; *Tiferet Yisrael*). This interpretation can be accepted only according to the second opinion mentioned in the Gemara, that the *tanna* of the mishna enumerates those who lived in his generation, and thus bore the names associated with their offices. According to the other opinion, that the names of particularly righteous officials are listed, then the officials must have had individual names.

Petaḥya was responsible for the pairs – פְּתַחְיָה עַל הַקִּינִּין: Because Petaḥya is identified with Mordecai, whose father was from the tribe of Benjamin and mother was from Judah (*Megilla* 12b). Some later commentaries conclude that these officials did not have to be from the tribe of Levi (Rav Ya'akov Emden on *Menaḥot* 65a).

It was necessary to appoint a great scholar, such as Mordecai, over the distribution of pairs of birds because the *halakhot* for when the *zav*, *zava*, and a woman after childbirth bring offerings are numerous and complex. Another explanation is that a great scholar was required for this position because it was sometimes unclear from the statements of those bringing these offerings if the offerings were for their ritual purification or intended as the thanks-offering of a poor person (*Maharsha*).

The pairs of birds – הַקִּינִּין: There are several cases in which one must bring a pair of birds, consisting of either turtledoves or pigeons. One bird is sacrificed as a burnt-offering, while the other is a sin-offering. These offerings must be brought in specific situations, e.g., the sin-offering of a poor person (Leviticus 5:7–10), a poor woman after childbirth (Leviticus 12:8), a poor leper (Leviticus 14:22), and a *zav* (Leviticus 15:14–15) or *zava* (Leviticus 15:29–30) who have undergone ritual purification.

That he would open difficult topics and interpret them – שֶׁהָיָה פּוֹתֵחַ דְּבָרִים וְדוֹרְשָׁן: The later commentaries note that, according to *Tosafot* (*Menaḥot* 64b), the name Mordecai from the book of Esther was given to all those who fulfilled this function in the Temple. Since the original Mordecai was described as "interpreting for the good of his people" (Esther 10:3), all officials named after him were expected to be able to interpret complex issues (*Iyyun Ya'akov* on *Menaḥot* 65a).

And he knew all seventy languages – וְיוֹדֵעַ בְּשִׁבְעִים לָשׁוֹן: The Gemara (*Menaḥot* 65a) asks: What was exceptional about Mordecai? After all, every member of the Sanhedrin had to know all seventy languages. The Gemara explains that Mordecai was exceptional in that he could even mix other languages and interpret, i.e., he knew all those languages well enough to pun on the various meanings of their words (see 13b; see *Menaḥot* 64b).

All seventy languages known at the time – בְּשִׁבְעִים לָשׁוֹן: Although there are many more than seventy languages in the world, the commentators note that these seventy were the basic, primary ones. At the time of the Tower of Babel, God mixed all the languages so that many additional ones developed from the original seventy (*Tiferet Yisrael*).

PERSONALITIES

Neḥunya the well digger – נְחוּנְיָה חוֹפֵר שִׁיחִין: The formal position of Neḥunya the well digger was to take care of the water supply for Jerusalem, especially for those visiting the capital on the pilgrimage Festivals. The Gemara mentions that Neḥunya was an expert in locating water sources and would dig wells along the water channels so that they drew water from underground sources in addition to collecting rainfall. The Gemara further praises him for transferring the ownership of these wells to the public domain.

HALAKHA

Temple crier – כָּרוֹז: This was the official responsible for the Temple timetable. At the appropriate time, he or one of his staff announced: Arise, priests, to your service; and Levites to your platform to sing; and Israelites to your watch; as a group of Israelites represented the entire nation at the sacrifice of the communal offerings. Upon hearing this announcement, each group went to their designated duty (Rambam *Sefer Avoda, Hilkhot Kelei HaMikdash* 7:2).

BACKGROUND

Preparation of the shewbread – מַעֲשֵׂה לֶחֶם הַפָּנִים: Due to its unique shape, special skill was needed for its preparation.

Priests replacing the shewbread

בֶּן אֲחִיָּיה עַל חוֹלֵי מֵעַיִים, נְחוּנְיָה חוֹפֵר שִׁיחִין, גְּבִינֵי כָּרוֹז, בֶּן גֶּבֶר עַל נְעִילַת שְׁעָרִים,

The mishna resumes the list of officials. **Ben Aḥiyya** was responsible **for** the care of the priests who suffered from **intestinal disease. Neḥunya** was the **well digger**[P] for pilgrims on their way to Jerusalem for the Festivals. **Gevini** was the Temple **crier**[HN] who would awaken the priests and the Levites for their Temple duties. **Ben Gever** was responsible **for locking the** Temple **gates** in the evening and for unlocking them in the morning.

בֶּן בֵּבַי מְמוּנֶּה עַל הַפָּקִיעַ, בֶּן אַרְזָא עַל הַצִּלְצָל, הוּגְרַס בֶּן לֵוִי עַל הַשִּׁיר,

Ben Bevai was **appointed over the shreds** of garments,[N] which were formed into wicks for the Temple candelabra. He also supervised the twisting of those wicks into the appropriate thickness for the various nights during the different seasons of the year. **Ben Arza** was responsible **for the cymbal,** which was rung as a signal that the Levites should commence their song. **Hugras ben Levi** was responsible **for the song.** He taught and conducted the singers in the Temple.

בֵּית גַּרְמוּ עַל מַעֲשֵׂה לֶחֶם הַפָּנִים, בֵּית אַבְטִינָס עַל מַעֲשֵׂה הַקְּטוֹרֶת, וְאֶלְעָזָר עַל הַפָּרוֹכֶת, וּפִנְחָס הַמַּלְבִּישׁ.

The house of Garmu was responsible **for the preparation of the shewbread;**[B] **the house of Avtinas** was responsible **for the preparation of the incense; and Elazar** was responsible **for** weaving **the** Temple **curtains; and Pineḥas** was **the valet,** who assisted the priests in fitting their clothes and dressing themselves for their Temple service.

גמ׳ רַבִּי חִזְקִיָּה אָמַר רַבִּי סִימוֹן וְרַבָּנַן, חַד אָמַר: כְּשֵׁירֵי דוֹר וָדוֹר בָּא לִמְנוֹת עֲלֵיהֶן, וְחָרָנָה אָמַר: מִי שֶׁהָיָה בְּאוֹתוֹ דוֹר מָנָה מַה שֶּׁבְּדוֹרוֹ.

GEMARA The mishna lists fifteen names of officials who filled specific positions in the Temple, despite the fact that during the many years of the Temple there must have been far more than fifteen officials who served those functions. **Rabbi Ḥizkiyah said** that **Rabbi Simon and the Rabbis** disagreed as to why the mishna mentions only these fifteen names. **One** of them **said:** The mishna **comes to enumerate those** who were the most **fit** of all the officials who served in each position, **from whatever generation** they were from. **And the other said:** The *tanna* **who was in that generation enumerated those** functionaries **who** served **in his generation.**

מַאן דְּאָמַר כְּשֵׁירֵי כָּל דוֹר וָדוֹר בָּא לִמְנוֹת – עַל כּוּלָּן הוּא אוֹמֵר ״זֵכֶר צַדִּיק לִבְרָכָה״.

Several of these officials are also mentioned in the mishna in Yoma, some for praise (37a), and others for censure (38a). The Gemara notes that this issue is related to the aforementioned dispute. **The one who said** that the mishna **comes to enumerate the** most **fit** of those who served **from whatever generation** claims that when the mishna in *Yoma* **says: "The memory of a righteous person shall be for a blessing"** (Proverbs 10:7) it is **in reference to all of them.** According to this opinion, the *tanna* in *Yoma* maintains that the reason these officials did not teach their specialties to others was because they wanted to prevent their knowledge from being used for idol worship. The only officials censured are those like ben Kamtzar, who refused to divulge their secrets for unworthy reasons, but these people are not mentioned in the mishna.

מַאן דְּאָמַר מִי שֶׁהָיָה בְּאוֹתוֹ דוֹר מָנָה מַה שֶּׁבְּדוֹרוֹ – עַל כּוּלָּן הוּא אוֹמֵר ״וְשֵׁם רְשָׁעִים יִרְקָב״. וְעַל מִי נֶאֱמַר ״זֵכֶר צַדִּיק לִבְרָכָה״ – עַל בֶּן קָטִין וַחֲבֵירָיו.

Conversely, **the one who said** that the *tanna* **who was in that generation enumerated those** officials **who** served **in his generation,** he claims that the mishna in *Yoma* **says: "But the name of the wicked shall rot"** (Proverbs 10:7) **in reference to all of them. And with regard to whom is** the *tanna* in *Yoma* **speaking** when he cites the verse: **"The memory of a righteous person shall be for a blessing"?** He is referring only **to ben Katin,** who improved the basin for the priests in the Temple, **and his colleagues.**

NOTES

Gevini the crier – גְּבִינֵי כָּרוֹז: The *Me'iri*, in his commentary on *Yoma* 28a, explains that Gevini the Temple crier stood on the Temple roof every morning at daybreak to determine when the sky was sufficiently bright and the time of the slaughter of the daily offering had arrived. At the appropriate moment, he would proclaim: *Barkai*; it is light! In the Jerusalem Talmud it is asked how they could rely upon a single witness in this regard, as slaughtering the daily offering at the wrong time violates a prohibition. The Gemara there answers that even a single witness is trusted with regard to a matter whose truth can easily be verified (Jerusalem Talmud, *Yoma* 3:1).

Over the shreds [*pakia*] of garments – עַל הַפָּקִיעַ: The interpretation in the commentary is in accordance with the statement (14a) that a fixed amount of oil, i.e., a half-*log*, was placed in each cup of the candelabrum throughout the year. Consequently, it was necessary to adjust the thickness of the wicks so that the half-*log* of oil would last the entire night during all seasons of the year. Thicker wicks caused the oil to burn more quickly.

The Babylonian Talmud (*Yoma* 23a) interprets this phrase entirely differently. According to the Gemara there, *pakia* means lashes. This official, whom the Gemara calls Biva'i, was in charge of the physical punishment meted out to those who were negligent in their Temple duties.

אָמַר רַבִּי יוֹנָה: כְּתִיב "לָכֵן אֲחַלֶּק לוֹ בָרַבִּים וְאֶת עֲצוּמִים יְחַלֵּק שָׁלָל" – זֶה רַבִּי עֲקִיבָא שֶׁהִתְקִין מִדְרַשׁ הַהֲלָכוֹת וְהַגָּדוֹת.

§ After recording the praises of certain historical figures, the Gemara continues in a similar vein. **Rabbi Yona said** that **it is written: "Therefore will I divide him a portion among the great, and he shall divide the spoil with the mighty;** because he bared his soul until death, and was numbered with the transgressors" (Isaiah 53:12). **This** verse **is referring to Rabbi Akiva,**[PN] **who** conveyed the Oral Law to the people by **arranging the halakhic and homiletic midrash.**

וְיֵשׁ אוֹמְרִים: אֵלּוּ אַנְשֵׁי כְּנֶסֶת הַגְּדוֹלָה תִּיקְּנוּ, אֶלָּא מַה תִּיקֵּן זֶה? כְּלָלוֹת וּפְרָטוֹת.

And some say that **the members of the Great Assembly arranged** these compilations of Torah knowledge. **But** if so, **what did this** Sage, Rabbi Akiva, **arrange?** He arranged the interpretive method of **generalizations and details.**

אָמַר רַבִּי אַבָּהוּ: כְּתִיב "מִשְׁפְּחוֹת סוֹפְרִים יוֹשְׁבֵי יַעְבֵּץ" מַה תַּלְמוּד לוֹמַר "סוֹפְרִים" – אֶלָּא שֶׁעָשׂוּ אֶת הַתּוֹרָה סְפוּרוֹת סְפוּרוֹת:

Rabbi Abbahu said: The lineage of Salma, son of Caleb, son of Hur, is listed in the book of Chronicles. **It is written** there: **"And the families of scribes that dwelt at Jabez:** The Tirathites, the Shimeathites, the Sucathites; these are the Kenites that came of Hammath, the father of the house of Rechab" (I Chronicles 2:55). **What** is the meaning when **the verse states** the word **scribes,** literally, counters? It does not mean that they were scribes; **rather,** it means **that they crafted** the *halakhot* of **the Torah** into **numbered groups.** They categorized and brought together disparate *halakhot* into a mnemonic device to assist learners.

חֲמִשָּׁה לֹא יִתְרוֹמוּ תְּרוּמָה, חֲמִשָּׁה דְּבָרִים חַיָּיבִין בְּחַלָּה, חֲמֵשׁ עֶשְׂרֵה נָשִׁים פּוֹטְרוֹת צָרוֹתֵיהֶן, שְׁלֹשִׁים וְשֵׁשׁ כְּרֵיתוֹת בַּתּוֹרָה, שְׁלֹשׁ עֶשְׂרֵה דָּבָר נֶאֶמְרוּ בְּנִבְלַת הָעוֹף הַטָּהוֹר, אַרְבַּע אֲבוֹת נְזִיקִין, אֲבוֹת מְלָאכוֹת אַרְבָּעִים חָסֵר אַחַת.

The Gemara lists some examples of this numerical categorization: **Five** categories of people may **not separate *teruma*; five types** of grain **require** the separation **of *ḥalla*** from their dough; **fifteen** categories of **women exempt their co-wives** from levirate marriage and *ḥalitza* if they were both married to the same man who died childless; **thirty-six** transgressions for which one is liable to receive *karet* are listed **in the Torah; thirteen matters are stated with regard to the unslaughtered carcass of a kosher bird;** there are **four primary categories of damages;** and the number of **primary categories of labor** prohibited on Shabbat **is forty-less-one.**

אָמַר רַבִּי אֱלִיעֶזֶר: כְּתִיב "לְעֶזְרָא הַכֹּהֵן הַסּוֹפֵר" מַה תַּלְמוּד לוֹמַר "סוֹפֵר"? אֶלָּא כְּשֵׁם שֶׁהָיָה סוֹפֵר בְּדִבְרֵי תוֹרָה כָּךְ הָיָה סוֹפֵר בְּדִבְרֵי חֲכָמִים.

The Gemara cites a different interpretation for the Hebrew word for scribe. **Rabbi Eliezer said: It is written:** "Now this is the copy of the letter that the king Artaxerxes gave **to Ezra the priest the scribe,** a scribe of the words of the mitzvot of the Lord, and of His statutes to Israel" (Ezra 7:11). **What** is the meaning when **the verse states** the word **scribe** [***sofer***][L] twice? "Scribe" can be interpreted as scholar. The verse is not redundant; **rather,** it means that **just as** Ezra **was a scholar in matters of Torah, so was he a scholar in matters of the Sages,**[N] i.e., the Oral Law.

PERSONALITIES

Rabbi Akiva – רַבִּי עֲקִיבָא: Akiva ben Yosef was one of the greatest of the *tanna'im* from just after the destruction of the Second Temple until the bar Kokheva revolt.

According to legend, Rabbi Akiva began his studies at the age of forty, when Rachel, the daughter of the wealthy Kalba Savua, agreed to marry him on condition that he would go and study Torah. Rabbi Akiva became the student of Rabbi Eliezer ben Hyrcanus and Rabbi Yehoshua ben Ḥananya. Ultimately, he became a great scholar, with 24,000 students of his own.

Rabbi Akiva's foremost students included Shimon ben Azzai and Shimon ben Zoma, with whom he studied esoteric elements of the Torah. Later, he taught Rabbi Meir and Rabbi Shimon bar Yoḥai, among others. He supported bar Kokheva's revolt against the Roman authorities, declaring him the Messiah. Even when Hadrian banned the study of Torah, Rabbi Akiva continued gathering Jews and teaching Torah. Finally, he was captured and executed. He is listed as one of the ten martyrs.

Rabbi Akiva collected early rabbinic teachings and worked to organize the Oral Torah systematically. The work done by Rabbi Akiva and his students served as the basis for the Mishna that was later redacted by Rabbi Yehuda HaNasi and his disciples.

LANGUAGE

Scribe [*sofer*] – סוֹפֵר: The word for a scribe in the language of the Sages bears several related meanings. One of these denotations is a Torah scholar, one who understands the sacred books. The title Ezra the Scribe is referring to his status as a Torah scholar. The Sages sometimes refer to rabbinic law in general as matters of the scribes, for the same reason. Another meaning of this word is closer to the English meaning of the term scribe: One who prepares documents and books, not only sacred writings, but also contracts, bills of divorce, and the like, both for the use of the courts and for private citizens. A third meaning of this word is a children's teacher who instructs them how to read.

NOTES

Therefore will I divide him a portion among the great…this is Rabbi Akiva – לָכֵן אֲחַלֶּק לוֹ בָרַבִּים...זֶה רַבִּי עֲקִיבָא: The later commentaries explain why this verse is a particularly apt description of Rabbi Akiva. The phrase: "Therefore will I divide him a portion among the great," is interpreted as referring to God's promise to allocate a portion in paradise to Rabbi Akiva and his 24,000 students who died in a plague (see *Yevamot* 62b and *Bereishit Rabba* 61:3). The statement: "And he shall divide the spoil with the mighty," is referring to the martyrs of Lod, the brothers Pappas and Lulianus, who were called mighty because they falsely confessed to killing a princess and delivered themselves over to execution, thereby saving the rest of the Jews from a decree of persecution (see *Pesaḥim* 50a and Rashi there). The verse is hinting that Rabbi Akiva will share the spoils of the heavenly rewards with these righteous men.

The subsequent phrase: "Because he bared his soul until death," relates to Rabbi Akiva's sacrifice of his life when he violated the imperial decree and taught Torah in public. Finally, the phrase: "And was numbered with the transgressors," is an allusion to his place amongst those martyred by the Roman empire, a list that also includes Rabban Shimon ben Gamliel and Rabbi Yishmael. This last phrase of the verse alludes to Rabbi Yishmael's comment to Rabban Shimon ben Gamliel after their arrest: Do not suppose that I am crying over our execution; I am crying only over the fact that we are to be executed like murderers and Shabbat transgressors (*Semaḥot* 8:8; see *Avot DeRabbi Natan* 41).

Just as he was a scholar in matters of Torah, so was he a scholar in matters of the Sages – כְּשֵׁם שֶׁהָיָה סוֹפֵר בְּדִבְרֵי תוֹרָה כָּךְ הָיָה סוֹפֵר בְּדִבְרֵי חֲכָמִים: According to some commentaries, this statement is also based on the meaning of scribe as a counter. The phrase: Just as he was a scholar in matters of Torah, means that he counted the letters of the Written Law and thereby established the accurate text, while the phrase: So was he a scholar in matters of the Sages, means that he tallied the Sages' halakhic rulings (*Korban HaEida*).

רַבִּי חַגַּי בְּשֵׁם רַבִּי שְׁמוּאֵל בַּר נַחְמָן: הָרִאשׁוֹנִים חָרְשׁוּ וְזָרְעוּ, נִיכְּשׁוּ, כִּיסְּחוּ, עִדְּרוּ, קָצְרוּ, עִמְּרוּ, דָּשׁוּ, זָרוּ, בֵּרְרוּ, טָחֲנוּ, הִרְקִידוּ, לָשׁוּ, קִיטְּפוּ, וְאָפוּ. וְאָנוּ אֵין לָנוּ מַה לֶּאֱכוֹל.

Rabbi Ḥaggai said **in the name of Rabbi Shmuel bar Naḥman: The former** Sages, i.e., the scholars of earlier generations, metaphorically **plowed and planted, weeded, cleared** thorns, **hoed, harvested, gathered** sheaves into a pile, **threshed** the sheaves, **winnowed** the threshed grain, **separated** the bad grain form the good, **ground** the remainder into flour, **sifted** the flour in a sieve, **kneaded** the dough, **smoothed** the surface of the unbaked loaves with liquid, **and baked** the bread. They prepared everything so that we should be able to grasp Torah concepts; **and yet,** after all that, **we have nothing to eat,** as we are still unable to understand the Torah properly.

רַבִּי אַבָּא בַּר זְמִינָא בְּשֵׁם רַבִּי זְעֵירָא: אִין הֲווֹן קַדְמָאִין מַלְאָכִין – אֲנַן בְּנֵי אֱנָשׁ, וְאִין הֲווֹן בְּנֵי אֱנָשׁ – אֲנַן חֲמָרִין. אָמַר רַבִּי מָנָא: בְּהַהִיא שַׁעְתָּא אָמְרִין: אֲפִילּוּ כַּחֲמָרְתֵיהּ דְּרַבִּי פִּינְחָס בֶּן יָאִיר לָא אִידַּמִּינוּן.

The Gemara cites another metaphor with regard to the relationship between the earlier and later generations. **Rabbi Abba bar Zemina** said **in the name of Rabbi Ze'eira: If the former** generations **were akin to angels,**[N] **we are akin to humans; and if they were akin to humans, we are akin to donkeys. Rabbi Mana said: At that hour,** when the previous statement was issued, **they** also **said: We are not even comparable to the female donkey of Rabbi Pineḥas ben Yair.**

חֲמָרְתֵיהּ דְּרַבִּי פִּינְחָס בֶּן יָאִיר גְּנַבְתָּה לִיסְטָאֵי בְּלֵילְיָא. עֲבָדַת טְמִירָא גַּבּוֹן תְּלָתָא יוֹמִין וְלָא טָעֲמָה כְּלוּם. בָּתַר תְּלָתָא יוֹמִין אִימְלְכוּן מַחֲזַרְתָּהּ. אָמְרִי: אַפְּקִינוּן מִן הָכָא, דְּלָא תֵימוּת גַּבָּן. אַפְּקוּנָהּ, אָזְלַת וְקָמַת לָהּ עַל תַּרְעָא דְּמָרָהּ, שָׁרְיַית מְנַהֲקַת. אָמַר לוֹן: פִּתְחוּן לְהָדָא עֲלוּבְתָּא דְּאִית לָהּ תְּלַת יוֹמִין דְּלָא טָעֲמָה כְּלוּם. פָּתְחִין לָהּ וְעָלַת לָהּ.

§ The Gemara explains the reference to this particular donkey. **The donkey of Rabbi Pineḥas ben Yair was stolen by robbers one night. It was kept hidden by them for three days, and** yet **it did not eat anything. After three days, they reconsidered** and decided to **return it. They said: Let's get it out of here, so that it shouldn't die in our possession** and leave a stench in our cave. When **they set it free it went and stood by its master's gate** and **began braying.** Rabbi Pineḥas **said to** the members of his household: **Open up for that poor** creature, **which has gone three days without eating anything. They opened** the gate **for it, and it entered** Rabbi Pineḥas' courtyard.

אָמַר לוֹן: יְהָבוּ לָהּ כְּלוּם תֵּיכוּל. יְהָבוּן קוֹמָהּ שְׂעוֹרִין וְלָא בָּעֵית לְמֵיכַל. אָמְרִין לֵיהּ: רַבִּי, לָא בָּעֵית לְמֵיכַל. אָמַר לוֹן: מְתַקְּנִין אִינּוּן? אָמְרוּ לֵיהּ: אִין. אָמַר לוֹן: וְאַרֵימְתּוּן דְּמָיֵין?

He told them: Give it something to eat. They placed barley before it, but it would not eat. They said to him: Rabbi, it will not eat. He said to them: Has the barley been tithed so that it is fit to eat? **They replied: Yes. He** then **asked them: And have you separated their doubtfully tithed produce?** Did you tithe the grain about which there is doubt as to whether it has been tithed properly?

אָמְרוּן לֵיהּ: לָא כֵן אַלְפוֹן רַבִּי, הַלּוֹקֵחַ זֶרַע לִבְהֵמָה, קֶמַח לְעוֹרוֹת, שֶׁמֶן לְאוֹר – פָּטוּר מִן הַדְּמַאי? אָמַר לוֹן: מַה נֶּעֱבַד לָהּ לְהָדָא עֲלוּבְתָּא דְּהִיא מַחְמְרָה עַל גַּרְמָהּ סַגִּין. וַאֲרִימוּן דְּמָיֵין, וַאֲכָלַת.

They replied: Didn't you teach us the following, Rabbi: One who purchases grain for feeding **an animal,**[H] **or flour for** processing animal **hides, or oil for lighting** a lamp, **is exempt from** separating **doubtfully tithed produce?** There is no need to separate tithes from doubtfully tithed produce to feed a donkey. **He said to them: What can we do for that poor** creature, **which is very strict with itself** and will not eat even from doubtfully tithed produce, despite this exemption? **And they** therefore **separated** tithes from the **doubtfully tithed produce, and the** donkey finally **ate** the barley grains.

"פְּתַחְיָה עַל הַקִּינִּין". בֹּא וּרְאֵה מַה גָּדוֹל הוּא כֹּחוֹ שֶׁל אוֹתוֹ הָאִישׁ פּוֹתֵחַ דְּבָרִים וְדוֹרְשָׁן. "יוֹדֵעַ בְּשִׁבְעִים לָשׁוֹן". תָּנֵי: סַנְהֶדְרִין שֶׁיֵּשׁ בָּהּ שְׁנַיִם שֶׁיְּכוֹלִין לְדַבֵּר וְכוּלָּן רָאוּיִן לִשְׁמוֹעַ – הֲרֵי זוֹ רְאוּיָה לְסַנְהֶדְרִין,

§ The mishna states that **Petaḥya** was responsible **for the pairs** of birds. The Gemara mentions some of the talents of this Petaḥya. **Come and see how great was the skill of that man.** He could **open,** i.e., elucidate, difficult **topics and interpret them.** As mentioned in the mishna, **he understood** all **seventy languages.** The Gemara adds: **It was taught in a *baraita*: A Sanhedrin that includes two** members **who are able to speak** all the seventy languages, **and all** of its members **are** at least **capable of understanding** those languages, this court is minimally **fit to** serve as **a Sanhedrin.**

שְׁלֹשָׁה – הֲרֵי זוֹ בֵּינוֹנִית, אַרְבָּעָה – הֲרֵי זוֹ חֲכָמָה. וּבְיַבְנֶה הָיוּ בָהּ אַרְבָּעָה: בֶּן עַזַּאי, וּבֶן זוֹמָא, וּבֶן חֲכִינַאי, וְרַבִּי אֶלְעָזָר בֶּן מַתְיָה.

If it has **three** who can speak those languages, **it is a medium** level Sanhedrin. If it has **four, it is a wise** Sanhedrin. **In Yavne,** the Sanhedrin **included four** who could speak all seventy languages: **Ben Azzai,**[P] **ben Zoma,**[P] **ben Ḥakhinai,**[P] **and Rabbi Elazar ben Matya.**

NOTES

The former were akin to angels, etc. – הֲוֹון קַדְמָאִין מַלְאָכִין וכו׳: One explanation of this metaphor is that if the former generations are considered by us as angels, i.e., if we relate to their statements as sacred, as though they were issued by heavenly angels, we can be considered human. However, if we consider the former generations as merely human, appointing ourselves as the judges of possible errors in their statements and rulings, we have placed ourselves on the level of donkeys (*Ḥut HaMeshulash*, citing Rabbi Akiva Eiger).

HALAKHA

One who purchases grain for feeding an animal, etc. – הַלּוֹקֵחַ זֶרַע לִבְהֵמָה וכו׳: For certain items, the Sages did not require the separation of tithes from doubtfully tithed produce. Examples of such produce include grain purchased for planting or for animal fodder, flour for processing animal hides or for medicinal purposes, oil for lighting a lamp or for polishing utensils, and wine for healing the eyes. If an *am ha'aretz*, one who is ignorant and neglectful about tithes, states that tithes have been separated from this produce, his claim is accepted and one need not separate tithes (Rambam *Sefer Zera'im, Hilkhot Ma'aserot* 13:14).

PERSONALITIES

Ben Azzai – בֶּן עַזַּאי: Shimon ben Azzai was one of the *tanna'im* in the city of Yavneh. Although he did not received formal ordination, which is why he is never referred to with an honorific but only by his name, and often only by his father's name, he was respected as one of the great Torah scholars of his generation.

It appears that ben Azzai did not study Torah in his youth until he met the daughter of Rabbi Akiva, who promised to marry him if he were to commit himself to learn Torah. He began his studies with Rabbi Yehoshua and Rabbi Yishmael and ultimately became a devoted student and colleague of Rabbi Akiva, whom he considered the leading sage of the generation. His devotion to Torah study was so complete that he was unable to live a normal family life and either he never actually married Rabbi Akiva's daughter or perhaps he married her but only lived with her for a brief period.

We find ben Azzai's teachings in both *halakha* and *aggada* throughout the Talmud, and he served as a mentor for such students as Rabbi Meir and Rabbi Shimon.

Aside from his study of the revealed Torah, ben Azzai was involved in the study of its esoteric traditions. According to the Gemara, together with Rabbi Akiva, ben Zoma, and Elisha ben Avuya, ben Azzai entered the Pardes, i.e., delved into esoteric mystical matters, with only Rabbi Akiva surviving unscathed while ben Azzai is described as having gazed and died (*Ḥagiga* 14b). With regard to him the verse states, "Precious in the eyes of God is the death of His pious ones" (Psalms 116:15).

Ben Zoma – בֶּן זוֹמָא: Shimon, son of Zoma, was a disciple of Rabbi Yehoshua and a student and colleague of Rabbi Akiva. Ben Zoma was considered one of the great Sages of his time, but he never received formal ordination, apparently due to his youth. For this reason, he is not referred to by the honorific Rabbi, but only by his father's name. Many of his statements are found in both *halakha* and *aggada* throughout the Talmud, and he was particularly acclaimed for his sermons on the Bible, to the extent that it is stated: Upon ben Zoma's death the sermonizers came to an end (*Sota* 49a).

Ben Ḥakhinai – בֶּן חֲכִינַאי: Rabbi Ḥannanya, or Ḥannina, son of Ḥakhinai, was one of those who deliberated before the Sages in Yavne and was identified as one of those who knew seventy languages. Ben Ḥakhinai was an especially devoted student of Rabbi Akiva. Traditions reported in his name can be found throughout the Mishna, the *Tosefta*, various compilations of halakhic midrash, and the Talmud. In one midrash he is listed among the renowned ten martyrs.

אָמַר רַבִּי חִסְדָּא: פַּעַם אַחַת יָבְשָׁה אֶרֶץ יִשְׂרָאֵל וְלֹא יָדְעוּ מֵהֵיכָן לְהָבִיא עוֹמֶר.

The Gemara cites a story that exemplifies Petaḥya's skills at understanding linguistic allusions. **Rabbi Ḥisda said: Once Eretz Yisrael dried up.** There was a drought, no grain grew there, **and the** Sages **did not know from where they could bring the** ***omer*****,** the measure of barley brought as a communal offering on the sixteenth of Nisan.

וַהֲוָה תַּמָּן חַד אִלֵּם, דַּהֲוָה יָהֵיב חַד יְדֵיהּ עַל גַּגּוֹת, וְחַד יְדֵיהּ עַל צְרִיפִים. אַיְיתוּנֵיהּ קַמֵּיהּ דִּפְתַחְיָה. אֲמַר לְהוּ: אִית אֲתַר דְּמִתְקַרְיָא גַּגּוֹת צְרִיפִין אוֹ צְרִיפִין גַּגּוֹת? אֲזַלִין לְתַמָּן וְאַשְׁכַּחַן.

And there was a mute present **there who** knew where barley was growing that year. He came to the Sages **and** gestured to them with his hands. He **placed one of his hands on roofs** [*gagot*] **and the other hand on huts** [*tzerifin*], alluding to the name of the place where barley could be found. Since they did not understand his allusions, **they brought Petaḥya before him,** who observed the actions of the mute and **said to them: Is there a place called Gagot Tzerifin**[B] **or Tzerifin Gagot?** They remembered that there was indeed such a place. **They went there and found** barley for the *omer* offering.

אָמַר רַבִּי יוֹסֵה בֵּי רַבִּי בּוּן: פַּעַם אַחַת נִשְׁדַּף כָּל הָעוֹלָם כּוּלּוֹ וְלֹא הָיוּ יוֹדְעִין מֵהֵיכָן לְהָבִיא הָעוֹמֶר. וַהֲוָה תַּמָּן חַד אִילֵּם, דַּהֲוָה יָהֵיב יְדֵיהּ עַל עֵינֵיהּ וִידֵיהּ עַל סוֹכְרָא. אַיְיתוּנֵיהּ לְגַבֵּי פְּתַחְיָה, אֲמַר לוֹן: אִית אֲתַר דְּמִיתְקַרְיָא עֵין סוֹכֵר אוֹ סוֹכֵר עֵין? וַאֲזַלוֹן תַּמָּן וְאַשְׁכְּחוֹן.

The Gemara relates a similar story. **Rabbi Yosei, son of Rabbi Bun, said:** Once all the grain in **the entire world was blighted, and the** Sages **did not know from where they could bring** barley for **the** ***omer*****.** And again **there was a mute** present **there who** knew where barley was growing. He came before the Sages and gestured to them with his hands. He **placed one hand on his eye and the other hand on a doorjamb** [*sokhara*].[L] Since the Sages were unable to understand his allusions, **they brought Petaḥya before him, who** observed his actions and **said to them: Is there a place called Ein Sokher**[B] **or Sokher Ein?** They remembered that there was indeed such a place. **They went there and found** barley for the *omer* offering.

שָׁלֹשׁ נָשִׁים הֵבִיאוּ קִינֵּיהֶן, אַחַת אוֹמֶרֶת "לְעֵינָתִי" וְאַחַת אוֹמֶרֶת "לְיַמָּתִי" וְאַחַת אוֹמֶרֶת "לְזִיבָתִי".

The Gemara cites yet another story that exemplifies Petaḥya's deciphering skills. There were **three women**[N] who **brought their** own **pair** of birds to the Temple. It was not clear which type of offering each of them intended to bring. **One of the women said:** This pair of birds is **for my fountain; and** the second **one said:** It is **for my sea; and** the third **one said:** It is **for my** ***ziva*****.**

זוֹ שֶׁאוֹמֶרֶת "לְעֵינָתִי" סָבְרִין מֵימַר: שׁוֹפַעַת כְּמַעְיָן. אֲמַר לוֹן: בְּעֵיינָא סַכְּנַת.

With regard to **that** woman **who said: For my fountain,** the Rabbis **thought to say** that she meant that her post-menstrual blood was **flowing like a fountain.**[N] She was therefore bringing the pair of birds of a *zava*, as a sin-offering and a burnt-offering for her ritual purity. However, Petaḥya **said to them: She was endangered in a fountain.** She has brought this pair of birds as a thanks-offering for her escape from that life-threatening situation.

BACKGROUND

Gagot Tzerifin – גַּגּוֹת צְרִיפִין: An alternate version of the text reads: The gardens of Tzerifin. Either way, this place is generally identified with modern-day Tzerifin, a name preserved in Arabic as صرفند العمار, *ṣarafand al-'amār*, which was a village east of Rishon LeTzion, along the road from Ramle to Jaffa.

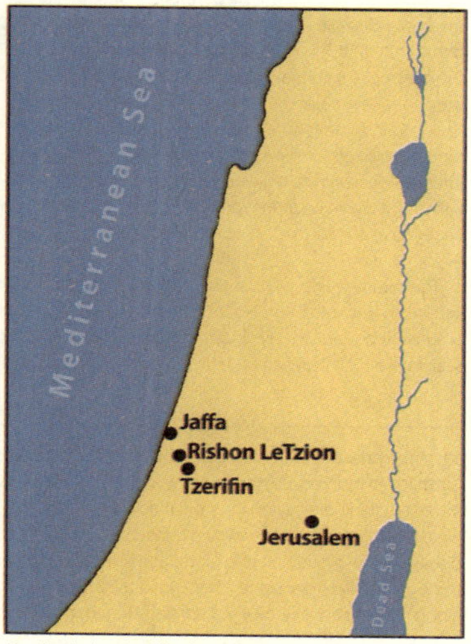

Map showing location of Tzerifin and the surrounding area

Ein Sokher – עֵין סוֹכֵר: The accepted identification of Ein Sokher is the valley called in Arabic سهل عسكر, *sahl 'askar*. It is located southwest of Mount Ebal, and the main road from Shechem to Jerusalem runs through it. The name is apparently derived from a deep well [*ein*] located in a neighboring village.

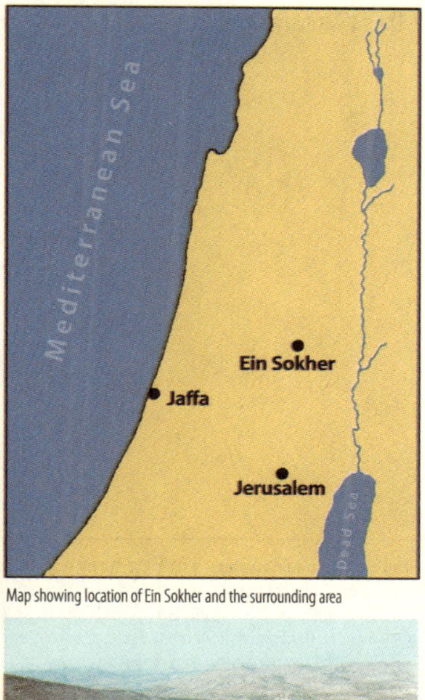

Map showing location of Ein Sokher and the surrounding area

Mikhmetet Valley, which includes the valley of Ein Sokher

LANGUAGE

Doorjamb [*sokhara*] – סוֹכְרָא: Several interpretations have been suggested for this Aramaic term. Some say it is referring to the hole in the doorpost into which the bolt is inserted, as it is spelled similarly to the Aramaic root *sgr*, which means to close (Rashi; *Sefer HaArukh*). Another interpretation is that it means a dam that stops the flow of water in a river (*Tosafot*). Alternatively, it means a grave (*Tosafot*).

Roman dam near Mérida, in Extremadura, Spain, dating from the first or second century CE

NOTES

Three women – שָׁלֹשׁ נָשִׁים: This incident is cited to teach that Petaḥya not only understood many languages, he also was acquainted with the dialects and idioms used in different communities. Consequently, even when the other Sages understood the literal meaning of what each woman said, he alone perceived that each woman actually had an entirely different intention in mind.

Flowing like a fountain – שׁוֹפַעַת כְּמַעְיָן: In the Babylonian Talmud the text reads: For my period [*onati*], which the other Sages thought was a reference to the time for her offering, i.e., the eighth day of purity after she had been a *zava* (*Menaḥot* 64b; and see Rashi there). Petaḥya explained that the woman was actually referring to her delivery from a life-threatening infection of her eye [*einati*].

זוֹ שֶׁאוֹמֶרֶת ״לְיַמָּתִי״ סָבְרִין מֵימַר שׁוֹפַעַת כַּיָּם, אֲמַר לוֹן: בְּיַמָּה סַכָּנְתָּ.

With regard to **that** woman **who said: For my sea,**[N] the Rabbis **thought to say** that she meant that her post-menstrual blood was **flowing like the sea,** which likewise means that she was a *zava* bringing her offerings for ritual purity. But Petaḥya **said to them: She was endangered in the sea,** so she too has brought this pair of birds as a thanks-offering.

זוֹ שֶׁאוֹמֶרֶת ״לְזִיבָתִי״ סָבְרִין מֵימַר זָבָה מַמָּשׁ, אֲמַר לוֹן: זְאֵב בָּא לִיטּוֹל אֶת בְּנָהּ.

Finally, with regard to **that** woman **who said: For my** ***ziva,*** the Rabbis **thought to say** that she meant that she was **an actual** ***zava,*** and she was therefore bringing an offering for ritual purity. But Petaḥya **said to them: A wolf** [*ze'ev*], a word that is similar to the one she used, **came** and attempted **to snatch her son,** but he was ultimately saved. She, too, has brought this pair of birds as a thanks-offering.

״בֶּן אֲחִיָּה״ וכו׳. עַל יְדֵי שֶׁהָיוּ הַכֹּהֲנִים מְהַלְּכִין יְחֵפִים עַל הָרִצְפָּה, וְהָיוּ אוֹכְלִין בָּשָׂר וְשׁוֹתִין מַיִם, הָיוּ בָּאִין לִידֵי חוֹלִי הַמֵּעַיִם, וַהֲוָה יָדַע הַאי דֵּין חֲמַר טַב לְמֵעַיָּא, וְהַאי דֵּין חֲמַר סָמָם לְמֵעַיָּיא.

§ The mishna states that **ben Aḥiyya** was appointed to treat those priests who suffered from intestinal disease. The Gemara explains why priests were particularly susceptible to this ailment. **Since the priests would walk barefoot**[H] **on the floor,** even when it was cold, as their feet had to be in contact with the stones of the Temple floor, **and** since **they would eat** a lot of **meat** from the offerings **and drink** a lot of **water, they would contract intestinal disease.**[N] And ben Aḥiyya **knew** that **this** particular type of **wine was good for** healing **the intestines, and** that **this** other type of **wine was** effective **intestinal medicine.**

״נְחוּנְיָא חוֹפֵר שִׁיחִין״. שֶׁהָיָה חוֹפֵר שִׁיחִין וּמְעָרוֹת, וַהֲוָה יָדַע

The mishna states that **Neḥunya** was **the well digger.** The Gemara explains **that he would dig wells and caves,** where rainwater would collect, for pilgrims to use on their way to Jerusalem for the Festivals. **And he knew**

NOTES

For my sea – **לְיַמָּתִי**: Some commentaries explain that because the term for sea is similar to the word for day [*yom*], the Sages took her statement to mean that she had completed the days of her *zava* status and was now bringing the offerings for her ritual purity (Rabbeinu Gershom on *Menaḥot* 64b).

Since the priests would walk barefoot…they would contract intestinal disease – **עַל יְדֵי שֶׁהָיוּ הַכֹּהֲנִים מְהַלְּכִין יְחֵפִים...הָיוּ בָּאִין לִידֵי חוֹלִי הַמֵּעַיִם**: The later commentaries are puzzled as to how the priests could contract illnesses, as the verse states: "One who keeps a mitzva shall know no evil thing" (Ecclesiastes 8:5). This seems to indicate that no harm will befall someone who is performing a sacred service. Even if one would say that a miraculous intervention would be necessary to prevent barefoot priests from falling ill, it would be fitting for this to occur in the Temple, as the Sages have stated that miracles occurred regularly there (see *Avot* 5:5).

The commentaries explain that it is God's will that the Temple service should entail some suffering. Alternatively, only priests who were not absolutely sincere but were haughty and profit seeking would fall prey to these illnesses (*Minḥat Elazar*).

HALAKHA

Since the priests would walk barefoot, etc. – **עַל יְדֵי שֶׁהָיוּ הַכֹּהֲנִים מְהַלְּכִין יְחֵפִים וכו׳**: Because the priests serving in the Temple would invariably stand directly on the stone floor, eat a lot of meat, and wear a single garment, they would frequently contract intestinal disease. Consequently, an official was appointed over this matter to heal their sicknesses and constantly look after their welfare, along with a specially designated staff (Rambam *Sefer Avoda, Hilkhot Kelei HaMikdash* 7:14).

Perek **V**
Daf **14** Amud **a**

הַאי דֵּין כֵּיף מְקוֹרֵר מַיָּא, וְהַאי דֵּין כֵּיף אִית בֵּיהּ שְׁרַבְרוּבֵי, וְעַד הֵיכָן שְׁרַבְרוּבוּתֵיהּ מָטְיָא. אָמַר רַבִּי אֱלִיעֶזֶר: וּמֵת בְּנוֹ בַּצָּמָא.

which rock contains water,[N] **and which rock contains fissures** in which water may be found, **and how far those fissures extend.** This would enable him to calculate how deep he had to dig to reach water. **Rabbi Eliezer said: And his son died of thirst.**[N]

אָמַר רַבִּי חֲנִינָא: מַאן דְּאָמַר רַחֲמָנָא וַותְּרָן – יִתְוַותְּרוּן בְּנֵי מֵעוֹי. אֶלָּא מַאֲרִיךְ רוּחֵיהּ וְגָבֵי דִּידֵיהּ.

Since the previous passage mentioned God's rigorously exacting attitude toward righteous people like Neḥunya, the Gemara discusses how God relates to sinners. **Rabbi Ḥanina said: Whoever says that the Merciful One overlooks**[N] the punishment due to sinners, **his intestines will be overlooked,** i.e., cease functioning. The reason sinners often appear to go unpunished is **rather** that God **extends His patience** with evildoers to give them a chance to repent, **but** eventually He **collects His due** and punishes the wicked.

NOTES

Which rock contains water – **הַאי דֵּין כֵּיף מְקוֹרֵר מַיָּא**: An alternative explanation of the phrase is: Which rock produces cold water, with the next phrase reading: And which stone produces hot water. The third phrase is: And how far does its heat extend, i.e., what is the temperature of the water (*Korban HaEida*; *Tiklin Ḥadatin*).

And his son died of thirst – **וּמֵת בְּנוֹ בַּצָּמָא**: A similar incident is reported at length in the Babylonian Talmud (*Bava Kama* 50a; *Yevamot* 121b): The daughter of Neḥunya the well digger fell into a great water pit, and people came and notified Rabbi Ḥanina ben Dosa. After one hour, he said to them: She is at peace, unharmed, in the pit. After two hours, he told them: She is still at peace. After three hours, he declared: She has ascended from the pit. Later, they asked her: Who pulled you up? She replied: A ram happened by, led by a certain elderly man. The Gemara adds that they asked Rabbi Ḥanina ben Dosa whether he was a prophet, as he could accurately report on the girl from so far away. He replied: I am neither a prophet nor the son of a prophet, but I simply reasoned that the offspring of that righteous man could not possibly come to harm through the very object over which he takes so much trouble for the public benefit.

The obvious question is why his merit was to no avail in the situation mentioned in the Gemara here, where his son died. Some explain that Rabbi Ḥanina's logical reasoning actually included a prayer to God. In other words, it was not only Neḥunya's own merit that caused his daughter's salvation, but also Rabbi Ḥanina's mention of his good deeds in his prayers. However, no one prayed for Neḥunya's son, and since God is exacting with the righteous, that misfortune came upon him (Rabbi Yeshaya in the *Shita Mekubbetzet*; *Penei Yehoshua*). Others maintain that the two incidents are not precisely the same, as pits, which are the very objects that Neḥunya dug, could never cause his offspring harm, whereas dehydration is not identical to anything Neḥunya himself dealt with, and therefore his offspring could be injured in this manner (see *Tosafot*).

The Merciful One overlooks – **רַחֲמָנָא וַותְּרָן**: Although God defers his anger toward evildoers, and sometimes it appears as though He were not repaying them their due, this is not because He overlooks their misdoings. Rather, judgment is rendered for every action, as God will ultimately punish every transgressor appropriately for each of his sins.

אָמַר רַבִּי אַחָא: כְּתִיב ״וּסְבִיבָיו נִשְׂעֲרָה מְאוֹד״ – מְדַקְדֵּק עִמָּהֶן כְּחוּט הַשַּׂעֲרָה.

The Gemara explains the harsh judgment inflicted on the righteous Neḥunya. **Rabbi Aḥa said** that **it is written:** “Our God comes and does not keep silence; a fire devours before Him, **and His surroundings storm** [*nis’ara*] **mightily**” (Psalms 50:3). The Hebrew spelling of the word *nis’ara* is very similar to the word *sa’ara*, hair. This hints that God **is exacting with** the righteous, who are close to Him and can be called His surroundings, **up to a hairsbreadth.**[N] Even slight deviations from the proper path can elicit punishment.

אָמַר רַבִּי יוֹסֵי: לֹא מִטַּעַם הַזֶּה, אֶלָּא מִן מַה דִּכְתִיב ״וְנוֹרָא הוּא עַל כָּל סְבִיבָיו״ – מוֹרָאוֹ עַל הַקְּרוֹבִים יוֹתֵר מִן הָרְחוֹקִים.

Rabbi Yosei said: This idea is derived **not through that source,** but **rather from that which is written** about God: **“And dreadful is He upon all of His surroundings”** (Psalms 89:8),[N] which indicates that **His dread is upon those close** to Him, i.e., the righteous, **more than** upon **those distant** from Him, i.e., the sinful.

רַבִּי חַגַּיי בְּשֵׁם רַבִּי שְׁמוּאֵל בַּר נַחְמָן: מַעֲשֶׂה בְּחָסִיד אֶחָד שֶׁהָיָה חוֹפֵר בּוֹרוֹת שִׁיחִין וּמְעָרוֹת לָעוֹבְרִים וְשָׁבִים, פַּעַם אַחַת הָיְתָה בִּתּוֹ עוֹבֶרֶת לְהִנָּשֵׂא וּשְׁטָפָהּ נָהָר, וַהֲווֹן כָּל עַמָּא עֲלָלִין לְגַבֵּי, בְּעוֹן מְנַחְמָתֵיהּ וְלָא קִיבֵּל עֲלוֹי מִתְנַחֲמָא.

The Gemara cites a related story. **Rabbi Ḥaggai** said **in the name of Rabbi Shmuel bar Naḥman:** There was **an incident involving a certain pious man who would dig pits, wells, and caves** to collect water **for passersby. Once his daughter was passing over** a river **for** the purpose of **marriage, and the river washed her away. And all the people came to console him, but he refused to accept their condolences.**

עָאל רַבִּי פִּנְחָס בֶּן יָאִיר לְגַבֵּיהּ, בְּעֵי מְנַחְמָתֵיהּ וְלָא קִיבֵּל עֲלוֹי מִתְנַחֲמָא. אֲמַר לוֹן: דֵּין הוּא חֲסִידְכוֹן? אָמְרוּ לֵיהּ: רַבִּי, כָּךְ וְכָךְ הָיָה עוֹשֶׂה וְכָךְ וְכָךְ אֵירַע לֵיהּ.

Rabbi Pineḥas ben Yair came to visit **him to console him, but he refused to accept condolences** even from Rabbi Pineḥas. Rabbi Pineḥas **said to** the people of that community: Is **this your righteous man,** who will not be consoled and accept God’s judgment? **They said to him: Rabbi, he would perform such and such** acts of righteousness, by supplying water, **and** yet **such and such** tragedy, the drowning of his daughter, **occurred to him.**

אָמַר: אֶפְשָׁר שֶׁהָיָה מְכַבֵּד אֶת בּוֹרְאוֹ בַּמַּיִם וְהוּא מְקַפְּחוֹ בַּמַּיִם? מִיָּד נָפְלָה הֲבָרָה בָּעִיר: בָּאת בִּתּוֹ שֶׁל אוֹתוֹ הָאִישׁ. אִית דְּאָמְרֵי בְּסוּכָתָא אִיתְעֲרִית, וְאִית דְּאָמְרֵי מַלְאָךְ יָרַד כִּדְמוּת רַבִּי פִּנְחָס בֶּן יָאִיר וְהִצִּילָהּ.

Rabbi Pineḥas **said:** Is it **possible that he honors his Creator with water, and** yet his Creator **strikes him with water? Immediately** thereafter, **a report spread throughout the city: The daughter of that** righteous **man has arrived,** as she did not actually drown. **Some say she grasped a branch** and pulled herself out of the river, **and some say an angel in the form of Rabbi Pineḥas ben Yair descended** from heaven **and rescued her.**

״גְּבִינִי כָּרוֹז״. שֶׁהָיָה מַכְרִיז בְּבֵית הַמִּקְדָּשׁ. מֶה הָיָה אוֹמֵר: עִמְדוּ הַכֹּהֲנִים לַעֲבוֹדָה, וּלְוִיִּים לְדוּכָנָן, וְיִשְׂרָאֵל לְמַעֲמָדָן. אַגְרִיפָּס הַמֶּלֶךְ שָׁמַע קוֹלוֹ עַד שְׁמוֹנֶה פַּרְסָאוֹת, וְנָתַן לוֹ מַתָּנוֹת הַרְבֵּה.

§ The mishna states that **Gevini** was the **Temple crier.** The Gemara cites a *baraita* that states **that** Gevini **would issue an announcement** every morning **in the Temple. What would he say** in his announcement? **Arise, priests, to service; and Levites to their platform** to sing; **and Israelites,** i.e., the group of Israelites who represented the entire community at the sacrifice, **to their watch.** Gevini’s voice was so powerful that **King Agrippa**[LP] once **heard his voice as far** away **as eight parasangs,**[N] **and** Agrippa **gave him many gifts** as a sign of his appreciation.

NOTES

Up to a hairsbreadth – כְּחוּט הַשַּׂעֲרָה: In other words, God is exacting with the righteous even for sins that are not considered serious for another person, as the demands upon the righteous increase with their greatness. The Sages express this idea in various forms on different occasions, and it is likewise stated in a verse: “You only have I known of all the families of the earth; therefore I will visit upon you all your iniquities” (Amos 3:2).

Some commentaries explain this idea by means of a parable: God is exacting with the righteous up to a hairsbreadth because they are the foundation of the world. This is similar to a builder who erects a very tall building. He must be especially exacting in his construction of its foundations, as even a small deviation there can cause enormous distortions as he proceeds to the upper levels (Rabbi Shalom Schwadron, citing Rabbi Yosef Ḥayyim Sonnenfeld). Others state that, as opposed to ordinary people, the righteous are fully aware of God’s greatness. Therefore, even a slight deviation from the correct path is considered insolence toward God (*Panim Yafot, parashat Tetzave*).

Another explanation is that since the righteous have a clearer perception of the Divine, even a minor sin is considered far more consequential than the width of a hair. They interpret that this hairsbreadth is referring to the significance of a sin to those who lack a clear perception of God’s greatness; but for the righteous, this act is considered a major transgression (*Darkhei Mussar*)

And His surroundings storm mightily…and dreadful is He upon all of His surroundings – וּסְבִיבָיו נִשְׂעֲרָה מְאוֹד... וְנוֹרָא הוּא עַל כָּל סְבִיבָיו: The commentaries on *Yevamot* 121b have noted that the two derivations of the idea that God is more exacting with the righteous have somewhat different implications. According to the first source, God is more exacting with the righteous, as He punishes them even for the few minor sins they commit. According to the second derivation, there are even times when God punishes the righteous in this world solely to cleanse them through ordeals of love. This suffering serves to sanctify His name. It has been suggested that the deaths of the sons of Aaron is an instance of this phenomenon.

A minor sin committed by a righteous person can have a stronger impact than more serious sins committed by others, both in the material world, because of the desecration of God’s name entailed, as well as in the lofty spiritual worlds (*Iyyun Ya’akov* on *Yevamot* 121b). Furthermore, when God is very strict with the righteous, other people realize how much more deserving of punishment they are themselves, and proceed to mend their ways (*Maharsha* on *Yevamot* 121b).

As far as eight parasangs – עַד שְׁמוֹנֶה פַּרְסָאוֹת: Although the Gemara here speaks of eight parasangs, in tractate *Tamid* (30b) it is stated that Gevini’s voice could be heard in Jericho, which, as stated in tractate *Yoma* (39b), is ten parasangs from Jerusalem. A parasang is approximately 4.5 km. It appears that the reason for this discrepancy is simply that the incident here occurred when King Agrippa was only eight parasangs from Jerusalem (*Tiklin Ḥadatin*).

LANGUAGE

Agrippa – אַגְרִיפָּס: Ἀγρίππας, *Agrippas*, is the Greek form of this king’s name. In Hebrew it is also pronounced Agrippas.

PERSONALITIES

King Agrippa – אַגְרִיפָּס הַמֶּלֶךְ: This story is probably referring to King Agrippa I, the grandson of Herod and Miriam the Hasmonean, who died in the year 44 CE. He spent his youth in Rome, in the dissolute and intrigue-filled society of the emperor’s court. Still, when he finally came home to Eretz Yisrael, upon his appointment as ruler over all of the areas governed by Herod, Agrippa appears to have undergone a spiritual awakening that drew him into a positive relationship with the Sages and a practical commitment to the mitzvot. Although the Sages never acknowledged him as the legitimate king, they treated him with respect, and several of his good deeds are mentioned in the Talmud.

Ancient coin bearing the profile of King Agrippa I

BACKGROUND

Kufra – **כּוּפְרָה**: This is a neighborhood in the region of Tiberias. According to the Jerusalem Talmud (*Megilla* 4:5), it is referring to the location of ancient Tiberias, Rabbi Hillel of Kipra's place of origin.

Cymbal – **צִלְצָל**: This is a metallic percussion instrument. Several musical instruments with similar names are mentioned in the Bible, e.g., "loud-sounding cymbals" and "clanging cymbals" (Psalms 150:5), but their precise identity has yet to be determined. The apparatus pictured here is probably the *sistrum* from the Roman period, a wooden-handled instrument with an arched top and metal tablets.

Egyptian *sistrum* dating from between 380 and 250 BCE

"בֶּן גֶּבֶר עַל נְעִילַת שְׁעָרִים". תִּירְגֵּם רַב קוֹמֵי דְּבֵית רַבִּי שֵׁילָא: קָרָא גַּבְרָא – אַכְרֵיז כָּרוֹזָא.

The mishna states that **ben Gever** was responsible **for locking** the Temple **gates** in the evening and opening them in the morning. The Gemara cites an incident involving ben Gever. It is taught in a mishna (*Yoma* 20a): On each day, the ashes are removed from the altar at the calling of the *gever* or near this time. The Sages dispute whether the term *gever* in this context means man or rooster. The Gemara relates that when Rav went to visit Rabbi Sheila, he would serve as his interpreter, explaining his lectures to the public. On one occasion, after Rabbi Sheila had explicitly stated that *gever* means a rooster, **Rav** nevertheless **interpreted in the study hall of Rabbi Sheila** that the phrase: ***Gever* cried out**, means: **The crier announced.**

אָמַר לֵיהּ: אֱמוֹר קָרָא תַּרְנְגוֹלָא! אֲמַר לֵיהּ: וְהָתְנֵינַן בֶּן גֶּבֶר אִית לָךְ לְמֵימַר בַּר תַּרְנְגוֹלָא?!

Rabbi Sheila **said to him: Say** that this expression means: **The rooster cried out.** Rav **said to him: But we learned** in a mishna above (13a) that there is a man called **ben Gever. Could you** possibly **say** that his name means **son of a rooster?**[N] In this context, *gever* must mean man, not rooster. Therefore, in *Yoma* as well it must indicate that a man issued an announcement.

"בֶּן בֵּבַי עַל הַפָּקִיעַ". שֶׁהָיָה מְזַיֵּיג פְּתִילוֹת. רַבִּי יוֹסֵי עָאל לְכוּפְרָה, בְּעוּ מְמַנַּיָּיא עֲלֵייהוֹן פַּרְנָסִים וְלָא קִיבְּלוֹן מִינְהָן.

The mishna states that **ben Bevai** was responsible **for the shreds** of garments. The Gemara explains **that he would braid** shreds together to prepare **wicks**[N] for the candelabrum that were of the appropriate thickness, so that they would burn the entire night during each period of the year. The Gemara relates that **Rabbi Yosei came to** the town of **Kufra**[B] and **wanted to appoint** community **leaders for them** to care for the needs of the community and the provisions of the poor. **However,** those who were selected **would not accept** the appointment **from them,** i.e., from Rabbi Yosei, because they deemed this job beneath their dignity.

עָאל וַאֲמַר קוֹמֵיהוֹן: בֶּן בֵּבַי עַל הַפָּקִיעַ. וּמָה אִם זֶה שֶׁנִּתְמַנָּה עַל הַפְּתִילוֹת זָכָה לְהִימָּנוֹת עִם גְּדוֹלֵי הַדּוֹר, אַתֶּם שֶׁאַתֶּם נִתְמַנִּין עַל חַיֵּי נְפָשׁוֹת לֹא כׇּל שֶׁכֵּן.

Rabbi Yosei **came and said to them: Ben Bevai,** was responsible **for** the lowly function of **the shreds** of garments, **and if this** man, **who was appointed** to deal **with the wicks, merited to be listed with the greatest of that generation, you, who are appointed for life-sustaining** matters, **all the more so** are you **not** honored by the position? You should therefore accept the request without hesitation.

"בֶּן אַרְזָה עַל הַצִּלְצָל". כִּי הָא דִּתְנַן תַּמָּן: הֵנִיף הַסְּגָן בַּסּוּדָרִין, וְהִקִּישׁ בֶּן אַרְזָה עַל הַצִּלְצָל.

The mishna further taught that **ben Arza** was responsible **for the cymbal.**[B] The Gemara explains that this is referring to **that which we learned** in a mishna **there** (*Tamid* 33b): When the High Priest bent over to pour the wine libation, the **deputy** High Priest **waved the scarves** as a signal **and ben Arza beat upon the cymbal.**

"הוּגְרַס בֶּן לֵוִי עַל הַשִּׁיר". אָמַר רַבִּי אַחָא: נְעִימָה יְתֵירָה הָיָה יוֹדֵעַ. וְאָמְרוּ עָלָיו עַל הוּגְרַס בֶּן לֵוִי שֶׁהָיָה מַנְעִים אֶת קוֹלוֹ בַּזֶּמֶר, וּכְשֶׁהָיָה נוֹעֵץ גּוּדָלוֹ בְּתוֹךְ פִּיו הָיָה מוֹצִיא כַּמָּה מִינֵי זֶמֶר, וְהָיוּ כׇּל אֶחָיו הַכֹּהֲנִים נִזְקָרִין לוֹ בְּבַת רֹאשׁ.

The mishna states that **Hugras ben Levi** was responsible **for the song. Rabbi Aḥa said: He knew an extraordinary manner of singing. And they said of Hugras ben Levi that he would make his voice pleasant in song, and when he would stick his thumb into his mouth he could produce several types of music** simultaneously, **and all of his fellow priests would lurch toward him all at once,**[N] from the intensity and the charm of the sound.

NOTES

***Gever* cried out…the son of a rooster** – **קָרָא גַּבְרָא...בַּר תַּרְנְגוֹלָא**: This incident is cited at greater length in the Babylonian Talmud (*Yoma* 20b). Some commentaries maintain that it is simply a dispute concerning terminology that has no practical ramifications. Other authorities claim that this dispute bears on the precise time for the removal of the ashes from the altar in the Temple, as the rooster's cry occurs much earlier in the morning than the Temple crier's announcement (*Me'iri* on *Yoma* 20b). Although this issue is left undecided in tractate *Yoma*, here Rav cites a proof that the word means a man, as the official responsible for the Temple gates would certainly not be called the son of a rooster. Some derive from the ruling in the mishna (*Bava Kama* 79b) that roosters may not be raised in Jerusalem that there could not have been roosters in the capital, and therefore the phrase must refer to the Temple crier's announcement (see Rabbi Yair Bakhrakh on *Yoma* 20b).

Braid shreds together to prepare wicks – **מְזַיֵּיג פְּתִילוֹת**: Another interpretation is that ben Bevai was proficient at ensuring that all the wicks were of equal length (*Tiklin Ḥadatin*).

All at once – **בְּבַת רֹאשׁ**: This phrase literally means: With one head. Alternatively, it is explained that when Hugras, who supervised the other singers, would produce his extraordinary music, the other priestly singers would join in, bending back their heads in an effort to raise their voices. This explains the reference to their heads (*Maharsha* on *Yoma* 38b).

״בֵּית גַּרְמוּ עַל מַעֲשֵׂה לֶחֶם הַפָּנִים״. בֵּית גַּרְמוּ הָיוּ בְּקִיאִין בְּמַעֲשֵׂה לֶחֶם הַפָּנִים וּבִרְדִיָּיתוֹ, וְלֹא רָצוּ לְלַמֵּד.

§ The mishna mentioned that **the house of Garmu** was responsible **for the preparation of the shewbread,** which is the bread baked each week in a special form and displayed for a week on the designated table in the Sanctuary. The Gemara relates a story from a *baraita* about the house of Garmu and their talent in baking. **The house of Garmu was proficient in the preparation of the shewbread and in its removal** from the oven without ruining it, **but they did not want to teach** these skills to others.

שָׁלְחוּ חֲכָמִים וְהֵבִיאוּ אוּמָּנִים מֵאֲלֶכְּסַנְדְּרִיאָה, שֶׁהָיוּ בְּקִיאִין בְּמַעֲשֵׂה לֶחֶם הַפָּנִים, וּבִרְדִיָּיתוֹ לֹא הָיוּ בְּקִיאִין.

Therefore, **the Sages sent** messengers **and brought in craftsmen from Alexandria,**[B] **who were** also **proficient in the preparation of the shewbread,** in an attempt to replace the house of Garmu. **However, they were not as proficient as** the house of Garmu **in its removal** from the oven. The complex form of the shewbread rendered it very difficult to remove from the oven without its breaking.

בֵּית גַּרְמוּ הָיוּ מַסִּיקִין מִבִּפְנִים וְרוֹדִין מִבַּחוּץ וְלֹא הָיְתָה מִתְעַפֶּשֶׁת, וְאֵלּוּ הָיוּ מַסִּיקִין מִבִּפְנִים וְרוֹדִין מִבִּפְנִים, וְהָיְתָה מִתְעַפֶּשֶׁת.

The Gemara clarifies the difference between the two manners of preparation. **The house of Garmu would ignite** the fire **within** the oven, bake the shewbread in a mold, **and remove** the bread from the mold only **outside** the oven, after it was fully baked. **And,** as they would remove it from the mold at this late stage, **it would not spoil. Whereas these** Egyptian craftsmen **would ignite** the fire **within** the oven and bake the shewbread in the mold, **but,** out of fear that it would break when removed from the mold, they would **remove** it from the mold **inside** the oven before it was fully baked. **And** the result was that the bread **would spoil.**

כֵּיוָן שֶׁיָּדְעוּ חֲכָמִים בַּדָּבָר הַזֶּה, אָמְרוּ: כָּל מַה שֶּׁבָּרָא הַקָּדוֹשׁ בָּרוּךְ הוּא – לִכְבוֹדוֹ בְּרָאוֹ, שֶׁנֶּאֱמַר ״כֹּל פָּעַל ה׳ לַמַּעֲנֵהוּ״.

Once the Sages realized this matter, that their replacement shewbread was flawed, **they said: Everything that the Holy One, Blessed be He, created, He created for His glory,** as it **is stated: "The Lord has made everything for His own purpose"** (Proverbs 16:4). Since spoiled shewbread does not promote the glory of God, we must forgo our honor and request the services of the house of Garmu once again.

שָׁלְחוּ אַחֲרֵיהֶם וְלֹא רָצוּ לָבֹא עַד שֶׁכָּפְלוּ לָהֶם שְׂכָרָן. שְׁנֵים עָשָׂר מָנֶה הָיוּ נוֹטְלִים, וְנָתְנוּ לָהֶם עֶשְׂרִים וְאַרְבָּעָה, רַבִּי יְהוּדָה אוֹמֵר: עֶשְׂרִים וְאַרְבָּעָה הָיוּ נוֹטְלִים, וְנָתְנוּ לָהֶן אַרְבָּעִים וּשְׁמוֹנָה.

Therefore, the Sages **sent for** the house of Garmu, **but they did not want to come** back to bake **until** the Sages **doubled their compensation. They had been receiving twelve** *maneh,* **and** now **they gave them twenty-four. Rabbi Yehuda says: They had been receiving twenty-four** *maneh,* **and** now **they gave them forty-eight.**

אָמְרוּ לָהֶן: מִפְּנֵי מָה אֵין אַתֶּם רוֹצִים לְלַמֵּד? אָמְרוּ לָהֶן: מָסוֹרֶת הִיא בְּיָדֵינוּ מֵאֲבוֹתֵינוּ שֶׁהַבַּיִת הַזֶּה עָתִיד לֵיחָרֵב, שֶׁלֹּא יִלְמְדוּ אֲחֵרִים וְיַעֲשׂוּ לִפְנֵי עֲבוֹדָה זָרָה שֶׁלָּהֶן. בִּדְבָרִים הַלָּלוּ מַזְכִּירִין אוֹתָן לְשֶׁבַח: שֶׁלֹּא יָצָא בְּיַד בְּנֵיהֶם פַּת נְקִיָּה מֵעוֹלָם, שֶׁלֹּא יְהוּ אוֹמְרִים מִמַּעֲשֵׂה לֶחֶם הַפָּנִים הֵן אוֹכְלִים.

The Sages **said to them: For what** reason **don't you want to teach** the art of shewbread baking to others? The house of Garmu **said to them: We have a tradition from our fathers that this House,** the Temple, **will be destroyed.** We do not want to teach our method, so **that others should not learn** this art and unscrupulously **perform** it **for their idolatry.** Although their reason for refraining from teaching their method to others was not accepted, **on this** other **matter** the Sages **did mention them with praise: That refined bread was never found in their children's possession at all,** so that people **should not say** that **they feast upon their shewbread labor.**

BACKGROUND

Alexandria – **אֲלֶכְּסַנְדְּרִיאָה:** This port city, which lies west of the Nile delta, was founded by Alexander the Great in 332 BCE. In its glory days, during the Ptolemaic rule in Egypt and until the end of the mishnaic period, Alexandria was one of the largest cities and cultural centers in the world. The greatest scientists, doctors, and artisans of the time lived in Alexandria, and Alexandrian doctors were renowned throughout the entire world. The Sages of the Talmud were very familiar with Alexandrian doctors and held them in high regard, often praising the medical accomplishments of this important urban center.

Bust of Alexander the Great near the Alexandria Library

Alexandria in relation to Eretz Yisrael and the lands surrounding it

Panoramic view of Alexandria

“בֵּית אַבְטִינָס עַל מַעֲשֵׂה הַקְּטוֹרֶת”. שֶׁל בֵּית אַבְטִינָס הָיוּ בְּקִיאִין עַל מַעֲשֵׂי פִּיטּוּם הַקְּטוֹרֶת וּבְמַעֲלֶה הֶעָשָׁן, וְלֹא רָצוּ לְלַמֵּד.

The mishna states that **the house of Avtinas** was responsible **for the preparation of the incense.** The Gemara relates a similar story from a *baraita* concerning the house of Avtinas and their knowledge of the incense preparation: **The house of Avtinas was proficient in the preparations of the incense mixture,** which included grinding the incense herbs and blending them together. And they were also expert in identifying the so-called **smoke raiser,**[BN] a plant that caused the incense smoke to rise upward in a straight line to the ceiling, **but they did not want to teach** these skills to others.

שָׁלְחוּ וְהֵבִיאוּ אוּמָּנִין מֵאָלֶכְּסַנְדְּרִיאָה שֶׁל מִצְרַיִם וְהָיוּ בְּקִיאִין בְּפִיטּוּם הַקְּטוֹרֶת, וּבְמַעֲלֶה עָשָׁן לֹא הָיוּ בְּקִיאִין. שֶׁל בֵּית אַבְטִינָס הָיְתָה מִתַּמֶּרֶת וְעוֹלָה כְּמַקֵּל וּפוֹסָה וְיוֹרֶדֶת. וְשֶׁל אֵלּוּ הָיְתָה פּוֹסָה מִיָּד.

Therefore, the Sages **sent** out messengers **and brought in craftsmen from Alexandria in Egypt. And** these craftsmen **were proficient in the incense mixture, but they were not proficient** in identifying **the smoke raiser.**[N] The incense smoke **of the house of Avtinas would rise straight up like a staff** to the ceiling, **and** from there it would **spread out** and **descend, whereas** the incense smoke **of these** Egyptian craftsmen **would** not rise but **would** simply **spread out immediately.**

כֵּיוָן שֶׁיָּדְעוּ חֲכָמִים בַּדָּבָר אָמְרוּ: כָּל מַה שֶּׁבָּרָא הַקָּדוֹשׁ בָּרוּךְ הוּא – לִכְבוֹדוֹ בָּרָא, שֶׁנֶּאֱמַר ״כֹּל הַנִּקְרָא בִשְׁמִי וְלִכְבוֹדִי בְּרָאתִיו״ וגו׳. שָׁלְחוּ אַחֲרֵיהֶם וְלֹא רָצוּ לָבֹא, עַד שֶׁכָּפְלוּ לָהֶן שְׂכָרָן. שְׁנֵים עָשָׂר מָנֶה הָיוּ נוֹטְלִין, וְנָתְנוּ לָהֶן עֶשְׂרִים וְאַרְבָּעָה. רַבִּי יְהוּדָה אוֹמֵר: עֶשְׂרִים וְאַרְבָּעָה הָיוּ נוֹטְלִין וְנָתְנוּ לָהֶן אַרְבָּעִים וּשְׁמוֹנָה.

Once the Sages realized this matter, that this incense smoke was flawed, **they said: Everything that the Holy One, Blessed be He, created, He created for His glory, as it is stated: “Everything that is called by My name, and I have created for My glory,** I have formed it and even made it” (Isaiah 43:7). Since incense smoke that rises straight up is superior, we must forgo our honor and request the services of the house of Avtinas once again. The Sages **sent for them, but they did not want to come back until they doubled their compensation. They had been receiving twelve *maneh,* and** now **they gave them twenty-four. Rabbi Yehuda says: They had been receiving twenty-four *maneh,* and** now **they gave them forty-eight.**

אָמְרוּ לָהֶן: מִפְּנֵי מָה אֵין אַתֶּם רוֹצִין לְלַמֵּד? אָמְרוּ לָהֶן: מָסוֹרֶת הִיא בְּיָדֵינוּ מֵאֲבוֹתֵינוּ שֶׁהַבַּיִת הַזֶּה עָתִיד לֵיחָרֵב, שֶׁלֹּא יִלְמְדוּ אֲחֵרִים וְיִהְיוּ עוֹשִׂין כֵּן לִפְנֵי עֲבוֹדָה זָרָה שֶׁלָּהֶן.

The Sages **said to them: For what** reason **don't you want to teach** the art of incense preparation to others? The house of Avtinas **said to them: We have a tradition from our fathers that this House,** the Temple, **will be destroyed.** We do not want to teach our method, so **that others should not learn** these skills **and prepare this** incense **for their idolatry.**

בַּדְּבָרִים הַלָּלוּ מַזְכִּירִין אוֹתָן לִשְׁבָח: שֶׁלֹּא יָצָאת אִשָּׁה מִשֶּׁל אֶחָד מֵהֶן מְבוּשֶּׂמֶת מֵעוֹלָם, וְלֹא עוֹד אֶלָּא כְּשֶׁהָיָה אֶחָד מֵהֶן נוֹשֵׂא אִשָּׁה מִמָּקוֹם אַחֵר הָיָה פּוֹסֵק עִמָּהּ עַל מְנָת שֶׁלֹּא תִּתְבַּשֵּׂם, שֶׁלֹּא יְהוּ אוֹמְרִים מִמַּעֲשֵׂה פִּיטּוּם הַקְּטוֹרֶת הֵן מִתְבַּשְּׂמוֹת, לְקַיֵּים מַה שֶּׁנֶּאֱמַר ״וִהְיִיתֶם נְקִיִּים מֵה׳ וּמִיִּשְׂרָאֵל״.

Although their reason for refraining from teaching their method to others was not accepted, **on these** other **matters** the Sages **did mention them with praise: That never did the wife of** any **one of them leave** her house **perfumed; and not only that, but when one of them would marry a woman from elsewhere, he would stipulate with her** that the marriage was **on condition that she** may **not perfume herself, so that** people **should not say** that **they perfume themselves from the preparation of the incense mixture.** They did so **to fulfill that which is stated: “Then you shall be clear before the Lord and before Israel”** (Numbers 32:22).

BACKGROUND

Smoke raiser – מַעֲלֵה עָשָׁן: As stated in the Gemara, the secret of this herb was guarded by the Avtinas family, and it was apparently lost in the years after the destruction of the Second Temple. A few attempts have been made to identify this plant, and the accepted view is that it is the plant called the desert smoke raiser, *Leptadenia pyrotechnica*. This bush has thin, green branches and is almost completely lacking in leaves. It grows up to 5 m in height and is found in the south of Eretz Yisrael, the southern Jordan Valley, and northern Sinai. The gray-white flowers of the desert smoke raiser are arranged in groups on one stem, called an inflorescence, and they bloom in the spring. Since the plant ignites extremely easily, Arabs once used it as gunpowder for rifles and cannons. If even one branch is lit, the entire bush ignites with astounding speed and creates an enormous flame that can reach up to a height of 10 m. It is conceivable that adding branches of this type to the incense would cause the smoke to rise vertically in a straight line, as depicted in the Talmud.

Desert smoke raiser

NOTES

Smoke raiser – מַעֲלֶה הֶעָשָׁן: This herb was known only to a few people, in particular the Avtinas family, as depicted here and in the Babylonian Talmud (*Yoma* 38a). The herb would cause the incense smoke to rise vertically in a straight line. The smoke raiser was used to fulfill an allusion from a verse that deals with Yom Kippur service: “For I appear in the cloud upon the Ark cover” (Leviticus 16:2). The Sages derived from here that the incense of the entire year must form a cloud over the Ark. Some later authorities maintain that the smoke raiser is an essential ingredient in the incense and one is liable to receive death at the hand of Heaven for leaving it out of the recipe, despite the fact that it is not listed in the verse (Exodus 30:35) among the ingredients of the incense (see *Yoma* 53a; *Mishne LaMelekh* on Rambam *Sefer Avoda, Hilkhot Kelei HaMikdash* 2:3).

And they were proficient in the incense mixture, but they were not proficient in the smoke raiser – וְהָיוּ בְּקִיאִין בְּפִיטּוּם הַקְּטוֹרֶת וּבְמַעֲלֶה עָשָׁן לֹא הָיוּ בְּקִיאִין: It has already been noted that it is inconceivable that these craftsmen were entirely unaware of the smoke raiser plant, as the Gemara (*Yoma* 38a) clearly states that any incense that lacks the smoke raiser is disqualified (*Tosafot Yeshanim* on *Yoma* 38a). However, it is possible that they did not know how to prepare the smoke raiser properly, or perhaps there were several plants suitable for this purpose and only the Avtinas family knew which was the best (see *Tosefot HaRosh* on *Yoma* 38a).

אָמַר רַבִּי יוֹסֵי: פַּעַם אַחַת הָיִיתִי עוֹמֵד בִּירוּשָׁלַיִם וּמָצָאתִי תִּינוֹק אֶחָד מִשֶּׁל בֵּית אַבְטִינָס, אָמַרְתִּי לוֹ: בְּנִי, מֵאֵיזוֹ מִשְׁפָּחָה אַתְּ? אָמַר לִי: מִמִּשְׁפַּחַת פְּלוֹנִי, אָמַרְתִּי לוֹ: בְּנִי, אֲבוֹתֶיךָ לְפִי שֶׁנִּתְכַּוְּונוּ לְרַבּוֹת כְּבוֹדָן וּלְמַעֵט כְּבוֹד שָׁמַיִם – לְפִיכָךְ כְּבוֹדָם נִתְמַעֵט, וּכְבוֹד שָׁמַיִם נִתְרַבָּה.

Rabbi Yosei said: Once I was standing in Jerusalem, and I found a certain child from the house of Avtinas. I said to him: My son, from which family are you? He said to me: I am **from a particular family,** i.e., the house of Avtinas. **I said to him: My son,** I will say this about **your forefathers: Since they intended to increase their own glory** by ensuring that none were as proficient as they at preparing incense and by demanding double their previous wages, **and they sought to reduce of the glory of Heaven** by taking money from the Temple coffers, **therefore** they were punished and ultimately **their glory was diminished,** as after the destruction of the Temple they lost their importance. **But the glory of Heaven increased,** for God's honor is not dependent upon the existence of the Temple.

אָמַר רַבִּי עֲקִיבָא: שָׂח לִי שִׁמְעוֹן בֶּן לוֹגָא, מְלַקֵּט הָיִיתִי עֲשָׂבִים אֲנִי וְתִינוֹק אֶחָד מִשֶּׁל בֵּית אַבְטִינָס וְרָאִיתִי אוֹתוֹ שֶׁבָּכָה, וְרָאִיתִי אוֹתוֹ שֶׁשָּׂחַק. אָמַרְתִּי לוֹ: בְּנִי, לָמָּה בָּכִיתָה? אָמַר לִי: עַל כָּבוֹד שֶׁל בֵּית אַבָּא שֶׁנִּתְמַעֵט. וְלָמָּה שָׂחַקְתָּה? אָמַר לִי: עַל הַכָּבוֹד הַמְתוּקָּן לַצַּדִּיקִים לֶעָתִיד לָבֹא.

Rabbi Akiva said: Shimon ben Loga told me: Once **I and a certain child from the house of Avtinas were collecting herbs, and I saw him crying,** and later **I saw him laughing. I said to him: My son, why did you cry? He said to me:** I cried **for the glory of my father's house, which has been diminished** after the destruction of the Temple. I subsequently asked him: **And why did you laugh? He said to me:** I laughed with joy **over the glory prepared for the righteous in the future,** when my family will have its role restored to them in the rebuilt Temple.

וּמָה רָאִיתָ – מַעֲלֶה עָשָׁן לְנֶגְדִּי. נוּמֵיתִי לוֹ: בְּנִי, הַרְאֵהוּ לִי! אָמַר לִי: רַבִּי, מָסוֹרֶת בְּיָדִי מֵאֲבוֹתַי שֶׁלֹּא לְהַרְאוֹתוֹ לַבְּרִיָּה.

Shimon ben Loga added that he asked that child further: **And what did you see** that brought these things to mind? He replied: I saw the **smoke raiser before me,** among the herbs we were collecting. **I said to him: My son, show it to me,** and I will keep its identity secret so that no one will be able to use it for idolatry. **He said to me: Rabbi, I have a tradition from my forefathers not to show it to a soul.**

אָמַר רַבִּי יוֹחָנָן בֶּן נוּרִי: (מְלַקֵּט הָיִיתִי עֲשָׂבִים אֲנִי וְזָקֵן אֶחָד) פָּגַע בִּי זָקֵן אֶחָד מִשֶּׁל בֵּית אַבְטִינָס וּמְגִילַּת סַמָּנִים בְּיָדוֹ, אָמַר לִי: רַבִּי, לְשֶׁעָבַר הָיוּ בֵּית אַבָּא צְנוּעִין וְהָיוּ

Similarly, **Rabbi Yoḥanan ben Nuri said:** Once **I and a certain elderly man were collecting herbs. I encountered a certain elderly man from the house of Avtinas with a scroll in his hand** with instructions on how to identify **herbs** for the Temple incense and how to prepare it. That elderly man **said to me: Rabbi, in the past** the members of my **father's house were discreet** [*tzenu'in*][N] and cautious. **And they would**

NOTES

Discreet [*tzenu'in*] – צְנוּעִין: The principal meaning of this Hebrew term is to hide or be discrete, which fits the context here. It has expanded to mean those who practice humility and modesty.

Perek **V**
Daf **14** Amud **b**

מוֹסְרִין אֶת הַמְּגִילָּה הַזֹּאת אֵלּוּ לְאֵלּוּ, וְעַכְשָׁיו שֶׁאֵינָן בֵּית אַבָּא נֶאֱמָנִים – הֵילָךְ אֶת הַמְּגִילָּה, וְהִזָּהֵר בָּהּ.

transfer this scroll only **to one another,** so that it would not come into the possession of anyone who might misuse its information. **And now that** the members of my **father's house are not reliable,** I am concerned that they might pass the scroll to the wrong person. I will not give it to one of them but only to someone whom I judge to be completely trustworthy. Therefore, **here** it is **for you,** as I can trust you to take **the scroll and be careful with it,** so that it will not reach anyone who might misuse its information.

וּכְשֶׁבָּאתִי וְהִרְצֵיתִי הַדְּבָרִים לִפְנֵי רַבִּי עֲקִיבָא זָלְגוּ עֵינָיו דְּמָעוֹת, וְאָמַר: מֵעַתָּה אֵין אָנוּ צְרִיכִין לְהַזְכִּירָן לִגְנַאי.

Rabbi Yoḥanan ben Nuri continued: **And when I came and recounted these matters to Rabbi Akiva, his eyes shed tears, and he said: From now on, we should not mention** the members of the house of Avtinas **unfavorably,** as it is evident that the only reason they did not teach their skills to others was due to the fear that someone might misuse them for idolatrous purposes.

"אֶלְעָזָר עַל הַפָּרוֹכֶת" – שֶׁהָיָה מְמוּנֶּה עַל אוֹרְגֵי פָּרוֹכֶת. "פִּנְחָס הַמַּלְבִּישׁ" – שֶׁהָיָה מַלְבִּישׁ בִּגְדֵי כְּהוּנָּה גְּדוֹלָה. מַעֲשֶׂה בְּכֹהֵן אֶחָד שֶׁהִלְבִּישׁ לְאִיסְטְרַטְיוֹת אֶחָד, וְנָתַן לוֹ שְׁמוֹנָה זְהוּבִים. וְאִית דְּאָמְרִין תְּרֵי עֲשַׂר יְהַב לֵיהּ.

The mishna states that **Elazar** was responsible **for the** Temple **curtains.** The Gemara explains **that** this means **he** was **the supervisor of** the Temple **curtain weavers.**[H] The mishna further teaches that **Pineḥas** was **the valet.** The Gemara states **that he would dress**[N] the High Priest in **the High Priestly vestments.**[HBN] The expertise of those appointed to this position was so great that there was **an incident involving a certain** valet **priest who dressed a certain** Roman **army officer** [*isteratiyot*],[LN] and the officer was so impressed with the manner in which he dressed him that **he gave him eight gold coins. And some say he gave him twelve** gold coins.

הלכה ב מתני׳ אֵין פּוֹחֲתִין מִשִּׁבְעָה אֲמַרְכּוֹלִין וּשְׁלֹשָׁה גִּזְבָּרִין. וְאֵין עוֹשִׂין שְׂרָרָה עַל הַצִּבּוּר פָּחוֹת מִשְּׁנַיִם. חוּץ מִבֶּן אֲחִיָּה שֶׁעַל חוֹלֵי מֵעַיִם, וְאֶלְעָזָר שֶׁעַל הַפָּרוֹכֶת, שֶׁאוֹתָן קִיבְּלוּ רוֹב הַצִּבּוּר עֲלֵיהֶן.

HALAKHA 2 · MISHNA **There must be no fewer than seven trustees** [*amarkolin*][L] **and three treasurers**[HN] appointed over the Temple administration. **And we do not appoint an authority over the public** comprised **of fewer than two**[H] people, **except for ben Aḥiyya,**[N] who was responsible **for** healing priests who suffered from **intestinal disease, and Elazar, who** was responsible **for the** weaving **of the** Temple **curtains.** The reason for these exceptions is **that the majority of the public accepted these men upon themselves** as officials who served without the assistance of even a single partner.

HALAKHA

Supervisor of the Temple curtain weavers – מְמוּנֶּה עַל אוֹרְגֵי פָּרוֹכֶת: The supervisor of the Temple curtains was in charge of all the curtain weavers and embroiderers. His job was to ensure that the curtains were ready for use in the Sanctuary and on the gates (Rambam *Sefer Avoda, Hilkhot Kelei HaMikdash* 7:16).

Dress him in the High Priestly vestments – מַלְבִּישׁ בִּגְדֵי כְּהוּנָּה גְּדוֹלָה: The supervisor of the priestly vestments would prepare the vestments of both common priests and the High Priest, and he was also in charge of the weaving of their garments. This supervisor had an office in the Temple. The Ra'avad identifies the holder of this office as Pineḥas the valet (Rambam *Sefer Avoda, Hilkhot Kelei HaMikdash* 7:20).

There must be no fewer than seven trustees and three treasurers – אֵין פּוֹחֲתִין מִשִּׁבְעָה אֲמַרְכּוֹלִין וּשְׁלֹשָׁה גִּזְבָּרִין: The authorities must appoint trustees, who are responsible for opening the Sanctuary, as well as treasurers, who are in charge of the collection and redemption of consecrated property. There must be no less than seven trustees and three treasurers. The Radbaz writes that this is merely the number of treasurers appointed over the collection of consecrated property, as the Rambam explicitly states. However, there were also thirteen officials responsible for the Temple gates, in accordance with the number of gates, as stated in the Gemara here and in tractate *Tamid* 27a (Rambam *Sefer Avoda, Hilkhot Kelei HaMikdash* 4:17).

And we do not appoint an authority over the public of fewer than two – וְאֵין עוֹשִׂין שְׂרָרָה עַל הַצִּבּוּר פָּחוֹת מִשְּׁנַיִם: With regard to money matters, e.g., the collection of charity for the indigent, the court may not appoint an authority over the public of fewer than two members. Since this prohibition is not due to a lack of trust, it is permitted to appoint one man as the treasurer for the charity fund after it has been collected. Furthermore, two brothers may be appointed as treasurers (Rambam *Sefer Zera'im, Hilkhot Mattenot Aniyyim* 9:5; *Shulḥan Arukh, Yoreh De'a* 256:3).

BACKGROUND

The High Priestly vestments – בִּגְדֵי כְּהוּנָּה גְּדוֹלָה: The garments worn by the High Priest were referred to as the eight vestments or the golden vestments (see Exodus 28). Four of them, the breastplate, the *ephod*, the robe, and the frontplate, were unique to the High Priest. The High Priest's other four vestments, the trousers, the tunic, the belt, and the miter, were similar to those worn by common priests. The Sages dispute whether the belt worn by the High Priest was identical to the one worn by common priests. It appears that the miters of the two types of priests differed, at least in the manner in which they were worn.

High Priest wearing the eight vestments

LANGUAGE

Roman army officer [*isteratiyot*] – אִיסְטְרַטְיוֹת: From the Greek στρατεία, *strateia*, whose many meanings include a group of soldiers, each of whom serve at a specific time, and army units sent to perform particular tasks in a war.

Trustees [*amarkolin*] – אֲמַרְכּוֹלִין: Apparently from the Persian hamārakara, an accountant. This official's job is to collect taxes and the like. Even in ancient times, this term probably referred not only to a treasurer but to any important official. Indeed, this is the meaning of the word in Aramaic translations of the Bible and in mishnaic Hebrew.

NOTES

That he would dress, etc. – שֶׁהָיָה מַלְבִּישׁ וכו׳: One interpretation is that Pineḥas would dress them in a most becoming manner, and this special method of dressing others was his unique area of expertise (*Penei Moshe*; *Shiklei Yosef*). Alternatively, Pineḥas was a tailor by trade. He would perform alterations on the priestly vestments in accordance with the precise measurements of each individual priest, so that the priests would appear like angels (Rash Sirilio).

That he would dress him in the High Priestly vestments – שֶׁהָיָה מַלְבִּישׁ בִּגְדֵי כְּהוּנָּה גְּדוֹלָה: The Rambam, in his Commentary on the Mishna, and Rabbi Ovadya Bartenura indicate that Pineḥas would also dress the other priests and was responsible for undressing them when they completed their Temple service. Likewise, he stored their garments, as can be inferred from a mishna (*Middot* 1:4; see Rash Sirilio; see Rosh; Rambam *Sefer Avoda, Hilkhot Kelei HaMikdash* 7:20). Other commentaries maintain that Pineḥas was responsible only for dressing the High Priest (*Yefe Mareh*).

Who dressed a certain Roman army officer [*isteratiyot*] – שֶׁהִלְבִּישׁ לְאִיסְטְרַטְיוֹת אֶחָד: Although there is a general principle that one who makes personal use of the priesthood has misused consecrated property (see Jerusalem Talmud, *Berakhot* 8:5), this priest was permitted to use his unique skills and dress the military officer because the priest may waive the right not to have to serve others when he benefits from the use of his services (*Matta Dirushalem*). Nevertheless, this case remains problematic, as the dressing of a Roman soldier in priestly vestments should certainly be considered misuse of consecrated property. Some commentaries explain that the priest did not in fact dress the soldier in priestly vestments, but rather dressed him in his own military uniform, but in such a special manner that the soldier was impressed and paid him a large sum of money. Yet others interpret the term *isteratiyot* differently, claiming that it refers to the priestly vestments. In their opinion, the Gemara is speaking of a priest who dressed the High Priest in his vestments, and therefore there is no question of any misuse of consecrated property (*Rabbeinu Meshullam*; *Talmid HaRashbash*).

Trustees [*amarkolin*]…treasurers – אֲמַרְכּוֹלִין...גִּזְבָּרִין: Trustees and treasurers are the names of Temple officials who supervise the safeguarding of Temple property and its treasuries. The Sages derived from the verse: "That they may be joined to you, and minister to you" (Numbers 18:2), that one must appoint trustees and treasurers (*Sifrei*, *Koraḥ* 116). The treasurer is subordinate to the trustee, and sometimes several treasurers are subordinate to a single trustee.

The word in Aramaic for a trustee, *amarkolin*, is interpreted homiletically to mean: He who decrees all [*amar kol*] (*Horayot* 13a). See Rashi in *Horayot*, who states that the *amarkolin* is the highest supervisor, and no one has authority to contradict his words. Alternatively, *amarkolin* can be read as *mar al kol*, master of all (*Tosefta*, *Shekalim* 2:15), an interpretation that emphasizes his executive position. Indeed, there is a dispute between the Babylonian Talmud and the Jerusalem Talmud with regard to whether the trustee, who was a permanent official, outranked the head of the priestly watch of any particular week or the head of the family serving on a particular day. According to the Jerusalem Talmud (*Horayot* 3:5), the trustee is subordinate to the head of the watch and to the head of the patrilineal family, while the Babylonian Talmud (*Horayot* 13a) states that the trustee is the more senior position. The Rambam rules according to the latter opinion (*Sefer Avoda, Hilkhot Kelei HaMikdash* 4:19).

And we do not appoint an authority…fewer than two except for ben Aḥiyya, etc. – וְאֵין עוֹשִׂין שְׂרָרָה...פָּחוֹת מִשְּׁנַיִם חוּץ מִבֶּן אֲחִיָּה וכו׳: Apart from ben Aḥiyya and Elazar, all the other officials mentioned in the mishna served along with at least one other official, although the mishna lists only the most important of them (Rash Sirilio; *Tiklin Ḥadatin*).

גמ׳ ״אין פוחתין משלשה גזברין ומשבעה אמרכולין״. תני: משני כתליקין.

GEMARA The mishna states that **there must be no fewer than three treasurers and seven trustees.** The Gemara states that **it was** likewise **taught** in a *baraita* that there must be no fewer **than two executive supervisors** [***katalikin***].[LH]

הדא הוא דכתיב ״ויחיאל ועזזיהו ונחת״ – גזברין, ״ועשהאל וירימות ויזבד ואליאל ויסמכיהו ומחת ובניהו״ – אמרכולין, ״פקידים מיד כוננהו ושמעי אחיו״ – קתיליקין, ״במפקד יחזקיהו המלך ועזריהו נגיד בית אלהים״ – המלך וכהן גדול.

This is as it is written in the verse that lists the men who supervised the receipt of *teruma* and tithes from the public and their distribution to the priests and the Levites, as well as the receipt of items dedicated to the Temple: **"And Jehiel, and Azaziah, and Nahath,"** these were the **treasurers; "and Asahel, and Jerimoth, and Jozabad, and Eliel, and Ismachiah, and Mahath, and Benaiah,"** these were the **trustees; "overseers under the hand of Conaniah and Shimei his brother,"** these were **executive supervisors; "by the appointment of Hezekiah the king and Azariah the ruler of the House of God,"** they were **the king and the High Priest**, the most senior officials (II Chronicles 31:13).

כשהוא חותם – הגזבר חותם ונותנו לאמרכול, אמרכל חותם ונותנו לקתליקון, קתליקון חותם ונותנו לכהן גדול, כהן גדול חותם ונותנו למלך.

These officials participated in the supervision of the Temple assets, according to the level and status of their positions. **When he would seal** an item to store in the treasury until it would be needed, **the treasurer** would first **seal** it with his own seal; **and** subsequently **give it to a trustee;** the **trustee** would **seal** it **and give it to an executive supervisor;** the **executive supervisor** would **seal** it **and give it to the High Priest;** and the **High Priest** would **seal** it **and give it to the king,** who would place the final seal.

וכשהוא מתיר, המלך רואה חותמו ומתיר, כהן גדול רואה חותמו ומתיר, קתליקין רואה חותמו ומתיר, אמרכל רואה חותמו ומתיר, גזבר רואה חותמו ומתיר.

And when a treasurer wanted to **release** an item for usage, the reverse order was followed: First **the king** would **examine his seal and release** the restriction on the item; the **High Priest** would **examine his seal and release** it; the **executive supervisor** would **examine his seal and release** it; the **trustee** would **examine his seal and release** it; and finally the **treasurer** would **examine his seal and release** it.

״אין עושין שררה על הצבור בממון פחות משנים״. רב נחמן בשם רבי מנא: על שם ״והם יקחו את הזהב ואת התכלת ואת הארגמן״.

The mishna states that **we do not appoint an authority over the public, in monetary matters,** comprised **of fewer than two** appointees. **Rav Naḥman** said **in the name of Rabbi Mana:** This principle is derived **on the basis of** a verse that is referring to those engaged in building the Tabernacle and weaving the priestly vestments, who received the community's donations: **"And they shall take the gold, and the sky blue wool, and the purple wool"** (Exodus 28:5). The plural "they" indicates that this authority must consist of at least two people.

אמר רבי חמא בי רבי חנינא: מפסולת של לוחות העשיר משה, הדא הוא דכתיב ״פסל לך שני לוחות אבנים״ – פסל לך, שתהא הפסולת שלך. אמר רבי חנין: מחצב של אבנים טובות ומרגליות ברא לו הקדוש ברוך הוא מתוך אהלו, וממנו העשיר משה.

Rabbi Ḥama, son of Rabbi Ḥanina, said: Although Moses supervised the building of the Tabernacle, he took nothing for himself from the community donations, as **Moses grew wealthy**[N] only **from the shavings** that broke off during the chiseling process **of the** second **tablets.**[N] **This is as it is written: "Hew for yourself two tablets of stone"** (Exodus 34:1). **"Hew [*pesol*] for yourself"** indicates that **the shavings [*pesolet*] shall be yours. Rabbi Ḥanin said: The Holy One, Blessed be He, created a quarry of precious stones and pearls for** Moses **inside his tent, and** Moses **grew wealthy from that** source.

כתיב ״והביטו אחרי משה עד בואו האוהלה״ תרין אמוראין, חד אמר לגנאי וחד אמר לשבח.

It is written: "And it came to pass when Moses went out to the Tent, that all the people rose up, and stood, every man at his tent door, **and looked after Moses, until he had gone into the Tent"** (Exodus 33:8). **Two** *amora'im* interpreted this verse with regard to Moses' wealth, but in opposite ways. **One said:** The people looked at Moses **unfavorably; while the other said:** The people looked at Moses **favorably.**

LANGUAGE

Executive supervisors [*katalikin*] – כתליקין: From the Greek καθολικός, *katholikos*, meaning the supervisor or general. In the Roman Empire, this term referred to the senior supervisor of the treasury and economic matters. In this context, it indicates a supervisor who is superior to the trustees and is responsible for the Temple treasury.

HALAKHA

Two executive supervisors – שני כתליקין: In addition to the trustees and the treasurers, the authorities would also appoint executive supervisors who ranked just below the deputy High Priest. There must be at least two executive supervisors (Rambam *Sefer Avoda, Hilkhot Kelei HaMikdash* 4:17).

NOTES

Moses grew wealthy – העשיר משה: The reason it is necessary for a prophet to be rich is to ensure that he will have influence on people and will not be ignored, as King Solomon stated: "The poor man's wisdom is despised, and his words are not heard" (Ecclesiastes 9:16; see Rabbi Zalman Sorotzkin, *Oznayim LaTorah*).

Moses grew wealthy from the shavings of the tablets – מפסולת של לוחות העשיר משה: The commentaries wonder: How, then, could Moses have served as a prophet before he became rich? Doesn't the Gemara state that God selects as His prophet only one who is brave, rich, wise, and modest, and this idea is derived from the case of Moses (*Nedarim* 38a)? The answer given is that Moses was indeed wealthy before he chiseled the tablets, but when he learned of the donations necessary for the construction of the Tabernacle and its vessels he gave all his wealth to that cause, as described in the midrash. Consequently, Moses required the shavings of the tablets to grow wealthy once again (*Ya'arot Devash*, part 1, lecture 2).

מַאן דְּאָמַר לִגְנַאי: חֲמוּן שָׁקִין, חֲמוּן כְּרָעִין, חֲמוּן קוּפָּד, אָכֵיל מִן דִּיהוּדָאֵי וְשָׁתֵי מִן דִּיהוּדָאֵי, כָּל מַדְלֵיהּ מִן דִּיהוּדָאֵי. וּמַאן דְּאָמַר לִשְׁבָח: מֶחֱמֵי צַדִּיקַיָּא וּמְזַכֵּי טוּבַיָּא דְּזָכַת לְמֶיחֱמֵי יָתֵיהּ.

He who said that the people looked at Moses **unfavorably** maintains that they said: **Look at his legs, look at his feet, look at his flesh.** See how healthy they are. All that **he eats** comes **from us Jews,** all that **he drinks** comes **from us Jews,** and **all of his assets** are taken **from us Jews. And the one who said** that they looked at Moses **favorably** maintains that the people were not responding to Moses' wealth but simply wanted to see the righteous man, saying: We desire to **view the righteous, and one who merits to view** Moses **earns great** rewards.

הלכה ג מתני׳ אַרְבָּעָה חוֹתָמוֹת הָיוּ בַּמִּקְדָּשׁ וְכָתוּב עֲלֵיהֶן: עֵגֶל, זָכָר, גְּדִי, וְחוֹטֵא. בֶּן עַזַּאי אוֹמֵר: חֲמִשָּׁה הָיוּ, וַאֲרָמִית כָּתוּב עֲלֵיהֶן: עֵגֶל, דְּכַר, גְּדִי, חוֹטֵא דַּל, וְחוֹטֵא עָשִׁיר.

HALAKHA 3 · MISHNA This mishna provides details of the functions performed by Yoḥanan ben Pineḥas and Aḥiyya, the officials mentioned in the first mishna of this chapter, which concerns the seals and libations. **There were four seals in the Temple**[H] that confirmed that the bearer had paid for the libations that accompanied his offering. **And** one of the following inscriptions was **written on them: Calf; male,**[N] i.e., a ram; **kid; and sinner,**[N] i.e., a leper, as leprosy is a punishment for one of seven sins (see *Arakhin* 16a). Conversely, **ben Azzai says: There were five** seals, **and** the following was **written upon them** in **Aramaic,** not Hebrew: **Calf, male, kid, poor sinner, and rich sinner.**

עֵגֶל מְשַׁמֵּשׁ עִם נִסְכֵּי בָקָר, גְּדוֹלִים וּקְטַנִּים, זְכָרִים וּנְקֵבוֹת. גְּדִי מְשַׁמֵּשׁ עִם נִסְכֵּי הַצֹּאן, גְּדוֹלִים וּקְטַנִּים, זְכָרִים וּנְקֵבוֹת, חוּץ מִשֶּׁל אֵילִים. אַיִל מְשַׁמֵּשׁ עִם נִסְכֵּי אֵילִים בִּלְבַד. חוֹטֵא מְשַׁמֵּשׁ עִם נִסְכֵּי שָׁלֹשׁ בְּהֵמוֹת שֶׁל מְצוֹרָע.

The mishna explains the significance of each of the four aforementioned seals. The **calf** seal **serves** as a payment receipt **for libations of cattle** offerings, whether they are **large or small, male or female,** as all offerings from the cow family are accompanied by the same libation. The **kid** seal **serves for libations of sheep** or goat offerings, whether **large or small, male or female, except for those of rams** aged thirteen months and older. The **ram** seal, which was earlier called the male seal, **serves exclusively for ram libations.** The **sinner** seal **serves for libations of the three animal** offerings **of a leper,** for the completion of his purification.

מִי שֶׁהוּא מְבַקֵּשׁ נְסָכִים הוֹלֵךְ לוֹ אֵצֶל יוֹחָנָן שֶׁהוּא מְמוּנֶּה עַל הַחוֹתָמוֹת. וְנוֹתֵן לוֹ מָעוֹת וּמְקַבֵּל מִמֶּנּוּ חוֹתָם. בָּא לוֹ אֵצֶל אֲחִיָּיה שֶׁהוּא מְמוּנֶּה עַל הַנְּסָכִים, וְנוֹתֵן לוֹ חוֹתָם וּמְקַבֵּל מִמֶּנּוּ נְסָכִים.

One who seeks libations for his offering **goes**[H] **to Yoḥanan,** the official **who was responsible for the seals, and gives him** the appropriate sum of **money and receives a seal from him.** With that seal **he** subsequently **comes to Aḥiyya, who was responsible for the libations, and gives him** Yoḥanan's **seal and receives** his **libations from him.**

לָעֶרֶב בָּאִין זֶה אֵצֶל זֶה, וַאֲחִיָּיה מוֹצִיא אֶת הַחוֹתָמוֹת וּמְקַבֵּל כְּנֶגְדָּן מָעוֹת. אִם פָּחֲתוּ – פָּחֲתוּ לוֹ, וִישַׁלֵּם יוֹחָנָן מִבֵּיתוֹ. וְאִם הוֹתִירוּ – הוֹתִירוּ לַהֶקְדֵּשׁ, שֶׁיַּד הֶקְדֵּשׁ עַל הָעֶלְיוֹנָה.

In the evening, Yoḥanan and Aḥiyya **would get together** to reconcile their accounts, **and Aḥiyya would take out the seals** he had received **and accept the money** Yoḥanan had received **in exchange for them. If** the money **was less** than the value of the seals, **they were less to him,** i.e., Yoḥanan would bear the loss, **and Yoḥanan would** have to **pay** the difference to the Temple treasury **from his own** property. **And if** there was some money **left over,** i.e., the total money was greater than the value of the seals, **they were left over to** the benefit of **the Temple treasury of consecrated property, as the Temple treasury** always **has the upper hand.**

מִי שֶׁאָבַד חוֹתָמוֹ מַמְתִּינִין לוֹ עַד הָעֶרֶב, וְאִם מָצְאוּ לוֹ כְּדֵי חוֹתָמוֹ – נוֹתְנִין לוֹ. וְאִם לָאו – לֹא הָיוּ נוֹתְנִין לוֹ וְשֵׁם הַיּוֹם כָּתוּב עֲלֵיהֶן, מִפְּנֵי הָרַמָּאִין.

With regard to **one who lost his seal** that he purchased from Yoḥanan, Yoḥanan and **Aḥiyya would wait to** resolve **his** problem **until the evening. And** when they added their accounts in the evening, **if they found for him** a surplus of money **equivalent to** the value of **his seal, they would give him** the corresponding libations. **And if not, they would not give him** libations. **And the name of the day** of the week **was written upon** the seals **because of the cheats.** They might try to use old seals that had been lost by the Temple officials or by someone who had brought an offering at an earlier date, so as to receive libations in a deceitful manner.

HALAKHA

There were four seals in the Temple, etc. – **אַרְבָּעָה חוֹתָמוֹת הָיוּ בַּמִּקְדָּשׁ וכו׳**: There were four seals in the Temple. On the first, the word calf was inscribed; on the second, male; on the third, kid; and on the fourth, sinner. This is in accordance with the opinion of the first *tanna* (Rambam *Sefer Avoda, Hilkhot Kelei HaMikdash* 7:11).

One who seeks libations goes, etc. – **מִי שֶׁהוּא מְבַקֵּשׁ נְסָכִים הוֹלֵךְ וכו׳**: Any individual who brought a private offering to the Temple would pay libation fees to the official responsible for the seals. That official would give him the appropriate seal for his offering. For example, if he brought the offerings of a rich leper, the official would give him a seal on which was written: Sinner. He would take that seal to the official responsible for the libations, who would give him the corresponding libations.

Every evening these two officials would meet and compare the number of seals with the total amount of money. If there was a surplus of money, it was used for the benefit of the Temple treasury of consecrated property. If money was missing, the official responsible for the seals would pay the difference to the Temple treasury from his own pocket. If someone lost their seal, he had to wait until the evening for the two officials to compare their accounts. If they found a surplus of money equal to the value of the seal he claimed he lost, they would give him libations of the value of that seal. If not, they would not give him anything. The name of the day of the week was written on each seal, to prevent cheats from acquiring seals when libations are inexpensive and storing them until they increased in value (Rambam *Sefer Avoda, Hilkhot Kelei HaMikdash* 7:12).

NOTES

Calf, male, etc. – **עֵגֶל זָכָר וכו׳**: Since the amounts of the libation offerings, which included fine flour, wine, and oil, were not identical for the various types of offerings, a separate seal was required for each type. The calf seal entitled its bearer to a meal-offering of three *isaron* of fine flour and one half of a *hin* each of wine and oil. The male seal entitled its bearer to a meal-offering of two *isaron* of fine flour and one-third of a *hin* each of wine and oil. Finally, the kid seal entitled its bearer to a meal-offering of one *isaron* of fine flour and one quarter of a *hin* each of wine and oil.

Sinner [*ḥoteh*] – **חוֹטֵא**: Another interpretation is that this term is referring to *ḥitui*, ritual purification, e.g., "And he shall take to purify [*leḥatei*] the house" (Leviticus 14:49) and "And he shall purify [*veḥitei*] the house" (Leviticus 14:52).

גמ׳ וּכְבֶן עַזַּאי חוֹטֵא דַּל לָמָּה? הָיָה מֵבִיא לוּגּוֹ עִמּוֹ. בְּרַם כְּרַבָּנַן, מֵבִיא גְּדִי.

GEMARA The Gemara asks: **And according to** the opinion of **ben Azzai, why** was it necessary to have a seal labeled **poor sinner?** The Gemara answers: Ben Azzai maintains that a poor leper **would** have to **bring his** *log*[B] of oil **with him.** This is referring to the additional oil required for the leper's purification (Leviticus 14:15–18), some of which is sprinkled on the altar while the rest is applied to the leper's ear, thumb, big toe, and head. According to ben Azzai, a leper would purchase this additional oil from Aḥiyya, and therefore he required a separate seal for each *log* of oil. **However, according to** the opinion of **the Rabbis,** a poor leper **brings** only the **kid** seal purchased from Yoḥanan, by which he receives the oil for his meal offering, and he must use his own private oil for the additional *log*.

BACKGROUND

Log – לוֹג: This is the basic liquid measure used by the Sages. It is equivalent to the volume of six eggs, one quarter of a *kav*, or one twenty-fourth of a *se'a*. A range of modern opinions estimates this volume to be 300–600 ml.

נִסְכֵּי רָחֵל מָה? מִן מַה דְּתָנֵינַן גְּדִי מְשַׁמֵּשׁ נִסְכֵּי צֹאן גְּדוֹלִים וּקְטַנִּים זְכָרִים וּנְקֵבוֹת, הָדָא אָמְרִי נִסְכֵּי רָחֵל כְּנִסְכֵּי גְּדִי. דִּכְתִיב ״כָּכָה יֵעָשֶׂה לַשּׁוֹר הָאֶחָד אוֹ לָאַיִל הָאֶחָד אוֹ לַשֶּׂה בַכְּבָשִׂים אוֹ בָעִזִּים״,

The mishna mentions only the libations for kids, referring to both sheep and goats that are less than one year old, and for rams, which are adult male sheep. The Gemara asks: **What** amounts are brought for **the libations of a lamb,** i.e., a female sheep in its second year? Are they the same as those of a kid or a ram? The Gemara answers that this *halakha* may be inferred **from that which we learned** in the mishna, that the **kid** seal **serves for libations of sheep** offerings, whether **large or small, male or female. That** ruling **says,** i.e., indicates, that **the libations of a lamb are like the libations of a kid.** The Gemara adds that this is derived from a verse that equates the two libations, **as it is written: "Thus shall it be done for each bull, or for each ram, or for each of the lambs, or of the kids"** (Numbers 15:11).

״לַשּׁוֹר הָאֶחָד״ לָמָּה נֶאֱמַר – מַגִּיד שֶׁלֹּא חִילֵּק בֵּין נִסְכֵּי עֵגֶל לְנִסְכֵּי שׁוֹר. שֶׁהָיָה בַּדִּין בֶּן הַצֹּאן טָעוּן נְסָכִים וּבֶן הַבָּקָר טָעוּן נְסָכִים, אִם מָצָאנוּ שֶׁחִילֵּק בֵּין נִסְכֵּי כֶּבֶשׂ לְנִסְכֵּי אַיִל,

The Gemara inquires further: **Why is it stated: For each bull?** The verse **teaches that** The Torah **does not differentiate between the libations of a calf,** which is less than a year old, **and the libations of a bull,** which is at least one year old. The Gemara explains: This is **because it was fitting** to differentiate between them, in light of the fact that both **the offspring of a sheep requires libations and the offspring of a cow requires libations. If we find that** the Torah **differentiates between the libations of a sheep** in its first year, whose meal offering is one *isaron* of fine flour, **and the libations of a ram,** a male sheep thirteen months old and older, whose meal-offering is two *isaron*,

Perek **V**
Daf **15** Amud **a**

לְכָךְ נַחֲלוֹק בֵּין נִסְכֵּי עֵגֶל לְנִסְכֵּי שׁוֹר, תַּלְמוּד לוֹמַר ״כָּכָה יֵעָשֶׂה לַשּׁוֹר הָאֶחָד״ – מַגִּיד שֶׁלֹּא חִילֵּק בֵּין נִסְכֵּי עֵגֶל לְנִסְכֵּי שׁוֹר,

then we should likewise **differentiate between the libations of** a **calf and the libations of a bull.** In order to indicate that this is not the case, **the** aforementioned **verse states: "Thus shall it be done for each bull,"** which **teaches that** the Torah **does not differentiate between the libations of a calf and the libations of a bull.**

״אוֹ לָאַיִל״ לָמָּה נֶאֱמַר? שֶׁהָיָה בְּדִין, אִם מָצָאנוּ שֶׁחִילֵּק בֵּין נִסְכֵּי בֶּן שָׁנָה לְנִסְכֵּי בֶּן שְׁנָתַיִים, לְכָךְ נַחֲלוֹק בֵּין נִסְכֵּי שְׁנָתַיִים לְנִסְכֵּי שָׁלֹשׁ – תַּלְמוּד לוֹמַר ״אוֹ לָאַיִל הָאֶחָד״.

The Gemara asks: **Why does** the verse **state: "Or for each ram,"** as the details of the ram libations were specified in the previous verses (Numbers 15:6–7)? The Gemara explains that this verse is necessary **because it would be fitting** to argue as follows: **If we have found that** the Torah **differentiated between the libations of a one-year-old** sheep **and the libations of a two-year-old** sheep, i.e., a sheep in its second year, which is already called a ram, **then we** should **differentiate between the libations of** a two-year-old **and the libations of** a three-year-old ram. In order to indicate that this is not the case, **the verse states: "Or for each ram,"** which teaches that the libations for rams of all ages are identical.

״אוֹ לַשֶּׂה בַכְּבָשִׂים״ לָמָּה נֶאֱמַר? שֶׁהָיָה בְּדִין, אִם מָצָאנוּ שֶׁחִילֵּק בֵּין נִסְכֵּי כֶּבֶשׂ לְנִסְכֵּי אַיִל, לְכָךְ נַחֲלוֹק בֵּין נִסְכֵּי כִּשְׂבָּה לְנִסְכֵּי רָחֵל – תַּלְמוּד לוֹמַר ״אוֹ לַשֶּׂה בַכְּבָשִׂים״.

The Gemara similarly asks: **Why does** the verse **state: "Or for each of the lambs,"** as the details of the lamb libations were provided in the previous verses (Numbers 15:4–5)? The Gemara explains that this phrase is necessary **because it would be fitting** to argue as follows: **If we have found that** the Torah **differentiated between the libations of a lamb** in its first year **and the libations of ram** that is thirteen months or older, **then we** should likewise **differentiate between the libations of** a full-grown ewe in its second year **and the libations of a female lamb** in its first year. In order to indicate that this is not the case, **the verse states: "Or for each of the lambs,"** which teaches that the libations for female sheep of all ages are identical.

״אוֹ בָעִזִּים״ לָמָּה נֶאֱמַר? שֶׁהָיָה בַדִּין, אִם מָצָאנוּ שֶׁחִלֵּק בֵּין נִיסְכֵי כֶבֶשׂ לְנִסְכֵי אַיִל, לְכָךְ נַחֲלוֹק בֵּין נִסְכֵי גְּדִי לְנִסְכֵי תַיִשׁ – תַּלְמוּד לוֹמַר ״אוֹ בָעִזִּים״ – הִקִּישׁ קָטָן שֶׁבָּעִזִּים לְגָדוֹל שֶׁבַּתְּיָשִׁים, מַה זֶּה בִּשְׁלֹשֶׁת לוּגִּין אַף זֶה בִּשְׁלֹשֶׁת לוּגִּין.

The Gemara continues: **Why does the verse state: "Or of the goats,"** which are also part of the sheep family? The Gemara explains that this phrase is necessary **because it would be fitting** to argue as follows: **If we have found that** the Torah **differentiated between the libations of a lamb** in its first year **and the libations of a ram** that is thirteen months or old, **then we** should likewise **differentiate between the libations of a kid,** a young goat, **and the libations of a full-grown goat.** In order to indicate that this is not the case, **the verse states: "Or of the kids,"** and thereby **juxtaposes** the libations for **the youngest of the kids and** those of **the oldest of the goats: Just as** the libations of **this** young kid consist **of three *log*** of wine, **so too,** the libations of **that** full-grown goat consist **of three *log*.**

״וְשֵׁם הַיּוֹם כָּתוּב״ כו׳. הַגַּע בְּעַצְמְךָ שֶׁזִּיֵּיג אוֹתוֹ הַיּוֹם! ״שֵׁם מִשְׁמָר הָיָה כָּתוּב עָלָיו״.

The mishna states: **And the name of the day** of the week **was written** upon the seals, to deter cheats. The Gemara points out a problem: **Consider** the following situation **yourself.** Suppose **that** a cheat found a seal and circumvented this precaution by waiting until the same day the next week, at which point he could **match up** [*ziyyeig*][L] his seal with **that day.** He would be able to collect the libations deceitfully a week later. The Gemara answers: **The name of the priestly watch**[N] that served in the Temple that week **was** also **written on it,** as each watch serves in the Temple only twice a year.

הַגַּע בְּעַצְמְךָ שֶׁזִּיֵּיג אוֹתוֹ הַמִּשְׁמָר! שֵׁם הַיּוֹם, שֵׁם שַׁבָּת, שֵׁם חוֹדֶשׁ הָיָה כָּתוּב עֲלֵיהֶן. אֲפִילוּ רוֹצֶה לְזַיֵּיג אֵין מָצוּי לְזַיֵּיג.

The Gemara retorts that even this is not a sufficient precaution. After all, **consider** for **yourself that** a cheat can wait half a year and **match up** with **that watch** and collect the libations. The Gemara explains that **the name of the day; the name,** i.e., the number, **of the week** within the month; and **the name of the month were** all **written on it.** Consequently, **even if** a cheat **wanted to match up** the seal with a similar day, **there is no** identical day to be **found** with which **to match** it **up.**

הלכה ד מתני׳ שְׁתֵּי לְשָׁכוֹת הָיוּ בַּמִּקְדָּשׁ, אַחַת לִשְׁכַּת חֲשָׁאִין וְאַחַת לִשְׁכַּת הַכֵּלִים. לִשְׁכַּת חֲשָׁאִין – יִרְאֵי חֵטְא נוֹתְנִין לְתוֹכָהּ בַּחֲשַׁאי, וַעֲנִיִּים בְּנֵי טוֹבִים מִתְפַּרְנְסִין מִתּוֹכָהּ בַּחֲשַׁאי.

HALAKHA 4 · MISHNA **There were two** special **chambers in the Temple, one** called **the chamber of secret** gifts **and the** other **one** called **the chamber of vessels.**[H] The mishna explains the purpose of these chambers. In **the chamber of secret** gifts, **sin-fearing people put** money **secretly and poor people of noble descent support themselves from it secretly.**

לִשְׁכַּת הַכֵּלִים – כָּל מִי שֶׁהוּא מִתְנַדֵּב כְּלִי זוֹרְקוֹ לְתוֹכָהּ. וְאַחַת לִשְׁלֹשִׁים יוֹם הַגִּזְבָּרִין פּוֹתְחִין אוֹתָהּ, וְכָל כְּלִי שֶׁמָּצְאוּ בוֹ צוֹרֶךְ לְבֶדֶק הַבַּיִת – מַנִּיחִין אוֹתוֹ, וְהַשְּׁאָר נִמְכָּרִין וּדְמֵיהֶן נוֹפְלִין לְבֶדֶק הַבַּיִת.

With regard to **the chamber of vessels, anyone who donates a vessel** to the Temple **drops it inside** that chamber, **and once every thirty days the treasurers open it. And any vessel that they found for it a use for Temple maintenance, they leave it** for that purpose, **and the rest are sold, and their monetary** value is **allocated to Temple maintenance.**

גמ׳ רַבִּי יַעֲקֹב בַּר אִידִי וְרַבִּי יִצְחָק בַּר נַחְמָן הֲווֹן פַּרְנָסִים, וַהֲווֹן יָהֲבִין לְרַבִּי חָמָא אֲבוֹי דְּרַבִּי יְהוֹשַׁעְיָה דִּינָר, וְהוּא יָהֵיב לֵיהּ לְחוֹרָנִין.

GEMARA Apropos the topic of charity given anonymously, the Gemara cites several stories on that theme and the mitzva of charity in general. **Rabbi Ya'akov bar Idi and Rabbi Yitzḥak bar Naḥman were supporters** of the indigent, i.e., they were responsible for a charity fund. **And** so as not to embarrass the poor, **they would give a dinar to Rabbi Ḥama, father of Rabbi Yehoshaya, and he would give it to** impoverished **others** surreptitiously, so that neither the givers nor the receivers were aware of one another's identity.

רַבִּי זְכַרְיָה חַתְנֵיהּ דְּרַבִּי לֵוִי הָיוּ הַכֹּל מְלִיזִין עָלָיו, אָמְרִין דְּלָא צָרִיךְ וְהוּא נָסַב. מִן דִּדְמָךְ בָּדְקִין וְאַשְׁכְּחִין דַּהֲוָה מְפַלֵּיג לֵיהּ לְחוֹרָנִין.

The Gemara similarly relates with regard to **Rabbi Zekharya, son-in-law of Rabbi Levi, that everyone would malign him. They would say that he does not need** charity, and yet **he takes** money from the charity fund. **After he died, they investigated and found that he had** discreetly **been distributing** all the charity money he received **to others** in actual need.

רַבִּי חִינְנָא בַּר פַּפָּא הֲוָה מְפַלֵּיג מִצְוָה בְּלֵילְיָא, חַד זְמַן פָּגַע בֵּיהּ רַבְּהוֹן דְּרוּחַיָּיא. אָמַר לֵיהּ: לָא כֵן אַלְפָן רַבִּי ״לֹא תַסִּיג גְּבוּל רֵעֲךָ״.

Rabbi Ḥinnana bar Pappa[P] **would distribute mitzva** money,[N] i.e., charity, **at night. Once the leader of** the evil **spirits encountered him.** The evil spirit **said to him: Didn't the rabbi,** i.e., you, **teach** that the verse: **"You shall not trespass upon your neighbor's border"** (Deuteronomy 19:14) indicates that one should not enter the domain of another, and the night belongs to evil spirits?

LANGUAGE

Match up [*ziyyeig*] – זַיֵּיג: This term is derived from a root meaning to attach or to connect. In this context, it is referring to falsely matching the seal of one day to another that has the same data written upon it, with the aim of using it in a deceitful manner.

NOTES

Priestly watch – מִשְׁמָר: All the priestly families were divided into twenty-four watches at a very early period in Jewish history. They were already mentioned in the days of King David (I Chronicles 24:1–18). Likewise, there were twenty-four priestly watches in the Second Temple, although this required a redivision of the four watches that returned from the Babylonian exile. Each priestly watch came to Jerusalem to serve in the Temple for a week, according to a predetermined schedule, so that each watch served approximately two weeks a year. Every watch was divided into six families, each of which served in the Temple on a specific day of the week. Every year, each family typically performed two days of service in the Temple. If the Temple service on a particular day was more than the family performing the service on that day could handle, another family helped. On Shabbat, the entire watch served together. For the three pilgrimage Festivals, namely Passover, *Shavuot*, and *Sukkot*, all twenty-four priestly watches came to Jerusalem and served together.

Would distribute mitzva money – הֲוָה מְפַלֵּיג מִצְוָה: The term mitzva in this context means charity. In the *aggada*, when the Sages use the term mitzva without further specification, they are typically referring to an act of charity (see Rashi on *Shabbat* 156a; see *Torat Ḥayyim* on *Avoda Zara* 4a).

HALAKHA

There were two chambers in the Temple, one the chamber of secret gifts and the other one the chamber of vessels – שְׁתֵּי לְשָׁכוֹת הָיוּ בַּמִּקְדָּשׁ, אַחַת לִשְׁכַּת חֲשָׁאִין וְאַחַת לִשְׁכַּת הַכֵּלִים: There were two special chambers in the Temple, one which was called the chamber of secret gifts, and the other called the chamber of vessels. The chamber of secret gifts was the place where sin-fearing people placed money discreetly so that poor people of noble descent could be supported secretly (see Rambam *Sefer Zera'im*, *Hilkhot Mattenot Aniyyim* 10:8). With regard to the chamber of vessels, anyone who wanted to donate a vessel to the Temple dropped it in there. The treasurers opened this chamber once every thirty days. Vessels for which they found a use in the maintenance of the Temple were so used. The rest were sold, with the proceeds placed in the chamber for funds for Temple maintenance (Rambam *Sefer Hafla'a*, *Hilkhot Arakhin VaḤaramim* 2:12).

PERSONALITIES

Rabbi Ḥinnana bar Pappa – רַבִּי חִינְנָא בַּר פַּפָּא: Rabbi Ḥinnana bar Pappa was an *amora* of the third generation of Eretz Yisrael *amora'im*. In the Babylonian Talmud, he is called Ḥanina, and he is possibly the student of Rabbi Yoḥanan called Ḥanina bar Pappi, a peer of Rabbi Abbahu and Rabbi Yitzḥak Nafḥa. He is mostly quoted in aggadic portions of the Talmud, in which he is described as a righteous man of exemplary character traits. According to one story, he maintained an ongoing dialogue with the Angel of Death. It is related that due to his great righteousness and holiness, a pillar of fire separated his bier from the public at the time of his death.

אֲמַר לֵיהּ: וְלָא כֵן כְּתִיב ״מַתָּן בַּסֵּתֶר יִכְפֶּה אָף״. וַהֲוָה מִסְתְּפֵי מִינֵּיהּ, וַעֲרַק מִן קוֹמוֹי.

Rabbi Ḥinnana **said to him: And isn't it written** elsewhere: **"A gift in secret pacifies anger"** (Proverbs 21:14)? Since I am busy giving secret charity, I have no fear that the Divine Wrath will permit evil spirits to harm me. **And** upon hearing this, the evil spirit **grew afraid of him and fled from his presence.**

אָמַר רַבִּי יוֹנָה: ״אַשְׁרֵי נוֹתֵן לְדַל״ אֵין כְּתִיב כָּאן, אֶלָּא ״אַשְׁרֵי מַשְׂכִּיל אֶל דָּל״ – זֶה שֶׁהוּא מִסְתַּכֵּל בַּמִּצְוָה הֵיאַךְ לַעֲשׂוֹתָהּ.

Rabbi Yona said: Happy is he who gives to the poor, is not written here; rather: "Happy is he who considers the poor" (Psalms 41:2) is written, which indicates that one must consider his actions carefully and act wisely in giving charity. **This** is referring to one **who scrutinizes the mitzva** of charity and considers **how to perform it** in the most appropriate manner to avoid embarrassing the poor.

כֵּיצַד הָיָה רַבִּי יוֹנָה עוֹשֶׂה כְּשֶׁהָיָה רוֹאֶה עָנִי בֶּן טוֹבִים שֶׁיָּרַד מִנְּכָסָיו, הָיָה אוֹמֵר לוֹ: בְּנִי, בִּשְׁבִיל שֶׁשָּׁמַעְתִּי שֶׁנָּפְלָה לָךְ יְרוּשָּׁה מִמָּקוֹם אַחֵר, טוֹל וְאַתְּ פּוֹרֵעַ. מִן דַּהֲוָה נְסֵיב הֲוָה אָמַר לֵיהּ: מַתָּנָה הִיא לָךְ.

How would Rabbi Yona himself **behave when he would see a poor person of noble descent, who** was once wealthy but **had lost his assets?** Rabbi Yona wanted to assist him but feared he would be too ashamed to accept charity. **He would say to him: My son, since I heard that you have come into an inheritance in another place, take** this money now **and you** can **pay**[N] it back when you receive the inheritance. **When** the poor person **would take** the money from him **he would tell him:** This money **is a gift to you,** and you do not have to repay it.

חִיָּיא בַּר אַדָּא: אִית הֲוָה סָבִין בְּיוֹמֵינוּן, מַאן דַּהֲוָה יָהֵיב לְהוֹן מִבֵּין רֵישׁ שַׁתָּא לְצוֹמָא רַבָּא – הֲוֹן נָסְבִין, מִן בָּתַר כֵּן – לָא הֲוֹן נָסְבִין. אָמְרִין: דְּשַׁתָּן גַּבָּן.

The Gemara cites a story involving people who did not want to receive charity from others, but preferred to rely on God's bounty. **Ḥiyya bar Adda** related: **In our days, there were** some **elderly people** who acted as follows. If **someone would give them** charity **between Rosh HaShana and the Great Fast,** i.e., Yom Kippur, **they would accept**[N] it, but **after that period they would not accept** it. **They would say:** The money **that is for this year** is already **with us,** i.e., our income for the entire year has already been decreed between Rosh HaShana and Yom Kippur (see *Beitza* 16a).

נְחֶמְיָה אִישׁ שִׁיחִין פָּגַע בּוֹ יְרוּשַׁלְמִי אֶחָד. אָמַר לֵיהּ: זְכֵה עִמִּי חֲדָא תַּרְנְגוֹלְתָא. אָמַר לֵיהּ: הֵא לָךְ טוּמִיתֵיהּ דְּקוּפָד. וּזְבִין קוּפָד, וְאָכִיל וּמִית. וְהָיָה צוֹוֵחַ וְאָמַר: בּוֹאוּ וְסִפְדוּ לַהֲרוּגוֹ שֶׁל נְחֶמְיָה.

Neḥemya the well digger[P] **encountered a certain Jerusalemite, who said to him: Give me one chicken** as charity. Neḥemya **said to him: Here is the** monetary **value of a piece of meat for you,** as meat was cheaper than chicken. **And** the beggar **bought meat** with the money he accepted from Neḥemya, **and ate it, and died** because his constitution was extremely sensitive to meat. **And** Neḥemya **cried out and said: Come and eulogize the one killed by Neḥemya,** as he felt guilty over the beggar's demise.

נַחוּם אִישׁ גַּם זוֹ הָיָה מוֹלִיךְ דּוֹרוֹן לְבֵית חָמִיו, פָּגַע בּוֹ מוּכֵּה שְׁחִין אֶחָד. אָמַר לֵיהּ: זְכֵה עִמִּי מִמַּה דְּאִית גַּבָּךְ! אָמַר לֵיהּ: מֵיחוֹר. חָזַר וְאַשְׁכְּחֵיהּ מֵית.

Naḥum of Gam Zo[P] **was bringing a gift to his father-in-law's house**[N] when a man **afflicted with boils met him** on the way. **He said to** Naḥum: **Give me** charity **from that which** you have brought **with you.** Naḥum **said to him: When I return,** I will give you something. After visiting his father-in-law's house, Naḥum **returned and found** the man **dead.** He realized that when he had first met him, this boil-afflicted man must have been on the verge of death from starvation.

וַהֲוָה אָמַר לְקִיבְלֵיהּ: עֵינַיָּא דַּחֲמִינָךְ וְלָא יְסִבּוּן לָךְ – יִסְתַּמְיָין, יְדַיָּה דְּלָא פַּשְׁטָן מֵיתַּן לָךְ – יִתְקַטְּעוּן רַגְלַיָּא דְּלָא רָהֲטָן לְמֵיתַּן לָךְ – יִתְּבְרוּן. וּמְטָתֵיהּ כֵּן.

And in his guilt over failing to provide immediate relief for his hunger, Naḥum **said about** the boil-afflicted man: **The eyes that saw you,** i.e., my own eyes, **and did not give you** food **should be blinded; the hands that did not stretch forth to give you** food **should be cut off; the feet that did not run to give you** food **should be broken. And** later all of **these** calamities actually **befell him.**

סְלִיק לְגַבֵּיהּ רַבִּי עֲקִיבָא, אָמַר לֵיהּ: אִי לִי שֶׁאֲנִי רוֹאֶה אוֹתְךָ בְּכָךְ. אָמַר לֵיהּ: אִי לִי שֶׁאֵין אֲנִי רוֹאֶה אוֹתְךָ בְּכָךְ. אָמַר לֵיהּ: מָה אַתְּ מְקַלְּלֵנִי?! אָמַר לֵיהּ: וּמָה אַתְּ מְבַעֵט בְּיִסּוּרִין?

Rabbi Akiva, Naḥum's disciple, **came to** visit and console **him.** Rabbi Akiva **said to him: Woe is me, that I see you like this.** Naḥum **said to him: Woe is me, that I do not see you like this.** Rabbi Akiva **said to him: Why do you curse me?** Naḥum **said to him: And why do you reject suffering?** You should not do so, as the Sages have said that suffering atones for sins like the sacrifice of offerings (*Mekhilta* of Rabbi Yishmael).

NOTES

You have come into an inheritance in another place, take this money now and you can pay – שֶׁנָּפְלָה לָךְ יְרוּשָּׁה מִמָּקוֹם אַחֵר טוֹל וְאַתְּ פּוֹרֵעַ: According to one interpretation, Rabbi Yona meant that everyone's livelihood comes to him through the influence of someone else. This might be his father, by means of an inheritance, as in the verse: "House and riches are the inheritance of fathers" (Proverbs 19:14). If his father cannot provide for him, someone else might perhaps be the instrument of his livelihood. Since Rabbi Yona realized that this pauper had to be provided for, he told him that he had to accept his livelihood in this manner. When he told the poor man that he can repay, Rabbi Yona did not mean this as a request for actual payment; rather, he was referring to the statement of the Sages that poverty is a wheel that turns in the world (*Shabbat* 151b). In other words, as this pauper might himself grow wealthy in the future, he should view the gift as a loan that he can repay by giving charity himself when his turn arrives (*Tiklin Ḥadatin*).

Between Rosh HaShana and the Great Fast they would accept, etc. – מִבֵּין רֵישׁ שַׁתָּא לְצוֹמָא רַבָּא הֲוֹן נָסְבִין וכו׳: Some commentaries maintain that those elderly people accepted charity between Rosh HaShana and Yom Kippur so as to increase the merits of the givers, to protect them during that period of judgment. For this reason, they were not concerned about the verse "But he who hates gifts shall live" (Proverbs 15:27), which teaches that one should not accept gifts (*Gilyonei HaShas* of Rabbi Yosef Engel on *Megilla* 28a).

Naḥum of Gam Zo was bringing a gift to his father-in-law's house – נַחוּם אִישׁ גַּם זוֹ הָיָה מוֹלִיךְ דּוֹרוֹן לְבֵית חָמִיו: This story is also cited, with certain differences, in the Babylonian Talmud (*Ta'anit* 21a). The Gemara there states that this gift was so large it had to be carried by three donkeys. One donkey carried the regular food, another carried the drink, while a third carried sweet delicacies.

PERSONALITIES

Neḥemya the well digger – נְחֶמְיָה אִישׁ שִׁיחִין: Neḥemya was a *tanna* from the third generation of *tanna'im* and a student of Rabbi Akiva. He originated from the village of Shiḥin in the western Galilee, just north of Tzippori, which was the dwelling place of the Yeshevav priestly family. The word *shiḥin* can mean wells, which is how his name is translated here, but it is also possible he was called Neḥemya of Shiḥin because of his hometown.

Naḥum of Gam Zo – נַחוּם אִישׁ גַּם זוֹ: Naḥum of Gam Zo was a *tanna* who lived at the time of the destruction of the Second Temple. Apparently, he came from the town of Gimzo in Judea, which is the source of his name. Aside from what is related here and in stories of Naḥum's righteousness that appear elsewhere (see *Ta'anit* 21a), his student, Rabbi Akiva, learned the halakhic interpretative method of amplification and restriction from him. It also seems that the difference in interpretive methods between Rabbi Akiva and Rabbi Yishmael derives from an earlier period and is grounded in the methods of Naḥum of Gam Zo and Rabbi Neḥunya ben Hakana (see *Shevuot* 26a).

רבי הושעיה רבה הוה רביה דבריה חד סגי נהורא, והוה יליף אכול עימיה בכל יום. חד זמן הוה ליה אורחין ולא מטא מיכול עימיה. ברמשא סליק לגביה, אמר ליה: לא יכעוס מרי עלי, בגין דהוה לי אורחין יומא דין, דאמרית דלא ליבזוי ביקרא דמרי יומא דין, בגין כן לא אכלית עם מרי יומא דין.

Rabbi Hoshaya the Great[P] **was the master,** i.e., the teacher, **of the son of a certain blind man and was accustomed to eat with** the blind man **every day. Once** Rabbi Hoshaya **had guests, and he** did not **invite** the blind man **to eat with him. In the evening,** Rabbi Hoshaya **went up to** visit the blind man and **said to him:** I request that **my master,** i.e., you, **not be angry with me, as I had guests today.** I therefore **said** to myself that I will not invite you **today,** so **as not to demean my master's dignity.** You sometimes spill food on yourself and they might have mocked you. **For this reason, I did not eat with my master today.**

אמר ליה: אתה פייסתה למאן דמתחמי ולא חמי – דין דחמי ולא מתחמיים יקבל פיוסך. אמר ליה: הדא מנא לך? אמר ליה: מרבי אליעזר בן יעקב.

The blind man **said to him:** Since **you appeased one who is seen but does not see, that** Holy **One, Who sees but is not seen, should accept your appeasement,** i.e., God should accept your prayers. Rabbi Hoshaya **said to him: From where** did **you** hear **that** metaphorical statement? The blind man **replied:** I learned that idea **from** a story involving **Rabbi Eliezer ben Ya'akov**[P] and a blind man.

דרבי אליעזר בן יעקב עאל חד דסגי נהורא לקרתיה, יתב ליה רבי אליעזר בן יעקב לרע מיניה. דיימרון: דאילולי דהוה בר נשא רבא – לא יתב ליה רבי אליעזר בן יעקב לרע מיניה. עבדין ליה פרנסה דאיקר.

As it is told **of Rabbi Eliezer ben Ya'akov** that **a blind man** once **came to his city,** and **Rabbi Eliezer ben Ya'akov sat below him,** so **that** the people of the city **would say that if he,** i.e., the blind man, **were not a great man, Rabbi Eliezer ben Ya'akov would not have sat below him.** When the people of the city saw this, **they gave** the blind man a very **respectable livelihood.**

אמר לון: מהו הכין? אמרון ליה: רבי אליעזר בן יעקב יתב לרע מינך, וצלוי עלוי הדא צלותא: אתה גמלתה חסד למאן דמתחמי ולא חמי, דין דחמי ולא מתחמי יגמול יתך חסד.

The blind man **asked them: What is this** situation? Why are you paying me such a high salary? **They said to him:** Since **Rabbi Eliezer ben Ya'akov sat below you,** we honor you. **And** the blind man **prayed this prayer with regard to** Rabbi Eliezer ben Ya'akov: **You rendered kindness to one who is seen but does not see.** Therefore, **that** Holy **One, Who sees but is not seen, should render kindness to you.**

רבי חמא בר חנינה ורבי הושעיא הוו מטיילין באילין כנישתא דלוד, אמר רבי חמא בר חנינא לרבי הושעיא: כמה ממון שיקעו אבותי כאן! אמר ליה: כמה נפשות שיקעו אבותיך כאן. לא הוה אית בני נש דילעון באורייתא? רבי אבון עבד אילין תרעייה

Rabbi Ḥama bar Ḥanina and Rabbi Hoshaya were once **touring the synagogues of Lod.**[B] **Rabbi Ḥama bar Ḥanina said to Rabbi Hoshaya: How much money my forefathers invested** in building synagogues **here!** Rabbi Hoshaya **said to him: How many souls your forefathers invested** in building synagogues **here!** The money they spent actually harmed people spiritually rather than helping them. Rabbi Hoshaya explained his comment: **Weren't there people who would have exerted themselves in** the study of **Torah** if only the money used for the construction of these buildings had been donated to them instead? In another case, **Rabbi Avun** donated money for **building the gates**

Perek **V**
Daf **15** Amud **b**

דסדרא רבא. אתא רבי מנא לגביה, אמר ליה: חמי מאי עבדית! אמר ליה: "וישכח ישראל את עושהו ויבן היכלות" לא הוה בני נש דילעון באורייתא?

of the great study hall. When **Rabbi Mana came to** visit **him,** Rabbi Avun, proud of his donation for this building, **said to him: Look at what I did** and the greatness of my contribution. Rabbi Mana **said to him:** Your attitude reminds me of the verse: **"For Israel has forgotten his Maker, and built palaces"** (Hosea 8:14). How could you focus upon the gates? **Weren't there people who would have exerted themselves in** the study of **Torah** if they only had the money? You could have given them that money instead of using it to build structures.

PERSONALITIES

Rabbi Hoshaya the Great – רבי הושעיה רבה: This Sage, who is called Rabbi Oshaya in the Babylonian Talmud, was one of the greatest scholars of the last generation of *tanna'im*. Rabbi Hoshaya was the third generation in a family of scholars, the son of Rabbi Ḥama, son of Rabbi Bisa. He studied Torah with his father, with the *tanna* bar Kappara, and with Rabbi Ḥiyya, with whom he had a relationship of disciple-colleague. His great work was the organization of the *baraitot*. It is said that any *baraita* not redacted in the study hall of Rabbi Ḥiyya and Rabbi Hoshaya is unreliable.

Rabbi Hoshaya maintained close ties with the house of the *Nasi*, the leader of the Jews in Eretz Yisrael, and he was a close friend of Rabbi Yehuda Nesia, the grandson of Rabbi Yehuda HaNasi. Rabbi Hoshaya had many students, the greatest of whom was Rabbi Yoḥanan, who studied Torah under him for many years. Rabbi Hoshaya apparently had a son, Rabbi Marinus, who was also a Torah scholar and continued his father's close ties with the house of the *Nasi*.

Rabbi Eliezer ben Ya'akov – רבי אליעזר בן יעקב: Two *tanna'im* are known by this name, one from the generation that lived during the destruction of the Second Temple and the other a student of Rabbi Akiva. The saying: The teachings of Rabbi Eliezer ben Ya'akov measure a *kav*, but are clean (*Eiruvin* 62b; *Bekhorot* 23b), i.e., his body of work is small in quantity but clear and complete, was apparently stated with regard to the earlier *tanna* of that name. The first Rabbi Eliezer ben Ya'akov saw the Second Temple before its destruction and transmitted many *halakhot* about the details of its structure. He is traditionally considered the author of tractate *Middot*.

BACKGROUND

Lod – לוד: One of the oldest towns in Judea, Lod grew in significance toward the end of the Second Temple period and served as an important cultural center for many generations after the destruction of the Temple. Some of the greatest *tanna'im* lived there, including Rabbi Eliezer ben Hyrcanus, also known as Rabbi Eliezer the Great; Rabbi Tarfon; and others. Several important ordinances were instituted in the so-called upper chamber of the house of Nitza in Lod. After the bar Kokheva revolt, the town remained an important Torah center, as it became the focal point for scholars of the south. Among the great *amora'im* who lived there were Rabbi Yehoshua ben Levi, Rabbi Simlai, Rabbi Yitzḥak bar Naḥmani, Rabbi Shimon ben Pazi, his son Rabbi Yehuda, and Rabbi Aḥa.

תָּנֵי: קׇדְשֵׁי הַמִּזְבֵּחַ מוֹצִיאִין אֶת הָרָאוּי לָהֶן מִקׇּדְשֵׁי בֶּדֶק הַבַּיִת,

§ With regard to the vessels donated for the Temple maintenance, which are mentioned in the mishna, the Gemara cites a *baraita* in which **it was taught:** If the shekels collected for the purchase of articles **consecrated for the altar,** i.e., communal offerings, are not enough to purchase them and the items that accompanied them, e.g., their libations, the funds **required for** purchasing the remainder **are taken from the funds consecrated for Temple maintenance.**

אֵין קׇדְשֵׁי בֶּדֶק הַבַּיִת מוֹצִיאִין אֶת הָרָאוּי לָהֶן מִקׇּדְשֵׁי מִזְבֵּחַ.

However, the converse is not the case: If there is a need for **funds consecrated to Temple maintenance, that which is required for it is not taken from funds consecrated for the altar.** The reason for this difference is that an item may be changed from a lesser to a greater sanctity, but not vice versa.

וְהָא תְּנַן: כְּלִי שֶׁמָּצְאוּ בּוֹ צוֹרֶךְ לְבֶדֶק הַבַּיִת מַנִּיחִין אוֹתוֹ, וְהַשְּׁאָר נִמְכָּרִין וּדְמֵיהֶן נוֹפְלִין לְבֶדֶק הַבַּיִת!

The Gemara notes an apparent contradiction. **But didn't we learn** in the mishna: **A vessel that they found for it a use for Temple maintenance, they leave it** for that purpose; **and the rest are sold, and their monetary** value **is allocated to Temple maintenance.** This statement indicates that this money could be used only for Temple maintenance, not for items consecrated for the altar. This contradicts the *baraita* cited above.

אָמַר רַבִּי חִזְקִיָּה: כֵּינֵי מַתְנִיתָא, לְלִשְׁכַּת בֶּדֶק הַבַּיִת.

In resolution of this contradiction, **Rabbi Ḥizkiya said: This is** the intent of **the mishna:** Donated items and, likewise, any money received as payment for sale of an item are physically taken **to the chamber for the Temple maintenance.** From there they may be removed for any Temple purpose, either for the maintenance of the Temple or for articles consecrated for the altar.

הדרן עלך אלו הן הממונין

Summary of **Perek V**

It is unclear whether the list of Temple officials provided in this chapter consists of names from a particular generation or whether it lists the names of unique individuals who served in these posts over the years. It can be inferred from the stories related by the Gemara that not all the officials were from the same era, although it is possible that the holder of a certain position would be referred to by the name of an important personage who once filled that position, instead of by his own name.

In any case, this chapter provided some detail of the functions, as well as the names, of some of the men who served in these positions, particularly those whose conduct was considered somewhat dubious. It is likely that there were other administrative posts in the Temple, apart from those listed in our chapter.

The discussion in the Gemara indicates that there were several levels of functionaries who managed the Temple finances. The senior official in the Temple was the High Priest. In certain periods he was subservient to the king, who would make good any financial discrepancies from his own pocket. The High Priest was in charge of two executive supervisors, seven trustees, and three treasurers. These officers would manage a complex accounting system designed to ensure that the treasury money was not used for unsuitable purposes.

It was further explained in this chapter that not all offerings were brought to the Temple by private individuals; rather, many animals were prepared by the Temple staff, and those who wished to sacrifice these offerings would purchase them from the appropriate officer. Basically, one treasurer was in charge of collecting the payment while a different treasurer would supply the offerings to the buyers. The first treasurer would give the purchaser a receipt, which he would subsequently transfer to the one appointed over the supply of animals. This would ensure that the Temple would suffer no losses from these transactions.

Incidentally, the mishna mentions two Temple chambers, the chamber of secret gifts, through which paupers who were ashamed to accept money any other way could receive charity, and the chamber of vessels, where all vessels donated to the Temple were placed. Some of these vessels were actually used in the Temple while others were sold, with the proceeds allocated to Temple maintenance.

The mention of the chamber of secret gifts led to a discussion in the Gemara of the mitzva of charity, particularly with regard to the degree that one must exert oneself to aid those in need, as well as the proper respect that must be paid to the indigent. It is not sufficient merely to give money to the poor; they must be treated with the dignity they deserve.

Introduction to **Perek VI**

This chapter opens with a topic that is somewhat related to the shekels, namely the Temple collection baskets, also called horns, in which the shekels and other donations were placed. This quickly leads to a discussion of other Temple vessels, as well as certain practices that were performed in particular areas of the Temple, or in memory of certain historical events.

Apparently, there were several vessels in the Temple, certainly in the First Temple and possibly in the Second Temple as well, that served mainly decorative purposes. For example, they did not make do with one table for the shewbread, but added a further ten similar tables. Likewise, an additional ten candelabras were placed in the Sanctuary. This chapter discusses where exactly these supplementary vessels were placed and how they were used in practice.

This chapter also includes a lengthy discussion of the Ark of the Covenant, citing statements of both *aggada* and *halakha*. As is well known, there was no Ark in the Second Temple; inside the Holy of Holies there was merely an empty space where the Ark should have been. There is a dispute as to the fate of the Ark of the Covenant, whether it was plundered along with the other Temple vessels or hidden somewhere in the tunnels beneath the Temple.

Another issue raised in this chapter is the manner of the placement of the stone tablets in the Ark. The Gemara also debates the possibility that in certain periods there was a second Ark, without the tablets, which the Jewish people would take with them into battle. Another topic briefly addressed is that of donations to the Temple, and the smallest amounts of different gifts that could be given for the special requirements of the Temple.

There is a great deal of aggadic material in this chapter, including a section that comments on the prophecies about the river that will in the future emerge from the House of God.

הלכה א מתני׳ שְׁלֹשָׁה עָשָׂר שׁוֹפָרוֹת, שְׁלֹשָׁה עָשָׂר שׁוּלְחָנוֹת, שְׁלֹשׁ עֶשְׂרֵה הִשְׁתַּחֲוָיוֹת הָיוּ בַּמִּקְדָּשׁ.

HALAKHA 1 · MISHNA **There were thirteen** collection **horns,**[H] narrow at the top and wide at the bottom, into which were placed the shekels that were collected for the various needs of the Temple. There **were** also **thirteen tables**[B] for various purposes, and **thirteen prostrations in the Temple.**

שֶׁל בֵּית רַבָּן גַּמְלִיאֵל וְשֶׁל בֵּית רַבִּי חֲנַנְיָה סְגַן הַכֹּהֲנִים הָיוּ מִשְׁתַּחֲוִים בְּאַרְבַּע עֶשְׂרֵה. וְהֵיכָן הָיְתָה יְתֵירָה – כְּנֶגֶד דִּיר הָעֵצִים, שֶׁכֵּן מְסוֹרֶת בְּיָדָן מֵאֲבוֹתֵיהֶן שֶׁשָּׁם הָאָרוֹן נִגְנַז.

The members **of the household of Rabban Gamliel and** the members **of the household of Rabbi Ḥananya, the deputy High Priest, would prostrate** themselves **in fourteen** places. **And where was** this extra location? It was **facing the wood depository,**[N] **as there was a tradition** handed down **to them from their fathers that the Ark was sequestered there.**[N]

מַעֲשֶׂה בְּכֹהֵן אֶחָד שֶׁהָיָה מִתְעַסֵּק, וְרָאָה אֶת הָרִצְפָּה שֶׁהִיא מְשׁוּנָּה מֵחֲבֵרוֹתֶיהָ, בָּא וְאָמַר לַחֲבֵירוֹ. לֹא הִסְפִּיק לִגְמוֹר אֶת הַדָּבָר עַד שֶׁיָּצְתָה נִשְׁמָתוֹ. וְיָדְעוּ בְּיִיחוּד שֶׁשָּׁם הָאָרוֹן גָּנוּז.

The mishna relates that there was **an incident involving a certain priest who was going about** his duties **and saw a certain flagstone that was different from the others.**[N] He noticed that one of the stones was slightly raised above the others, indicating that it had been removed and returned to its place. The priest understood that this was the opening to an underground tunnel where the Ark was concealed. **He came and said to his fellow** that he had noticed this deviation in the floor. **He did not manage to conclude** relating **the incident before his soul left him,** i.e., he died. Following this event, **they knew with certainty that the Ark was sequestered there** and that God had prevented that priest from revealing its location.

גמ׳ תָּנֵי: הַשּׁוֹפָרוֹת הַלָּלוּ עֲקוּמוֹת הָיוּ, צָרוֹת מִלְּמַעְלָן וּרְחָבוֹת מִלְּמַטָּן, מִפְּנֵי הָרַמָּאִין.

GEMARA **It was taught** in a *baraita*: **Those** collection **horns were asymmetrical.** They were **narrow at the top and wide at the bottom.** Why were they shaped like that? It was **due to cheaters,** to prevent them from inserting their hands on the pretense of adding shekels and removing them instead.

תָּנֵי בְּשֵׁם רַבִּי אֶלְעָזָר: הָאָרוֹן גָּלָה עִמָּהֶן לְבָבֶל, מַאי טַעְמָא – ״לֹא יִוָּתֵר דָּבָר אָמַר ה׳״, אֵין דָּבָר אֶלָּא שֶׁהַדִּיבְּרוֹת לְתוֹכוֹ.

The Gemara cites a *baraita* that expounds a tannaitic dispute with regard to the sequestering of the Ark, a topic mentioned in the mishna: **It was taught in the name of Rabbi Elazar: The Ark was exiled with** the Jews **to Babylonia.** When the Jews were exiled to Babylonia, they took the Ark with them. **What is the source** for this statement? When Isaiah prophesied about the exile before King Hezekiah, he stated: "Behold, the days come, that all that is in your house, and that which your fathers have stored up until this day, shall be carried to Babylon; **no item shall be left, said the Lord**" (II Kings 20:17). The **item** [*davar*] referred to in the verse can **only be** an item **that contains the commandments** [*dibrot*]. That is the Ark, which contains the two tablets upon which the Ten Commandments are carved.

וְכֵן הוּא אוֹמֵר ״וְלִתְשׁוּבַת הַשָּׁנָה שָׁלַח הַמֶּלֶךְ נְבוּכַדְנֶאצַּר וַיְבִאֵהוּ בָבֶלָה עִם כְּלֵי חֶמְדַּת בֵּית ה׳״. אֵיזֶהוּ כְּלֵי חֶמְדַּת בֵּית ה׳ – זֶה הָאָרוֹן.

And, so too, it says: "And at the return of the year, King Nebuchadnezzar sent, and brought him to Babylon, with the desired vessels of the House of the Lord, and made Zedekiah his brother king over Judah and Jerusalem" (II Chronicles 36:10). **What is** referred to by the phrase **"the desired vessels of the House of the Lord"? This is the Ark,** in which the Tablets of the Law were placed. The Torah is a desirable object for the Jews, as it is stated, "More to be desired are they than gold, indeed, than much fine gold" (Psalms 19:11).

HALAKHA

Thirteen collection horns – שְׁלֹשָׁה עָשָׂר שׁוֹפָרוֹת: In the Temple, the following thirteen containers collected donations. The shape of each one was like a horn, narrow at the top and wide at the bottom. Each one was designated for a specific type of donation: (1) Shekels of the current year; (2) shekels of the previous year; (3) money for a pair of birds. Anyone liable to bring an offering of two birds, i.e., one for a sin-offering and the other for a burnt-offering, would deposit the cost of these offerings in this horn; (4) money for a burnt-offering of fowl, without the accompanying sin-offering; (5) money for the wood of the altar fire; (6) money for frankincense; (7) donations of gold, or money to buy it, for the Ark cover; (8) money left over from that set aside for sin-offerings; (9) money left over from that set aside for guilt-offerings; (10) money left over from that set aside for the offerings of a *zav*, a *zava*, or a woman after childbirth; (11) money left over from that set aside for the offerings of a nazirite; (12) money left over from that set aside for the guilt-offering of a leper; and (13) donations for a burnt-offering of an animal, as opposed to one of a fowl (*Rambam Sefer Zemanim, Hilkhot Shekalim* 2:1–2).

BACKGROUND

Thirteen tables – שְׁלֹשָׁה עָשָׂר שׁוּלְחָנוֹת: The following are the tables found in the Temple: (A) Eight marble tables in the slaughtering area; (B) one marble table to the west of the ramp of the altar; (C) one silver table to the west of the ramp of the altar; (D) one silver table at the doorway to the Entrance Hall; (E) one gold table at the doorway to the Entrance Hall; (F) and one gold table in the Sanctuary.

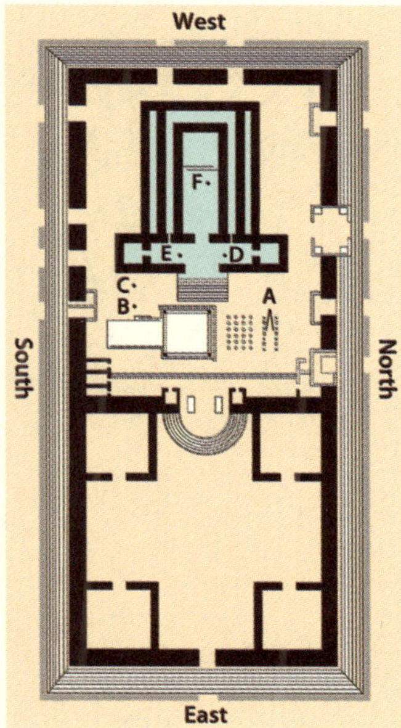

Location of the thirteen tables in the Temple

NOTES

The wood depository – דִּיר הָעֵצִים: The storage room for wood was the chamber located in the northeastern corner of the Women's Courtyard (see *Middot* 2:5). In this chamber, wood was stored to be used as fuel on the altar. Blemished priests were assigned the task of checking the wood for worms, as worm-infested wood is disqualified for use on the altar (see *Menaḥot* 85b).

That the Ark was sequestered there – שֶׁשָּׁם הָאָרוֹן נִגְנַז: There was no Ark in the Second Temple, as explained in *Yoma* 52b. The Gemara there cites a tannaitic dispute as to the whereabouts of the Ark that is parallel to the dispute recorded here. It is clear from the mishna here that the families of Rabban Gamliel and Rabbi Ḥananya, the deputy High Priest, had a tradition that the Ark was sequestered in the Temple and that its location was in the tunnels under the wood depository. Out of respect for this place, they performed an additional prostration facing that chamber.

And he saw a certain flagstone that was different from the others – וְרָאָה אֶת הָרִצְפָּה שֶׁהִיא מְשׁוּנָּה מֵחֲבֵרוֹתֶיהָ: It is explained that one of the stones was raised above the others. An alternative explanation is that the color of the stone was a different shade than the others, due to the sanctity of the Ark located beneath it (Rabbeinu Meshulam).

רַבִּי שִׁמְעוֹן בֶּן לָקִישׁ אוֹמֵר: בִּמְקוֹמוֹ הָיָה הָאָרוֹן נִגְנַז. הֲדָא הוּא דִכְתִיב ״וַיַּאֲרִיכוּ הַבַּדִּים וַיֵּרָאוּ רָאשֵׁי הַבַּדִּים אֶל הַקֹּדֶשׁ אֶל פְּנֵי הַדְּבִיר וְלֹא יֵרָאוּ הַחוּצָה״.

Rabbi Shimon ben Lakish differs and **says: The Ark** was not sent into exile, but rather **was sequestered in its place,**[H] i.e., buried in the Holy of Holies. **This is as it is written: "And the staves were so long that the ends of the staves were seen from the holy place, even before the Sanctuary; but they could not be seen without;** and there they are until this day" (1 Kings 8:8). The phrase "until this day" means forever, as "this day" can refer to any point in time. Consequently, this verse indicates that the Ark was sequestered in its place.

כְּתִיב ״וַיֵּרָאוּ״ וְאַתְּ אָמְרַתְּ ״וְלֹא יֵרָאוּ״? אֶלָּא, נִרְאִין וְלֹא נִרְאִין, בּוֹלְטִין וְיוֹצְאִין כִּשְׁנֵי דַּדֵּי הָאִשָּׁה.

Having cited this verse, the Gemara proceeds to further explain it, by pointing out an internal contradiction in the verse. Initially, **it is written:** "The ends of the staves **were seen," and you say,** in the continuation of the verse, **"but they could not be seen."** How can that be? **Rather,** the verse should be understood as follows: The staves **could be seen and** they **could not be seen, as they protruded outward** through the curtain **like the two breasts of a woman.** The staves themselves could not be seen, but their position was discernible from the protrusion of the curtain.

וְרַבָּנַן אָמְרֵי: בְּלִשְׁכַּת דִּיר הָעֵצִים הָיָה הָאָרוֹן גָּנוּז. מַעֲשֶׂה בְּכֹהֵן אֶחָד בַּעַל מוּם שֶׁהָיָה עוֹמֵד וּמְפַצֵּל עֵצִים בְּלִשְׁכַּת דִּיר הָעֵצִים, וְרָאָה אֶת הָרִצְפָּה שֶׁהִיא מִשְׁתַּנָּה מֵחַבְרוֹתֶיהָ. בָּא וְאָמַר לַחֲבֵירוֹ: בֹּא וּרְאֵה אֶת הָרִצְפָּה הַזֹּאת שֶׁהִיא מִשְׁתַּנָּה מֵחַבְרוֹתֶיהָ. לֹא הִסְפִּיק לִגְמוֹר אֶת הַדָּבָר עַד שֶׁיָּצְתָה נִשְׁמָתוֹ. וְיָדְעוּ בְּיִחוּד שֶׁשָּׁם הָאָרוֹן גָּנוּז. תָּנֵי רַבִּי הוֹשַׁעְיָא: הִקִּישׁ עָלֶיהָ בְּקוּרְנָס וְיָצְאת אֵשׁ וּשְׂרָפַתּוּ.

The Gemara returns to the discussion of the location of the Ark during the Second Temple period. **And the Rabbis say: The Ark was sequestered in the wood depository chamber.** The Gemara relates that there was **an incident involving a certain blemished priest who was standing and splitting wood in the wood depository chamber** in order to verify that the wood was not infested with worms. **And he saw the flagstone that was different from the others. He came and said to his fellow: Come and see that this flagstone differs from the others. He did not manage to conclude** relating **the incident before his soul left him. And they knew with certainty that the Ark was sequestered there. Rabbi Hoshaya taught** a slightly different version of the story in a *baraita*: **He tapped** on the stone **with a mallet** [*kurenas*][LN] to determine if it was hollow underneath the stone, **and fire came out and burned him.**[N]

תָּנֵי רַבִּי יְהוּדָה בֶּן לָקִישׁ אָמַר: שְׁנֵי אֲרוֹנוֹת הָיוּ מְהַלְּכִין עִם יִשְׂרָאֵל בַּמִּדְבָּר, אֶחָד שֶׁהָיְתָה הַתּוֹרָה נְתוּנָה בְתוֹכוֹ, וְאַחֵר שֶׁהָיוּ שִׁבְרֵי לוּחוֹת נְתוּנִין בְּתוֹכוֹ. זֶה שֶׁהָיְתָה הַתּוֹרָה נְתוּנָה בְּתוֹכוֹ הָיָה מוּנָּח בְּאֹהֶל מוֹעֵד, הֲדָא הוּא דִכְתִיב ״וַאֲרוֹן בְּרִית ה׳ וּמֹשֶׁה לֹא מָשׁוּ מִקֶּרֶב הַמַּחֲנֶה״. זֶה שֶׁהָיוּ שִׁבְרֵי לוּחוֹת נְתוּנִין בְּתוֹכוֹ – הָיָה נִכְנָס וְיוֹצֵא עִמָּהֶן, וּפְעָמִים שֶׁהָיָה מִתְרָאֶה עִמָּהֶן.

The Gemara elaborates on the topic of the Ark of the Covenant. **It was taught** that **Rabbi Yehuda ben Lakish said: Two Arks would travel with Israel in the desert: One, in which the Torah,** i.e., the second tablets that were given to Moses after he broke the first ones, **was placed, and the other, in which the shards of** the first **tablets were placed. That in which the Torah was kept,** was the Ark that **was placed in the Tent of Meeting,** in the Holy of Holies. **This is as it is written: "And the Ark of the Covenant of the Lord, and Moses, departed not out of the camp"** (Numbers 14:44). **The one in which the shards of** the **tablets were placed would embark and return with them** when they went to war. Consequently, **there were times that it would be seen among them.**

וְרַבָּנַן אָמְרֵי: אָרוֹן אֶחָד הָיָה, וּפַעַם אַחַת יָצָא בִּימֵי עֵלִי וְנִשְׁבָּה. קְרָייָא מְסַייֵעַ לְהוּ לְרַבָּנַן ״אוֹי לָנוּ מִי יַצִּילֵנוּ מִיַּד הָאֱלֹהִים הָאַדִּירִים הָאֵלֶּה״, מִילָּה דְּלָא חֲמוּן מִן יוֹמֵיהוֹן.

And the Rabbis say: There was only **one Ark,** not two, kept in the Holy of Holies. **And one time it went out** with the nation to battle **in the days of Eli and it was captured.** The Gemara notes that **a verse supports** the opinion of **the Rabbis:** When the Philistines who captured the Ark saw it, they said: **"Woe unto us! Who shall deliver us out of the hand of these mighty gods?"** (1 Samuel 4:8). It is clear that they were very frightened, and it would seem that this was due to the fact that the Ark was **something that they had never seen in all their days.**

קְרָייָא מְסַייֵעַ לְרַבִּי יוּדָה בֶּן לָקִישׁ ״וַיֹּאמֶר שָׁאוּל לַאֲחִיָּה הַגִּישָׁה אֲרוֹן הָאֱלֹהִים״. וַהֲלֹא אָרוֹן בְּקִרְיַת יְעָרִים הָיָה!

There is also **a verse** that **supports** the opinion of **Rabbi Yuda ben Lakish** that there were two Arks, one that they took with them into battle and one that remained in its place. Apropos the battle of King Saul with the Philistines, the verse states: **"And Saul said unto Ahijah: Bring here the Ark of God,** for the Ark of God was there at that time with the children of Israel" (1 Samuel 14:18). This is puzzling. **Wasn't the Ark in Kiryat Ye'arim** at the time (see 1 Samuel 7:1–2)? Therefore, it is clear that there were two Arks, one that resided in Kiryat Ye'arim and a different one that they took with them to battle.

HALAKHA

The Ark was sequestered in its place – בִּמְקוֹמוֹ הָיָה הָאָרוֹן נִגְנַז: In the First Temple, the Ark of the Covenant was placed on a stone located in the western part of the Holy of Holies. The canister containing manna from the desert and Aaron's staff were set before it. Tradition has it that at the time that Solomon built the Temple, he knew that it would eventually be destroyed. Therefore, he built a hiding place in the tunnels underneath the Temple to serve as a storage place for the Ark. King Josiah commanded that the Ark be concealed in the place that Solomon had prepared, along with Aaron's staff, the canister of manna, and the anointing oil. None of these items was recovered during the time of the Second Temple. This determination of the fate of the Ark is in accordance with the opinion of Rabbi Shimon ben Lakish (Rambam *Sefer Avoda*, *Hilkhot Beit HaBeḥira* 4:1)

LANGUAGE

Mallet [*kurenas*] – קוּרְנָס: Apparently from the Greek **κάρνον**, *karnon*, meaning a ram or horn.

NOTES

He tapped on the stone with a mallet – הִקִּישׁ עָלֶיהָ בְּקוּרְנָס: There is an explanation that the priest was tapping in order to determine if the ground under the stone was hollow. A different explanation is that he tapped with a mallet in order to make this stone level with the others (Rash Sirilio).

And fire came out and burned him – וְיָצְאת אֵשׁ וּשְׂרָפַתּוּ: One explanation is that the fire consumed the priest. Others explain that the fire consumed the mallet (*Talmid HaRashbash*).

מָה עַבְדִּין לֵיהּ רַבָּנַן – הַגִּישָׁה אֵלַי הַצִּיץ. קְרָיָא מְסַיֵּיעַ לְרַבִּי יוּדָא בֶּן לָקִישׁ ״הָאָרוֹן וְיִשְׂרָאֵל וִיהוּדָה יוֹשְׁבִים בַּסּוּכּוֹת״

What do the Rabbis do with this verse so that it does not contradict their opinion? The Rabbis would interpret the verse as follows: Saul said, **"Bring here"** the container that contains the eight priestly garments, among them **the frontplate.**[B] The verse is referring to this container, not the Ark. A different **verse supports** the opinion of **Rabbi Yuda ben Lakish** that there were two Arks: When Uriah explains to King David why he will not return to his house while there is a war with the children of Ammon, he says: **"The Ark, and Israel, and Judah, abide in booths;** and my lord Joab, and the servants of my lord, are encamped in the open field; shall I then go into my house, to eat and to drink, and to lie with my wife?" (II Samuel 11:11).

BACKGROUND

Frontplate – צִיץ: The frontplate of the High Priest was a plate of gold on which the words "Sacred to the Lord" (Exodus 28:36) were engraved. This plate was tied to the forehead of the High Priest, adjacent to where his hairline began.

The frontplate was one of the eight priestly vestments that made up the raiment of the High Priest. It is one of the four vestments that are called the golden vestments. The High Priest would wear all eight vestments year round, except during part of the Yom Kippur service, when he would wear only the four white vestments that all priests wore.

Frontplate

Perek **VI**
Daf **16** Amud **a**

וַהֲלֹא אָרוֹן בְּצִיּוֹן הָיָה!

But wasn't the Ark in Zion, i.e., Jerusalem, at the time, and not in a booth at the battlefield? Rather, there must have been two Arks; one remained in Jerusalem and the other went out with the Jews to the battlefield.

מָה עַבְדִּין לֵיהּ רַבָּנַן – סְכַךְ שֶׁהוּא כְּקֵירוּי, שֶׁעֲדַיִין לֹא נִבְנָה בֵּית הַבְּחִירָה.

What do the Rabbis do with this verse? How would they interpret it according to their opinion that there was only one Ark, and it remained in Jerusalem? The word for booth, *sukka*, is related to the word ***sekhakh*, which is** temporary **roofing** for a structure. The verse, in mentioning that the Ark was in a booth, is not implying that it was with the army at the battlefield, but merely that the Ark was in a temporary structure, **as the Temple had not yet been built.**

מִשֶּׁנִּגְנַז הָאָרוֹן נִגְנַז עִמּוֹ צִנְצֶנֶת הַמָּן, וּצְלוֹחִית שֶׁמֶן הַמִּשְׁחָה, וּמַקְּלוֹ שֶׁל אַהֲרֹן וּפְרָחָיו וּשְׁקֵדָיו, וְאַרְגָּז שֶׁהֵשִׁיבוּ פְּלִשְׁתִּים אָשָׁם לֵאלֹהֵי יִשְׂרָאֵל.

§ As the mishna mentions the subject of concealing the Ark, the Gemara cites a further *baraita* on this topic: **When the Ark was sequestered, sequestered along with it was the canister of manna**[B] that Moses placed before God to be kept throughout the generations (see Exodus 16:32–34); **the flask of the anointing oil; Aaron's staff with its blossoms and berries,** which were placed before the Ark (see Numbers 17:23); **and the box that the Philistines returned** together with the Ark that was captured during the war, which they filled with golden vessels **as a guilt-offering to the God of Israel,** as the verse says: "And put the jewels of gold, which you return Him for a guilt-offering, in a coffer by the side thereof" (I Samuel 6:8).

Rock of the Dome of the Rock, viewed from above

BACKGROUND

When the Ark was sequestered, sequestered along with it was the canister of manna – מִשֶּׁנִּגְנַז הָאָרוֹן נִגְנַז עִמּוֹ צִנְצֶנֶת הַמָּן: The Ark was placed on a slab of bedrock, called the foundation rock, that was in the Holy of Holies. The canister of manna and Aaron's staff were set before it. King Josiah commanded that the Ark be concealed along with the canister of manna, the anointing oil, and Aaron's staff in the tunnels under the Temple that Solomon had constructed for this purpose (Rambam *Sefer Avoda*, *Hilkhot Beit HaBeḥira* 4:1).

The Radbaz writes in his responsa (2:691) that the rock in the Dome of the Rock is unquestionably the foundation rock.

מִי גְּנָזוֹ – יֹאשִׁיָּהוּ גְּנָזוֹ. כֵּיוָן שֶׁרָאָה שֶׁכָּתוּב "יוֹלֵךְ ה' אוֹתְךָ וְאֶת מַלְכְּךָ אֲשֶׁר תָּקִים עָלֶיךָ אֶל גּוֹי אֲשֶׁר לֹא יָדַעְתָּ אַתָּה וַאֲבוֹתֶיךָ" – עָמַד וּגְנָזוֹ.

Who sequestered the Ark? **Josiah,** king of Judah, sequestered it. **Since he saw that it is written,**[N] **"The Lord will bring you and your king, whom you shall set over you, to a nation that you have not known, you nor your fathers"** (Deuteronomy 28:36), **he arose and sequestered it,**[N] so that it would not be sent into exile with the Jews.

הָדָא הוּא דִּכְתִיב "וַיֹּאמֶר לַלְוִיִּם הַמְּבִינִים לְכָל יִשְׂרָאֵל הַקְּדוֹשִׁים לַה' תְּנוּ אֶת אֲרוֹן הַקֹּדֶשׁ בַּבַּיִת אֲשֶׁר בָּנָה שְׁלֹמֹה בֶן דָּוִיד מֶלֶךְ יִשְׂרָאֵל אֵין לָכֶם מַשָּׂא בַּכָּתֵף". אָמַר לָהֶם: אִם גּוֹלֶה הוּא עִמָּכֶם לְבָבֶל – אֵין אַתֶּם מַחֲזִירִין אוֹתוֹ עוֹד לִמְקוֹמוֹ, אֶלָּא "עַתָּה עִבְדוּ אֶת ה' אֱלֹהֵיכֶם וְאֶת עַמּוֹ יִשְׂרָאֵל".

This is as it is written: "And he said unto the Levites who taught all Israel, who were holy unto the Lord: Put the Holy Ark in the house which Solomon the son of David king of Israel did build; there shall no more be a burden upon your shoulders; now serve the Lord your God, and His people Israel" (II Chronicles 35:3). The Gemara explains: Josiah **said to** the Levites: **If** the Ark **is exiled with you to Babylonia,** there is a real concern that **you will never return it to its place. Rather,** I am concealing it so you will no longer need to carry it. **"Now serve the Lord your God, and His people Israel"** (II Chronicles 35:3) in the other tasks that are incumbent upon you.

פִּטּוּם שֶׁמֶן הַמִּשְׁחָה "וְאַתָּה קַח לְךָ וגו' וְקִדָּה חֲמֵשׁ מֵאוֹת וגו'" – שֶׁהֵן אֶלֶף וַחֲמֵשׁ מֵאוֹת מָנִים. "שֶׁמֶן זַיִת הִין" – שְׁנֵים עָשָׂר לוֹג שֶׁבּוֹ שׁוֹלְקִין אֶת הָעִיקָּרִין, דִּבְרֵי רַבִּי מֵאִיר.

§ Apropos the anointing oil mentioned among the items sequestered with the Ark, the Gemara elaborates: The types and quantities of spices that were used in the **blending of the anointing oil** are detailed in the verses: **"Take you also unto yourself** the chief spices, of flowing myrrh five hundred shekels, and of sweet cinnamon half so much, even two hundred and fifty, and of sweet calamus two hundred and fifty, **and of cassia [*kidda*]**[B] **five hundred,** after the shekel of the Sanctuary" (Exodus 30:23–24). All together, **they total 1,500 *maneh*.** The Gemara explains in a *baraita* how this was done: **"And of olive oil a *hin*"** (Exodus 30:24), this *hin* equals **twelve *log*** of oil **in which they would cook the roots**[H] of the plants mentioned in the verse above, so that the oil would absorb their fragrance; **this is the statement of Rabbi Meir.**

NOTES

He saw that it is written, etc. – **שֶׁרָאָה שֶׁכָּתוּב וכו'**: Some commentaries wonder: As King Josiah was righteous and involved in learning Torah, wasn't he aware of this verse beforehand? They explain that when Hilkiah, the High Priest, found the Torah scroll in the Temple, it was open to this verse. Therefore, Josiah saw this as a warning and an instruction that in the near future the Jewish nation would go into exile, and he decided to conceal the Ark (*Yefei Mareh*; *Be'er Sheva* on *Horayot* 12a).

He arose and sequestered it – **עָמַד וּגְנָזוֹ**: The commentaries add that one can even find a hint to this in Solomon's prayer at the inauguration of the Temple. Solomon said: "And there have I set a place for the Ark," (I Kings 8:21) to indicate that he had made an additional place for the Ark of the Covenant to be buried when the need arose.

HALAKHA

They would cook the roots – **שׁוֹלְקִין אֶת הָעִיקָּרִין**: How did Moses prepare the anointing oil? He would pulverize each of the elements separately, then mix them together and soak them in pure, sweet water until all of the essence was extracted. He would then pour a *hin*, i.e., twelve *log*, of olive oil onto the water and boil it all on a fire until the water evaporated, leaving only the oil, which was then stored in a container for future generations (Rambam *Sefer Avoda*, *Hilkhot Beit HaBeḥira* 4:1).

BACKGROUND

Cassia [*kidda*] – **קִידָּה**: In the Septuagint, *kidda* is translated as cassia, apparently referring to *Cinnamomum cassia*. It is a tall tree whose height extends up to 10 m, native to East Asia where it is grown for its bark, flower buds, and the oil that is extracted from it. The Ramban (Exodus 30:34) identified it as the Indian tree *Aquilaria agallocha*, a tall tree with a wide trunk that contains very fragrant sap. Josephus identifies it as the iris. The *Iris florentina*, a species of iris, is used to produce perfume.

Aquilaria agallocha

Iris florentina in Monte Solaro, Italy

רַבִּי יְהוּדָה אוֹמֵר: שׁוֹלְקָן הָיָה בְּמַיִם, וְנוֹתֵן שֶׁמֶן עַל גַּבֵּיהֶן. מִשֶּׁהָיָה קוֹלֵט אֶת הָרֵיחַ הָיָה מַעֲבִירוֹ, כְּדֶרֶךְ שֶׁהַפַּטָּמִין עוֹשִׂין. הָדָא הוּא דִּכְתִיב "שֶׁמֶן מִשְׁחַת קֹדֶשׁ" וגו'.

Rabbi Yehuda says: That is not how it was prepared. Rather, the priest who prepared the oil **would cook** the roots **in water,** such that the fragrant essence would rise to the top, **and** he would then **place oil on top of** the water.[B] **When it had** completely **absorbed the fragrance, he would remove** the oil from the water, **in the manner that the perfumers prepare** fragrant oils. The accepted way of extracting fragrances was to boil the plants in water and then place the oil on top to absorb the fragrance essences. **This is as it is written:** "And you shall make it **a holy anointing oil,** a perfume compounded after the art of the perfumer; it shall be a holy anointing oil" (Exodus 30:25). "After the art of the perfumer" indicates that it should be prepared in the manner of those who make such perfumes.

תָּנֵי רַבִּי יְהוּדָה בֵּי רַבִּי אִילְעַי: שֶׁמֶן הַמִּשְׁחָה שֶׁעָשָׂה מֹשֶׁה בַּמִּדְבָּר מַעֲשֵׂה נִסִּים נַעֲשָׂה בּוֹ מִתְּחִלָּה וְעַד סוֹף, שֶׁמִּתְּחִלָּה לֹא הָיָה בּוֹ אֶלָּא שְׁנֵים עָשָׂר לוֹג, שֶׁנֶּאֱמַר "שֶׁמֶן זַיִת הִין", אִם לָסוּךְ בּוֹ אֶת הָעִיקָּרִין לֹא הָיָה בּוֹ סִפֵּק, עַל אַחַת כַּמָּה וְכַמָּה שֶׁהָאוּר בּוֹלֵעַ, וְהָעֵצִים בּוֹלְעִים, וְהַיּוֹרָה בּוֹלַעַת. וּמִמֶּנּוּ נִמְשְׁחוּ הַמִּשְׁכָּן וְכׇל כֵּלָיו, הַשּׁוּלְחָן וְכׇל כֵּלָיו, הַמְּנוֹרָה וְכׇל כֵּלֶיהָ, וּמִמֶּנּוּ נִמְשְׁחוּ אַהֲרֹן כֹּהֵן גָּדוֹל וּבָנָיו כׇּל שִׁבְעַת יְמֵי הַמִּלּוּאִים, וּמִמֶּנּוּ נִמְשְׁחוּ כֹּהֲנִים גְּדוֹלִים וּמְלָכִים.

Continuing on the subject of the anointing oil, **Rabbi Yehuda, son of Rabbi Elai, taught: The anointing oil that Moses prepared in the desert was a miraculous feat from beginning to end. At the outset, there were only twelve** ***log***[N] of oil, **as it is stated: "And of olive oil a** ***hin,***" and a *hin* is twelve *log*. **If there** initially **wasn't** even **enough** oil **to pour over the roots,**[B] **all the more so after the fire absorbs** some oil, as it reduces the amount of oil through cooking, **and the wood,** i.e., the roots from which the fragrant essence was extracted, **absorbs** some oil, **and the pot** in which the roots were cooked absorbs some oil as well. **Yet from this** small amount **were anointed the Tabernacle and all its vessels, the table and all its vessels, and the candelabrum and all its vessels. And from that** oil **Aaron the High Priest and his sons were anointed during all the seven days of consecration, and from that** oil **the High Priests and kings** throughout all the generations **were anointed.**[N]

מֶלֶךְ בַּתְּחִלָּה – טָעוּן מְשִׁיחָה, מֶלֶךְ בֶּן מֶלֶךְ – אֵין טָעוּן מְשִׁיחָה. מַאי טַעְמָא? "קוּם מְשָׁחֵהוּ כִּי זֶה הוּא" – זֶה טָעוּן מְשִׁיחָה, וְאֵין בְּנוֹ טָעוּן מְשִׁיחָה.

The *baraita* goes on to discuss those who were anointed with the anointing oil. **A king at the outset,** i.e., when his appointment as king begins a dynasty, **requires anointing** with the anointing oil. **A king** who is the **son of a king,**[H] who stands to reign in his father's place, **does not require anointing. What is the source** for this ruling? God instructed Samuel with regard to David: **"Arise, anoint him; for this is he"** (I Samuel 16:12). Only **"this"** one, i.e., David, **requires anointing,** as his monarchy begins a dynasty, **but his son does not require anointing.**

BACKGROUND

He would place oil on top of the water – נוֹתֵן שֶׁמֶן עַל גַּבֵּיהֶן: The Rambam rules that the essence of the various roots and spices was extracted by means of Rabbi Yehuda's method. This was the accepted method of producing perfumed oils throughout the generations, and is still used to this day. The plant used to produce the pleasant fragrance was boiled or soaked in water to extract the fragrance-producing substance, usually essential oils. As the density of these substances is less than that of water, it would float on the surface. Oil could then be poured onto that surface, into which the fragrance would be absorbed. This fragrant oil that was produced could be used for various perfumes.

There wasn't enough to pour over the roots – לָסוּךְ בּוֹ אֶת הָעִיקָּרִין לֹא הָיָה בּוֹ סִפֵּק: As the Gemara details here, the total weight of the roots was 1,500 shekel. Opinions are divided as to the exact weight of the biblical shekel. According to *ge'onim* and the Rambam, it was equivalent to 14.2 g, while according to Rashi it was 11.75 g. Therefore, according to the Rambam, the total weight of the roots comes to 24.850 kg; according to Rashi, it comes to 20.562 kg. Though there is a range of opinion with regard to the size of the *log*, such that 12 *log* of oil could be between 3.6 and 7.2 ℓ, it is clear that according to all the opinions this quantity of oil was insufficient to pour over all the roots.

HALAKHA

A king, son of a king – מֶלֶךְ בֶּן מֶלֶךְ: One does not anoint a king who is the son of a king. However, if there is a dispute over the succession, he is anointed in order to resolve the dispute and publicize that he is the king (Rambam *Sefer Shofetim, Hilkhot Melakhim UMilhemoteihem* 1:12).

NOTES

At the outset there were only twelve ***log*** **– שֶׁמִּתְּחִלָּה לֹא הָיָה בּוֹ אֶלָּא שְׁנֵים עָשָׂר לוֹג:** The quantity is based on the verse that explicitly states: "And of olive oil a *hin*," and a *hin* is a liquid measurement of volume that is equivalent to twelve *log*. Later on, the Gemara derives the measurement of twelve from the numerical value of the word *zeh*, twelve. It maintains there were always twelve *log* of anointing oil, regardless of how much was used.

And from that oil the High Priests and kings were anointed – וּמִמֶּנּוּ נִמְשְׁחוּ כֹּהֲנִים גְּדוֹלִים וּמְלָכִים: In the Torah, the commandment to anoint with the anointing oil is mentioned only with regard to Aaron and his sons. However, the verse in I Kings states explicitly that Solomon was anointed with the anointing oil, as it is written, "And Zadok the priest took the horn of oil out of the Tent, and anointed Solomon" (I Kings 1:39). The following question has been raised: The verse states concerning the anointing oil: "Whoever put any of it upon a non-priest [*zar*], he shall be cut off from his people" (Exodus 30:33). Since the king is not a priest, how could they use this oil to anoint kings? Ibn Ezra claims that the anointing of Solomon was a provisional edict issued in exigent circumstances. The discussion in the Gemara, however, appears to contradict this claim (Ramban). Rav Sa'adia Gaon holds that there was a tradition passed down to anoint David and his descendants. The Ramban (Exodus 30:33) explains that the verse's mention of the prohibition against anointing a *zar* is not referring to a non-priest but to one who is not in the service of God. Both kings and High Priests are considered the anointed ones of God, as it is written, "I have found David My servant; with My holy oil have I anointed him" (Psalms 89:21).

אֲבָל כֹּהֵן גָּדוֹל בֶּן כֹּהֵן גָּדוֹל, אֲפִילּוּ עַד עֲשָׂרָה דּוֹרוֹת – טָעוּן מְשִׁיחָה. וְכוּלּוֹ קַיָּים לֶעָתִיד לָבֹא, הֲדָא הוּא דִּכְתִיב ״שֶׁמֶן מִשְׁחַת קוֹדֶשׁ יִהְיֶה זֶה לִי לְדוֹרוֹתֵיכֶם״.

In contrast to the anointing of kings, with regard to **a High Priest, son of a High Priest,**[H] **even up to ten generations** or more of High Priests of fathers and sons, each one **requires anointing,** as the position of High Priest is not passed as an inheritance from father to son like the monarchy. Rabbi Yehuda concludes his statement about the miraculous nature of the anointing oil, adding that despite the reduction in the amount of oil during its preparation process, as well as its multiple uses throughout history, **it all** will remain **intact in the future** that will surely **come. This is as it is written: "This [*zeh*] shall be a holy anointing oil unto Me throughout your generations"** (Exodus 30:31). The word *zeh* has a numerical value of twelve, which teaches that the original twelve *log* of oil that existed at the outset will remain throughout all the generations.

אֵין מוֹשְׁחִין הַמְּלָכִים אֶלָּא עַל גַּבֵּי הַמַּעְיָין, שֶׁנֶּאֱמַר ״וְהִרְכַּבְתֶּם אֶת שְׁלֹמֹה בְנִי עַל הַפִּרְדָּה אֲשֶׁר לִי וְהוֹרַדְתֶּם אוֹתוֹ אֶל גִּיחוֹן וּמָשַׁח אוֹתוֹ שָׁם צָדוֹק הַכֹּהֵן וְנָתָן הַנָּבִיא לְמֶלֶךְ עַל יִשְׂרָאֵל״.

§ The Gemara continues the discussion of anointing kings, citing an additional *baraita* on the subject. **One** may **anoint kings only next to a spring.**[H] It is a fortuitous sign that their monarchy should continue uninterrupted just as the waters of the spring flow uninterrupted throughout the year, **as it is stated** with regard to the coronation of Solomon in the days of King David: "And the king said unto them: Take with you the servants of your lord, **and cause Solomon my son to ride upon my own mule, and bring him down to Giḥon.**[B] **And let Zadok the priest and Nathan the prophet anoint him there king over Israel"** (I Kings 1:33–34). From this verse, the Sages learned that all kings should be anointed near a spring, just as David instructed that the anointing of Solomon take place near the Giḥon spring.

אֵין מוֹשְׁחִין מֶלֶךְ בֶּן מֶלֶךְ אֶלָּא מִפְּנֵי הַמַּחֲלוֹקֶת. מִפְּנֵי מָה נִמְשַׁח שְׁלֹמֹה – מִפְּנֵי מַחֲלוֹקְתּוֹ שֶׁל אֲדוֹנִיָּהוּ, יוֹאָשׁ – מִפְּנֵי עֲתַלְיָהוּ, יְהוֹאָחָז – מִפְּנֵי יְהוֹיָקִים אָחִיו שֶׁהָיָה גָּדוֹל מִמֶּנּוּ שְׁתֵּי שָׁנִים, יֵהוּא מִפְּנֵי יוֹרָם.

Another *baraita* states: **One** only **anoints a king, son of a king, due to a dispute**[N] over the monarchy. For example, **why was Solomon anointed,** despite the fact that he was the son of a king? It was **because of the dispute** over the throne instigated **by** his older brother **Adonijah,**[N] who attempted to usurp the monarchy. Similarly, **Joash,** son of Ahaziah, was anointed as king (see II Kings 11:12) **due to** the threat of **Athaliah,** his paternal grandmother, who attempted to seize the monarchy for herself (II Kings 11:1–3). **Jehoahaz,** son of Josiah, was anointed (II Kings 23:30) **due to** the competition from **Jehoiakim, his brother, who was older than him by two years.**[N] Ordinarily, the older brother should have succeeded their father, but Jehoahaz was more worthy of the throne. **Jehu,** son of Jehoshaphat, was anointed **due to Joram,**[N] son of Ahab, who was the incumbent king, and Jehu rebelled against his rule (see II Kings 9:6).

HALAKHA

A High Priest, son of a High Priest – כֹּהֵן גָּדוֹל בֶּן כֹּהֵן גָּדוֹל: When the anointing oil was available, they would use it to anoint the High Priest, as all High Priests require anointing, even if the High Priest is the son of a High Priest and is serving in his father's place.

One may anoint kings only next to a spring – אֵין מוֹשְׁחִין הַמְּלָכִים אֶלָּא עַל גַּבֵּי הַמַּעְיָין: Kings from the house of David must be anointed near a spring (Rambam *Sefer Avoda, Hilkhot Kelei HaMikdash* 1:11 and *Sefer Shofetim, Hilkhot Melakhim UMilḥemoteihem* 1:11).

BACKGROUND

Giḥon – גִּיחוֹן: Hezekiah's tunnel leads from the Giḥon spring to the Pool of Siloam.

Hezekiah's tunnel

NOTES

Due to a dispute – מִפְּנֵי הַמַּחֲלוֹקֶת: The Rambam writes that the purpose of anointing in this situation is in order to resolve the dispute and inform all that this is the one and only king (*Sefer Avoda, Hilkhot Kelei HaMikdash* 1:11). Alternatively, Rashi explains that in the case of a dispute, the dynastic succession has been interrupted such that the resolution of the dispute amounts to the inauguration of a new dynasty, the first of which requires anointing. Others write that the reason for anointing is due to the fact that this inheritance is not similar to the inheritance of property, but rather it is a right that is given to the king from the nation and for their benefit. However, in a case where his appointment is done against the will of the nation or a significant portion of the nation, the rights of inheritance are canceled, and the right to appoint the king reverts to the entire nation through their spiritual leaders, i.e., the Sanhedrin, who are the instructors of the nation (*She'elot UTeshuvot Mishpetei Uziel* 2, *Yoreh De'a* 42).

The dispute instigated by Adonijah – מַחֲלוֹקְתּוֹ שֶׁל אֲדוֹנִיָּהוּ: Some ask: Why did the Gemara state that Solomon was anointed for this reason? It could simply have stated that they anointed him because he had older brothers who were candidates for the throne? Some explain that Solomon was appointed to the monarchy by his father David, and a king has the right to appoint any son he chooses as his successor. Therefore, there was a need to anoint Solomon only because of Adonijah's dispute over the monarchy (*Magen Giborim*).

Despite the fact that the succession is hereditary, with the caveat that the king can choose to pass on the monarchy to whichever son he chooses, its validity is dependent on whether the king is accepted by the people. If the nation does not wish to accept someone as king, he can be dismissed from his position, returning him to the status of a regular citizen. Such was King David's status when he was forced to flee Jerusalem due to Absalom's rebellion.

Older than him by two years – גָּדוֹל מִמֶּנּוּ שְׁתֵּי שָׁנִים: Jehoahaz was twenty-three years old when he began his rule, and he ruled for three months (II Kings 23:30). In his place, Jehoiakim was appointed king when he was twenty-five years old. This indicates that he was two years older than Jehoahaz, as is explained in *Seder Olam* (see *Be'er Sheva*).

Jehu was anointed due to Joram – יֵהוּא מִפְּנֵי יוֹרָם: The Babylonian Talmud (*Horayot* 11b; *Keritot* 5b) asks why the *baraita* had to resort to this reason for Jehu's anointing. Jehu wasn't the son of a king; therefore, it is clear that he required anointing just as with any king who begins a dynasty. The Gemara there answers that Jehu didn't need anointing because only kings from the Davidic dynasty are anointed, not those of the kingdom of Israel, as is explained later in the Gemara. Consequently, Jehu, who was a candidate for the monarchy in the kingdom of Israel, would not have needed anointing if not for the dispute with Joram.

לא כן כתיב "קום משחהו כי זה הוא" זה טעון משיחה ואין מלכי ישראל טעונין משיחה! אלא, יהואחז מפני יהויקים אחיו שהיה גדול ממנו שתי שנים. ולא יאשיהו גנזו? הדא אמרה: באפרסמון נמשח.

The Gemara presents a difficulty concerning the latter example cited previously: Why was Jehu anointed as king? **Isn't it written** with regard to the anointing of David: **"Arise, anoint him; for this is he"** (I Samuel 16:12)? **This** king, i.e., any king from the house of David, **requires anointing, but the kings** from the kingdom **of Israel,** who were not descendants of the house of David, **do not require anointing.**[N] Jehu, a king of Israel, should not have required anointing. The Gemara presents a counter-question: According to that line of reasoning, there is a further difficulty in the *baraita*. How can one explain that **Jehoahaz** was anointed **due to** the competition from **Jehoiakim his brother, who was older than him by two years? Didn't Josiah,** their father, **sequester** the anointing oil as was explained previously? How then was there oil available to anoint Jehoahaz, his son? Rather, when the *baraita* says that Jehoahaz was anointed, **that is to say** that **he was anointed with balsam**[B] oil[H] and not with the anointing oil. Similarly, one can say that Jehu was also anointed with balsam oil and not with the anointing oil.

אין מושחין המלכים אלא מן הקרן. שאול ויהוא נמשחו מן הפך – היתה מלכותן מלכות עוברת, דוד ושלמה נמשחו מן הקרן – היתה מלכותן מלכות קיימת.

It was further taught that **one** may **anoint kings only** with anointing oil that is poured **from a horn,** and not any other vessel. **Saul and Jehu were anointed from** oil poured from an earthenware **cruse,** and **their monarchy was a temporary monarchy. David and Solomon were anointed** with oil poured **from a horn,** and **their monarchy was a monarchy that was established** for many generations.

אין מושחין כהנים מלכים. אמר רבי יודה ענתונדרייא: על שם "לא יסור שבט מיהודה". אמר רבי חייא בר אדא "למען יאריך ימים על ממלכתו הוא ובניו בקרב ישראל" מה כתיב בתריה – "לא יהיה לכהנים הלוים".

One may **not anoint priests** to serve **as kings**[N] *ab initio*. **Rabbi Yuda Antondraya said** that this rule is **on account of** the verse that states: **"The scepter shall not depart from Judah"** (Genesis 49:10), i.e., the scepter of monarchy will forever belong to the tribe of Judah and not to any other tribe. Therefore, the priests who are from the tribe of Levi may not be appointed as kings. **Rabbi Ḥiyya bar Adda said** that this rule is derived from a different verse, as it is written: **"To the end that he may prolong his days in his kingdom, he and his children, in the midst of Israel"** (Deuteronomy 17:20). **What is written** in the **subsequent** verse? **"The priests the Levites, even all the tribe of Levi, shall have no** portion nor inheritance with Israel" (Deuteronomy 18:1). This implies that the priests will have no part in that which is referred to previously, i.e., the monarchy.

אמר רבי יוחנן: הוא יוחנן הוא יהואחז. והא כתיב "הבכור יוחנן"? בכור למלכות. אמר רבי יוחנן: הוא שלום הוא צדקיהו. והכתיב "השלישי צדקיהו והרביעי שלום"! שלישי לתולדות רביעי למלכות.

It was taught previously that Jehoahaz was anointed king, despite the fact that his brother Jehoiakim was older. **Rabbi Yoḥanan said:** The one who is called **Johanan** in the verse, "And the sons of Josiah: The firstborn Johanan, the second Jehoiakim, the third Zedekiah, the fourth Shallum" (I Chronicles 3:15), **he** is the same as the one called **Jehoahaz. But isn't it written** in that verse **"the firstborn Johanan,"** and it was just stated that Jehoiakim was two years older than Jehoahaz? The Gemara explains that in calling Jehoahaz firstborn, the verse means that he was the **first** to rise **to the monarchy. Rabbi Yoḥanan** continued and **said: He** who is called **Shallum** is the same as **he** who is called **Zedekiah.** The Gemara challenges this statement: **But isn't it written: "The third Zedekiah, the fourth Shallum,"** indicating that these are two different people? The Gemara explains the verse is as follows: He was the **third in birth position, but he was fourth to** achieve **kingship,** as his two brothers, Jehoahaz and Jehoiakim, as well as his nephew, Jehoiachin, all ruled before him.

צדקיהו – שצידק עליו מדת הדין, שלום – שבימיו שלמה מלכות בית דוד. (ריש לקיש אמר) לא שלום הוה שמיה ולא צדקיהו הוה שמיה, אלא מתניה, הדא הוא דכתיב "וימלך מלך בבל את מתניה דודו תחתיו ויסב את שמו צדקיהו".

The Gemara cites an additional *baraita* that discusses these names: He was called **Zedekiah because he accepted** [*tzideik*] **upon himself the attribute of judgment** when the king of Babylonia had Zedekiah's sons slaughtered in front of him and then proceeded to have his eyes gouged out. Zedekiah justified the punishment that God had inflicted upon him. He was called **Shallum** because **in his days the kingdom of the house of David was completed** [*shalma*], as he was the last king in King David's dynasty. **Reish Lakish said: His name was not Shallum and his name was not Zedekiah; rather,** his name was **Mattaniah. This is as it is written: "And the king of Babylon made Mattaniah, his father's brother, king in his stead and changed his name to Zedekiah"** (II Kings 24:17). This verse indicates that the king of Babylonia changed his name to Zedekiah, but it was not his original name.

NOTES

But the kings of Israel do not require anointing – ואין מלכי ישראל טעונין משיחה: The commentaries are divided with regard to the question of whether King Saul was anointed with the anointing oil. According to the opinion of the Radak, he was anointed with balsam oil. However, from the discussion of Rashi and *Tosafot*, it appears that King Saul was indeed anointed with the anointing oil, and only after the coronation of David was the use of that oil limited to members of the Davidic line (see *Ḥok Natan* and others).

One may not anoint priests as kings – אין מושחין כהנים מלכים: This does not mean that one may instead coronate them in a different manner. Rather, it means that they should not be appointed as kings at all.

BACKGROUND

Balsam – אפרסמון: This is apparently the plant *Commiphora opobalsamum*, a bush or low tree 3–5 m in height, with thin branches and compound leaves. The best quality perfume drips from the edges of the stems in small drops, while most of the perfume is extracted by boiling the branches. Although balsam oil also served for medicinal purposes, its primary use was for incense and perfumed oil. Balsam was so valuable in the ancient world that its price was equal its weight in gold.

Detail from Madaba Map depicting a branch of balsam (circled)

HALAKHA

He was anointed with balsam oil – באפרסמון נמשח: Kings from the house of David must be anointed with the anointing oil. Kings of Israel are anointed only with balsam oil (Rambam *Sefer Avoda, Hilkhot Kelei HaMikdash* 1:7, 11 and *Sefer Shofetim, Hilkhot Melakhim UMilḥemoteihem* 1:10).

אָמַר רַבִּי יוֹחָנָן: בְּאַמָּה שֶׁל שִׁשָּׁה טְפָחִים הָיָה הָאָרוֹן עָשׂוּי. מַאן תַּנָּא בְּאַמָּה שֶׁל שִׁשָּׁה טְפָחִים – רַבִּי מֵאִיר הִיא. דִּתְנַן, רַבִּי מֵאִיר אוֹמֵר: כָּל הָאַמּוֹת הָיוּ בְּבֵינוֹנִית. רַבִּי יְהוּדָה אוֹמֵר: אַמּוֹת הַבִּנְיָן שִׁשָּׁה, שֶׁל כֵּלִים חֲמִשָּׁה.

§ The Gemara turns to a discussion of the measurements of the Ark. **Rabbi Yoḥanan said: The Ark was constructed with a cubit of six handbreadths.** The unit of measurement used in the Torah to describe the Ark, the cubit, equaled six handbreadths. **Who is the *tanna*** that holds that the Ark was constructed **using cubits of six handbreadths? It is Rabbi Meir, as we learned** in a mishna: **Rabbi Meir says: All the cubits that** are mentioned in the Torah **were medium**-sized cubits six handbreadths in length. **Rabbi Yehuda says** that **cubits** used for measuring **the building,** such as the walls or the gates, were of **six** handbreadths. However, cubits used for measuring **the vessels,** such as the Ark, were of **five** handbreadths.

עַל דַּעְתֵּיהּ דְּרַבִּי מֵאִיר דְּאָמַר בְּאַמָּה שֶׁל שִׁשָּׁה טְפָחִים הָיָה הָאָרוֹן עָשׂוּי, אוֹרְכּוֹ שֶׁל אָרוֹן חֲמִשָּׁה עָשָׂר טְפָחִים, דִּכְתִיב ״אַמָּתַיִם וָחֵצִי אָרְכּוֹ״ אַמְּתָא אַשִּׁיתָא, וְאַמְּתָא אַשִּׁיתָא, וּפַלְגוּת אַמְּתָא תְּלָתָא.

According to the opinion of Rabbi Meir, who said that **the Ark was constructed using a cubit of six handbreadths, the length of the Ark was fifteen handbreadths, as it is written: "Two cubits and a half shall be the length thereof"** (Exodus 25:10). **A cubit is six** handbreadths, **and** another **cubit is six** handbreadths, **and a half-cubit is three** handbreadths. This totals fifteen handbreadths.

וְאַרְבָּעָה לוּחוֹת הָיוּ בּוֹ, שְׁנַיִם שְׁלֵמִים וּשְׁנַיִם שְׁבוּרִים, דִּכְתִיב ״אֲשֶׁר שִׁבַּרְתָּ וְשַׂמְתָּם בָּאָרוֹן״. הַלּוּחוֹת הָיוּ כָּל אֶחָד וְאֶחָד אׇרְכּוֹ שִׁשָּׁה טְפָחִים רׇחְבּוֹ שִׁשָּׁה. וְתֵן אׇרְכָּן שֶׁל לוּחוֹת לְאוֹרְכּוֹ שֶׁל אָרוֹן – נִשְׁתַּיֵּיר שָׁם שְׁלֹשָׁה טְפָחִים.

And four tablets were placed **in** the Ark, **two** tablets were **whole and two** tablets were **broken, as it is written:** "And I will write on the tablets the words that were on the first tablets **which you did break, and you shall put them in the Ark"** (Deuteronomy 10:2). The juxtaposition of these phrases teaches that the broken tablets were also placed in the Ark. **The length of each one of the tablets was six handbreadths, and its width was six handbreadths. Lay the length of the tablets across the length of the Ark,** and **three handbreadths remain there.** The length of the Ark was fifteen handbreadths, and the length of the two tablets together was twelve handbreadths; there were three remaining handbreadths available at the end of the Ark.

Perek **VI**
Daf **16** Amud **b**

LANGUAGE

Handling [*shilut*] – שִׁילוּט: From the Hebrew root *shalat*, šalṭu in Akkadian, meaning mastery, or grasping and holding.

NOTES

Where the Torah scroll was placed – שֶׁסֵּפֶר תּוֹרָה מוּנָּח: Rabbeinu Tam (*Sefer HaYashar*) argues that the Gemara's use of the term placed is evidence for his opinion that a Torah scroll must be placed in the Ark lying down and not standing up, as this is the position in which the Torah scroll was placed in the Ark of the Covenant.

תֵּן מֵהֶם חֲצִי טֶפַח לְכָל כּוֹתֶל – נִשְׁתַּיֵּיר שְׁנֵי טְפָחִים לְסֵפֶר תּוֹרָה.

Give, i.e., subtract, **from** those remaining three handbreadths **a half-handbreadth for** the width of **each wall** of the Ark. **There remain two handbreadths** in which to place **the Torah scroll** that Moses wrote (see *Bava Batra* 14a).

רׇחְבּוֹ שֶׁל אָרוֹן תִּשְׁעָה טְפָחִים, דִּכְתִיב ״אַמָּה וָחֵצִי רׇחְבּוֹ״ אַמְּתָא אַשִּׁיתָא, וּפַלְגוּת אַמְּתָא תְּלָתָא. וְאַרְבָּעָה לוּחוֹת הָיוּ בּוֹ, שְׁנַיִם שְׁלֵימִים וּשְׁנַיִם שְׁבוּרִים, דִּכְתִיב ״אֲשֶׁר שִׁבַּרְתָּ וְשַׂמְתָּם בָּאָרוֹן״.

The width of the Ark was nine handbreadths, as it is written: "And a cubit and a half the breadth thereof" (Exodus 25:10). **A cubit is six** handbreadths, **and a half-cubit is three** handbreadths. Therefore, the total width of the Ark is nine handbreadths. **And four tablets were** placed **in** the Ark, **two** tablets were **whole and two** tablets were **broken.** What is the source for the fact that the broken tablets were placed in the Ark? **As it is written:** "And I will write on the tablets the words that were on the first tablets **which you did break, and you shall put them in the Ark"** (Deuteronomy 10:2).

הַלּוּחוֹת הָיוּ כָּל אֶחָד וְאֶחָד אׇרְכָּן שִׁשָּׁה טְפָחִים וְרׇחְבָּן שִׁשָּׁה טְפָחִים, תֵּן רׇחְבָּן שֶׁל לוּחוֹת לְרוֹחְבּוֹ שֶׁל אָרוֹן – נִשְׁתַּיֵּיר שָׁם שְׁלֹשָׁה טְפָחִים, חֲצִי טֶפַח מִכָּאן לְכוֹתֶל זֶה, וַחֲצִי טֶפַח מִכָּאן לְכוֹתֶל זֶה, וּטְפָחַיִים לְשִׁילוּט מָקוֹם שֶׁסֵּפֶר תּוֹרָה מוּנָּח.

The length of each one of the tablets was six handbreadths and their width was six handbreadths. If one **lays the width of the tablets across the width of the Ark, three handbreadths remains there: A half-handbreadth from here,** on one side, **for** the thickness of **this wall, and a half-handbreadth from here,** on the other side, **for** the thickness of **that wall, and two handbreadths for handling** [*shilut*][L] **in the place where the Torah scroll was placed.**[N] It was necessary to leave this space around the Torah scroll in order to allow the insertion and removal of the Torah scroll with ease. This is the opinion of Rabbi Meir that is adopted by Rabbi Yoḥanan.

רַבִּי שִׁמְעוֹן בֶּן לָקִישׁ אָמַר: בְּאַמָּה בַּת חֲמִשָּׁה טְפָחִים הָיָה הָאָרוֹן עָשׂוּי. מַאן תָּנָא בְּאַמָּה בַּת חֲמִשָּׁה טְפָחִים – רַבִּי יְהוּדָה. דִּתְנַן תַּמָּן: רַבִּי יְהוּדָה אוֹמֵר: אַמַּת הַבִּנְיָן שִׁשָּׁה, שֶׁל הַכֵּלִים חֲמִשָּׁה. וְהָהֵן אָרוֹן – כְּלִי הוּא.

Rabbi Shimon ben Lakish disagrees with Rabbi Yoḥanan's opinion. He **said: The Ark was constructed using a cubit of five handbreadths. Who is the *tanna*** that holds that the Ark was constructed **using a cubit of five handbreadths?** It is **Rabbi Yehuda. As we learned** in a mishna **there** (*Kelim* 17:10): **Rabbi Yehuda says:** The **cubit** used as the unit of measurement for **the construction** of the walls and the gates was of **six** handbreadths; the cubit for **the vessels** was of **five** handbreadths. **And this Ark is a vessel.** Therefore, **it** was constructed with a cubit of five handbreadths.

עַל דַּעְתֵּיהּ דְּרַבִּי יְהוּדָה דּוּ אָמַר בְּאַמָּה שֶׁל חֲמִשָּׁה טְפָחִים – הָיָה אוֹרְכּוֹ עָשׂוּי שְׁנֵים עָשָׂר טֶפַח וּמֶחֱצָה, דִּכְתִיב ״אַמָּתַיִם וָחֵצִי אׇרְכּוֹ״ אַמְּתָא חֲמִשָּׁה וְאַמְּתָא חֲמִשָּׁה וּפַלְגּוּת אַמְּתָא תְּרֵי וּפַלְיג.

According to the opinion of Rabbi Yehuda, who said that unit of measurement for **the Ark was a cubit of five handbreadths, it was constructed to a length of twelve and a half handbreadths, as it is written: "Two cubits and a half shall be the length thereof"** (Exodus 25:10). **A cubit is five** handbreadths, **and** another **cubit is five** handbreadths, **and a half-cubit is two and a half** handbreadths, which totals twelve and a half handbreadths.

וְאַרְבָּעָה לוּחוֹת הָיוּ בוֹ שְׁנַיִם שְׁלֵימִים וּשְׁנַיִם שְׁבוּרִים, דִּכְתִיב ״אֲשֶׁר שִׁבַּרְתָּ וְשַׂמְתָּם בָּאָרוֹן״ וְהַלּוּחוֹת הָיָה כׇּל אֶחָד וְאֶחָד אׇרְכָּן שִׁשָּׁה טְפָחִים וְרׇחְבָּן שִׁשָּׁה טְפָחִים, תֵּן אׇרְכָּן שֶׁל לוּחוֹת לְאׇרְכּוֹ שֶׁל אָרוֹן וְנִשְׁתַּיֵּיר שָׁם חֲצִי טֶפַח. אֶצְבַּע לְכוֹתֶל מִכָּאן, וְאֶצְבַּע לְכוֹתֶל מִכָּאן.

And four tablets were placed **in** the Ark, **two** tablets were **whole and two** tablets were **broken, as it is written:** "And I will write on the tables the words that were on the first tables **which you did break, and you shall put them in the Ark"** (Deuteronomy 10:2). **Each one of the tablets' length was six handbreadths, and its width was six handbreadths.** If one **lays the length of the tablets across the length of the Ark, a half-handbreadth remains there.** This leaves **a fingerbreadth,** equal to a quarter of a handbreadth, **for the wall from here,** on one side, and **a fingerbreadth for the wall from there,** on the other side. According to this opinion, the Torah scroll was not placed in the Ark.

רוֹחְבּוֹ שֶׁל אָרוֹן שִׁבְעָה טְפָחִים וּמֶחֱצָה, דִּכְתִיב ״אַמָּה וָחֵצִי רׇחְבּוֹ״ אַמְּתָא חֲמִשָּׁה וּפַלְגּוּת אַמְּתָא תְּרֵי וּפַלְיג, וְאַרְבָּעָה לוּחוֹת הָיוּ בוֹ שְׁנַיִם שְׁלֵימִים וּשְׁנַיִם שְׁבוּרִים, דִּכְתִיב ״אֲשֶׁר שִׁבַּרְתָּ וְשַׂמְתָּם בָּאָרוֹן״.

The width of the Ark was seven and a half handbreadths, as it is written: "And a cubit and a half the breadth thereof" (Exodus 25:10). **A cubit is five** handbreadths, **and a half-cubit is two and a half** handbreadths, which totals seven and a half handbreadths. **And four tablets were** placed **in** the Ark, **two** tablets were **whole and two** tablets were **broken, as it is written:** "And I will write on the tables the words that were on the first tables **which you did break, and you shall put them in the Ark"** (Deuteronomy 10:2).

הַלּוּחוֹת הָיָה כׇּל אֶחָד וְאֶחָד אׇרְכָּן שִׁשָּׁה טְפָחִים וְרׇחְבָּן שִׁשָּׁה טְפָחִים. תֵּן רׇחְבָּן לְרוֹחְבּוֹ שֶׁל אָרוֹן וְנִשְׁתַּיֵּיר שָׁם טֶפַח וּמֶחֱצָה, אֶצְבַּע לְכוֹתֶל מִכָּאן וְאֶצְבַּע לְכוֹתֶל מִכָּאן, חֲצִי טֶפַח מִכָּאן וַחֲצִי טֶפַח מִכָּאן לְשִׁילּוּט.

The length of each one of the tablets was six handbreadths, and their width was six handbreadths. If one **lays the width of the tablets across the width of the Ark, one and a half handbreadths remains there: A fingerbreadth for the wall from here,** on one side, **and a fingerbreadth for the wall from there,** on the other side, as well as **a half-handbreadth from here,** on one side, **and a half-handbreadth from here,** on the other side, **for handling** the tablets.

כֵּיצַד עָשָׂה בְּצַלְאֵל אֶת הָאָרוֹן? רַבִּי חֲנִינָא אָמַר: שָׁלֹשׁ תֵּיבוֹת עֲשָׂאוֹ, שְׁתַּיִם שֶׁל זָהָב וְאַחַת שֶׁל עֵץ. נָתַן שֶׁל זָהָב בְּשֶׁל עֵץ, וְשֶׁל עֵץ בְּשֶׁל זָהָב, וְצִיפָּהוּ, דִּכְתִיב ״וְצִפִּיתָ אוֹתוֹ זָהָב טָהוֹר מִבַּיִת וּמִחוּץ״. מַה תַּלְמוּד לוֹמַר ״תְּצַפֶּנּוּ״ – לְהָבִיא שְׂפָתוֹ הָעֶלְיוֹנָה.

The Gemara continues its discussion of the Ark. **How did Bezalel construct the Ark? Rabbi Ḥanina said: He constructed it of three boxes,** each one larger than the previous one (see *Yoma* 72b). **Two** of them were made **of gold** and **one** was made **of wood. He placed** the smallest box, which was made **of gold, in** the box **of wood, and** he placed the box **of wood in** the box **of gold,** the largest box. **And** he then **overlaid** the lip of the box of wood with gold as well, **as it is written: "And you shall overlay it with pure gold, within and without** shall you overlay it" (Exodus 25:11). The verse already stated: "You shall overlay it." **What** is the added meaning when **the verse states: "Shall you overlay it?"** The added words **convey** that **the upper lip** of the wooden box was also covered in gold.

LANGUAGE

Cube [*tatroga*] – **טַטְרוֹגָה**: From the Greek τετράγωνος, *tetragonos*, meaning with four angles or squared.

Beryl [*tarshish*] – **תַּרְשִׁישׁ**: This word has a number of different meanings. Some say the sea referred to in the Gemara was found near a place on the coast of the Mediterranean that exported precious metals and gems. It is not clear precisely where it was, as there was more than one locale with markets in precious metals and gems, and they all had similar names. Examples of these are Tarsus in Cilicia on the southern coast of Asia Minor, and Tartessos in southern Spain. Another option, mentioned by some biblical commentaries, is that it refers to the sea near Tzor, in modern-day Lebanon, near Rosh Hanikra on Israel's northeastern border.

Tarshish is also the name of one of the gemstones that was set in the breastplate of the High Priest (Exodus 28:20). According to the classic Aramaic translations of the Bible, it is to be identified with the *khrom yama*, meaning the color of the sea. This is a green-blue stone, similar to the color of seawater. It is called aquamarine in Latin, and the Septuagint translates it as chrysolite.

Aquamarine

רַבִּי שִׁמְעוֹן בֶּן לָקִישׁ אָמַר: תֵּיבָה אַחַת עֲשָׂאוֹ וְצִיפָּהוּ, דִּכְתִיב ״וְצִפִּיתָ אוֹתוֹ זָהָב טָהוֹר מִבַּיִת וּמִחוּץ״. מַה תַּלְמוּד לוֹמַר ״תְּצַפֶּנּוּ״? אָמַר רַבִּי פִּנְחָס לְהָבִיא בֵּין נֶסֶר לְנֶסֶר.

Alternatively, Rabbi Shimon ben Lakish said: **He constructed one box and overlaid it** on all sides with gold, **as it is written: "And you shall overlay it with pure gold, within and without** shall you overlay it" (Exodus 25:11). According to this explanation, **what** is the added meaning when **the verse states: "Shall you overlay it"? Rabbi Pineḥas said:** The added words **convey** that the area **between each board**[N] needed to be covered in gold as well, to insure that no part of the Ark lacked a gold covering.

כֵּיצַד הָיוּ הַלּוּחוֹת כְּתוּבִים? רַבִּי חֲנִינָה בֶּן גַּמְלִיאֵל אוֹמֵר: חֲמִשָּׁה עַל לוּחַ זֶה וַחֲמִשָּׁה עַל לוּחַ זֶה, הֲדָא הוּא דִּכְתִיב ״וַיִּכְתְּבֵם עַל שְׁנֵי לוּחוֹת אֲבָנִים״, חֲמִשָּׁה עַל לוּחַ זֶה וַחֲמִשָּׁה עַל לוּחַ זֶה. וְרַבָּנַן אָמְרִי: עֲשָׂרָה עַל לוּחַ זֶה וַעֲשָׂרָה עַל לוּחַ זֶה, הֲדָא הוּא דִּכְתִיב ״וַיַּגֵּד לָכֶם אֶת בְּרִיתוֹ אֲשֶׁר צִוָּה אֶתְכֶם לַעֲשׂוֹת עֲשֶׂרֶת הַדְּבָרִים״ – עֲשָׂרָה עַל לוּחַ זֶה וַעֲשָׂרָה עַל לוּחַ זֶה. רַבִּי שִׁמְעוֹן בֶּן יוֹחַאי אוֹמֵר: עֶשְׂרִים עַל לוּחַ זֶה וְעֶשְׂרִים עַל לוּחַ זֶה, דִּכְתִיב ״וַיִּכְתְּבֵם עַל שְׁנֵי לוּחוֹת אֲבָנִים״ עֶשְׂרִים עַל לוּחַ זֶה, וְעֶשְׂרִים עַל לוּחַ זֶה. רַבִּי סִימַאי אָמַר: אַרְבָּעִים עַל לוּחַ זֶה, וְאַרְבָּעִים עַל לוּחַ זֶה, דִּכְתִיב ״מִזֶּה וּמִזֶּה הֵם כְּתוּבִים״ – טַטְרוֹגָה.

The Gemara continues with discussion of the two tablets. **How were the tablets written? Rabbi Ḥanina ben Gamliel says: Five on this tablet and five on that tablet. This is as it is written: "And He wrote them upon two tablets of stone"** (Deuteronomy 4:13), i.e., **five** of the Ten Commandments **on this tablet and five on that tablet. But the Rabbis say:** All of the **Ten** Commandments were written **on this tablet and** the same **ten were written on that tablet.**[N] **This is as it is written: "And He declared unto you His covenant, which He commanded you to perform, even the ten words"** (Deuteronomy 4:13). This teaches that there were **ten on this tablet and ten on that tablet. Rabbi Shimon ben Yoḥai says: Twenty on this tablet and twenty on that tablet,**[N] **as it is written: "And He wrote them upon two tablets of stone"** (Deuteronomy 4:13). This teaches that there **were twenty on this tablet and twenty on that tablet. Rabbi Simai said: Forty on this tablet and forty on that tablet, as it is written: "On the one side and on the other were they written"** (Exodus 32:15), as **a cube** [*tatroga*].[L]

חֲנַנְיָה בֶּן אֲחִי רַבִּי יְהוֹשֻׁעַ אוֹמֵר: בֵּין כָּל דִּבּוּר וְדִבּוּר דִּקְדּוּקֶיהָ וְאוֹתִיּוֹתֶיהָ שֶׁל תּוֹרָה, דִּכְתִיב ״מְמוּלָּאִים בַּתַּרְשִׁישׁ״ – כְּיַמָּא רַבָּא.

Ḥananya, nephew of Rabbi Yehoshua, says: Between each and every statement that was written on the tablets, **its precise** details **and** the explanation of **its letters** were written as well, **as it is written: "Filled with beryl** [*tarshish*]" (Song of Songs 5:14).[L] *Tarshish* is the name of a sea, or more likely, an area of the Mediterranean. The verse is indicating that the Torah is filled with all of these details, **like the great sea** is filled with waves.

רַבִּי שִׁמְעוֹן בֶּן לָקִישׁ כַּד הֲוָה מָטֵי הָדֵין קְרָייה הֲוָה אָמַר: יָפֶה לִמְּדַנִי חֲנַנְיָה בֶּן אֲחִי רַבִּי יְהוֹשֻׁעַ, מַה הַיָּם הַזֶּה בֵּין גַּל גָּדוֹל לְגַל גָּדוֹל גַּלִּים קְטַנִּים – כָּךְ בֵּין כָּל דִּבּוּר וְדִבּוּר דִּקְדּוּקֶיהָ וְאוֹתִיּוֹתֶיהָ שֶׁל תּוֹרָה.

When Rabbi Shimon ben Lakish would reach this verse, "Filled with beryl," **he would say:** The parable that **Ḥananya, nephew of Rabbi Yehoshua, taught me is appropriate. Just as between** one **large wave and** another **large wave there are smaller waves in this sea, so too, the precise** details **and the explanations of the letters of the Torah** were written **between each and every commandment.**

NOTES

The area between each board – **בֵּין נֶסֶר לְנֶסֶר**: The sides of the Ark were made of a number of attached boards. The verse teaches that the fissure between the boards also had to be covered in gold, even if the fissure was indiscernible (Rabbi Eliyahu Fulda; Rash Sirilio)

Ten commandments were written on this tablet and the same ten were written on that tablet – **עֲשָׂרָה עַל לוּחַ זֶה וַעֲשָׂרָה עַל לוּחַ זֶה**: An alternative understanding is that the same text was not written on each of the two tablets. Rather, one tablet contained the Ten Commandments as they appear in Exodus (20:2–14), while the other tablet contained the version that appears in Deuteronomy (5:6–18) (*Ḥatam Sofer*; Ibn Ezra's long commentary on Exodus 20:1 and short commentary on Exodus 34:38).

Twenty on this tablet and twenty on that tablet – **עֶשְׂרִים עַל לוּחַ זֶה וְעֶשְׂרִים עַל לוּחַ זֶה**: Some commentaries explain that the Ten Commandments were written twice on each tablet, once on each side (Rash Sirilio). Others explain that they were written only on one side of the tablets, but they were written twice on that side (Rash Sirilio in a second explanation; *Hakotev* in the *Ein Ya'akov*). A third opinion maintains that they were written only one time on each tablet and only on one side, yet miraculously the writing could be read from the other side. Therefore, it appeared as if the Ten Commandments were written on both sides (*She'elot UTeshuvot Radbaz* 3:549; see Rashi on Exodus 32:15).

אָמַר רַבִּי תַּנְחוּמָא אִיתְקַשְׁיַית קוֹמֵי רַבִּי פִּנְחָס: אָתְיָא כְּרַבִּי יְהוּדָה וְלָא אָתְיָא כְּרַבִּי מֵאִיר. מַאי טַעְמָא דְּרַבִּי יְהוּדָה – דִּכְתִיב "לָקוֹחַ אֵת סֵפֶר הַתּוֹרָה הַזֶּה וְשַׂמְתֶּם אוֹתוֹ מִצַּד אֲרוֹן בְּרִית ה׳ וגו׳" עַל דַּעֲתֵיהּ דְּרַבִּי יְהוּדָה דּוּ אֲמַר הֵיכָן הָיָה סֵפֶר תּוֹרָה נָתוּן – כְּמִין גְּלוּסְקְיָיא עָשׂוּי לוֹ מִבַּחוּץ, וְהָיָה סֵפֶר תּוֹרָה נָתוּן בְּתוֹכוֹ.

Due to the differing opinions with regard to the length of the cubit, there are differing opinions with regard to the size of the Ark. It follows that, according to the opinion of Rabbi Meir, the Torah scroll was placed in the Ark, while according to the opinion of Rabbi Yehuda, it was not placed there. **Rabbi Tanḥuma said: I raised the** following **difficulty in the presence of Rabbi Pineḥas.** The next verse **conforms to** the opinion of **Rabbi Yehuda and does not conform to** the opinion of **Rabbi Meir. What is the source** for the opinion of **Rabbi Yehuda? As it is written: "Take this book of the law, and put it by the side of the Ark of the Covenant of the Lord your God"** (Deuteronomy 31:26). This verse indicates that the Torah scroll was placed next to the Ark and not inside it. This is **in accordance with the opinion of Rabbi Yehuda, who said: Where was the Torah scroll placed? A box-like** container [*gluskiyya*][L] **was made for it on the outside, and the Torah scroll was placed inside it.**

מַאי טַעְמָא דְּרַבִּי מֵאִיר – דִּכְתִיב "וְנָתַתָּ אֶת הַכַּפֹּרֶת עַל הָאָרוֹן מִלְמָעְלָה וְאֶל הָאָרוֹן תִּתֵּן אֶת הָעֵדוּת אֲשֶׁר אֶתֵּן אֵלֶיךָ".

What is the source for the opinion of **Rabbi Meir** that the Torah scroll was placed inside the Ark? It is **as it is written, "And you shall put the Ark cover upon the Ark from above; and in the Ark you shall put the testimony that I shall give you"** (Exodus 25:21). This verse indicates that first the Ark cover was placed on the Ark, and only subsequently was the testimony, i.e., the tablets, placed inside. Since a previous verse (Exodus 25:16) already commands to put the tablets in the Ark, this second instruction to place the testimony must be referring to the Torah scroll rather than the tablets. This reading is supported by the fact that the instruction to place the testimony follows the instruction to place the Ark cover. The Ark cover must have been put in place first, as the complete Torah scroll did not exist until the end of the fortieth year in the desert, long after the assembly of the Tabernacle and the Ark.

עַל דַּעֲתֵיהּ דְּרַבִּי (מֵאִיר) יְהוּדָה דּוּ אֲמַר אֵין מוּקְדָּם וּמְאוּחָר בַּתּוֹרָה אֶלָּא "וְאֶל הָאָרוֹן תִּתֵּן אֶת הָעֵדוּת אֲשֶׁר אֶתֵּן אֵלֶיךָ" וְאַחַר כָּךְ "וְנָתַתָּ אֶת הַכַּפֹּרֶת עַל הָאָרוֹן מִלְמָעְלָה".

According to the opinion of Rabbi Yehuda,[N] who stated that **there is no absolute chronological order in the Torah,** the verse can be understand that testimony always refers to the tablets. **Therefore,** the verse may be understood that first it states: **"And in the Ark you shall put the testimony that I shall give you,"** and only **afterward** it states: **"And you shall put the Ark cover upon the Ark from above."**

רַבִּי פִּנְחָס בְּשֵׁם רַבִּי שִׁמְעוֹן בֶּן לָקִישׁ: הַתּוֹרָה שֶׁנָּתַן לוֹ הַקָּדוֹשׁ בָּרוּךְ הוּא לְמֹשֶׁה נִתְּנָה לוֹ אֵשׁ לְבָנָה חֲרוּתָה בְּאֵשׁ שְׁחוֹרָה, הִיא אֵשׁ מוּבְלֶלֶת בְּאֵשׁ, חֲצוּבָה מֵאֵשׁ, וּנְתוּנָה מֵאֵשׁ, דִּכְתִיב "מִימִינוֹ אֵשׁ דָּת לָמוֹ".

Apropos the discussion of the tablets and the Torah, the Gemara cites a further statement on the subject. **Rabbi Pineḥas** said **in the name of Rabbi Shimon ben Lakish: The Torah that the Holy One,** Blessed be He, **gave to Moses** on Mount Sinai **was given to him** as **white fire engraved with black fire.[N] It,** the Torah itself, **is fire mixed with fire, carved from** beneath the throne of glory, which is **fire, and given from** the One who is **fire, as it is written: "At His right hand was a fiery law unto them"** (Deuteronomy 33:2).

הלכה ב מתני׳ הֵיכָן הָיוּ הִשְׁתַּחֲוָיוֹת הָאֵלוּ? אַרְבַּע בַּצָּפוֹן, וְאַרְבַּע בַּדָּרוֹם, שָׁלֹשׁ בַּמִּזְרָח וּשְׁתַּיִם בַּמַּעֲרָב, כְּנֶגֶד שְׁלֹשָׁה עָשָׂר שְׁעָרִים, דְּרוֹמִיִּים סְמוּכִים לַמַּעֲרָב – שַׁעַר הָעֶלְיוֹן, שַׁעַר הַדֶּלֶק, שַׁעַר הַבְּכוֹרוֹת, שַׁעַר הַמַּיִם. וְלָמָּה נִקְרָא שְׁמוֹ שַׁעַר הַמַּיִם – שֶׁבּוֹ מַכְנִיסִין צְלוֹחִית

HALAKHA 2 · MISHNA The previous mishna mentioned that there were thirteen prostrations in the Temple. **Where were these prostrations?** There were **four in the north** of the courtyard, **four in the south, three in the east and two in the west,** as the thirteen prostrations were **facing the thirteen gates** of the Temple courtyard. The thirteen gates were as follows: **The southern ones,** listed in order, beginning with the one **adjacent to the western** side, were **the Upper Gate,** and the topography of the courtyard was such that there was an incline on the east-west plane, therefore the gate farthest to the west was higher than the other gates; **the Gate of Kindling,[N]** through which the priests would bring the wood for the arrangement of fire on top of the altar; **the Gate of the Firstborn,** through which priests would bring the ritually pure firstborn animals to be sacrificed, as it is permitted to slaughter firstborn animals on the southern side of the courtyard; and **the Gate of Water.** The mishna elaborates: **And why was it named the Gate of Water? Since through it they would bring in the vial**

LANGUAGE

Box-like container [*gluskiyya*] – גְּלוּסְקְיָיא: Perhaps from the Greek, γλωσσόκομον, *glossokomon*, meaning case or box. Different versions of this word appear throughout the Talmud, such as *deluskama* and *geluskema*, which usually refers to an ossuary, a container used for storing bones after decomposition.

Ossuary

NOTES

According to the opinion of Rabbi Yehuda – עַל דַּעֲתֵיהּ דְּרַבִּי (מֵאִיר) יְהוּדָה: In the Vilna edition of the Jerusalem Talmud Rabbi Meir is written instead of Rabbi Yehuda. However, both the *Korban HaEida* and the *Tiklin Ḥaditin* conclude that the text should be emended to read Rabbi Yehuda instead of Rabbi Meir, and that is how it appears in the translation. Rabbi Meir derives support for his opinion that the Torah scroll was placed in the Ark from the seeming oddity that the verse repeats the instruction to place the testimony in the Ark after the instruction to place the Ark cover. The invocation of the principle that there is no absolute chronological order in the Torah therefore makes sense only as an explanation of Rabbi Yehuda's lack of concern with the instruction to place the testimony in the Ark after the Ark was already closed.

White fire engraved with black fire – אֵשׁ לְבָנָה חֲרוּתָה בְּאֵשׁ שְׁחוֹרָה: The *Korban HaEida* offers two competing readings. Either the divine Torah is written with white fire engraved in a black background, or the opposite, which matches the image of our Torah scrolls.

The Gate of Kindling – שַׁעַר הַדֶּלֶק: Some explain that this was not the gate through which wood was brought for the altar but rather the gate through which the fire was brought (*Tosefot Yom Tov* on *Middot* 1:4).

שֶׁל נִיסּוּךְ הַמַּיִם בֶּחָג. רַבִּי אֱלִיעֶזֶר בֶּן יַעֲקֹב אוֹמֵר: בּוֹ הַמַּיִם מְפַכִּים וַעֲתִידִין לִהְיוֹת יוֹצְאִין מִתַּחַת מִפְתַּן הַבַּיִת.

of water for **the water libation**[N] **on the festival** of *Sukkot*, as they would ceremoniously draw the water from the Pool of Siloam and bring it to the altar through this gate. **Rabbi Eliezer ben Ya'akov says:** There was a different reason for this name. It was called the Gate of Water because **through it the water would trickle** [*mefakim*],[N] **and in the future** this water will increase and **go out from under the threshold of the House.**

לְעוּמָּתָן בַּצָּפוֹן סְמוּכִים בַּמַּעֲרָב: שַׁעַר יְכָנְיָה, שַׁעַר הַקָּרְבָּן, שַׁעַר הַנָּשִׁים, שַׁעַר הַשִּׁיר.

Facing these gates were the ones **in the north,** listed in order from the one **closest to the west: The Gate of Jeconiah; the Gate of the Offering,** through which they would bring the offerings of the most sacred order, as these could be slaughtered only in the northern part of the courtyard; **the Gate of Women,** where women would enter the courtyard to place their hands on the heads of their offerings; and **the Gate of Song,** through which they would bring the musical instruments into the courtyard.

וְלָמָּה נִקְרָא שְׁמוֹ שַׁעַר יְכָנְיָה – שֶׁבּוֹ יָצָא יְכָנְיָה בְּגָלוּתוֹ.

The mishna asks: **And why was it called the Gate of Jeconiah?** The reason is **that through it Jeconiah went out to his exile.**[N] Before Jeconiah was exiled by Nebuchadnezzar to Babylon he came to take leave of the Temple, and he left through this gate.

שֶׁבַּמִּזְרָח שַׁעַר נִקָּנוֹר, וּשְׁנֵי פִשְׁפָּשִׁין הָיוּ לוֹ אֶחָד מִימִינוֹ וְאֶחָד מִשְּׂמֹאלוֹ, וּשְׁנַיִם בַּמַּעֲרָב וְלֹא הָיָה לָהֶן שֵׁם.

The mishna resumes the list with the gates **that are in the east: the Gate of Nicanor,**[B] which was named after Nicanor, who brought the doors of this gate from Egypt (see *Yoma* 38a). **And** the Gate of Nicanor **had two wickets [*pishpeshin*],**[NLH] **one on its right and one on its left. And there were two** gates **in the west that did not have a name,** making a total of thirteen gates.

גמ׳ מַתְנִיתִין אַבָּא יוֹסֵה בֶּן יוֹחָנָן הִיא, דְּאָמַר כְּנֶגֶד שְׁלֹשָׁה עָשָׂר שְׁעָרִים. בְּרַם כְּרַבָּנַן שִׁבְעָה שְׁעָרִים הָיוּ בָּעֲזָרָה. עַל דַּעְתַּיְיהוּ דְּרַבָּנַן הֵיכָן הָיוּ הִשְׁתַּחֲוָואוֹת הַלָּלוּ?

GEMARA The mishna taught that there were thirteen gates in the courtyard. The Gemara notes that **the mishna is** in accordance with the opinion of **Abba Yosei ben Yoḥanan, who said** in *Middot* 2:6 that the thirteen prostrations were performed **opposite** the **thirteen gates.**[B] **However, according to** the opinion of **the Rabbis,** in *Middot* 1:4, **there were** only **seven gates in the courtyard.**[H] Consequently, **according to** the opinion of **the Rabbis, where were these** thirteen **prostrations**[N] performed, if there weren't a corresponding number of gates?

BACKGROUND

The Gate of Nicanor – שַׁעַר נִקָּנוֹר: The Gate of Nicanor was well known, both for the beauty of its copper doors as well as for the miracles that occurred during its transport from Egypt. This gate, located at the main entrance to the courtyard, served many purposes, often involving cases when someone needed to be as close to the courtyard as possible without actually entering the Temple area (see *Nazir* 45a).

The thirteen gates in the Temple – שְׁלֹשָׁה עָשָׂר הַשְּׁעָרִים שֶׁבַּמִּקְדָּשׁ:

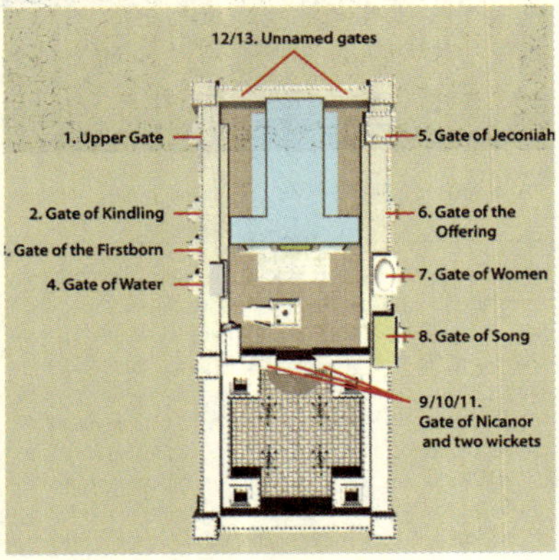

Diagram of the Temple showing the locations of the thirteen gates

LANGUAGE

Wickets [*pishpeshin*] – פִּשְׁפְּשִׁין: This word exists in Syriac with the same meaning, a small door within a larger door. Some maintain that it is from the Greek ψῆφος, *psèfos*, meaning pebble or small stone, such as those used in a mosaic. Just as one tile is set within the others in a mosaic, so too this door is set within the framework of the larger door.

HALAKHA

And the Gate of Nicanor had two wickets – וּשְׁנֵי פִשְׁפָּשִׁין הָיוּ לוֹ: There was a wicket on each side of the large gate which stood in the middle of the Sanctuary, one to the north and the other to the south. The one to the south was never used: "This gate shall be shut; it shall not be opened" (Ezekiel 44:2). The one to the north was used as an entrance to the Sanctuary, as follows: The priest who was appointed to open the doors to the Sanctuary entered this wicket and continued walking between the two walls until he reached an area that opened onto the courtyard on his left. He would then enter the Sanctuary and continue to the large gate and open it from the inside (see *Middot* 2:6; Rambam *Sefer Avoda, Hilkhot Beit HaBeḥira* 4:6).

There were seven gates in the courtyard – שִׁבְעָה שְׁעָרִים הָיוּ בָּעֲזָרָה: There were seven gates to the courtyard. Three were on the northern side, close to the western end of the courtyard, and three were on the southern side, also close to the west. The seventh gate was in the east, opposite the center of the Holy of Holies (see *Middot* 1:4; Rambam *Sefer Avoda, Hilkhot Beit HaBeḥira* 5:4).

NOTES

The water libation – נִיסּוּךְ הַמַּיִם: The mitzva to pour wine on the altar during the sacrifice of the offerings is stated explicitly in the Torah. In contrast, pouring of water is not mentioned in the Torah; rather, it is a *halakha* transmitted to Moses from Sinai that for the seven days of the festival of *Sukkot* a water libation accompanies the regular wine libation. The Gemara in tractate *Sukka* describes how the water was brought from the Pool of Siloam to the Temple and how the water libation was performed.

Trickle [*mefakim*] – מְפַכִּים: See Ezekiel 47:2: "And, behold, there trickled forth [*mefakim*] waters on the right side." The Radak and Targum Yonatan on this verse translate this term as "go out." In Rashi's commentary on that verse, in *Yoma* 78a, and in Rabbeinu Meshulam's commentary here, the following interpretation is provided: The etymology of the word *mefakim* is from the word *pakh*, a cruse. In other words, the water flow was the width of the opening of a cruse.

That through it Jeconiah went out to his exile – שֶׁבּוֹ יָצָא יְכָנְיָה בְּגָלוּתוֹ: As the Temple, including this gate, stood for over four hundred years prior to Jeconiah's exile, it would appear that the gate could not originally have been named for this event. However, it is possible that when King Solomon built the Temple he saw by divine inspiration that Jeconiah would be exiled through this gate in a public manner. He therefore named the gate Jeconiah in reference to this future event (*Siftei Tzaddik* of Rabbi Pineḥas Menaḥem Elazar of Piltz).

And the Gate of Nicanor had two wickets – וּשְׁנֵי פִשְׁפָּשִׁין הָיוּ לוֹ: Some say that these two wickets were located within the doors of the gates themselves. They were used as entrances because they were easier to open than the larger gate. Others explain that these wickets opened on either side of the larger gate (Rambam's Commentary on the Mishna; *Me'iri*; Rosh).

Where were these prostrations – הֵיכָן הָיוּ הִשְׁתַּחֲוָואוֹת הַלָּלוּ: The discussion in the Gemara assumes that there was no dispute with regard to the number of prostrations, as both the Rabbis and Abba Yosei ben Yoḥanan agreed that there were thirteen prostrations. The Gemara therefore inquires about the location of these prostrations, instead of suggesting that according to the Rabbis there were only seven prostrations (*Korban HaEida*).

כִּי הַהִיא דִּתְנַן תַּמָּן: שְׁלֹשׁ עֶשְׂרֵה פְּרָצוֹת הָיוּ בּוֹ שֶׁפְּרָצוּם מַלְכֵי יָוָן וְחָזְרוּ וּגְדָרוּם בְּנֵי חַשְׁמוֹנַאי, וְגָזְרוּ כְּנֶגְדָּן שְׁלֹשׁ עֶשְׂרֵה הִשְׁתַּחֲוָאוֹת.

The Gemara answers that the prostrations correspond **to that which we learned** in a mishna **there** (see *Middot* 2:3): **There were thirteen breaches** in the *soreg*, the lattice fence between the walls of the courtyard and the Temple Mount, **that the kings of Greece breached.** They did this to allow foreigners to enter the courtyard and to demonstrate that this area was not reserved exclusively for priests. **And the sons of the Hasmonean** dynasty[B] **returned and fenced in** those breaches, **and decreed** that **thirteen prostrations** should be performed **opposite them.** Anyone who encircled the courtyard and passed by one of the places where a breach had been sealed would prostrate in gratitude to God for removing Greek control and the decrees against the Jews of Eretz Yisrael.

כְּתִיב ״וְהָיָה בַּיּוֹם הַהוּא יֵצְאוּ מַיִם חַיִּים מִירוּשָׁלַיִם וגו׳״. תָּנֵי: מִבֵּית קָדְשֵׁי קָדָשִׁים עַד הַפָּרוֹכֶת – כְּקַרְנֵי סִילַי וְכִילַיי,

The Gemara expands upon the idea expressed by Rabbi Eliezer ben Ya'akov that in the future the water from the Gate of Water will increase and emerge from under the threshold of the House: It is written in a prophecy concerning the end of days: **"And it shall come to pass in that day, that living waters shall go out from Jerusalem:** Half of them toward the eastern sea, and half of them toward the western sea; in summer and in winter shall it be" (Zechariah 14:8), and **it was taught** in a *baraita*: **From the house of the Holy of Holies to the curtain,** the stream of water will be as thin **as the antennae of *silai* and *khilai*,** two types of snails.

מִן פָּרוֹכֶת עַד מִזְבַּח הַזָּהָב – כְּקַרְנֵי חֲגָבִים. מִמִּזְבַּח הַזָּהָב עַד עֲזָרוֹת – כְּחוּט שֶׁל שְׁתִי, מִן הָעֲזָרוֹת עַד מִפְתַּן הַבַּיִת – כְּחוּט שֶׁל עֵרֶב. מִיכָּן וְאֵילָךְ כְּמִפִּי הַפַּךְ.

From the curtain to the golden altar the stream of water will increase slightly until it is **like the antennae of grasshoppers. From** the place of **the golden altar to the courtyards** it will further increase to the thickness **of a thread of the warp** of a loom. **From the courtyards to the threshold of the House** the stream will widen to the size **of a thread of the woof,**[B] which was thicker than the thread of the warp. **From here onward** the stream will reach the width of **a stream of liquid poured from the mouth of a cruse.**

כְּתִיב ״וְהִנֵּה מַיִם מְפַכִּים מִן הַכָּתֵף הַיְמָנִית בְּצֵאת הָאִישׁ קָדִים וְקָו בְּיָדוֹ וַיָּמָד אֶלֶף בָּאַמָּה וַיַּעֲבִירֵנִי בַמַּיִם מֵי אָפְסָיִם״ – עַד קַרְסוּלָה. ״וַיָּמָד אֶלֶף וַיַּעֲבִירֵנִי בַמַּיִם מֵי בִּרְכָּיִם״ – עַד בִּרְכַּיָּיה,

The Gemara cites another *baraita* on this topic. **It is written: "And, behold, there trickled forth waters on the right side. When the man went forth eastward with the line in his hand, he measured a thousand cubits, and he caused me to pass through the waters, waters that were to the ankles"** (Ezekiel 47:2–3). This verse teaches that at a distance of a thousand cubits the height of the water was **up to the ankles.** The next verse states: **"Again he measured a thousand, and caused me to pass through the waters, waters that were to the knees,"** which indicates that after an additional thousand cubits the water was **up to the knees.**

״וַיָּמָד אֶלֶף וַיַּעֲבִירֵנִי מֵי מָתְנָיִם״ – עַד מָתְנַיָּיא, מִכָּאן וְאֵילָךְ ״וַיָּמָד אֶלֶף נַחַל אֲשֶׁר לֹא אוּכַל לַעֲבוֹר״ אֲפִילּוּ לַבִּירָנִין גְּדוֹלָה אֵינָהּ יְכוֹלָה לַעֲבוֹר בּוֹ.

The verse continues: **"Again he measured a thousand, and caused me to pass through waters that were to the loins"** (Ezekiel 47:4), which teaches that after the next thousand cubits the height of the water rose **until the loins. From here onward** the water continued to rise, until **"he measured a thousand; and it was a river that I could not pass through"** (Ezekiel 47:5). After the last thousand cubits the water was so high that **even a large Liburnian ship,** a type of a warship, **could not pass through** the current.[N]

מַאי טַעְמָא – ״וְצִי אַדִּיר לֹא יַעַבְרֶנּוּ״. מִפְּנֵי מָה – ״כִּי גָאוּ הַמַּיִם מֵי שָׂחוּ״ מַהוּ מֵי שָׂחוּ – מִלָּשׁוּט. אָמַר רַב הוּנָא בְּאַתְרִין קָרוּ לְשַׁיְיטָא שָׁחוּנָא ״וּפֵרַשׂ יָדָיו בְּקִרְבּוֹ כַּאֲשֶׁר יְפָרֵשׂ הַשּׂוֹחֶה לִשְׂחוֹת״.

What is the explanation of the verse: **"Neither shall gallant ship pass thereby"** (Isaiah 33:21). **Why? "For the waters were risen, waters to swim in** [*mei sahu*], a river that could not be passed through" (Ezekiel 47:5). **What is the meaning of the phrase *mei sahu*?** It means that the water flowed so fast and high it prevented one **from swimming.** Similarly, **Rav Huna said** to clarify the meaning of the word "*sahu*": **In our locale they call swimming *sahona,*** as in the verse: **"And when he shall spread forth his hands in its midst, as he who swims spreads forth his hands to swim** [*hasoheh lishot*]" (Isaiah 25:11).

מַהוּ ״לִשְׂחוֹת״? אָמַר רַבִּי יוֹסֵי בֵּי רַבִּי בּוּן מַיִין דְּמִתְמַלְּלִין בְּעָלְמָא.

The Gemara presents an alternate explanation for this verse. **What is** the meaning of **"waters to swim in** [**sahu**]"? **Rabbi Yosei, son of Rabbi Bun, said: Water that is discussed in the world.** The term *sahu* is associated with *siha*, which means discussion or conversation. The verse indicates that this river will be the topic of every discussion, due to its high waters and strong current.

BACKGROUND

The sons of the Hasmonean dynasty – בְּנֵי חַשְׁמוֹנַאי: Despite the fact that the entire dynasty is referred to in our own sources as the Hasmonean house, the identity of the original member of the family bearing that name is not clear. One theory is that Hasmonean was the appellation of Shimon, the son of Matityahu and brother of Judah Maccabee, whose descendants served as the Hasmonean kings for many generations.

Thread of the warp...thread of the woof – ...חוּט שֶׁל שְׁתִי חוּט שֶׁל עֵרֶב: Even when the weaving was done evenly, and the threads of the warp, i.e., those set in the loom, were of the same type as the threads of the woof, there was still a certain difference between them, in accordance with their specific functions. The threads of the warp were usually both thinner and stronger than those of the woof.

NOTES

Even a large Liburnian ship could not pass through the current – אֲפִילּוּ לַבִּירָנִין גְּדוֹלָה אֵינָהּ יְכוֹלָה לַעֲבוֹר בּוֹ: As large ships regularly traverse the sea even thousands of miles, clearly a ship could also traverse a river, even one that was wide and deep. The Gemara means that ships will be unable to cross the river due to the strength of the current (Maharsha on *Yoma* 77b).

LANGUAGE

Slopes [*ketafrisot*] – קְטַפְרִיסוֹת: From the Greek καταφερής, *kataferès*, meaning inclined or going down.

כְּתִיב "בַּיּוֹם הַהוּא יִהְיֶה מָקוֹר נִפְתָּח לְבֵית דָּוִיד וּלְיוֹשְׁבֵי יְרוּשָׁלַיִם לְחַטֵּאת וּלְנִדָּה".

The Gemara continues to discuss this river. It is written: **"In that day there shall be a fountain opened to the house of David and to the inhabitants of Jerusalem, for purification and for sprinkling"** (Zechariah 13:1). This river will be used for the purification of the house of David and the inhabitants of Jerusalem. The Gemara asks: Since this river can serve to purify any member of the Jewish people, why did the verse single out the house of David and the inhabitants of Jerusalem?

רַבִּי שְׁמוּאֵל בַּר נַחְמָן בְּשֵׁם רַבִּי יוֹנָתָן: מִבֵּית דָּוִד וְעַד יוֹשְׁבֵי יְרוּשָׁלַיִם – כְּשֵׁרִים לְנִדָּה וּלְחַטָּאת, מִכָּאן וְאֵילָךְ מֵי תַעֲרוֹבוֹת הֵם, כְּשֵׁרִים לְנִדָּה וּפְסוּלִים לְמֵי חַטָּאת.

The Gemara answers: The verse is not listing those who are fit to be purified by this river. Rather, it is delineating the various parts of this river that serve different functions. As **Rabbi Shmuel bar Naḥman** explained **in the name of Rabbi Yonatan: From** the dwelling place of **the house of David until** the residences of **the inhabitants of Jerusalem,** the water in this river is considered running spring water, which **is fit for** the purpose of purifying **a menstruating woman,** as well as for use in the waters of **purification,** i.e., spring water that was mixed with the ashes of the Red Heifer. **From here onward it is** considered **combined water,** a mixture of spring and rain water, which is **fit for** the purification of **a menstruating woman but unfit for the waters of purification.**[H]

אָמַר רַבִּי אֶלְעָזָר: מִבֵּית דָּוִד וְעַד יוֹשְׁבֵי יְרוּשָׁלַיִם כְּשֵׁרִים לְנִידָּה וּלְחַטָּאת, מִכָּאן וְאֵילָךְ – מֵי קְטַפְרִיסוֹת הֵן, פְּסוּלִין לְנִדָּה וּלְחַטָּאת.

The Gemara presents an alternate explanation of the verse. **Rabbi Elazar said: From** the palace of **the house of David until** the residences of **the inhabitants of Jerusalem,** the water is **fit for** the purification of **a menstruating woman** as well as for the waters of **purification. From here onward, it is** considered **water** running down **slopes** [*ketafrisot*],[L] **and is unfit**[H] both **for** the purification of **a menstruating woman and for** the waters of **purification.**

כְּתִיב "וַיֹּאמֶר אֵלַי הַמַּיִם הָאֵלֶּה יוֹצְאִים אֶל הַגְּלִילָה הַקַּדְמוֹנָה" – זֶה יָם שֶׁל סַמְכוּ, "וְיָרְדוּ אֶל הָעֲרָבָה" – זֶה יָם שֶׁל טְבֶרְיָא.

In Ezekiel's prophecy concerning this river, **it is** further **written: "Then he said to me: These waters issue forth toward the eastern region,** and shall go down into the Arabah; and when they shall enter into the sea, into the sea of the putrid waters, the waters shall be healed" (Ezekiel 47:8). **This** eastern region mentioned in this verse **is the Sea of Samkhu,** which is the modern Hula Lake in the northern Galilee. **"And shall go down into the Arabah," this** phrase refers to **the Sea of Tiberias,** i.e., the Sea of Galilee.

"וּבָאוּ הַיָּמָּה" – זֶה יָם הַמֶּלַח, "אֶל הַיָּמָּה הַמּוּצָאִים" – זֶה הַיָּם הַגָּדוֹל, וְלָמָּה נִקְרָא שְׁמוֹ "מוּצָאִים" – כְּנֶגֶד שְׁתֵּי פְּעָמִים שֶׁיָּצָא, אֶחָד בְּדוֹר אֱנוֹשׁ וְאֶחָד בְּדוֹר הַפַּלָּגָה.

"And when they shall enter into the sea," this is the Dead Sea. "Into the sea of the putrid waters [*mutza'im*]," this is the Great Sea, the Mediterranean Sea. **And why was it called *mutza'im*,** which literally means taken out? This **corresponds to the two occasions that** the sea **went out** and overran the dry land, **once in the Generation of Enosh,** when idolatry proliferated, **and once in the Generation of the Dispersion,** i.e., that of the Tower of Babel.

HALAKHA

Water running down slopes is unfit – מֵי קְטַפְרִיסוֹת הֵן פְּסוּלִין: Rainwater that runs down a slope may be used for immersion only once it collects in one place, even if the entire flow contains the requisite forty *se'a* of water. This ruling is in accordance with the opinion of Beit Hillel (*Mikvaot* 5:6; Rambam *Sefer Tahara, Hilkhot Mikvaot* 9:16).

But unfit for the waters of purification – וּפְסוּלִים לְמֵי חַטָּאת: A mixture of water that includes water not drawn from a spring is unfit for sanctifying the ashes of the Red Heifer. The water of marshes, the water of the Jordan River, and the water of the Yarmouk River are all mixed waters and consequently unfit for this purpose (see *Para* 8:10; Rambam *Sefer Tahara, Hilkhot Para Aduma* 6:13).

רַבִּי לְעָזָר בְּשֵׁם רַבִּי חֲנִינָה: בָּרִאשׁוֹנָה יָצָא עַד קַלַבְרִיאָה וּבַשְּׁנִיָּה יָצָא עַד כֵּיפֵי בַּרְבַּרִיאָה, רַבִּי אַחָא בְּשֵׁם רַבִּי חֲנִינָה: בָּרִאשׁוֹנָה יָצָא עַד כֵּיפֵי בַּרְבַּרִיאָה, וּבַשְּׁנִיָּה יָצָא עַד עַכּוֹ וְעַד יָפוֹ.

Until where did the sea overrun the dry land? **Rabbi Elazar** said **in the name of Rabbi Ḥanina: In the first instance,** the Generation of Enosh, it **went out until Calabria,**[B] in southern Italy, **and in the second instance,** the Generation of Dispersion, it **went out until the rocks of Barbary**[B] in North Africa. **Rabbi Aḥa** said **in the name of Rabbi Ḥanina: In the first instance** the sea **went out until the rocks of Barbary, and in the second instance it went out until Akko**[B] **and until Jaffa.**

״עַד פֹּה תָבֹא וְלֹא תוֹסִיף״ – עַד עַכּוֹ תָּבֹא וְלֹא תוֹסִיף. ״וּפֹה יָשִׁית בִּגְאוֹן גַּלֶּיךָ״ – עַד יָפוֹ אָשִׁית גְּאוֹן גַּלֶּיךָ.

The Gemara adds that there is support for this claim from the verse: **"Thus far [*ad po*] you shall come, but no further,** and here your proud waves shall be stayed" (Job 38:11). The phrase *ad po* is similar in meaning to *ad ko*, which alludes to the city of Akko. The verse is saying that **until Akko you shall come, but no further.** Likewise, in the last part of the verse: **"And here [*ufo*] your proud waves shall be stayed,"** the similarity between the words *ufo* and *Yafo*, Jaffa, hints that **until Jaffa your proud waves shall be stayed.**

נִיחָא, יַמָּא רַבָּא וְיַמָּא דְּמִילְחָא – בִּשְׁבִיל לְמִיתְקַן. יַמָּא דִּטְבֶרְיָא יַמָּא דְּסַמְכוֹ –

The Gemara stated above that the waters of the river that emerge from the Temple Mount will reach four seas: The Sea of Samkhu, the Sea of Tiberias, the Dead Sea, and the Mediterranean Sea. The Gemara asks: **It works out well** that the river will reach the **Great Sea,** i.e., the Mediterranean Sea, and the **Dead Sea, in order to sweeten them,** and render them drinkable, as they contain saltwater. However, with regard to **the Sea of Tiberias, and the Sea of Samkhu,** whose water is already sweet, for what purpose will this river reach them?

BACKGROUND

Calabria – קַלַבְרִיאָה: A geographic region in southern Italy, north of Sicily. A mostly mountainous area, Calabria's rocky beaches serve as a kind of natural sea barrier that blocks the currents coming from the Atlantic Ocean in the west. This accounts for the Gemara's statement that the sea, i.e., the Atlantic, broke into the Mediterranean basin and initially reached Calabria.

Beach on the western coast of Calabria

Akko – עַכּוֹ: Although this ancient and significant port city is included in the boundaries of Eretz Yisrael as described in the Torah, it was never actually conquered by the Jewish people and remained under the jurisdiction of the rulers of Sidon. Even during the Second Temple period, when the Hasmonean dynasty was at its zenith, Akko remained under foreign control.

Since it was not under Jewish control, Akko was not consecrated as part of Eretz Yisrael for the purposes of the mitzvot that are dependent on the Land. The outskirts of the city were under Jewish control and thus were considered consecrated by the Jews returning from the Babylonian exile. The Jerusalem Talmud provides highly specific demarcations of which areas form part of Eretz Yisrael. Despite its unconsecrated status, there were periods in which Akko contained a significant Jewish community that produced many illustrious Sages.

Akko beach

BACKGROUND

Barbary – בַּרְבַּרִיאָה: From the Greek βαρβαρία, *barbaria*, meaning foreign place. Those who didn't speak Greek were called barbarians by the Greeks because their language sounded to unaccustomed ears as if they were saying *barbarbar*. The Greeks referred to the Romans as barbarians, and ironically the Romans took up the same practice and called whoever was not Roman a barbarian. Consequently the term barbarian has come to refer to uncultured people in general. The natives of the North African coast were thus called barbarians and the area became known as the Barbary Coast. This name has been preserved through the generations in various languages with only slight changes, and is now associated with the local North African tribes, the Berbers.

Jebel Musa, the rocky mountain in Morocco, on the southern side of the Strait of Gibraltar

Above: Rock of Gibraltar on the northern side of the strait

Left: Strait of Gibraltar and the Barbary Coast, as seen from space. Africa is below and Europe is above.

BACKGROUND

Sidon – **צַיְידָן**: Sidon, which is referred to in other sources as Beit Tzayda, or Bethsaida, was a village on the northern side of the Sea of Galilee, adjacent to the estuary of the Jordan River. The Sages of Tiberias would occasionally meet there to issue various halakhic rulings.

Remains of the entrance to Beit Tzayda

לְרַבּוֹת דְּגָתָם, דִּכְתִיב בֵּיהּ ״לְמִינָה תִּהְיֶה דְגָתָם״ – לְמִינֵי מִינִים תִּהְיֶה דְגָתָם. תַּנְיָא, אָמַר רַבָּן שִׁמְעוֹן בֶּן גַּמְלִיאֵל: מַעֲשֶׂה שֶׁהָלַכְתִּי לְצַיְידָן וְהֵבִיאוּ לְפָנַי יוֹתֵר מִשְּׁלֹשׁ מֵאוֹת מִינֵי דָגִים בְּתַמְחוּי אֶחָד.

The Gemara responds that when the water of this river reaches these seas, their waters will be blessed **by an increase** in the number of **their fish, as it is written with regard to** this river: **"Their fish shall be after their kinds"** (Ezekiel 47:10). This verse teaches that **their fish will be of multiple kinds,** great in number and variety. **It was** likewise **taught** in a *baraita* that **Rabban Shimon ben Gamliel said:** There was **an incident in which I went to Sidon,**[B] north of the Sea of Galilee, **and they brought before me more than three hundred kinds of fish in one pot.**

״וְנִרְפְּאוּ הַמָּיִם״ ״בִּצָּאתָיו וּגְבָאָיו וְלֹא יֵרָפְאוּ לְמֶלַח נִתָּנוּ״, כְּתִיב ״וְנִרְפְּאוּ הַמָּיִם״ וְאַתְּ אָמְרַתְּ וְלֹא יֵרָפְאוּ הַמָּיִם? מָקוֹם הוּא וּשְׁמוֹ ״וְלֹא יֵרָפְאוּ״.

The Gemara continues to interpret the verses in Ezekiel: **"And the waters shall be healed…But its miry places and its marshes shall not be healed; they shall be given for salt"** (Ezekiel 47:8–11). The Gemara points out an apparent contradiction: It is written: **"And the waters shall be healed," and** yet **you say that the waters shall not be healed?** The Gemara responds that **it is a place called Velo Yerafu,** which means: They will not be healed. This verse is detailing the locations where the waters will heal, namely the miry places, the marshes, and a place called Velo Yerafu.

כְּתִיב ״וְעַל הַנַּחַל יַעֲלֶה עַל שְׂפָתוֹ מִזֶּה וּמִזֶּה כָּל עֵץ מַאֲכָל לֹא יִבּוֹל עָלֵהוּ וְלֹא יִתֹּם פִּרְיוֹ לָחֳדָשָׁיו יְבַכֵּר״.

It is further **written** there: **"And by the river upon its bank, on this side and on that side, shall grow every tree for food, whose leaf shall not wither, neither shall its fruit fail; it shall bring forth new fruit every month,** because its waters issue out of the Temple; and its fruit shall be for food, and its leaf for healing" (Ezekiel 47:12). What is the meaning of the phrase "it shall bring forth new fruit every month"?

תַּנְיָא: אָמַר רַבִּי יְהוּדָה: לְפִי שֶׁבָּעוֹלָם הַזֶּה תְּבוּאָה עוֹשָׂה לְשִׁשָּׁה חֳדָשִׁים וְאִילָן עוֹשֶׂה לִשְׁנֵים עָשָׂר חוֹדֶשׁ, אֲבָל לֶעָתִיד לָבוֹא הַתְּבוּאָה עוֹשָׂה לְחוֹדֶשׁ אֶחָד וְאִילָן עוֹשֶׂה לִשְׁנֵי חֳדָשִׁים.

It was taught in a *baraita* that **Rabbi Yehuda said:** The meaning of the verse is **that in this world, grain produces** a crop **six months** after it is planted, **and a tree produces fruit twelve months** after its fruit is harvested. **However, in the future, grain will produce** crops **in one month, and a tree will produce** fruit **in two months.**

מַאי טַעְמָא – ״לָחֳדָשָׁיו יְבַכֵּר״.

What is the explanation of the words in the verse: **"It shall bring forth new fruit every month [*ḥodashav*]?"** The term *ḥodashav*, which incorporates the plural of the word month, indicates that the fruit will grow in two months. As the time required for grain to ripen is half the time of that of fruit, grain will ripen in a single month.

אָמַר רַבִּי יוֹסֵי: לְפִי שֶׁבָּעוֹלָם הַזֶּה הַתְּבוּאָה עוֹשָׂה לְשִׁשָּׁה חֳדָשִׁים וְאִילָן עוֹשֶׂה לִשְׁנֵים עָשָׂר חֹדֶשׁ, אֲבָל לֶעָתִיד לָבֹא הַתְּבוּאָה עוֹשָׂה לַחֲמִשָּׁה עָשָׂר יוֹם וְאִילָן עוֹשֶׂה לְחֹדֶשׁ אֶחָד. שֶׁכֵּן מָצִינוּ שֶׁעָשְׂתָה הַתְּבוּאָה בִּימֵי יוֹאֵל לַחֲמִשָּׁה עָשָׂר יוֹם וְקָרַב מִמֶּנָּה הָעוֹמֶר,

This Gemara presents a dissenting opinion. **Rabbi Yosei said:** The meaning of the verse is **that in this world grain produces a** crop **six months** after it is planted, **while a tree produces fruit twelve months** after its fruit is harvested. **However, in the future, grain will produce** crops **in fifteen days, and a tree will produce** fruit **in one month, as we found that grain produced** a crop **in the days of Joel** that ripened **in fifteen days, and the *omer*** offering **was brought from** that grain on the sixteenth of Nisan. In that year they brought the *omer* offering from grain fifteen days after it was sown.

מַאי טַעְמָא ״וּבְנֵי צִיּוֹן גִּילוּ וְשִׂמְחוּ בַּה׳ אֱלֹהֵיכֶם כִּי נָתַן לָכֶם אֶת הַמּוֹרֶה לִצְדָקָה וַיּוֹרֶד לָכֶם גֶּשֶׁם מוֹרֶה וּמַלְקוֹשׁ בָּרִאשׁוֹן״.

What is the explanation of the verse: **"Be glad then, you children of Zion, and rejoice in the Lord your God; for He gives you the first rain in just measure, and He causes the rain to come down for you, the first rain and the latter rain, at the first"** (Joel 2:23)? The Sages explain that there was a severe drought that year, and the first rains fell only on the first of Nisan (see *Ta'anit* 5a). The prophet commanded the people to plant their fields, and they found sufficient seeds to sow the fields. The second rains fell on the fifth of Nisan, and miraculously the grain ripened so quickly that they were able to bring the *omer* offering from that grain on the sixteenth of the month. In the future the grain will ripen as quickly as it did then.

וּמַה מְקַיֵּים רַבִּי יוֹסֵי ״לָחֳדָשָׁיו יְבַכֵּר״ – בְּכָל חוֹדֶשׁ וְחוֹדֶשׁ יִהְיֶה מְבַכֵּר.

The Gemara asks: **And how does Rabbi Yosei establish** the meaning of the verse: **"It shall bring forth new fruit every month,"** which apparently indicates that fruit will grow in two months? He explains that the verse means **that each and every month the tree will bring forth fruit.**

״וְעָלֵהוּ לִתְרוּפָה״ רַבִּי יוֹחָנָן אָמַר: תַּרְפֵּיה, מֵצִיץ עָלֶיהָ וְתָרַף מְזוֹנָה.

The aforementioned verse states: "**And its leaf for healing** [*terufa*]" (Ezekiel 47:12). The Sages dispute the meaning of this phrase. **Rabbi Yoḥanan said:** The word *terufa* with a *tav* is similar to *terufa* with a *tet*, which means food. Therefore the verse means: For **its food he sucks the leaves** of the tree that grows on the banks of that river, **and ingests their sustenance,** as the leaves of this tree nourish as much as its fruit.

רַב וּשְׁמוּאֵל חַד אָמַר: לְהַתִּיר פֶּה שֶׁלְּמַעְלָן, וְחַד אָמַר: לְהַתִּיר פֶּה שֶׁלְּמַטָּן. רַבִּי חֲנִינָה וְרַבִּי יְהוֹשֻׁעַ בֶּן לֵוִי, חַד אָמַר: לְהַתִּיר פֶּה עֲקָרוֹת, וְחַד אָמַר: לְהַתִּיר פֶּה אִלְּמִים.

Rav and Shmuel both interpreted *terufa* as an allusion to *lehatir pe*, to release the mouth, but differed over the exact meaning. **One said** it means **to release the upper mouth,** i.e., to open the mouth of a mute person, such that he will be able to speak if he eats from the fruit of this tree. And the other **one said** it means **to release the lower mouth,** a reference to the womb; a barren woman who eats from this tree will be able to conceive. **Rabbi Ḥanina and Rabbi Yehoshua ben Levi** disagree in a similar manner. **One said** the verse means **to release the mouth of infertility,** and the other **one said** it means **to open the mouth of the mute.**

״וּלְעֻמָּתָן בַּצָּפוֹן״ וכו׳. אַתְּ מוֹצֵא בְּשָׁעָה שֶׁעָלָה נְבוּכַדְנֶאצַּר לְכָאן בָּא וְיָשַׁב לוֹ בְּדוֹפְנֵי שֶׁל אַנְטוֹכְיָא, וְיָצְאָה סַנְהֶדְרִין גְּדוֹלָה לִקְרָאתוֹ, וְאָמְרָה לוֹ: הִגִּיעַ זְמַן הַבַּיִת הַזֶּה לֵיחָרֵב? אָמַר לָהֶן: אוֹתוֹ שֶׁהִמְלַכְתִּי עֲלֵיכֶם תְּנוּהוּ לִי וַאֲנִי הוֹלֵךְ.

In its list of the gates in the Temple, the mishna stated: **Facing** the gates in the south were additional gates **in the north, etc.** One of the gates in the north was the Gate of Jeconiah, through which this king departed for exile. The Gemara relates that **you find at the time that Nebuchadnezzar ascended to** Eretz Yisrael to remove Jeconiah, Jehoiachin, from his throne, three months after he had crowned him instead of his father Jehoiakim. **He came and settled in Dofnei of Antioch,**[B] where he set up his camp. **And the Great Sanhedrin came out to greet him and said to him: Has the time come for this House to be destroyed?** Is that the purpose for which you have arrived? **He said to them: The king that I crowned** to rule **over you, give him to me** as a captive **and I will go.**

בָּאוּ וְאָמְרוּ לִיהוֹיָכִין מֶלֶךְ יְהוּדָה: נְבוּכַדְנֶאצַּר בָּעֵי לָךְ. כֵּיוָן שֶׁשָּׁמַע מֵהֶן כָּךְ נָטַל מַפְתְּחוֹת שֶׁל בֵּית הַמִּקְדָּשׁ עָלָה לְגַגּוֹ שֶׁל הֵיכָל, אָמַר לְפָנָיו: רִבּוֹנוֹ שֶׁל עוֹלָם, לְשֶׁעָבַר הָיִינוּ נֶאֱמָנִים לְךָ וְהָיוּ מַפְתְּחוֹתֶיךָ מְסוּרִין לָנוּ, עַכְשָׁיו שֶׁאֵין אָנוּ נֶאֱמָנִים – הֲרֵי מַפְתְּחוֹתֶיךָ מְסוּרִין לְךָ. תְּרֵין אֲמוֹרָאִין, חַד אָמַר: זְרָקָן וְעוֹד לֹא יָרְדוּ, וְחַד אָמַר: בָּאָה כְּמִין יָד וּנְטָלָתַן מִיָּדוֹ. כֵּיוָן שֶׁרָאוּ כָּל

They came and said to Jehoiachin, king of Judea: Nebuchadnezzar requires that you be taken into captivity to Babylon. **When he heard this from them, he took the keys of the Temple** and **ascended to the roof of the Sanctuary and said before Him: Master of the Universe, in the past we were faithful to You and Your keys were handed over to us. Now that we are not faithful, Your keys are handed over to You. Two** ***amora'im*** dispute what happened next: **One said** that Jehoiachin took the keys and **threw them** up to the heavens **and they have not yet descended** from there. **And one said** that **the likeness of a hand came and took them from his hand. When all**

BACKGROUND

Antioch – אַנְטוֹכְיָא: This was one of the most important cities in the ancient Middle East. Seleucus I established it and named for his father, Antiochus, in approximately 300 BCE. The city was located on the eastern side of the Orontes River, in the shadow of the Taurus Mountains to the northwest, approximately 25 km from the Mediterranean Sea. Situated at a major crossroads, Antioch was a key trade center for hundreds of years. The ruins of ancient Antioch can be found near modern Antakya, in the Hatay province of Turkey.

Antioch was a significant Jewish center from the time of its founding and throughout the Roman and Byzantine periods. The Jews there maintained contact with the Jewish community and leaders in Eretz Yisrael.

Map showing location of Antioch

Perek **VI**
Daf **17** Amud **b**

חוֹרֵי יְהוּדָה כֵּן – עָלוּ לְרֹאשׁ גַּגּוֹתֵיהֶן וְנָפְלוּ וּמֵתוּ. הֲדָא הוּא דִּכְתִיב ״מַשָּׂא גֵּיא חִזָּיוֹן מַה לָּךְ אֵיפוֹא כִּי עָלִית כּוּלָּךְ לַגַּגּוֹת. תְּשׁוּאוֹת מְלֵאָה עִיר הוֹמִיָּה וגו׳״.

the nobles of [*ḥorei*][L] **Judea saw** what had occurred, **they went up to the top of their roofs and fell and died. This is as it is written: "The burden concerning the Valley of Vision.**[N] **What ails you now, that you have wholly gone up to the housetops, you that are full of uproar, a tumultuous city,** a joyous town? Your slain are not slain with the sword, nor dead in battle" (Isaiah 22:1–2). Isaiah prophesies about Jerusalem, the Valley of Vision, which will be conquered by Nebuchadnezzar, crying: What ails you, Jerusalem, that your nobles will go up to the rooftops and fall to their deaths? Your dead will not be slain with the sword or in battle; they will die by falling from the rooftops.

LANGUAGE

Nobles of [*ḥorei*] – חוֹרֵי: The word *ḥorim* means dignitaries, nobles, ministers, and deputies. See Nehemiah 13:7; I Kings 21:8 and the Radak on that verse; see also Isaiah 34:12, where *ḥorim* is the parallel term for ministers. It is also possible that *ḥorim* is a term for freemen who were exempt from royal taxes.

NOTES

The Valley of Vision – גֵּיא חִזָּיוֹן: Jerusalem is known as the Valley of Vision because all eyes look toward it (Rashi, *Ta'anit* 29a). However, in his commentary on Isaiah 22:1, Rashi writes that Jerusalem is known by this name because most prophetic visions mention Jerusalem.

הלכה ג מתני׳ שְׁלֹשָׁה עָשָׂר שֻׁלְחָנוֹת הָיוּ בַּמִּקְדָּשׁ. שְׁמוֹנָה שֶׁל שַׁיִישׁ בְּבֵית הַמִּטְבָּחַיִים, שֶׁעֲלֵיהֶן מְדִיחִין אֶת הַקְּרָבַיִים.

HALAKHA 3 · MISHNA This mishna details the exact location and purpose of the thirteen tables in the Temple. There **were thirteen tables in the Temple. Eight**[H] of them were made **of marble** and were located **in the slaughtering area,**[B] north of the altar, where the priests would slaughter the offerings of the most sacred order. **Upon these** tables **they would wash the innards** of the offerings, as the marble was cool and preserved the freshness of the meat.

וּשְׁנַיִם בְּמַעֲרַב הַכֶּבֶשׁ, אֶחָד שֶׁל שַׁיִישׁ וְאֶחָד שֶׁל כֶּסֶף. עַל שֶׁל שַׁיִישׁ נוֹתְנִין אֶת הָאֵבָרִים, וְעַל שֶׁל כֶּסֶף כְּלֵי שָׁרֵת.

And there were **two** more tables **on the western** side **of the ramp,**[H] south of the altar, **one of marble and one of silver. On** the table **of marble they would place the limbs** before they were sacrificed, and from there the priests would bring them up to the altar. **On** the table made **of silver** they would place the ninety-three **sacred vessels**[N] brought out from the Chamber of Vessels each morning for the services of that day.

וּשְׁנַיִם בָּאוּלָם מִבִּפְנִים עַל פֶּתַח הַבַּיִת, אֶחָד שֶׁל שַׁיִישׁ וְאֶחָד שֶׁל זָהָב. עַל שֶׁל שַׁיִישׁ נוֹתְנִין לֶחֶם הַפָּנִים בִּכְנִיסָתוֹ, וְעַל שֶׁל זָהָב בִּיצִיאָתוֹ,

And there were **two** tables **in the Entrance Hall** to the Sanctuary, **on the inside**[H] of the Entrance Hall, **near the opening to the Temple, one of marble and one of gold. On** the table **of marble they would put the shewbread before its entrance** to the Sanctuary after it was baked on the eve of Shabbat. **And** they would place the old shewbread **on** the table **of gold upon its exit** from the Sanctuary, to be divided among the priests.

שֶׁמַּעֲלִין בַּקּוֹדֶשׁ וְלֹא מוֹרִידִין.

The reason the shewbread was placed on a marble table before being brought into the Sanctuary and on a golden one upon when removed from there is **that one elevates** to a higher level **in** matters of **sanctity and one does not downgrade.** Since it had been placed on the golden Shewbread table all week inside the Sanctuary, upon its removal it could not be derogated to a marble table and so was placed on a different golden table in the Entrance Hall.

אֶחָד שֶׁל זָהָב מִבִּפְנִים שֶׁעָלָיו לֶחֶם הַפָּנִים תָּמִיד.

Finally, there was **one** table **of gold inside** the Sanctuary, i.e., the Shewbread table, **upon which the shewbread** was placed **always.**

גמ׳ תָּנֵי: עַל שֶׁל כֶּסֶף. רַבִּי יוֹסֵי בְּשֵׁם רַבִּי שְׁמוּאֵל בַּר רַב יִצְחָק רַבִּי חֲנַנְיָה מָטֵי בָהּ בְּשֵׁם רַבִּי יוֹחָנָן: לֵית כָּאן שֶׁל כֶּסֶף, מִפְּנֵי שֶׁהוּא מַרְתִּיחַ.

GEMARA The mishna stated that the shewbread was placed on a marble table when it was brought into the Sanctuary. The Gemara cites a different opinion: As it **was taught** in a *baraita*: When the shewbread was brought into the sanctuary it was placed **on** a table **of silver.**[N] In accordance with the opinion stated in the mishna, that the bread was placed on a marble table, **Rabbi Yosei** said **in the name of Rabbi Shmuel bar Rav Yitzḥak,** who said that **Rabbi Ḥananya cites this** tradition **in the name of Rabbi Yoḥanan: There was no** table **of silver here, as it boils,** i.e., it heats articles placed upon it, which could cause the shewbread to grow moldy.

לֹא כֵן תָּנֵי: זֶה אֶחָד מִן הַנִּסִּים שֶׁנַּעֲשׂוּ בְּבֵית הַמִּקְדָּשׁ, שֶׁכְּשֵׁם שֶׁהָיוּ מַנִּיחִין אוֹתוֹ חוּם כָּךְ הָיוּ מוֹצִיאִין אוֹתוֹ חוּם, שֶׁנֶּאֱמַר ״לָשׂוּם לֶחֶם חֹם בְּיוֹם הִלָּקְחוֹ״.

The Gemara raises a difficulty: **Wasn't it taught** in a *baraita* **as follows: This was one of the miracles that were performed in the Temple, that just as they would place** the shewbread **hot** as it came out of the oven, **so too they would remove it hot, as it is stated: "To put hot bread in the day when it was taken away"** (I Samuel 21:7). When they removed the shewbread after seven days on the golden table, it was as hot as it was when they originally placed it there. Why, then, were they concerned about placing the shewbread on a silver table, if it would remain warm in any event?

HALAKHA

Eight tables – שְׁמוֹנָה שֻׁלְחָנוֹת: There were eight marble tables in the Temple slaughtering area upon which the pieces of meat from the offerings were placed. The priests would wash the meat on these tables before eating it (Rambam *Sefer Avoda, Hilkhot Beit HaBeḥira* 5:13).

And two on the western side of the ramp – וּשְׁנַיִם בְּמַעֲרַב הַכֶּבֶשׁ: There were two tables on the western side of the altar: One of marble, upon which the priests placed the limbs of the offerings, and one of silver, where they placed the sacred vessels (Rambam *Sefer Avoda, Hilkhot Beit HaBeḥira* 2:15).

And two in the Entrance Hall on the inside – וּשְׁנַיִם בָּאוּלָם מִבִּפְנִים: There were two tables on the inside of the Entrance Hall, near the entrance to the Temple. One was made of marble, upon which the shewbread was placed when it was brought into the Sanctuary. The other was made of gold, for the shewbread on its exit from the golden table in the Sanctuary. This is due to the principle that in matters of sanctity one elevates to a higher level rather than downgrades to a lower one (Rambam *Sefer Avoda, Hilkhot Beit HaBeḥira* 3:16).

BACKGROUND

The slaughtering area – בֵּית הַמִּטְבָּחַיִים:

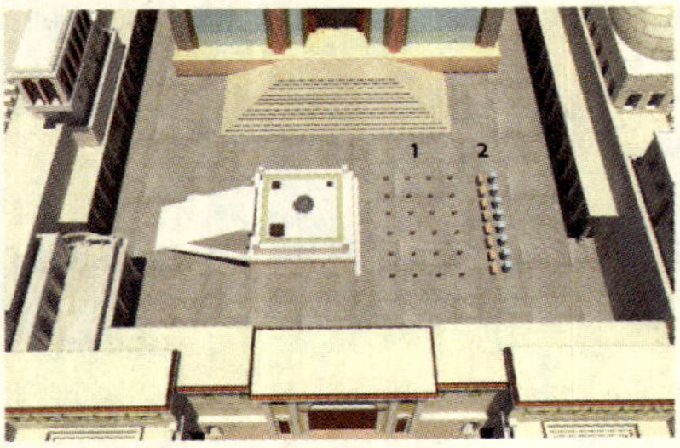

(1) Slaughtering area
(2) Tables and columns

NOTES

On the table of silver they would place sacred vessels – עַל שֶׁל כֶּסֶף כְּלֵי שָׁרֵת: The early commentaries explain that this refers to the ninety-three sacred vessels that were taken out at the start of the day for the services of the day (Rosh, *Tamid* 31b). The later commentaries note that it is unclear how all ninety-three vessels could fit on a single table. They further question the very placement of the vessels on this table, as this is not the appropriate place for them. Rather, they belong at the entrance to the courtyard, so that they are available for all of the services of the offerings. These commentaries therefore explain that that those vessels were placed in a vestibule, while the silver table served to hold the vessels that the priests used for the services on the altar, e.g., the burning of the incense or the pouring of the libations. If the priest needed to rest during these services, he would place the vessels on this table. Some suggest that the priest would also mix the meal offerings on this table (*Hiddushim UBiurim*).

It was taught, on a table of silver – תָּנֵי עַל שֶׁל כֶּסֶף: The priests would transfer the shewbread from this silver table to the golden table, in accordance with the principle that in matters of sanctity one elevates to a higher level rather than downgrades to a lower one. The opinion of this *tanna* that they would use a silver table is based upon the principle that there is no poverty in a place of wealth. In other words, the Temple is the glory of Israel, and the community is responsible for providing its needs. Since the community is not a pauper, it is unbecoming to the Temple to treat it frugally. Therefore, all the requirements of the Temple were provided generously and with splendor, including this table. Consequently, the table was made of silver, not marble.

רַבִּי יְהוֹשֻׁעַ בֶּן לֵוִי אָמַר: אֵין מַזְכִּירִין מַעֲשֵׂה נִסִּים.

The Gemara answers that **Rabbi Yehoshua ben Levi said: One does not mention miraculous events.** Despite the fact that miracles occur, one should not rely on them, but rather act according to the laws of nature. Therefore the priests did not place the bread on a silver table that could have spoiled the shewbread through natural causes.

בְּעוֹן קוֹמֵי רַבִּי אִילָא: לֹא הָיָה שָׁם לֶחֶם מַהוּ לְהָנִיחוֹ לְשַׁבָּת הַבָּאָה? אֲמַר לוֹן: כְּתִיב ״וְנָתַתָּ עַל הַשּׁוּלְחָן לֶחֶם פָּנִים לְפָנַי תָּמִיד״ – לֶחֶם פָּנִים אֲפִילּוּ פָּסוּל.

They raised a dilemma before Rabbi Ila: If one week **there was no** new **bread** to replace the old bread on the shewbread table, **what is** the *halakha* with regard to **leaving** the old shewbread **until the next Shabbat?**[H] On the one hand, as the time has arrived for the bread to be removed and divided among the priests, if it remains after this time it could be considered *notar*, left over, and disqualified by remaining overnight. On the other hand, as there is no new bread to replace it, perhaps this bread would still be considered the shewbread of the table and would not be disqualified until new bread would be brought. Rabbi Ila **said to them** that **it is written: "And you shall set upon the table shewbread before Me always"** (Exodus 25:30). There should always be **shewbread** on the table, **even if it is disqualified.**[N]

עֲשָׂרָה שֻׁלְחָנוֹת עָשָׂה שְׁלֹמֹה, דִּכְתִיב ״וַיַּעַשׂ שׁוּלְחָנוֹת עֲשָׂרָה וַיַּנַּח בַּהֵיכָל חֲמִשָּׁה מִיָּמִין וַחֲמִשָּׁה מִשְּׂמֹאל״.

The Gemara cites a *baraita* that discusses the shewbread table: **Solomon built ten tables**[N] for the Temple, modeled after the shewbread table. **As it is written: "He made also ten tables, and placed them in the Temple, five on the right side and five on the left"** (II Chronicles 4:8).

אִין תֵּימַר חֲמִשָּׁה בַּדָּרוֹם וַחֲמִשָּׁה בַּצָּפוֹן – וַהֲלֹא אֵין הַשֻּׁלְחָן כָּשֵׁר אֶלָּא בַּצָּפוֹן, שֶׁנֶּאֱמַר ״וְאֶת הַשֻּׁלְחָן תִּתֵּן עַל צֶלַע צָפוֹן״, מַה תַּלְמוּד לוֹמַר ״חֲמִשָּׁה מִיָּמִין וַחֲמִשָּׁה מִשְּׂמֹאל״ אֶלָּא, חֲמִשָּׁה מִימִין שֻׁלְחָנוֹ שֶׁל מֹשֶׁה וַחֲמִשָּׁה מִשְּׂמֹאלוֹ.

The Gemara asks: **If you say** that right and left refer to the sides of the entrance to the Sanctuary, which means that Solomon set up **five** tables **in the southern** side of the Sanctuary to the left of its entrance, **and five in the northern** side of the Sanctuary to the right, this is difficult. The Gemara explains the difficulty: **Isn't the table fit only** if it is **in the northern** part of the Sanctuary, **as it is stated: "And you shall put the table on the north side"** (Exodus 26:35)? If so, **what is** the meaning when **the verse states: "Five on the right side and five on the left"? Rather,** it must mean that the table prepared by Moses was positioned in the proper place in the Sanctuary, and **five** of the tables made by Solomon were placed **to the right of the table of Moses, and five to its left.**

אַף עַל פִּי כֵן לֹא הָיָה מְסַדֵּר אֶלָּא בְּשֶׁל מֹשֶׁה בִּלְבָד, שֶׁנֶּאֱמַר ״אֶת הַשֻּׁלְחָן אֲשֶׁר עָלָיו לֶחֶם הַפָּנִים״, רַבִּי יוֹסֵי בֵּי רַבִּי יְהוּדָה אוֹמֵר: עַל כּוּלָּן הָיָה מְסַדֵּר, שֶׁנֶּאֱמַר ״אֶת הַשּׁוּלְחָנוֹת וַעֲלֵיהֶם לֶחֶם הַפָּנִים״.

Even so, despite the fact that there were so many tables in the Sanctuary, the priest **would arrange** the shewbread **only on the table of Moses alone, as it is stated:** "And Solomon made all the vessels that were in the House of the Lord, the golden altar, **and the table whereupon the shewbread was,** of gold" (I Kings 7:48). The use of the definite article "the" to describe the table indicates that there was one unique table upon which the shewbread was arranged, the table of Moses. Conversely, **Rabbi Yosei, son of Rabbi Yehuda, says: He would arrange** the shewbread **on all of** the tables, each one in turn, **as it is stated: "And the tables upon which was the shewbread"** (II Chronicles 4:19). This verse indicates that the shewbread was placed on all the tables.

תָּנֵי: מִזְרָח וּמַעֲרָב הָיוּ נְתוּנִין דִּבְרֵי רַבִּי, רַבִּי אֶלְעָזָר בֵּי רַבִּי שִׁמְעוֹן אוֹמֵר: צָפוֹן וְדָרוֹם הָיוּ נְתוּנִין.

The Gemara continues to discuss the shewbread table. **It was taught** in a *baraita*: All the tables, both of Moses and Solomon, **were positioned** from **east to west,** in the northern part of the Sanctuary, so that their length ran parallel to the length of the Sanctuary. This is **the statement of Rabbi** Yehuda HaNasi. **Rabbi Elazar, son of Rabbi Shimon, says: They were placed** from **north to south,** and their length was to the width of the Sanctuary.

מַאן דְּאָמַר מִזְרָח וּמַעֲרָב – נִיחָא, כּוּלְּהֶן רְאוּיִין לְשֵׁירוּת. מַאן דְּאָמַר צָפוֹן וְדָרוֹם – נִמְצָא שֻׁלְחָן בַּדָּרוֹם

According to **the one who said** that the tables were placed from **east to west it works out well, as they are all suitable for service.** The tables were positioned in a manner that rendered them all fit for service, as the table could be used only in the northern part of the Sanctuary, in accordance with the verse: "And you shall put the table on the north side" (Exodus 26:35). However, according to **the one who said** that they were placed from **north to south, the table,** i.e., five of the tables, are **found in the southern** part of the Sanctuary,

HALAKHA

If there was no new bread, what is the *halakha* with regard to leaving it until the next Shabbat – לֹא הָיָה שָׁם לֶחֶם מַהוּ לְהָנִיחוֹ לְשַׁבָּת הַבָּאָה: If the shewbread, along with the bowls of frankincense, is left on the golden table for a few weeks and not exchanged for new ones, no prohibition has been violated (Rambam *Sefer Avoda, Hilkhot Temidin UMusafin* 5:13).

NOTES

What is the *halakha* with regard to leaving it until the next Shabbat…even if it is disqualified – מַהוּ לְהָנִיחוֹ לְשַׁבָּת הַבָּאָה...אֲפִילּוּ פָּסוּל: Some commentaries explain that if there is no new shewbread available for the new week, the shewbread from the previous week is left on the table until the next Shabbat. According to this explanation, the phrase: Even if it is disqualified, is imprecise, as leaving the shewbread on the table does not disqualify it. If this were the case and the shewbread were actually disqualified, there would be no point in leaving it on the table, as the mitzva of the shewbread could not be fulfilled in this manner. Rather, the phrase means: Even if it could be rendered disqualified, by removing it from the table and leaving it on the floor until nightfall, as long as it has not been removed from the table it can remain there until new bread is brought (*Talmid HaRashbash; Har Efrayim*; see also Rabbeinu Meshulam, and Rash Sirilio in his second explanation).

Others claim that the Gemara's description of the shewbread as disqualified should be taken at face value. Since shewbread is fit for one week from when it is first placed on the table, as soon as this time has passed, the bread is rendered disqualified. Therefore, when it is removed from the table the following week it must be taken out and burned, as is the case for all disqualified offerings. However, if there is no new shewbread available, it is best to keep the old bread on the table, as this fulfills the mitzva of ensuring that there is bread continuously present on the shewbread table. The requirement that there always be bread on the shewbread table can be fulfilled even with disqualified bread (*Korban HaEida* in his second explanation; Mahara Fulda).

Solomon built ten tables – עֲשָׂרָה שֻׁלְחָנוֹת עָשָׂה שְׁלֹמֹה: Despite the indication in the mishna that there was only one table in the Temple for the shewbread, the commentaries explain that this *baraita* does not contradict the mishna. The reason is that the mishna counts only those tables that were present in the Second Temple, where there was only one shewbread table, as in the Tabernacle.

Some commentaries have found this explanation difficult in light of the Gemara in *Yoma* 51b, which indicates that even in the Second Temple there were ten additional tables, as explained by Tosafot there (see Rashi). The anonymous commentary in tractate *Tamid* resolves this difficulty by explaining that the *tanna* of the mishna counts only the table upon which the shewbread was actually placed, not the other tables. According to this opinion, the other nine tables in the Temple were for show and were never used, in accordance with the statement of the first *tanna* in the *baraita* here.

וּמְנוֹרָה בַּצָּפוֹן. וְהָא תָּנֵי: הַשֻּׁלְחָן הָיָה נָתוּן מֵחֲצִי הַבַּיִת וְלִפְנִים. מָשׁוּךְ מִן הַכּוֹתֶל שְׁתֵּי אַמּוֹת וּמֶחֱצָה כְּלַפֵּי הַצָּפוֹן, וּמְנוֹרָה כְּנֶגְדּוֹ בַּדָּרוֹם.

and the candelabrum in the north of the Sanctuary. **But wasn't it taught**[N] in a *baraita*: The shewbread **table was situated**[N] **from** the **halfway** point **of the House and inward,** in the inner half of the Sanctuary, **drawn two and a half cubits** away **from the wall to the north.** The priests who arranged the shewbread on the table would stand in this space. **And the candelabrum** was situated **opposite it, in the south** of the Sanctuary, likewise two and a half cubits from the wall.

מִזְבַּח הַזָּהָב הָיָה נָתוּן בְּאֶמְצַע הַבַּיִת, חוֹלֵק אֶת הַבַּיִת מֵחֶצְיוֹ וְלִפְנִים, מָשׁוּךְ קִימְעָא כְּלַפֵּי חוּץ, וְכוּלָּהֶן הָיָה נָתוּן מִשְּׁלִישׁ הַבַּיִת וְלִפְנִים.

The golden altar was situated in the middle of the House, dividing the House from its **halfway** point **and inward,** i.e., equidistant from the north and south walls, **slightly drawn** back[HN] from the place of the table and the candelabrum **toward the outside.** Since the length of the entire area was sixty cubits, twenty for the Holy of Holies, and forty for the Sanctuary, **all** the vessels **were situated from a third of the entire House and inward,** i.e., the vessels were all contained in the second third of the entire area.[B]

עֶשֶׂר מְנוֹרוֹת עָשָׂה שְׁלֹמֹה, שֶׁנֶּאֱמַר ״וַיַּעַשׂ אֶת מְנֹרוֹת הַזָּהָב עֶשֶׂר כְּמִשְׁפָּטָם וַיִּתֵּן בַּהֵיכָל חָמֵשׁ מִיָּמִין וְחָמֵשׁ מִשְּׂמֹאל״. אִין תֵּימָר חָמֵשׁ בַּצָּפוֹן וְחָמֵשׁ בַּדָּרוֹם –

King **Solomon constructed ten candelabra,**[NB] modeled after the one that Moses crafted, **as it is stated: "And he made the ten candlesticks of gold according to the ordinance concerning them; and he set them in the Sanctuary, five on the right, and five on the left"** (II Chronicles 4:7). Before completing its citation of the *baraita*, the Gemara asks: **If you say** that right and left refer to the sides of the entrance to the Sanctuary, which would mean that Solomon set up **five** candelabra **in the north** of the Sanctuary, to the left of its entrance, **and five in the south** of the Sanctuary, to the right of its entrance, this is difficult.

וַהֲלֹא אֵין הַמְּנוֹרָה כְּשֵׁירָה אֶלָּא בַּדָּרוֹם, שֶׁנֶּאֱמַר ״וְאֶת הַמְּנֹרָה נֹכַח הַשֻּׁלְחָן עַל יֶרֶךְ הַמִּשְׁכָּן תֵּימָנָה״. מָה תַּלְמוּד לוֹמַר חָמֵשׁ מִיָּמִין וְחָמֵשׁ מִשְּׂמֹאל, אֶלָּא חָמֵשׁ מִימִין מְנוֹרָתוֹ שֶׁל מֹשֶׁה וְחָמֵשׁ מִשְּׂמֹאלָהּ.

The Gemara explains the difficulty: **Isn't the candelabrum fit only** if it is **in the south of the Sanctuary, as it is stated: "And the candelabrum over against the table on the side of the Tabernacle toward the south"** (Exodus 26:35). **What,** then, is the meaning when **the verse states: "Five on the right, and five on the left"? Rather,** it must mean that the candelabrum that Moses made was located in the Sanctuary, while **five** of the candelabra that Solomon crafted were placed **to the right of the candelabrum of Moses, and five to its left.**

HALAKHA

The placement of the candelabrum, shewbread table, and incense altar – מְקוֹם הַנָּחַת הַמְּנוֹרָה, שׁוּלְחַן הַפָּנִים וּמִזְבַּח הַקְּטוֹרֶת: The candelabrum was situated in the south of the Sanctuary on the left side of the entrance, while the shewbread table was on the right. They both were located outside the Holy of Holies, with the incense altar between them, slightly further to the outside, as stated in the *baraita* (Rambam *Sefer Avoda, Hilkhot Beit HaBeḥira* 1:7).

BACKGROUND

The Temple – הַמִּקְדָּשׁ:

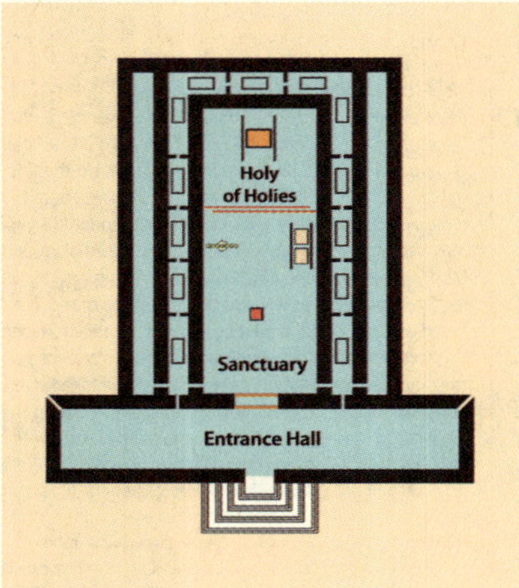

Position of the vessels in the Sanctuary

King Solomon constructed ten candelabra – עֶשֶׂר מְנוֹרוֹת עָשָׂה שְׁלֹמֹה: The ten candelabra that Solomon constructed were in addition to the candelabrum created by Moses. Five were placed to the right of the candelabrum of Moses and five were placed to the left.

Candelabra in the Sanctuary

NOTES

But wasn't it taught – וְהָא תָּנֵי: The explanation of the Gemara presented here is in accordance with a version of the text that omits the phrase: But wasn't. In other words, this *baraita* is cited in support of the previous claim, not as an objection (see *Tiklin Ḥadatin* and *Yefe Einayim*).

The shewbread table was situated – הַשֻּׁלְחָן הָיָה נָתוּן: All the measurements in this *baraita*, as well as the location of the Temple vessels, are based on the following verses: "And the House which King Solomon built for the Lord, its length was sixty cubits, and its breadth twenty cubits, and its height thirty cubits. And the porch before the Sanctuary of the House, its length was twenty cubits, according to the breadth of the House; and ten cubits was its breadth before the House" (I Kings 6:2–3). According to this description, the Temple was divided into three sections: the Entrance Hall, which was the outermost section; the Sanctuary; and finally, the Holy of Holies, which was the innermost section. The *baraita* discusses the Sanctuary and the Holy of Holies, as well as the location of the vessels inside this combined area, which was sixty by twenty cubits. The Sanctuary measured forty by twenty cubits, while the Holy of Holies was twenty by twenty cubits.

Slightly drawn back – מָשׁוּךְ קִימְעָא: The Gemara in tractate *Yoma* (33b) explains why the altar was slightly drawn back. The verse states: "And you shall set…the candelabrum opposite the table" (Exodus 26:35). Since the candelabrum and the table had to be positioned opposite one another, the altar was not placed directly between them, so as not to separate them.

King Solomon constructed ten candelabra – עֶשֶׂר מְנוֹרוֹת עָשָׂה שְׁלֹמֹה: King Solomon placed ten candelabra and ten tables in the Temple because the area of the Sanctuary he built was more than ten times larger than that of the Tabernacle. The Tabernacle was thirty by ten cubits. Solomon's Sanctuary was sixty by twenty cubits. Consequently, whereas one candelabrum sufficed for the Tabernacle, the Temple required eleven. Furthermore, as the Torah dictates that the candelabrum in the Tent of Meeting was to be situated opposite the table, an equivalent number of tables in the Temple was required (*Meshekh Ḥokhma, Parashat Tetzave*).

אַף עַל פִּי כֵן לֹא הָיָה מַבְעִיר אֶלָּא שֶׁל מֹשֶׁה בִּלְבָד, שֶׁנֶּאֱמַר "וּמְנוֹרַת הַזָּהָב וְנֵרוֹתֶיהָ לְבָעֵר בָּעֶרֶב בָּעֶרֶב". רַבִּי יוֹסֵה בֵּי רַבִּי יְהוּדָה אוֹמֵר: עַל כּוּלָּן הָיָה מַבְעִיר, שֶׁנֶּאֱמַר "וְאֶת הַמְּנוֹרוֹת וְנֵרוֹתֵיהֶם לְבָעֲרָם כַּמִּשְׁפָּט לִפְנֵי הַדְּבִיר זָהָב סָגוּר".

Even so, i.e., despite the fact that there were so many candelabra in the Sanctuary, the priest **would kindle only** the candelabrum **of Moses alone, as it is stated: "And the candelabrum of gold with its lamps, to burn every evening"** (II Chronicles 13:11). The singular form indicates that only one candelabrum was lit. Conversely, **Rabbi Yosei, son of Rabbi Yehuda, says: He would kindle all** eleven candelabra, one of Moses and ten of Solomon, each one in turn, **as it is stated: "And the candelabra with their lamps, that they should burn according to the ordinance before the Sanctuary, of pure gold"** (II Chronicles 4:20).[N] The plural "candelabra" indicates that they were all lit.

"וְהַפֶּרַח וְהַנֵּרוֹת וְהַמֶּלְקָחַיִם זָהָב הוּא מִכְלוֹת זָהָב" – הֵן כִּילּוּ זְהָבוֹ שֶׁל שְׁלֹמֹה.

The *baraita* analyzes the subsequent verse: **"And the flowers, and the lamps, and the tongs, of gold, and that perfect gold [*mikhelot zahav*]"** (II Chronicles 4:21). This means that the candelabrum completely **depleted [*killu*] the gold of Solomon.**[N] As the gold was repeatedly purified until it reached the required level of purity, a large quantity of gold evaporated.

תָּנֵי רַב יְהוּדָה בְּשֵׁם אַסִּי הָיָה שְׁלֹמֹה נוֹטֵל אֶלֶף כִּכְּרֵי זָהָב וּמַכְנִיסָן לַכּוּר וּמוֹצִיאָן, עַד שֶׁהוּא מַעֲמִידָן עַל אֶחָד, לְקַיֵּים מַה שֶּׁנֶּאֱמַר "כִּכָּר זָהָב טָהוֹר עָשָׂה אוֹתָהּ וגו'".

The Gemara cites a related *baraita*. **Rav Yehuda taught in the name** of the Sage **Asi: Solomon would take a thousand talents of gold and insert them into the crucible**[B] **and remove them.** He repeated this process **until** the gold was so refined that **he established** its weight **as one** talent of gold, **to fulfill that which is stated** about the original candelabrum in the Tabernacle: **"Of a talent of pure gold made he it, etc."** (Exodus 37:24).

תַּנְיָא: אָמַר רַבִּי יוֹסֵי בֵּי רַבִּי יְהוּדָה: מַעֲשֶׂה בִּמְנוֹרַת זָהָב שֶׁעָשָׂה מֹשֶׁה בַּמִּדְבָּר וְהָיְתָה יְתֵירָה דִּינַר זָהָב, וְהִכְנִיסוּהָ לַכּוּר שְׁמוֹנִים פַּעַם וְלֹא חָסְרָה כְּלוּם.

It was taught in a *baraita* that **Rabbi Yosei, son of Rabbi Yehuda, said:** There was **an incident involving the candelabrum of gold that Moses made in the desert,**[N] **which exceeded** the weight set by the Torah, one talent, **by one dinar of gold. And they inserted it into the crucible eighty times,** to further refine it and reduce its weight, **but it was not reduced** by **anything.**

וְיָאוּת, עַד דְּלָא יָקוּם עַל בְּרָיֵיהּ – הֲוָה חֲסַר סַגִּין, מִן דּוּ קַיֵּים עַל בְּרָיֵיהּ – לָא חֲסַר כְּלוּם.

And this is proper, for **as long as it had not achieved its correct** state of purity, **it would decrease greatly,** as its refinement in the crucible removed all the impurities, thereby reducing its weight. However, **from when it had achieved its correct** state of purity, **it was not reduced at all.** Unlike the gold of Moses, the gold Solomon used was not originally free of impurity and therefore required refinement.

הלכה ד מתני' שְׁלֹשָׁה עָשָׂר שׁוֹפָרוֹת הָיוּ בַּמִּקְדָּשׁ, וְכָתוּב עֲלֵיהֶן: תִּקְלִין חֲדַתִּין, וְתִקְלִין עַתִּיקִין, קִנִּין, וְגוֹזְלֵי עוֹלָה, עֵצִים, לְבוֹנָה, זָהָב לְכַפּוֹרֶת, שִׁשָּׁה לִנְדָבָה.

HALAKHA 4 · MISHNA There were thirteen collection **horns in the Temple, and** the intended use of the funds **was written upon** each one, as follows: **New shekels, old shekels, pairs** of birds, **fledglings** designated for **burnt-offerings, wood** for the arrangement on the altar, **frankincense** that accompanied meal-offerings, and **gold** donated **for the Ark cover.**[N] The remaining **six horns** were designated for communal **free-will offerings.**

BACKGROUND

Crucible for gold – כּוּר זָהָב:

Molten gold being poured from a crucible into a mold

NOTES

Pure gold – זָהָב סָגוּר: This gold was exceptionally pure. It was called *zahav sagur*, literally, closed gold. One explanation of this name is that anyone who sold such gold would drive out of business others who sold regular gold, thereby forcing them to close their shops (*Yoma* 45a; see Rashi; Rashi on *Menaḥot* 26a). In his commentary to I Kings 7:49, the Ralbag explains that this expression means refined gold. It was called closed gold because it was closed in a crucible with substances that removed its impurities.

Depleted the gold of Solomon – כִּילּוּ זְהָבוֹ שֶׁל שְׁלֹמֹה: The version that reads: The gold of Solomon, instead of: The gold of Moses, as appears in some texts, is in accordance with the Gemara in *Menaḥot* 29b, as well as certain printed versions of the Gemara here.

An incident involving the candelabrum of gold that Moses made in the desert, etc. – מַעֲשֶׂה בִּמְנוֹרַת זָהָב שֶׁעָשָׂה מֹשֶׁה בַּמִּדְבָּר וכו': The explanation of the Gemara accords with the version of the text here (see *Dikdukei Sofrim*). However, there are variant texts that read: There was an incident involving the candelabrum of the Temple that exceeded the weight of the candelabrum that Moses made in the desert. According to this version, the discussion of the Gemara proceeds as follows: The weight of the golden candelabrum in the Temple exceeded that of the candelabrum of Moses by one gold dinar. They repeatedly inserted it into the crucible to refine it, but the weight was not diminished at all. If the refinement of the gold in the crucible did not cause it to decrease in weight at all, how then was the gold of Solomon reduced to one-thousandth of its original weight?

Gold for the Ark cover – זָהָב לְכַפּוֹרֶת: Rashi (*Temura* 23b) cites two explanations for the purpose of these funds. The first is that this horn was designated for gold intended for any of the Temple vessels. The second is that one who obligates himself to donate a sacred vessel to the Temple without specifying which one must bring a basin. The basins are referred to as *keforei zahav* (Ezra 1:10), similar to the term *zahav lakapporet*, the phrase written on the collection horn. Rashi prefers the second explanation, because, as consecrated funds for Temple maintenance were brought not to the Temple itself but directly to the treasurer, there was no need to designate a collection horn for them. Others explain that these funds were used for the gold cover for the Holy of Holies, which was called the house of the Ark cover, as it is stated elsewhere that leftover donations were used for this purpose (*Tosefot Yeshanim* on *Yoma* 55b; Rambam's Commentary on the Mishna; Rambam *Sefer Zemanim*, *Hilkhot Shekalim* 12:1; *Me'iri*; Rash Sirilio).

תִּקְלִין חֲדַתִּין – שֶׁבְּכׇל שָׁנָה וְשָׁנָה, וְעַתִּיקִין – מִי שֶׁלֹּא הֵבִיא אֶשְׁתָּקַד שׁוֹקֵל לְשָׁנָה הַבָּאָה.

The horn labeled **new shekels** was designated for the half-shekel donation **that** was brought **every year** for the needs of that year. The horn labeled **old shekels** was for **one who did not bring** his half-shekel **the previous year,** who would **contribute his shekel for the following year.**

קִינִּין הֵן תּוֹרִין, וְגוֹזְלֵי עוֹלָה הֵן בְּנֵי יוֹנָה, כּוּלָּן עוֹלוֹת, דִּבְרֵי רַבִּי יְהוּדָה.

The funds in the horn labeled **pairs** of birds **are** designated for the **turtledoves** used for bird-offerings, and the one labeled **fledglings** for **burnt-offerings are** used to purchase **young pigeons** as burnt-offerings. **All of these,** i.e., the funds in both horns, were used exclusively for voluntary **burnt-offerings.** This is **the statement of Rabbi Yehuda.**

וַחֲכָמִים אוֹמְרִים: קִינִּין – אֶחָד חַטָּאת וְאֶחָד עוֹלָה, גּוֹזְלֵי עוֹלָה – כּוּלָּן עוֹלוֹת.

And the Rabbis say: The funds in both the horn labeled pairs of birds and the horn labeled fledglings were for young pigeons and turtledoves. The distinction between them is that the funds in the horn labeled **pairs** of birds were designated for the obligatory offerings of a *zav*, a *zava*, a woman after childbirth, and a leper. These offerings included a pair of birds, **one** brought for **a sin-offering, and** the other **one** brought for **a burnt-offering.** Conversely, the funds in the horn labeled **fledglings** for **burnt-offerings** were **all** used exclusively for voluntary **burnt-offerings.**[N]

הָאוֹמֵר ״הֲרֵי עָלַי עֵצִים״ – לֹא יִפְחוֹת מִשְּׁנֵי גְּזִירִין, לְבוֹנָה – לֹא יִפְחוֹת מִקּוֹמֶץ, זָהָב – לֹא יִפְחוֹת מִדִּינַר זָהָב.

One who says: It is incumbent **upon me** to donate **wood** to the Temple, must donate **no fewer than two logs**[H] for the arrangement on the altar. One who says: It is incumbent upon me to donate **frankincense,**[H] must donate **no less than a handful** of frankincense, the amount brought with a meal-offering. One who says: It is incumbent upon me to donate **gold,** must donate **no less than a dinar of gold.**

שִׁשָּׁה לִנְדָבָה. נְדָבָה מָה הָיוּ עוֹשִׂין בָּהּ? לוֹקְחִים בָּהּ עוֹלוֹת, הַבָּשָׂר לַשֵּׁם וְעוֹרוֹת לַכֹּהֲנִים.

It was stated that **six horns** were designated **for** communal **free-will offerings.** The mishna asks: With regard to the money designated for communal **free-will offerings, what would they do with this** money? The mishna answers that they used **it to purchase** animals for **burnt-offerings,** as **the meat** from these offerings was offered on the altar **to God and the hides** were given **to the priests.**

זֶה מִדְרָשׁ דָּרַשׁ יְהוֹיָדָע כֹּהֵן גָּדוֹל: ״אָשָׁם הוּא אָשׁוֹם אָשַׁם לַה׳״.

This midrash was taught by **Jehoiada the High Priest:**[N] There is an apparent contradiction between two verses. With regard to the guilt-offering, the verse states: **"It is a guilt-offering; he is certainly guilty before the Lord"** (Leviticus 5:19). This verse indicates that the guilt-offering goes to God, not the priests. However, a different verse states: "As is the sin-offering, so is the guilt-offering; there is one law for them; the priest who makes atonement with it, he shall have it" (Leviticus 7:7). This verse indicates that the offering is designated for the priests alone. How can these two verses be reconciled?

זֶה הַכְּלָל: כֹּל שֶׁהוּא בָּא מִשּׁוּם חַטָּאת וּמִשּׁוּם אַשְׁמָה – יִלָּקַח בָּהֶן עוֹלוֹת, הַבָּשָׂר לַשֵּׁם וְהָעוֹרוֹת לַכֹּהֲנִים. נִמְצְאוּ שְׁנֵי כְתוּבִין קַיָּימִין אָשָׁם לַה׳ וְאָשָׁם לַכֹּהֵן.

The mishna explains that **this is the principle: Any** funds **that come due to a sin-offering or due to a guilt-offering,** i.e., leftover coins designated for one of these offerings, **they** should be used for the **purchase of animals for a** voluntary **burnt-offering,** as **the meat** will be offered on the altar **to God, and the hides** will go **to the priests.** In this manner **the two verses are found** to be **fulfilled,** as it is both **a guilt-offering to God as well as a guilt-offering to the priest.**

וְאוֹמֵר ״כֶּסֶף אָשָׁם וְכֶסֶף חַטָּאוֹת לֹא יוּבָא בֵּית ה׳ לַכֹּהֲנִים יִהְיוּ״.

And this *halakha* also explains the verse that **says: "The guilt-offering money and the sin-offering money was not brought into the House of the Lord; it was for the priests"** (II Kings 12:17). This verse is understood to refer to the hides given to the priests.

גמ׳ תַּנְיָא, אָמַר רַבִּי יְהוּדָה: לֹא הָיָה שׁוֹפָר שֶׁל קִינִּין בִּירוּשָׁלַיִם מִפְּנֵי הַתַּעֲרוֹבוֹת שֶׁמָּא תָּמוּת אַחַת, וְנִמְצְאוּ דְּמֵי חַטָּאוֹת מֵיתוֹת מְעוֹרָבוֹת בָּהֶן.

GEMARA It was taught in a *baraita* that **Rabbi Yehuda said: There was no** collection **horn for pairs** of birds in the Temple in **Jerusalem, due to the mixtures.** The concern was that **perhaps** one of the women obligated to bring a pair of birds **would die** after putting her money in the horn. **And** if that happens, it would **turn out** that **the funds for sin-offerings left to die are mixed with** the rest of the money in the horn. When the owner of funds designated for a sin-offering passes away, the designated money must be destroyed. Since there is no way to distinguish between the coins, all the money is prohibited.

NOTES

Pairs of birds and fledglings for burnt-offerings – קִינִּין וְגוֹזְלֵי עוֹלָה: The money placed in these horns was used for the purchase of offerings for the atonement of particular individuals. At the time of the actual sacrifice, the owner's identity was unknown to the priests performing the rite, since all the money was mixed together in the horn. However, this did not invalidate the offerings, as the priests who brought them intended that each bird would be used to fulfill the obligation of whoever placed money in the horn. The owners of these sacrifices relied upon the priests to bring the offerings at the soonest possible time.

This midrash was taught by Jehoiada the High Priest – זֶה מִדְרָשׁ דָּרַשׁ יְהוֹיָדָע כֹּהֵן גָּדוֹל: The reference is to Jehoiada, the High Priest who reorganized the collection of funds for the Temple and its maintenance during the reign of King Jehoash.

The early commentaries differ with regard to the basis of this midrash. Some commentaries explain that it is derived from an apparent contradiction between two verses: "The guilt-offering money and the sin-offering money was not brought into the House of the Lord; it was for the priests" (II Kings 12:17), and: "The priest who makes atonement with it, he shall have it" (Leviticus 7:7). Others explain that the verse "It is a guilt-offering; he is certainly guilty before the Lord" (Leviticus 5:19) is self-contradictory. "It is a guilt offering" (Leviticus 5:19) indicates that it is like any other guilt-offering, which is eaten by priests, whereas the phrase: "He is certainly guilty before the Lord" indicates that it is all for the Lord. The explanation is that this verse does not mean that the money intended for offerings goes to the priests; rather, the hides of the burnt-offerings, which come from the remainder of the money for the sin-offerings and the guilt-offerings, belong to the priests.

The early commentaries also differ concerning the novelty in the teaching of Jehoiada the High Priest. Some claim that his essential point was that the remainder is given as a free-will offering (Rashi on *Zevaḥim* 11b), while others contend that he taught that the hide of this burnt-offering, like all others, goes to the priests (Ra'avad).

HALAKHA

It is incumbent upon me to donate wood to the Temple, must donate no fewer than two logs – הֲרֵי עָלַי עֵצִים, לֹא יִפְחוֹת מִשְּׁנֵי גְּזִירִין: One who donates wood to the Temple must give no fewer than two logs that are a cubit long and as wide as the tool used to level the *se'a* measure (Rambam *Sefer Avoda, Hilkhot Ma'aseh HaKorbanot* 16:13).

It is incumbent upon me to donate frankincense – הֲרֵי עָלַי...לְבוֹנָה: One who donates frankincense to the Temple must give no less than a handful (Rambam *Sefer Avoda, Hilkhot Ma'aseh HaKorbanot* 16:13).

וְהָתַנְיָא: הָאִשָּׁה שֶׁאָמְרָה ״הֲרֵי עָלַי קֵן״ – מְבִיאָה דְּמֵי קֵן וְנוֹתַנְתּוֹ בַּשּׁוֹפָר,

The Gemara raises a difficulty against this conclusion. **But wasn't it taught** in a *baraita* that with regard to **a woman who said:** It is incumbent **upon me** to bring **a pair** of birds, that **she brings the funds for** the purchase of **a pair** of birds to the Temple **and places them in the** collection **horn?**

Perek **VI**
Daf **18** Amud **b**

וְאוֹכֶלֶת בַּקֳּדָשִׁים. וְאֵינָהּ חוֹשֶׁשֶׁת שֶׁמָּא נִתְעַצֵּל בָּהֶן. וְאֵין הַכֹּהֵן חוֹשֵׁשׁ שֶׁמָּא דְּמֵי חַטָּאוֹת מֵיתוֹת מְעוֹרָבוֹת בָּהֶן.

And after she has ritually immersed for her purification and the sun has set, **she** may **eat consecrated** foods. **And she need not be concerned that perhaps** the priest **was lazy**[H] and neglected to sacrifice her offering, which would cause her to lack atonement and be prohibited from eating sacrificial food. **And the priest need not be concerned that perhaps** one of the women who placed funds in this horn has died, which would mean that **the funds for sin-offerings left to die are mixed with** the rest of the coins. Since this ruling is undisputed, it is evidently accepted by all the Sages, including Rabbi Yehuda. If so, how can it be claimed that Rabbi Yehuda said there were no horns for obligatory pairs of birds due to the concern that one of the women who placed money there had died?

כִּי קָאָמְרִינַן בְּחַטָּאוֹת שֶׁמֵּתוּ בַּעֲלֵיהֶן וַדַּאי.

The Gemara answers: **When we say** this opinion of Rabbi Yehuda, we are referring to a case where it is known that one of the women had died, which means that the funds she gave have the status **of a sin-offering whose owner had certainly died.** In this case the coins definitely cannot be used for an offering, and they invalidate the other coins with which they are mingled in the horn. To avoid this scenario, Rabbi Yehuda maintains that there was no horn for obligatory pairs of birds.

וְאִי אָמְרִינַן נִבְרוֹר אַרְבָּעָה זוּזֵי וְנִישְׁדֵי בְּנַהֲרָא וְאִידָךְ לִישְׁתְּרוּ,

The Gemara asks: **But** even **if we say** that there is a concern that the horn contains invalidated coins, the following remedy can be applied: **Let us select four *zuz*,**[N] the value of one pair of birds (see *Keritot* 1:7), and declare that these are the invalidated coins, **and throw them into the river** so that they will be destroyed, **and the remainder will be permitted.** If so, even according to the opinion of Rabbi Yehuda, there should be no problem with a horn for pairs of birds.

הָא אָמְרִינַן בְּעָלְמָא: רַבִּי יְהוּדָה לֵית לֵיהּ בְּרֵירָה.

The Gemara answers: This is not an effective solution according to the opinion of Rabbi Yehuda, because **we generally say: Rabbi Yehuda does not accept** the principle of **retroactive designation.** According to Rabbi Yehuda, a doubtful state of affairs cannot be clarified retroactively. Consequently, one cannot resolve this problem by setting aside four *zuz*, and he maintains that there was no horn for obligatory pairs of birds.

רַבִּי יוֹסֵה בֵּי רַבִּי בּוּן אָמַר רַבִּי בָּא בַּר מָמֶל בָּעֵי: דְּאָמַר ״הֲרֵי עָלַי עֵץ״ – מֵבִיא גֵּיזֶר אֶחָד.

§ It was taught in the mishna that if one said: It is incumbent upon me to donate wood, he must donate no fewer than two logs. The Gemara addresses a similar case: **Rabbi Yosei, son of Rabbi Bun, said that Rabbi Ba bar Memel raised a dilemma:** What is the ruling if **one said:** It is incumbent **upon me** to donate a log of **wood?**[H] Does **he bring** only **one log?**

אָמַר רַבִּי לְעָזָר: מַתְנִיתָא אֲמָרָהּ כֵּן, שֶׁזֶּה קָרְבָּן בִּפְנֵי עַצְמוֹ וְזֶה קָרְבָּן בִּפְנֵי עַצְמוֹ.

Rabbi Elazar said: The Mishna says so; i.e., a mishna provides a solution to our dilemma. We learned that the two logs added each day to the arrangement on the altar, before the daily morning offering and before the daily afternoon offering, were not considered one offering, **as this** log **was an offering to itself and that** log **was an offering to itself.** Since each log was a separate offering, evidently one may donate even a single log.

HALAKHA

And she need not be concerned that perhaps the priest was lazy – וְאֵינָהּ חוֹשֶׁשֶׁת שֶׁמָּא נִתְעַצֵּל: A woman after childbirth and a *zava* bring their funds to the Temple and place them in the horn specified for that purpose. After ritual immersion, she is permitted to eat consecrated food that evening, as she may assume that her purification offering was sacrificed (Rambam *Sefer Korbanot, Hilkhot Meḥusrei Kappara* 1:12).

It is incumbent upon me to donate a log of wood – הֲרֵי עָלַי עֵץ: One who pledges wood to the Temple must bring a log one cubit in length. If he prefers, he may instead donate the value of this log (Rambam *Sefer Avoda, Hilkhot Ma'aseh HaKorbanot* 16:13).

NOTES

Let us select four *zuz* – נִבְרוֹר אַרְבָּעָה זוּזֵי: The early commentaries ask: Even according to those who accept the principle of retroactive designation, this principle cannot be used to identify prohibited items in a mixture and thereby render the other articles permitted. Therefore, these commentaries explain that a horn can be designated for obligatory pairs of birds in the following manner: Everyone who inserts money into this horn should make a condition at the time of his donation that if his money is thrown into the river due to the death of someone who put money into the horn, the money he is now giving should belong to that person, and if he himself dies, the money that is thrown away should be his. This condition need not be formulated verbally (*Tosefot Yom Tov*). In this manner, all the money in the horn will belong to those who are alive, and will be fit for a sin-offering. Even so, this condition is effective only for those who accept the principle of retroactive designation, as it is the act of throwing the coins into the river that determines whose money was donated in the name of the dead from the outset.

LANGUAGE

Scale [*turtanei*] – טוּרְטָנֵי: From the Greek τρυτάνη, *trutanè*, meaning a balance or a pair of scales. Here it refers to one rod hanging from another rod, as on a scale.

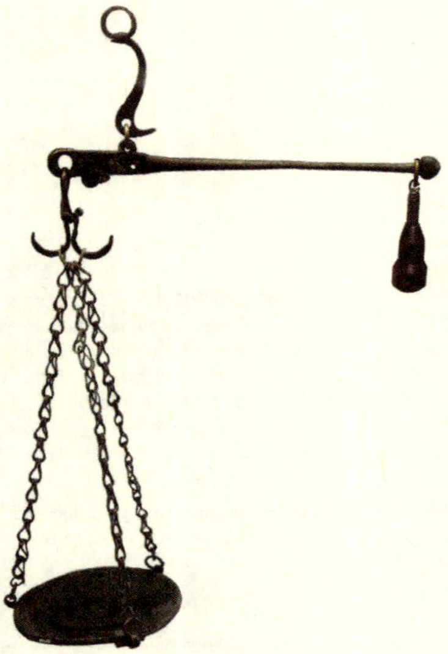

Roman steelyard balance, a type of scale used since antiquity

BACKGROUND

The altar – הַמִּזְבֵּחַ:

(1) Base of the altar
(2) Surrounding ledge
(3) Red line encircling the Temple altar at precisely half its height
(4) The arrangement, three cubits in height
(5) Corners
(6) Rim that served as a walkway for the priests

כְּהַאי דְּתָנֵינַן תַּמָּן: הַשְּׁנַיִם בְּיָדָם שְׁנֵי גִּזְרֵי עֵצִים.

Where was this ruling taught? **As we learned in a mishna there,** with regard to the order of the daily afternoon offering: **Two** priests ascended to the altar, and **in their hands** were **two logs of wood** for the arrangement, each holding one log in his hand. This statement indicates that each log was a separate offering, as each was held by a different priest.

וּ״קָרְבָּן״ – לְרַבּוֹת אֶת הָעֵצִים.

The Gemara asks: From where is it derived that even an individual can pledge wood for the arrangement? From the verse: "And when any one brings a meal-offering to the Lord" (Leviticus 2:1). The word **offering** comes **to include the wood,** which is also referred to as an offering in the verse: "And we cast lots, the priests, the Levites, and the people, for the wood-offering" (Nehemiah 10:35). Furthermore, the phrase "any one" teaches that even an individual can pledge wood.

רַבִּי יְהוֹשֻׁעַ בֶּן לֵוִי אָמַר: עוֹבְיָין אַמָּה בְּאַמָּה שׂוֹחֶקֶת, וְאָרְכָּן בְּאַמָּה גְּדוּמָה. רַבִּי חוֹנִי בְּשֵׁם רַבִּי אַמִּי: כְּמִין טוּרְטָנֵי.

As the Gemara is discussing the donation of logs for the arrangement, it mentions their measurements. **Rabbi Yehoshua ben Levi said: The thickness** of this wood **was a cubit of the expanded cubits, and their length** was measured **by the shortened cubits. Rabbi Ḥoni** said **in the name of Rabbi Ammi:** The measurement of their thickness was **as on a scale** [***turtanei***],[L] i.e., it was exactly one cubit.

אָמַר רַבִּי שְׁמוּאֵל בַּר רַב יִצְחָק: לְפִי שֶׁלֹּא הָיָה מְקוֹם הַמַּעֲרָכָה אֶלָּא אַמָּה עַל אַמָּה, לְפִיכָךְ לֹא הָיָה בּוֹ אֶלָּא אַמָּה גְּדוּמָה. וְתָנֵי כֵן: אַמָּה הַיְּסוֹד, אַמָּה סוֹבֵב, אַמָּה כַּרְכּוֹב, וְאַמָּה קְרָנוֹת, וְאַמָּה מַעֲרָכָה.

Rabbi Shmuel bar Rav Yitzḥak explained why a shortened cubit was used for the measurement of the wood and **said: As the area of the arrangement** on the bronze altar built by Moses **was only one cubit by one cubit,**[N] **therefore,** the length of the log **was only a shortened cubit,** as it would otherwise protrude from the arrangement. **And it was likewise taught** in a *baraita*: The breadth of **the base** of the altar[B] made by Moses was **a cubit, the surrounding ledge** was **a cubit,**[N] **the rim a cubit, the corners a cubit,** and the breadth of the place of the **arrangement** was likewise **a cubit.**

לְבוֹנָה לֹא יִפְחוֹת מִקּוֹמֶץ. נֶאֱמַר כָּאן ״אַזְכָּרָה״ וְנֶאֱמַר לְהַלָּן ״אַזְכָּרָה״,

§ It was taught in the mishna that if one pledges **frankincense** without specifying an amount, he must donate **no less than a handful.** The Gemara cites the verbal analogy that is the source for this *halakha*. **It is stated here:** "And you shall put pure frankincense with each row, that it may be to the bread for a **memorial-part**" (Leviticus 24:7). **And it is stated there,** with regard to the meal-offering of a sinner: "And the priest shall take his handful of it as its **memorial-part**" (Leviticus 5:12).

NOTES

As the area of the arrangement was only one cubit by one cubit – לְפִי שֶׁלֹּא הָיָה מְקוֹם הַמַּעֲרָכָה אֶלָּא אַמָּה עַל אַמָּה: The Sages derived this from the verse: "And Aaron's sons, the priests, shall lay the pieces, and the head, and the suet, in order upon the wood that is on the fire which is upon the altar" (Leviticus 1:8). The Sages learned from the seemingly superfluous words "Which is upon the altar" that the wood must be placed on the altar without protruding. Therefore, the logs must be slightly less than a cubit long (*Korban HaEida*; *Tiklin Ḥadatin*; *Penei Zaken*).

The Rambam states that the measurement of one cubit by one cubit was established for all generations. Although the size of the arrangement later increased, and in the Second Temple its area was twenty-four by twenty-four cubits, the measure for the size of the wood remained one cubit by one cubit (*Sefer Avoda, Hilkhot Issurei Mizbe'aḥ* 7:3).

The base was a cubit, the surrounding ledge was a cubit, etc. – אַמָּה הַיְּסוֹד, אַמָּה סוֹבֵב וכו׳: The altar was built such that it was widest at its base and indented a cubit at intervals, creating at the indentation a cubit-wide ledge. What is called the base of the altar was the altar up to the height of one cubit, which appeared as a cubit-wide protrusion below the rest of the altar that rose above it. This ledge did not extend around the entire altar, but only on its northern and western sides, plus one additional cubit both at the northernmost point of the eastern side and at the westernmost point of the southern side (see *Zevaḥim* 53b).

At the height of six cubits, the altar was indented a cubit width all around, creating the surrounding ledge. According to most opinions, the rim of the altar was the cubit-wide strip around the outer edge of the top of the altar. It served as a walkway for the priests. However, see *Zevaḥim* 62a, where an opinion is cited that identifies the rim with the surrounding ledge. The corners refers to the four corners of the altar where an area of one square cubit was elevated one cubit.

מָה "אַזְכָּרָה" הָאָמוּר לְהַלָּן מְלֹא קוֹמֶץ – אַף "אַזְכָּרָה" הָאָמוּר כָּאן מְלֹא קוֹמֶץ.

The Gemara interprets the verbal analogy: **Just as** the term **"memorial-part" that is stated below** must be **a handful, so too,** the term **"memorial-part" that is stated here,** with regard to the frankincense brought with the shewbread, must be **a handful.** This shows that when an unspecified amount of frankincense is pledged as an independent free-will offering, the obligation is to bring a handful.

אִי מָה "אַזְכָּרָה" הָאֲמוּרָה לְהַלָּן – שְׁנֵי קוֹמְצִין, אַף "אַזְכָּרָה" הָאֲמוּרָה כָּאן שְׁנֵי קוֹמְצִין!

The Gemara asks: **If** so, one can derive the opposite conclusion from the same verbal analogy: **Just as the memorial-part that is stated below,** by the shewbread, must be **two handfuls,** one for each arrangement of bread, **so too** the term **memorial-part stated here,** with regard to the free-will offering of frankincense, should be a measure of **two handfuls.**

אָמַר רַבִּי אִילָא: כְּלוּם לָמְדוּ לַקּוֹמֶץ אֶלָּא מִמִּנְחַת חוֹטֵא, מַה לְּהַלָּן קוֹמֶץ הֶחָסֵר פָּסוּל – אַף כָּאן קוֹמֶץ הֶחָסֵר פָּסוּל.

Rabbi Ila said in response: **Didn't we** derive the measurement of a handful of frankincense **only from the meal-offering of a sinner? Just as there,** in the case of the meal-offering of a sinner, **an incomplete handful is invalid, so too, here,** with regard to frankincense of the shewbread, **an incomplete handful** should be **invalid.** It is possible to invalidate the frankincense of the shewbread only if each handful is considered an independent mitzva. If the two handfuls together were considered one mitzva, they would remain valid even if one of them were incomplete, as they contain a total amount greater than a handful. This proves that each handful is an independent mitzva, which means that if one of them is incomplete, the second does not complete it and it is invalidated. From here it can be inferred that every measurement of the frankincense, including a free-will offering of frankincense, requires a handful.

אָמַר רַבִּי יוֹסֵה מִילְּתָא דְּרַבִּי אִילָא אֲמָרָה: הַמִּתְנַדֵּב לְבוֹנָה, מְבִיאָהּ בְּקוּמְצוֹ שֶׁל כֹּהֵן (גָּדוֹל). רַבִּי חִזְקִיָּה בְּשֵׁם רַבִּי יִרְמְיָה: וַאֲפִילּוּ בַּקּוֹמֶץ הַבְּעָלִים.

Rabbi Yosei said: From the **statement of Rabbi Ila,** that the measurement of a handful of frankincense for a free-will offering is derived from the handful that came with the shewbread, which is measured according to the handful of the largest of the priests, it can be **said** that **one who donates incense brings it** according to the measure **of the handful of a priest** who has the **largest** hands,[N] not the handful of the one who brings it. **Rabbi Ḥizkiya** said **in the name of Rabbi Yirmeya:** One who donates incense can approximate the handful of any priest, **and even** use **the handful of the owners.**

זָהָב לֹא יִפְחוֹת כו׳. אָמַר רַבִּי אֶלְעָזָר: וְהוּא שֶׁהִזְכִּיר צוּרָה, אֲבָל אִם לֹא הִזְכִּיר צוּרָה – מֵבִיא אֲפִילּוּ צִינּוֹרָה.

The mishna taught that one who pledges **gold** without specifying the amount must donate **no less** than a dinar of gold. **Rabbi Elazar said: And this is** the case **if he mentioned a form**[H] by saying: It is incumbent upon me to bring a gold coin. **However, if he did not mention a form,** but merely said: It is incumbent upon me to bring gold, **he** may **bring even a** small **hook** of any size.

שִׁשָּׁה לִנְדָבָה. חִזְקִיָּה אָמַר: כְּנֶגֶד שִׁשָּׁה בָּתֵּי אָבוֹת.

The mishna states that there were **six** collection horns **for** communal **free-will offerings,** in which the remainder of the funds for sin-offerings and burnt-offerings were placed, for the purchase of free-will offerings. **Ḥizkiya said:** There six horns **correspond to the six** extended **patrilineal families**[B] of priests who served each week in the Temple. There was one collection horn for each family, to prevent quarrels among the priests.

בַּר פְּדָיָה אָמַר: כְּנֶגֶד שֵׁשׁ בְּהֵמוֹת: פָּר, וְעֵגֶל, וְשָׂעִיר, אַיִל, גְּדִי, וְטָלֶה. שְׁמוּאֵל אָמַר: כְּנֶגֶד שִׁשָּׁה קָרְבָּנוֹת (קִנֵּי זָבִים וְקִנֵּי זָבוֹת קִנֵּי יוֹלְדוֹת) חַטָּאוֹת, וַאֲשָׁמוֹת, הַמְּנָחוֹת, וַעֲשִׂירִית הָאֵיפָה.

Bar Pedaya said: The six horns **correspond to the six** types of **animals** from which burnt-offerings can be brought: **Bulls, calves, goats, rams, kids, and lambs.** Each collection horn was for the funds designated for a particular type of animal. **Shmuel said:** They **correspond to the six** obligatory **offerings** whose leftover funds were used for the purchase of burnt-offerings: (1) **Pairs** of birds offered in the purification ritual **of a** ***zav*****, pairs** of birds **of a** ***zava*****;** (2) **pairs** of birds **of a woman after childbirth;** (3) **sin-offerings;** (4) **guilt-offerings;** (5) **meal-offerings** of a sinner; **and** (6) **the tenth part of an ephah** brought each day by the High Priest as a meal-offering.

אָמַר רַבִּי יוֹחָנָן: עַל יְדֵי שֶׁהַנְּדָבָה מְרוּבָּה רִיבּוּ לָהּ שׁוֹפָרוֹת הַרְבֵּה.

Rabbi Yoḥanan said: Since the free-will offerings are plentiful, i.e., much money was donated for this purpose, there was a concern that if too many coins were placed in one horn, only the uppermost coins would be taken and the bottom ones would deteriorate. Therefore **they instituted many horns,** so that each horn contained fewer coins and the funds would be preserved properly.

NOTES

Of a priest who has the largest hands – בְּקוּמְצוֹ שֶׁל כֹּהֵן גָּדוֹל: The reason for this is that the service of the shewbread, including the taking of the handful of frankincense and offering it upon the altar, was divided among the priests by means of a lottery. Since the priest with the largest hands could be appointed to perform this task, the frankincense must be brought in this measure.

HALAKHA

And this is the case if he mentioned a form – וְהוּא שֶׁהִזְכִּיר צוּרָה: If one says: It is incumbent upon me to bring silver, or: It is incumbent upon me to bring gold, without mentioning the word coin, he is obligated to bring silver or gold as follows: He adds to the measure until he can definitively state: I did not intend to bring that much. The *halakha* is in accordance with the opinion of Rabbi Elazar (Rambam *Sefer Hafla'a, Hilkhot Arakhin VaḤaramim* 2:10).

BACKGROUND

Six patrilineal families – שִׁשָּׁה בָּתֵּי אָבוֹת: Even before the construction of the Temple was completed, there were already more priests than necessary to perform the sacred service. Therefore, King David and the prophet Samuel established priestly watches (see I Chronicles 24). The priests were grouped into twenty-four watches, each of which served in the Temple for one week twice a year. It was only during the pilgrim Festivals, when the entire nation ascended to Jerusalem, that all of the priests came to the Temple. During the Second Temple period, the watches were divided afresh; however, the basic divisions remained intact. Each watch was divided into six families, corresponding to the days of the week, so that all of the members of the watch served one day. The changing of the watch took place each Shabbat.

כְּתִיב: "וּכְכַלּוֹתָם הֵבִיאוּ לִפְנֵי הַמֶּלֶךְ וִיהוֹיָדָע" וגו׳ רַבִּי שִׁמְעוֹן בַּר נַחְמָן בְּשֵׁם רַבִּי יוֹנָתָן אָמַר: שְׁתֵּי נְדָבוֹת עָשָׂה,

The Gemara discusses the midrash of Jehoiada the High Priest mentioned in the mishna. **It is written: "And when they had made an end, they brought the rest of the money before the king and Jehoiada,** from which they made vessels for the house of the Lord, even vessels used in the Temple service" (II Chronicles 24:14). In explanation of this verse, **Rabbi Shimon bar Naḥman said in the name of Rabbi Yoḥanan: Jehoiada made two** chests[NS] for two different types of **voluntary donations,** one for maintaining the Temple and the other for free-will offerings.

תָּנֵי דְּבֵי רַבִּי יִשְׁמָעֵאל: נְדָבָה אַחַת. דִּכְתִיב "וַיֹּאמֶר הַמֶּלֶךְ וַיַּעֲשׂוּ אֲרוֹן אֶחָד" וַיִּתְּנֻהוּ בְּהֵיכַל בֵּית ה׳ "וַיִּקֹּב חוֹר בְּדַלְתּוֹ".

A dissenting opinion **was taught** in a *baraita* **of the school of Rabbi Yishmael:** Jehoiada prepared a single chest for **one free-will offering, as it is written: "So the king commanded, and they made a chest"** (II Chronicles 24:8). The verse specifically states that Jehoiada made only one chest. This is the same chest mentioned elsewhere: **And he placed it in the Sanctuary of the House of God, "and he bored a hole in its lid"** (II Kings 12:10).

וְהָא דִכְתִיב "וַיֹּאמֶר הַמֶּלֶךְ וַיַּעֲשׂוּ אֲרוֹן אֶחָד וַיִּתְּנֻהוּ בְּשַׁעַר בֵּית ה׳ חוּצָה"!

The Gemara asks: **But isn't it written: "So the king commanded, and they made a chest, and set it without, at the gate of the House of the Lord"** (II Chronicles 24:8)? This indicates that that there was an additional chest that was placed outside the Temple.

אָמַר רַב חוּנָא: מִפְּנֵי הַטְּמֵאִים.

Rav Ḥuna said: There was only one chest, which was originally located inside the Temple by Jehoiada's command. Afterward, however, he instructed that it should be placed outside the Temple **because of** those people who were **ritually impure** by contact with a corpse or a dead creeping animal. These people were unable to enter the Temple to insert their money for free-will offerings.

רַבִּי חֲנִינָא בְּשֵׁם רַבִּי יוֹסֵף: "אַךְ לֹא יֵעָשֶׂה בֵּית ה׳ סִפּוֹת כֶּסֶף מְזַמְּרוֹת" וגו׳.

Rabbi Ḥanina said **in the name of Rabbi Yosef:** There were two free-will offerings in the Temple, as it is written: **"But there were not made for the House of the Lord cups of silver, snuffers,** basins, trumpets, any vessels of gold, or vessels of silver, of the money that was brought into the House of the Lord; for they gave that to them who did the work, and repaired with it the House of the Lord" (II Kings 12:14). These were for the repairs of the Temple, not for making sacred serving vessels. Conversely, the verses in II Chronicles discuss the construction of the vessels, as it is written: "From which they made vessels for the House of the Lord" (II Chronicles 24:14). As this verse refers to a different chest and a separate free-will offering, it shows that there were in fact two chests.

הדרן עלך
שלשה עשר שופרות

Summary of **Perek VI**

This chapter elaborated on certain set quantities connected to some of the permanent features of the Temple. One recurring figure is that of the number thirteen, as that is the number of collection baskets, obligatory bowings, tables, and gates, at least according to some opinions. Another prominent number is ten, as there were ten additional tables and candelabras in the First Temple, some of which were found in the Second Temple as well. The chapter also addressed in detail the minimum amounts of the various donations to the Temple, as one must provide gifts of a respectable size. To this end, several minimum sizes are provided for donations of gold and silver, and even of logs.

However, the two main topics of the Gemara of this chapter are only peripherally addressed by the Mishna. One is the Ark of the Covenant, as the Gemara discusses its fate, whether it was exiled to Babylonia with the other Temple vessels or sequestered; and if it was sequestered, where it was buried. Likewise, the Gemara analyzed in detail the contents of the Ark, and what objects were either placed in it or attached to its side, in accordance with the various opinions.

The other main topic of this chapter, which is also discussed at some length, likewise belongs to the realm of *aggada*. It concerns the prophecy of the water that will emerge from the Holy of Holies and flow at least as far as the Dead Sea, changing the nature of the entire region. In addition to these central matters, this chapter naturally addressed other minor issues as well.

Introduction to **Perek VII**

This chapter deals primarily with found items whose precise halakhic status is not known. It addresses what must be done with money that was found among the collection horns in the Temple, when it is not clear to which category it belongs. Likewise, there is a discussion of money that was found in the city of Jerusalem, where there is a reasonable possibility that it had been set aside for the purchase of sacrifices and thus consecrated. So too with regard to animals that were found in proximity to Jerusalem, as there is a reasonable possibility that they had been designated as sacrifices and subsequently strayed or ran away. The found animals are assumed to have been consecrated, and the question arises what to do with them, when it is not evident to what category of consecrated animals they belong. The clarification of these questions in the realm of consecrated items leads to a discussion of several matters relating to found objects in general, especially the question how one is to know whether a found food item is permitted or forbidden to be eaten.

The end of the chapter deals with an issue that is only slightly connected to the previous *halakhot*, namely, the ordinances that were instituted by the court with regard to a situation where certain elements of a sacrifice, e.g., the associated libations or meal-offerings, are missing. In some cases the missing elements are filled in with money taken from the Temple treasury. There is also a more detailed discussion concerning the wafer-offering brought by the High Priest, that goes beyond the issue of when the meal-offering is purchased with public funds, and addresses the specifics about how this meal-offering was prepared.

הלכה א מתני׳ מָעוֹת שֶׁנִּמְצְאוּ בֵּין הַשְּׁקָלִים לִנְדָבָה, קָרוֹב לַשְּׁקָלִים – יִפְּלוּ לַשְּׁקָלִים, לַנְּדָבָה – יִפְּלוּ לַנְּדָבָה, מֶחֱצָה לְמֶחֱצָה – יִפְּלוּ לַנְּדָבָה.

HALAKHA 1 · MISHNA If **money was found** on the floor of the Temple **between** one of **the** collection horns marked **shekels and the** collection horn marked **free-will offerings,**[H] that is to say, between the first and the thirteenth collection horns, in which funds contributed to the Temple were stored, the following distinctions apply: If the money was found **closer to the** horn marked **shekels, it is allocated to the shekels;**[N] if it was found **closer to the** horn marked **free-will offerings, it is allocated to free-will offerings;** and if it was **equidistant** from the horn marked shekels and the horn marked free-will offerings, **it is allocated to free-will offerings.**

בֵּין עֵצִים לִלְבוֹנָה, קָרוֹב לָעֵצִים – יִפְּלוּ לָעֵצִים, לַלְּבוֹנָה – יִפְּלוּ לַלְּבוֹנָה, מֶחֱצָה לְמֶחֱצָה – יִפְּלוּ לַלְּבוֹנָה.

If the money was found **between** the horn marked **wood and** the horn marked **frankincense**, that is, between the fifth and sixth horns, if it was **closer to the** horn marked **wood, it is allocated to wood;** if it was closer to **the** horn marked **frankincense, it is allocated to frankincense;** and if it was found **equidistant** from both, **it is allocated to frankincense.**

בֵּין קִינִּין לְגוֹזְלֵי עוֹלָה, קָרוֹב לַקִּינִּין – יִפְּלוּ לַקִּינִּין, קָרוֹב לְגוֹזְלֵי עוֹלָה – יִפְּלוּ לְגוֹזְלֵי עוֹלָה, מֶחֱצָה לְמֶחֱצָה – יִפְּלוּ לְגוֹזְלֵי עוֹלָה.

If the money was found **between** the horn marked **pairs** of bird-offerings **and** the horn marked **doves for burnt-offerings**, i.e., between the third and the fourth horns, if it is **closer to the** horn marked **pairs** of bird-offerings, **it is allocated to pairs** of bird-offerings; if it was found **closer to** the horn marked **doves for burnt-offerings, it is allocated to doves for burnt-offerings;** and if it was found **equidistant** from both, **it is allocated to doves for burnt-offerings.**

בֵּין חוּלִּין לְמַעֲשֵׂר שֵׁנִי, קָרוֹב לַחוּלִּין – יִפְּלוּ לַחוּלִּין, לְמַעֲשֵׂר שֵׁנִי – יִפְּלוּ לְמַעֲשֵׂר שֵׁנִי, מֶחֱצָה לְמֶחֱצָה – יִפְּלוּ לְמַעֲשֵׂר שֵׁנִי. זֶה הַכְּלָל: הוֹלְכִין אַחַר הַקָּרוֹב לְהָקֵל, מֶחֱצָה לְמֶחֱצָה לְהַחְמִיר.

And similarly, if money was found anywhere else **between** a container for ordinary, **non-sacred** money **and** one containing **second-tithe**[N] money,[H] the following distinctions apply: If the money was found **closer to the non-sacred** money, **it is allocated to the non-sacred** money; if it was found closer to **second-tithe** money, **it is allocated to second-tithe** money; and if it was found **equidistant** from both, **it is allocated to second-tithe** money. **This is the principle:** In cases of doubt, the ruling **follows whichever is closer,** even if this involves **being lenient,** but if the money was found **equidistant** from both, the ruling follows whichever allocation involves **being stringent.**

גמ׳ לָא הוּצְרְכָה דְּלָא בֵּין שְׁקָלִים לְקִינִּים?

GEMARA The mishna taught the *halakha* governing the case where money was found between the horn marked shekels and a horn marked free-will offerings. The Gemara asks: Addressing this case **was not necessary,** as these horns were not adjacent to one another; the one marked shekels was the first horn and the last six were marked free-will offerings. Why should it be presumed that money found in the middle belongs to one or the other and not to one of the horns in between? **Rather** [*dela*],[L] the mishna should have addressed the case where money was found **between** the horn marked old **shekels and** the horn marked **pairs** of bird-offerings, as they are adjacent to one another.

רַבִּי אָבוּן בְּשֵׁם רַבִּי פִּנְחָס: כְּמִין בּוּכְלִיָּאר הָיוּ עֲשׂוּיִן.

Rabbi Avun said **in the name of Rabbi Pinehas:** The contribution horns in the Temple **were arranged like a circle** [*bukhliyar*].[L] The horns did not stand in a straight row, but rather in a circle, such that the horn marked new shekels and the horn marked free-will offerings were adjacent to one another from the other side.

NOTES

It is allocated to the shekels – **יִפְּלוּ לַשְּׁקָלִים**: The *halakha* recorded in the mishna that money found is allocated to the closest horn addresses only a situation in which the same number of coins is found in each of the horns. If, however, one of the horns has more coins than the other, the money is allocated to the horn with the greater number of coins, even if it was closer to a different horn. The Sages conclude elsewhere (see *Bava Batra* 23b) that the principle that uncertainty is resolved by following the majority trumps the principle articulated here that it should be resolved based on proximity.

The other cases in the mishna that rely on proximity to resolve the uncertainty should also be understood in this light (Rosh; *Talmid HaRashbash*; Rabbi Ovadya Bartenura). Some, however, argue that since the number of coins in each horn does not remain fixed over the course of the day and the situation can change at any time, the majority is unstable. In such a case, the principle that the majority trumps proximity in resolving uncertainties does not apply and the cases in the mishna are resolved as it says, based upon proximity (*Talmid HaRashbash*; see also *Tiferet Yisrael*).

Second tithe – **מַעֲשֵׂר שֵׁנִי**: The second tithe was one-tenth of the produce that remained after *teruma* had been given to the priests and the first tithe had been given to the Levites. The second tithe was separated during the first, second, fourth, and fifth years of the Sabbatical cycle. After the second tithe was set aside, it was brought to Jerusalem to be consumed there by its owner. If the journey to Jerusalem was too long, so that it would be difficult to carry the entire amount of second tithe there, or if the produce became ritually impure, it could be redeemed for an equivalent sum of money. If the owner redeemed his own produce he had to add one-fifth of its value. This redemption money was brought to Jerusalem, where it could be spent only to purchase food.

LANGUAGE

Rather [*dela*] – **דְּלָא**: An abbreviated form of *da ela*. The expression here, *lo hutzrekha dela*, is similar to the common expression in the Babylonian Talmud, *lo nitzrekha ela*: It was only necessary…rather.

Circle [*bukhliyar*] – **בּוּכְלִיָּאר**: The correct pronunciation appears to be *kukhliyar*, derived from the Greek κοχλιάριον, *kokhliarion*, spoon, made in the shape of a shell, a cochlea, or in a spiral.

Twisted snail shells, known in Latin as cochlea

HALAKHA

If money was found between the shekels and the free-will offerings – **מָעוֹת שֶׁנִּמְצְאוּ בֵּין הַשְּׁקָלִים לִנְדָבָה**: If money was found in the Temple treasury between the horn marked shekels and the horn marked free-will offerings, closer to the horn marked shekels, it is allocated to the shekels. If it was found closer to the horn marked free-will offerings, it is allocated to free-will offerings. If it was found equidistant from both, it is allocated to free-will offerings. The same *halakha* applies to any money found between the various horns located in the Temple treasury, i.e., it is allocated to the closest horn. If it was found equidistant from the horn marked wood and the horn marked frankincense, it is allocated to frankincense; between the horn marked pairs of bird-offerings and the horn marked doves for burnt-offerings, it is allocated to doves for burnt-offerings. This is the principle: In all cases, the money is allocated to the closest horn, and if it was found equidistant from two horns, it is allocated to the horn which leads to greater stringency. This ruling follows the mishna (Rambam *Sefer Zemanim*, *Hilkhot Shekalim* 3:14–15).

Between non-sacred money and second-tithe money – **בֵּין חוּלִּין לְמַעֲשֵׂר שֵׁנִי**: If money was found between a container for non-sacred money and one containing second-tithe money, it is allocated to whichever is closer. If it was found equidistant from both, one must be stringent and treat it like second-tithe money (Rambam *Sefer Zera'im*, *Hilkhot Ma'aser Sheni* 6:12).

מֶחֱצָה לְמֶחֱצָה יִפְּלוּ לִנְדָבָה (לָא צוֹרְכָה דְּלָא מֶחֱצָה לְמֶחֱצָה יִפְּלוּ לִשְׁקָלִים).

The mishna teaches that if money was found **equidistant** from the horn marked shekels and the horn marked free-will offerings, **it is allocated to free-will offerings.** The Gemara asks: The mishna **should not have** said that the money is allocated to free-will offerings. **Rather,** it should have said that when money is found **equidistant** from both, **it is allocated to shekels.** For the *halakha* governing the money in the horn marked shekels is more stringent, as the regular communal offerings are bought with that money, whereas the money in the horn marked free-will offerings is used only to buy offerings for those times when there are no regular offerings being sacrificed.

אִית דְּבָעֵי מֵימַר: שֶׁמָּא יִפְּלוּ לִשְׁיָרֵי הַלִּשְׁכָּה,

The Gemara answers: **Some wish to say** that the *halakha* governing the money in the horn marked shekels is less stringent because **perhaps** the money allocated would not be used for the purchase of offerings, and consequently **it would be allocated to the remainders of the chamber** funds, i.e., those left over after the public offerings have been bought with the half-shekels collected in the chamber. Such money would be used for repairing the walls and towers of Jerusalem, and not for offerings. It is consequently preferable that the money be allocated to free-will offerings, and therefore be used for offerings.

אִית דְּבָעֵי מֵימַר: מֶחֱצָה לְמֶחֱצָה כְּמִי שֶׁמֵּת. אָמַר רַבִּי יֵסָא: עַד דַּאֲנָא תַּמָּן שְׁמָעִית קַל רַב יְהוּדָה שְׁאַל לִשְׁמוּאֵל: הִפְרִישׁ שִׁקְלוֹ וָמֵת? אֲמַר לֵיהּ: יִפְּלוּ לִנְדָבָה.

And **some wish to say** that money that is found **equidistant** from both is treated like money that has no owner, i.e., **like** money that was set aside by **someone who** subsequently **died,** and the Sages said that such money is allocated to free-will offerings. As **Rabbi Yesa said: While I was there** in Babylonia, **I heard the voice of Rav Yehuda who asked Shmuel** the following question: If someone **set aside his shekel and** subsequently **died,**[H] what is to be done with the money? Shmuel **said to him: It is allocated to free-will offerings.**

עֲשִׂירִית הָאֵיפָה שֶׁלּוֹ, רַבִּי יוֹחָנָן אָמַר: יוֹלִיכֵם לְיָם הַמֶּלַח, רַבִּי לְעָזָר אָמַר: יִפְּלוּ לִנְדָבָה.

The Gemara now asks a similar question: The High Priest could set aside money to be used for the purchase of **his** daily griddle-cake offering made from **one-tenth of an ephah**[H] of flour, half in the morning and half in the evening. If he died before the flour had been bought, what is to be done with the money? **Rabbi Yoḥanan said:** The money must be **cast into the Dead Sea,** i.e., so that it is destroyed. **Rabbi Elazar** disagreed and **said:** The money **is allocated to free-will offerings.**

וְקַשְׁיָא: וְיֵשׁ חַטָּאת קְרֵיבָה עוֹלָה!

The mishna taught that if the money was found equidistant from the horn marked pairs of bird-offerings, i.e., one burnt-offering and one sin-offering, and the horn marked doves for burnt-offerings, it is allocated to doves for burnt-offerings. **And this is difficult: Is a sin-offering brought as a burnt-offering?**[N] Surely it is possible that the money fell from the horn marked pairs of bird-offerings, and is therefore partially designated for the purchase of sin-offerings.

חִזְקִיָּה בְּשֵׁם רַבִּי שִׁמְעוֹן בֶּן לָקִישׁ: תְּנַאי בֵּית דִּין הוּא עַל הַמּוֹתָרוֹת שֶׁיִּקָּרְבוּ עוֹלוֹת.

Ḥizkiya said **in the name of Rabbi Shimon ben Lakish: A condition of the court stipulates with regard to the remainder** of the money originally consecrated for sin-offerings **that it is brought** as **burnt-offerings.** Even if the one who consecrated the money did not state such a condition explicitly, he is regarded as having done so, as it is presumed that the money was consecrated in accordance with the court's stipulation.

הָאִשָּׁה הַזֹּאת בְּמָה הִיא מִתְכַּפֶּרֶת?

The Gemara asks: If so, **with what does this woman,** who had placed the money for her offering in the horn marked pairs of bird-offerings, **achieve atonement?** A woman who had given birth or is a *zava* must bring a pair of bird-offerings, one as a burnt-offering and the other as a sin-offering, as part of her purification process. If that money has been allocated to doves for burnt-offerings, she has not completed the process.

אָמַר רַבִּי יִצְחָק: תְּנַאי בֵּית דִּין הוּא, הַמְסַפֵּק אֶת הַקִּינִּין – הוּא מְסַפֵּק אֶת הַפְּסוּלוֹת.

Rabbi Yitzḥak said: A condition of the court stipulates: Whoever supplies the Temple with **the pairs** of birds, **he** also **supplies** extra birds to replace those birds that are **disqualified.**[H] If one of the birds is disqualified or missing, he provides another bird in its place, and so in any event the woman will have brought both a burnt-offering and a sin-offering.

HALAKHA

If someone set aside his shekel and died – הִפְרִישׁ שִׁקְלוֹ וָמֵת: If someone set aside his shekel and then died, the shekel is allocated to free-will offerings, in accordance with the ruling in the *baraita* (Rambam *Sefer Zemanim*, *Hilkhot Shekalim* 3:12).

His one-tenth of an ephah – עֲשִׂירִית הָאֵיפָה שֶׁלּוֹ: Any extra meal left over from the tenth of the ephah of the High Priest's griddle-cake offering must be left to rot, in accordance with the mishna (Rambam *Sefer Avoda*, *Hilkhot Pesulei HaMukdashin* 5:8).

Whoever supplies the pairs of birds, he also supplies extra birds to replace those that are disqualified – הַמְסַפֵּק אֶת הַקִּינִּין הוּא מְסַפֵּק אֶת הַפְּסוּלוֹת: If one who was appointed to supply the birds needed for bird-offerings sold someone a bird that was disqualified or became so before it was sacrificed, he must provide another in its place (Rambam *Sefer Avoda*, *Hilkhot Kelei HaMikdash* 7:9).

NOTES

Is a sin-offering brought as a burnt-offering – וְיֵשׁ חַטָּאת קְרֵיבָה עוֹלָה: The Gemara did not ask the corresponding question with regard to the earlier ruling, i.e., that if the money was found closer to the horn marked doves for burnt-offerings than to the horn marked pairs of bird-offerings, would it be allocated to doves for burnt-offerings? Yet a corresponding difficulty does exist: As every pair of bird offerings includes a sin-offering, there is a chance that money that was meant for a sin-offering would be used to buy a burnt-offering. Why is this not a concern?

The explanation lies in the distinction between the resolution based on proximity and the merely procedural resolution of allocating the money to the more stringent use in the case of equidistance. In cases where the uncertainty is resolved based on proximity, the resolution is determinate and the *halakha* regards it as a certainty. In contrast, in the case where the money is equidistant from two different horns, the resolution is merely procedural and the Gemara's objection makes sense. It is then reasonable to ask about the possibility that the money fell from the other horn, i.e., from that marked pairs of bird-offerings, and if so, how can a sin-offering be brought as a burnt-offering (*Penei Zaken*).

This explanation applies as well to the Gemara's question below, with regard to a woman who needs to sacrifice both a sin-offering and a burnt-offering: How does this woman achieve atonement? That question is raised only if the money was found equidistant from the horn marked pairs of bird-offerings and the horn marked doves for burnt-offerings, and is allocated to doves for burnt-offerings. Since the money was equidistant from both horns, the uncertainty remains. However, were the money found closer to one rather than the other, the resolution is determinate and there is no longer any uncertainty; every offering that was required is presumed to have been brought (Rosh; *Talmid HaRashbash*; *Tiklin Ḥadatin*).

לָא צוֹרְכָה דְּלָא בֵּין קְטוֹרֶת לָעֵצִים, לִלְבוֹנָה, לְזָהָב לְכַפּוֹרֶת?

The mishna did not consider all the possible places that money could be found between different horns, and so the Gemara asks: **Shouldn't** the mishna **also** discuss additional cases, like where the money was found between the fourth and fifth horns, i.e., **between** the horn marked **incense and** the horn marked **wood,** or between the sixth and seventh horns, i.e., between the horn marked **frankincense and** the horn marked **gold for the Ark cover?**

וּתְנִיתָה בְּסוֹפָהּ: זֶה הַכְּלָל, הוֹלְכִין אַחַר הַקָּרוֹב, מֶחֱצָה לְמֶחֱצָה לְהַחְמִיר.

The Gemara answers: In fact, this mishna addresses these cases as well, **as it teaches at its end: This is the principle:** In cases of doubt, the ruling **follows whichever is closer,** even if this involves being lenient; but if the money was found **equidistant** from both, the ruling follows whichever attribution involves **being stringent.**

הלכה ב מתני׳ מָעוֹת שֶׁנִּמְצְאוּ לִפְנֵי סוֹחֲרֵי בְהֵמָה – לְעוֹלָם מַעֲשֵׂר,

HALAKHA 2 · MISHNA This mishna considers other situations in which something is found and its source is unknown. **Money found before animal merchants** in Jerusalem is **always** presumed to be second-**tithe** money.[NH] The presumption is based on the fact that in Jerusalem, most of the animals are bought with second-tithe money and sacrificed as peace-offerings.

וּבְהַר הַבַּיִת – חוּלִּין. וּבִירוּשָׁלַיִם, בִּשְׁאָר כׇּל יְמוֹת הַשָּׁנָה – חוּלִּין. וּבִשְׁעַת הָרֶגֶל – הַכֹּל מַעֲשֵׂר.

and money found **on the Temple Mount** is presumed to be **non-sacred** money. **And** with regard to money found **in** the rest of **Jerusalem,** the following distinction applies: If it was found **during the rest of the days of the year,** it is presumed to be **non-sacred** money, **but** if it was found **during the time of a pilgrim Festival,** it is **all** presumed to be second-**tithe** money, because most of the money found in Jerusalem at the time of a Festival is second-tithe money.

בָּשָׂר שֶׁנִּמְצָא בָּעֲזָרָה, אֵיבָרִים – עוֹלוֹת, וַחֲתִיכוֹת – חַטָּאוֹת. וּבִירוּשָׁלַיִם – זִבְחֵי שְׁלָמִים. זֶה וָזֶה תְּעוּבַּר צוּרָתוֹ וְיֵצֵא לְבֵית הַשְּׂרֵיפָה.

The mishna continues: With regard to **meat that was found in the** Temple **courtyard,**[H] and it is not known from whence it came, the *halakha* is as follows: If it is whole **limbs** of the animal, in the manner that burnt-offerings are brought to the altar, it is presumed to be **burnt-offerings. And** if it is in small **pieces,** it is presumed to be **sin-offerings. And** if the meat, in whatever form, is found **in** the city of **Jerusalem,** as opposed to the courtyard, it is presumed to be the meat of **peace-offerings,** as most of the meat in Jerusalem is the meat of peace-offerings. Since it is possible that the time during which it is permitted to eat any of it has already passed, both **this and that,** whether it is determined to be the meat of burnt-offerings or the meat of peace-offerings, **its form** must be allowed **to decay,**[N] i.e., it must be left until it is definitely disqualified, **and then it must be taken out to the place of burning,** where offerings that have become disqualified are burned.

נִמְצָא בַּגְּבוּלִין, אֵיבָרִים – נְבֵילוֹת, וַחֲתִיכוֹת – מוּתָּרוֹת.

With regard to meat **found in the outlying areas,** outside of Jerusalem, if it is in the form of whole **limbs,** the meat presumably comes from **carcasses** of animals that were not properly slaughtered, for meat unfit for eating was generally cut up into full limbs, to be fed to dogs or sold to gentiles. **But** if it is in small **pieces,** it is presumably kosher and **permitted** to be eaten, as kosher meat was ordinarily cut up into small pieces.

NOTES

Money found before animal merchants is always presumed to be second-tithe money – מָעוֹת שֶׁנִּמְצְאוּ לִפְנֵי סוֹחֲרֵי בְהֵמָה לְעוֹלָם מַעֲשֵׂר: The Gemara (*Pesaḥim* 7a; see Rashi there) explains as follows: If money was found in the market where animals were sold in Jerusalem, it was presumed to be second-tithe money, because most of the animals bought in Jerusalem were purchased with second-tithe money. This was true both on the Festivals and throughout the year, as any second-tithe money that was not spent on the Festivals was left in Jerusalem, where most of it was used to purchase peace-offerings.

If, however, the money was found on the Temple Mount, it was presumed to be non-sacred money, even on a Festival. When one entered the Temple Mount, he had presumably already purchased whatever he would need for his Temple service. Some commentaries explain that money found on the Temple Mount was presumed to be non-sacred money because one must not enter the Temple Mount with money. Therefore, money found there was assumed to have belonged to the Temple treasury and was used for the purchase of sacred objects, in the process of which the money lost its consecrated status (Ra'avad; *Me'iri*; *Pesaḥim* 7a).

With regard to money found elsewhere in Jerusalem, if it was on a Festival, when the city was filled with pilgrims who had brought their second-tithe money with them, the money was presumed to be second-tithe money. Throughout the year, however, it was presumed to be non-sacred money, as most of the money in Jerusalem was non-sacred. Since the streets of Jerusalem were swept every day, and any money that had been lost by the pilgrims would have been found by the sweepers, it may be supposed that any money found was lost that day.

Its form must be allowed to decay – תְּעוּבַּר צוּרָתוֹ: In Mishna tractate *Pesaḥim* (7:9), the Rambam glosses this phrase as *ta'avor tzurato*; that is, the meat should be left until its form has changed by its becoming spoiled. After the meat has been left past the time it is permitted to eat it, it is referred to as being left over, and is disqualified and must be burned (see Rash and Rabbeinu Ḥananel on *Pesaḥim* 34a). Some Mishna commentaries indicate that decay of form actually means leaving it past the time permitted for consumption, so that it is no longer fit for its intended purpose. This is apparently based on the Gemara in tractate *Menaḥot* 46b, and so too it would appear from the Rambam's Commentary on the Mishna, tractate *Zevaḥim* 34a. Most sacrificial meat becomes left over the following morning, but when the meat comes from a peace-offering, it is considered left over only once a night and a day have passed subsequent to the day on which the offering was sacrificed. Only then may it be burned.

HALAKHA

Money found before animal merchants is always second-tithe money – מָעוֹת שֶׁנִּמְצְאוּ לִפְנֵי סוֹחֲרֵי בְהֵמָה לְעוֹלָם מַעֲשֵׂר: If money was found in Jerusalem when the Temple was standing, in front of a place where sacrificial animals are sold, it is presumed to be second-tithe money and must be treated accordingly. If it was found on the Temple Mount, it is presumed to be ordinary, non-sacred money. Anywhere else in Jerusalem, if the money was found on one of the Festivals, it is presumed to be second-tithe money. At any other time of the year it is presumed to be non-sacred money. Since the streets of Jerusalem are swept every day, the money that was found must have been lost that day (Rambam *Sefer Zera'im, Hilkhot Ma'aser Sheni* 6:9–10).

Meat that was found in the Temple courtyard – בָּשָׂר שֶׁנִּמְצָא בָּעֲזָרָה: With regard to meat found in the Temple courtyard, if it was in the form of whole limbs it is presumably the meat of a burnt-offering; if it was cut up into small pieces it is presumably the meat of a sin-offering. If the meat was found elsewhere in the city of Jerusalem, it is presumably the meat of a peace-offering. Such meat must be left over past the time permitted for its consumption and then taken out to the place of burning, as per the ruling in the mishna.

Since none of this meat is actually sacrificed, the determination that it belongs to a burnt-offering, a sin-offering, or a peace-offering is relevant only with regard to liability for misuse of consecrated articles. If the meat was found in Jerusalem, since it is presumed to be the meat of a peace-offering, whose consumption is permitted to non-priests, one who eats it transgresses but is not liable for misuse of consecrated articles. Similarly, if it was found in the Temple courtyard cut up into small pieces, since it is presumed to be the meat of a sin-offering, and a sin-offering may be eaten by priests, there is no liability for misuse of consecrated articles. But if it was found cut up in limbs, since it is presumed to be the meat of a burnt-offering, and a burnt-offering may not be eaten, one who eats it is liable for misuse of consecrated articles (Rambam *Sefer Avoda, Hilkhot Pesulei HaMukdashin* 19:4).

NOTES

If one diverted his attention – הִסִּיעַ דַּעַת: In the Babylonian Talmud (*Pesaḥim* 34a), the *amora'im* disagree about the nature of the disqualification stemming from diverting one's attention from a sacred object. According to Rabbi Yoḥanan, this is a disqualification of impurity, i.e., there is a concern that perhaps the object contracted ritual impurity without anyone knowing, and the disqualification is based on this uncertainty. According to Reish Lakish, it is an intrinsic disqualification, i.e., owing to a special stringency applying to consecrated objects, diversion of attention in itself disqualifies the object. In practice, both agree that if the object was sacrificial meat it must be burned. The difference between them is that according to Rabbi Yoḥanan, since the disqualification is based on an uncertainty, the meat is burned only after its form has decayed, whereas according to Reish Lakish, it can be burned immediately, even before its form has decayed.

Rabbi Hoshaya, who was Rabbi Yoḥanan's teacher (*Mishnat Eliyahu*), agrees with him that diversion of attention is only a disqualification of impurity, and therefore the meat must undergo decay of form before it can be burned.

Decay of form – עִיבּוּר צוּרָה: Rashi explains (see *Pesaḥim* 73b) that decay of form means that the meat of the offering is left overnight past its normal time limit, at which point it acquires the status of leftover sacrificial meat and should be burned. Rabbeinu Ḥananel and the Rambam appear to have understood the phrase literally: The disqualified meat is left until it rots or decays and no longer looks like regular meat.

וּבִשְׁעַת הָרֶגֶל, שֶׁהַבָּשָׂר מְרוּבֶּה – אַף אֵיבָרִים מוּתָּרוֹת.

And if meat is found **at the time of a Festival, when meat is plentiful,** so that it is generally not cut up into small pieces, then **even** whole **limbs are permitted** to be eaten.

גמ׳ לָא צוֹרְכָה דְּלָא בְּהַר הַבַּיִת קוֹדֶשׁ?

GEMARA The mishna teaches that money found on the Temple Mount is presumed to be non-sacred money. The Gemara asks: **Shouldn't the mishna** have said that the money found **on the Temple Mount** is treated as **consecrated** money? Most of the money on the Temple Mount is consecrated money, and even if it were not, one ought to be stringent and regard any found money as such.

רַבִּי בָּא רַבִּי חִיָּיה בְּשֵׁם רַבִּי יוֹחָנָן: חֲזָקָה שֶׁאֵין הַכֹּהֵן מוֹצִיא מִן הַלִּשְׁכָּה מָעוֹת עַד שֶׁהוּא מְחַלְּלָן עַל הַבְּהֵמָה.

The Gemara answers: **Rabbi Ba** said that **Rabbi Ḥiyya** said **in the name of Rabbi Yoḥanan:** There is **a presumption that the priest** who is in charge **does not remove money from the chamber until he desacralizes it** by transferring its consecrated status **onto the animals** that he purchases for offerings. Therefore, any money that is found on the Temple Mount is presumably non-sacred money.

בָּשָׂר שֶׁנִּמְצָא כו׳. רַבִּי לְעָזָר בְּשֵׁם רַבִּי הוֹשַׁעְיָה: הִסִּיעַ דַּעַת טָעוּן עִיבּוּר צוּרָה.

The mishna teaches that **meat found** in the rest of the city of Jerusalem, cut into whole limbs or small pieces, is presumably from a peace-offering. However, it may not be eaten and its form must be allowed to decay, after which it is burned. The Gemara now cites what **Rabbi Elazar** said **in the name of Rabbi Hoshaya** and a proof for his opinion from the mishna: If **one diverted** his **attention**[N] from sacrificial meat such that it was not protected from ritual impurity, even though the meat is disqualified, it is not burned immediately. Rather, it **must** be left over past the time permitted for its consumption in order that its **form decays.**[N]

אָמַר רַבִּי הוֹשַׁעְיָה: מַתְנִיתִין אָמְרָה כֵּן: תְּעוּבַּר צוּרָתוֹ וְיֵצֵא לְבֵית הַשְּׂרֵיפָה.

Rabbi Hoshaya said: The mishna says like that with regard to meat that was found in Jerusalem, i.e., that **its form** must first be allowed **to decay and** then **it is taken out to the place of burning.** As the meat was lost, clearly its owner's attention was diverted from it, and the meat became disqualified. The mishna rules that nevertheless it must be kept left over before it is burned, therefore supporting Rabbi Hoshaya's ruling that meat from which one's attention was diverted is not burned immediately but must be left over. The disqualification stems from the uncertainty whether the meat became impure, and the meat cannot be burned until its disqualification is certain.

אָמַר רַבִּי יוֹסֵי: וְיָאוּת, לְאָכְלוֹ אֵין אַתְּ יָכוֹל – שֶׁמָּא נִתְקַלְקֵל צוּרָתוֹ, לְפוּם כֵּן צָרִיךְ מֵימַר – תְּעוּבַּר צוּרָתוֹ וְיֵצֵא לְבֵית הַשְּׂרֵיפָה.

Rabbi Yosei said: The *halakha* of the mishna is indeed **correct,** but not for this reason. With regard to the meat that one found in Jerusalem, the reason **you may not eat it** is that **perhaps its form had** already **decayed.** Perhaps before it was found the time permitted for eating it had already elapsed. **Therefore, one must say** that **its form must** be allowed to **decay,** lest the allotted time has not elapsed, **and** only then **is it taken out to the place of burning.** The requirement that its form decay has nothing to do with the fact that the meat might have become impure. Since the meat was lost in Jerusalem, which is a public domain, it cannot become disqualified because of doubtful ritual impurity, as the principle is that any doubt about ritual impurity that arises in a public domain is declared ritually pure (*Teharot* 4:7).

נִמְצָא בַּגְּבוּלִין כו׳. רַבִּי קְרִיסְפָּא בְּשֵׁם רַבִּי יוֹסֵי בְּרַבִּי חֲנִינָה: אֵיבָרִים נְבֵילוֹת, לוֹקִין עֲלֵיהֶן מִשּׁוּם נְבֵילָה.

The mishna taught that with regard to meat **found in the outlying areas,** outside of Jerusalem, if it was whole limbs, the meat is presumably that of carcasses and therefore forbidden, but if it was found in small pieces it is presumably kosher and permitted to be eaten. **Rabbi Krispa** said **in the name of Rabbi Yosei, son of Rabbi Ḥanina:** When the mishna says that **whole limbs are** presumed to come from **carcasses,** that presumption is determinate, to the extent that one who eats this meat **receives lashes for** eating the meat of unslaughtered **carcasses.**

מַתְנִיתָא אָמְרָה כֵּן: אֵיבְרֵי נְבֵילוֹת, וַחֲתִיכוֹת מוּתָּרוֹת. חֲתִיכוֹת מוּתָּרוֹת לֹא מַמָּשׁ? וּדְכְוָותָהּ אֵיבָרִים נְבֵילוֹת – לוֹקִין עֲלֵיהֶן מִשּׁוּם נְבֵילָה.

The Gemara comments: **The mishna** itself **says this,** i.e., the wording of the mishna implies this, for the mishna teaches: With regard to meat found in the outlying areas, outside of Jerusalem, if it is in the form of whole **limbs,** the meat presumably comes from **carcasses. And** if it is in small **pieces,** it is presumably kosher and **permitted** to be eaten. When the mishna says that **small pieces are permitted,** does it **not** mean that they are **actually** permitted, i.e., the mishna permits the eating of the small pieces of meat and does not regard it as an uncertainty? **In a corresponding manner,** when the mishna says that meat found in the form of **limbs** is presumably that of **carcasses,** this is regarded as a certainty, such that one who eats this meat **is flogged for** having violated the prohibition against eating the meat of **a carcass** that was not properly slaughtered.

רַבִּי קְרִיסְפָּא בְּשֵׁם רַבִּי יוֹסֵי בְּרַבִּי חֲנִינָה: אִם הָיוּ מַחֲרוּזוֹת – מוּתָּרוֹת.

Rabbi Krispa said further **in the name of Rabbi Yosei, son of Rabbi Ḥanina,** with regard to meat that was found in the form of whole limbs: **If** the meat **was** found strung together on strings like **beads,** it may be presumed that the meat is kosher, and it is therefore **permitted.**

תֵּשַׁע חֲנוּיוֹת מוֹכְרוֹת בְּשַׂר נְבֵילָה וְאַחַת מוֹכֶרֶת בְּשַׂר שְׁחוּטָה, נִתְחַלְּפוּ לוֹ, חוֹשֵׁשׁ. וְלַנִּמְצֵאת הוֹלְכִין אַחַר הָרוֹב.

It was further taught in a *baraita* with regard to meat of an unknown source: If one bought meat in a town that has ten stores, **nine stores selling** the non-kosher **meat of a carcass and one** store **selling the meat of a** properly **slaughtered** animal, **and he was confused about them,** not remembering from which store he made his purchase, **he must be concerned** that perhaps he bought non-kosher meat. However, the meat is forbidden only because of an uncertainty, and if he ate it he is not liable to receive lashes. **And** if a piece of meat **was found** in the marketplace and it is not known from which store the meat came, **one follows the majority** of meat stores. Since in this scenario the majority of stores sell non-kosher meat, the found meat is presumed to be non-kosher.[H]

תֵּשַׁע חֲנוּיוֹת מוֹכְרוֹת בְּשַׂר שְׁחוּטָה וְאַחַת מוֹכֶרֶת בְּשַׂר נְבֵילָה, נִתְחַלְּפוּ לוֹ – חוֹשֵׁשׁ, וְלַנִּמְצֵאת הוֹלְכִין אַחַר הָרוֹב.

As for the reverse case, if **nine stores**[N] **were selling the meat of a** properly **slaughtered** animal **and one** store **was selling** the non-kosher **meat of a carcass, and** one bought meat in one of the stores but **was confused about them,** not remembering from which store he made his purchase, **he must be concerned** that perhaps he bought non-kosher meat. **And** if a piece of meat **was found** in the marketplace and it is not known from which store the meat came, **one follows the majority** of meat stores, and presume that the meat is kosher.

אָמַר רַבִּי יוֹחָנָן: הַנִּמְצָא בְּיַד גּוֹי כַּנִּמְצָא בִּפְלַטְיָא. רַבִּי לְעָזָר בֵּי רַבִּי חַגַּיי הֲוָה מִסְמַךְ לְרַבִּי מָנָא. חָמָא לְחַד אַרְמַאי מְקַטֵּעַ מִן סוּסְיָה וּמַפֵּיק לְבָרָא, אֲמַר לֵיהּ: הָדָא הִיא דְּאָמַר רַבִּי יוֹחָנָן: הַנִּמְצָאָה בְּיַד גּוֹי – כַּנִּמְצָא בִּפְלַטְיָא. אֲמַר לֵיהּ: כֵּן אָמַר רַבִּי יוֹסֵי רַבִּי: וְהֵן שֶׁרָאוּ אוֹתוֹ יוֹצֵא מִמַּקּוּלִין שֶׁל יִשְׂרָאֵל.

Rabbi Yoḥanan said: Meat **that is found in the hand of a gentile** is regarded **as if it were found in a large public square** [*pelatya*],[LB] and so its status is determined in accordance with the majority of stores in the town. It is related that **Rabbi Elazar, son of Rabbi Ḥaggai, was supporting Rabbi Mana,** helping him walk, when **he saw a certain Roman** [*Armai*][L] **lopping off** a piece of flesh **from his horse and taking it out** for sale. Rabbi Elazar **said to** Rabbi Mana: **Is this what Rabbi Yoḥanan** meant when he **said:** Meat **that is found in the hand of a gentile** is regarded **as if it were found in a large public square,** and so one follows the majority of stores in the town? If so, then if the majority of the town's stores are owned by Jews, this meat should be treated as kosher. But surely it isn't, as we saw where it came from. Rabbi Mana **said to** Rabbi Elazar: **Thus said Rabbi Yosei my teacher** about Rabbi Yoḥanan's ruling: **This** ruling of Rabbi Yoḥanan's applies only **where they saw** the gentile **exiting from a butcher shop belonging to a Jew** with a piece of meat in his hand.

HALAKHA

Nine stores – תֵּשַׁע חֲנוּיוֹת: If meat was found lying in the marketplace, its status is determined in accordance with the majority, as per the principle that anything separated out is presumed to be from the majority. Therefore, if the majority of meat sellers in that town are gentiles, the meat is prohibited. If the majority are Jews, it is permitted.

The same *halakha* applies to meat that is found in the possession of a gentile and it is not known from whom it was purchased. If the majority of meat sellers in that town are Jews, by Torah law the meat is permitted to be eaten. The Sages, however, rendered prohibited any meat that was found, whether in the marketplace or in the hand of a gentile, even if all the slaughterers and all the meat sellers in the town are Jews. This ruling is in accordance with the opinion of Rabbi Yehuda HaNasi, based on the Gemara in tractate *Ḥullin* (Rambam *Sefer Kedusha, Hilkhot Ma'akhalot Assurot* 8:11; *Shulḥan Arukh, Yoreh De'a* 63:1, 110:3).

NOTES

Nine stores – תֵּשַׁע חֲנוּיוֹת: According to a straightforward reading of the Gemara, and according to the Gemara in tractate *Ketubot* 15a, the reason that the meat is forbidden and is not judged according to the majority of nine stores that sell kosher meat is that any doubt that arises concerning the status of something while it is fixed in its place is considered an evenly balanced doubt, and these stores are considered fixed in their place. However, some commentaries explain that improperly slaughtered meat is generally sold at a lower price than properly slaughtered meat, and therefore even though the majority of stores sell kosher meat, there is still room for concern that this person bought from a store that sells non-kosher meat (Rabbeinu Ḥananel on *Ketubot* 15a).

LANGUAGE

Large public square [*pelatya*] – פְּלַטְיָא: From the Greek πλατεία, *plateia*, meaning broad, wide, or flat.

Roman [*Armai*] – אַרְמַאי: In its narrow and precise sense, this word refers to Arameans, speakers of the Aramaic language. However, the meaning of the term expanded, perhaps because Babylonia, the main area of Jewish settlement in the Persian Empire, was officially called Bei Armai, the house of Armai. Ultimately, the term was used in reference not only to the Aramaic speakers, but to all the gentile peoples in Babylonia.

BACKGROUND

Large public square [*pelatya*] – פְּלַטְיָא: A *pelatya* was a large public square in which great numbers of people could be assembled and through which they passed. It serves as a classic example of a public domain, as it meets all the criteria set down for its inclusion in that category.

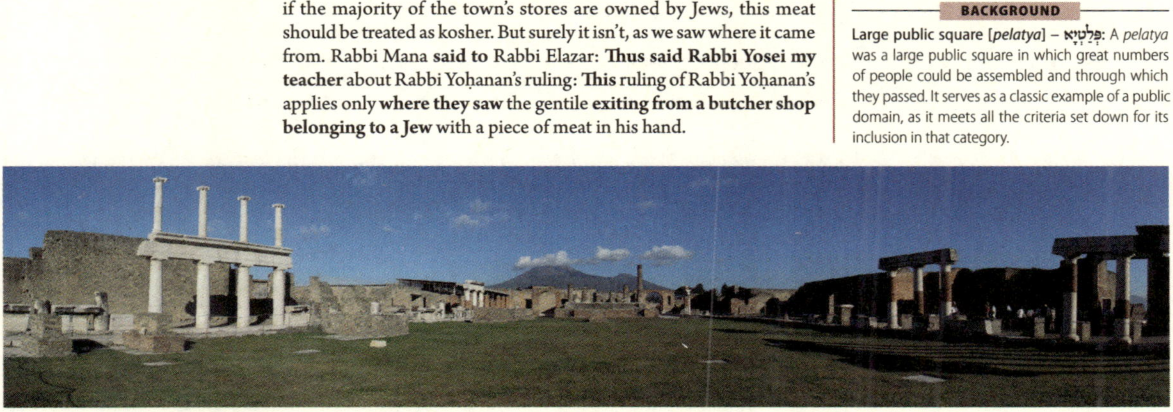

The Forum in Pompeii, Italy. The volcano Mount Vesuvius can be seen in the background.

חַד בַּר נַשׁ בְּצִיפּוֹרִין אֲזַל בְּעֵי מִיזְבּוֹן קוּפָד מִן טַבָּחָא וְלָא יְהַב לֵיהּ. אֲמַר לֵיהּ לְחַד רוֹמַי, וְאַיְיתֵי לֵיהּ. אֲמַר לֵיהּ: לָא נְסַבִית עַל כָּרְחֵיהּ? אֲמַר לֵיהּ: וְלָאו בְּשַׂר דִּנְבֵילָה יְהָבִית לֵיהּ? רַבִּי יִרְמְיָה בְּשֵׁם רַבִּי חֲנִינָה: מַעֲשֶׂה בָּא לִפְנֵי רַבִּי, וְאָמַר: לָא כּוּלָּא מִינֵּיהּ מֵיסַר מַקּוּלִין דְּצִיפּוֹרִין.

It is further related that **a certain man in Tzippori was walking** and **he wanted to buy a piece of meat** [*kufad*][L] **from the butcher, but** the butcher **did not give him** the meat, as they were at odds with each other. The man **asked a certain Roman** to buy the meat on his behalf, **and he brought him** the meat. The man later **said to** the butcher: **Did I not** in the end **take** the meat from you **against your will?** The butcher **said to him: Did I not give him the** non-kosher **meat of a carcass,** and so the meat you received from him was not kosher? **Rabbi Yirmeya** said **in the name of Rabbi Ḥanina: An incident** like this **came before Rabbi** Yehuda HaNasi, who **said** about this: **It is not within his power to prohibit all the** butcher **shops** [*makkulin*][L] **of Tzippori**[N] on that day; since the majority of meat shops in that city belong to Jews, the butcher's claim that he gave the Roman non-kosher meat is not to be believed.

רַב נְחַת לְתַמָּן חֲמָתוּן מְקִילִין, וְחוֹמֶר עֲלֵיהֶן. חַד בַּר נַשׁ אֲזַל

It is related that **Rav went down there** to Babylonia and **saw that they were lenient** about meat of unknown origin, **and he was stringent with them.** The Gemara now reports what it is that Rav saw: **A certain man went**

LANGUAGE

Piece of meat [*kufad*] – **קוּפָד**: From the Greek, possibly through Syriac, κοπάδιον, *kopadion*, derived from κόπαιον, *kopaion*, and meaning a slice of meat, fish, etc.

Shops [*makkulin*] – **מַקּוּלִין**: From the Latin macellum, meaning butcher's stall or a meat market.

Carved stone images used to support tables in the meat market of Jerash, Jordan

NOTES

It is not within his power to prohibit all the butcher shops of Tzippori – לָא כּוּלָּא מִינֵּיהּ מֵיסַר מַקּוּלִין דְּצִיפּוֹרִין: It was the custom in Tzippori that when an animal slaughtered in one of the local slaughterhouses was found to be ritually unfit for consumption, a public announcement was made to that effect, so that the Jewish residents of the city would not buy meat from gentiles on that day. In the absence of such an announcement, there was no concern that non-kosher meat would be found in the marketplace (Rashi on *Ḥullin* 95a).

Rabbi Yehuda HaNasi did not prohibit all the meat in all the butcher shops in Tzippori on that day, despite the fact that the butcher had sold non-kosher meant to a gentile without the requisite announcement, and possibly sold non-kosher meat to others as well. One explanation for this is that the majority of butchers in Tzippori were Jews, and therefore Rabbi Yehuda HaNasi relied on the majority and permitted the meat in the other meat shops (*Tiklin Ḥadatin*; *Mishnat Eliyahu*, based on the Gemara in tractate *Ḥullin* 95a). Others explain that he did not prohibit all the meat sold that day in Tzippori because he holds that the butcher was not to be believed with regard to his claim that he had sold non-kosher meat to the gentile. It stands to reason that he said he had sold the gentile non-kosher meat only because of his animosity toward the man to whom he had refused to sell any meat (*Me'iri*).

Modern-day Tzippori, as seen from its ancient ruins

בעי משיזגה אסקופתיה בגו נהרא ואינשתה, ואזיל ליה. חזר בעי מיסבינה. אמר ליה רב: אסור לך, דנא אמר: ההיא שטף נהרא ואייתי חורי דנבילה תחתוי.

and **wanted to rinse his hat** [*askuptei*][N] **in the river.** While doing so, the piece of kosher meat he was carrying **fell and** the man **went** on his way. Afterward, **he returned** to that very place and found a piece of meat identical to the one that he had dropped, **and he wanted to take it. Rav,**[P] however, **said to him:** This meat **is forbidden for you** to eat, **as I can say:** It is possible that **the river swept away that** piece of meat, **and brought in its place a different** piece of **non-kosher meat** that had fallen into the water somewhere else.

חד בר נש הוה מהלך בשוקא טעין קופד, אתא דייתא וחטפתיה מיניה, וטלקתיה. חזר בעי מיסבינא. אמר ליה רב: אסור לך, דנא אמר בשר דנבילה הוות טעינא, וטלקתיה ונסבה ההוא אוחרנא.

The Gemara relates another incident where Rav was stringent about meat of doubtful provenance. **A certain man was walking in the market, carrying a piece of** kosher **meat. A kite**[B] bird **came and snatched it from him, and** later **cast it** away elsewhere. The man **returned** and **wanted to take** the piece of meat from the place where he saw the bird drop it. **Rav,** however, **said to him:** This meat **is forbidden for you** to eat, **as I can say:** It is possible the kite **was carrying non-kosher meat and** that is what **it cast** away in this place. It then **took away the other** piece of meat that it snatched from you.

גינאי שטף זיקין, אתא עובדא קומי רבי יצחק ברבי אלעזר ואמר: יתחכמון שפייא קיטרהון.

It is further related that the **Gina'ei**[B] River once **swept away wineskins**[N] belonging to Jews, and the wineskins were later found along the riverbank. **The incident came before Rabbi Yitzḥak, son of Rabbi Elazar, who said: Let the** Jewish **wine-dealers** come and **examine the knots** on the wineskins. If they recognize the knots as theirs, the wineskins are presumably theirs, and the wine and the wineskins are permitted.

נקוניקה אשתכח בכנישתא דבולי, אתא עובדא קומי רבי ירמיה, אמר: יתחכמון סקורייא עבידתהון.

It once happened that **a** wine **container** [*nekonika*][N] **was found in the synagogue of the** city **council** [*bulei*],[L] **and the incident came before Rabbi Yirmeya** for a ruling. **He said: Let the** Jewish **markers,** i.e., those who paint the markings on the containers, **examine their work.** Only if they recognize it as theirs, is the wine permitted.

LANGUAGE

Council [*bulei*] – **בולי**: From the Greek βούλη, *bulei*, meaning council. In most places in the Talmud it is referring to the city council, a local senate that administered the city's affairs.

BACKGROUND

Kite – **דייתא**: The kite is a medium-sized bird of prey of the Accipitridae family. Kites are opportunistic hunters and the behavior described in the Gemara is typical. There have been reports of kites grabbing food from people in modern times as well.

Black-shouldered kite descending toward its prey

Gina'ei – **גינאי**: From the Greek Γιναή, *Ginaei*. Some point to a village by this name mentioned in the writings of Josephus, located on the site of the present-day city of Jenin, on the border between the Jezreel Valley and Samaria, through which passes one of the major tributaries of the Kishon River.

View of Jenin from Mount Gilboa

Kishon River emptying into the Mediterranean

NOTES

His hat [*askuptei*] – **אסקופתיה**: Rash Sirilio writes that the man went down to rinse his hat in the river, and as he was washing it, a piece of meat inside it fell into the river. According to the *Penei Moshe*, however, this word is referring to an animal's head, leg, and intestines which were sold together.

Swept away wineskins – **שטף זיקין**: Some understand that these wineskins were filled with wine, and the concern was that the wineskins found along the riverbank were other wineskins filled with wine belonging to gentiles, which is forbidden for Jews to consume (Rabbeinu Meshulam). Others suggest that these wineskins were empty, and the concern was that the wineskins found belonged to gentiles and were therefore prohibited because they had previously been used for non-kosher wine (see *Avoda Zara* 29b; *Talmid HaRashbash*).

Container [*nekonika*] – **נקוניקה**: Some authorities hold that the word *nekonika* is not a container but rather a kind of sausage made from ox intestines filled with small pieces of meat (*Sefer HaMa'arikh*, s.v. *nekonika*). Others suggest that the reference here is to a lung together with the intestines (*Penei Moshe*). According to both explanations, the butchers would apparently mark these parts with special symbols.

PERSONALITIES

Rav – **רב**: Rav, whose full name was Rabbi Abba bar Ivu, was the first, and perhaps the greatest, of the Babylonian *amora'im*. Known as Abba Arikha because of his great height, Rav established the academy in Sura that lasted for over eight hundred years, through the period of the *ge'onim*. Aside from the visiting students who attended the academy only during the *yarḥei kalla* months of Adar and Elul, the Gemara reports that 1,200 full-time students learned in the academy throughout the year.

In his youth, Rav traveled to Eretz Yisrael with his uncle, Rabbi Ḥiyya, where he studied under Rabbi Yehuda HaNasi, the redactor of the Mishna. He traveled back and forth between Israel and Babylonia until he settled in Babylonia in the year 219 CE. Rav's greatness is apparent not only in the large number of *amora'im* who were his students and who quote him throughout the Gemara, but also by the fact that he is recognized as the last of the *tanna'im*, and is permitted to disagree with tannaitic rulings.

Rav's teachings are found throughout both the Jerusalem Talmud and the Babylonian Talmud. Among his many rulings are several that deal with issues of marriage, such as his ruling that man cannot marry a woman without first meeting her, and the requirement that underage girls cannot be married until they are old enough to state whom they want to marry. His rulings in the area of ritual law were invariably accepted, although the rulings of his colleague and adversary, Shmuel, were accepted in criminal and financial matters.

Rav's son, Rabbi Ḥiyya, followed in his father's footsteps and became a great scholar; his other son, Ivu, was a merchant.

גְּדִי צְלִי אִשְׁתַּכַּח בְּאִסְרָטֵי דְּגוּפְתָא וְהִתִּירוּהוּ מִשּׁוּם שְׁנֵי דְבָרִים, מִשּׁוּם מְצִיאָה וּמִשּׁוּם רוֹב מְהַלְּכֵי דְרָכִים.

It is further related that **a roasted goat was** once **found in the street** in the town of **Gufta, and** the Rabbis **permitted it** to be eaten **based on two considerations:** First, **because of found property;** that is to say, they allowed the finder to keep it. Secondly, **because of the majority of traffic,** i.e., the majority of people passing through that street were Jews.

מִשּׁוּם מְצִיאָה – דְּתָנֵי: הַמַּצִּיל מִיַּד הָאֲרִי, מִיַּד הַגַּיִּס, מִשּׁוּנִת הַיָּם, וּמִשּׁוּנַת הַנָּהָר, וּמֵאִיסְרַטְיָא גְּדוֹלָה, וּמִפְּלַטְיָא גְּדוֹלָה – הֲרֵי אֵלּוּ שֶׁלּוֹ, מִפְּנֵי שֶׁהַבְּעָלִים מִתְיָיאֲשִׁין מֵהֶן.

The Gemara explains: **Because of found property, as it was taught** in a *baraita*: **One** who rescues an article from a lion,[H] from an enemy army [*gayyis*],[L] from rocks in the **sea** [*shunit hayam*],[N] **or from rocks in a river, or from a large** public **street** [*isratya*],[L] **or from a large** public **square;** in all these cases, **these** articles **belong to him,** even if they have an identifying mark on them, **because the owners have given up hope of** ever recovering **them.** For this reason the Rabbis ruled that the goat belonged to its finder, as it was found on the street.

מִשּׁוּם רוֹב מְהַלְּכֵי דְרָכִים – מִשּׁוּם שְׁחִיטַת גּוֹי. וְאִשְׁתַּכַּח מִן דְּבֵית רַבִּי.

The Rabbis also permitted the goat **because of the majority of traffic.**[H] Since most of the people who passed through that street were Jews, it stands to reason that a Jew had lost the roast goat, and the Rabbis were not concerned **that** it was the product of **gentile slaughter** and therefore not kosher. The Gemara adds that in the end, the goat **was found** to be **from the house of Rabbi** Yehuda HaNasi, and indeed kosher.

עִיגּוּל דְּגוּבְנָא אִשְׁתַּכַּח בְּפוּנְדְּקָא דְּלֵוִי וְהִתִּירוּהוּ מִשּׁוּם שְׁנֵי דְבָרִים מִשּׁוּם מְצִיאָה וּמִשּׁוּם רוֹב מְהַלְּכֵי דְרָכִים.

The Gemara relates that **a wheel of cheese was** once **found in an inn** [*pundaka*][L] belonging **to Levi, and the Rabbis permitted it** to be eaten **based on two considerations: Because of found property** and **because of the majority of traffic.**

מִשּׁוּם מְצִיאָה – דְּתָנֵי: הַמַּצִּיל מִיַּד הַגַּיִּס, מִיַּד הָאֲרִי, מִשּׁוּנַת הַיָּם, וּמִשּׁוּנַת הַנָּהָר, מֵאִיסְרַטְיָא גְּדוֹלָה, וּמִפְּלַטְיָא גְּדוֹלָה – הֲרֵי אֵלּוּ שֶׁלּוֹ, מִפְּנֵי שֶׁהַבְּעָלִים מִתְיָיאֲשִׁין מֵהֶן.

The Gemara explains: **Because of found property, as it was taught** in a *baraita*: **One who rescues** an article **from an enemy army, from a lion, from rocks in the sea, or from rocks in a river, from a large** public **street, or from a large** public **square;** in all these cases, **these** articles **belong to him,** even if they have an identifying mark on them, **because the owners have given up hope of** ever recovering **them.** The same applies to something that was found in an inn, which is also a public area; its owner presumably gave up hope of getting it back, and so the finder is entitled to keep it for himself.

מִשּׁוּם רוֹב מְהַלְּכֵי דְרָכִים – מִשּׁוּם גְּבִינַת גּוֹי. וְאִשְׁתַּכַּח מִן דְּרַבִּי אֶלְעָזָר בְּר׳ יוֹסֵי.

The problem that was overcome **because of the majority of traffic,** was that perhaps the cheese should have been prohibited **because** it was **the cheese of a gentile.** Since the majority of the guests at the inn were Jews, this was not a concern. The Gemara notes that, in the end the wheel of cheese **was found** to be **from** the house of **Rabbi Elazar, son of Rabbi Yosei,** and was indeed kosher.

אָמַר רַבִּי מָנָא קוֹמֵי רַבִּי יוֹסֵי: וַאֲנַן חָמְיָין רַבָּנַן מַכְרִיזִין. אֲמַר לֵיהּ: אַתְּ אִין הֲוֵיתָה מַשְׁכַּח לָא נָסְבַתְּ. רַבִּי יוֹנָה אֲבוּךְ לֹא אָמַר כֵּן, אֶלָּא אָמַר: הַלְוַאי כַּד נַשְׁכַּח נִשְׁכַּח מִן פִּיּוּסָא וּלְגָוָא אֲפִילוּ כֵּן אַשְׁכַּח וְלָא נְסֵיב.

Rabbi Mana said in the presence of Rabbi Yosei: But I saw the Rabbis announcing that they had found lost property, even when the item was found in a public area. Rabbi Yosei **said to him: If you were to find** an article in a public area, **you would not take** it either. **Rabbi Yona, your father, did not say this, but said: If only that when we find** some item, **we should find it** in a place that will not require us to announce its discovery, e.g., **from the gate outward,** in a public area. The Gemara notes that **even so,** when Rabbi Yona **found** a lost article in a crowded public place, **he did not take** it for himself, but rather announced that he had found it, so that he could locate its original owner.

LANGUAGE

Army [*gayyis*] – **גַּיִּיס:** From the Aramaic *gaysa*, meaning army. Also related to the Arabic جيش, *jaysh*, meaning army or band of soldiers.

Large street [*isratya*] – **אִיסְרַטְיָא:** From the Latin strata, meaning street or public road. Etymologically speaking, there is a link to the Greek στρατός, *stratos*, the meaning of which is linked to soldiers and military camps but not street.

Inn [*pundaka*] – **פּוּנְדְּקָא:** From the Greek πανδοκεῖον, *pandokeion*, meaning inn. From this word is also derived the term for innkeeper, *pundaki*. It should be noted that the Hebrew term *zona*, meaning harlot, is often translated into Aramaic as *pundakita*, apparently on the assumption that a female innkeeper gives herself over to harlotry with her guests (see Radak on Joshua 2:1).

NOTES

Rocks in the sea [*shunit hayam*] – שׁוּנַת הַיָּם: The mishna in *Oholot* 18:6 states: What is a *shunit*? It is any place to which the sea rises when it is stormy. *Talmid HaRashbash* renders this phrase as a rock in the sea or the force of the sea.

HALAKHA

One who rescues an article from a lion – הַמַּצִּיל מִיַּד הָאֲרִי: An article that was lost under circumstances where it was irretrievable by anyone, e.g., it was swept away by the sea or a river, or was about to be burned in a fire or eaten by a beast, belongs to the finder even if it has an identifying sign. This is the case even if the original owner has not yet despaired of finding it, and even if he is standing there shouting that it is his. The Rema writes that in any event it is good and proper to return the article to its original owner. If, however, the lost article was not irretrievable, and it was possible to save it in some manner, it does not belong to the finder if it has an identifying sign (*Bava Kamma* 114a; Rambam *Sefer Nezikim*, *Hilkhot Gezeila VaAveda* 6:2, 11:10; *Shulḥan Arukh*, *Ḥoshen Mishpat* 259:7).

Because of the majority of traffic – מִשּׁוּם רוֹב מְהַלְּכֵי דְרָכִים: If one's lambs or chickens are stolen or lost, and he finds them ritually slaughtered in proper fashion, the following distinction applies: If the majority of the local inhabitants are Jews, the slaughtered animals are permitted to be eaten, whether they are found in the market place or they are found on the garbage dump at home. But if they are found on the garbage dump in the marketplace, they are forbidden (Rambam *Sefer Kedusha*, *Hilkhot Sheḥita* 4:8; *Shulḥan Arukh*, *Yoreh De'a* 1:4).

הלכה ג מתני׳ בְּהֵמָה שֶׁנִּמְצֵאת מִירוּשָׁלַיִם וְעַד מִגְדַּל עֵדֶר, וּכְמִדָּתָהּ לְכׇל רוּחַ, זְכָרִים – עוֹלוֹת, נְקֵבוֹת – זִבְחֵי שְׁלָמִים. רַבִּי יְהוּדָה אוֹמֵר: הָרָאוּי לִפְסָחִים לִפְסָחִים, קוֹדֶם לָרֶגֶל שְׁלֹשִׁים יוֹם.

HALAKHA 3 · MISHNA If **an animal** that is fit for the altar **was found** straying, **from Jerusalem**[H] **and as far as Migdal Eder,**[B] **and** similarly if it was found **within that distance** from Jerusalem **in any** other **direction,** it is presumed that the animal came from Jerusalem. Most of the animals in Jerusalem were designated for offerings, and presumably this one was as well. **Males** are presumed to be **burnt-offerings,** as only males are brought as burnt-offerings. **Females** are presumed to be **peace-offerings,** as it is permitted to bring a female peace-offering. **Rabbi Yehuda says:** An animal **that is fit for the Paschal offering,** i.e., a one-year-old male lamb or kid, is presumed to be **a Paschal offering,**[N] provided that it was found **within thirty days before the Festival**[N] of Passover.

בָּרִאשׁוֹנָה הָיוּ מְמַשְׁכְּנִין אֶת מוֹצְאֶיהָ עַד שֶׁהוּא מֵבִיא (עִמָּהּ) נִסְכֶּיהָ. חָזְרוּ לִהְיוֹת מַנִּיחִין אוֹתָהּ וּבוֹרְחִין. הִתְקִינוּ בֵּית דִּין שֶׁיְּהוּ נִסְכֶּיהָ בָּאִין מִשֶּׁל צִבּוּר.

Originally, the court **would seize collateral from one who found** such an animal, as security **until he would bring with it the libations** associated with this offering, as if the found animal were his own and he had committed himself to bring the libations. This brought about a situation in which those who found the animals **began leaving them** where they found them, **and absconding,** so as not to become liable for the libations. **The court** therefore **instituted that the libations** accompanying these offerings **would come from public** funds, that is, from the Temple treasury.

אָמַר רַבִּי שִׁמְעוֹן: שִׁבְעָה דְּבָרִים הִתְקִינוּ בֵּית דִּין, וְזֶה אֶחָד מֵהֶן. גּוֹי שֶׁשָּׁלַח עוֹלָתוֹ מִמְּדִינַת הַיָּם וְשָׁלַח עִמָּהּ נְסָכִים – קְרֵיבִין מִשֶּׁלּוֹ, וְאִם לָאו – קְרֵיבִין מִשֶּׁל צִבּוּר.

Rabbi Shimon said: The court instituted seven ordinances with regard to the financial aspects of offerings and consecrations. **And this** ordinance, namely, that the cost of the libations accompanying the sacrifice of a found animal is borne by the public, **is one of them.** These are the other ordinances: If **a gentile sent his burnt-offering**[N] **from abroad,** outside Eretz Yisrael, **and he sent with it** money for the purchase of the **libations** that must accompany it, the libations **are offered at his** expense. **And if** the gentile **did not** cover the cost of the libations, it is a condition of the court that the libations are **sacrificed at the public's** expense, with funds taken from the Temple treasury.[H]

וְכֵן גֵּר שֶׁמֵּת וְהִנִּיחַ זְבָחִים, אִם יֵשׁ לוֹ נְסָכִים – קְרֵיבִין מִשֶּׁלּוֹ, וְאִם לָאו – קְרֵיבִין מִשֶּׁל צִבּוּר.

And likewise, in the case of **a convert who died** without heirs **and left** animals that he had designated as **offerings. If he has the libations,** i.e., if he also had set aside libations or money for that purpose, the libations **are sacrificed from his** estate. **And if** he did **not** do so, the libations **are sacrificed from public** funds.[H]

HALAKHA

An animal that was found straying from Jerusalem – בְּהֵמָה שֶׁנִּמְצֵאת מִירוּשָׁלַיִם: If an animal was found in Jerusalem or its environs, as far as Migdal Eder or the equivalent distance in any other direction, it is presumed to be a consecrated animal that ran away. Because it is assumed that the animal had been consecrated, it must be treated in a special way based on its age and gender, so that it will be possible to use it as an offering (Rambam *Sefer Avoda, Hilkhot Pesulei HaMukdashin* 6:18; *Sefer Zemanim, Hilkhot Shekalim* 4:3).

If a gentile sent his burnt-offering – גּוֹי שֶׁשָּׁלַח עוֹלָתוֹ: If a gentile sent his burnt-offering from overseas, but failed to send money for the required libations along with it, the libations are sacrificed at the public's expense with funds taken from the Temple treasury, in accordance with the opinion of Rabbi Shimon (Rambam *Sefer Zemanim, Hilkhot Shekalim* 4:3).

A convert who died and left offerings – גֵּר שֶׁמֵּת וְהִנִּיחַ זְבָחִים: If a convert died without heirs and left animals designated as offerings, and he also left wine or money for their libations, the libations are sacrificed from what he designated. If he did not leave the libations or the money for their purchase, they are sacrificed from public funds taken from the Temple treasury, in accordance with the statement of Rabbi Shimon (Rambam *Sefer Zemanim, Hilkhot Shekalim* 4:4).

BACKGROUND

Migdal Eder – מִגְדַּל עֵדֶר: This place is mentioned in Genesis 35:21. From the context it seems to be located between Bethlehem and Hebron. The author of the *Kaftor VaFeraḥ* maintains that it is situated west of Hebron, whereas others think that it is just south of Bethlehem, and about 15 km south of Jerusalem.

NOTES

An animal that is fit for the Paschal offering is presumed to be a Paschal offering – הָרָאוּי לִפְסָחִים לִפְסָחִים: Even though such an animal could also be the guilt-offering of a nazirite or a leper, as they too are brought from one-year-old animals, since these offerings were relatively uncommon, and especially since the animal was found within thirty days before Passover, it is reasonable to assume that it had been set aside as a Paschal lamb (Rav Yehuda ben Rav Binyamin HaRofeh).

Within thirty days before the Festival – קוֹדֶם לָרֶגֶל שְׁלֹשִׁים יוֹם: Since questions begin to be asked and lectures begin to be delivered about the *halakhot* of Passover thirty days before the Festival (see *Pesaḥim* 6a), people at that time began to buy lambs to consecrate them as Paschal offerings. It is therefore reasonable to assume that this animal that had been found was consecrated for that purpose and not as something else, such as a burnt-offering or a peace-offering (Rosh; *Talmid HaRashbash*; *Tiklin Ḥadatin*).

The Gemara (*Kiddushin* 55b) offers an explanation of the anonymous first *tanna*'s opinion, which does not distinguish between the period prior to Passover and other times, and presumes all one-year-old male animals to be burnt-offerings: Since people are especially careful to ensure that their Paschal offerings will not become lost, there is no reason to suspect that that the found animal is a Paschal lamb.

If a gentile sent his burnt-offering – גּוֹי שֶׁשָּׁלַח עוֹלָתוֹ: Even though gentiles are not commanded to bring offerings, and obligatory offerings may not be accepted from them, gentiles can bring free-will offerings, which are accepted and sacrificed in the Temple. The Gemara (*Menaḥot* 73b) records a dispute as to whether only burnt-offerings are accepted from them or also peace-offerings.

An offering brought by a gentile requires libations just like an offering brought by a Jew, as the obligation to bring a libation depends on the offering, regardless of who brings it. Therefore, if the gentile failed to send money for his libations, they are sacrificed from public funds (Rashi; Rambam).

וּתְנַאי בֵּית דִּין הוּא עַל כֹּהֵן גָּדוֹל שֶׁמֵּת שֶׁתְּהֵא מִנְחָתוֹ קְרֵיבָה מִשֶּׁל צִבּוּר. רַבִּי יְהוּדָה אוֹמֵר: מִשֶּׁל יוֹרְשִׁין, וּשְׁלֵימָה הָיְתָה קְרֵיבָה.

And another ordinance: **It is a condition of the court with regard to a High Priest who died,** and a new High Priest had not yet been appointed in his place, **that his meal-offering,** i.e., the griddle-cake offering that the High Priest would bring each day from one-tenth of an ephah of flour, would be **sacrificed from public** funds.[HN] **Rabbi Yehuda says:** It was brought **from** the property of the High Priest's **heirs,**[N] i.e., his estate,[N] and not from public funds.[N] In any event, the offering was not brought as it would have been brought by the High Priest himself were he still alive, half in the morning and half in the evening, **but** rather **it was sacrificed** all at once, from a **whole** one-tenth of an ephah.[H]

עַל הַמֶּלַח וְעַל הָעֵצִים שֶׁיְּהוּ הַכֹּהֲנִים נֵאוֹתִין בָּהֶן.

The fourth ordinance was **about the salt** in the Temple that was designated for salting the offerings, **and** the fifth was **about the wood** that was used for the burning of the offerings. These ordinances decreed **that the priests may use them** also to prepare the meat of the offerings that they eat.[H]

וְעַל הַפָּרָה שֶׁלֹּא יְהוּ מוֹעֲלִין בְּאֶפְרָהּ.

And the sixth ordinance **concerned the** red **heifer, that** deriving benefit **from its ashes is not considered misusing** consecrated property.[H]

וְעַל הַקִּינִּין הַפְּסוּלוֹת שֶׁיְּהוּ בָּאוֹת מִשֶּׁל צִבּוּר. רַבִּי יוֹסֵי אוֹמֵר: הַמְסַפֵּק אֶת הַקִּינִּין הוּא מְסַפֵּק אֶת הַפְּסוּלוֹת.

And the seventh ordinance was **about disqualified pairs** of bird-offerings: It ruled **that** their replacements **should come from public** funds. **Rabbi Yosei** disagreed and **says:** The expense does not fall upon the public, but rather upon **whoever supplies** all **the pairs** of bird-offerings to the Temple; **he must** also **supply,** at no additional charge, the replacements for **the disqualified** birds.[H]

HALAKHA

A High Priest who died – כֹּהֵן גָּדוֹל שֶׁמֵּת: If a High Priest died and a new High Priest was not yet appointed in his place, the griddle-cake offering was sacrificed from public funds taken from the Temple treasury, in accordance with the statement of Rabbi Shimon (Rambam *Sefer Zemanim, Hilkhot Shekalim* 4:4; see *Kesef Mishne* to *Halakha* 3). Elsewhere, however, the Rambam rules in accordance with the opinion of Rabbi Yehuda, that in such a case the griddle-cake offering is brought from the property of the High Priest's heirs (Rambam *Sefer Avoda, Hilkhot Temidin UMusafin* 3:22; see *Leḥem Mishne* there).

It was sacrificed from a whole one-tenth – שְׁלֵימָה הָיְתָה קְרֵיבָה: If the High Priest died in the morning before bringing the griddle-cake offering and another High Priest had not yet been appointed in his place, his heirs bring a whole one-tenth of an ephah in the morning and a whole one-tenth of an ephah in the evening. The amount of oil and the frankincense sacrificed with it was not doubled even though the amount of flour was doubled. Instead, a *log* and a half of oil and half a handful of frankincense were brought with the one-tenth of an ephah sacrificed in the morning, and a *log* and a half of oil and half a handful of frankincense were brought with the one-tenth of an ephah sacrificed in the afternoon, in accordance with the opinion of the Sages elsewhere (*Menaḥot* 52a; Rambam *Sefer Avoda, Hilkhot Temidin UMusafin* 3:22).

About the salt and about the wood – עַל הַמֶּלַח וְעַל הָעֵצִים: It is a condition of the court that priests may benefit from consecrated salt and wood while preparing the offerings granted to them as their portion. They may not, however, use the consecrated salt on their ordinary food (Rambam *Sefer Avoda, Hilkhot Me'ila* 8:6).

Concerned the red heifer – עַל הַפָּרָה: The prohibition against misusing consecrated property applied to the red heifer from the time it was consecrated until the time it was burned to ashes. It is a condition of the court that once the heifer is burned and reduced to ashes, making use of the ashes is not a violation of the prohibition against misuse of consecrated property. This is in accordance with Rabbi Shimon's statement (Rambam *Sefer Avoda, Hilkhot Me'ila* 2:5).

Disqualified pairs of bird-offerings – הַקִּינִּין הַפְּסוּלוֹת: If a pair of bird-offerings was found to be unfit or was otherwise disqualified before it was sacrificed, the one appointed to supply the pairs of birds must provide the Temple with another pair in its place. This is in accordance with the opinion of Rabbi Yosei (Rambam *Sefer Avoda, Hilkhot Kelei HaMikdash* 7:9).

NOTES

From public funds…from the heirs – מִשֶּׁל צִבּוּר...מִשֶּׁל יוֹרְשִׁין: The opinion of the anonymous first *tanna* here is the same as that of Rabbi Shimon quoted in the *baraita* and in tractate *Menaḥot*. The later commentaries on *Menaḥot* point out that Rabbi Shimon's wording could be understood to mean only that it is permissible to draw on public funds for the purpose of the griddle-cake offering, in order to overcome the negligence of the heirs. However, Rabbi Shimon's wording at the end of the discussion both here and in tractate *Menaḥot* make it clear that his opinion is not based on the avoidance of negligence, but rather is derived from the verse dealing with the daily offering. Accordingly, it is an obligation, not an option, that this offering be brought from the public funds taken from the Temple treasury.

From the heirs – מִשֶּׁל יוֹרְשִׁין: Later commentaries wondered: How can the heirs bring this offering when they are in a state of acute mourning, when it is prohibited to bring an offering? They answer that since the purpose of the offering is to atone for the High Priest who died, rather than for his heirs now in mourning, their status as acute mourners does not disqualify it (*Minḥat Aharon*).

From the heirs, i.e., his estate – מִשֶּׁל יוֹרְשִׁין: Rabbi Yehuda, in both the mishna and the *baraita*, speaks of heirs, without defining who these heirs are. The verse from which Rabbi Yehuda derives his position: "And the anointed priest that shall be in his stead from among his sons shall offer it" (Leviticus 6:15), implies that the relevant heirs are specifically his sons. Later commentaries disagree on this point. Some argue that since Rabbi Yehuda uses the general term, heirs, this includes even heirs who are Israelites. They can bring the griddle-cake offering, because an heir does not bring it in his own name, but rather to atone for the High Priest who had died (*Minḥat Ḥinukh*; Rabbi Shmuel Shtrason; Rabbi Yitzḥak Ze'ev Soloveitchik). Others insist that the term heirs refers specifically to the sons of the High Priest who are priests themselves (*Mikdash David*; *Ḥazon Ish*; *Sefat Emet*).

And not from public funds – וְלֹא מִשֶּׁל צִבּוּר: The High Priest's griddle-cake offering is not a voluntary offering but rather his personal obligation. Later commentaries discuss the question of how the public could bring this offering since they are not obligated to do so, at least according to Rabbi Yehuda. They explain that the public as a whole has an obligation that the griddle-cake offering be brought every day, but that obligation is not tied to anyone in particular. Rabbi Yehuda and Rabbi Shimon disagree only with regard to the question of whose responsibility it is to bring the offering in such a case (*Ḥazon Ish*).

גמ׳ רַבִּי הוֹשַׁעְיָא רַבָּה אָמַר: לְבָא בִּדְמֵיהֶן שָׁנוּ.

GEMARA The mishna taught that if a male animal was found near Jerusalem, it is presumed to have been consecrated as a burnt-offering. Given that a male animal could just as easily be a peace-offering, and as such, most of its meat is meant to be eaten and it is prohibited to burn it on the altar, how can the found animal be sacrificed as a burnt-offering? In answer to this question, **Rabbi Hoshaya Rabba said: They taught** the *halakha* that it is presumed to be a burnt-offering only **with regard to one who comes with its money,**[N] i.e., the money with which the animal was redeemed. One who finds such an animal near Jerusalem may not bring it as a burnt-offering, as it might be a peace-offering. He must redeem the animal for its monetary value, and in addition he must consecrate the same sum again, from his own money. He then stipulates the following: If the animal is a burnt-offering, let it be redeemed on the first sum, and let the second sum be used for a free-will peace-offering. If this animal is a peace-offering, let it be redeemed on the second sum, and let the first sum be used for a free-will burnt-offering. He then purchases a burnt-offering with the first sum and a peace-offering with the second sum.

אֲמַר לֵיהּ רַבִּי יוֹחָנָן: אוֹמְרִים לוֹ לָאָדָם צֵא וּמְעוֹל בְּקָדָשִׁים?

Rabbi Yoḥanan said to him: Does one say to a person that he should **go out and misuse consecrated animals?** If one redeems a consecrated animal that is still fit for the altar, the redemption is valid; the animal is no longer consecrated and the money is now sacred in its place and must be used to buy other offerings. This redemption, however, is valid only after the fact; it is considered misuse to redeem an unblemished animal and prohibited to do so *ab initio*.

אֶלָּא, הִילְכוּ בָּהֶן אַחַר הָרוֹב, אִם רוֹב זְכָרִים – עוֹלוֹת, אִם רוֹב נְקֵבוֹת – זִבְחֵי שְׁלָמִים.

Rather, the mishna must be understood differently. **In their regard, follow the majority. If the majority** of the animals found **are males,** they are determined to be **burnt-offerings,** for most male animals brought as offerings are burnt-offerings. And **if the majority** of the animals found **are females,** they are determined to be **peace-offerings,** for most female animals brought as offerings are peace-offerings.

וְאֵין הַשְּׁלָמִים בָּאִין מִן הַזְּכָרִים וּמִן הַנְּקֵבוֹת?

The Gemara asks: **But are peace-offerings not brought** both **from males and from females?** Therefore, it is possible that the male animals that were found are not burnt-offerings, but rather peace-offerings.

כֵּיצַד הוּא עוֹשֶׂה? מוֹצִיאָן לְחוּלִּין, וְחוֹזֵר וְעוֹשֶׂה אוֹתָן

Rather, Rabbi Yoḥanan's words must be understood as follows: If one finds animals near Jerusalem, even though they are presumed to be offerings, he cannot sacrifice the animals themselves on the altar. **What** then **does he do? He must** wait until the animals develop blemishes and only then redeem them, and thereby **remove** their consecrated status and restore them **to their non-sacred state. He then goes back and** ensures that he makes them

NOTES

They taught this with regard to one who comes with its money – לְבָא בִּדְמֵיהֶן שָׁנוּ: This explanation is difficult in light of the mishna's earlier point that those who found such animals would abscond, so as not to become liable for the libations. Why then would the finder be willing to consecrate money of his own of the same value as the animal that he found? The *Tiferet Yisrael* (*Yakhin*, on *Shekalim* 7:5) suggests that people would abscond only in situations where after they set aside an additional animal, the court would insist that they fund the libations as well, and even seize collateral to that effect. The ordinance that the libations would be funded from communal funds was instituted in this context.

An alternative explanation is that the finder would object only to the expense of the libations, as with regard to the animals themselves he did not suffer any loss. When he would sacrifice the animal bought with the value of the found animal that he redeemed, he would stipulate that if what he had found was not a burnt-offering, then the present offering would be his own burnt-offering. The opportunity for the finder to bring his own offering is not a loss. The additional animal of equal value that he would consecrate was also not a loss for him; in exchange he received the animal that he found, as with its redemption it became non-sacred property and he acquired it. Consequently, the only added expense was that of the libations of the offering that was brought for the owner who had lost the animal (Rabbi Ḥayyim Kanievsky, *Shekel HaKodesh*).

HALAKHA

If one set aside his shekel and died – **הִפְרִישׁ שִׁקְלוֹ וּמֵת**: If one set aside his shekel and then died, the shekel is used for the purchase of free-will burnt-offerings (Rambam *Sefer Zemanim, Hilkhot Shekalim* 3:12).

Leftover money from one-tenth of an ephah – **מוֹתַר עֲשִׂירִית הָאֵיפָה**: The leftovers from the High Priest's griddle-cake offering are destroyed, in accordance with the opinion of Rabbi Yoḥanan (Rambam *Sefer Avoda, Hilkhot Pesulei HaMukdashin* 5:8).

The High Priest's one-tenth of an ephah – **עֲשִׂירִית הָאֵיפָה שֶׁל כֹּהֵן גָּדוֹל**: How was the High Priest's griddle-cake offering prepared? He would consecrate a whole one-tenth of an ephah of flour and then divide it in half using the half-tenth measure in the Temple. Even though it was sacrificed in half portions, it was not consecrated in half portions, in accordance with the opinion of Rabbi Yoḥanan in tractate *Menaḥot*, where the opinions of Rabbi Yoḥanan and Reish Lakish are reversed, i.e., Rabbi Yoḥanan's opinion in *Menaḥot* is that of Reish Lakish here (Rabbi Yosef Korkos; Rambam *Sefer Avoda, Hilkhot Ma'aseh HaKorbanot* 13:2).

He sacrifices one half, and the second half is destroyed – **מַקְרִיב מֶחֱצָה וּמֶחֱצָה אָבֵד**: If the High Priest brought half of his griddle-cake offering in the morning and then died, became ritually impure, or developed a blemish, and another High Priest was appointed in his place, the successor does not sacrifice in the evening a half-tenth from his own property, nor does he sacrifice the second half-tenth of his predecessor. Rather, he brings a whole one-tenth, divides it into two equal portions, offers one half, and leaves the second half to be destroyed. How is it destroyed? Its form is left overnight and allowed to decay, and then it is taken out to the place of burning in the Temple courtyard. Therefore, two half-tenths are brought, and two half-tenths are destroyed, in accordance with the mishna (Rambam *Sefer Avoda, Hilkhot Temidin UMusafin* 3:20–21).

עוֹלוֹת.

burnt-offerings. He does this by taking two unblemished animals and stipulating as follows: If the animal that was found was a burnt-offering, let the first animal be a burnt-offering in its place, and let the second be a peace-offering. And if the animal that was found was a peace-offering, let the second animal be peace-offering, and let the first be a free-will burnt-offering.

אָמַר רַבִּי זְעִירָא: כְּמָה דְאַתְּ אָמַר תַּמָּן תְּנַאי בֵּית דִּין הוּא עַל הַמּוֹתָרוֹת שֶׁיִּקָרְבוּ עוֹלוֹת, כֵּן אַתְּ מַר אוּף הָכָא: תְּנַאי בֵּית דִּין הוּא עַל הָאוֹבְדוֹת שֶׁיִּקָרְבוּ עוֹלוֹת.

Rabbi Zeira offers a different explanation of the *halakha* in the mishna: Male animals found near Jerusalem are sacrificed as burnt-offerings, even though they may have been designated as peace-offerings. He **says: Just as you say there** (19a) in the name of Reish Lakish that **it is a condition of the court** that stipulates **with regard to funds left over** from what had originally been consecrated for sin-offerings that they **are brought as burnt-offerings; so too, you say here** that **it is a condition of the court with regard to** animals that were **lost** and later found, that even though they may be peace-offerings, they **are brought as burnt-offerings.**

אָמַר רַבִּי יוֹסֵי לְרַבִּי יַעֲקֹב בַּר אַחָא: אֵין זֶה מֵזִיד?

Rabbi Yosei said to Rabbi Yaakov bar Aḥa: Is this not a case of **intentional** change of an offering's purpose? A condition of the court can allocate leftover money that had originally been consecrated for sin-offerings to the purchase of a burnt-offering, but that does not mean that one can intentionally change the sanctity of the animal itself from that of a peace-offering to that of a burnt-offering.

אָמַר לֵיהּ: מִכֵּיוָן שֶׁהוּא תְּנַאי בֵּית דִּין אֵין זֶה מֵזִיד.

Rabbi Yaakov bar Aḥa **said to** Rabbi Yosei: **Since it is a condition of the court, it is not** considered a case of **intentional** change of an animal's purpose. Even if the animal had initially been consecrated as a peace-offering, that consecration is regarded as conditional in accordance with the court's stipulation. Consequently, the animal can now be sacrificed as a burnt-offering *ab initio*.

אָמַר רַבִּי יֵסָא: עַד דַּאֲנָא תַמָּן שְׁמָעִית קָל רַב יְהוּדָה שָׁאַל לִשְׁמוּאֵל: הִפְרִישׁ שִׁקְלוֹ וּמֵת? אָמַר לֵיהּ: יִפְּלוּ לִנְדָבָה.

§ Since the mishna mentioned the griddle-cake offering of a High Priest who had died, the Gemara records what **Rabbi Yesa said** about similar matters: **While I was there** in Babylonia, **I heard the voice of Rav Yehuda asking Shmuel:** If one **set aside his shekel and** then **died**[H] before handing it over to the treasurer, what is to be done with the shekel? Shmuel **said to him: It is allocated to free-will offerings** and is used for the purchase of free-will burnt-offerings.

וּמוֹתַר עֲשִׂירִית הָאֵיפָה שֶׁלּוֹ, רַבִּי יוֹחָנָן אָמַר: יוֹלִיכֵם לְיָם הַמֶּלַח. רַבִּי אֶלְעָזָר אָמַר: יִפְּלוּ לִנְדָבָה.

It was further asked: What is to be done with **leftover** money that a High Priest set aside for the purchase of his griddle-cake offering made from **one-tenth of an ephah** of flour? If a High Priest designated money for the purchase of flour for his meal-offering and it turns out that he set aside too much money, what is to be done with the extra money? **Rabbi Yoḥanan said:** The money **goes to the Dead Sea,**[H] meaning, it is destroyed. **Rabbi Elazar** disagreed and **said:** The money **is allocated to free-will offerings.**

עֲשִׂירִית הָאֵיפָה שֶׁל כֹּהֵן גָּדוֹל. רַבִּי יוֹחָנָן אָמַר: חוֹצֶה אוֹתָהּ וְאַחַר כָּךְ מְקַדְּשָׁהּ. רַבִּי שִׁמְעוֹן בֶּן לָקִישׁ אָמַר: מְקַדְּשָׁהּ וְאַחַר כָּךְ חוֹצֶה אוֹתָהּ.

The Gemara continues its discussion of the High Priest's griddle-cake offering. The mishna in *Menaḥot* 4:5 teaches that it was divided in two; half of it was sacrificed in the morning and half in the evening. The Gemara records a dispute among the *amora'im*: With regard to **the High Priest's one-tenth of an ephah, Rabbi Yoḥanan said: He divides it** into two equal portions in two non-sacred vessels, **and afterward he consecrates** each half by itself before it is sacrificed.[H] **Rabbi Shimon ben Lakish said: He** must first **consecrate** the entire one-tenth of an ephah, **and** only **afterward does he divide it** into two equal portions.

מַתְנִיתָא פְלִיגֵי עַל רַבִּי יוֹחָנָן: מַקְרִיב מֶחֱצָה וּמֶחֱצָה אָבֵד.

The Gemara comments: **A mishna** seems to **disagree with** the opinion of **Rabbi Yoḥanan,** as the mishna (*Menaḥot* 4:5) teaches that if the High Priest sacrificed half of his griddle-cake offering in the morning and then died, and another High Priest was appointed in his place, the successor does not bring the second half that evening. Instead **he** consecrates a whole one-tenth of an ephah and divides it into two equal portions. He then **sacrifices** one **half, and the** second **half is destroyed.**[H] According to Rabbi Yoḥanan, who says that the High Priest consecrates each half by itself, why must the second half be destroyed? It had never been consecrated for the altar, and so it can still be redeemed.

פָּתַר לָהּ שֶׁכֵּן אֲפִילּוּ מָעוֹת יֵלְכוּ לְיַם הַמֶּלַח.

Rabbi Yoḥanan **solves it,** i.e., resolves the difficulty: The mishna maintains that even though the second half is consecrated only for its value and not for the altar, it still must be destroyed. **As even** what is left over from the **money** that a High Priest set aside for the purchase of his griddle-cake offering **goes to the Dead Sea,** although it had never been consecrated for the altar.

מַתְנִיתָא פְּלִיגִי עַל רַבִּי שִׁמְעוֹן בֶּן לָקִישׁ: נִמְצְאוּ שְׁנֵי חֲצָאִין קְרֵיבִין וּשְׁנֵי חֲצָאִין אֲבוּדִין,

The Gemara notes that **the** same **mishna** also seems to **disagree with** the opinion of **Rabbi Shimon ben Lakish.** The mishna teaches that in the aforementioned case where the High Priest dies before sacrificing the second half of his griddle-cake offering and is succeeded on the same day, **it turns out that two halves** of the griddle-cake offering **are sacrificed,** i.e., the first half from the deceased High Priest and the first half from his successor, **and two halves are destroyed,** i.e., the second half of each offering.

וְתָנֵי עֲלָהּ: מֶחֱצָה רִאשׁוֹן וּמֶחֱצָה שֵׁנִי – תְּעוּבַּר צוּרָתָן וְיֵצְאוּ לְבֵית הַשְּׂרֵיפָה.

And it was taught about this mishna in a *baraita*: The **half of the first** High Priest **and the half of the second** High Priest that are destroyed, i.e., that which is left over once each of them has sacrificed half of one-tenth of an ephah, **their form** must first be allowed **to decay,** i.e., they must be left overnight until they are disqualified, **and** only then **are they taken out to the place of burning.** According to the opinion of Rabbi Shimon ben Lakish that the High Priest consecrates for the altar the entire one-tenth of an ephah before dividing it, there is no reason to wait for the form to decay. The principle is that if anything becomes intrinsically disqualified such that it cannot be sacrificed, it is burned immediately (*Pesaḥim* 34b). Therefore, it should be possible to immediately burn each disqualified, leftover half from each High Priest, and not wait for their forms to decay.

פָּתַר לָהּ כְּרַבִּי יִשְׁמָעֵאל, דְּאָמַר: עִשָּׂרוֹן מְקַדֵּשׁ.

Rabbi Shimon ben Lakish **solves** this difficulty by arguing that the mishna, and his own opinion, which is an interpretation of the mishna, does not accord with the *baraita* but rather **with** the opinion of **Rabbi Yishmael** (*Menaḥot* 90a), **who says** that **the one-tenth** of an ephah **measure** is regarded as a sacred service vessel that **consecrates** its contents. The flour is therefore consecrated for the altar at the original measuring of the one-tenth of the ephah. Accordingly, the remaining half of each one-tenth of an ephah is destroyed immediately without decay of form. The *baraita*, on the other hand, does not consider the one-tenth of an ephah measure to be a sacred service vessel, and therefore the measure does not consecrate the flour. As long as the remaining halves have not been consecrated for the altar, they are consecrated only for their value and require decay of form before they are burned.

כְּשֶׁהַכֹּהֵן מִתְקָרֵב תְּחִילָּה לַעֲבוֹדָה מֵבִיא עֲשִׂירִית הָאֵיפָה שֶׁלּוֹ וְעוֹבְדָהּ בְּיָדוֹ. אֶחָד כֹּהֵן גָּדוֹל וְאֶחָד כֹּהֵן הֶדְיוֹט שֶׁעָבְדוּ עַד שֶׁלֹּא הֵבִיאוּ עֲשִׂירִית הָאֵיפָה שֶׁלָּהֶם – עֲבוֹדָתָן כְּשֵׁירָה.

§ As the topic of the griddle-cake offering brought each day by the High Priest has been raised, the Gemara elaborates on it and on the inaugural meal-offering brought by each and every priest the first time that he serves in the Temple. It was taught in a *baraita*: **When a priest approaches** the altar **for the first time to** perform **the service, he brings his** meal-offering from **one-tenth of an ephah** of flour **and he performs the service himself,** and in this way he inaugurates himself for service. Nevertheless, for **both a High Priest and an ordinary priest who performed the** sacrificial **service before bringing their** meal-offerings from **one-tenth of an ephah** of flour as their inaugural meal-offerings, **their service is valid,**[H] as the absence of a priest's inaugural meal-offerings does not invalidate his service.

רַבִּי מָנָא בָּעֵי מֵימַר: בּוֹ בַּיּוֹם שֶׁנִּתְקָרֵב תְּחִילָּה לַעֲבוֹדָה בּוֹ בַּיּוֹם נִתְמַנָּה לִהְיוֹת כֹּהֵן גָּדוֹל – מֵבִיא שְׁתַּיִם, אַחַת לְחִינּוּכוֹ וְאַחַת לְחוֹבַת הַיּוֹם.

Rabbi Mana wanted to say the following *halakha*: If **on the same day that** a priest **approached** the altar **to** perform **the service for the first time, on that same day he was** also **appointed to be the High Priest,**[H] **he must bring two** meal-offerings, each one-tenth of an ephah of flour; **one for his inaugural** meal-offering **and one for the obligation of the day,** i.e., for the griddle-cake offering that the High Priest must bring every day.

HALAKHA

When a priest approaches for the first time to perform the service – כְּשֶׁהַכֹּהֵן מִתְקָרֵב תְּחִילָּה לַעֲבוֹדָה: Neither the High Priest nor an ordinary priest may perform the Temple service for the first time until he brings a meal-offering of one-tenth of an ephah of flour from his own property and offers it himself. If an ordinary priest performed any part of the Temple service before bringing this meal-offering, or if the High Priest served as the High Priest before bringing this meal-offering, his service is still valid (Rambam *Sefer Avoda, Hilkhot Kelei HaMikdash* 5:16).

On the same day that a priest approached the altar to perform the service for the first time, he was also appointed to be the High Priest – בּוֹ בַּיּוֹם שֶׁנִּתְקָרֵב תְּחִילָּה לַעֲבוֹדָה בּוֹ בַּיּוֹם נִתְמַנָּה לִהְיוֹת כֹּהֵן גָּדוֹל: If a priest who had never before performed the Temple service was appointed as the High Priest, he was required to bring three meal-offerings, each of one-tenth of an ephah. The first would be his inaugural meal-offering like any ordinary priest who begins his service. He would then bring a second one-tenth of an ephah as the inaugural meal-offering of a High Priest. Finally, he would bring a third one-tenth of an ephah as the daily griddle-cake offering of the High Priest. All three are sacrificed in the identical manner (Rambam *Sefer Avoda, Hilkhot Kelei HaMikdash* 5:17).

"תּוּפִינֵי" – בְּשַׁעַת הֲבָאָה תּוּפִינֵי, וְאֵין בְּשַׁחֲרִית תּוּפִינֵי.

The Gemara records another *halakha* with regard to the daily griddle-cake offering brought by the High Priest. Concerning this offering, the verse states: "On a griddle it shall be made with oil; when it is soaked, you shall bring it in; and **baked pieces** of the meal-offering shall you offer for a sweet savor unto the Lord" (Leviticus 6:14). The juxtaposition of the words "you shall bring it in" to the words "and baked pieces" teaches that **at the time** that the meal-offering **is brought,** it is made into **baked pieces,** i.e., during that same day, **and not before daybreak** is it made into **baked pieces.**

וְהָא תָּנֵינַן: הֶעֱמִידוּ עוֹשֵׂה חֲבִיתִּין לַעֲשׂוֹת חֲבִיתִּין! אָמַר רַבִּי חִיָּיא בַּר אַחָא: לַעֲשׂוֹת חַמִּין לִרְבוּכָה.

The Gemara asks: **But didn't we learn** in a mishna (*Tamid* 1:3) that every day before the removal of the ashes from the altar, which was before daybreak, **they assigned whoever made the griddle-cake offerings to make,** i.e., bake, **griddle-cakes?**[NH] **Rabbi Ḥiyya bar Aḥa said:** All that they assigned him to do was **to heat water for the boiling** of the dough as part of the preparation of the griddle-cakes for the day.

"תּוּפִינֵי", רַבִּי יֵסָא בְּשֵׁם רַבִּי חֲנִינָה: מְטַגְּנָהּ וְאַחַר כָּךְ אוֹפֶה אוֹתָהּ, רַבִּי אַחָא בְּשֵׁם רַבִּי חֲנִינָה: אוֹפֶה אוֹתָהּ וְאַחַר כָּךְ מְטַגְּנָהּ.

Having mentioned the baking of the High Priest's griddle-cake offering, the Gemara addresses the various stages in the preparation of the offering. The verse implies that the offering must be fried, as it says: "On a griddle it shall be made with oil"; it also indicates that it must be scalded in water, as it says: "When it is soaked"; and it further teaches that it must be baked, as it says: "And **baked pieces** of the meal-offering shall you offer for a sweet savor unto the Lord." As for the order of these procedures, **Rabbi Yesa** said **in the name of Rabbi Ḥanina: He** first **fries it, and afterward he bakes it. Rabbi Aḥa** said **in the name of Rabbi Ḥanina: He** first **bakes it, and** only **afterward does he fry it.**

"תּוּפִינֵי" – תֵּאָפֶנָה נָא. רַבִּי אוֹמֵר: תֵּאָפֶינָה נָאָה. רַבִּי דוֹסָא אוֹמֵר: תֵּאָפֶנָה רִיבָּה.

The Gemara notes that this dispute depends on another tannaitic dispute, as it was taught in a *baraita* that says with regard to the High Priest's griddle-cake offering: "And **baked pieces** [*tufinei*] of the meal-offering" (Leviticus 6:14). This word is interpreted as **it shall be baked when** it is already **half done** [*te'afena na*], meaning that it is fried before it is baked. **Rabbi** Yehuda HaNasi **says:** The word for baked pieces [*tufinei*] should be understood as meaning **it must be baked when** still **beautiful** [*te'afena na'a*],[H] i.e., before it is fried. **Rabbi Dosa says: It shall be baked in an amplified** manner, i.e., more than once.

אָתְיָין אִלֵּין פַּלְגְּוָותָא כְּהִינֵין פַּלְגְּוָותָא. מַאן דְּאָמַר תֵּאָפֶינָה נָאָה – כְּמַאן דְּאָמַר אוֹפָה וְאַחַר כָּךְ מְטַגְּנָהּ. וּמַאן דְּאָמַר תֵּאָפֶינָה נָא – כְּמַאן דְּאָמַר מְטַגְּנָהּ וְאַחַר כָּךְ אוֹפָה.

The Gemara explains: **These disputes follow,** i.e., match, **those disputes** mentioned earlier. **The one who says,** i.e., understands *tufinei* to mean that **it must be baked when** still **beautiful** [*te'afena na'a*] **is like the one who says** that **he** first **bakes it, and afterwards fries it. And the one who says** *tufinei* should be interpreted as baked **when half done** [*te'afena na*] **is like the one who says** that **he** first **fries it, and** only **afterward does he bake it.**

לֹא סוֹף דָּבָר שֶׁמֵּת? אֶלָּא אֲפִילוּ נִטְמָא.

The Gemara above cited the mishna in tractate *Menaḥot* that teaches that in the event of the death of the High Priest after having brought his morning griddle-cake offering, if another High Priest is appointed that same day, the successor brings one-tenth of an ephah of his own, divides it into two, and offers one half for the evening griddle-cake offering. The Gemara clarifies this matter: **Is this not the end of it,** that is to say, is the *halakha* not restricted to the case **where** the High Priest **died?**[N] **Rather, even if** he **became** ritually **impure** after having brought the morning griddle-cake offering, another High Priest must bring a whole one-tenth of an ephah, divide it into two equal portions, and then sacrifice one half as the evening griddle-cake offering. And all the more so is this true, in accordance with this ruling, if the first High Priest was permanently disqualified because he became disfigured by a blemish.

וַאֲפִילוּ נִדְחָה מִמּוּם.

The Gemara suggests an alternative: The mishna's ruling extends **even** to cases where the first High Priest is found **unfit because of a** permanent **blemish.** This scenario would require his successor to bring a new one-tenth of an ephah. However, in accordance with this ruling, temporary disqualification due to ritual impurity would not require the temporary High Priest to bring a separate meal-offering.

NOTES

They assigned whoever made the griddle-cake offerings to make griddle-cakes – הֶעֱמִידוּ עוֹשֵׂה חֲבִיתִּין לַעֲשׂוֹת חֲבִיתִּין: The griddle-cake offering was prepared prior to the removal of the ashes from the altar. The mishna in tractate *Tamid* does not state explicitly when the ashes were removed from the altar. According to Rashi (*Yoma* 20b) and *Tosafot* (*Yoma* 27b), the ashes were removed from the altar before the break of dawn, whereas according to the Rambam this took place only after daybreak. The Gemara indicates that the actual baking of the griddle-cake offering must take place during the day. According to the Rambam, this could still be possible before the removal of the ashes (Rambam *Sefer Avoda, Hilkhot Temidin UMusafin* 2:11; *Gevurat Yitzḥak*).

Is this not the end of it, where the High Priest died – לֹא סוֹף דָּבָר שֶׁמֵּת: Some explain that the Gemara's question: Is this not the end of it, means that not only is this the *halakha* when the High Priest died, but even when he became ritually impure; the question is whether the same is true in the case where he developed a permanent blemish. It then resolves its doubt based on the words of Rabbi Yehuda bar Pazzi of Bar Delaya, who states that the same *halakha* applies in the case where the High Priest developed a blemish (*Korban HaEida*; see Rambam *Sefer Avoda, Hilkhot Temidin UMusafin* 3:2).

HALAKHA

They assigned whoever made the griddle-cake offerings to make griddle-cakes – הֶעֱמִידוּ עוֹשֵׂה חֲבִיתִּין לַעֲשׂוֹת חֲבִיתִּין: In the morning, shortly before dawn, the priest appointed to this task would knock on the door of the Chamber of the Hearth, and the priests would open the door for him. He took the key and opened the small gate between the Chamber of the Hearth and the Temple courtyard, and entered the courtyard. The other priests went in after him, holding two torches. They divided into two groups, one going around the courtyard to the east and the other to the west. They would check the entire courtyard for anything irregular, until the two groups reached the Chamber of the Bakers of the Griddle-cake offerings. When both groups arrived there, they would declare to one another: Peace; everything is at peace. They then set the bakers of the griddle-cake offerings at their work, in accordance with the mishna (Rambam *Sefer Avoda, Hilkhot Beit HaBeḥira* 8:11).

Baked when half done [*te'afena na*]…baked when still beautiful [*te'afena na'a*] – תֵּאָפֶנָה נָא...תֵּאָפֶינָה נָאָה: Each of the loaves of the High Priest's griddle-cake offering would be baked somewhat and afterward fried in a frying pan with the remainder of its quarter-*log* of oil. The initial baking should be between fully baked and half-baked, as it says "*tufinei*." This is in accordance with the opinion of Rabbi Yosei, who is referred to as the one whose explanation is always with him, meaning, his opinions are always well justified (Rambam *Sefer Avoda, Hilkhot Ma'aseh HaKorbanot* 13:3; see *Kesef Mishne* there).

תָּנֵי רַבִּי יְהוּדָה בַּר פַּזִּי דְּבַר דְּלָיָה: וַאֲפִילּוּ נִדְחָה מִמּוּם.

Rabbi Yehuda bar Pazzi of Bar Delaya[B] **taught: Even** the first High Priest being found **unfit because of a** permanent **blemish** would require his successor to bring a new one-tenth of an ephah. However, if the first High Priest became ritually impure and only temporarily suspended from his position, the second High Priest may use the first High Priest's leftover half-tenth of an ephah for the evening griddle-cake offering.

מִנַּיִן לְכֹהֵן גָּדוֹל שֶׁמֵּת וְלֹא מִינּוּ אַחֵר תַּחְתָּיו שֶׁתְּהֵא מִנְחָתוֹ קְרֵיבָה מִשֶּׁל יוֹרְשִׁים? תַּלְמוּד לוֹמַר: "מִבָּנָיו יַעֲשֶׂה אוֹתָהּ". יָכוֹל יְבִיאֶנָּה לַחֲצָיִים – תַּלְמוּד לוֹמַר "אוֹתָהּ" – כּוּלָּהּ אָמַרְתִּי, דִּבְרֵי רַבִּי יְהוּדָה.

The mishna records a dispute among *tanna'im* with regard to the case of a High Priest who died. The first opinion is that until a new High Priest has been appointed, the griddle-cake offering is brought from public funds. Rabbi Yehuda disagrees, and argues that it should come from the property of the High Priest's heirs. The Gemara recounts a *baraita* about this issue: **From where is it derived that** if **the High Priest died and another** High Priest **had not** yet **been appointed in his place, that his meal-offering should be brought from** the property of **the** High Priest's **heirs? The verse states** with regard to this offering: "And the anointed priest that shall be in his stead **from among his sons shall bring it**" (Leviticus 6:15). That is to say, he sacrifices it from the property of the sons of the High Priest. I **might** have thought that the heirs **should bring** this meal-offering **in halves,** half in the morning and half in the evening, as it is ordinarily brought by the High Priest. Therefore, **the verse states:** "Shall bring **it**" (Leviticus 6:15); **I said** that he should bring **all of** it as a single offering, and not in halves. This is **the statement of Rabbi Yehuda.**

רַבִּי שִׁמְעוֹן אוֹמֵר: אֵינָהּ בָּאָה אֶלָּא מִשֶּׁל צִבּוּר, שֶׁנֶּאֱמַר "חֹק עוֹלָם" – מִי שֶׁהַבְּרִית כְּרוּתָה לוֹ.

Rabbi Shimon says: It comes only from public funds collected in the Temple treasury, **as it is stated:** "It is a **statute forever** to the Lord" (Leviticus 6:15), to be brought from **those with whom a covenant was made,**[N] i.e., from the community with whom God entered into a covenant.

"כָּלִיל תָּקְטָר" – כָּלִיל לְהַקְטָרָה.

The verse continues: **"It shall be wholly burnt,"** from which it may be derived that the griddle-cake offering is **to be burnt in its entirety.** In contrast to most meal-offerings, a handful of flour is not separated to be burned on the altar and no part of it is eaten by the priests, but rather the entire offering is burned on the altar.

"כֹּהֵן גָּדוֹל שֶׁמֵּת" וְכוּ'. רַבִּי בָּא בַּר מֶמֶל בְּעֵי: מְחַלְּפָה שִׁיטָּתֵיהּ דְּרַבִּי שִׁמְעוֹן, תַּמָּן אָמַר: מִשֶּׁל יוֹרְשִׁין, וְהָכָא אָמַר: מִשֶּׁל צִבּוּר!

Returning to the dispute with regard to a **High Priest who died, etc.,** whether the griddle-cake offering is brought from the his estate or comes from public funds, **Rabbi Ba bar Memel,** in the context of a parallel discussion (*Menaḥot* 51b), **raised a difficulty:** It would seem that the attribution of **the opinion of Rabbi Shimon is reversed. There,** that is, according to the mishna in *Shekalim*, **he says** that the original, Torah law was that the griddle-cake offering should be brought **from** the property of the late High Priest's **heirs.** This is indicated by the fact that according to Rabbi Shimon, the griddle-cake offering is brought from public funds only by rabbinic ordinance as a condition of the court, implying that prior to the institution of the ordinance, the *halakha* was that it be brought from the late High Priest's estate. **Whereas here,** that is, in the *baraita* above and in tractate *Menaḥot*, Rabbi Shimon **says** that by Torah law it comes **from public** funds, as according to his opinion it is derived from the wording of the Torah: "It is a statute forever."

אָמַר רַבִּי חִיָּיה

Rabbi Ḥiyya

BACKGROUND

Bar Delaya – בַּר דְּלָיָה: Rabbi Yehuda bar Pazzi and other Sages apparently lived in Bar Delaya. The name appears in the Jerusalem Talmud in several versions: Rav Delaya (*Shabbat* 1:5); Bardelaya (*Beitza* 4:4); and Barzila (*Megilla* 1:6). The place is identified today with the Arab village of Bardala, about 14 km south of Beit She'an.

Others identify Bar Delaya with the village of Beit Dali mentioned in the Mishna (*Yevamot* 16:7) or Badela, according to the reading of the Jerusalem Talmud, which was located along the road to Babylonia and is apparently the village of Dali near Ḥuran in the Golan Heights.

Bardala, Israel, as seen from Route 90

Golan Heights as seen from west of the Sea of Galilee

NOTES

Those with whom a covenant was made – מִי שֶׁהַבְּרִית כְּרוּתָה לוֹ: Early commentaries explain that Rabbi Shimon derives the *halakha* governing the griddle-cake offering from the *halakha* governing the shewbread, by way of a verbal analogy between two instances of the phrase, "a statute forever" [*ḥok olam*]. With regard to the griddle-cake offering it says: "And the anointed priest that shall be in his stead from among his sons shall bring it; it is a statute forever [*ḥok olam*] to the Lord" (Leviticus 6:15). With regard to the shewbread it says: "And it shall be for Aaron and his sons, and they shall eat it in a holy place; for it is most holy unto him of the offerings of the Lord made by fire, a statute forever [*ḥok olam*]" (Leviticus 24:9). Since with regard to the shewbread it says: "It is from the children of Israel, an everlasting covenant" (Leviticus 24:8), that is to say, the bread is brought from the children of Israel to Him Who entered into an everlasting covenant with them, so too the griddle-cake offering is brought from the children of Israel, i.e., from the communal treasury, in certain situations, e.g., where the High Priest died and a substitute had not yet been appointed in his place (Ra'avad, commentary to *Torat Kohanim*).

בַּר בָּא: וְלָא יָאוּת הוּא מַקְשֶׁה?

bar Ba said: Isn't the difficulty raised by Rabbi Ba bar Memel **legitimate?**[N]

אֲתָא רַבִּי יַעֲקֹב בַּר אָחָא רַבִּי אַבָּהוּ בְּשֵׁם רַבִּי יוֹחָנָן: דְּבַר תּוֹרָה הוּא שֶׁתְּהֵא בָּאָה מִן הַצִּבּוּר. הָיִיתִי אוֹמֵר יִגְבּוּ לָהּ (מִן הַיּוֹרְשִׁין) – הִתְקִינוּ שֶׁתְּהֵא בָּאָה מִתְּרוּמַת הַלִּשְׁכָּה.

The Gemara answers that when **Rabbi Yaakov bar Aḥa came,** he said that **Rabbi Abbahu** said **in the name of Rabbi Yoḥanan:** In the case where the High Priest has died and not yet been replaced, **by Torah law,** the griddle-cake offering **comes from public** funds, as is derived from the words: "It is a statute forever." Rabbi Shimon did not mean to imply otherwise. As it is not a public offering but the High Priest's personal one, **I might have said** that it should be **collected from the heirs'** property. Therefore, to ensure compliance with the Torah law, the Sages **instituted that it should come from the collection of the** Temple treasury **chamber.**

רַבִּי יוֹסֵה אָמַר רַבִּי יוֹחָנָן בָּעֵי: מַהוּ שְׁלֵימָה בְּשַׁחֲרִית וּשְׁלֵימָה בֵּין הָעַרְבַּיִם? אוֹ שְׁלֵימָה בְּשַׁחֲרִית וּבְטֵילָה בֵּין הָעַרְבַּיִם?

§ The mishna taught that a griddle-cake offering that was brought in the interim between the tenures of two High Priests was not brought in halves, morning and evening. Instead, a whole one-tenth of an ephah was sacrificed. **Rabbi Yosei said** that **Rabbi Yoḥanan raised a dilemma: What** does this mean? Is a **whole** one-tenth of an ephah brought **in the morning, and** then a **whole** one-tenth of an ephah again **in the evening?**[N] **Or** was a **whole** one-tenth of an ephah brought **in the morning,** and since they already brought one-tenth of an ephah that day, it **was canceled in the evening?**

כַּד תְּהֵא פְּשִׁיטָא לֵיהּ, דִּכְתִיב "מִנְחַת תָּמִיד".

When that question **was resolved for him,** it gave rise to other questions. The original question was resolved by reference to the verse, **as it is written:** "This is the offering of Aaron and of his sons, which they shall offer unto the Lord in the day when he is anointed: The tenth part of an ephah of fine flour for a **meal-offering perpetually,** half of it in the morning, and half thereof in the evening" (Leviticus 6:13). The word "perpetually" indicates that the griddle-cake offering is always brought both in the morning and in the evening.

שְׁלֹשֶׁת לוּגִּין מַה הֵן, שְׁלֹשֶׁת לוּגִּין שַׁחֲרִית וּשְׁלֹשֶׁת לוּגִּין בֵּין הָעַרְבַּיִם, אוֹ לוֹג וּמֶחֱצָה שַׁחֲרִית וְלוֹג וּמֶחֱצָה בֵּין הָעַרְבַּיִם?

A further question: **What is** the *halakha* with regard to the **three** ***log*** of oil that the High Priest would bring every day together with his griddle-cake offering, half in the morning and half in the evening? Is the *halakha* with regard to the oil the same, i.e., that **three** ***log*** of oil were brought in the **morning and three** ***log*** of oil were brought again **in the evening? Or** was only **a** ***log*** **and a half** brought in the **morning and** another ***log*** **and a half** brought **in the evening?**

אָמַר רַבִּי חִזְקִיָּה: אוּף הָדָא צְרִיכָה לֵיהּ: שְׁנֵי קוֹמְצִין מַה הֵן, שְׁנֵי קוֹמְצִין בְּשַׁחֲרִית וּשְׁנֵי קוֹמְצִין בֵּין הָעַרְבַּיִם, אוֹ קוֹמֶץ אַחַת בְּשַׁחֲרִית וְקוֹמֶץ אַחַת בֵּין הָעַרְבַּיִם.

Rabbi Ḥizkiya said that Rabbi Yoḥanan **also wonders about this: What is** the *halakha* with regard to the **two handfuls** of frankincense that were ordinarily brought every day together with the High Priest's griddle-cake offering, one with the morning offering and the other together with the evening offering? Is the *halakha* with regard to the frankincense the same as that of the griddle-cake offering, i.e., that **two handfuls** of frankincense were brought **in the morning and two handfuls** of frankincense were brought again **in the evening? Or** was only **one handful** brought **in the morning and one handful** brought **in the evening?**

אָמַר רַבִּי יוֹסֵה: כְּלוּם לָמְדוּ לְקוֹמֶץ – לֹא מִמִּנְחַת חוֹטֵא, מַה לְהַלָּן שְׁנֵי קוֹמְצִין – אַף כָּאן שְׁנֵי קוֹמְצִין.

Rabbi Yosei said: Didn't they learn (18b) that the amount of frankincense brought along with a meal-offering must be **a handful** by way of analogy **to** the handful of flour that must be taken **from a sinner's meal-offering?** This being the case, the *halakha* in the issue under discussion should also be learned from the *halakha* governing meal-offerings in general. **Just as there,** when the quantity of flour is doubled **two handfuls** of frankincense are required, **here too,** since two-tenths of an ephah are brought, the measure of the frankincense must also be doubled, that is to say, **two handfuls** are required.

NOTES

Isn't the difficulty legitimate – וְלָא יָאוּת הוּא מַקְשֶׁה: This sentence can be understood in two different ways. The first is that Rabbi Ḥiyya bar Ba posed this as a question, expressing his agreement with the question raised by Rabbi Ba bar Memel. What he meant is: Is there anybody who says that Rabbi Ba bar Memel did not ask a proper question? The alternative is that it is an assertion that Rabbi Ba bar Memel did not ask a good question, as in Rabbi Ḥiyya bar Ba's opinion there is no contradiction. This is immediately explained in the Gemara (*Korban HaEida*, second explanation).

A whole one-tenth in the morning and a whole one-tenth in the evening – שְׁלֵימָה בְּשַׁחֲרִית וּשְׁלֵימָה בֵּין הָעַרְבַּיִם: The later commentaries disagree with regard to the manner in which this whole one-tenth of an ephah was brought. Some suggest that the whole one-tenth was not sacrificed in the same way as the half-tenth brought by the High Priest himself. The High Priest would bring twelve loaves made from one-tenth of an ephah of flour, divide them into two, and sacrifice six loaves in the morning and six loaves in the evening. But when a whole one-tenth of an ephah was brought in the morning and a whole one-tenth of an ephah was brought in the evening, twelve loaves would be sacrificed on each occasion (*Tiferet Yisrael*). Others say that the whole one-tenth was brought in the same way as the half-tenth: in both cases six loaves were brought in the morning and six loaves were brought in the evening, though obviously if it was from a whole tenth, the loaves were twice the size (*Minḥat Ḥinukh*).

(מַה תַּמָּן צְרִיכָה לֵיהּ אַף הָכָא צְרִיכָה לֵיהּ).

The Gemara rejects this proof: Whether the measure of frankincense is doubled when a meal-offering is doubled is not completely clear: **Just as there,** with regard to meal-offerings in general, **he requires** a resolution, i.e., he does not know the answer as to whether a double measure of frankincense is required when the quantity of flour is doubled, **so too here,** with regard to the High Priest's griddle-cake offering, **he requires** a resolution as to whether a double measure is required.

אָמַר רַבִּי חִזְקִיָּה: כְּלוּם לָמְדוּ שְׁלֹשֶׁת לוּגִּין לֹא מִתָּמִיד שֶׁל בֵּין הָעַרְבַּיִם. מַה לְהַלָּן שְׁלֹשֶׁת לוּגִּין – אַף כָּאן שְׁלֹשֶׁת לוּגִּין.

Rabbi Ḥizkiya addresses the previous question about the three *log* of oil brought as part of the High Priest's griddle-cake offering. He **said: Didn't they learn** that **three** *log* of oil must be brought along with the griddle-cake offering **from the daily evening offering,** as this is the measure of oil that must be brought as part of this offering? Accordingly, **just as there,** in the case of the daily evening offering the measure of oil is **three** *log* per one-tenth of an ephah of flour, **so too** in the case where the griddle-cake offering is brought from a whole one-tenth of an ephah, it is accompanied by **three** *log* of oil both in the morning and in the evening.

וּמַה תַּמָּן צְרִיכָה לֵיהּ – אַף כָּאן צְרִיכָה לֵיהּ.

The Gemara rejects this proof as well: **And just as there,** when the daily meal offering is doubled **he requires** a resolution with regard to the measure of oil, **here too** with regard to the High Priest's griddle-cake offering, **he requires** a resolution as to whether only the original three *log* are brought, or whether three *log* are brought for each measure of one-tenth of an ephah of flour.

שֶׁלֹּא יִהְיֶה כו׳. רַבִּי שִׁמְעוֹן בַּר נַחְמָן בְּשֵׁם רַבִּי יוֹנָתָן: בְּדִין הָיָה שֶׁיִּמְעֲלוּ בָהּ, וְהֵן גָּזְרוּ שֶׁלֹּא יִמְעֲלוּ בָהּ.

§ The mishna taught that one who derives benefit from the ashes of a red heifer **is not** liable for misusing property consecrated to the Temple. **Rabbi Shimon bar Naḥman** said **in the name of Rabbi Yonatan: By** Torah **law** one **should be liable for misusing it,** i.e., the ashes of a red heifer, as it is consecrated to the Temple, **but** the Sages **decreed that one is not liable.**

וְהָא תָּנֵי: ״חַטָּאת״ – מְלַמֵּד שֶׁמּוֹעֲלִין בָּהּ! – בָּהּ מוֹעֲלִין וְאֵין מוֹעֲלִין בְּאֶפְרָהּ.

This, however, is difficult, **as it was taught** otherwise in the following *baraita*: With regard to a red heifer, the verse states: "It is **a sin-offering**" (Numbers 19:9), which **teaches** that a red heifer is treated like a sin-offering in that **one is liable for misusing** consecrated property **with it,** i.e., the animal itself. Only **with it,** the animal itself, is one **liable**[N] **for misusing** consecrated property, **but he is not liable for misusing** consecrated property **with its ashes.**[N] Therefore, it is clear from the *baraita* that by Torah law one is not liable for misusing the ashes of a red heifer.

NOTES

With it is one liable – בָּהּ מוֹעֲלִין: In the parallel passage in the Babylonian Talmud (*Menaḥot* 51b), *Tosafot* write that the word: Sin-offering was not needed to derive the that a red heifer is subject to the *halakhot* of misusing consecrated property. Rather, it was only meant to teach that there can be further liability for misusing the red heifer even after it had already been misused. Since a red heifer is considered property consecrated for Temple maintenance, there was no need to teach that it is subject to the *halakhot* of misuse, as all property consecrated for Temple maintenance is subject to those *halakhot*. However, it was necessary to teach that it is subject to the *halakhot* of misuse after misuse, in contrast to ordinary property consecrated for Temple maintenance for which the first misuse already removes it from its sacred status. This is not true of property consecrated to the altar, for there the misuse does not remove the property from its sacred status, and so the second misuse was also performed on consecrated property.

Some later commentaries argue that the derivation was needed to teach that a red heifer is subject to the *halakhot* of misuse, as without it one might have thought that a red heifer is not even considered property consecrated for Temple maintenance. It is only a means for purification, and so it should be treated like public ritual baths, which do not have the sanctity of property consecrated to the Temple treasury (*Sefat Emet*; Rabbi Yitzḥak Ze'ev Soloveitchik; *Korban Aharon*; *Ḥazon Ish*).

As for the assumption in *Tosafot* that a red heifer is considered property consecrated to the Temple treasury, the later commentaries discuss at length whether a red heifer is considered property consecrated for Temple maintenance or property consecrated to the altar. Some distinguish between its status before it is slaughtered, when it has only the sanctity of property consecrated for Temple maintenance and consequently can be redeemed, and its status after it is slaughtered, when it is considered property consecrated to the altar and consequently can no longer be redeemed (Rabbi Yitzḥak Ze'ev Soloveitchik).

But he is not liable for misusing consecrated property with its ashes – וְאֵין מוֹעֲלִין בְּאֶפְרָהּ: The Gemara here mentions only the word sin-offering, but elsewhere (*Menaḥot* 52a) it brings the full derivation, which is based on the word: It. *Tosafot* in *Menaḥot* ask: Given the general principle that the ashes of consecrated objects are permitted (*Temura* 34a), why is it necessary to derive from the word: It, that the status of the ashes of a red heifer differs from that of the red heifer itself, such that by Torah law they are not subject to the *halakhot* of misusing consecrated property? They explain that the principle applies only to cases where the burning of the consecrated object was a case of misuse of consecrated property, so that it reverted to a non-sacred state. In the case of a red heifer, however, the burning of the animal is not a case of misuse of consecrated property, and the ashes ought not to become non-sacred. A special derivation from the word: It, is consequently required to teach that they nevertheless do become non-sacred.

Tosafot add that the special derivation might be required for another reason: One might have thought that the ashes of the red heifer are different from the ashes of other consecrated property, since they come into being through a mitzva. The nature of the red heifer is that it is designated to be reduced to ashes through burning, and one might have thought that its sanctity would be preserved in its ashes. *Tosafot* further distinguish between other ashes, where the mitzva associated with them has already been completed, and the ashes of a red heifer, where the mitzva associated with them has not yet been performed, namely, to be mixed with water and sprinkled on the ritually impure as part of the purification process.

אָמַר רַבִּי אַבָּהוּ: בָּרִאשׁוֹנָה הָיוּ מִשְׁתַּקְשְׁקִין בָּהּ וְנוֹתְנִין אוֹתָהּ עַל גַּבֵּי מַכּוֹתֵיהֶן, וְגָזְרוּ שֶׁיִּמְעֲלוּ בָּהּ. כֵּיוָן שֶׁנִּגְדְּרוּ – גָּזְרוּ שֶׁלֹּא יִמְעֲלוּ בָּהּ.

Rabbi Abbahu said: Indeed, there is no liability by Torah law for misusing the ashes of a red heifer. **At first,** however, the priests would treat the sanctity of the ashes lightly and **would clean themselves** [*mishtakshekin*][N] **with them and** even **apply them to their wounds**[N] as medicine. **And** the Sages therefore **decreed that one becomes liable for misusing** consecrated property **with them,** the ashes.[N] But **when** they saw that the priests **restrained themselves** and no longer used the ashes for anything except purification water, the Sages reverted to the Torah law and **decreed that one does not become liable for misusing** consecrated property if he derives benefit from a red heifer's ashes.[N]

וְעַל הַקִּינִּין כו׳.

§ The mishna taught, **with regard to** the replacements for **disqualified pairs** of bird-offerings, that they should come from public funds. Rabbi Yosei disagreed and said that whoever supplies all the pairs of bird-offerings to the Temple must also supply, at no extra charge, the replacements for the disqualified birds. Having mentioned the pairs of bird-offerings, the Gemara repeats the discussion from earlier in the chapter. The mishna there (19a) taught that if money was found between the horn marked pairs of bird-offerings and the horn marked doves for burnt-offerings, it is allocated to doves for burnt-offerings, and is used exclusively for that purpose.

הָאִשָּׁה הַזֹּאת בַּמֶּה הִיא מִתְכַּפֶּרֶת?

The Gemara asks: If so, **how does this woman,** who had placed the money for her offering in the horn marked pairs of bird-offerings, **achieve atonement?** A woman who gave birth or is a *zava* must bring a pair of bird-offerings, one as a burnt-offering and the other as a sin-offering, as part of her purification process. If that money has now been allocated to doves for burnt-offerings, she has not completed the process.

אָמַר רַבִּי יִצְחָק: תְּנַאי בֵּית דִּין הוּא: הַמְסַפֵּק אֶת הַקִּינִּין הוּא מְסַפֵּק אֶת הַפְּסוּלוֹת וְאֶת הָאוֹבְדוֹת.

Rabbi Yitzḥak said: It is a condition of the court that whoever **supplies** the Temple with **the pairs** of birds, **he** also **supplies** extra birds to replace those birds that are **disqualified or lost.** Therefore, in any event the woman will have brought both a burnt-offering and a sin-offering.

הדרן עלך מעות שנמצאו

NOTES

They would clean themselves [*mishtakshekin*] – הָיוּ מִשְׁתַּקְשְׁקִין: This word denotes washing, cleaning, and scouring (see *Bereishit Rabba, Vayeitzei* 69:5). It may be derived from the word *shikhshukh*, which is referring to moving a part of the body or an object in water.

And apply them to their wounds – וְנוֹתְנִין אוֹתָהּ עַל גַּבֵּי מַכּוֹתֵיהֶן: Rav Ashi (*Menaḥot* 52a) maintains that applying ashes to a wound is permitted even though it might appear to involve a prohibition, as the ashes may look like a tattoo and consequently be included in the prohibition: "You shall not make any cuttings in your flesh for the dead, nor imprint any marks upon you" (Leviticus 19:28; *Makkot* 21a). This is because it is clearly evident that the ashes are being applied for a healing purpose. However, although applying the ashes of the red heifer on wounds was technically permitted, it smacked of disrespect for consecrated objects (*Tosafot* on *Menaḥot* 52a).

The Sages decreed that one becomes liable for misusing with them – גָּזְרוּ שֶׁיִּמְעֲלוּ בָּהּ: The early authorities (on *Menaḥot* 52a) disagree with regard to the nature of this decree. Some say that when the Sages saw that people were treating the ashes of a red heifer lightly, they decreed that the ashes are subject to the *halakhot* of misusing consecrated property, even though according to Torah law they are not subject to these *halakhot* (Rashi). Others maintain that the Sages decreed that the ashes are consecrated with sanctity that inheres in their value. Once this consecration is in effect, one who derives benefit from the ashes is liable by Torah law for misusing consecrated property (*Shita Mekubbetzet*, citing Rashi).

They decreed that one does not become liable…from the ashes – גָּזְרוּ שֶׁלֹּא יִמְעֲלוּ בָּהּ: In the wake of the rabbinic decree, not only did people stop using the ashes for medicinal purposes, they even began to avoid using the ashes to purify doubtful cases of ritual impurity, lest they misuse them. When the Sages saw that their decree had undesirable consequences, they canceled it and reverted to the Torah law, according to which the ashes of a red heifer are not subject to the *halakhot* of misusing consecrated property (Rambam's Commentary on the Mishna, *Shekalim*). Later commentaries note that this conclusion may be applied to other rabbinic decrees, so that if the Sages issued a certain decree for some reason, and the decree achieved its purpose so that the reason was no longer relevant, there is room for the Sages to cancel the decree as it is no longer needed (*Korban Aharon*).

Summary of **Perek VII**

This chapter dealt primarily with questions that arise when an object is found and its status needs to be determined. The chapter began with a discussion of money found between different collection horns; the Gemara determined where it should be allocated based on proximity, while in cases where the proximate source cannot easily be established the money is treated in accordance with the more stringent possibility. A similar question arose with regard to money found in the city of Jerusalem. As the site of the Temple, a large portion of the money reaching the city was consecrated money, and this must be taken into account. Similarly, the question of both animals and pieces of meat found either in Jerusalem or its proximity was addressed, with attention to the fact that in and around the Temple these were likely to be consecrated. The discussion then proceeded to touch on the general case of found foodstuffs, both with regard to whether the finder can take possession of them and whether he can assume that they are kosher.

In this context, the Gemara also addressed the issue of kosher meat that has been left unobserved, such that it is at least possible that it was replaced with non-kosher meat. Some authorities were very stringent with regard to such meat, even when there is no reasonable concern that the meat is not kosher, while others were lenient when it is reasonable to assume that the meat is kosher and belongs to a Jew.

Another topic that was dealt with at length in this chapter is that of a wafer-offering, the special meal-offering brought each day by the High Priest. This offering occupies a unique position in that, on the one hand, it is a personal obligation of the High Priest, while, on the other hand, it is a general communal obligation as part of the fixed sacrificial service in the Temple. When a High Priest dies, and his successor has yet to be appointed, the question arises as to how this offering is brought and who is responsible for it. The Gemara also considered the extent to which the manner of sacrificing the wafer-offering is affected by these circumstances.

Introduction to **Perek VIII**

This chapter focuses on matters of ritual purity. In a sense, it continues a theme from the previous chapter in that it begins with a discussion of found items, though here it is with regard to their status as ritually pure or impure. From there the Gemara addresses the difficulties involved given that many people in Jerusalem needed to remain ritually pure in order to enter the Temple, yet they lived alongside others who were impure. Since it was not always possible to know who was pure and who was impure, the Gemara also deals with questions of contact with other people and objects whose status with regard to ritual impurity is unclear.

The Gemara then proceeds to discuss how to relate to consecrated items or the flesh of offerings that have become impure. With regard to vessels and the like, the question is whether to purify them on Temple grounds or outside; with regard to the flesh of offerings, the question is whether to burn them in the Temple or outside it. There is an additional discussion regarding the places where the parts of the offerings are placed before they are put on the altar to be burnt.

Eventually the Gemara returns to the main theme of this tractate and raises the question of what to do with funds collected as shekels and other Temple donations once the Temple was destroyed. One part of this discussion focuses on funds consecrated while the Temple still stood that remained after the destruction. The chapter, and the entire tractate, closes with the topic of consecration of money or objects in the present day, as they cannot be used in the absence of the Temple. The Gemara considers the extent to which such consecrations are effective and, when they are, whether one should refrain entirely from imparting sanctity to objects, money, and animals, as people are liable to misuse them.

הלכה א מתני׳ כָּל הָרוּקִּין הַנִּמְצָאִין בִּירוּשָׁלַיִם טְהוֹרִין, חוּץ מִשֶּׁל שׁוּק הָעֶלְיוֹן, דִּבְרֵי רַבִּי מֵאִיר.

HALAKHA 1 · MISHNA The mishna discusses the ritual purity of items found either in the Temple or in Jerusalem and its environs, in continuation of the previous chapter's discussion of found money, animals, or meat. **All the spittle**[N] **that is found in Jerusalem**[H] **is ritually pure.**[N] Since neither ritually impure people nor gentiles were commonly present in Jerusalem, the Sages decreed an exception to the rule that spittle that is found is ritually impure since it presumably comes from one of those groups. This is the case **except for** spittle found **in the upper marketplace,** where gentiles and ritually impure Jews were likely to be present. This is **the statement of Rabbi Meir.**

רַבִּי יוֹסֵי אוֹמֵר: בִּשְׁאָר כָּל יְמוֹת הַשָּׁנָה, שֶׁבָּאֶמְצַע – טְמֵאִין, שֶׁבַּצְּדָדִין – טְהוֹרִין. וּבִשְׁעַת הָרֶגֶל – שֶׁבָּאֶמְצַע טְהוֹרִין שֶׁבַּצְּדָדִין – טְמֵאִין, מִפְּנֵי שֶׁהַמּוּעוּטִין מִסְתַּלְּקִין לַצְּדָדִין.

Rabbi Yosei says: On all the other days of the year, i.e., any day that is not on one of the three pilgrim Festivals, Passover, *Shavuot*, and *Sukkot*, spittle **that** is found **in the middle** of the street **is ritually impure,** and spittle **that** is found on **the sides** of the street **is ritually pure.** According to Rabbi Yosei, it was common for people who were ritually impure to be present in the streets of Jerusalem. They would be careful to walk in the middle of the street, while the ritually pure who wished to remain so would walk on the sides. Therefore, it is reasonable to presume that spittle found in the middle of the street is from one who is impure, while spittle found on the side of the street is from one who is pure. **But during the time of the Festival,** when most of the people in Jerusalem were there for the Festival and were ritually pure, the spittle found **in the middle** of the street was **ritually pure,** and that found on **the sides** of the street was **ritually impure.** The difference is **due to** the fact **that** at the time of the Festival, **the** ritually impure **minority moves to the sides** of the streets.

כָּל הַכֵּלִים הַנִּמְצָאִין בִּירוּשָׁלַיִם דֶּרֶךְ יְרִידָה לְבֵית הַטְּבִילָה – טְמֵאִין, וְדֶרֶךְ עֲלִיָּה – טְהוֹרִין, שֶׁלֹּא כִּירִידָתָן עֲלִיָּיתָן, דִּבְרֵי רַבִּי מֵאִיר. רַבִּי יוֹסֵי אוֹמֵר: כּוּלָּן טְהוֹרִין, חוּץ מִן הַסַּל וְהַמַּגְרֵיפָה וְהַמְּרִיצָה הַמְיוּחָדִין לַקְּבָרוֹת.

The mishna continues: **All the vessels that are found in Jerusalem**[N] on the **way down into the bathhouse,** wherein one purifies vessels in a ritual bath, are **ritually impure, and** those that are found on the **way up**[N] are **ritually pure.** The mishna explains: **Their descent** into the bathhouse **is not** by the same route **as their ascent** out of it, and it can be assumed that those found on the way down have not yet been immersed, while those found on the way up have been. This is **the statement of Rabbi Meir.** However, **Rabbi Yosei says: They are all ritually pure, except for the basket, and the shovel,**[B] **and the *meritza*,**[B] **which are specifically used for graves,** to gather up the bones of the dead. These tools must be presumed to be ritually impure, but in general, vessels are presumed to be pure.

HALAKHA

Spittle that is found in Jerusalem – הָרוּקִּין הַנִּמְצָאִין בִּירוּשָׁלַיִם: The Sages decreed that on any day of the year besides the pilgrim Festivals, spittle found in the middle of the streets of Jerusalem is impure like spittle found anywhere else. However, spittle found on the side of the street is ritually pure, since those who were vigilant about the *halakhot* of ritual purity would walk on the sides of the street in order not to be rendered ritually impure by coming into contact with an *am ha'aretz*, who was not so careful. During the pilgrim Festivals, spittle found in the middle of Jerusalem's streets is ritually pure, for all the Jews are ritually pure during the Festival and they walk down the middle of the street. Spittle found on the sides of the streets is impure, for those who are ritually impure are the minority, and therefore they walk on the sides of the street. This ruling is in accordance with Rabbi Yosei's opinion (Rambam *Sefer Tahara, Hilkhot She'ar Avot HaTumot* 13:8).

BACKGROUND

Shovel – מַגְרֵיפָה: This is referring to several possible tools. When it is associated with a basket, as it is here, it means a shovel with a wide head and a long handle, held in both hands, used for digging as well as the collection of bones for burial. It was additionally used to shovel dried figs (Rashi, *Shabbat* 122b). This shovel could be made of metal or wood.

***Meritza* – מְרִיצָּה:** In modern Hebrew, a *meritza* is a wheelbarrow, but that is not what the Gemara is referring to here. In this context, *meritza* means a tool similar to a pickax, also called a dolabra, with which one could extract large stones and then push them into place to close a burial cave.

Roman dolabras

NOTES

All the spittle – כָּל הָרוּקִּין: The mishna (*Teharot* 4:5) explains that the Sages decreed that spittle found in the markets and streets is ritually impure out of concern that it came from people who were ritually impure as a result of impurity due to bodily emissions, i.e., a *zav*, a *zava*, a menstruating woman, and a woman after childbirth. Similarly, the Sages decreed that a gentile has the impurity of a *zav* or *zava*, even though biblically there is no ritual impurity for gentiles. The Sages also decreed that the spittle of an *am ha'aretz* must be avoided, as he cannot be expected to be careful about ritual impurity. The spittle found in Jerusalem has a different status, as the Gemara explains.

Spittle that is found in Jerusalem is ritually pure – הָרוּקִּין הַנִּמְצָאִין בִּירוּשָׁלַיִם טְהוֹרִין: This leniency is based upon the fact that only a minority of the people in Jerusalem were ritually impure. In other places, the impure were presumably also a minority; nevertheless, the Sages decreed ritual impurity on spittle found in any other place, since there was a significant minority who were impure (*Tosafot*, *Avoda Zara* 40b, s.v. *kol hatzelamim*). In Jerusalem the impure were an insignificant minority, as one who was classified as a *zav* would refrain from entering the city. Furthermore, although a significant minority of women were impure due to menstruation, women did not frequent the streets and markets, as "all the glory of the king's daughter is on the inside" (Psalms 45:14; *Tiferet Yisrael*).

The vessels that are found in Jerusalem – הַכֵּלִים הַנִּמְצָאִין בִּירוּשָׁלַיִם: The mishna (*Teharot* 4:5) explains that the Sages decreed that all vessels found in the markets and streets are ritually impure, out of concern that they had been rendered impure by contact with a corpse. The streets of Jerusalem are an exception to this rule.

The way down …and the way up – דֶּרֶךְ יְרִידָה...וְדֶרֶךְ עֲלִיָּה: Some explain that vessels that had already been immersed would be positioned in a different manner than those that had not. According to this interpretation, Rabbi Meir's statement that their descent into the bathhouse is not the same as their ascent out of it is referring to the vessels' position (*Me'iri*). Others explain that there were two paths into the bathhouse: The entrance, or way down, for the impure, and the exit, or way up, for those who had already immersed themselves. This would help ensure that the ritually pure would avoid coming into contact with the impure. According to this reading, Rabbi Meir's statement is referring to the distinct entrances and exits (Rosh; Rav Yehuda ben Rav Binyamin HaRofeh; Rabbi Ovadya Bartenura).

Ancient ritual bath in Jerusalem with two openings

סַכִּין שֶׁנִּמְצֵאת בְּאַרְבָּעָה עָשָׂר – שׁוֹחֵט בָּהּ מִיָּד. בִּשְׁלֹשָׁה עָשָׂר – שׁוֹנֶה וּמַטְבִּיל.

The mishna continues with another ruling about ritual purity: One may **slaughter immediately with a knife that was found**[N] **on the fourteenth**[HN] of Nisan, i.e., the day the Paschal lamb is slaughtered, and need not be concerned that it is ritually impure. Presumably it was immersed the day before so that it could be used to slaughter the Paschal offering. If he found it **on the thirteenth**[H] of Nisan, he **immerses it again.**[N] Perhaps its owners had not yet immersed it, since they still had time to do so before the evening.

קוֹפִיץ – בָּזֶה וּבָזֶה שׁוֹנֶה וּמַטְבִּיל. חָל אַרְבָּעָה עָשָׂר לִהְיוֹת בַּשַּׁבָּת – שׁוֹחֵט בָּהּ מִיָּד.

If one finds a **cleaver** [*kofitz*],[L] which is used to slaughter an animal and break its bones, whether it was **on this** day, i.e., the fourteenth, or **on that** day, i.e., the thirteenth, **he immerses it again**[N] out of doubt. Since breaking the bones of the Paschal lamb is prohibited, its owners would have no need for it on the fourteenth, and it cannot be presumed that it has already been immersed to make it ritually pure. However, if the **fourteenth occurs on Shabbat,** he may **slaughter with** the cleaver **immediately.** Since immersing a vessel is prohibited on Shabbat, and presumably the owner of the cleaver wants it to be ritually pure on the fifteenth, one can assume that he immersed it already on Friday, the thirteenth of Nisan. It is therefore ritually pure.

HALAKHA

The vessels that are found in Jerusalem…a knife that was found on the fourteenth – הַכֵּלִים הַנִּמְצָאִין בִּירוּשָׁלַיִם...סַכִּין שֶׁנִּמְצֵאת בְּאַרְבָּעָה עָשָׂר: All the vessels that are found in Jerusalem are ritually pure, even if they were found on the way down to the place of immersion, except for vessels used to deal with the bones of a corpse. The Sages decreed that vessels found in Jerusalem are ritually pure except for knives used to slaughter offerings, due to the gravity with which offerings are regarded. However, if the knife is found on the fourteenth of Nisan, it can be used to slaughter an offering immediately, even if the fourteenth of Nisan occurs on Shabbat, as the Sages did not decree knives found on the fourteenth of Nisan to be ritually impure. This ruling is in accordance with Rabbi Yosei's opinion (Rambam *Sefer Tahara, Hilkhot She'ar Avot HaTumot* 13:5; Ra'avad; *Kesef Mishne*).

A knife that was found…on the thirteenth – סַכִּין שֶׁנִּמְצֵאת...בִּשְׁלֹשָׁה עָשָׂר: If one finds a knife on the thirteenth of Nisan, one sprinkles purification water on it and immerses it before using it. According to the Ra'avad, there is no need to sprinkle it; it is sufficient just to immerse it (Rambam *Sefer Tahara, Hilkhot She'ar Avot HaTumot* 13:6).

LANGUAGE

Cleaver [*kofitz*] – קוֹפִיץ: From the Greek κοπίς, *kopis*, a person, tool, or machine that chops. Typically, it is a large knife used to slice or chop up hard items.

A large chopping knife, or cleaver, used to cut meat

NOTES

A knife that was found – סַכִּין שֶׁנִּמְצֵאת: The *Me'iri* (*Pesaḥim* 70a) explains why the principle that vessels found in Jerusalem are presumed to be pure does not apply to knives: Since most vessels are carried together in a bag or a basket, people ensure that they are ritually pure so that they do not render one another impure. Knives are generally not carried together in a basket with other vessels, so it is conceivable that one would not takes pains to ensure that a knife does not become impure.

One may slaughter immediately with a knife that was found on the fourteenth – סַכִּין שֶׁנִּמְצֵאת בְּאַרְבָּעָה עָשָׂר שׁוֹחֵט בָּהּ מִיָּד: After immersion, a person or a vessel does not become fully pure until the conclusion of the day upon which the immersion took place. Until dark such a person is called a *tevul yom*, i.e., one who immersed that day. By Torah law, one who immersed himself that day does not render items fully impure, in that they cannot subsequently render other things impure, but he does render them unfit for consecrated use. However, the Sages decreed that one who immersed that day does render items impure. According to the opinion of Abba Shaul, he confers first-degree ritual impurity, and according to the opinion of the Rabbis, he confers second-degree impurity (*Me'ila* 8a).

A knife that was found on the fourteenth of Nisan can be presumed to have been immersed by its owners the day before, so that it will become ritually pure at nightfall of the thirteenth, enabling its use in time for the slaughtering of the Paschal lamb on the fourteenth. If the knife were found on the thirteenth, there are no grounds for such a presumption. The owners may not yet have immersed it, as there is still time left to do so before sunset.

He immerses it again – שׁוֹנֶה וּמַטְבִּיל: The Rambam explains that this phrase means to sprinkle purification water on the knife to remove any possible ritual impurity imparted from a corpse, and then to immerse it. In his opinion, the instruction could not mean merely to immerse it again, since the motivation for immersing at all is the presumption that it has not yet been immersed.

A cleaver…whether it was on this day or on that day, he immerses it again – קוֹפִיץ בָּזֶה וּבָזֶה שׁוֹנֶה וּמַטְבִּיל: Since it is prohibited to break the bones of the Paschal lamb, there is no presumption that the cleaver was immersed in time for use on the fourteenth. The Gemara (*Pesaḥim* 70a–b) asks: Since it was customary to bring a Festival peace-offering along with the Paschal lamb to ensure that there was enough meat to satisfy the entire group, and it is permitted to break the bones of a Festival peace-offering, why do we not presume that a cleaver found on the fourteenth was purified in order to use it to cut up the Festival peace-offering?

The Gemara there offers two answers: First, it answers that the mishna is in accordance with the opinion of ben Teima that the Festival peace-offering of the fourteenth takes on some of the *halakhot* of the Paschal lamb and it is forbidden to break its bones as well.

Second, the Gemara points out that even if one subscribes to the Rabbis' opinion, that a Festival peace-offering on the fourteenth is no different from any other Festival peace-offering and its bones may be broken, there are two overlapping doubts with regard to whether the owner of the cleaver would sacrifice a Festival peace-offering. First, the owner's group may not require an additional offering if it is small enough that the Paschal lamb will suffice. Second, it is possible that most of the populace will become impure; this would be the case if, for example, the *Nasi* would die and everyone was obligated to occupy themselves with his burial. In such a situation, the Paschal lamb is nevertheless sacrificed, but it is prohibited to add the Festival peace-offering, since it may not be offered when one is impure. In such a case of two overlapping doubts, it cannot be presumed that there would be a Festival peace-offering and that therefore the cleaver was immersed on the thirteenth.

בַּחֲמִשָּׁה עָשָׂר שׁוֹחֵט בָּהּ מִיָּד. נִמְצְאָה קְשׁוּרָה לַסַּכִּין – הֲרֵי הִיא כַּסַּכִּין.

If the cleaver was found **on the fifteenth** of Nisan, i.e., if it was found on the Festival itself, he may **slaughter with it immediately**. The owners of the cleaver would have immersed it so that they could use it on the fifteenth to cut up the bones of a Festival peace-offering. If the cleaver **was found attached to a knife,**[H] **it is like a knife,** i.e., if it was found on the thirteenth of Nisan it is presumed impure, and if it was found on the fourteenth he may slaughter with it immediately, as it was certainly immersed on the day before.

גמ׳ רַבִּי אָבִין בְּשֵׁם רַבִּי יְהוֹשֻׁעַ בֶּן לֵוִי: קַצְרָן שֶׁל נׇכְרִים הָיָה שָׁם.

GEMARA The mishna taught that according to Rabbi Meir, all spittle that is found in Jerusalem is ritually pure, except if it were found in the upper marketplace. With regard to this, **Rabbi Avin in the name of Rabbi Yehoshua ben Levi** explains: **A fortress [*katzran*] of gentiles was there**[N] in the upper marketplace. The Sages decreed that gentiles have the ritual impurity of a *zav* (see *Shabbat* 17b and *Nidda* 34a), therefore their spittle is impure. The Roman soldiers were gentiles, so any spittle found in the upper marketplace was presumably theirs.

אָמַר רַבִּי חֲנִינָה: עֲרוֹדוֹת הָיוּ נוֹחֲרִין בִּירוּשָׁלַיִם, וְהָיוּ עוֹלֵי רְגָלִים מִשְׁתַּקְּעִין בְּדָם עַד אַרְכּוּבוֹתֵיהֶן. וּבָאוּ לִפְנֵי חֲכָמִים וְלֹא אָמְרוּ לָהֶן דָּבָר. (רַבִּי שִׁמְעוֹן בַּר אַבָּא בְּשֵׁם רַבִּי חֲנִינָה: קַצְרָן שֶׁל נׇכְרִים הָיָה שָׁם.)

The Gemara recounts an incident about this fortress. **Rabbi Ḥanina said:** Once **they were killing wild donkeys**[B] **in Jerusalem,** to feed the lions in the circus (see *Menaḥot* 103b), **and the pilgrims** coming to Jerusalem to celebrate **the Festival were wading in blood up to their ankles** from the large amount of blood coming from the wild donkeys. **And they came before the Sages** to find out if they had been rendered ritually impure, **and they,** the Sages, **did not say anything,** as the blood of an animal carcass does not render one ritually impure, even though the carcass itself does. Where did this story take place? **Rabbi Shimon bar Abba said in the name of Rabbi Ḥanina: There was a gentile,** i.e., Roman, **fortress there,** in the upper marketplace of Jerusalem, and that was where they were killing the wild donkeys.

רַבִּי סִימוֹן בְּשֵׁם רַבִּי יְהוֹשֻׁעַ בֶּן לֵוִי: מַעֲשֶׂה בְּפִרְדָּה מִשֶּׁל בֵּית רַבִּי שֶׁמֵּתָה, וְטִהֲרוּ אֶת דָּמֶיהָ מִשּׁוּם נְבֵילָה. רַבִּי אֶלְעָזָר שָׁאֵיל לְרַבִּי סִימוֹן: עַד כַּמָּה? וְלָא אֲגִיבֵיהּ. שָׁאֵיל לְרַבִּי יְהוֹשֻׁעַ בֶּן לֵוִי: אֲמַר לֵיהּ: עַד רְבִיעִית – טָהוֹר, יוֹתֵר מִיכֵּן – טָמֵא. וּבָאֵשׁ לְרַבִּי לְעָזָר דְּלָא חֲזַר לֵיהּ רַבִּי סִימוֹן שְׁמוּעָתָא.

Apropos the ritual impurity of blood from an animal carcass, the Gemara recounts that **Rabbi Simon** said **in the name of Rabbi Yehoshua ben Levi:** There was **an incident** with regard to **a mule from Rabbi** Yehuda HaNasi's **household that died, and** the Sages **ruled its blood to be ritually pure** and not subject to the impurity imparted by an animal **carcass.** On this topic, **Rabbi Elazar asked Rabbi Simon: Up to how much** blood from an animal carcass does not render one ritually impure? **And he did not answer him. He** then went and **asked Rabbi Yehoshua ben Levi.** Rabbi Yehoshua ben Levi, **said to him: Up to** the size of a **quarter-*log***[N] **is ritually pure; more than that is ritually impure. And Rabbi Elazar was annoyed that Rabbi Simon did not respond with the *halakha*** that the minimal size for ritual impurity is a quarter-*log*, as he certainly heard it from Rabbi Yehoshua ben Levi.

HALAKHA

If the cleaver were found attached to a knife – נִמְצְאָה קְשׁוּרָה לַסַּכִּין: If one found, whether on the Festival or not, one knife attached to another knife, then if the state of purity is known with regard to one of them, then the other has the same status, be it pure or impure. This ruling is in accordance with the mishna (Rambam *Sefer Tahara, Hilkhot She'ar Avot HaTumot* 13:7).

BACKGROUND

Wild donkeys – עֲרוֹדוֹת: The wild donkey or onager, *Equus hemionus*, is an untamed animal that lives in the desert. Nowadays it survives mostly in the Asian deserts, and it is often mentioned in the Bible as a symbol of freedom and lack of inhibition.

Onagers

NOTES

A fortress [*katzran*] of gentiles was there – קַצְרָן שֶׁל נׇכְרִים הָיָה שָׁם: An alternate explanation interprets the word *katzran* to mean launderers rather than fortress. Accordingly, the upper marketplace was populated by gentile launderers, and therefore any spittle found there was presumed impure, as the Sages decreed that gentiles have the ritual impurity of a *zav* (*Korban Netanel*; *Tiklin Ḥaditin*).

Up to the size of a quarter-*log* – עַד רְבִיעִית: The opinion that a quarter-*log* of the blood of an animal carcass confers ritual impurity is that of Beit Hillel according to Rabbi Yehuda (*Eduyyot* 5:1). A different mishna records Rabbi Yehoshua ben Beteira's testimony that the blood of an animal carcass is ritually pure (*Eduyyot* 8:1). The minimal measure of a quarter-*log* is derived from the fact that that amount of blood, when dried, measures approximately an olive-bulk. Ra'avad explains (*Eduyyot* 5:1) that since dried blood is similar to the meat of the animal, the Sages decreed that it imparts ritual impurity as well. They further decreed that even in liquid form, the same amount of blood will confer impurity. Later authorities inferred from Ra'avad's explanation that the blood of an animal carcass is a source of ritual impurity only by rabbinic law. This is evident from the fact that the minimal measure is a quarter-*log*. If it were the case that animal carcass blood conferred impurity by Torah law, then the minimum amount would be an olive-bulk, as an olive-bulk is the standard minimal measure (*Avi Ezri*).

רב ביבי הוה יתיב מתני הדין עובדא. אמר ליה רבי יצחק בר ביסנא: עד כמה? אמר ליה: עד רביעית – טהור, יותר מיכן – טמא. ובעט ביה.

The Gemara continues: **Rav Beivai was sitting and teaching this story** of the mule from Rabbi Yehuda HaNasi's household, in which the Sages ruled that the blood of a carcass does not render one impure. **Rabbi Yitzḥak bar Bisna said to him: Up to how much** blood from an animal carcass does not render one ritually impure? Rav Beivai **said to him: Up to a quarter-*log*[B] is ritually pure; more than that is impure. And** then **he kicked him.**

אמר ליה רבי זריקא: בגין דהוה שאיל לך את בעיט ביה? אמר ליה: בגין דלא הוות דעתי בי, דאמר רבי חנין: "והיו חייך תלואים לך מנגד" – זה שהוא לוקח לו חטין לשנה, "ופחדת לילה ויומם" – זה שהוא לוקח מן הסדקי, "ולא תאמין בחייך" – זה שהוא לוקח מן הפלטור. ואנא סמיך אפלטירא.

Rabbi Zerika said to Rav Beivai: **You kicked him because he asked you a question? He said to** Rabbi Zerika: **Because my mind was unsettled,** and not because he did anything wrong. **As Rabbi Ḥanin said** in expounding the verse: "And your life shall hang in doubt before you; and you shall fear night and day, and shall have no assurance of your life" (Deuteronomy 28:66). **"And your life shall hang in doubt before you"; this is one who buys for himself wheat for a year,** who has no financial security with regard to the following year. **"And you shall fear night and day"; this** is one who is so poor that **he buys** wheat **from the storekeeper** a bit at a time, with the attendant concern that he might not have enough for the morrow. **"And shall have no assurance of your life"; this is one who** is so poor **he buys from the baker** and cannot afford to buy wheat in advance to assure even one future meal. **And I rely on the baker,** i.e., I am on this lowest level of poverty, and therefore I do not have the presence of mind to answer his questions.

מאי כדון, העיד רבי יהושע בן פתורה על דם נבילות שהוא טהור. מהו טהור – טהור מלהכשיר, הא ליטמות – מטמא.

The Gemara asks: **What then** is the halakhic ruling regarding the ritual impurity of the blood of an animal carcass? In response, the Gemara quotes a mishna (*Eduyyot* 8:1): **Rabbi Yehoshua ben Petora testified that the blood of animal carcasses is ritually pure,** which implies that it is ritually pure regardless of the amount, even more than a quarter-*log*. The Gemara rejects this answer: **What** does the mishna mean by **ritually pure?** That such blood is **ritually pure** in that it does not **render** an item **susceptible** to impurity.[N] Even though blood is one of the seven liquids that render an item susceptible to ritual impurity, the blood of an animal carcass is not deemed blood for this purpose. **Nevertheless, with regard to conferring impurity,** such blood **does render something ritually impure.**

תמן תנינן: דם השרץ מטמא כבשרו, מטמא ואינו מכשיר, ואין לנו כיוצא בו.

The Gemara asks: Didn't **we learn** in a mishna **there** (*Makhshirin* 6:5): **The blood of a creeping animal**[H] **confers ritual impurity, as does its flesh? It confers impurity, but does not render an item susceptible** to impurity, **and we have nothing** else **like it** that confers impurity but does not render something susceptible to impurity. The implication is that the blood of an animal carcass would either both confer impurity and render an item susceptible to impurity or do neither.

ואין לנו כיוצא בו כשיעור טומאתו, אבל דמו מטמא כבשרו.

The Gemara answers: When the mishna said that we have nothing else like it, it meant that **we have nothing else like it with regard to the measure** required for this substance **to confer impurity.** The measure of both the blood and the flesh of a creeping animal required for conferring impurity is a lentil-bulk. Creeping animals are unique in this regard, since the measures of blood and flesh that confer impurity from an animal carcass are different. An olive-bulk of flesh is sufficient to confer impurity, while a quarter-*log* of blood is required. **However,** the Gemara concludes, **its blood,** i.e., that of an animal carcass, nevertheless **confers impurity like its flesh.**

אמר רבי יוסי: פליגי בה תרין אמוראין, חד אמר: טמא, וחד אמר: טהור.

Rabbi Yosei said: Two *amora'im* disputed this point, whether the blood of an animal carcass confers ritual impurity. **One said** a quarter-*log* of this blood renders one **ritually impure, and one said** that even after contact with this blood, one remains **ritually pure.**

מאן דאמר טמא – כרבי יהודה, ומאן דאמר טהור – כרבי יהושע בן פתורה.

The one who said ritually impure holds **like the opinion of Rabbi Yehuda** as it appears in a mishna (*Eduyyot* 5:1). Rabbi Yehuda asserts there that this issue is the subject of a dispute between Beit Shammai and Beit Hillel. The *halakha* would follow the opinion of Beit Hillel, which is that carcass blood does confer impurity. **And the one who said ritually pure** holds **like** the opinion of **Rabbi Yehoshua ben Petora,** who testified (*Eduyyot* 8:1) that the blood of an animal carcass is ritually pure. It appears that this *amora* interprets Rabbi Yehoshua ben Petora's statement literally, implying that even more than a quarter-*log* of blood does not confer impurity.

BACKGROUND

Quarter-*log* – רביעית: A unit of liquid measurement. In Hebrew, it is literally a quarter. Unless indicated otherwise, a quarter refers to a quarter-*log*. The *log* is a talmudic measurement of volume equal to six egg-bulks, which is equivalent to approximately 346 ml according to Rabbi Ḥayyim Na'e's standard method of converting talmudic measurements. A quarter-*log* measures approximately 86.5 ml, or slightly less than half a cup.

The quarter-*log* is a standard unit of measurement in certain matters. For example, a quarter-*log* is the minimum amount of wine over which *kiddush* may be recited, the amount of wine for which a nazirite is punished for drinking, and the minimum quantity of certain edible liquids for which one is liable for violating the prohibition against transferring objects from one domain to another on Shabbat. A quarter-*log* of blood from a corpse confers ritual impurity.

NOTES

Ritually pure in that it does not render an item susceptible to impurity – טהור מלהכשיר: A food item does not become susceptible to ritual impurity unless it comes into contact with water, or one of six other liquids. The seven liquids that cause an item to become susceptible to impurity are wine, honey, oil, milk, dew, blood, and water (*Makhshirin* 6:4). Once it has come into contact with one of these liquids, food is susceptible to impurity, even if it subsequently becomes dry. Only these seven liquids can confer susceptibility to impurity, as it appears from the Gemara's interpretation of the testimony of Rabbi Yehoshua ben Petora that animal carcass blood does not render food susceptible to impurity.

HALAKHA

The blood of a creeping animal – דם השרץ: Blood of a creeping animal has the same status as its flesh and the two combine to form the requisite lentil-bulk for ritual impurity as long as it is attached to the flesh. This is in accordance with the mishna (Rambam *Sefer Tahara, Hilkhot She'ar Avot HaTumot* 4:7).

אֲמַר לֵיהּ רַב אַבְדּוּמָה דְּמִן נְחוֹתָה: וְיָאוּת, דְּרַבִּי יְהוּדָה מוֹרַיְינָא דְּבֵי נְשִׂיאָה הֲוָה.

Rav Avduma of the descenders, i.e., travelers from Eretz Yisrael to Babylonia, bringing with them the Torah taught in Eretz Yisrael, **said to him: And it is right,** that which you explained is correct, **as Rabbi Yehuda was the halakhic authority for the house of the** ***Nasi***. Rabbi Yehuda ruled then that the blood of the dead mule was pure only because there was less than a quarter-*log* of it.

״כָּל הָרוּקִין״ וכו׳: לֹא כֵן אָמַר רַבִּי אַבָּהוּ בְּשֵׁם רַבִּי יוֹסֵי בֶּן חֲנִינָה: לֹא גָּזְרוּ עַל הָרוּקִין שֶׁבִּירוּשָׁלַיִם! הָא אִיתְּמַר עֲלֵיהּ, רַבִּי אָבִין בְּשֵׁם רַבִּי יְהוֹשֻׁעַ בֶּן לֵוִי: קַצְרָן שֶׁל גּוֹיִם הָיָה שָׁם.

§ The mishna states that according to Rabbi Meir's opinion, **all the spittle** found in Jerusalem is pure, except for spittle found in the upper marketplace. The Gemara asks: **Didn't Rabbi Abbahu say this in the name of Rabbi Yosei ben Ḥanina:** The Sages **did not decree the spittle** found **in Jerusalem** to be ritually impure? If so, why is the spittle found in the upper marketplace ritually impure? The Gemara answers: **But wasn't it stated with regard to** that marketplace that **Rabbi Avin said in the name of Rabbi Yehoshua ben Levi: A fortress of gentiles was there,** and since the Sages decreed that gentiles have the ritual impurity of a *zav*, any spittle found there must be from them and therefore is ritually impure.

בִּשְׁאָר יְמוֹת הַשָּׁנָה הַטְּמֵאִין מְהַלְּכִין שִׁיבּוֹלֶת וְהַטְּהוֹרִין מְהַלְּכִין מִן הַצַּד, וְהַטְּהוֹרִין מְהַלְּכִין סְתָם, וְהַטְּמֵאִים אוֹמְרִין לָהֶן ״פְּרוֹשׁוּ״. בִּשְׁעַת הָרֶגֶל הַטְּהוֹרִים מְהַלְּכִין שִׁיבּוֹלֶת, וְהַטְּמֵאִין מְהַלְּכִין מִן הַצַּד, הַטְּמֵאִין מְהַלְּכִין סְתָם, וְהַטְּהוֹרִין אוֹמְרִים לָהֶן ״פְּרוֹשׁוּ״.

The mishna also states Rabbi Yosei's opinion that for most of the year, all spittle found in the middle of the street was impure and spittle found on the sides was pure; during the pilgrim Festival, the spittle in the middle was pure and that on the sides was impure. The Gemara discusses a *baraita* that explains this opinion: **On the rest of the days of the year, the ritually impure proceed** down the middle of the street **in a group,**[H] **and the pure proceed on the side** to avoid contact that would render them impure. **And the ritually pure proceed ordinarily**[N] and don't warn the ritually impure not to touch them, while the **impure** are the ones who **say to** those who are ritually pure: **Stay away. During the period of the pilgrim Festival the ritually pure proceed in a group** in the middle of the street **and the impure proceed on the side** of the street. **The impure proceed ordinarily** and do not warn the ritually pure not to touch them, **and the ritually pure** are the ones who **say to** those who are impure: **Stay away,** i.e., be careful not to touch us and render us impure.

״וְכָל הַכֵּלִים הַנִּמְצָאִים״ כו׳. לֹא כֵן אֲמַר רַבִּי אַבָּהוּ בְּשֵׁם רַבִּי יוֹחָנָן לֹא גָּזְרוּ עַל הַכֵּלִים שֶׁבִּירוּשָׁלַיִם? מִכֵּיוָן שֶׁנִּמְצְאוּ דֶּרֶךְ יְרִידָה לְבֵית הַטְּבִילָה – נַעֲשׂוּ הוֹכִיחַ,

§ The mishna further states: **And all the vessels that are found** in Jerusalem, if they are found on the way down to the **bathhouse,** where one purifies vessels in a ritual bath, they are ritually impure, and if they are found on the way up, they are ritually pure. The Gemara asks: **Didn't Rabbi Abbahu say this in the name of Rabbi Yoḥanan:** The Sages **did not decree** ritual impurity **with regard to the vessels** found in **Jerusalem?** The Gemara answers: **Since they were found on the way down to the bathhouse, it becomes** as if it had been conclusively **demonstrated** that they are ritually impure, for one does not bring a vessel to be immersed if it is not ritually impure.

אַבָּא שָׁאוּל הָיָה קוֹרֵא אוֹתָן צִיפּוֹרִין. מַאן דְּאָמַר צִיפּוֹרִין – שֶׁהָיָה דּוֹמֶה לְצִיפּוֹרִין, מַאן דְּאָמַר מְרִיצָה – שֶׁמְּרִיצָה אֶת הָאֶבֶן לְבֵית הַקְּבָרוֹת.

The mishna also states that Rabbi Yosei is of the opinion that all vessels that are found in Jerusalem are ritually pure, except for the basket, the shovel, and the *meritza*, which are specifically used for graves. The Gemara recounts that **Abba Shaul,** who was a gravedigger and regularly used such tools, **would call them,** the tools referred to by the name *meritza*, **fingernails** [***tzipporin***]. The Gemara explains: **The one who said** to call it *tzipporin* did so because this tool **was similar** in appearance to a **fingernail,** with a sharp point. **The one who said** to call it a ***meritza***, literally, a runner, did so because it is a tool with which **one runs,** i.e., moves **the stone** used to close the entrance to the burial cave **to the cemetery.**

קוֹפִיץ וכו׳. תָּנֵי: הַסַּכִּין קְשׁוּרָה לָהּ – הֲרֵי זוֹ כְּמוֹתָהּ.

The mishna also states that if the **cleaver** is found tied to a knife, it has the same rule as the knife with regard to ritual impurity. The Gemara quotes: **It was taught** in a *baraita* that disagrees with the *halakha* in the mishna, and in its view, if **the knife were tied to** the cleaver, **it has the same** ***halakha*** **as** the cleaver, and if the cleaver is ritually impure, the knife is also ritually impure.

HALAKHA

On the rest of the days of the year the ritually impure proceed down the middle of the street in a group – בִּשְׁאָר יְמוֹת הַשָּׁנָה הַטְּמֵאִין מְהַלְּכִין שִׁיבּוֹלֶת: On days that are not pilgrim Festivals, spittle found in the middle of the street is ritually impure by decree of the Sages, as is the *halakha* for spittle in any other place. However, in Jerusalem, spittle found on the sides of the street is ritually pure. Those who were vigilant about ritual purity would walk on the sides of the street in order to avoid contact with an *am ha'aretz*, and presumably the spittle on the sides comes from the ritually pure. This ruling is in accordance with the opinion of Rabbi Yosei (Rambam *Sefer Tahara, Hilkhot She'ar Avot HaTumot* 13:8).

NOTES

And the ritually pure proceed ordinarily – וְהַטְּהוֹרִין מְהַלְּכִין סְתָם: The text of the Gemara is in accordance with that of Rav Yehuda ben Rav Binyamin HaRofeh. However, some versions of the text have: The ritually impure proceed ordinarily, while the ritually pure tell them to stay away…the ritually pure proceed ordinarily, while the ritually impure tell them to stay away (Venice edition, and that of Rambam, Rosh, *Talmid HaRashbash*, Rash Sirilio, and the Vilna Gaon). According to that version, the warning to stay away lest the pure be rendered impure is always the task of whoever proceeds along the sides of the street, whether it is the impure during the Festival or the ritually pure during the rest of the year. Those who walk in the middle simply proceed ordinarily.

LANGUAGE

Bench [*itztabba*] – **אִיצְטַבָּא**: From the Greek στοά, *stoa*, meaning roofed colonnade or cloister. In *Kiddushin* 70a it refers to a row of pillars, but also to a covering on top of such pillars, whence developed the meaning used by the Rabbis. In the vernacular it is anything that juts out, even a bench.

HALAKHA

A curtain that became ritually impure from a secondary source of impurity – פָּרוֹכֶת שֶׁנִּטְמֵאת בְּוָלָד הַטּוּמְאָה: If the curtain of the Temple became ritually impure from a secondary source of ritual impurity, it is immersed in the courtyard. If it is removed from the Temple in order to immerse it, it is brought back inside immediately after immersion, as there is no need to wait until dark.

If it became ritually impure from a primary source of ritual impurity, it is immersed outside the Temple and is spread out to dry on the rampart, as it becomes ritually pure only once it is dark. If it is a new curtain, it is spread out to dry on the bench so that the nation will see that its work is beautiful. This ruling is in accordance with the mishna (Rambam *Sefer Avoda Hilkhot Kelei HaMikdash* 7:18).

The curtain has the thickness of a handbreadth – פָּרוֹכֶת עוֹבְיָהּ טֶפַח: Two curtains each year were made to separate between the Sanctuary and the Holy of Holies. The curtain was woven from four different types of yarn: Fine linen, sky-blue wool, purple wool, and scarlet wool. Each strand was made of six threads of each, for a total of twenty-four threads. The curtain was woven in seventy-two looms and was one handbreadth thick. It was forty cubits long and twenty cubits wide. This ruling is in accordance with the mishna (Rambam *Sefer Avoda Hilkhot Kelei HaMikdash* 7:16).

הלכה ב מתני׳ פָּרוֹכֶת שֶׁנִּטְמֵאת בְּוָלָד הַטּוּמְאָה – מַטְבִּילִין אוֹתָהּ בִּפְנִים, וּמַכְנִיסִין אוֹתָהּ מִיָּד.

HALAKHA 2 · MISHNA With regard to **a curtain that became ritually impure from a secondary source of impurity,** since its ritual impurity is by rabbinic law and not Torah law, there is no need to remove it from the Temple. Rather, **it is immersed inside** the Temple. **And** if it were removed to outside the courtyard in order to immerse it, **it** can **be brought** back into the courtyard **immediately.** Since it is ritually impure only by rabbinic law, there is no need to wait until sunset before returning it.

וְשֶׁנִּטְמֵאת בְּאַב הַטּוּמְאָה – מַטְבִּילִין אוֹתָהּ בַּחוּץ, וְשׁוֹטְחִין אוֹתָהּ בַּחֵיל, מִפְּנֵי שֶׁהִיא צְרִיכָה הֶעֱרֵב שֶׁמֶשׁ. אִם הָיְתָה חֲדָשָׁה – שׁוֹטְחִין אוֹתָהּ עַל גַּג הָאִיצְטַבָּא, כְּדֵי שֶׁיִּרְאֶה הָעָם אֶת מְלַאכְתָּהּ שֶׁהִיא נָאָה.

But **if it became impure from a primary source of impurity,** e.g., it came into contact with the carcass of one of the eight creeping animals that confer impurity by Torah law, **it is immersed outside** the courtyard **and is spread out** to dry **on the rampart.** This is the low wall surrounding the Temple courtyard and the buildings within it, which has a lower level of holiness than the courtyard. The reason for this policy is **because the sun needs to set on it.** Immersion does not confer ritual purity on an item that became impure by Torah law until after the sun has set. And **if** this curtain **were new, it is spread out** to dry **on top of the bench** [*itztabba*],[L] a prominent place on the Temple Mount, **so that the people** will **see its craftsmanship and perceive its beauty.**[H]

רַבָּן שִׁמְעוֹן בֶּן גַּמְלִיאֵל אוֹמֵר מִשּׁוּם רַבִּי שִׁמְעוֹן בֶּן הַסְּגָן: פָּרוֹכֶת עוֹבְיָהּ טֶפַח עַל שִׁבְעִים וּשְׁתַּיִם נִימִים נֶאֱרֶגֶת עַל כָּל נִימָה וְנִימָה עֶשְׂרִים וְאַרְבָּעָה חוּטִין. אׇרְכָּהּ אַרְבָּעִים אַמָּה וְרׇחְבָּהּ עֶשְׂרִים, וּמִשְּׁמוֹנִים וּשְׁתַּיִם רִבּוֹא הָיְתָה נַעֲשֵׂית, וּשְׁתַּיִם עוֹשִׂין בְּכׇל שָׁנָה, וּשְׁלֹשׁ מֵאוֹת כֹּהֲנִים מַטְבִּילִין אוֹתָהּ.

The Gemara discusses the aforementioned curtain that separated the Holy of Holies from the Sanctuary. **Rabban Shimon ben Gamliel says in the name of Rabbi Shimon the son of the deputy** High Priest: The **curtain** has the **thickness of a handbreadth,**[H] and **it is woven from seventy-two strands** of yarn. And **each and every strand** from those seventy-two is made from **twenty-four threads.**[N] The curtain was made from four materials: Sky-blue wool, purple wool, scarlet wool, and fine linen, and a strand was made up of six threads of each type of material. And with regard to the dimensions of the curtain, **its length** was **forty cubits,** as the height of the ceiling of the Sanctuary; **and its width** was **twenty** cubits, to match the width of the entrance; **and it was made from eighty-two ten-thousands,**[N] i.e., 820,000 golden dinar. **And they** used to **make two** new curtains **every year.**[N] **And** the curtain was so heavy that they needed **three hundred priests** to carry it when they would **immerse it.**[N]

NOTES

Twenty-four threads – עֶשְׂרִים וְאַרְבָּעָה חוּטִין: The Sages derived that every time a verse uses the term *sheish* with regard to sacred garments or cloth, that material is linen, and each thread of it is in turn spun from six smaller threads. As the curtain is made up of four materials, fine linen, purple wool, scarlet wool, and sky-blue wool, it is clearly understood, or in the Gemara's terminology: There is no ruling and there is no judge that can argue otherwise, that it is woven from twenty-four threads (*Yoma* 71b–72a).

And the curtain was made from eighty-two ten-thousands – וּמִשְּׁמוֹנִים וּשְׁתַּיִם רִבּוֹא הָיְתָה נַעֲשֵׂית: The text follows the interpretation of the Rambam that this number is referring to the cost of the curtain. Other commentaries claim that it is referring to the number of young girls who have not yet menstruated and are therefore certainly ritually pure, who were needed to weave the curtain. Weaving was traditionally women's work, and in the Temple women would weave the curtain and were paid to do so (see Commentary on tractate *Tamid*). According to this view, the text should read eighty-two *rivot*, meaning girls, rather than *ribo*, meaning ten-thousands. Some explain that the number is referring to the number of threads that were in the curtain (Rabbeinu Barukh).

And they used to make two new curtains every year – וּשְׁתַּיִם עוֹשִׂין בְּכׇל שָׁנָה: Some explain that this is referring to the two curtains that separated the Holy of Holies and the Sanctuary in the Second Temple. These were spaced a cubit apart, and they replaced the cubit-width dividing wall, called the *amma traksin*, of the First Temple. The wall was replaced by curtains because the Second Temple was much taller than the first (most sources say it was one hundred cubits high, or forty cubits high according to Rashi on *Bava Batra* 3a), and they could not build a self-supporting wall that was only one cubit wide to that height. They also could not widen the space allotted for the wall, as the verse states, "All this [do I give you] in writing, as the Lord has made me wise by His hand upon me, even all the works of this pattern" (I Chronicles 28:19), i.e., every detail in the Temple is set by prophecy and may not be changed (*Eiruvin* 104a). Therefore, they made two curtains, side by side with some space between, whose entire width was one cubit. As each curtain was one handbreadth thick, the space between them of four handbreadths allowed a priest to walk between them (see Commentary on tractate *Tamid*). An alternate explanation of the two curtains is that one is for the Holy of Holies and the other for the Entrance Hall (Rashi on *Ḥullin* 90b). Some explain that they needed new ones each year, because the curtains were ruined by the large quantity of smoke produced from the incense (Rosh).

They would immerse it – מַטְבִּילִין אוֹתָהּ: The early authorities discussed the reason for this immersion. Some said that it was a custom that the last step in the creation of a ritually pure vessel for consecrated use was to immerse it in a ritual bath (Rosh). Others question this explanation, as the curtain cannot become ritually impure, since it is part of a building and not meant for human use, and therefore it has the same status as a building, which cannot become impure (see *Shevi'it* 10:7).

Some explain that even though the curtain is considered attached to the earth, it may nevertheless become impure in that it is in one aspect a tent, as the verse says about the curtain: "And you shall screen [*vesakota*] the Ark with the curtain" (Exodus 40:3). In explanation of this verse, the Sages said that the curtain should not be completely straight, but rather should be slightly horizontal at its top. The horizontal portion of the curtain is based on an analogy to the roofing of a *sukka*, which comes from the same root as *vesakota* (*Sukka* 7b). There are consequently early authorities who believe that the curtain can be rendered impure, and they understand that this immersion took place only when that happened (Rosh; Rashi on *Ḥullin* 90b).

Other authorities claim that when they immersed the curtain after it was woven, before hanging it, one of the weavers became ritually impure from menstruation and inadvertently rendered the curtain ritually impure while she worked on it (see Commentary on tractate *Tamid*). Even though, as mentioned, the weavers were young girls who did not yet menstruate, it was not impossible that that might occur.

גמ׳ אִילּוּ אָמַר חוּט – אֶחָד, כָּפוּל – לִשְׁנַיִם, שָׁזוּר – לִשְׁלֹשָׁה, מָשְׁזָר – לְשִׁשָּׁה. אַרְבַּע מִכָּאן – הָא עֶשְׂרִים וְאַרְבָּעָה.

GEMARA The mishna stated that every one of the strands of yarn used to weave the curtain was made of twenty-four threads. The Gemara explains the biblical source for this: The verse says: "And you shall make a curtain of sky-blue wool, purple wool, scarlet wool, and fine twined linen" (Exodus 26:37). **Had** the verse about the curtain **said a thread,** it would mean **one** thread. Had it said **doubled,** it would be expanded **to two** threads. **Twisted** would be increased **to three** threads. **Twined,** which is what the verse in fact says, must mean double that, i.e., **to six** threads. Since the curtain was woven from **four** types of thread, i.e., sky-blue wool, purple wool, scarlet wool, and fine linen, **from here this** count tells us that each strand used in the curtain was made from **twenty-four** threads.

תָּנֵי: שְׁלֹשִׁים וּשְׁתַּיִם, אִילּוּ אָמַר חוּט – אֶחָד, כָּפוּל – לִשְׁנַיִם, שָׁזוּר – לְאַרְבַּע, מָשְׁזָר – לִשְׁמוֹנָה, אַרְבַּע מִכָּאן – הָא תְּלָתִין וּתְרֵין.

Another opinion was **taught** in a *baraita*: Each strand of the curtain was made from **thirty-two** threads. This is how that *tanna* expounds the verse: **Had** the verse about the curtain **said a thread,** it would mean **one** thread. Had it said **doubled,** it would be expanded **to two** threads. **Twisted** would be increased **to four** threads. **Twined,** which is what the verse in fact says, must mean double that, i.e., **to eight** threads. Since the curtain was woven from **four** types of thread, **from here this** count tells us that each strand used in the curtain was made from **thirty-two** threads.

תָּנָא אַרְבָּעִים וּשְׁמוֹנָה, אִילּוּ אָמַר חוּט – אֶחָד, כָּפוּל – לִשְׁנַיִם, קְלִיעָה – לִשְׁלֹשָׁה, שָׁזוּר – לְשִׁשָּׁה, מָשְׁזָר – לִשְׁנֵים עָשָׂר, אַרְבָּעָה מִיכָּן – הָא אַרְבָּעִים וּתְמַנְיָא.

Another *baraita* **taught:** Each strand of the curtain was made from **forty-eight** threads. That *tanna* expounds the verse as follows: **Had** the verse about the curtain **said a thread,** it would mean **one** thread. Had it said **doubled,** it would be expanded **to two** threads. **Wound** would be increased **to three** threads. **Twisted** would be increased **to six** threads. **Twined,** which is what the verse in fact says, must mean double that, i.e., **to twelve** threads. Since the curtain was woven from **four** types of thread, **from here this** count tells us that each thread used in the curtain was made from **forty-eight** threads.

כָּתוּב אֶחָד אוֹמֵר "מַעֲשֵׂה רוֹקֵם" וְכָתוּב אֶחָד אוֹמֵר "מַעֲשֵׂה חוֹשֵׁב". "מַעֲשֵׂה רוֹקֵם" – פַּרְצוּף אֶחָד, "מַעֲשֵׂה חוֹשֵׁב" – שְׁנֵי פַּרְצוּפוֹת.

The Gemara compares the workmanship of the curtain, which separated the Holy of Holies from the Sanctuary, with that of the screen, which was hung at the entrance to the Sanctuary: **One verse,** about the screen, **says** that it is **"the work of the embroiderer"** (Exodus 26:36), **and one verse,** about the curtain, **says** that it is **"the work of the skillful workman"** (Exodus 26:31).[H] The Gemara explains: **"The work of the embroiderer"** means **one face** was on both sides of the curtain; **"the work of the skillful workman"** means there were **two** different **faces,** one on each side.

רַבִּי יְהוּדָה וְרַבִּי נְחֶמְיָה, חַד אָמַר: "מַעֲשֵׂה רוֹקֵם" – אֲרִי מִכָּאן וַאֲרִי מִכָּאן, "מַעֲשֵׂה חוֹשֵׁב" – אֲרִי מִכָּאן וְחָלָק מִכָּאן. וְחָרָנָה אָמַר: "מַעֲשֵׂה רוֹקֵם" – אֲרִי מִכָּאן וְחָלָק מִכָּאן, "מַעֲשֵׂה חוֹשֵׁב" – אֲרִי מִכָּאן וְנֶשֶׁר מִכָּאן.

Rabbi Yehuda and Rabbi Neḥemya disagreed about this: **One said** that **"the work of the embroiderer"** means that there was an image embroidered that could be seen from both sides, e.g., **a lion from here,** on one side, **and a lion from there,** on the other side. **"The work of the skillful workman"** means that the lion could be seen **from here,** from one side, **and** it was **smooth** with no image **from there,** on the other side. **And the other said: "The work of the embroiderer"** means that there was an image like a **lion from here,** on one side, **and smooth** without an image **from there. "The work of the skillful workman"** means that from each side a different image could be seen, e.g., **a lion from here and an eagle from there.**

בִּשְׁמוֹנִים וּשְׁתַּיִם רִבּוֹא הָיְתָה נַעֲשֵׂית וְכוּ׳. רַבִּי יִצְחָק בַּר בִּיזְנָא בְּשֵׁם שְׁמוּאֵל: גּוּזְמָא. תַּמָּן תְּנִינָן: פְּעָמִים הָיָה עָלֶיהָ כִּשְׁלֹשׁ מֵאוֹת כּוֹר. רַבִּי יוֹסֵי בֵּי רַבִּי בּוּן בְּשֵׁם שְׁמוּאֵל: גּוּזְמָא.

The mishna stated that the curtain **was made from eighty-two ten-thousands,** i.e., 820,000 golden dinar, and that it needed three hundred priests in order to immerse it. **Rabbi Yitzḥak bar Bizna** said **in the name of Shmuel:** Three hundred priests is an **exaggeration** [*guzma*],[L] and really a much smaller number of priests were needed. Similarly, **we learned** in a mishna **there** (*Tamid* 28b) with regard to the pile of ash on the altar, that **at times there was on it as much** as **three hundred** *kor*.[B] Regarding this, **Rabbi Yosei, son of Rabbi Bun,** said **in the name of Shmuel:** This is an **exaggeration.**

HALAKHA

The work of the embroiderer…the work of the skillful workman – מַעֲשֵׂה רוֹקֵם...מַעֲשֵׂה חוֹשֵׁב: Any place in the Torah where it says "the work of the embroiderer," it is referring to images made by weaving that can be seen from only one side of the cloth. When it says "the work of the skillful workman," it is referring to images that can be seen from both sides of the cloth. This ruling is in accordance with Rabbi Neḥemya's opinion (*Yoma* 72b; *Kesef Mishne*; Rambam *Sefer Avoda, Hilkhot Kelei HaMikdash* 8:15).

LANGUAGE

Exaggeration [*guzma*] – גּוּזְמָא: The source of this term is not clear. Possibly this meaning is a development of the root *gazam*, meaning cut, which in turn came to mean, in rabbinic Hebrew, a threat or an attempt to frighten. From there, perhaps, it came to refer to any statement that is made merely to make an impression, without being taken literally.

BACKGROUND

***Kor* – כּוֹר:** A *kor* is a measure of volume equaling 30 *se'a*, which is about 250 ℓ according to the mainstream opinion.

NOTES

It all should be burned inside except for that which became impure from a primary source of ritual impurity outside – הַכֹּל יִשָּׂרֵף בִּפְנִים חוּץ מִשֶּׁנִּטְמָא בְּאַב הַטּוּמְאָה בַּחוּץ: Even though it is prohibited by Torah law to bring a ritually impure item into the Temple or to leave such an item there, this *halakha* does not refer to impure food, including the flesh of offerings. Only an item that became a primary source of ritual impurity, or that can become ritually pure by immersion in a ritual bath (see *Eiruvin* 104b) is prohibited by Torah law from entering the Temple. The flesh of an offering, like other foods, can never become ritually impure beyond first-degree ritual impurity, and it also cannot be rendered pure by immersion (Rav Yehuda ben Rav Binyamin HaRofeh; *Tiklin Ḥaditin*, citing the Vilna Gaon). However, even though the consecrated flesh that has been rendered ritually impure may be burned in the Temple courtyard according to Torah law, the Sages prohibited allowing it into the courtyard except under certain circumstances (Ra'avad on *Torat Kohanim*, *Parashat Tzav*, 8:6–7). The Sages disagree in the mishna as to what those circumstances are.

הלכה ג מתני׳ בְּשַׂר קָדְשֵׁי קָדָשִׁים שֶׁנִּטְמָא, בֵּין בְּאַב הַטּוּמְאָה בֵּין בִּוְלַד הַטּוּמְאָה, בֵּין בִּפְנִים בֵּין בַּחוּץ, בֵּית שַׁמַּאי אוֹמְרִים: הַכֹּל יִשָּׂרֵף בִּפְנִים, חוּץ מִשֶּׁנִּטְמָא בְּאַב הַטּוּמְאָה בַּחוּץ. בֵּית הִלֵּל אוֹמְרִים: הַכֹּל יִשָּׂרֵף בַּחוּץ, חוּץ מִשֶּׁנִּטְמָא בִּוְלַד הַטּוּמְאָה בִּפְנִים.

HALAKHA 3 · MISHNA With regard to **the flesh of offerings of the most sacred order that became impure, whether** it became impure **from a primary source of impurity or from a secondary source of impurity, whether** it became impure **inside** the courtyard **or outside,** it must be burned. There is a dispute among the *tanna'im* with regard to where it is burned. **Beit Shammai say: It all should be burned inside** the Temple courtyard, **except for that which became impure from a primary source of ritual impurity outside,**[N] as under such circumstances, it is not appropriate to bring it inside the Temple. **Beit Hillel say: It all should be burned outside** the Temple courtyard, **except for that which became ritually impure by a secondary source of impurity inside.** In such a case the flesh need not be removed from the courtyard and is burned there.

Perek **VIII**
Daf **22** Amud **a**

HALAKHA

That became ritually impure – שֶׁנִּטְמָא: There is a positive commandment to burn all consecrated meats that become ritually impure, as the verse states: "And the flesh that touches any unclean thing shall not be eaten; it shall be burnt with fire" (Leviticus 7:19). Where is it burnt? If it became ritually impure inside, it is burnt inside, and if it became ritually impure outside, it is burnt outside; this is the case whether it became ritually impure from a primary source of ritual impurity or a secondary source of ritual impurity. This ruling is in accordance with the view of Rabbi Akiva (Rambam *Sefer Avoda, Hilkhot Pesulei HaMukdashin* 19:1 and 19:6).

רַבִּי אֱלְעָזָר אוֹמֵר: שֶׁנִּטְמָא בְּאַב הַטּוּמְאָה, בֵּין בִּפְנִים בֵּין בַּחוּץ – יִשָּׂרֵף בַּחוּץ, שֶׁנִּטְמָא בִּוְלַד הַטּוּמְאָה בֵּין בַּחוּץ בֵּין בִּפְנִים – יִשָּׂרֵף בִּפְנִים. רַבִּי עֲקִיבָא אוֹמֵר: מְקוֹם טוּמְאָתוֹ שָׁם שְׂרֵיפָתוֹ.

Rabbi Elazar says: Flesh from offerings of the most sacred order **that became** ritually **impure from a primary source of ritual impurity, whether** it became so **inside** the courtyard **or outside, is burned outside.** Since its ritual impurity is of the most stringent type, it is not be brought into the courtyard, or allowed to remain there. However, an item **that became ritually impure from a secondary source of ritual impurity, whether** it became ritually impure **outside or inside, is burned inside.** Since its ritual impurity is of a lenient type, it can be brought into the courtyard in order to be burned. **Rabbi Akiva says: The place of its impurity is where its burning should occur.** Therefore, regardless of whether the source is primary or secondary, such flesh is burned wherever it presently is.[H]

גמ׳ בַּר קַפָּרָא אָמַר: אַב הַטּוּמְאָה – דְּבַר תּוֹרָה, וְלַד הַטּוּמְאָה – מִדִּבְרֵיהֶם. רַבִּי יוֹחָנָן אָמַר: בֵּין זֶה בֵּין זֶה דְּבַר תּוֹרָה.

GEMARA The opinions in the mishna, with the exception of that of Rabbi Akiva, distinguish between impurity conferred by a primary source and that conferred by a secondary source. The Gemara presents a dispute as to the nature of this distinction. **Bar Kappara said: The primary source of ritual impurity** mentioned in the mishna is referring to a scenario where the flesh of the offering became impure by **Torah law,** and **the secondary source of ritual impurity** mentioned in the mishna is referring to impurity **by** rabbinic **ordinance. Rabbi Yoḥanan said: Both this and that,** both the primary and secondary sources of ritual impurity mentioned, refer to cases of impurity by **Torah law.**

וְקַשְׁיָא דְּרַבִּי יוֹחָנָן עַל דְּבֵית שַׁמַּאי, דְּבֵית שַׁמַּאי אוֹמְרִים: הַכֹּל יִשָּׂרֵף בִּפְנִים, חוּץ מִשֶּׁנִּטְמָא בְּאַב הַטּוּמְאָה בַּחוּץ. מַה בֵּין אָב הַטּוּמְאָה בַּחוּץ מַה בֵּין וְלַד הַטּוּמְאָה בַּחוּץ, זֶה וָזֶה לֹא דְּבַר תּוֹרָה הוּא?

The Gemara asks: **And there is a difficulty with Rabbi Yoḥanan's** opinion that arises from **Beit Shammai's** opinion in the mishna. It was taught in the mishna that **Beit Shammai say: It all should be burned inside** the courtyard of the Temple, **except for that which became impure from a primary source of impurity outside.** In accordance with the opinion of Rabbi Yoḥanan, **what is** the distinction **between a primary source of impurity outside** and **a secondary source of impurity outside?** After all, are not **this and that,** both the flesh that became impure from the primary source and that which became impure from the secondary source, impure by **Torah law?**

וַאֲפִילוּ עַל דְּבֵית הִלֵּל לָא מִקַּשְׁיָא, דְּבֵית הִלֵּל אָמַר: הַכֹּל יִשָּׂרֵף בַּחוּץ – חוּץ מַה שֶּׁנִּטְמָא בִּוְלַד הַטּוּמְאָה בִּפְנִים. מַה בֵּין וְלַד הַטּוּמְאָה בִּפְנִים מַה בֵּין אַב הַטּוּמְאָה בִּפְנִים, זֶה וָזֶה לֹא דְּבַר תּוֹרָה הוּא?

And is this not difficult even according to the opinion of **Beit Hillel?** As the mishna stated **that Beit Hillel said: It all should be burned outside** the courtyard of the Temple, **except for what became ritually impure by a secondary source of impurity inside.** In accordance with the opinion of Rabbi Yoḥanan, **what is** the distinction **between** consecrated flesh that became ritually impure from a **secondary source of impurity inside** and consecrated flesh that became ritually impure from a **primary source of impurity inside?** Are **not this and that Torah law,** and shouldn't the principle be the same?

לָא הָווּ בָּהּ רַבָּנַן אֶלָּא עַל דְּבַר קַפָּרָא. וְקַשְׁיָא דְּבַר קַפָּרָא עַל דְּבֵית שַׁמַּאי. דְּבֵית שַׁמַּאי אוֹמְרִים: הַכֹּל יִשָּׂרֵף בִּפְנִים חוּץ מִשֶּׁנִּטְמָא בְּאַב הַטּוּמְאָה בַּחוּץ, מַה בֵּין אַב הַטּוּמְאָה בֵּין בַּחוּץ בֵּין בִּפְנִים, זֶה וָזֶה לֹא דְּבַר תּוֹרָה הוּא?

The Gemara proceeds to ignore these questions with regard to Rabbi Yoḥanan's opinion, explaining that **the Sages did not discuss** the mishna except **in accordance with** the opinion of **bar Kappara. And** there is also **a difficulty in accordance with** the opinion of **bar Kappara with** the statement of **Beit Shammai.** For it was taught in the mishna that **Beit Shammai say: It all should be burned inside** the courtyard of the Temple, **except for that which became impure from a primary source of ritual impurity outside.** In accordance with the opinion of bar Kappara, **what is** the distinction, with regard to flesh that became impure by a **primary source of impurity, between whether** it occurred **outside** the Temple courtyard **or inside?** In accordance with the opinion of bar Kappara, are **not this and that Torah law** and shouldn't the rule be the same? Accordingly, why distinguish between them with regard to where the flesh must be burned?

בְּגִין דְּרַבִּי עֲקִיבָא אָמַר מְקוֹם טוּמְאָתוֹ שָׁם תְּהֵא שְׂרֵיפָתוֹ.

The Gemara answers: The reason that Beit Shammai distinguish between impurity that occurred inside the Temple courtyard and that which occurred outside is **because** they accepted the reasoning of **Rabbi Akiva,** who **said** in the mishna: **The place of its impurity is where its burning should occur.** Beit Shammai, however, do not completely agree with Rabbi Akiva. With regard to items that became impure by Torah law, their opinion is in accordance with the opinion of Rabbi Akiva, meaning that the items should be burned wherever they are. However, if an item became impure by rabbinic ordinance, Beit Shammai maintain, against the opinion of Rabbi Akiva, that it is brought into the courtyard to be burned.

וַאֲפִילוּ עַל דְּבֵית הִילֵּל לָא מִקַּשְׁיָא. דְּבֵית הִלֵּל אָמַר: הַכֹּל יִשָּׂרֵף בַּחוּץ חוּץ מִשֶּׁנִּטְמָא בְּוְלַד הַטּוּמְאָה בִּפְנִים, מַה בֵּין וְלַד הַטּוּמְאָה בֵּין בִּפְנִים בֵּין בַּחוּץ זֶה וָזֶה לֹא מִדִּבְרֵיהֶם הוּא?

The Gemara continues to question the opinion of bar Kappara: **And is this not difficult even according to** the opinion **of Beit Hillel?** As the mishna stated **that Beit Hillel said: It all should be burned outside** the courtyard of the Temple, **except for that which became ritually impure by a secondary source of impurity inside.** According to bar Kappara **what is between,** why is there a distinction, with regard to flesh that became impure by a **secondary source of impurity between whether** it occurred **outside** the Temple courtyard **or inside? Aren't both this and that** instances where the impurity **is by rabbinic ordinance?**

בְּגִין דְּרַבִּי שִׁמְעוֹן אָמַר: מַאֲכָלוֹ וּמַשְׁקוֹ שֶׁל מְצוֹרָע מִשְׁתַּלְּחִין חוּץ לְשָׁלֹשׁ מַחֲנוֹת.

The Gemara answers: Beit Hillel distinguish between impurity that occurred inside the Temple courtyard and impurity that occurred outside **due to that** which **Rabbi Shimon said: The food and drink of a leper is banished from all three** of the **camps** in which the Children of Israel lived in the desert. These are the camp of the Divine Presence, i.e., the Tabernacle; the camp of the Levites, who were encamped around the Tabernacle; and the camp of Israel, where the rest of the nation lived. Once food and drink has become impure through contact with a leper, it is banned from all three camps, like the leper himself. If it became impure outside the camps, it should not be brought inside. Beit Hillel follow the same rationale, that an item rendered impure outside, even if by rabbinic ordinance, may not be brought into the Temple even for the purpose of burning it.

הלכה ד מתני׳ אֵיבְרֵי הַתָּמִיד נִיתָּנִין מֵחֲצִי כֶּבֶשׁ וּלְמַטָּה. שֶׁל מוּסָפִין – נִיתָּנִין מֵחֲצִי כֶּבֶשׁ וּלְמַטָּה בַּמִּזְרָח. שֶׁל רָאשֵׁי חֳדָשִׁים נִיתָּנִין עַל כַּרְכּוֹב הַמִּזְבֵּחַ מִלְּמַעְלָן.

HALAKHA 4 · MISHNA The **limbs of the daily offering** were not placed directly on the altar fire. Instead, after cutting up the offering, its limbs **were placed** first on the **ramp** of the altar, **from the halfway point and below,**[NH] on the lower sixteen cubits of the ramp, **on** its **western** side. Limbs **of the additional** offerings of the Shabbat and Festivals **were placed on the ramp from the halfway point and below on** its **eastern** side. **Additional New Moon offerings were placed on top of the upper part of the edge** [*karkov*] **of the altar.**

NOTES

From the halfway point and below – מֵחֲצִי כֶּבֶשׁ וּלְמַטָּה: Some of the early commentaries explain that the limbs were placed specifically on the lower half of the ramp, so that when the priests would transfer the limbs to the fire on the altar after the incense was offered, this transfer would be recognized as a significant rite. Another explanation is that if the limbs were too close to the fire, it could lead to a mistake, as they might be improperly placed on the fire before the incense was offered in the Sanctuary (Commentary on tractate *Tamid*). Some later commentaries address the question of whether transferring the limbs from the ramp is part of the sacrificial rite of transferring, which usually refers to the blood of the sacrifice, or is part of the rite of sacrificing (Rabbi Yitzḥak Ze'ev Soloveitchik; Ḥazon Ish).

HALAKHA

The limbs of the daily offering were placed first on the ramp, from the halfway point and below – אֵיבְרֵי הַתָּמִיד נִיתָּנִין מֵחֲצִי כֶּבֶשׁ וּלְמַטָּה: The limbs of the daily burnt-offering were placed on the ramp of the altar, from halfway up the ramp and below, on its western side. Limbs of the additional offerings of Shabbat and Festivals were placed on the ramp of the altar, from halfway up the ramp and below, on its eastern side. Additional New Moon offerings were placed on the upper part of the altar, between the horns, in the place of the priests' passageway. This was done to publicize the New Moon, in accordance with the mishna (Rambam *Sefer Avoda, Hilkhot Temidin UMusafin* 6:3).

הַשְּׁקָלִים וְהַבִּיכּוּרִים אֵינָן נוֹהֲגִין אֶלָּא בִּפְנֵי הַבַּיִת, אֲבָל מַעְשַׂר דָּגָן וּמַעְשַׂר בְּהֵמָה וּבְכוֹרוֹת – נוֹהֲגִין בֵּין בִּפְנֵי הַבַּיִת וּבֵין שֶׁלֹּא בִּפְנֵי הַבַּיִת. הַמַּקְדִּישׁ שְׁקָלִים וּבִיכּוּרִים – הֲרֵי זֶה קוֹדֶשׁ. רַבִּי שִׁמְעוֹן אוֹמֵר: הָאוֹמֵר בִּיכּוּרִים קוֹדֶשׁ – אֵינָן קוֹדֶשׁ.

Another law: The obligation to give **half-shekels**[H] each year and to offer **the first fruits**[HN] **is practiced only in the presence of the Temple,** as fulfillment of these mitzvot is only possible then. **But** the mitzvot of produce tithes and **grain tithes**[HN] **and of animal tithes**[HN] **and of** the sanctified **firstborn** animals[H] **are practiced whether** one is **in the presence of the Temple, or** one is **not in the presence of the Temple.** Although animal tithes and firstborn cannot be sacrificed without a Temple, once they develop a blemish, they may be eaten by their owners. If, in the present time when there is no Temple, **one consecrates shekels** for the mitzva of the half-shekel **or** fruits for the mitzva of **first fruits, they are consecrated,** and it is prohibited to derive benefit from them. **Rabbi Shimon says: One who declared first fruits to be consecrated,** in the present time, does not give them that status and they are **not consecrated.**

גמ׳ אֵיזֶהוּ כַּרְכּוֹב הַמִּזְבֵּחַ – אַמָּה בֵּין קֶרֶן לְקֶרֶן, מְקוֹם הִילּוּךְ רַגְלֵי כֹּהֲנִים.

GEMARA The mishna states that additional New Moon offerings were placed on the *karkov*. **What is the *karkov* of the altar?**[N] It is the **cubit**-wide area **between one horn and the other**[N] on the top surface of the altar, and **the place allocated for the priests' passage** when they move about the altar performing their duties.

HALAKHA

Half-shekels – הַשְּׁקָלִים: The obligation to give a half-shekel coin is only when the Temple is standing, in accordance with the mishna (Rambam *Sefer Zemanim, Hilkhot Shekalim* 1:8).

The first fruits – הַבִּיכּוּרִים: The obligation to bring first fruits is only when the Temple is standing and only applies to produce of Eretz Yisrael, in accordance with the mishna (Rambam *Sefer Zera'im, Hilkhot Bikkurim* 2:1).

Grain tithes – מַעְשַׂר דָּגָן: *Terumot* and tithes are Torah laws that apply only to the produce of Eretz Yisrael, whether or not the Temple is standing, in accordance with the mishna (Rambam *Sefer Zera'im, Hilkhot Terumot* 1:1).

Animal tithes – מַעְשַׂר בְּהֵמָה: Animal tithes are a Torah law that applies both in Eretz Yisrael and outside of it, whether or not the Temple is standing (see *Bekhorot* 53a). The Sages prohibit the tithing of animals in the present day. They decreed that it should be done only when there is a Temple, lest one mistakenly eat it and thereby violate the prohibition against slaughtering consecrated animals outside of the Temple, which is punishable by *karet*. However, if one went ahead and separated animal tithes in the present day, the animal is consecrated as a tithe and can only be eaten after it develops a blemish, in accordance with the mishna (Rambam *Sefer Korbanot, Hilkhot Bekhorot* 6:2).

Firstborn animals – בְּכוֹרוֹת: This mitzva applies whether or not there is a Temple, like tithes of grain, in accordance with the mishna (Rambam *Sefer Korbanot, Hilkhot Bekhorot* 1:5).

NOTES

The first fruits – הַבִּיכּוּרִים: The mitzva of the first fruits is elaborated in Deuteronomy 26 and mentioned in several other places in the Torah, and the details of the mitzva are explained in tractate *Bikkurim*. The first fruits come from the seven species that are identified as the produce of Eretz Yisrael, and they are the first produce separated from the harvest, even before *teruma* and tithes. They are brought by the landowner to the Temple, and the priest waves them in front of the owner before the altar while the owner recites the verses about the first fruits (Deuteronomy 26:5–10) and then gives them to the priests. The Mishna explains that there are also cases in which one offers the first fruits but does not read the verses, due to the irrelevance of certain passages in the verses to his individual situation.

Procession with the first fruits on the way to the Temple

Grain tithes – מַעְשַׂר דָּגָן: The Gemara (*Yevamot* 81a) records a dispute with regard to whether *teruma* in the present day is a rabbinic or Torah law. This is an ancient dispute that begins among the *tanna'im* but continues, in various forms, amongst the *amora'im* and early commentaries. One understanding of this issue is that *teruma* in the present day is not in force by Torah law, because the sanctity of Eretz Yisrael is no longer in effect by Torah law. Nevertheless, the people took upon themselves to continue to observe mitzvot that are dependent on the land.

As such, the sanctity of the land regarding *teruma* and tithes is not dependent on the presence of the Temple, but on whether the majority of Jews live in Eretz Yisrael. According to this view, as explained by the Rambam, the laws of *teruma* and tithes did not have force as Torah law even during the time of the Second Temple; rather, it was the Jews who had accepted upon themselves to observe the laws of *teruma*. The basis for this understanding comes from the book of Nehemiah (chapter 9). The Gemara discusses in depth what exactly can be learned from this chapter.

Animal tithes – מַעְשַׂר בְּהֵמָה: Animal tithes were separated from kosher, domesticated animals, i.e., oxen, sheep, and goats, that are born each year. The animals from which the tithe had not been taken were placed together in a corral and removed one at a time. When the count reached ten, that animal would customarily be marked with red dye, and it became the tithe. If the animal were unblemished, it would be offered as a sacrifice and eaten by its owners in Jerusalem. The tithe was consecrated and it was prohibited to use it for any purpose until it developed a blemish.

Though the mishna says that animal tithes are still practiced in the present day, this is only by Torah law. Out of concern that one may come to use a consecrated animal, to shear its wool or for labor, the Sages canceled the law of animal tithes (Rosh; Rabbi Ovadya Bartenura based on *Bekhorot* 53a). The Sages have the power to uproot a positive commandment, despite its status as Torah law, so long as it involves passively refraining from action as opposed to committing an infraction (see *Yevamot* 90a). *Tosefot Yom Tov* adds that the ability of the Sages to cancel this mitzva relies on the fact that untithed animals, as opposed to untithed produce, are not prohibited (see *Bekhorot* 57b–58a).

What is the *karkov* of the altar – אֵיזֶהוּ כַּרְכּוֹב הַמִּזְבֵּחַ: Rashi (*Zevaḥim* 62a) explains that a *karkov* is a groove that surrounds a structure and is usually there for beauty. According to the opinion of Rabbi Yosei bar Rabbi Yehuda, there was a cubit-wide groove around the edge of the altar, with a narrow curb at its edge to prevent the priests from falling off the altar. According to Rabbi Yehuda HaNasi, it was not a groove but some sort of molding that was made around the altar as decoration. Some explain that according to Rabbi Yehuda HaNasi the *karkov* was purely for decoration, while according to Rabbi Yosei bar Rabbi Yehuda it served as a walkway for the priests (see the classical commentaries on Exodus 27:5).

Between one horn and the other – בֵּין קֶרֶן לְקֶרֶן: The Gemara (*Zevaḥim* 62a) points out that this cubit cannot be the place the priests walked, as their passage would be blocked by the horns of the altar. It therefore concludes that the *karkov* was actually two cubits wide, including a cubit-wide area for the priests' passage. See the commentary of Rabbi Avraham ben HaRambam, who quotes an early view of Rabbi Ḥefetz that suggests that the *karkov* was a gutter that surrounded the altar (see *Kenesset HaRishonim*).

מוּסְפֵי שַׁבָּת מוּסְפֵי רֹאשׁ חוֹדֶשׁ מִי קוֹדֵם? רַבִּי יִרְמְיָה סָבַר מֵימַר: מוּסְפֵי שַׁבָּת וּמוּסְפֵי רֹאשׁ חוֹדֶשׁ – מוּסְפֵי רֹאשׁ חוֹדֶשׁ קוֹדְמִין. חֵיילֵיהּ דְּרַבִּי יִרְמְיָה מִן הָדָא: שִׁירוֹ שֶׁל שַׁבָּת וְשִׁירוֹ שֶׁל רֹאשׁ חוֹדֶשׁ – שִׁירוֹ שֶׁל רֹאשׁ חוֹדֶשׁ קוֹדֵם.

While on the topic, the Gemara asks: When the New Moon falls on Shabbat and both the **additional Shabbat offerings** and the **additional New Moon offerings**[NH] must be offered, **which** of them **takes precedence? Rabbi Yirmeya thought to say** that when **additional Shabbat offerings and additional New Moon offerings** are both sacrificed, the **additional New Moon offerings take precedence** and are offered first. The Gemara comments: **The strength** of, or support for, **Rabbi Yirmeya's** opinion comes **from that** which was taught in a *baraita*: When the New Moon falls on Shabbat, **the song** sung by the Levites in the Temple **of Shabbat and the song of** the **New Moon**[H] both need to be sung; **the song of** the **New Moon takes precedence,** and likewise, the additional offering of the New Moon is offered first.

אָמַר רַבִּי יוֹסֵה: שַׁנְיָיא הִיא תַּמָּן, דְּאָמַר רַבִּי חִיָּיא בְּשֵׁם רַבִּי יוֹחָנָן: כְּדֵי לְפַרְסְמוֹ וּלְהוֹדִיעַ שֶׁהוּא רֹאשׁ חוֹדֶשׁ.

Rabbi Yosei said: The *halakha* **is different there** in the case of the Levites' song, as **Rabbi Ḥiyya said in the name of Rabbi Yoḥanan:** The reason that the song of the New Moon takes precedence over the song of Shabbat is **in order to publicize** the occasion **and to inform** everyone **that it is** the **New Moon.** Since the New Moon originally depended upon the Sanhedrin establishing its exact date, there was a need to publicize which day was the first of the month.

כֵּיצַד הָיָה עוֹשֶׂה? שׁוֹחֵט מוּסְפֵי שַׁבָּת וְאוֹמֵר עֲלֵיהֶן שִׁירוֹ שֶׁל רֹאשׁ חוֹדֶשׁ. בְּרַם הָכָא – מוּסְפֵי שַׁבָּת וּמוּסְפֵי רֹאשׁ חוֹדֶשׁ – מוּסְפֵי שַׁבָּת קוֹדְמִין, עַל שֵׁם כָּל הַתָּדִיר מֵחֲבֵירוֹ קוֹדֵם אֶת חֲבֵירוֹ.

How precisely **would it be done?** When would they sing the song for the New Moon, while preserving the precedence of the additional Shabbat offerings? The priest would **slaughter** the **additional Shabbat offerings and** the Levites would then **sing the song for the New Moon. However** [*beram*][L] **here,** with regard to **the additional Shabbat offerings and** the **additional New Moon offerings** rather than the songs, the **additional Shabbat offerings take precedence, following** the principle: When **a frequent** practice and **an infrequent** practice clash, **the frequent practice takes precedence** over **the other,** the infrequent, practice. Therefore, the Sages said to slaughter the additional Shabbat offering before the additional New Moon offering.

״שְׁקָלִים וּבִיכּוּרִים״ וכו׳. הָא שְׁקָלִים קָדְשׁוּ. רַבִּי שִׁמְעוֹן בֶּן יְהוּדָה מִשּׁוּם רַבִּי שִׁמְעוֹן: בֵּין אֵלּוּ וּבֵין אֵלּוּ לֹא קָדְשׁוּ.

§ The mishna stated that the obligation to give half-shekels each year and to offer the first fruits is only practiced in the presence of the Temple. However, if one consecrates shekels or first fruits in the present day, they are consecrated, and it is prohibited to derive benefit from them. Rabbi Shimon disagrees and says such an attempt to consecrate the first fruits would not be effective. The Gemara points out: Even according to Rabbi Shimon, **this** indicates that **shekels would be consecrated** if one did so in the present day. **Rabbi Shimon ben Yehuda in the name of Rabbi Shimon** says, contrary to this implication: **Both these,** first fruits, **and those,** shekels, **are not consecrated.**

תָּנֵי: גֵּר בַּזְּמַן הַזֶּה צָרִיךְ לְהָבִיא קִינּוֹ רִיבְעִית כֶּסֶף. אָמַר רַבִּי שִׁמְעוֹן: בִּיטְּלָהּ רַבִּי יוֹחָנָן בֶּן זַכַּאי מִפְּנֵי הַתַּקָּלָה.

The Gemara continues with a discussion of consecrated items in the present day, in the absence of the Temple. **It was taught** in a *baraita*: A **convert** who converts **in the present day**[H] **is obligated to set aside,** in lieu of **his pair** of doves, **a quarter-**dinar **of silver,**[N] for that is the cheapest price at which one can purchase them. A convert at the time of the Temple was obligated to offer two doves or pigeons as the conclusion of the conversion process. **Rabbi Shimon said: Rabbi Yoḥanan ben Zakkai voided** that obligation **due to the** potential for a **mishap,** since that money would be consecrated and there is a high risk that it would be misused.

מַהוּ מִפְּנֵי הַתַּקָּלָה – כַּהֲדָא דְּתָנֵי: אֵין מַקְדִּישִׁין וְלֹא מַעֲרִיכִין וְלֹא מַחֲרִימִין וְלֹא מַגְבִּיהִין תְּרוּמוֹת וּמַעַשְׂרוֹת בַּזְּמַן הַזֶּה,

What is meant by: **Due to the** potential for a **mishap?** Where can it be seen that the Sages were concerned about the possibility of such mishaps? **Like that** which **was taught** in a *baraita*: **One may not consecrate** an item, **or take a valuation vow,** i.e., vow that one's value is dedicated to the Temple, **or consecrate** objects for use by the priests or the Temple,[H] **or separate** ***terumot*** or **tithes in the present day** when there is no Temple, lest there be a mishap and one derive prohibited benefit from any of those items.

NOTES

Additional Shabbat offerings and the additional New Moon offerings – מוּסְפֵי שַׁבָּת מוּסְפֵי רֹאשׁ חוֹדֶשׁ: The mishna (*Zevaḥim* 89a) states that additional Shabbat offerings take precedence over additional New Moon offerings based on the principle that more frequent practices take precedence over less frequent practices. Nevertheless, the Gemara here raises this question. Furthermore, Rabbi Yirmeya maintains that the additional New Moon offerings take precedence. The commentaries explain that Rabbi Yirmeya bases his opinion on the *baraita* quoted here, which he understands as disagreeing with the mishna in *Zevaḥim* (Rash Sirilio; *Shayarei HaKorban*).

A convert who converts in the present day is obligated to set aside, in lieu of his pair of doves, a quarter-dinar of silver – גֵּר בַּזְּמַן הַזֶּה צָרִיךְ לְהָבִיא קִינּוֹ רִיבְעִית כֶּסֶף: A pair of doves could not be bought for less than a quarter-dinar (*Keritot* 10b). The requirement to set aside funds to buy an offering applies only to a convert, as the offering is part of what allows him to join the congregation. Others who require atonement as part of a purification process, such as a woman after childbirth, were not required by the Sages to set money aside, as the offering is required only to permit the eating of consecrated meat and in the absence of the Temple there is no need for it (*Tosafot Yeshanim*, *Keritot* 9a).

HALAKHA

Additional Shabbat offerings and the additional New Moon offerings – מוּסְפֵי שַׁבָּת מוּסְפֵי רֹאשׁ חוֹדֶשׁ: When a New Moon falls on Shabbat, the additional Shabbat offerings are offered first and only after their completion are the additional New Moon offerings sacrificed, in accordance with the principle that frequent practices take precedence over the infrequent practices. This ruling is in accordance with Rabbi Yosei's opinion (Rambam *Sefer Avoda, Hilkhot Temidin UMusafin* 9:2).

The song of Shabbat and the song of the New Moon – שִׁירוֹ שֶׁל שַׁבָּת וְשִׁירוֹ שֶׁל רֹאשׁ חוֹדֶשׁ: When a New Moon falls on Shabbat, the song of the New Moon supersedes the song of Shabbat in order to publicize that it is a New Moon, in accordance with the *baraita* (Rambam *Sefer Avoda, Hilkhot Temidin UMusafin* 6:10).

A convert who converts in the present day – גֵּר בַּזְּמַן הַזֶּה: A non-Jew who converts today requires immersion and circumcision; and when the Temple is rebuilt, he should offer his sacrifice. The *halakha*, in accordance with Rabbi Yoḥanan ben Zakkai and in accordance with Rabbi Shimon (*Keritot* 9a), is that he does not set aside a quarter-dinar of silver for his offering, but nevertheless he must bring an offering once the Temple is rebuilt (Rambam *Sefer Kedusha, Hilkhot Issurei Bia* 13:5; *Maggid Mishne* there).

One may not consecrate an item, or take a valuation vow, or consecrate objects for the Temple – אֵין מַקְדִּישִׁין וְלֹא מַעֲרִיכִין וְלֹא מַחֲרִימִין: Consecrating items, taking dedicatory vows of valuation, or consecrating objects for use of the priests or the Temple is not done in the present day when there is no Temple to maintain. If one does consecrate an item, if it is an animal, he must lock it up until it dies of its own accord. If it is produce, an article of clothing, or a vessel, it must be left to rot. If it is money or a metal vessel, it must be thrown into the Dead Sea or Mediterranean Sea and lost. All of this applies if the owner does not want to redeem the item; but if he does want to redeem it, he can do so with a *peruta*, and instead throw that *peruta* into the oblivion of the Dead Sea (Rambam *Sefer Hafla'a, Hilkhot Arakhin VaḤaramim* 8:8; Ra'avad there).

LANGUAGE

However [*beram*] – בְּרַם: This Aramaic word appears in the book of Daniel. Usually it means but, however, or only. Some think that it comes from the same root as *berar*, meaning choose or differentiate, and others think it is a shortened version of *bar min*, meaning except for.

BACKGROUND

Antodarya – ענתודרייא: Antodarya is the name of a place. The name appears in the Talmud also as Antoraya, but that could be a mistake. Researchers are unsure as to its identity. Some identify it as a place near Kfar Yehoshua in the Jezreel Valley called Ein Tora or Tel Tora, which may be a corrupted form of Antotya, or Ein Totiya, meaning the fountain or spring of the strawberry.

ואם הקדיש או העריך או החרים או הגביה – הכסות תישרף, הבהמה – תיעקר. כיצד? נועל בפניה הדלת והיא מתה מאיליה. והמעות ילכו לים המלח.

And if he violated this rule, and **consecrated** an item, **or took a valuation vow, or consecrated** an object for use by the priests or the Temple, **or separated** *terumot* or tithes, **the clothing** that was consecrated **is burnt, the animal is destroyed. How** is it destroyed? The door of its stall is locked **in front of it and it dies by itself,** of hunger, as it is prohibited to actively destroy consecrated items. **And the money** that was consecrated **goes to the Dead Sea,** i.e., is abandoned where no one will ever find it.

עבר והקדיש, מן מה דאמר רבי שמעון ביטלה רבן יוחנן בן זכאי מפני התקלה – הדא אמרה עבר והקדיש קדשו.

Rabbi Yoḥanan ben Zakkai voided the convert's obligation to set aside money for a pair of doves. The Gemara asks: If the convert **transgressed** and ignored the instructions of Rabbi Yoḥanan ben Zakkai **and consecrated** money for a pair of doves, is it effective? The answer to this question can be inferred **from that which Rabbi Shimon said** in that same *baraita*: **Rabbi Yoḥanan ben Zakkai voided** that obligation **due to the** potential for a **mishap. That is to say,** from the fact that the potential for a mishap exists, one can infer that if one **transgressed and consecrated** the money, **it is** nevertheless **consecrated.**

רבי יודה ענתודרייא בעי קומי רבי יוסי: הכא את

Rabbi Yodeh Antodarya[B] **asked in the presence of Rabbi Yosei: Here** in the *baraita* **you**

Perek **VIII**
Daf **22** Amud **b**

NOTES

The *halakha* is in accordance with the opinion of Rabbi Shimon – הלכה כרבי שמעון: The Rambam appears to rule like Rabbi Shimon with regard to both first fruits and the quarter-dinar of silver set aside for the convert's offering. Hence, if one consecrated first fruits in the present day, they are not consecrated at all. Additionally, though one should not consecrate a quarter-dinar of silver for the convert's offering *ab initio*, if one did, it is consecrated.

HALAKHA

The *halakha* is in accordance with the opinion of Rabbi Shimon – הלכה כרבי שמעון: If one consecrates his shekel for Temple maintenance nowadays, it is consecrated. This is in accordance with Rabbi Shimon, for Rav decided the *halakha* according to Rabbi Shimon's view (Rambam *Sefer Hafla'a, Hilkhot Arakhin VaḤaramim* 6:16).

אמר קדשו, והכא את אמר לא קדשו! אמר ליה: תמן לכך אין מקדישין לכתחלה – לפי שמצוה להקריב מתרומה חדשה, והיאך הוה לה ישנה.

say that the money **has been consecrated; and here,** in the *baraita* mentioned before, **you say** that Rabbi Shimon ben Yehuda says in the name of Rabbi Shimon that if one consecrates shekels in the present day, they **are not consecrated.** He said to him: **There,** regarding the shekels, **one does not consecrate *ab initio* because the mitzva is to bring** the communal **offerings** each year **from the new collection** of half-shekels, those collected for that year, **and these** shekels, those consecrated in the present day, will necessarily be from the **old** collection, whenever the Temple is rebuilt, and as such have no use. For this reason, even if he consecrated shekels, they remain non-sacred.

והכא מאי אית לך למימר האי ישנה היא? לגבי הקדשות אחרים וקינו של גר אינו צריך חדשה, ואם הקדיש – קדוש, ויניחנה עד שיבנה בית המקדש.

And here, however, with regard to the convert's money set aside for his pair of doves, **what have you to say?** In what sense is **this** consecrated money **old?** The disqualification of the old collection only applies to shekels used to purchase communal offerings, **and other** private **consecrated items and a convert's pair** of doves **do not need** to be purchased from a **new** collection. Money consecrated now can be used to acquire a convert's pair of doves. **And** therefore, **if** he went ahead and **consecrated** a quarter-dinar of silver in order to acquire a pair of doves, it is **consecrated,** and he **should set it aside** until the Temple is rebuilt.

שמא יבנה הבית כבראשונה, ותתרם תרומת הלשכה מן החדשה בזמנה באחד בניסן. והכא מאי אית לך?

According to Rabbi Yosei's reasoning, the shekels are not consecrated because they have no use, as long as the Temple is not rebuilt this year. The Gemara asks: Why are they not consecrated? **Perhaps** the **Temple will** be **rebuilt** again **as at first, and the collection of the** Temple Treasury **chamber will be collected from the new** collection **in its** proper **time on the first of Nisan.** If that comes to pass, his shekels will be from the current year, and their consecration would have a point. **And here** too, **what have you** to say? What are the grounds for a distinction between the convert's offering whose illicit consecration is effective and the shekels whose illicit consecration is ineffective? The Gemara does not offer an answer.

רב המנונא ורב אדא בר אהבה בשם רב: הלכה כרבי שמעון.

Apropos the dispute in the mishna about someone who went ahead and consecrated first fruits in the present day, **Rav Hamnuna and Rav Adda bar Ahava** said **in the name of Rav: The *halakha* is in accordance with** the opinion of **Rabbi Shimon**[NH] that they are not consecrated.

הדרן עלך כל הרוקין
וסליקא לה מסכת שקלים

Summary of **Perek VIII**

The closing chapter of tractate *Shekalim* began with the topic of ritual purity. Given the need for those who came to visit or work in the Temple to remain ritually pure, the Gemara addressed situations in which there was some doubt as to an item's or a person's status as ritually pure or impure. Thus, there was a discussion of items found in Jerusalem and also a discussion of the traffic arrangements by means of which people could ensure not to come into contact with the ritually impure. The prescribed practice in such situations depended on circumstances: During the pilgrim Festivals, when most people were ritually pure, they would walk in the middle of the road, while the impure would walk along the sides. At other times, when most people were impure, the arrangement was reversed. Similarly, with regard to vessels found in Jerusalem, the Gemara determined that the status of a vessel depends upon the circumstances in which it is found. In this light, the Gemara distinguished between vessels found on the way to the ritual bath, which presumably have not been immersed, and vessels found on the way out of the ritual bath, which presumably have been.

A further discussion took place with regard to the proper treatment or disposal of objects that have been rendered impure. Impure vessels must be immersed, while impure offerings, or the meat thereof, must be burned. The question was raised as to what extent either its purification or disposal should be accomplished within the Temple courtyard or outside it. Most opinions concluded, at least with regard to meat that had been rendered impure, that it should be burnt wherever it is found, regardless of the level of impurity it had acquired.

The concluding section of the chapter and the whole tractate related to a question relevant in the present: In the absence of the Temple, how does one relate to the various mitzvot associated with consecrated items? In general, the Gemara concluded that those obligations and consecrations that are relevant only when there is a sacrificial rite are not practiced today. That is to say, one should not set aside items for consecration in the present day, and if one does so, then at least in some circumstances, the sanctity of such a consecration is null and void. However, other types of consecrations, such as tithing, are maintained in the present day. Since these can be dealt with in the absence of the Temple, though perhaps in a deficient manner, the Rabbis left the original *halakha* in place.

Image **Credits**

All images are copyright © Koren Publishers Jerusalem Ltd., except:

p116 © **courtesy of the Temple Institute**; **p119** left image © Charly Morlock, www.charlymorlock.com; **p119** bottom right© Daniel Ventura; **p121** © Mogador; **p122** © Walters Art Museum, Baltimore, MD, USA; **p123** bottom image © Wing; **p124** © Marco Schmidt; **p126** © **courtesy of the Temple Institute**; **p141** 1st image © **courtesy of the Temple Institute**; **p141** 2nd image © G. Eric and Edith Matson Photograph Collection; **p142** right image © Alessandra Perugi; **p145** © M. Disdero; **p144** © Max Richardson, courtesy of the archives of the City of David – Ancient Jerusalem; **p148** © Rob Lavinsky, iRocks.com; **p149** © Clara Amit, Yoram Lehman, Yael Yolovitch, Miki Koren, and Mariana Salzberger, courtesy of the Israel Antiquities Authority; **p153** bottom left © NASA; **p153** top middle © Hedwig Storch; **p153** bottom middle © Joe Vinent; **p153** top right © Nikater; **p153** bottom right © Dr. Avishai Teicher; **p154** © Hanay; **p158** 1st image © HaRav Menachem Makover, courtesy of *Harenu Bevinyano*; **p158** 2nd image © **courtesy of the Temple Institute**; **p159** © Andrey N. Bannov, www.shutterstock.com; **p156** © HaRav Menachem Makover, courtesy of *Harenu Bevinyano*; **p162** 2nd image © HaRav Menachem Makover, courtesy of *Harenu Bevinyano*; **p169** © H. Zell; **p173** © Gaiusiulianus; **p174** top image © Bernard Gagnon; **p174** bottom image © Almog; **p175** top image © Frankzed; **p175** middle image © Jusmine; **p175** bottom image © Zvi Roger; **p183** 1st image © Yaakov; **p183** 2nd image © Yuval Rosenberg; **p191** top image © Dr. K. Grote; **p193** © Kaczensky; **p200** © **courtesy of the Temple Institute.**

תורה אור

א"ר יוסי קייטתיה קרא רא"ר שמואל בשם ר' זעירא: כל שאינה יכולה ליקרב לא היא ולא דמיה — לא קדושה אלא הקדש דמים, ואת אמרת יאות, להקריבו אין את יכול — דכתיב "מבקר" ולא עופות, לפדותו אין את יכול — שאין לעוף פדיון, לפום כן צריך מימר לא קדושה אלא קדושת דמים. חברייא בשם רבי יוחנן, ר' איבו בר נגרי אמר קומי רבי אילא בשם רבי יוחנן: טעמא דהדין תנא "ואם כל בהמה טמאה אשר לא יקריבו ממנה קרבן לה'" מה ת"ל "טמאה"? אלא אפילו טמאה באותו השם. וקשיא: בדא כתיב "והעמיד והעריך". ר' זעירא בשם ר"א לא אמר כן, אלא: "ואם כל בהמה טמאה אשר לא יקריבו ממנה קרבן לה'" כל שאינה ראוי ליקרב לא כאן ולא במקום אחר אינו עושה תמורה, יצאת נקבה (שבעוף) לעולה, אע"פ שאינה ראויה ליקרב כאן — ראוי ליקרב במקום אחר. (א) רבי אבון ורבי בון בעון קומי רבי זעירא: הרי "הרובע והנרבע", שאינן ראוין ליקרב לא כאן ולא במקום אחר והרי הן עושין תמורה. אמר לון: אף אני לא אמרתי אלא טמאה ממש (ס"א מפום) וקשיא: בדא כתיב "והעמיד והעריך".

הלכה ה מתני' אחת לל' יום משערין את הלשכה. כל (ה) המקבל עליו לספק סלתות מארבע, עמדו משלש — יספק מד'. משלש ועמדו מד' — יספק מד' שיד הקדש על העליונה. אם התליעה סולת — התליעה לו, ואם החמיץ יין — החמיץ לו. אינו מקבל מעותיו עד שיהא המזבח מרצה. גמ' תני (ו) בשם ר"ש: כך היו מקבלין את מעותיהן, והכהנים זריזין הן.

הדרן עלך פרק התרומה

הלכה א מתני' [א]אלו הן הממונים שהיו במקדש: יוחנן בן פנחס על החותמות, אחייה על הנסכים, (ב) מתיה בן שמואל על הפייסות, פתחיה (ג) על הקנין פתחיה זהו מרדכי ולמה נקרא שמו פתחיה — שהיה פותח דברים ודורשן, ויודע בשבעים לשון. בן אחייה על חולי מעיים, נחוניה חופר שיחין, גביני כרוז, בן גבר על נעילת שערים, בן (ד) בבי ממונה על הפקיע, בן ארזא על הצלצל, הוגרס בן לוי על השיר, בית גרמו על מעשה לחם הפנים, בית אבטינס על מעשה הקטורת, ואלעזר על הפרוכת, ופנחס המלביש. (ה).§ **גמ'** ר' (ו) חזקיה א"ר סימון ורבנן, חד אמר: כשירי דור ודור בא למנות עליהן, וחרנה אמר: מי שהיה באותו דור מנה מה שבדורו. [א] (מאן דאמר כשירי כל דור ודור בא למנות — על כולן הוא אומר "זכר צדיק לברכה". מאן דאמר מי שהיה באותו דור מנה מה שבדורו — על כולן הוא אומר "ושם רשעים ירקב". ועל מי נאמר "זכר צדיק לברכה" — על בן קטין וחביריו) אמר

ריבב"ן

מתני' אלו הן הממונים. ירושלמי רבי חזקיה ורבנן חד אמר כשירי כל דור ודור בא למנות ותרנא אמר מי שהיה באותו הדור מנה מה שבדורו. על החותמות שהיה נותן חותם למי שרוצה סולת ויין ושמן מן הגזבר דדמיהן ידועין לכל ומי שבא לקנות מן ההקדש נותן מעות ליוחנן והוא נותן לו חותם והיה כתוב בו דמי נסכי כבש או איל או פר כדמפרש לקמן וכתב בו שם היום ושם הנאמר ואחיה היה נותן לו הסולת והיין והשמן: על הפייסות. כדמפרש ביומא פ"ב כשהיו באין להפיס זקן ויושב במערבה בלשכה חליה בגויה בקודש וחליה בגויה בחול ומלמד להם דרך הפיים א"נ הוא היה נוטל מצנפת מראשו של א' מהן וממנו היה מתחיל המנין כדמפרש התם: פתחיה זה מרדכי בלשן ולמה נקרא שמו פתחיה שהיה פותח דברים ודורשן ויודע בשבעים לשון. היכי דמי פותח דברים ודורשן כדאמר במנחות בפרק ר' ישמעאל (דף סד:) מעשה שבא העומר מגגות צריפין ושתי הלחם מבקעת עין סוכר אתא עומר לא הוו ידעי מהיכא איתויי אכרוז אתא ההוא חרשא אותיב חדא ידיה אאיגרא וחדא ידיה אצריפא אמר להו מרדכי מי איכא דוכתא דשמיה גגות צריפין או צריפין גגות דרוק ואשכח מטא לאתויי שתי הלחם לא הוו ידעי מהיכא איתויי מפרש בירושלמי לפי שכל התבואות נשדפו באותה שנה בארץ ישראל אכרוז אתא ההוא חרשא אותיב חדא ידיה אעיניה וחדא ידיה אסכרא אמר להו מרדכי מי איכא דוכתיה דשמיה עין סוכר או סוכר עין דרוק ואשכח הנהו ג' נשים דאתיין ג' קינין חדא אמרה לזיבתי וחדא אמרה לימתי וחדא אמרה לעיניתי. סבור זיבתי זיבה ממש לימתי שמפעה כים לעינתי שופעת כמעין דכלהו חדא לחטאת וחדא לעולה אמר להו מרדכי שמא בזוב סיכנה בים סיכנה בעינא סיכנה וכולן עולות דנדר הביאום בדוק ואשכח הייעו דתנן פתחיה על הקנין שהיה עומד לפרש כילד מביאות הנשים קיניהם: מתני' על חולי מעיים. ירושלמי על ידי שהכהנים הולכין יחפין על

הלכה א מתני' על החותמות. ועל הסלתות, כדמפרש לקמן במתני': על הפייסות. להורות סדר הגורל מי יזכה בעבודה זו ומי בזו, כמפורש במס' יומא: על הקינים. מחוסרי כפרה, כגון זב וזבה ויולדת שמביאין קני חובה, דהיינו תורים ובני יונה — נותנים מעותיהם לשופריי שבמקדש, והממונים על השופרות לוקחים המעות ומביאין בהן הקנים. והיה צריך שיתמנה על זה חכם גדול ובקי, כדאמרינן במסכת אבות: קנים ופתחי נדה הן הן גופי הלכות: שהיה פותח דברים וכו'. והוא מרדכי בלשן שעלה מן הגולה. ונקרא כן שהיה בולל לשונות הרבה, כדמפרש בגמרא: על חולי מעים. מפרש בגמרא: חופר שיחין. היה בקי במקורות שיחין כדמפרש בגמרא. והיה ממונה לחפור שיחין כדי שיהיו מים מצויין לעולי רגלים: גביני. כך שמו של האיש המכריז, כדמפרש בגמרא: על נעילת שערים. לנעול השערים בערב ולפתחן בבקר: על הפקיע. מפרש בגמ': צלצל. כלי שיר שיש לו קול גדול, לשון "תצלינה אזניו" צימבל"ו בלע"ז. וכשהיו שומעין קולו היו הלוים מתחילין בשיר: על השיר. להתחיל את השיר, וכשהיה מסיים היו כולן מסיימין: בית גרמו וכו'. כולה מפרש בגמרא: **גמ'** כשירי דור ודור בא למנות. שאי אפשר שאלו הנזכרים היו ממונים בכל זמן הבית. דבכל דור דור היו משתנים הממונים. לכן פירש דאותן הכשרים שבכל מינוי ומינוי מנה התנא במשנתנו: מי שהיה באותו הדור. כשעלו ישראל מן הגולה מנה אותן שהיו בדורו, ולא כל הממונים שהיו בזמן הבית: על כולן הוא אומר וכו'.

הנשים קיניהם: מתני' על חולי מעים. ירושלמי על ידי שהכהנים הולכין יחפין על / אסא דתנן בפ"ג דיומא בית גרמו: לא רצו ללמד על מעשה לחם הפנים, בית אבטינס לא רצו ללמד וכו', הוגרס בן לוי היה יודע פרק בשיר ולא רצה ללמדו, בן קמצר לא רצה ללמד

על מעשה הכתב. על הראשונים הוא אומר "זכר צדיק לברכה", ועל האחרונים הוא אומר "שם רשעים ירקב". וקאמר דלמ"ד דכשרים מנה התנא — א"כ ע"כ צומר דאף בית גרמו ובית אבטינס היו כשרים, שהרי מנה התנא אותם כאן, ו"שם רשעים ירקב" — אבן קמצר לחודיה קאי: על כולן הוא אומר "שם רשעים ירקב". אפילו על בית גרמו: על בן קטין וחביריו.

עין משפט נר מצוה

נוסחת הבבלי

הגהות הגר"א
[א] ה"ג תמן תנינן על הראשונים נאמר זכר צדיק לברכה ועל אלו נאמר שם רשעי' ירקב מ"ד כשירי דור ודור בא למנות עליהן הוא אומר זל"ע מ"ד מי שהיה באותו דור מנה מה שבדורו על מי נאמר זל"ל על בן קטין וחביריו כל"ל. והוא ביומא פ"ג וגי' הספרים משובשת ועי' בס' ת"ח טעם מרווח ועיין בק"ע שסביב הגמרא דיומא שם:

ציון ירושלים
הוגרס בן לוי על השיר. עי' תוספות יו"ט מ"ש בזה ועי' שו"ת (א) א"ז סימן טו בהגהה בנו הרב שם:

תקלין חדתין

מתני' אלו הן הממונים כו'. לשון רביע הגאון. כולם נקראו ע"ש הראשון. וכן במלכים פרעה ואבימלך ומלכי צדק, וכמ"ש במנחות במרדכי. ובירושלמי בפנחס המלביש: הפייסות. להורות סדר הגורלות, מי יזכה בעבודה זו ומי באחרת: הקנים. כגון זב וזבה ויולדת שמביאין קני חובה, נותנים מעותיהם לשופרות שבמקדש והממונים על השופרות לוקחים המעות ומביאין בהן קנין. והיה צריך שיתמנה על זה חכם גדול ובקי, כדתנן: קנין ופתחי נדה הן הן גופי הלכות: ויודע בשבעים לשון. הוא סיומא דמילתא. דלהכי מינוהו לזה, לפי שכל הנשים שמביאין הקינים לשום מסוים לארצותם ללשונותם ומשובם ג"כ, והוא היה מבין כל ע' לשון, וממילא הבין כל שינויי אותן הלשונות. וכמפרש בגמרא על אחת שאמרה לזיבתי ופירש הוא כוונתה שבא זאב ליטול את בנה: על חולי מעים. מפרש בגמרא: חופר שיחין. כדי שיהא מים מצויין לעולי רגלים: גביני. שם אדם המכריז: צלצל. צימב"ל בלע"ז. וכשהיו שומעין קולו היו מתחילין הלוים בשיר: בן לוי. משבט לוי, על השיר להתחיל, ובסיומו היו כולן מסיימין: **גמ'** בשרי בכל דור ודור. שלא מנה רק הכשרים המיוחדים, ולכן מנה אלו בלבד. אע"פ שהיו עוד בדורות אחרים ממונים אחרים — לא מנה אלא המעולים, כמ"ש ראיתי בני עליה והמה מועטים במספר: מי שהיה באותו הדור כו'. ולאו דוקא משום שהן כשרי כל דור, אלא המונה מנה אלו שהיה בדורו: ה"ג: תמן תנינן. ביומא פרק ג': עליהן הוא אומר זכר כו'. דאיהו ס"ל שכל המנויין כאן היו כשרים, וא"כ לדידיה צריך לפרושי מ"ש ביומא "על הראשונים נאמר זל"ל" — על כולם, גם אבית גרמו ובית אבטינס, אף שמוזכירים שם במשנה לגנאי. אך דבברייתא אמרו שמצאו תשובה לדבריהם. וכ"ה בסוגיין. ולכן נאמר גם עליהם זל"ל. ועל בן קמצר שלא מצא תשובה לדבריו נאמר "ושם רשעים" כו': מ"ד מי שהיה כו'. ול"ד כשרים, א"כ מתני' דיומא כפשטיה, דעל הראשונים קאי על בן קטין וחבריו דחשיב שם ברישא דמתני' דמוזכרין לשבח, עליהן קאי מ"ש זל"ל. וגירסת הספרים

הפנויים שם ברישא דמתני': "לכן אחלק לו ברבים ואת עצומים יחלק שלל תחת אשר הערה נפשו למות": שהתקין מדרש וכו'. שדורשין אותן ברבים. ואף זה שמוסר נפשו לה' יהיה לו חלק בתורת ה', כר"ע: ה"ג: "ואת עצומים" — אלו אנשי כנסת הגדולה שהתקינו כללין ופרטין בתורה: מה ת"ל "סופרים"? מאי רבותייהו, דשבחינהו קראי בהכי? ספורות. שקבלו בחכמתן כל החלוקות שבדינין, ושמו לכן מספר, ככל הנך דמייתי: חמשה לא יתרומו. בריש מסכת תרומות: ה' דברים חייבין בחלה. ריש פ"ק דחלה: ט"ו נשים. רפ"ק דיבמות. ל"ו כריתות. ריש כריתות: י"ג דבר וכו'. ריש טהרות: ד' אבות נזיקין. ריש בבא קמא: ל"ט אבות מלאכות. שבת פרק "כלל גדול": מה ת"ל סופר. דכתיב לעזרא הכהן סופר "סופר דברי מצות ה'", ו"סופר" בתרא ל"ל: אלא כשם שהיה סופר בדברי תורה. שמנה כל האותיות שבתורה שבכתב ועשה המסורת: כך היה סופר בדברי חכמים. למנות ההלכות: הראשונים חרשו כו'. איידי דמייתי שהראשונים עשו ספורות להקל על המעיינים, מייתי נמי הא דר' חגי: ואנו אין לנו מה לאכול. כלומר, אף על פי שהראשונים עשו כל הפעולות להקל עלינו, עדיין קשה עלינו להבין ד"ת על בוריין: אין הוון וכו'. אם היו הראשונים מלאכים אנו בני אדם, אבל אם היו הן בני אדם — אנחנו כחמורים, לרוב פחיתותינו: א"ר מנא, באותה שעה אמרו: אפי' לחמורו של ר"פ בן יאיר לא דמיין: חמרתא דר"פ בן יאיר. גנבוה לסטים בלילה, והיתה טמונה אצלם שלשה ימים ולא טעמה כלום: בתר שלשה ימים. נמלכו להחזירה, אמרו: הוציאוה מכאן שלא תמות אצלינו, ויהיה ניכר הגניבה: אפקונה. הוציאו אותה, והלכה מעצמה, ועמדה על פתח ביתו של ר"פ, והתחילה לנעוק: א"ל ר' פנחס. פתחו הדלת לעניה זו, דהא שלשה ימים שלא אכלה כלום: פתחין לה. ונכנסה: אמר להן. ר"פ: תנו לה לאכול, ונתנו לפניה שעורים, ולא רצתה לאכול: אמר לון ר"פ: וכי מתוקנים הם השעורים שאין בהם פסולת: וארימתון דמיין. הפרשתן מהם דמאי: אמרון ליה. לא כך למדתנו רבינו: הלוקח פירות מעם הארץ לזרע או להאכילן לבהמה פטורין מן הדמאי? דכיון דרוב עמי הארץ מעשרין הן — לא גזרו באלו, כיון שאינו אוכל מהן בעצמו: קמח לעורות. לעבדן, ושמן לנר — פטור מן הדמאי, וזו נמי למה אינה אוכלת: אמר לון ר"פ: מה נעשה לעניה זו שהיא מחמרת על עצמה הרבה, והפרישו דמאי ואכלה: שיודעין לדבר בשבעים לשון וכו'. ראויין לשמוע, שהן מבינין שבעים לשון, אע"פ שאינן יודעין להשיב: ה"ז ראויין לסנהדרין. וכשרה על צד הדוחק: שלשה. שיודעין לדבר: ארבעה שידעום לדבר — ה"ז מעולה: יבשה א"י. שלא ירדו הגשמים, ולא ידעו מאין להביא העומר: והוה תמן. שם: חד אלם. שאינו שומע ואינו מדבר: צריפין. הוא סוכה שאין לה גג, אלא חדה מלמעלה ועשויה מערבה: אייתוני' וכו'. הביאוהו לפני פתחיה, להבין ממנו באיזה מקום הוא: א"ל: מי איכא מקום בא"י ששמו 'גגות צריפין' או 'צריפין גגות'? והלכו לשם ומצאו: נשדף. נלקה בשדפון: סוכרא. חור שבמזוזות הדלת שבו תוחבים הבריח לנעול: שופעת דמים כמעיין. ומביאה קן אחד חובה, א' חטאת ואחד עולה כדין זבה: בעינה סיכנה. וזו קן נדבה, וכולן עולות: בים סכנה. בעברה תוך הים היתה בסכנה, וזו לנדרה ועולות הן: זאב בא ליטול את בנה. ונדרה קן אחד להצלת בנה: ע"י שהיו הכהנים וכו' והיו באין לידי חולי מעיים. לכך היו צריכין לרופא לרפאותן. והלכך אף הוא נחשב מהממונים שהיו במקדש, שאף הוא נטל שכרו מתרומת הלשכה. דצרכי קרבן הוא, שיאכלו הכהנים בשר קרבנות השמנים, ולא יבוא לידי נותר: ושותין מים. שאסורים לשתות יין בעזרה: והוה ידע. בן אחיה איזה יין יפה למעיים לעצרן, ואיזה יין טוב לרפאותן. שע"י הלינה המעיים מתרפאין או מתעצרים יותר מדאי: והוה ידע. איזה סלע מוציא מים צוננים ואיזהו מים חמים

תורה אור

אמר רבי יונה: כתיב "לכן אחלק לו ברבים ואת עצומים יחלק שלל" (ישעיה נג) — (א) זה ר"ע שהתקין מדרש ההלכות וההגדות. וייש אומרים: אלו אנשי כנסת הגדולה תיקנו, אלא מה תיקן — זה כללות ופרטות. אמר ר' אבהו: (ב) כתיב "משפחת סופרים יושבי יעבץ" (דה"א ב) מה ת"ל "סופרים" — אלא שעשו את התורה [א] סופיות ספורות חמשה לא יתרומו תרומה, ה' דברים חייבין בחלה, חמש עשרה נשים פוטרות צרותיהן, שלשים ושש כריתות בתורה, שלש עשרה דבר נאמרו בנבלת העוף הטהור, ד' אבות נזיקין, אבות מלאכות ארבעים חסר אחת. אמר רבי (אחא) אליעזר: כתיב "לעזרא הכהן הסופר" (עזרא ז) מה ת"ל "סופר"? אלא כשם שהיה סופר בדברי תורה כך היה סופר בדברי חכמים. ר' חגי בשם ר' שמואל בר נחמן: הראשונים חרשו וזרעו, ניכשו כיסחו, עדרו, קצרו, עמרו, דשו, זרו, ברו, טחנו, הרקידו, לשו, קיטפו, ואפו. ואנו אין לנו [א] מה לאכול. ר' אבא בר (יונה) זמינא בשם ר' זעירא: אין א) הוון קדמאין מלאכין — אנן בני אנש, ואין הוון בני אנש — אנן חמרין. א"ר מנא: בההיא שעתא אמרין: אפילו כחמרתיה דר' פנחס בן יאיר לא אידמינון. חמרתיה ב) דר"פ בן יאיר גנבתה ליסטאי בליליא. עבדת טמירא גבון תלתא יומין ולא טעמה (ג) כלום. בתר תלתא יומין אימלכון מחזרתה. אמרי: אפקינון מן הכא, דלא תימות גבן. אפקונה, אזלת וקמת לה על תרעא דמרה, שריית מנהקת. אמר לון: פתחון להדא עלובתא דאית לה תלת יומין דלא טעמה כלום. פתחין לה ועלת לה. אמר לון: יהבו לה כלום תיכול. יהבון קומה שעורין ולא בעית למיכל. אמרין ליה: רבי, לא בעית למיכל. אמר לון: מתקנין אינון? אמרו ליה: אין. אמר לון: וארימתון דמיין? אמרון ליה: לא כן אלפון רבי, אהלוקח ג) זרע לבהמה, קמח לעורות, שמן לאור — פטור מן הדמאי? אמר לון: [ב] מה נעבד לה להדא עלובתא דהיא מחמרה על גרמה סגין. וארימן דמיין, ואכלת.§ "פתחיה על הקינין".§ (ד) בא וראה מה גדול הוא כחו של אותו האיש פותח דברים ודורשן".§ "יודע בע' לשון".§ תני: ד) בסנהדרין שיש בה שנים שיכולין לדבר וכולן ראוין לשמוע — הרי זו ראויה לסנהדרין, ג' — הרי זו בינונית, ד' — הרי זו חכמה. וביבנה היו בה ד' בן עזאי, ובן זומא, ובן חכינאי, ור"א בן מתיה. (נ"א חנניה בן חנילאי) א"ר ה) חסדא: פעם אחת יבשה א"י ולא ידעו מהיכן להביא עומר. והוה תמן חד אלם, דהוה יהיב חד ידיה על גגות, וחד ידיה על צריפים. אייתוניה קמיה דפתחיה. אמר להו: אית אתר דמתקריא גגות צריפין או צריפין גגות? אזלינן לתמן ואשכחן. א"ר יוסה (ביבן) בי רבי בון: פעם אחת [ג] נשדף כל העולם כולו ולא היו יודעין מהיכן להביא העומר. והוה תמן חד אילם, דהוה יהיב ידיה על עיניה וידיה על סוכרא. אייתוניה לגבי פתחיה, אמר לון: אית אתר דמיתקריא עין סוכר או סוכר עין? ואזלון תמן ואשכחון. (ה) ג' נשים הביאו קיניהן, אחת אומרת "לעינתי" ואחת אומרת "לימתי" ואחת אומרת "לזיבתי". זו שאומרת "לעינתי" סברין מימר: שופעת כמעין. אמר לון: בעיינא סכנת. זו שאומרת "לימתי" סברין מימר שופעת כים, אמר לון: בימה סכנת. זו שאומרת "לזיבתי" סברין מימר זבה ממש, אמר לון: זאב בא ליטול את בנה.§ "בן אחיה" וכו'.§ געל ידי שהיו הכהנים מהלכין יחפים על הרצפה, והיו אוכלין בשר ושותין מים, היו באין לידי חולי המעים, והוה ידע האי דין חמר טב למעייא, והאי דין חמר סמם למעייא.§ "נחוניא חופר שיחין".§ דשהיה חופר שיחין ומערות, והוה ידע האי

ריבב"ן

על הרצפה ואוכלין בשר ושותין מים שאסורין לשתות יין כדכתיב יין ושכר אל תשת וכו' הוו באין לידי חולי מעיים והוו ידע הידין חמר טב למעיא: נחוניא חופר שיחין שיהיו מצויין מים לעולי רגלים. גביני כרוז היה משכים ואומר עמדו הכהנים לעבודתכם כו' כדאיתא ביומא פרק א' (דף כ:) ממונה על הפקיע. ירושלמי שהיה מזויג את הפתילות כדתנן מבלאי מכנסי כהנים ומהמייניהן היו מפקיעין ובהן היו מדליקין לשמחת בית השואבה וקשה דבבבלי ביומא [דף כג] מפרש מאי פקיע אמר רב יהודה*) מרעתרא מאי מרעתרא אמר רב פפא דתירקא דטייעי דפסיק רישיה כדתניא ולא עוד אלא שלוקה מן הממונה בפקיע: הצלצל. מלשון בצלצלי שמע כלי שיר על השיר נעימה יתירה היה יודע אמרו עליו על הוגרוס בן לוי שהיה מנעים את קולו בזמר וכשהיה נועץ גודלו לתוך פיו היה מוציא כמה מיני זמר והיו אחיו הכהנים נזקרין בבת ראש: על מעשה לחם הפנים. שאין אדם יודע לרדות כמותם כדאמר ביומא פ"ג: ובית אבטינס על מעשה הקטורת. שאין אדם יודע כמותן שיהא מתמר ועולה כמקל. על הפרוכת שהיה ממונה על אורגי פרוכת. פינחס המלביש שהיה מלביש בגדי כהונה גדולה לכהן גדול בשעת עבודה. ירושלמי מעשה בכהן אחד שהלביש לסרדיוט אחד ונתן לו ח' זהובים ותיקנו שיהיה נאמן ממונה עליהן שלא יהא כהן רשאי להלבישן לאחר ויש מפרשים שהיה מלבישן לכהן גדול ומתקנן שיעמדו נאין לו ואינו נ"ל:

תקלין חדתין

חסרה ומשובשת: אר"י כתיב כו'. איידי דנקט מעלות המוזכרין לשבח, וגם מעלת החכמים שמנו הכל, נקט לה הכא: אחלק לו ברבים. זה ר"ע. שרבים היו תלמידיו. כמ"ש בריש מגילה. וכולהו סתימתאי אליבא דר"ע. ואמרינן בגמ': והיה העולם שמם עד שבא ר"ע אצל רבותינו כו' והעמיד תלמידים הרבה. ולכן דריש עליו "אחלק לו ברבים" — חלק עולם הבא לו ותלמידיו, וסיפיה דקרא "ואת עצומים" קאי לפ"ז על הרוגי לוד שנתעלמו למסור נפשם על קידוש ה'. "יחלק שלל" שלל האויבים, כמ"ש "תחת רבי עקיבא וחביריו מה הן מביאין כו'". וזהו שנאמר "תחת אשר הערה למות נפשו" — שמסר נפשו למיתה. וכמו שאמר: בכל יום היה מצטער לקיים "ואהבת כו' בכל נפשך". וזה שאמר "נפשו", וזהו לישנא דקאמר "והערה" שעורר עליו שהיה מקהיל קהלות, "ואת פושעים נמנה" כמ"ש אוי לי כו' כמחללי שבתות כו': אנשי כנה"ג תיקנו. שהמשנה והמדרש היה מקובל מידם מימי אנשי כה"ג, כמ"ש הגאונים: כללים ופרטים. כללים — כמו "כלל אר"ע". וכלהו סתימתאי כללי הלכות ופרטות שהיה דורש על כל קוץ וקוץ תלי תלים של הלכות, שהיה אמיתו מתגין דאורייתא, מענין שהיה בן גרים: מה ת"ל סופרים. דכבר נקט משפחתו מפורש, וכולי קרא לדרשא: סופרים כו' ספורות. כדי שיהיו נגד עיני העוסקים בה זכור ושמור: חמשה לא יתרמו כו'. והא דלא חשיב אלא הני דברים לחודייהו, ולאו משום סמנא בעלמא — ליחשבו ד' או ג'. אלא דהוא כולל כל הש"ס, ומתחיל בסדר הראשון ונקט כסדר המספר. אלא דסמיך קדשים לטהרות ואבות לאבות: "לעזרא הכהן הסופר", מה ת"ל "סופר". דכתיב שם "אשר נתן המלך ארתחשסתא לעזרא הכהן הסופר סופר דברי מצות ה' וחקיו", וכיון דכתיב "הסופר" קמא מה ת"ל "סופר" בתרא?: כשם שהיה סופר בדברי תורה, כך היה סופר בדברי חכמים. וסיפא דקרא "דברי מצות ה'" — הוא תורה שבכתב, כמש"ש והוא סופר מהיר בתורת ה'. וחקיו על ישראל — זהו תורת שבע"פ. שתורה שבכתב גם לאומות נכתבה באר היטב בשבעים לשון. וכמ"ש: לעתיד מביא הקדוש ברוך הוא ספר תורה בחיקו כו' כלום יש בכם מגיד זאת, דקאי על תורה שבעל פה: הראשונים. אגב שזכר מעלת הראשונים הזכיר החילוק ביניהם לבינינו: חרשו כו'. חשיב ט"ו מלאכות הפת, לפי שהתורה נקראת "לחם", כמ"ש "לכו לחמו בלחמי". ועיין בקידושי על אגדות ענין הט"ו מלאכות בארוכה:

מסורת הש"ס

א) שבת קיב ב וירו' דמאי פ"א הל"ג: ב) ירושלמי שם ובה"ר פ' ס' ועי' חולין ז ב: ג) דמאי פ"א מ"ג: ד) עי' סנהדרין יז ב: ה) מנחות סד ב:

עין משפט נר מצוה

ב א מיי' פרק י"ג ממעשר הל"ד:
ג ב מיי' פרק א מסנהדרין הל"ו:
ד ג מיי' פ"ז מכלי המקדש הל"ד:
ה ד מיי' שם הלט"ו:

נוסחת הבבלי

(א) זה ר"ע שהתקין משנה ומדרש והלכות וכו': (ב) כתיב ומשפחות סופרים כו' סופרים שעשו כו' אמר רב אחא כתיב כו' סופר כשם כו' ר"ש בר נחמני כו' ר"א בר מונה בשם כו': (ג) כלום אמרו אפקנא מהכא כו' דמרה שריא מיתאנחת אמר ליה ר' פנחס בן יאיר פתחו לה לעלובה כו' ועיילה יהבן קמה שעורין ולא אכלת אמרו לי' ר' לא בעית למיכל אמר להון מתקנון אינון אמר ליה אין ארומתון דמאי א"ל לא כדין אלפינן הנותן זרע לבהמה פטור מן הדמאי אמר מה ניעבד לה דהיא מחמרא על נפשה ארומה דמאי ואכלת: (ד) תני פתחיה זה מרדכי בא וראה כמה גדול כחו של אותו האיש שפותח בדברים כו' סנהדרין שהיו בה שנים יודעין לדבר כו' זומא ור' אליעזר בן מתתיה וחנניה בן חנילאי פ"א כו' ולא היו יודעין להביא כו' א"ר יוסי בר ביבן פ"א נשדפה א"י ולא ידעו כו' יהיב חדא ידיה כו' וחדא על סוכרא אייתיניה קמיה דפתחיה אמר להו אית כו': (ה) ג' נשים הביאו שלש קינין כו':

משנת אליהו

שנים שיודעין לדבר. עיין סנהדרין י"ד ועיין תוספות מנחות ס"ה א' ד"ה ויודעים בשבעים לשון כו': אחת אומרת לעינתי כו'. בבבלי מנחות ס"ד ב' מובא זו הסוגיא וכתוב בגמ' וחדא אמרה לעונתי סבור מינה זיבתי זבה ממש לימתי ממש לעונתי לעונתה ממש ופרש"י שם על ימתה ששופעת כים ועל לעונתה פי' לעונת קרבן זיבת' ליום ח' שלה והיינו משום דהגי' לעונתי ולפי סוגיא דירושלמי הגירסא לעינתי ואפשר דכן צ"ל בבבלי וס"ל שופעת כמעין כמ"ש בירושלמי דלפ"ז הוי א"ש טפי מה דפתר שמה בעינה סיכנה משא"כ אי גרסינן לעונתי לא משתמע על עינה. ועל מ"ש שם שמא בזוב סיכנה פירש רש"י ג"כ שהיתה שופעת דם יותר ונסתכנה למות ונדבה לקונה להביא כו'. ובירושל' מפור' זאב בא ליטול את בנה והיה צריך להגיה בבבלי שם שמא בזאב סיכנה וממש כירושלמי דעובדא חדא הוי ולא מסתבר שיפלוגו בזה התלמודים:

הגהות הגר"א

[א] צ"ל אנו אין לנו פה לאכול. וכ"ה בעירובין פ"ה לחות האבן אם משים אדם לחייו כאבן הזה שאינו נימח וכמ"ש פתח פומך קרי וכו'. תני וכו'. שנא' כי חיים הם למוצאיהם למוציאיהם בפה ואנחנו מתעצלים בזה:

גליון הש"ס

[א] עי' תוספות קדושין ל ע"א ד"ה נקראו: [ב] עיין תוס' חולין דף ז ע"ב ד"ה הא: [ג] עי' תוס' מנחות דף סד ע"ב ד"ה ועל ותוס' ב"ק דף פב ע"ב ד"ה ועל:

אין לנו פה לאכול. כמ"ש בפ"ה דערובין: "לחת האבן": אם משים אדם לחייו כאבן הזה שאינה נמחית, וכמ"ש: פתח פומך קרי כו', תני כו', שנאמר "כי חיים הם למוצאיהם" — למוציאיהם בפה, ואנחנו מתעצלים בזה: אין קדמאין מלאכים. שהאדם תלוי מלאך מצד הנשמה ותלוי בבהמה מצד הגוף, כידוע. וכמה שהאריך הסמ"ג בהקדמתו לחלק עשין. והראשונים הגבירו כח המלאך לעשות רצון קונם: בני אנש. כמ"ש "בן חכם ישמח אב" וגו'. וכמ"ש רבינו הגאון שחלק אביו גורם חכמתו. וכן אמרו "קדשים תהיו" — המקדש עצמו כו'. וכמ"ש בזוהר: ווי למאן דבני בניינא כו'. וכמ"ש במ"ר ע"פ "כי אבי ואמי עזבוני". הן שבכח האדם להתגבר ולהרגיז יצר טוב על יצר הרע, כמ"ש דוד הרגו כו' וז"ש "בני אנש": ואי הוו ב"א. ואפ"ה זכו למדרגתם הנפלאה: אנן חמרין. שגבר החמר בגלות התורה ומצות, שאין לנו הרמ"ח לנלחם. כי נגרעו רובי מצות בגלות, וכן כתיב "מלכה ושריה בגוים אין תורה": חמרתיה דרפב"י גנבוהו לסטים. עבידת — היתה אצלם ג' ימים ולא טעמה כלום: מחזרתה. שנמלכו להחזירה: אפקנא. עליאה מכאן שלא תמות: תרעא. שער של רפב"י: מתקנין אינון. בלא פסולת: ארימתון. אם נתתם דמאי: לא כן אלפן. וכי לא למדתנו רבינו שהלוקח לבהמה פטור מדמאי? לפי שרוב עמי הארץ מעשרין הן, ולא גזרו כשאינו אוכל בעצמו: מחמרה על נפשה. שיקחו דמאי: בוא וראה כו'. לפי שמינויו היו על הקינין שהן גופי תורה. ונותן טעם למה שנקרא "פתחיה", שהיה פותח דברים הנסתרים וסגורים: שיודעין לדבר. בשבעים לשון: לשמוע. = להבין, אע"פ שא"י להשיב: חד אלם. שאינו שומע ואינו מדבר: צריפין. היא סוכה שאין לה גג, וחדה מלמעלה: גגות צריפין. לפי שהניח ידו תחלה על גגות, אמר תחלה "גגות צריפין": סוכרא. חור שבמזוזות הדלת, שבו תוחבים הבריח לנעול: עין סוכר כו'. כדפרישית: שופעת כמעיין. דמים, ומביאה ב' קינין: א' חטאת וא' עולה, כדין זבה: בעינא. בימא. והן לנדרה, ועולות הן: זאב בא ליטול כו'. ונדרה קן א' להצלת בנה. ומייתי לה שממוך שהיה חכם גדול ויודע טיב הלשונות הבין דבר זה, ואחר היה נכשל בזה: מים. שאסורין לשתות יין בעזרה: והוה ידע. בין אחיס: ממסמם. מרכך וממית ומזיק ולא ישמו ממנו. ומדאמר תחלה "דין חמר טב למעייא" משמע דממסמם רע למעיים, ולא כיש מפרשים

*) לפנינו ביומא שם איתא א"ר מדרא מאי מדרא אמר רב פפא מטרקי דטייעי וכו'.

ועד היכן מגיע חמימותיה: וותרן. לעבור על כל פשעם: יתוותרון בני מעוי. יוותרו קשרי בני מעיו, ויצאו בתחלואים. ל"א: יהיו לו בני מעים יתירים. שהוא מורה לבריות לחטוא, שסומכין שימחול להם המקום, ואינו כן אלא כל דרכיו משפט: אלא. שמאריך אפו וגובה חובו, אע"ג שאינו גובה אותו מיד: וסביביו. לצדיקים הנדבקים בו: נשערה מאוד. לשון "חוט השערה": "ונורא על כל סביביו". מטיל אימת משפטיו עליהם יותר מן הרחוקים: והוון כל עמא. והיה כל העם נכנסין אצל החסיד לנחמו, ולא רצה לקבל תנחומין: אמר להן: זהו חסידכם? בתמיה. הרי נוטע במידת הדין: והוא מקפחו במים. בתמיה. ו'קיפוח' הוא לשון חיתוך וקילור: מיד נפלה. קול בעיר: בסוכתא איתערית. בענף אחד אחזה עצמה ועלתה: קרא גברא. הא דתנן בפ"ק דיומא בכל יום תורמין את המזבח בקריאת הגבר, מהו "קריאת הגבר" — שהכריז הכרוז, והיינו שקרא גביני כרוז: אמרון ליה דבית ר' שילא שיתרגם "קרא התרנגול", שהוא נקרא "גבר": אית לך מימר "בר תרנגולא". בתמיה. אלא שם אדם שמו "גבר", ה"נ: קריאת הגבר — האדם קאי: ה"ג: שהיה מזווג את הפתילות. וכ"ה ביומא. וה"פ: שגדלן וקלען: בעי וכו'. רצה למנות עליהן פרנסים, ולא רצו לקבל על עצמן להיות פרנסים על הצבור, שאין זה כבודן: זכה להימנות עם גדולי הדור. עם הממונין החשובין שבישראל: כהאי דתנינן תמן. תמיד פ' בתרא: נזקרין לו בבת ראש. נרתעין מהכרעת קול: וברדייתו. ולרדות' מן התנור: היו מסיקין מבפנים. בתוך התנור ורודה מבחוץ לדפוס שהיה בתנור. שכך שנינו במנחות: ג' דפוסין היו שם. נותנו לדפוס ועדיין הוא בצק, כמין דפוס היה לה בתנור וכו', והיה הלחם דבוק מבחוץ לדפוס, והיה נאפה יפה, שחום התנור שולט בו: ואלו. אנשי אלכסנדריא לא היו בקיאין לרדותה מן התנור אם הוא דבוק חוץ לדפוס, והיו דובקין אותן בתוך הדפוס, ולא היה נאפה כל צרכו, מפני שעובי הדפוס מפסיק בין הבצק לתנור, ונתעפש: למענהו. לכבודו, שלא יהא לחם שולחנו מגוול בעיפוש: י"ב מנה היו נוטלים. כל יום מתרומת הלשכה: שלא יהיו אומרים ממעשה וכו'. וכתיב "והייתם נקיים מה' ומישראל": היתה מתמרת ועולה. היה העשן עולה זקוף כתמר, ומתפשט בשמי קורה, ואח"כ יורד: היתה. מתפשטת מיד למטה בתחילת עליית העשן: ממקום אחר. שלא ידעה מנהגם: היה פוסק עמה שלא תתבשם. דהמדיר את אשתו שלא תתקשט בא' מכל המינין — יוציא ויתן כתובה. לכך התנו עמה קודם הנישואין: לרבות כבודם. שלא ימלאו בקיאין זולתם: נתמעט כבודם. נחורבן הבית: וכבוד שמים נתרבה. שאמרו העשרת שבטים הא אלהינו הא קשוט, דאפי' לביתיה לא נסיב אפיה, וגם האומות אמרו כן: על הכבוד המתוקן לצדיקים. בבנין דלעתיד: הרי מעלה עשן לנגדי. ונזכרתי ע"י כן חורבן הבית. וגם בכבוד הצדיקים, שנאמר בישעיה "ועל כל מקראיה ענן יומם ועשן" וגו' ועשן זה ע"כ היה כמעלה עשן, דאל"כ האיך ישבו בחופה מפני העשן. אלא ודאי שהיה העשן מתפשט למעלה

נוסחאות ישנות

תורה אור

הַאי דֵּין כֵּיף מְקוֹרֵר מַיָּא, וְהַאי דֵּין כֵּיף אִית בֵּיהּ שְׁרַבְרוּבִי, וְעַד הֵיכָן שְׁרַבְרוּבוּתֵיהּ מָטֵי׳ א״ר אֱלִיעֶזֶר (אַחָא) וּמֵת בְּנוֹ בַּצָּמָא. אָמַר א) רַבִּי חֲנִינָא מַאן דְּאָמַר רַחֲמָנָא וַותְּרָן — יִתְוַותְּרָן בְּנֵי מֵעוֹיי. אֶלָּא מַאֲרִיךְ רוּחֵיהּ וְגָבֵי דִּידֵיהּ. א״ר אַחָא: כְּתִיב "וּסְבִיבָיו נִשְׂעֲרָה מְאוֹד" — מְדַקְדֵּק עִמָּהֶן כְּחוּט הַשַּׂעֲרָה. א״ר יוֹסֵי (בַּר אָבִין) לֹא מִטַּעַם הַזֶּה, אֶלָּא מִן מַה דִּכְתִיב "וְנוֹרָא הוּא עַל כָּל סְבִיבָיו" — מוֹרָאוֹ עַל הַקְּרוֹבִים יוֹתֵר מִן הָרְחוֹקִים. רַבִּי חַגַּיי בְּשֵׁם רַבִּי שְׁמוּאֵל בַּר נַחְמָן: מַעֲשֶׂה ב) בְּחָסִיד אֶחָד שֶׁהָיָה חוֹפֵר בּוֹרוֹת שִׁיחִין וּמְעָרוֹת לָעוֹבְרִים וְשָׁבִים, פַּעַם אַחַת הָיְתָה בִּתּוֹ עוֹבֶרֶת לְהִנָּשֵׂא וּשְׁטָפָהּ נָהָר, וַהֲוֹון כָּל עַמָּא עָלְלִין לְגַבֵּי, בְּעוֹן מְנַחֲמְתֵּיהּ וְלָא קִיבֵּל עָלוֹי מִתְנַחֲמָא. עָאל רַבִּי פִּנְחָס בֶּן יָאִיר לְגַבֵּיהּ, בְּעֵי מְנַחֲמְתֵּיהּ וְלָא קִיבֵּל עָלוֹי מִתְנַחֲמָא. אֲמַר לוֹן: דֵּין הוּא חֲסִידְכוֹן? אָמְרוּ לֵיהּ: רַבִּי, כָּךְ וְכָךְ הָיָה עוֹשֶׂה כָּךְ וְכָךְ אֵירַע לֵיהּ. אָמַר: אֶפְשָׁר שֶׁהָיָה מְכַבֵּד אֶת בּוֹרְאוֹ בַּמַּיִם וְהוּא מְקַפְּחוֹ בַּמַּיִם? מִיָּד נָפְלָה הֲבָרָה בָּעִיר: בָּאת בִּתּוֹ שֶׁל אוֹתוֹ הָאִישׁ. אִית דְּאָמְרֵי בְּסוּכָּתָא אִיתְעֲרִית, וְאִית דְּאָמְרֵי מַלְאָךְ יָרַד כִּדְמוּת ר׳ פִּנְחָס בֶּן יָאִיר וְהִצִּילָהּ.§ "גְּבִינֵי כָּרוֹז".§ שֶׁהָיָה ג) מַכְרִיז בְּבֵית הַמִּקְדָּשׁ. אֵימָה הָיָה אוֹמֵר: עִמְדוּ הַכֹּהֲנִים לַעֲבוֹדָה, וּלְוִיִּים לְדוּכָנָן, וְיִשְׂרָאֵל לְמַעֲמָדָן. אַגְרִיפָּס הַמֶּלֶךְ שָׁמַע קוֹלוֹ עַד ח׳ פַּרְסָאוֹת, וְנָתַן לוֹ מַתָּנוֹת הַרְבֵּה.§ "בֶּן גֶּבֶר עַל נְעִילַת שְׁעָרִים".§ תִּירְגֵּם ד) רַב קוּמֵי דְּבֵית ר׳ שֵׁילָא: קְרָא גַּבְרָא — אַכְרֵיז כָּרוֹזָא. *אָמַר לֵיהּ: אֱמוֹר קְרָא תַּרְנְגוֹלָא! א״ל וְהָתְנֵינַן בֶּן גֶּבֶר אִית לָךְ לְמֵימַר בַּר תַּרְנְגוֹלָא?!§ ב"בֶּן בֵּבַי עַל הַפָּקִיעַ".§ [א] שֶׁהָיָה (מְזַוֵּוג) מְזַיֵּיג פְּתִילוֹת. ר׳ ה) יוֹסֵי (אַסִּי) עָאל לְכוּפְרָה, בְּעוּ מְמַנֵּייא עֲלַיְיהוֹן פַּרְנָסִים וְלָא קִיבְּלוֹן מִינְהוֹן. (א) עָאל וַאֲמַר קוֹמֵיהוֹן: בֶּן בֵּבַי עַל הַפָּקִיעַ. וּמָה אִם זֶה שֶׁנִּתְמַנָּה עַל הַפְּתִילוֹת זָכָה לְהִימָּנוֹת עִם גְּדוֹלֵי הַדּוֹר, אַתֶּם שֶׁאַתֶּם נִתְמַנִּין עַל חַיֵּי נְפָשׁוֹת לכ״ש.§ "בֶּן אַרְזָה עַל הַצִּלְצָל".§ כִּי הָא דְּתַנֵּינַן ו) תַּמָּן: "הֵנִיף הַסְּגָן בַּסּוּדָרִין, וְהִקִּישׁ בֶּן אַרְזָה עַל הַצִּלְצָל.§ "הוּגְרַס בֶּן לֵוִי עַל הַשִּׁיר".§ (ב) אָמַר ז) ר׳ אַחָא: נְעִימָה יְתֵירָה הָיָה יוֹדֵעַ. וְאָמְרוּ עָלָיו עַל הוּגְרַס בֶּן לֵוִי שֶׁהָיָה מְנַעִים אֶת קוֹלוֹ בַּזֶּמֶר, וּכְשֶׁהָיָה נוֹעֵץ גּוּדָלוֹ בְּתוֹךְ פִּיו הָיָה מוֹצִיא כַּמָּה מִינֵי זֶמֶר, וְהָיוּ כָּל אֶחָיו הַכֹּהֲנִים נִזְקָרִין לוֹ בְּבַת רֹאשׁ.§ "בֵּית ח) גַּרְמוּ עַל מַעֲשֵׂה לֶחֶם הַפָּנִים".§ בֵּית גַּרְמוּ הָיוּ בְּקִיאִין בְּמַעֲשֵׂה לֶחֶם הַפָּנִים וּבִרְדִיָּיתוֹ, וְלֹא רָצוּ לְלַמֵּד. שָׁלְחוּ חֲכָמִים וְהֵבִיאוּ אוּמָּנִים (ג) מֵאֲלֶכְּסַנְדְּרִיאָה, שֶׁהָיוּ בְּקִיאִין בְּמַעֲשֵׂה לֶחֶם הַפָּנִים, וּבִרְדִיָּיתוֹ לֹא הָיוּ בְּקִיאִין. בֵּית (ד) גַּרְמוּ [א] הָיוּ מַסִּיקִין מִבִּפְנִים וְרוֹדִין מִבַּחוּץ וְלֹא הָיְתָה מִתְעַפֶּשֶׁת, וְאֵילּוּ הָיוּ מַסִּיקִין מִבִּפְנִים וְרוֹדִין מִבִּפְנִים, וְהָיְתָה מִתְעַפֶּשֶׁת. כֵּיוָן שֶׁיָּדְעוּ חֲכָמִים בַּדָּבָר הַזֶּה, אָמְרוּ: כָּל מַה שֶּׁבָּרָא הקב״ה — לִכְבוֹדוֹ בָּרָא, שֶׁנֶּאֱמַר "כֹּל פָּעַל ה׳ לַמַּעֲנֵהוּ". שָׁלְחוּ אַחֲרֵיהֶם וְלֹא רָצוּ לָבֹא עַד שֶׁכָּפְלוּ לָהֶם שְׂכָרָן. י״ב מָנֶה הָיוּ נוֹטְלִים, וְנָתְנוּ לָהֶם כ״ד ר׳ יְהוּדָה אוֹמֵר: כ״ד הָיוּ נוֹטְלִים, וְנָתְנוּ לָהֶן מ״ח אָמְרוּ לָהֶן: מִפְּנֵי מָה אֵין אַתֶּם רוֹצִים לְלַמֵּד? אָמְרוּ לָהֶן: מָסוֹרֶת הִיא בְּיָדֵינוּ מֵאֲבוֹתֵינוּ שֶׁהַבַּיִת הַזֶּה עָתִיד לֵיחָרֵב, שֶׁלֹּא יִלְמְדוּ אֲחֵרִים וְיַעֲשׂוּ לִפְנֵי ע״ז שֶׁלָּהֶן. בִּדְבָרִים הַלָּלוּ מַזְכִּירִין אוֹתָן לִשְׁבָח: שֶׁלֹּא יָצָא בְּיַד בְּנֵיהֶם פַּת נְקִיָּה מֵעוֹלָם, שֶׁלֹּא יְהוּ אוֹמְרִים מִמַּעֲשֵׂה לֶחֶם הַפָּנִים הֵן אוֹכְלִים.§ "בֵּית אַבְטִינָס עַל מַעֲשֵׂה הַקְּטוֹרֶת".§ שֶׁל בֵּית אַבְטִינָס הָיוּ בְּקִיאִין עַל מַעֲשֵׂי פִּיטּוּם הַקְּטוֹרֶת וּבְמַעֲלֵה הֶעָשָׁן, וְלֹא רָצוּ לְלַמֵּד. (ה) שָׁלְחוּ וְהֵבִיאוּ אוּמָּנִין מֵאֲלֶכְּסַנְדְּרִיאָה שֶׁל מִצְרַיִם וְהָיוּ בְּקִיאִין בְּפִיטּוּם הַקְּטוֹרֶת, וּבְמַעֲלֵה עָשָׁן לֹא הָיוּ בְּקִיאִין. שֶׁל בֵּית אַבְטִינָס הָיְתָה מִתַּמֶּרֶת וְעוֹלָה כְּמַקֵּל וּפוֹסָה וְיוֹרֶדֶת. וְשֶׁל אֵלּוּ הָיְתָה פּוֹסָה מִיָּד. כֵּיוָן שֶׁיָּדְעוּ חֲכָמִים בַּדָּבָר אָמְרוּ: כָּל מַה שֶּׁבָּרָא הקב״ה — לִכְבוֹדוֹ בָּרָא, שֶׁנֶּאֱמַר "כֹּל הַנִּקְרָא בִשְׁמִי לִכְבוֹדִי בְּרָאתִיו" וְגוֹ׳ (כ״א כָּל מַה שֶּׁפָּעַל הקב״ה לֹא פָּעַל אֶלָּא לְמַעֲנֵהוּ שֶׁנֶּאֱמַר "כֹּל פָּעַל ה׳ לַמַּעֲנֵהוּ") שָׁלְחוּ אַחֲרֵיהֶם וְלֹא רָצוּ לָבֹא, עַד שֶׁכָּפְלוּ לָהֶן שְׂכָרָן. י״ב מָנֶה הָיוּ נוֹטְלִין, וְנָתְנוּ לָהֶן כ״ד רַבִּי יְהוּדָה אוֹמֵר: כ״ד הָיוּ נוֹטְלִין וְנָתְנוּ לָהֶן מ״ח אָמְרוּ לָהֶן: מִפְּנֵי מָה אֵין אַתֶּם רוֹצִין לְלַמֵּד? אָמְרוּ לָהֶן: מָסוֹרֶת הִיא בְּיָדֵינוּ מֵאֲבוֹתֵינוּ שֶׁהַבַּיִת הַזֶּה עָתִיד לֵיחָרֵב, שֶׁלֹּא יִלְמְדוּ אֲחֵרִים וְיִהְיוּ עוֹשִׂין כֵּן לִפְנֵי ע״ז שֶׁלָּהֶן. בִּדְבָרִים הַלָּלוּ מַזְכִּירִין אוֹתָן לִשְׁבָח: שֶׁלֹּא יָצְאת אִשָּׁה מִשֶּׁל אֶחָד מֵהֶן מְבוּשֶּׂמֶת מֵעוֹלָם, וְלֹא עוֹד אֶלָּא כְּשֶׁהָיָה אֶחָד מֵהֶן נוֹשֵׂא אִשָּׁה מִמָּקוֹם אַחֵר הָיָה פּוֹסֵק עִמָּהּ ע״מ שֶׁלֹּא תִּתְבַּשֵּׂם, שֶׁלֹּא יְהוּ אוֹמְרִים מִמַּעֲשֵׂה פִּיטּוּם הַקְּטוֹרֶת הֵן מִתְבַּשְּׂמוֹת, לְקַיֵּים מַה שֶּׁנֶּאֱמַר "וִהְיִיתֶם נְקִיִּים מֵה׳ וּמִיִּשְׂרָאֵל". [ב] א״ר יוֹסֵי: פַּעַם אַחַת הָיִיתִי עוֹמֵד בִּירוּשָׁלַיִם וּמָצָאתִי תִּינוֹק אֶחָד מִשֶּׁל בֵּית אַבְטִינָס, אָמַרְתִּי לוֹ: בְּנִי, מֵאֵיזוֹ מִשְׁפָּחָה אַתְּ? אָמַר לִי: מִמִּשְׁפַּחַת פְּלוֹנִי, אָמַרְתִּי לוֹ: בְּנִי, אֲבוֹתֶיךָ לְפִי שֶׁנִּתְכַּוְּונוּ לְרַבּוֹת כְּבוֹדָן וּלְמַעֵט כְּבוֹד שָׁמַיִם — לְפִיכָךְ כְּבוֹדָם נִתְמַעֵט, וּכְבוֹד שָׁמַיִם נִתְרַבָּה. אָמַר ר״ע שָׂח לִי שִׁמְעוֹן בֶּן לוּגָא, מְלַקֵּט הָיִיתִי עֲשָׂבִים אֲנִי וְתִינוֹק אֶחָד מִשֶּׁל בֵּית אַבְטִינָס וְרָאִיתִי אוֹתוֹ שֶׁבָּכָה, וְרָאִיתִי אוֹתוֹ שֶׁשָּׂחַק. אָמַרְתִּי לוֹ: בְּנִי, לָמָּה בָּכִיתָ? אָמַר לִי: עַל כְּבוֹד שֶׁל בֵּית אַבָּא שֶׁנִּתְמַעֵט. וְלָמָּה שָׂחַקְתָּ? אָמַר לִי: עַל הַכָּבוֹד הַמְתוּקָּן לַצַּדִּיקִים לֶעָתִיד לָבֹא. וּמָה רָאִיתָ — מַעֲלֶה עָשָׁן לְנֶגְדִּי. נוֹמֵיתִי לוֹ: בְּנִי, הַרְאֵהוּ לִי! אָמַר לִי: רַבִּי, מָסוֹרֶת בְּיָדַי מֵאֲבוֹתַי שֶׁלֹּא לְהַרְאוֹתוֹ לִבְרִיָּיהוּ א״ר יוֹחָנָן בֶּן נוּרִי: (מְלַקֵּט הָיִיתִי עֲשָׂבִים אֲנִי וְזָקֵן א׳) פָּגַע בִּי זָקֵן א׳ מִשֶּׁל בֵּית אַבְטִינָס וּמְגִילַּת סַמָּנִים בְּיָדוֹ, אָמַר לִי: רַבִּי, לְשֶׁעָבַר הָיוּ בֵּית אַבָּא צְנוּעִין וְהָיוּ מוֹסְרִין

(margin: תהלים נ; שם פט; אמרון; משלי טז; ישעיה מג; במדבר לב)

תקלין חדתין

מפרשים ממשמש ג"כ לטובה לרפותן: כיף. סלע: מקרר. מוליא מים קרים: שרברוב. חמימות, ועד היכן החמימות מגיע: ומת בנו בצמא. כי במדה שאדם זהיר בה מאוד אם הוא פוגם קלת בזה נענש עליו ביותר. כדאיתא בפ"ז דב"מ פ"ד ב' בר"א בר"ש יומא חד תוא׳ דקא נפיק ריחשא מאוניה, אלש דעתאי כו'. א"ל: יומא חד שמעי בזילותא דצורבא מרבנן ולא מחאי כדבעי ליה כו'. והיינו לפי שהיה נזהר הרבה בזה, כדאמרינן במסכת מכות כ"ד א': "אוטם אזנו משמוע דמים" — כגון ראב"ש דלא שמיע ליה בזילותא דרבנן ושתיק. וכדפי' רש"י שם. ולכן אמר הכא בב"מ ולא מחאי כדאבעי לי. והכא נמי, שהיה אוחז במדה טובה זו להמציא מים לרבים וכשאירע לו דלא נזהר כמה דבעי — נענש בזה הענין גופיה: מ"ד רחמנא וותרן. מוותר על עבירות, דלא איכפת ליה: יתוותרן בני מעיא. דאמרינן בפ"ג דחולין ע"פ "הוא עשך ויכוננך": מלמד שעשה הקב"ה כוניות באדם, שאם נהפך א' מהם אינו יכול לחיות, והוא בני המעיים. כמ"ש הערוך: מלשון הדורא דכנתא. וראיה לדבריו דסמיך לה בסוגיא עובדא דההוא גברא דנפל מאיגרא ונפיק מעייניה כו'. וכמו שכל עיקר חיות האדם תלוי במעיו, כדקאמר: שאם נהפך כו', כן כל העולמות תלוים במעשי ב"א לבנותם או להרסם. וז"ש: שמי שאומר שמוותר הש"י על עבירה — יתוותרן כמו ויתר לבי כו'. שלא ישמש פעולתו, ואז היה נחרב העולם הקטן: מאריך רוחיה. הן מלאכיו. כמ"ש "עושה מלאכיו רוחות", ממיני הפורעניות, והם רצים, אך "והוא רחום יכפר וגו' והרבה להשיב אפו" — מלאך האף: וגבי דיליה. כמ"ש "צור ילדך תשי" — שמתישין כח פמליא של מעלה שהאדם נבנה מכולם, כמ"ש "כי בצלם אלהים עשה" וגו'. "ובו לדבר יחבל לו" בכל כח פוגם שרשו, וכל אחד גבי דיליה: כחוט השערה. כי יעקב איש חלק ועשו איש שעיר. ולדיקים הם יסודי עולם כוללים הרבה, ופגם קטן שלהן עושה רושם, והן נשפטין במדת אמת. ולכן היו יראים לדיקים הראשונים שמא יגרום החטא, אף חטא כל דהו. ומדקדק עמהם בעוה"ז כדי שלא יכנסו כלל ל"פתח חטאת רובץ": לעוברים ושבים. לזכות הרבים: ולא מקבל עליה תנחומין. שעל המת נגזר להשתכח מן הלב משא"כ על החי, כמ"ש "וימאן להתנחם" והיא היתה בחיים: אפשר הוה מכבד בוראו במים. אם היה מכבד הכל בזהירות וכבוד לשם שמים ולא פגם כלל והוא מקפחו במים? בתמיה. אלא ודאי תעלה: עלתה. שנזדמן לה גם שאחזה בענף אחד ועלתה: אגריפס המלך שמע קולו בשמנה פרסאות. אף דקולו של כ"ג היו שומעין עשרה פרסאות, כמ"ש מיריחו היו שומעין קולו של גביני כרוז (תמיד ל, ב), מ"מ ההיא עובדא הוה בסמוך שמנה פרסאות ושמע המלך שהיה שם אז: קרא גברא. היה מפרש מ"ש בפ"ק דיומא: ולא היתה קריאת הגבר מגעת כו'. הייני ש"קרא גברא ואכריז כרוזא" — האריך בלשונו דלא ליטעי שכוונתו תרנגולא, וגם הטמין כוונתו לראיה, מדאמר: גביני כרוז מה היה אומר, וז"ש "אכריז כרוזא". ובבבלי מסייע ליה מזה: א"ל קרא תרנגולא. משום דמלא ברייתא היולא לדרך קודם קריאת הגבר כו' בתרנגול בינוני כו' כדאמר ביומא (כ"א): והתנן בן גבר על כו'. אית לך למימר כו', אלא ע"כ "גבר" שניהם במשמע. ואינו ראיה מה שנמלא פעם "גבר" על תרנגול. ואידך ע"כ ס"ל דהכא ליכא למיטעי, אבל התם אי הוי שם אדם, ה"ל למינקט מפורש דלא ליטעי בתרנגולא. אלא ש"מ "קריאת הגבר" באמת תרנגולא, ועובדא דגביני כרוז מלתא אחריתי. ומה דאמר "ולא היה קריאת הגבר מגעת" — קאי על תרנגול, וג"מ בזמן: מזווג. רואה שיהא שוין משום הידור: ולא קבלון מיניה. משום "ושנא את הרבנות", ורצו לברוח מן הכבוד. א"נ: חרדו שלא יכשלו במ"ש פרנס המטיל אימה כו': חיי נפשות עאכ"ו. שדומה הכל, והמצוה רבה וראוי להכניס א"ע בזה: דתנינן תמן. פרק בתרא דתמיד: נזקרין. נרתעין מהכרעת הקול: של אלו. של אלכסנדריא: ה"ג: מבחוץ ואופין מבחוץ. וכ"ה בבבלי שם. ופי' רש"י: הללו שבאו מאלכסנדריא, לפי שלא היו יודעים לרדות מן התנור שלא יהא נשבר, לפי שהוא עשוי כמין תיבה פרולה כמין ספינה, והיו יראים לדבקם מבפנים לתנור, ואופין אותו מבחוץ. וגירסת הספרים משובש בתוספתא. והכא נמי האי שבשתא כיון דעל על: שכפלו להן. מתרומת הלשכה: בפטום. לכתוש הסממנין ולערבם יפה, כמו שאמר "ממולח": ובמעלה עשן. שלא היו מכירין בעשב שהוא מעלה עשן זוקף ומתמר כמקל: לשוק. כלומר, שלא היו מתבסמין כלל. ובבבלי אמר: לא יצאה כלה מבושמת מבתיהן. והכא נמי קאמר, ולא עוד כו': א"ר ישמעאל גרסינן: ונתרבה כבוד שמים. ובבבלי אמר כבוד המקום במקומו ומיעט כבודן: המתוקן לצדיקים לע"ל. והיינו שעתיד הקב"ה להחזיר לנו לע"ל. ובבבלי הלשון: שעתיד הקב"ה להחזיר לנו: מעלה עשן עומד לנגדי. עשב שמעלה עומד כנגדי, ורואיתיו ונזכרתי: הראהו לי. לי בלבדי, שאני בודאי אהיה זהיר שלא יגיע לע"ז, וליכא טעמא שמא יעשה לע"ז: מסורת בידי. ובבבלי: שבועה: לבריה. לשום אדם, משום גדר בדבר: רבי יוחנן. ובבבלי גרסינן "ר"י בן נורי" ו"רבי ישמעאל בן לוגא" במקום "שמעון ב"ל" לעיל: נאמנין

משנת אליהו

א"ל אפשר הוה מכבד בוראו. עיין מה שפירשתי בקונטרס ומזה מתורץ קושיית תוס' ב"ק דהא גבי נחוניא מת בנו בצמא דהתם היה לו איזה נדנוד חטא שנענש עבורו כמו דמייתי עלה בסוגיא מ"ד רחמנא ותרן כו' והקב"ה מדקדק עם הצדיקים כחוט השערה וכ"מ בסוגיא דב"ק שם וכאן ה"ק אפשר הוה מכבד בוראו הכל בכבוד בלי פגם בההוא חסידא ויקפחנו במים אלא בודאי תנצל ע"י נס וכן הוה: אגריפס המלך שמע קולו ברחוק ח' פרסה כו'. עמ"ש ולא סתרא הא לדתנן בתמיד שקולו היו שומעין מיריחו דבאמת הוא כן רק דעובדא דאגריפס שהיה אז רחוק ח' פרסה ושמע ונתשב לו לדבר נפלא ונתן לו מתנות אבל סוגיא דבבלי יומא כ' ע"ב קשה דקאמר והיה קולו נשמע בג' פרסאות דמשמע תמיד לא יותר וכן מצאתי בת"י דיומא שם שדמו בזה תירץ הרב יוסף בר"מ וגם תירץ התוס' דמו ע"ש ומסקי דפליגי הסוגיות ומ"ש התוי"ט דבתמיד מייתי לא קול של כ"ג רק של העם דוחק רב ותימה שלא הזכיר כלל לדברי התוספות דיומא:

מסורת הש"ס

א) בבלי ב"ק נ א ירושלמי ביצה פ"ג הל"ח ותענית פ"ג הל"א: ב) ב"ק דף נ א יבמות קכא ב וירושלמי דמאי פ"א הל"ג: ג) יומא כ ב: ד) יומא כ ב וירושל' סוכה פ"ה הל"ה: ה) ירושלמי יומא פ"ב הל"ב ירושלמי פאה פ"ח הלכה ו: ו) תמיד פרק ז: ז) יומא לח ב: ח) יומא לח א וירו' שם פ"ג הל"ט:

עין משפט נר מצוה

ו א מיי' פ"ז מכלי המקדש הל"ב:

ז ב שם הלכה ז ובהשגות וכ"מ:

ח ג מיי' שם הל"א ופ"ו מתמידין הל"ז:

נוסחת הבבלי

(א) פתח ואמר קמיהון כו' ומה זה שלא נתמנה אלא על הפתילו' זכה למנו' כו': (ב) א"ר אחיא נעימה יתירה היתה לו אמרו כו' נזקרין בבת ראש: (ג) מאלכסנדריא של מצרים שהיו כו' ורדייתן לא היו כו': (ד) בית גרמו היו מסיקין את התנור מבפנים כו' כיון ששמעו חכמי' כו' ולא רצו לחזור כו' לשבח אמרו לא נמצאת מעולם פת נקיה ביד בניהן כדי שלא יאמרו מלחם הפנים היו אוכלין: (ה) שלחו חכמים והביאו כו' כיון ששמעו חכמי' כו' ולא רצו לחזור עד כו' מעולם לא יצתה אשה מהם כשהיתה מתבסמת לשוק ולא עוד אלא כשהיו נושאין ממקום אחר פוסקין עמה ע"מ שלא תתבסם כדי שלא יהו אומרין כו' תינוק א' (ממשפחת פלוני) ואמרתי לו בני של מי אתה א"ל ממשפחת של בית אבטינס אני אמרתי לו ע"י שאבותיך בקשו להרבות בכבודם ולמעט בכבודו של מקום עכשיו נתמעט כבודם ונתרבה כבוד שמים אר"ע כו':

הגהות הגר"א

[א] ה"ג היו מסיקין את התנור מבפנים ואופין מבפנים ולא היתה מתעפשת של אלו היו מסיקין מבחוץ ואופין מבחוץ והיתה מתעפשת כצ"ל וכ"ה בבבלי שם ופי' רש"י הללו שבאו מאלכסנדריא לפי שלא היו יודעים לרדות מן התנור שלא יהא נשבר לפי שהיא עשויה כמין תיבה פרוצה כמין ספינה והיו יראים לדבקם מבפני' לתנור ואופין אותו מבחוץ. וגירסת הספרים משובש בתוספתא והכא נמי האי שבשתא כיון דעל על: [ב] אמר ר' ישמעאל גרסינן:

גליון הש"ס

[א] עי' מוהרש"פ ומדברי התוס' מנחו' דף פט ע"א ד"ה ושיעורו מוכח כפי' הק"ע דקאי על עובי הפתילה ודקות' ועי' ירושלמי יומא ועי' בת"י יומא טו ד"ה תן וריטב"א שם:

תורה אור

מוסרין את המגילה הזאת אלו לאלו, ועכשיו שאינן בית אבא (א) נאמנים — הילך את המגילה, והזהר בה. וכשבאתי והרציתי הדברים לפני ר"ע זלגו עיניו דמעות, ואמר: מעתה אין אנו צריכין (ראשין) להזכירן לגנאי.§ "אלעזר על הפרוכת"§ אשהיה ממונה על אורגי פרוכת.§ ב"פנחס המלביש"§ שהיה מלביש בגדי כהונה גדולה. מעשה בכהן א' שהלביש לאיסטרטיות א' ונתן לו שמונה זהובים. ואית דאמרין תרי עשרי יהב ליה.§

הלכה ב מתני' אין (א) פוחתין גמשבעה אמרכולין ושלשה גזברין.

דואין ג) עושין שררה על (ב) הצבור פחות משנים. חוץ מבן אחיה שעל חולי מעיים, ואלעזר שעל הפרוכת, שאותן קיבלו רוב הצבור עליהן.§ גמ' "אין פוחתין מג' גזברין ומז' אמרכולין". תני: המשני כתליקין. הדא הוא דכתיב "ויחיאל ועוזיהו ונחת" — גזברין, "ועשהאל וירימות ויוזבד ואליאל ויסמכיהו ומחת ובניהו" — אמרכולין, "פקידים מיד כונניהו ושמעי אחיו" — קתליקין, "במפקד יחזקיהו המלך ועזריהו נגיד בית אלהים" — המלך וכ"ג כשהוא חותם — הגזבר חותם ונותנו (ג) לאמרכול, אמרכל חותם ונותנו לקתליקון, קתליקון חותם ונותנו לכהן גדול, כ"ג חותם ונותנו למלך. וכשהוא מתיר, המלך רואה חותמו ומתיר, כ"ג רואה חותמו ומתיר, קתליקין רואה חותמו ומתיר, אמרכל רואה חותמו ומתיר, גזבר רואה חותמו ומתיר.§ "אין עושין שררה על הצבור בממון פחות משנים".§ רב ג) נחמן בשם רבי מנא על שם "והם יקחו את הזהב ואת התכלת ואת הארגמן". אמר ר' (נחמיה) חמא בי רבי חנינא: מפסולת של לוחות העשיר משה, הדא הוא דכתיב "פסל לך שני לוחות אבנים" — פסל ד) לך, שתהא הפסולת שלך. אמר ה) ר' חנין מחצב של אבנים טובות ומרגליות (גילה) ברא לו הקב"ה מתוך אהלו, וממנו העשיר משה. כתיב "והביטו אחרי משה עד בואו האהלה" תרין ו) אמוראין, ח"א לגנאי וח"א לשבח. מ"ד לגנאי: חמון שקין, חמון כרעין, (ד) חמון קופד, אכיל מן דיהודאי ושתי מן דיהודאי, כל מדליה מן דיהודאי. ומ"ד לשבח: מחמי צדיקיא ומזכי טוביא דזכת למיחמי יתיה.§

הלכה ג מתני' יד' חותמות היו במקדש וכתוב עליהן: עגל, זכר, גדי, וחוטא. בן

עזאי אומר: ה' היו, וארמית כתוב עליהן: עגל, דכר, גדי, חוטא דל, וחוטא עשיר. עגל ז) משמש עם נסכי בקר, גדולים וקטנים, זכרים ונקבות. גדי משמש עם נסכי הצאן, גדולים וקטנים, זכרים ונקבות, חוץ משל אילים. איל משמש עם נסכי אילים בלבד. חוטא משמש עם נסכי שלש בהמות של מצורע. זמי שהוא מבקש נסכים הולך לו אצל יוחנן שהוא ממונה על החותמות. ונותן לו מעות ומקבל ממנו חותם. בא לו אצל אחיה שהוא ממונה על הנסכים, ונותן לו חותם ומקבל ממנו נסכים. לערב באין זה אצל זה, ואחיי' מוציא את החותמות ומקבל כנגדן מעות. חאם פחתו — פחתו לו, וישלם יוחנן מביתו. ואם הותירו — הותירו להקדש, שיד הקדש על העליונה. מי שאבד חותמו ממתינין לו עד הערב, ואם מצאו לו כדי חותמו — נותנין לו. ואם לאו — לא היו נותנין לו ושם היום כתוב עליהן, מפני הרמאין.§

גמ' [א] וכבן עזאי חוטא דל למה היה מביא לוגו עמו? ברם כרבנן, מביא גדי נסכי רחל מה? מן מה דתנינן גדי משמש טנסכי צאן גדולים וקטנים זכרים ונקבות, הדא אמרי נסכי רחל כנסכי גדי. דכתיב "ככה יעשה לשור האחד או לאיל האחד או לשה בכבשים או בעזים", "לשור ח) האחד" למה נאמר — מגיד שלא חילק בין נסכי עגל לנסכי שור. שהיה בדין בן הצאן טעון נסכים ובן הבקר טעון נסכים, אם מצאנו שחילק בין נסכי כבש לנסכי איל, לכך

ריבב"ן

מתני' מז' מרכולין. תניא בתוספתא פ"ג גזברין מה הן עושין פודין את הערכין ואת החרמין ואת ההקדשות וכל מלאכות הקדש בידן מרכולין מה הן עושין ז' מפתחות עזרה בידן רצה אחד מהן לפתוח אינו יכול עד שיכנסו כולן מרכולין פותחין וגזברין נכנסין ויוצאין ולפי כבוד הנכנסין היו יוצאין אמר ר' יהודה למה נקרא שמו מרכול מפני שהוא מר על הכל פי' מר אדון לשון מרות ירושלמי תניא אין פוחתין מג' כתליקין הדא הוא דכתיב ויחיאל ועוזיהו ונחת גזברין ועשהאל וירימות ויוזבד ואליאל ויסמכיהו ומחת ובניהו מרכולין פקידים מיד כנניהו ושמעי אחיו מרכולין כשהוא חותם הגזבר נותנו למרכול מרכול חותם ונותנו לקתלקוס וקתלקוס לכ"ג וכ"ג למלך ואין עושין שררה פחות משנים בגבאות בתרא פרק א' דכתיב והם יקחו את הזהב:

מתני' ד' חותמות וכתוב עליהן עגל זכר גדי חוטא. מפרש ואזיל למה הוצרכו לפי שנסכיהן חלוקין זה מזה: ארמית. לפי שמלומדין בלשון כשדים בגלות בבל: חוטא דל וחוטא עשיר מצורע עני מצורע עשיר ותנן בערכין על ד' דברים הנגעים באין לפיכך נקרא חוטא. עני מביא תורין או בני יונה אחד לעולה ואחד לחטאת ואשם זה הכבש שהיה צריך נסכים אבל מצורע עשיר מביא ג' בהמות חטאת ועולה ואשם ואין חטאת ואשם טעונין נסכים אלא חטאתו ואשמו של מצורע לפי שאין באין על חטא דבנגעים איכפר ליה והמקריבים מאין בהן אין באין אלא להכשירו בקדשים: גדולים וקטנים. שאין חילוק בנסכים בין עגל לשור ולמה היו חותם אחד לאשם ולחטאת של מצורע והלא נסכיהן כשאר כבשין שבאין נדבה דשניהן היו כבשים שאשם מצורע טעון לוג שמן לבד ממה שמביא לשמן הוא אלא לפי שאשם מצורע טעון לוג שמן ליתן לבהונות לבד שמן שבא מן הנסכים:

מתני' לערב באין זה אצל זה. יוחנן אצל אחיה וכנגד החותמות שקיבל אחיה נותן [לו] יוחנן מעות אם פחתו פחתו ליוחנן אם הותירו הותירו להקדש: מתני' מי שאבד חותמו ממתינין לו עד הערב. שיוצא יוחנן אצל אחיה ויראה אם מלאו מעות יתירין כדי חותמו של זה שאבד נותן לו הנסכים ושם של היום פי' שם של היום כתוב ביום פ' נעשה חותם זה. מפני הרמאין שמא ימצאנו אדם אחר זמן וילך אצל אחיה ויתן לו סולת: ירושלמי הגע עצמך שזיוג אותו היום שם המשמר היה כתוב עליו הגע עצמך שזיוג אותו המשמר שם היום שם שבת שם חדש כתוב עליהן:

תקלין חדתין

נאמנים כו' אלו לאלו. ולא היה בא ליד אחר שאינו הגון: שאינן נאמנים. וירא אנכי שלא יגיע ליד אדם שאינו הגון: הא לך. שאתה נאמן, ותחזר בהם: בגנותן. שהרי טעמם אמת. שעכשיו שהיה צריך למסור מסר. ובגבלי: כ"ז שהיו בית אבא קיימין כו': מתני' אין פוחתין וכו'. גזברין הן שממונין הקדש בידם, והם פודין ערכין וחרמין וכל מלאכות הקדש נעשה על ידם: אמרכלין. למעלה מהגזברין, אמר על כולם: ואין עושין שררה כו'. לשון הגאון: דכל הממונים היו עמהן אחרים, לתתני' משל ראש הממונים לבד אלו השנים שהיו יחידים: גמ' תנא ברייתא מוספת שאין פוחתין מג' ממונים למעלה מן האמרכלין הדא הוא דכתיב. מסמיך בכתוב: ויחיאל וגו'. שם מיירי בתרומת הלשכה וקדשים כו', וזה יחיאל ועוזיהו ונחת אלו ג' גזברין שעסקו בערכין וחרמין שלריכין ודאי ג'. ואח"כ חשיב ז' אמרכלין מן ועשהאל וגו' עד ובניהו. וכנניהו ושמעי אחיו נקראו פקידים, והן ג' כתלקין: במפקד כו'. המלך וכ"ג, ש"נגיד בית אלהים" הוא כ"ג: כשהוא חותם. כשרולה לחתום

קרבן העדה

חוץ לנסכך: המגילה הזאת שכתובים בה סמני קטורת איך להכירם וסדר פיטומו: מעתה. אין להזכירם לגנאי. שהרי ניכר שכוונתם היתה לשמים, שהרי עכשיו מסרה להגון, אע"פ שאינו ממשפחתו: שהיה מלביש בגדי כ"ג. שיהיו נאין ומהודרין: לאיסטרטיאות. שר משרי החיילות:

הלכה ב מתני' גזברים. הם שממון הקדש תחת ידם, והם פודין ערכין וחרמין, וכל מלאכת ההקדש נעשה על ידם: אמרכלין. למעלה מן הגזברים. והוא נוטריקון "אמר על כלו". ובגמ' יליף לה דממונים אלו מקרא: גמ' כתיליקין. והוא שררה למעלה מן האמרכל: גזברין. אע"ג דבקרא לא כתיב גזברין, מסברא ידעינן שהיו גזברין

ג'. דהא פסקו שכר ולדקות ופדיית ערכין, וחרמי' לריכין ג' דהיינו דין. וכיון דקרא ממנה למעלה קחשיב — ש"מ שהראשונים הם הגזברין שהן למטה מהאמרכלין. והא דקחשיב בקרא כה"ג לסוף, אע"ג דהמלך גדול ממנו — היינו כדי לסיים נגיד בית האלהים, שיהיה השם בתר כולם. שהוא למעלה על כל: כשהוא חותם. הלכשה שהמעות נחתם. דהאי קרא בשמירת האוצרות איירי, וילפינן מיניה דלכך כתיבי כולהו, ללמד דכולם חותמין האוצרות. ולכדמסיק: והם יקחו את הזהב. מיעוט רבים שנים: שתהא הפסולת שלך. והלוחות של סנפירינון היו: מחצב. מקום שחולבין ממנו: חמון שקין וכו'. ראו השוקים, ראו הכרעיים, ראו בשרו, ראו ממה שהוא אוכל ושותה מן היהודים, וכל רכושו מן היהודים: מיחמי צדיקא וכו'. כדי לזכות בראיית הצדיק הביטו אחריו, דזכות גדול הוא שזוכה לראותו:

הלכה ג מתני' ד' חותמות היו במקדש. ג' לג' נסכים חלוקין של בהמות, חותם ראשון — לנסכי בקר, והן ג' עשרונים סולת בלול בחצי הין שמן ויין לנסך חצי ההין, וחותמו "עגל". והב' — "זכר", לנסכי איל, שתרגום "איל" — "דכרא". ונסכיו שתי עשרונים סולת בלול בשמן שלישית ההין, ויין לנסך שלישית ההין. והג' — "גדי", לנסכי כבש בן שנתו, והן עשרון סולת בלול ברביעית ההין שמן ויין לנסך רביעית ההין. והד' "חוטא" — והם נסכיו של מצורע עשיר שמביא ג' בהמות, ולריך עשרה לוגין מן תשעה לשלשה כבשים, ואחד למתן תנוך והבהונות. וקרי ליה "חוטא" משום דעל שבע עבירות נגעים באין: ה' היו. ב' חותמות היו למצורע: חוטא דל וחוטא עשיר. לפי שמצורע עני אינו מביא אלא בהמה אחת. ואם לא היה למצורע אלא חותם אחד — היו נותנים למצורע עני עשר לוגין. ות"ק סבר למצורע עני נותנין חותם גדי, ולוג רביעית היה מביא מביתו: וארמית כתוב עליהן. שהכל היה בלשון ארמי: זכרים ונקבות. בין לנסכי עולות שאינן באות אלא זכרים, בין נסכי שלמים שבאין זכרים ונקבות. ועולה ושלמים טעונין נסכים, דכתיב "עולה או זבח". כפי הנסכים שהוא לריך: בא לו אצל אחיה. שהיה ממונה לקנות יינות ושמנים וסלתות. שלא יהא כל מביא קרבן לריך לחזור אחר נסכים המעשין על טהרת הקדש: ואם הותירו הותירו להקדש. ולא אמרינן שמא מעותיו של יוחנן הם שנתערבו במעות של נסכים: ממתינים לו עד הערב, שיזדווגו יחד יוחנן ואחיה. אם נמלאו מעות יתירים ביד יוחנן כנגד החותם שאמר זה שנאבד ממנו — נותנים לו: ושם היום כתוב. על החותם יום פלוני בשבת: מפני הרמאין. שמא מלא חותם שנפל מחבירו או מאחיה או מיוחנן, ובא עכשיו ליקח. וביום שמוליאו אינו רשאי להוליאו, שהאובד מחזר אחריו. ועוד: יש לחוש שמא לקח חותם בשער הזול והלניעו עד שער היוקר: גמ' ופריך: ולבן עזאי חוטא דל למה ליה חותם בפני עצמו? היה לו להביא חותם "גדי"! ומשני: היה מביא לוגו עמו. כדי שיביא גם לוג שמן שלריך המצורע למתן תנוך והבהונות, והמותר נאכל לכהנים כדין קדשי הקדשים. ולריך שיהיה על טהרת הקדש, לפיכך נתנו לו חותם בפני עצמו, שהוא נסכי גדי וד' לוג שמן: ברם כרבנן. אבל לרבנן לא היו נותנין לחוטא דל אלא חותם של "גדי", ולוג שמן למתן בהונותיו היה מביא מביתו, קשיא: א"כ אף לחוטא עשיר לא היו לריכין לתתן חותם בפני עצמו שיכולין ליתן לו ג' חותמות "גדי"! נסכי רחל בכמה? שאינן מוזכרים במתני' ומשני: מן מה דתני במתני' גדי משמש לנסכי צאן וכו'. שמעינן דנסכי רחל כנסכי גדי: שהיה בדין. שיהא חילוק בין נסכי עגל לנסכי שור:

מסורת הש"ס

א) תמיד כו: ב) בבא בתרא ח כ: ג) שם: ד) נדרים לח א: ה) ויקרא רבה פ' לב: ו) בבלי קדושין לג ב ירושלמי בכורים פ"ג הל"ג ועי' שיר פ' נג: ז) מנחות לב: ח) מנחות לא כ:

עין משפט נר מצוה

ט א מיי' פ"ז מהל' המקדש הל"ז:
י ב מיי' שם הל"ב:
יא ג מיי' שם פ"ד הלכה יח:
יב ד מיי' פרק ט ממ"ע הלכה כ:
יג ה מיי' פ"ד מהל' המקדש הל"ד:
יד ו מיי' פ"ז שם הל"ח:
טו ז מיי' שם הל"ה:
טז ח מיי' שם הל"ג ובהשגות:
יז ט מיי' פרק ב ממעשה"ק הל"ד:

נוסחת הבבלי

(א) נאמנין הא לך זו כו' מעתה אין אנו רשאין לספר בגנותן של אלו: (ב) שררה על הצבור בממון פחות מב' כו' ואלעזר שעל הפרוכת כו': (ג) למלך המלך רואה כו': (ד) חמו קופריה אכיל כו' לשבח הלואי מחמו צדיקא כו':

הגהות הגר"א

[א] צ"ל ולבן עזאי חוטא דל למה מפני שמביא לוגו עמו ברם כרבנן וכו'. ועי' בקי"ע שמפרש גם כן על דרך הגס"ס זו:

מפני הרמאין. שם מיהו לא ענש ולא חסרה ואי כח העשה קורא בדוכתי, חוק לפריבס. אבל חותם חד למחוייב עשיר: ברם כרבנן מביא גדי. ...

תורה אור

לָכָךְ נַחֲלוֹק בֵּין נִסְכֵּי עֵגֶל לְנִסְכֵּי שׁוֹר, ת"ל "כָּכָה יֵעָשֶׂה לַשּׁוֹר הָאֶחָד" — מַגִּיד שֶׁלֹּא חִלֵּק בֵּין נִסְכֵּי עֵגֶל לְנִסְכֵּי שׁוֹר, "אוֹ לָאַיִל" לָמָּה נֶאֱמַר? שֶׁהָיָה בְּדִין, אִם מָצָאנוּ שֶׁחִלֵּק בֵּין נִסְכֵּי בֶּן שָׁנָה לְנִסְכֵּי בֶּן שְׁנָתַיִם, לָכָךְ נַחֲלוֹק בֵּין נִסְכֵּי שְׁנָתַיִם לְנִסְכֵּי שָׁלֹשׁ —
(במדבר טו) ת"ל "אוֹ לָאַיִל הָאֶחָד". "אוֹ לַשֶּׂה בַכְּבָשִׂים" לָמָּה נֶאֱמַר? שֶׁהָיָה בְּדִין, אִם מָצָאנוּ שֶׁחִלֵּק בֵּין נִיסְכֵּי כֶבֶשׂ לְנִסְכֵּי אַיִל, לָכָךְ נַחֲלוֹק בֵּין נִסְכֵּי כִשְׂבָּה לְנִסְכֵּי רָחֵל — ת"ל "אוֹ לַשֶּׂה בַכְּבָשִׂים". "אוֹ בָעִזִּים" לָמָּה נֶאֱמַר? שֶׁהָיָה בְּדִין, אִם מָצָאנוּ שֶׁחִלֵּק בֵּין נִיסְכֵּי כֶבֶשׂ לְנִסְכֵּי אַיִל, לָכָךְ נַחֲלוֹק בֵּין נִסְכֵּי גְדִי לְנִסְכֵּי תַיִשׁ — ת"ל "אוֹ בָעִזִּים" — הִקִּישׁ קָטָן שֶׁבָּעִזִּים לְגָדוֹל שֶׁבַּתְּיָשִׁים, מַה זֶּה בִּשְׁלֹשֶׁת לוּגִּין אַף זֶה בִּשְׁלֹשֶׁת לוּגִּין.§ "וְשֵׁם הַיּוֹם כָּתוּב" כו'.§ (א) הַגַּע בְּעַצְמְךָ שֶׁזֵּיֵּג אוֹתוֹ הַיּוֹם! "שֵׁם מִשְׁמָר הָיָה כָּתוּב עָלָיו". הַגַּע בְּעַצְמְךָ שֶׁזֵּיֵּג אוֹתוֹ הַמִּשְׁמָר! שֵׁם הַיּוֹם, שֵׁם שַׁבָּת, שֵׁם חוֹדֶשׁ הָיָה כָּתוּב עֲלֵיהֶן. אֲפִילּוּ רוֹצֶה לְזַיֵּיג אֵין מָצוּי לְזַיֵּיג.§

הלכה ד מתני' אשְׁתֵּי לְשָׁכוֹת הָיוּ בַּמִּקְדָּשׁ, אַחַת לִשְׁכַּת חֲשָׁאִין וְאַחַת לִשְׁכַּת הַכֵּלִים. לִשְׁכַּת חֲשָׁאִין — יִרְאֵי חֵטְא נוֹתְנִין לְתוֹכָהּ בַּחֲשַׁאי, וַעֲנִיִּים בְּנֵי טוֹבִים מִתְפַּרְנְסִין מִתּוֹכָהּ בַּחֲשַׁאי. לִשְׁכַּת הַכֵּלִים — כָּל מִי שֶׁהוּא מִתְנַדֵּב כְּלִי זוֹרְקוֹ לְתוֹכָהּ. וְאַחַת לִשְׁלֹשִׁים יוֹם הַגִּזְבָּרִין פּוֹתְחִין אוֹתָהּ, וְכָל כְּלִי שֶׁמָּצְאוּ בוֹ צוֹרֶךְ לְבֶדֶק הַבַּיִת — מַנִּיחִין אוֹתוֹ, וְהַשְּׁאָר (ב) נִמְכָּרִין וּדְמֵיהֶן נוֹפְלִין (לְלִשְׁכַּת) בדק הַבַּיִת.§ גמ' ר' א) יַעֲקֹב בַּר אִידִי ור' יִצְחָק בַּר נַחְמָן הֲווֹן פַּרְנָסִים, וַהֲווֹן יָהֲבִין לר' חָמָא אֲבוֹי (ג) דר' יְהוֹשֻׁעְיָה דִּינָר, וְהוּא יָהֵיב לֵיהּ לְחוֹרָנִין. רַבִּי זְכַרְיָה חַתְנֵיהּ דר' לֵוִי הָיוּ הַכֹּל מְלִיזִין עָלָיו, אָמְרִין דְּלָא צָרִיךְ וְהוּא נָסַב. מִן דִּדְמָךְ בָּדְקִין וְאַשְׁכְּחִין דַּהֲוָה מְפַלֵּיג לֵיהּ לְחוֹרָנִין. רַבִּי חִינְנָא בַּר פַּפָּא הֲוָה מְפַלֵּיג מִצְוָה בְּלֵילְיָא, חַד זְמַן פָּגַע בֵּיהּ רַבְּהוֹן
(דברים יט) דְּרוּחַיָּא. א"ל לֹא כֵן אַלְפָן ר' "לֹא תַסִּיג גְּבוּל רֵעֲךָ".
(משלי כא) א"ל וְלֹא כֵן כְּתִיב "מַתָּן בַּסֵּתֶר יִכְפֶּה אָף". וַהֲוָה מִסְתַּפֵּי מִינֵּיהּ, וַעֲרַק מִן קוֹמוֹי. אָמַר ג) רַבִּי יוֹנָה: "אַשְׁרֵי
(תהלים מא) נוֹתֵן לַדָּל" אֵין כְּתִיב כָּאן, אֶלָּא "אַשְׁרֵי מַשְׂכִּיל אֶל דָּל" — זֶה שֶׁהוּא מִסְתַּכֵּל בְּמִצְוָה הֵיאַךְ לַעֲשׂוֹתָהּ. כֵּיצַד הָיָה רַבִּי (יוֹחָנָן) יוֹנָה עוֹשֶׂה כְּשֶׁהָיָה רוֹאֶה עָנִי בֶּן טוֹבִים שֶׁיָּרַד מִנְּכָסָיו, הָיָה אוֹמֵר לוֹ: בְּנִי, בִּשְׁבִיל שֶׁשָּׁמַעְתִּי שֶׁנָּפְלָה לְךָ יְרוּשָּׁה מִמָּקוֹם אַחֵר, טוֹל וְאַתְּ פּוֹרֵעַ. מִן דַּהֲוָה נָסֵיב הֲוָה א"ל מַתָּנָה הִיא לָךְ. חִיָּיא בַּר אַדָּא: אִית הֲוָה סָבִין בְּיוֹמֵינוֹן, מַאן דַּהֲוָה יָהֵיב לְהוֹן מִבֵּין רֵישׁ שַׁתָּא לְצוֹמָא רָבָא — הֲווֹן נָסְבִין, מִן בָּתַר כֵּן — לָא הֲווֹן נָסְבִין. אָמְרִין: [א] דְּשַׁתָּן גַּבָּן. נְחֶמְיָה ג) אִישׁ שִׁיחִין פָּגַע בּוֹ יְרוּשַׁלְמִי א' א"ל זְכֵה עִמִּי חֲדָא תַּרְנְגוֹלְתָּא. א"ל הֵא לָךְ (ד) טוּמִיתֵיהּ דְּקוּפָּד. וְזַבֵּין קוּפָּד, וְאָכֵיל וּמִית. וְהָיָה צוֹוֵחַ וְאָמַר: בּוֹאוּ וְסִפְדוּ לַהֲרוּגוֹ שֶׁל נְחֶמְיָה. נַחוּם ד) אִישׁ גַּם זוֹ הָיָה מוֹלִיךְ דּוֹרוֹן לְבֵית חָמִיו, פָּגַע בּוֹ מוּכֵּה שְׁחִין א' א"ל זְכֵה עִמִּי מִמַּה דְּאִית גַּבָּךְ! אָמַר לֵיהּ: מֵיחְזוֹר. חָזַר וְאַשְׁכְּחֵיהּ
(יהבון) מִית. וַהֲוָה אָמַר לְקִיבְלֵיהּ: עַיְנַיָּא דַּחֲמִינָךְ וְלָא *יִסְבּוּן לָךְ — יִסְתַּמְּיָין, יָדַיָּה דְּלָא פַּשְׁטָן מֵיתַן לָךְ — יִתְקַטְּעוּן רַגְלַיָּא דְּלָא רָהֲטָן לְמֵיתַן לָךְ — יִתְבְּרוּן. וּמַטְתֵיהּ כֵּן. סְלֵיק לְגַבֵּיהּ ר' עֲקִיבָא, אָמַר לֵיהּ: אִי לִי שֶׁאֲנִי רוֹאֶה אוֹתְךָ בְּכָךְ. אָמַר לֵיהּ: אִי לִי שֶׁאֵין אֲנִי רוֹאֶה אוֹתְךָ בְּכָךְ. אָמַר לֵיהּ: מָה אַתְּ מְקַלְּלֵנִי?! אָמַר לֵיהּ: וּמָה אַתְּ מְבַעֵט בְּיִסּוּרִין? רַבִּי הוֹשַׁעְיָה רַבָּה הֲוָה רַבֵּיהּ דִּבְרֵיהּ חַד סַגֵּי נְהוֹרָא, וַהֲוָה יָלֵיף אֱכוֹל עִימֵּיהּ בְּכָל יוֹם. חַד זְמַן הֲוָה לֵיהּ אוֹרְחִין וְלָא מְטָא מֵיכוֹל עִימֵּיהּ. בְּרַמְשָׁא סְלֵיק לְגַבֵּיהּ, א"ל לֹא יִכְעוֹס מָרִי עֲלַי, בְּגִין דַּהֲוָה לִי אוֹרְחִין יוֹמָא דֵין, דַּאֲמָרִית דְּלָא לִיבְזוֹי בִּיקָרָא דְּמָרִי יוֹמָא דֵין, בְּגִין כֵּן לָא אֲכָלִית עִם מָרִי יוֹמָא דֵין. א"ל אַתָּה פַּיְיסְתָּה לְמַאן דְּמִתְחָמֵי וְלָא חָמֵי — דֵּין דְּחָמֵי וְלָא מִתְחָמֵיים יְקַבֵּל פִּיּוּסָךְ. א"ל הָדָא מְנָא לָךְ? א"ל מר"א בֶּן יַעֲקֹב. דר"א בֶּן יַעֲקֹב עָאל חַד דְּסַגֵּי נְהוֹרָא לְקַרְתֵּיהּ, יְתַב לֵיהּ ר"א בֶּן יַעֲקֹב לְרַע מִינֵּיהּ. דְּיֵימְרוּן: דְּאִילּוּלֵי דַּהֲוָה בַּר נָשָׁא רָבָא — לָא יְתַב לֵיהּ ר"א בֶּן יַעֲקֹב לְרַע מִינֵּיהּ. עֲבַדִין לֵיהּ פַּרְנָסָה דְּאִיקַּר. אֲמַר לוֹן: מַהוּ הָכֵין? אֲמַרוּן לֵיהּ: ר"א בֶּן יַעֲקֹב יְתַב לְרַע מִינָּךְ, וְצַלֵּי עֲלוֹי הָדָא צְלוֹתָא: אַתָּה גָּמַלְתָּה חֶסֶד לְמַאן דְּמִתְחָמֵי וְלָא חָמֵי, דֵּין דְּחָמֵי וְלָא מִתְחָמֵי יִגְמוֹל יָתָךְ חֶסֶד.§ (דִּלְמָא) רַבִּי חָמָא בַּר חֲנִינָה וְרַבִּי הוֹשַׁעְיָא (רַבָּה) הֲווּ מְטַיְילִין בְּאִילֵּין כְּנִישְׁתָּא דְּלוֹד, א"ר חָמָא בַּר חֲנִינָא לר' הוֹשַׁעְיָא: כַּמָּה מָמוֹן שִׁיקְּעוּ אֲבוֹתַי כָּאן! אָמַר לֵיהּ: כַּמָּה נְפָשׁוֹת שִׁיקְּעוּ אֲבוֹתֶיךָ כָּאן. הֲלָא הֲוָה אִית בְּנֵי נָשׁ דְּיִלְעוּן בְּאוֹרַיְיתָא? רַבִּי אָבוּן עֲבַד אִילֵּין תַּרְעַיָּה

קרבן העדה

בין נסכי כבש שהוא בן שנה, לנסכי איל שהוא בן שתי שנה: ת"ל "ככה יעשה לשור האחד". כל נסכי שור — אחד הן, ושור בן יומו קרוי "שור". ורש"י במנחות פי': דמיתורא דלשון קדריש שכבר כתיב "והקריב על בן הבקר מנחה". וכן דריש בכולן. והראשון נ"ל: ת"ל "או לאיל הא'". כיון שהוא איל — כל נסכיו אחד הן, בין זקן, או שהוא בין י"ג חדש: ת"ל "או לשה בכבשים". כל שה שבכבשים שוות הם בנסכיהם: בין נסכי גדי קטן לתיש גדול: הגע עצמך. ופריך: הגע עצמך, שהצניעו עד שיבוא היום ההוא בשבת הבאה, ומאי מהני שכתוב עליו שם היום?: ומשני: שם משמר. של אותו שבת נמי היה כתוב עליו: ופריך: הגע עצמך. שימתין אלי שנה עד שיבוא זמן המשמר שנית: ומשני: שם היום. כמה ימים בשבת: שם השבת. כמה שבת בחודש: שם החדש היה כתוב עליהן. וגם שם המשמר, שאינו מצוי שיזדמן שיהיו כולם ביום א' מכון אלא להרבה שנים:

נוסחאות ישנות

הלכה ד מתני' לשבת חשאים. על שם שהנותנין בתוכה נותנין בסתר, והמתפרנסים ממנה נוטלין בסתר: ללשבת בדק הבית. ללשכה שנותנים בה כל קדשי בדק הבית: גמ' הוון פרנסין. היו גבאי לדקה: והוה יהיב ליה. לאחרים שהיו העניים מתביישים לקבל מהגבאי: מליזין עליו. מדברין בו, ואמרו שאינו צריך ליטול לדקה ונוטל: מן דדמך. כשמת בדקו ומצאו שלא נהנה ממה שקיבל, אלא היה נותן לאחרים: הוה מפליג וכו'. היה מחלק לדקה בלילה ומוליכה אצל העניים, שלא לביישן: חד זמן. פעם אחת פגע בו שר של רוחות. וא"ל: לא כן למדתנו רבינו "לא תסיג גבול רעך" ולילה גבול של רוחות לילך, ואין לבני אדם לצאת אז: מתן בסתר יכפה אף. ויציאתו זו כדי ליתן לדקה בסתר ראוי הוא שיסתיר עצמו מפניו: והוה. הרוח מתיירא ממנו שלא יכפהו וברח מלפניו: זהו שמסתכל במצות. הלדקה היאך לעשותה, שלא יתבייש העני: טול ואתה פורע. כשתקבל ירושתך: ה"ג: א"ל: יהא לך במתנה. אר"ח בר אדא וכו'. וה"פ: והוה א"ל אם לא יהיה לך לשלם — הרי הוא לך במתנה. כי היה חושש אולי יתאמץ העני לפרוע לו כשיראה שלא נפלה לו ירושה, או כדי שלא יהיה לעני כגזל לפי דעתו: אית הוה סבין וכו'. היו זקנים בימינו, כל מה שהיו נותנין להם מר"ה עד יוה"כ היו מקבלין, ומשם ואילך לא היו מקבלין: אמרי דשתן גבן. מה שאנו צריכין לכל השנה כבר הוא אצלנו. שהיו נותנין להם בימים אלו די פרנסתן לכל השנה כך נ"ל. וה"יפה מראה" פי' בזה פירושים דחוקים: זכה עמי. עשה עמי לדקה ותן לי תרנגולת חדא: ה"ג: א"ל: הא לך טימיתא וזיל זבין קופד. וה"פ: הא לך מטבע זו וקנה לך בשר: ואבל בשר שור, ומת: להרוגו של נחמיה. שאילו נתן לו בשר תרנגולת שהיה רגיל בו, היה חי: א"ל: מיחזור. כשיחזור, יתן לו לאכול: אמר לנגד המת: עיניו שראו אותו ולא קבלוהו — יהיו סתומין: ידים דלא פשטו עצמן ליתן לעני — יתקטעון: רגלים שלא רצו לקראתך ליתן לך — ישברו: ומטתיה בן. ועלתה לו כך בעיניו וידיו ורגליו: א"ל רבי עקיבא: מה אתה מקללני?: א"ל נחום: ולמה אתה מבעט ביסורין, דקאמרת "אוי לי": הוה רביה דבריה. מלמד של בנו היה סגי נהור, והיה רגיל לאכול עם רבי הושעיא בכל יום: חד זמן וכו'. פעם אחת היה לו לר"ה אורחים, ולא קרא לסגי נהור שיאכל עמו: ברמשא. לערב: א"ל ר"ה: לא יכעוס אדוני עלי שלא זמנתיך שתאכל עמי היום, לפי שהיו אורחין אצלי, ואמרתי שלא לזלזל בכבודך שיביישוך. הלכך לא אכלתי עמך יום הזה: א"ל: אתה פייסת למי שנראה ואינו רואה, אותו שרואה ואינו נראה, והוא הקב"ה, יקבל פיוסך ותפלתך: א"ל: מנ"ל הא לברך כן: מראב"י. מעובדא דראב"י: דראב"י נכנס סגי נהור לעירו, ישב ראב"י למטה ממנו, שיאמרו הבריות: אילו לא היה סגי נהור זה גברא רבא לא הוה ראב"י יושב למטה ממנו. ועשו לו פרנסה ולדקה יקרה: אמר להון. הסגי נהור: מהו זה שנותנין לי כל כך?: וצלי עלוי. והתפלל סגי נהור זה על ראב"י האי תפלה: דלמא. מעשה: הוון מטיילין. בבתי כנסיות שבלוד: כמה ממון שיקעו אבותי בבאן. שהם בנו בתי כנסיות אלה משלהם: כמה נפשות שיקעו בבנין הזה. וכי לא היו בני אדם שיעסקו בתורה, והיה ראוי להוציא ממון זה עליהם לפרנסתם. ונראה שהיה ידוע לר' הושעיא שהיו עניים בני תורה בזמן ההוא שביטלו תורתם מדוחק הפרנסה, והיה ראוי לאבותיו של ר' חמא לפרנסם ולא יקפידו על הציור של בנין בהכ"נ: עבד. אלו

ריבב"ן

מתני' לשבות חדרים. חשאים על שם שעניים בני טובים מתפרנסין ממנה בחשאי בלנעא שלא יתביישו: כלי שמצאו בו צורך בדק הבית מניחין אותו. לבד"ה: ירושלמי תני קדשי מזבח מוציאין את הראוי להן מקדשי בדק הבית [ואין קדשי בה"ב] מוציאין את הראוי להן מקדשי מזבח. והתנינן כלי שמצאו בו צורך לבדק הבית מניחין אותו והשאר נמכרין ודמיהן נופלין ללשכת בדק הבית פ"ד אותן שהקדישו לקדשי מזבח הקדישו וקתני ודמיהן נופלין ללשכת בד"ה*). כלומר, בשעה שהקדישו עיקר קדושתן לב"ה:

תקלין חדתין

הכתוב כו' דכבש עשרון א' ואיל ב' עשרונים: ת"ל "ככה יעשה לשור האחד". דבין גדול בין קטן נסכיו שוין. א"נ: מהכא: דשור בן יומו קרוי "שור", כדכתיב "שור או כשב או עז כי יולד": "או לאיל" למה נאמר. והלא כבר נאמר "או לאיל תעשה מנחה": בן שנה. הוא כבש, בן שנתים הוא איל: לבן שלש. שיהיה נסכיו יותר: ת"ל או לאיל. מריבויא אשמועינן. א"נ מעת שקרוי איל הכל אחד, בן שנתים ובן ג': או לשה בכבשים למה נאמר כו'. והלא כבר נאמר "או לזבח לכבש האחד": כבשה. נקבה דכבשים. רחלה. נקבה דעזים: ת"ל "או" גו'. מריבויא: או בעזים. והלא עזים בכלל כבשים הם: גדי. היינו בחור: תיש. זקן: בג' לוגין. הוא רביעית ההין. שההין י"ב לוג, וכ"ה הסוגיא בבבלי (מנחות לא ב לג א): הגע עצמך כו'. אמתניתין מהדר. כלומר, מה בכך שהיה כתוב עליו שם היום? יכול הרמאי להמתין בשבוע האחרת, שיגיע יום זה הכתוב בחותם: שם משמר. ומשני: שהיה כתוב שם המשמר, ובשבוע האחרת משמר אחר ולא יהיה יכול לרמאות: ופריך: הרי יכול להמתין עד שיחזור חלילה זה המשמר וזה היום: ומשני: שם יום ושבת וחדש כתוב. שלא שייך שימתין זמן הרבה עד שיארע כך: מתני' לשבת חשאים. על שם שנותנין לתוכה בסתר, והמתפרנסים ממנה נוטלים בסתר: ללשבת בד"ה. ללשכה שנותנין בתוכה כל בד"ה: גמ' לאוחרנין. מפני שהיו מתביישים לקבל מיד הגבאי. ונתן להם מה שלקח, שהוא לא היה צריך: מלעיזין. לשון לעז: מפליג. ממה שהיה נוטל: מצוה. לדקה: בלילא. משום מתן בסתר שלא
(דברים יט) לביש המקבלים וכמ"ש טב דלא יהביה כו': לא תסיג.
(משלי כא) ובלילה זמן הרוחות. ואמרו: אל יצא ת"ח יחידי בלילה: מתן בסתר. וזה כל כוונתי בהליכתי בלילה, ושלוחי
(תהלים מא) מצוה אינן ניזוקין, ובפרט שכופה אף: שהוא מסתכל במצוה. בהשכל וחכמה שלא יהיה בה איזה פחיתות: שנפלה לך ירושה ממקום אחר. דכתיב "בית והון נחלת אבות". וכשנפסק זה, כגון זה שירד מנכסיו — ירושתו ממקום אחר להתפרנס מאחרים, המשפיעים לזה כאבותיו שהשפיעו לו: טול ואתה פורע. כדאמרי' בשבת (קנא, ב): כי אתא עניא, אקדים ליה ריפתא. כי היכי דליקדמו לבניך כו', גלגל הוא שחוזר בעולם כו'. שאם הוא לא בא בנו או בן בנו. ואמרו במ"ר: הקב"ה עושה סולמות, מוריש לזה ומעשיר לזה. וז"ש "ואתה פורע בזימנא אחריתי": מן דהוה נסיב כו'. כדי שלא יסבור כפשוטו שהוא בע"ח ויצטער, כמ"ש בריש ע"ז: בע"ח עלב כו': אית הוי סבין ביומינו. בימינו היו זקנים: מבין ריש שתא כו'. דגירסת הירושל' "כל מזונותיו של אדם קצובין מר"ה ועד יוה"כ". והיה דעתם בזה שמר"ה ועד יוה"כ הוא קצבת מזונם לכל השנה. ולכן, עד יוה"כ היו נוטלין, שעדיין לא נקצב להם במרום, ורשות בידם ליטול. משא"כ אחר יו"כ שכבר נקצב להם פרנסתם על כל השנה מהסיבה שהיה בידם, ולא היו רוצים ליטול.. וזהו "דשתא גבן" — של כל השנה אצלנו כבר: זכה עמי. עשה עמי לדקה. והוא כמ"ש: יותר ממה שבעל הבית עושה עם העני העני עושה עם בעל הבית, שנאמר "ושם האיש אשר עשיתי" וגו': הא לך. מטבע זו וקנה לך חילופה בשר: ואבל. בשר שור ומת: להרוגו של נחמיה. שאילו נתן לו בשר תרנגולת כהרגלו, היה חי: נחום איש גם זו. סוגיא זו איתמרא בבבלי במס' תענית (כא, א) וכאן יותר מדוקדקת: גם זו. שהיה אומר על כ"ד "גם זו לטובה": דורון. בבבלי מפורש: משא ג' חמורים, מאכל ומשתה ומגדים: מוכה שחין א'. שהיה נראה לעין חולה גדול וחלש: זכה עמי. לא אמר כמוכרת לזה מאד, אלא שתזכה עמי בנתינתך לי, ולא הפליג בקשתו. כההיא דאתיא לקמיה דבנימין הלדיק וא"ל: הרי הם מוטלים בסכנת מיתה. שבודאי היה מוזרז ליתן תכף. ועתה חשב בחזירתו יתן לו, ומשום כבוד חמיו היה אץ לדרכו, וז"ש "לבית חמיו": אשכחיה. בחזירתו דמית: קאים כו'. עמד לנגדו: עיני' דלא חמון כו'. האשים עצמו על שלא הביט גודל חוליו ותלישותו, וה"ל להזדרז: דלא פשטן. כמ"ש "פתוח תפתח את ידך" וגו': לך. שהיית נראה חולה גדול ופניו העידו בו: דלא רהטין. בתחילה. וגם אילו היה רך יותר בחזירתו מיראתו ודאגתו על העני היה מוצאו עדיין חי, והיה מצילו: רביה דבריה. מלמד של בנו היה סגי נהור, והיה רגיל לאכול עמו בכל יום משום כבודו: חד זמן כו'. פ"א היו לר' הושעיא אורחין ולא אכל עמו: לא יבעום. לא יתרעם אדוני עלי: דלא ליבזו. שלא יבזו כבודך, שאינם מכירים אותך: מנא לך. הא ברכתא, שהוא דרך חכמה: דראב"י. בא חד סגי נהור למקומו, וישב ר"א למטה הימנו, כדי שיאמרו: אילו לא היה סגי נהור זה גברא רבא לא היה יתיב רבי אליעזר בן יעקב למטה הימנו, ועשו לו פרנסה בכבוד: מהו הבין. שראה שהפריזו על המדה כפי ערכו, שהיו רגילים בני אדם ליתן לו: א"ל. רבי אליעזר בן יעקב יושב למטה ממך: וצלי כו'. התפלל הסגי נהור עליו: גמלת חסד. שישב למטה הימנו: שקעו אבותי. שבנו בתי כנסיות אלו: כמה נפשות כו'. וכי לא היו בני אדם שיפרנסו אותם שיעסקו בתורה?:

תרעייהו

*) נראה דחסר כאן וצ"ל ומשני כיני מתניתין לצורך בדק הבית כלומר בשעה שהקדישו וכו' כצ"ל ור"ל דהירושלמי משני דמתני' מיירי שעיקר קדושתן הי' לבה"ב:

מסורת הש"ס

א) ירושל' פאה פ"ח הל"ח: ב) ויק"ר פ' לד: ג) עי' כתובו' סז ב: ד) תעני' כא א:

עין משפט נר מצוה

יח א מיי' פרק ג מערכין הל"ב ופ"י ממ"ע הל"א:

יט ב טוש"ע יו"ד סי' רמט סט"ז:

נוסחת הבבלי

(א) הגע עצמך (ששירות אותו היום ממש) כו': (ב) נמכרין בדמיהן ונופלין ללשכת בדק הבית: (ג) דר' אושעיא (זיני) דינר כו' הוו מלעיזין כו' דל"צ למינסב והוא כו' דדמך אשכחיה דהוה יהיב מן דליה לאחרנין כו' אר"י אשרי משכיל אל דל אשרי נותן כו' זה המשתכל בצדקה כו' נסיב יהיב ליה במתנה א"ר חייא בר אבא כו' למימר רשותא גבן כו': (ד) טומיתא תיזיל ותיכול קופר אכל קופר ומית כו' זכה עמי א"ל כו' עינים דלא חמון לך יסתמון כו' סליק ר"ע לבקרו ליה א"ל כו' אורחין לא סליק לגביה לרמשא כו' חמי תיפיים מן דחמא ולא מיתחמי אמר ליה כו':

הגהות הגר"א

[א] ויש גורסין רשותא גבן ועוד חלופי גרסאות ועי' ביפ"מ סוף מס' פאה:

א) ע' תמורה לג א: ב) מדות פ"ב מ"ג: ג) יומא נד א: ד) תוספתא פרק ב ויומא נג ב: ה) שם נד א: ו) ירושלמי סוטה פ"ח הלכה ג ותוספתא סוטה פ"ז: ז) ספרי פ' בהעלותך:

הפתחים של בהמ"ד הגדול: **חמי מה דעבדית.** היה משבח עצמו: ראה מה שעשיתי: **וישכח ישראל וכו'.** טוב הוא ליתן לעניי תורה שעושין מלות בכל עת, משיבנו בניינים והיכלות: **מוציאין את הראוי להן מקדשי בדק הבית.** כגון אם הקדיש בהמה או אבנים לבדק הבית ולריכין אותן למזבח, נוטלין אותן למזבח. אבל הקדיש בהמה, אפי' בעלי מומים, או אבנים למזבח — אין מוליאין אותן לבדק הבית, אלא ימכרו, ודמיהן נופלין לבדק הבית: **כלי שמצאו בו צורך לבד"ה — מניחין אותו.** הא ראוי למזבח — מוכרין אותו. שמעינן: דקדשי בדק הבית, אף ע"פ שראוין למזבח — אין מוליאין מקדשי בדק הבית: **כיני מתנית'.** כן היא משנתנו: כלי שמלאו בו לורך, והיינו לצורך המזבח או לבד"ה ללשכת בד"ה — מניחין אותו, ומשם נוטלין אותו למה שלריכין אותו:

דִּסְדְרָא רַבָּא. אֲתָא ר' מָנָא לְגַבֵּיהּ, אֲמַר לֵיהּ: חֲמֵי מַאי עֲבַדִּית! א"ל "וַיִּשְׁכַּח יִשְׂרָאֵל אֶת עוֹשֵׂהוּ וַיִּבֶן הֵיכָלוֹת" הושע ח
לָא הֲוָה בְּנֵי נָשׁ [א] דִּילְעוֹן בְּאוֹרַיְיתָא? א) [א] תָּנֵי: אקָדְשֵׁי הַמִּזְבֵּחַ מוֹצִיאִין אֶת הָרָאוּי לָהֶן מִקָּדְשֵׁי (א) בֶּדֶק הַבַּיִת, אֵין קָדְשֵׁי בֶּדֶק הַבַּיִת מוֹצִיאִין אֶת הָרָאוּי לָהֶן מִקָּדְשֵׁי מִזְבֵּחַ. וְהָא תָּנֵינַן: כְּלִי שֶׁמָּצְאוּ בּוֹ צוֹרֶךְ לְבֶדֶק הַבַּיִת מַנִּיחִין אוֹתוֹ, וְהַשְּׁאָר נִמְכָּרִין וּדְמֵיהֶן נוֹפְלִין לְבֶדֶק הַבַּיִת! א"ר חִזְקִיָּה: כֵּינִי מתני' (לְצוֹרֶךְ) לְלִשְׁכַּת בֶּדֶק הַבַּיִת.§

הדרן עלך פרק אלו הן הממונים

הלכה א מתני'

בשְׁלֹשָׁה עָשָׂר שׁוֹפָרוֹת, שְׁלֹשָׁה עָשָׂר שׁוּלְחָנוֹת, שְׁלֹשׁ ג) עֶשְׂרֵה הִשְׁתַּחֲוָויוֹת הָיוּ בַּמִּקְדָּשׁ. שֶׁל בֵּית ר"ג וְשֶׁל בֵּית רַבִּי חֲנַנְיָה סְגַן הַכֹּהֲנִים הָיוּ מִשְׁתַּחֲוִים בְּאַרְבַּע עֶשְׂרֵה. וְהֵיכָן הָיְתָה יְתֵירָה — כְּנֶגֶד דִּיר הָעֵצִים, שֶׁכֵּן מָסוֹרֶת בְּיָדָן מֵאֲבוֹתֵיהֶן שֶׁשָּׁם הָאָרוֹן נִגְנַז. מַעֲשֶׂה ג) בְּכֹהֵן א' שֶׁהָיָה מִתְעַסֵּק, וְרָאָה אֶת הָרִצְפָּה שֶׁהִיא מְשׁוּנָּה מֵחַבְרוֹתֶיהָ, בָּא וְאָמַר לַחֲבֵירוֹ. לֹא הִסְפִּיק לִגְמוֹר אֶת הַדָּבָר עַד שֶׁיָּצְתָה נִשְׁמָתוֹ. וְיָדְעוּ בְּיִיחוּד שֶׁשָּׁם הָאָרוֹן גָּנוּז.§ **גמ'** תָּנֵי: גהַשּׁוֹפָרוֹת הַלָּלוּ עֲקוּמּוֹת הָיוּ, צָרוֹת מִלְּמַעְלָן וּרְחָבוֹת מִלְּמַטָּה מִפְּנֵי הָרַמָּאִין. תָּנֵי ד) בְּשֵׁם ר"א הָאָרוֹן גָּלָה עִמָּהֶן לְבָבֶל, מ"ט "לֹא יִוָּתֵר דָּבָר אָמַר ה'" אֵין דָּבָר אֶלָּא שֶׁהַדִּיבְּרוֹת לְתוֹכוֹ. מ"ב כ
וְכֵן הוּא אוֹמֵר "וְלִתְשׁוּבַת הַשָּׁנָה שָׁלַח הַמֶּלֶךְ נְבוּכַדְנֶצַּר וַיְבִיאֵהוּ בָבֶלָה עִם כְּלֵי חֶמְדַּת בֵּית ה'" איזהו כְּלֵי חֶמְדַּת בֵּית ה' — זֶה הָאָרוֹן (תָּנֵי ר"י בַּר אֶילְעַי) דרַבִּי שִׁמְעוֹן בֶּן לָקִישׁ אוֹמֵר: בִּמְקוֹמוֹ הָיָה הָאָרוֹן נִגְנַז. הָדָא הוּא דִּכְתִיב "וַיַּאֲרִיכוּ הַבַּדִּים וַיֵּרָאוּ רָאשֵׁי (ב) הַבַּדִּים אֶל הַקֹּדֶשׁ אֶל פְּנֵי הַדְּבִיר וְלֹא יֵרָאוּ הַחוּצָה". [ב] כְּתִיב ה) "וַיֵּרָאוּ" וְאַתְּ אָמַרְתְּ "וְלֹא יֵרָאוּ"? אֶלָּא, נִרְאִין וְלֹא נִרְאִין, בּוֹלְטִין וְיוֹצְאִין כִּשְׁנֵי דַדֵּי הָאִשָּׁה. וְרַבָּנַן אָמְרֵי: בְּלִשְׁכַּת דִּיר הָעֵצִים הָיָה הָאָרוֹן גָּנוּז. מַעֲשֶׂה בְּכֹהֵן אֶחָד בַּעַל מוּם שֶׁהָיָה עוֹמֵד וּמְפַצֵּל עֵצִים בְּלִשְׁכַּת דִּיר הָעֵצִים, וְרָאָה אֶת הָרִצְפָּה שֶׁהִיא מִשְׁתַּנָּה מֵחַבְרוֹתֶיהָ. בָּא וְאָמַר לַחֲבֵירוֹ: בֹּא וּרְאֵה אֶת הָרִצְפָּה הַזֹּאת שֶׁהִיא מִשְׁתַּנָּה מֵחַבְרוֹתֶיהָ. לֹא הִסְפִּיק לִגְמוֹר אֶת הַדָּבָר עַד שֶׁיָּצְתָה נִשְׁמָתוֹ. וְיָדְעוּ בְּיִיחוּד שֶׁשָּׁם הָאָרוֹן גָּנוּז.§ תָּנֵי (מִשּׁוּם) ר' הוֹשַׁעְיָא: הִקִּישׁ עָלֶיהָ בְּקוּרְנָס וְיָצָאת אֵשׁ וּשְׂרָפַתּוּ. תָּנֵי ו) רַבִּי יְהוּדָה (בַּר אֶילְעַי) בֶּן לָקִישׁ אָמַר: [ג] ב' אֲרוֹנוֹת הָיוּ מְהַלְּכִין עִם יִשְׂרָאֵל בַּמִּדְבָּר, [ג] אֶחָד שֶׁהָיְתָה הַתּוֹרָה נְתוּנָה בְּתוֹכוֹ, וְאַחֵר שֶׁהָיוּ שִׁבְרֵי לוּחוֹת נְתוּנִין בְּתוֹכוֹ. זֶה שֶׁהָיְתָה הַתּוֹרָה נְתוּנָה בְּתוֹכוֹ הָיָה מוּנָּח בְּאֹהֶל מוֹעֵד, הָדָא הוּא דִּכְתִיב "וַאֲרוֹן בְּרִית ה' וּמֹשֶׁה לֹא מָשׁוּ מִקֶּרֶב הַמַּחֲנֶה". זֶה ז) שֶׁהָיוּ שִׁבְרֵי לוּחוֹת נְתוּנִין בְּתוֹכוֹ — הָיָה נִכְנָס וְיוֹצֵא עִמָּהֶן, וּפְעָמִים שֶׁהָיָה מִתְרָאֶה עִמָּהֶן. במדבר יד
וְרַבָּנַן אָמְרֵי: אָרוֹן א' הָיָה, וּפַעַם אַחַת יָצָא בִּימֵי עֵלִי וְנִשְׁבָּה. קְרָיָיא מְסַיֵּיעַ לְהוּ לְרַבָּנַן "אוֹי לָנוּ מִי יַצִּילֵנוּ מִיַּד הָאֱלֹהִים הָאַדִּירִים הָאֵלֶּה", מִילָּה דְּלָא חֲמוּן מִן יוֹמֵיהוֹן. קְרָיָיא מְסַיֵּיעַ לר' יוּדָה בֶּן לָקִישׁ "וַיֹּאמֶר שָׁאוּל לַאֲחִיָּה הַגִּישָׁה אֲרוֹן הָאֱלֹהִים". וַהֲלֹא אָרוֹן בְּקִרְיַת יְעָרִים הָיָה! מָה עַבְדוּן לֵיהּ רַבָּנַן — הַגִּישָׁה אֵלַי הַצִּיץ. קְרָיָיא מְסַיֵּיעַ לר' יוּדָא (בַּר אֶילְעַי) בֶּן לָקִישׁ "הָאָרוֹן וְיִשְׂרָאֵל וִיהוּדָה יוֹשְׁבִין בַּסּוּכּוֹת" וַהֲלֹא ש"א ד / שם יד / ש"ב יא

הדרן עלך פרק אלו הן הממונין

הלכה א מתני' שלשה עשר שופרות. תיבות לרות מלמעלה ורחבות מלמטה, עקומות כעין שופר. מפני הרמאים, שלא יתנו ידן לתוכן להראות כאילו נותנין לתוכו, ויטלו מתוכן. ולקמן מפרש למה י"ג שופרות, וי"ג שולחנות, ובאיזה מקום מונחין: **י"ג השתחוויות.** לקמן מפרש היכן היו: **כנגד דיר העצים.** לשכה שבה היו נותנין כל עלי המערכה, והיא היתה במקצוע מזרחית לפונית של עזרת נשים: **ששם ארון נגנז.** ע"י יאשיהו, כדמפרש בגמרא: **שהיה מתעסק.** במלאכתו, מתליע את העלים. שאין לבעלי מומין מלאכה במקדש כי אם להכין עלים למערכה. דכל עץ שנמלא בו תולעת פסול למזבח: **שהיא משונה.** שלא היתה האבן שוה לשאר אבני הרלפה, והבין שנסתלק משם והוחזרה: **ביחוד.** בבירור: **גמ'** ה"ג: אלא הדברות שבתוכו: **ולא יראו החוצה.** סיפא דקרא "ויהיו שם עד היום הזה": **כתיב.** ברישא "ויראו" וכתיב בסיפא "ולא יראו", וקשיא אהדדי: **בולטין.** ודוחקין בפרוכת, ונראין כשני דדי אשה שבולטין מתחת חלוקה: **ומפצע.** ומבקע: **ביחוד.** בבירור: **הקיש עליה בקורנס** על המקום ההוא, ויצא אש ושרפו: **התורה.** ולוחות שניות מונחים בתוכו: **לא משו וכו'.** ואם"ד דהארון ההוא הוא שהיה הולך לפניהם במלחמה, מסתמא גם המעפילים היו נוטלים אותו עמהם במלחמה: **היה נכנס ויוצא עמהן.** כשנסעו במדבר נסע לפניהם, כדכתיב "וארון ברית ה' נוסע לפניהם": ה"ג: **ופעמים הוא מתראה עמהן במלחמה.** וי"ס דל"ג ליה, והוא הנכון. וכן הוא במס' סוטה: **מילה דלא חמון וכו'.** דבר שלא ראו מימיהם. ואם"ד שהיה יולא עמהן תמיד במלחמה — מאי יום מיומיים שהיו מתיראין עתה?: **והלא ארון בקרית יערים היה.** עד שבא דוד והעלוהו משם: ומשני: **הגישה אלי הציץ.** והארון הזה לאו ארון ברית ה', אלא הארון שהיה בו החשן והאפוד והאורים והתומים. ובבר הלין — לפי שאסור לשאול באורים כי אם בלבישת

משנת אליהו

ה"ג תני קדשי מזבח כו'. ועיין רמב"ם פ"ד מהלכות שקלים הלכה י' והראב"ד השיג עליו ועיין כ"מ שנדחק וכתב שהירושלמי הזה לריך לימוד ורבינו הגדול אנהריניהו לעיינין בגירסתו ממש כשיטת הרמב"ם דתני קדשי מזבח מוליאין הראוי להן מקדשי בדק הבית ומפרש בכה"ג שלא הספיקו שקלים לקרבנות כו' ול"ק קושית הראב"ד דמתני' דמיירי מלשכת כלים ומחלק בינייהו לגירסת רבינו מה דפריך גמרא ממתני' דלשכת הכלים קאי אמ"ש ולא קדשי בדק הבית מקדשי בד"ה וכדפרישית ובבא דקדשי בד"ה מבד"ה ג"כ לא הוא שיטת הרמב"ם בפירושו ולא כרש"י שם אלא דפירושו כפשטא כמו בקדשי מזבח מקדושה לקדושה בדידי' קאי ה"נ בקדשי בד"ה ומיהו דלפעמים מקדשי בד"ה מוליאין הראוי להן לקדשי מזבח כסוגיא דמעלין בקודש כו' וכדתנינא בתוספתא המתפיס תמימים לבד"ה כו' רק דחילוק דבקדשי מזבח אין משנין אף לקדושה חמורה משום שינוי אכילתו משא"כ בקדשי בד"ה לקדושה קלה הוא דאין משנין משא"כ לקדושה חמורה סימנו ולפ"ז מתורץ פסק הרמב"ם בפ"ד מהלכו' תמורה הלכ' י"א כילד אם הקדיש לבדק היכל לא ישנה לבדק המזבח וכן כל כיולא בזה וכל מה שהשיג עליו הראב"ד ל"ק כלל דפסק כשיטתו בפירושו וכגירסתו ולא קדשי בדק הבית מקדשי בד"ה והיינו היכא דהקדיש בהדיא לבדק ההיכל לא ישנה לבדק המזבח וכפירושו במתני' דתמורה (ל"ב א) ומדפריך עלה ממתני' דסוף פ"ה דשקלים ומשני כיני ללשכת בד"ה שכיון שאין לורך לבד"ה ונופלין ללשכה חוזרו ונתערבו כמחדש ורשאי לשנות לבד"ה אחר משא"כ לשנות מזה לזה אסור ומה שהקשה הראב"ד ממתני' דשקלים לשכות ועזרות באין מקדשי בד"ה אלמא דאין חילוק בין קדשי היכל לשאר עזרות לק"מ דהתם מסתמא דקדשי בד"ה והרמב"ם מיירי בהקדיש בהדיא לבדק ההיכל לכן אין משנין והוא דומיא דהקדיש כלי לבד"ה בזמן שיש לורך וגם כשאין לורך דוקא ללשכה הוא דנופלין. והא דהקשה הראב"ד דהרי מודה הרמב"ם דמשנין קדשי בד"ה ל"ק דזהו כללא דמעלין בקדש כו' רק בקדשי מזבח אף להעלות אסור משום שינוי אכילתן משא"כ בקדשי בדק הבית מעלין ולא מורידין ומפרשי ירושלמי בק"ע והרא"פ נלמוו יחד בשמוקים רבים: **ה"ג** תני ר"י בר אלעאי שני ארונות היו מהלכין כו' אחד שהיו הלוחות נתונין לתוכו ואחד שהיו שברי לוחות כו'. כ"ה גי' רבינו [illegible]

ריבב"ן

מתני' י"ג שופרות י"ג שולחנות. כלהו מפרש למאי אלטריכו: **כנגד דיר העצים.** מקום שהיו העלים לצורך המזבח: **ששם הארון נגנז.** שגנזו יאשיהו המלך כדאיתא ביומא (פ"ד) [פ"ה] (ד' נג) דכתיב (דה"ב לה) ויאמר ללוים המבינים לכל ישראל הקדושים לה' תנו את ארון הקודש בבית אשר בנה שלמה בן דוד מלך ישראל אין לכם משא בכתף. ירושלמי אמר להם אם גולה הוא עמכם לבבל אין עוד אתם מחזירין אותו למקומו אלא עבדו את ה' אלהיכם ואת עמו ישראל. תניא בתוספתא ר' יהודה אומר י"ג השתחויות כנגד י"ג פרלות. ירושלמי מתני' אבא יוסי בר חנין היא דאמר [אבא] יוסי בר חנין כנגד י"ג שערים ברם לרבנן ז' שערים הם בעזרה. על דעתיהון דרבנן היכן היו השתחויות הללו כהדא דתנינן י"ג פרלות היו בו שפרלום מלכי יון וחזרו וגדרום וכנגדן גזרו י"ג השתחויות: **מתני'** **שהיה מתעסק.** מפרש ביומא פ' הוליאו לו (ד' נד) מאי הוה עביד אמר ר' חלבו מתעסק בקרדומו הוה. תנא דר"י כהנים בעלי מומין היו מתליעין בעלים ונשמטה קרדומו של א' מהן ויצאתה האש ואכלתו ותנן במס' מדות (פ"ב מ"ה) ואיתא בפ"א דיומא (דף טז) ופ' כל קרבנות (דף פה) כל עץ שנמלא בו תולעת פסול ומפרש (שם) בפ' כל קרבנות ל"ש אלא לח אבל יבש גורדו וכשר: **משונה מחברותי'.** שהיתה גבוהה אותה טבלא של שיש שהיתה ברלפה והארון תחתיה ומת לפי שלא היה לו להראותו מקום הארון שמא ירגישו האומות: **ביחוד.** בבירור כדאי' בבילה פ"ב גבי אין אופין פת עבה ביו"ט:

תקלין חדתין

תרעייהו. שערי בהמ"ד הגדול: **חמי מאי עבדית.** מה עשיתי זה השער, והיה משבח עלמו: ה"ג: תני קדשי מזבח כו'. מוליאין את הראוי להן מקדשי בד"ה. כמ"ש בפרק ד': המקדיש נכסיו והיו בהן דברים הראוים למזבח כו' — יקרבו עולות. אע"ג דסתם הקדשות לבדק הבית. ותנינא בתוספתא פ"ק דתמורה: המקדיש תמימים לבד"ה — אין פודין אותן אלא למזבח. וז"ש "את הראוי להן": **אין קדשי בד"ה מוציאין את הראוי להן מקדשי מזבח.** דמקדושה חמורה לקדושה קלה אף בקדשי מזבח גופיה אסור לשנות. כדתנן בתמורה (לג, א): ה"ג: **ולא קדשי בד"ה מקדשי בדק הבית.** מתניתין היא בתמורה (לג, א): א' קדשי מזבח וא' קדשי בד"ה אין משנין אותן מקדושה לקדושה. ופירשה הרמב"ם ז"ל: כמו שאין משנין בקדשי מזבח גופיה משלמים לעולה וכן להיפך, כן אין משנין בבדק הבית מקדושה לקדושה. ופריך: **והא תנינן כו' והשאר נמכרין ודמיהן נופלין לבד"ה.** הרי דמשנין בבד"ה, שנמכרין ולוקחין לבד"ה מזה: ומשני: **כיני מתני' ללשכת בד"ה.** וה"ק: והשאר מה שאין לורך למה שהוקדשה כעת — נמכרין, ודמיהן נופלין ללשכת בד"ה. ומ"ש "ולא קדשי בד"ה מקדשי בד"ה" — היינו דומיא דאינך, שישנה מזה לבדק הבית. אבל ללשכה הוא אחר כך, כמו דבר חדש, כיון שאין לורך בזה כלל לבדק הבית. וגירסת הספרים חסרה ומשובשת:

הדרן עלך פרק אלו הן הממונים

שלשה עשר שופרות. תיבות לרות מלמעלה ורחבות מלמטה, ועקומות כשופר, וכדמפרש בגמ': י"ג השתחויות. ומפרש בגמרא היכן היו: **כנגד דיר העצים.** לשכה שבה היו נותנין כל עלי המערכה, והיא היתה במקצוע מזרחית לפונית של עזרת נשים: **ששם ארון נגנז.** על ידי יאשיהו, כדמפרש בגמרא: **שהיה מתעסק.** בקרדומות במלאכתו מתליע את העלים: **שהיא משונה.** שהיה גבוה אבן אחת משאר אבני הרלפה, והבין שנסתלקה משם והוחזרה: **ביחוד.** בבירור: **גמ'** **מפני הרמאים.** שלא יהיו הרמאים עושים את עלמם כמטילים לתוכם ויקחו מהם בנחת: **תני בשם ר"א וכו' אין דבר כו'.** דהא תחלה נאמר "כל אשר בביתך" והכל בכלל, ולמה ליה למימר "ולא יותר דבר"? אלא דקאי על הארון: **וכן הוא אומר ולתשובת וגו' בבלה.** בתוספתא שם נקט לה בשם ר"ש בפ"ע. והכא מביא לראיה דמקרא קמא אפשר לומר דנתבטלה הגזירה מרעה לטובה, כמ"ש: שאני גוזר גזירה ולדיק מבטלה. [illegible]

נוסחת הבבלי
(א) מקדשי בדה"ה (א"ר חייא בן הוא מתניתא קדשי מזבח מוציאין את הראוי להן לקדשי בדה"ה) אין קדשי בדה"ב כו': (ב) הבדים מן הקודש על פני הדביר כו' מסייע ליה לר"י בר אילעאי כו':

עין משפט נר מצוה
ב א מיי' פרק ג מערכין הלכה יג ובהשגות ופרק ד משקלים הל"י ובכ"מ ולח"מ:
א ב מיי' פרק ג משקלים הל"ב:
ב ג מיי' שם הל"א:
ג ד מיי' פ"ד מבית הבחירה הל"א:

הגהות הגר"א
[א] ה"ג תנן קדשי מזבח מוליאין את הראוי לקדשי בדה"ב אין מקדשי בדה"ב מוליאין את הראוי להן לקדשי בדק הבית מקדשי בדה"ב והא תנינן כלי שמלאו בו וכו'. [illegible] [ב] ה"ג ויאריכו הבדים [illegible] [ג] ה"ג אחד [illegible]

גליון הש"ס [א] ע' תשובת מהר"ם מרוטנבורג סימן תרלב: [ב] ע' תוספות פירובין דף סג ע"ב ד"ה כל וסוטה דף מג ע"ב ד"ה מפני:

תורה אור

וַהֲלֹא אָרוֹן בְּצִיּוֹן הָיָה! מָה עָבְדִין לֵיהּ רַבָּנָן — סָכָךְ שֶׁהוּא [א] כְּקִירוּי, שֶׁעֲדַיִין לֹא נִבְנָה בֵּית הַבְּחִירָה. מִשֶּׁנִּגְנַז א) הָאָרוֹן אנִגְנַז עִמּוֹ צִנְצֶנֶת הַמָּן, וּצְלוֹחִית שֶׁמֶן הַמִּשְׁחָה, וּמַקְלוֹ שֶׁל אַהֲרֹן וּפְרָחָיו וּשְׁקֵדָיו, וְאַרְגָּז שֶׁהֵשִׁיבוּ פְּלִשְׁתִּים אָשָׁם לֵאלֹהֵי יִשְׂרָאֵל. מִי גְּנָזוֹ — יֹאשִׁיָּהוּ גְּנָזוֹ. כֵּיוָן שֶׁרָאָה שֶׁכָּתוּב "יוֹלֵךְ ה' אוֹתְךָ וְאֶת מַלְכְּךָ אֲשֶׁר תָּקִים עָלֶיךָ אֶל גּוֹי אֲשֶׁר לֹא יָדַעְתָּ אַתָּה וַאֲבוֹתֶיךָ" — עָמַד וּגְנָזוֹ. הָדָא הוּא דִכְתִיב "וַיֹּאמֶר לַלְוִיִּם הַמְּבִינִים וּלְכָל יִשְׂרָאֵל הַקְּדוֹשִׁים לַה' תְּנוּ אֶת אֲרוֹן הַקֹּדֶשׁ בַּבַּיִת אֲשֶׁר בָּנָה שְׁלֹמֹה בֶן דָּוִיד מֶלֶךְ יִשְׂרָאֵל אֵין לָכֶם מַשָּׂא בַּכָּתֵף". אָמַר לָהֶם: אִם גּוֹלֶה הוּא עִמָּהֶם לְבָבֶל — [א] אֵין אַתֶּם מַחֲזִירִין אוֹתוֹ עוֹד לִמְקוֹמוֹ, אֶלָּא "עַתָּה עִבְדוּ אֶת ה' אֱלֹהֵיכֶם וְאֶת עַמּוֹ יִשְׂרָאֵל".§ [ב] פִּטּוּם שֶׁמֶן הַמִּשְׁחָה "וְאַתָּה קַח לְךָ וְגו' וְקִדָּה חֲמֵשׁ מֵאוֹת וְגו' שֶׁהֵן אֶלֶף וַחֲמֵשׁ מֵאוֹת מָנִים.§ "שֶׁמֶן זַיִת הִין" — שְׁנֵים ב) עָשָׂר לוֹג שֶׁבּוֹ שׁוֹלְקִין אֶת הָעִיקָּרִין, [ג] דִּבְרֵי ר"מ רַבִּי יְהוּדָה אוֹמֵר: בשׁוֹלְקָן הָיָה בְּמַיִם, וְנוֹתֵן שֶׁמֶן עַל גַּבֵּיהֶן. מִשֶּׁהָיָה קוֹלֵט אֶת הָרֵיחַ הָיָה מַעֲבִירוֹ, כְּדֶרֶךְ שֶׁהַפַּטָּמִין עוֹשִׂין. הָדָא הוּא דִכְתִיב "שֶׁמֶן מִשְׁחַת קֹדֶשׁ" וְגו'. תָּנֵי ג) רַבִּי יְהוּדָה בֵּי רַבִּי אִילְעַי: שֶׁמֶן הַמִּשְׁחָה שֶׁעָשָׂה מֹשֶׁה בַּמִּדְבָּר מַעֲשֶׂה נִסִּים נַעֲשָׂה בּוֹ מִתְּחִלָּה וְעַד סוֹף, שֶׁמִּתְּחִלָּה לֹא הָיָה בּוֹ אֶלָּא שְׁנֵים עָשָׂר לוֹג, שֶׁנֶּאֱמַר "שֶׁמֶן זַיִת הִין", אִם לָסוּךְ בּוֹ אֶת הָעִיקָּרִין לֹא הָיָה בּוֹ סִפֵּק, עַל אַחַת כַּמָּה וְכַמָּה שֶׁהָאוֹר בּוֹלֵעַ, וְהָעֵצִים בּוֹלְעִים, וְהַיּוֹרָה בּוֹלַעַת. וּמִמֶּנּוּ נִמְשְׁחוּ הַמִּשְׁכָּן וְכָל כֵּלָיו, הַשֻּׁלְחָן וְכָל כֵּלָיו, הַמְּנוֹרָה וְכָל כֵּלֶיהָ, וּמִמֶּנּוּ נִמְשְׁחוּ אַהֲרֹן כֹּהֵן גָּדוֹל וּבָנָיו כָּל שִׁבְעַת יְמֵי הַמִּלּוּאִ' וּמִמֶּנּוּ נִמְשְׁחוּ כֹּהֲנִים גְּדוֹלִים וּמְלָכִים. מֶלֶךְ בַּתְּחִלָּה — טָעוּן מְשִׁיחָה, [ד] מֶלֶךְ בֶּן מֶלֶךְ — גאֵין טָעוּן מְשִׁיחָה. מ"ט "קוּם מְשָׁחֵהוּ כִּי זֶה הוּא" — זֶה טָעוּן מְשִׁיחָה, וְאֵין בְּנוֹ טָעוּן מְשִׁיחָה. אֲבָל דכ"ג בֶּן כ"ג אֲפִי' עַד עֲשָׂרָה דוֹרוֹת — טָעוּן מְשִׁיחָה. וְכוּלּוֹ קַיָּים לֶעָתִיד לָבֹא, הה"ד "שֶׁמֶן מִשְׁחַת קוֹדֶשׁ יִהְיֶה זֶה לִי לְדוֹרוֹתֵיכֶם".§ אֵין ד) מוֹשְׁחִין הַמְּלָכִים האֶלָּא ע"ג הַמַּעְיָן, שֶׁנֶּא' "וְהִרְכַּבְתֶּם אֶת שְׁלֹמֹה בְנִי עַל הַפִּרְדָּה אֲשֶׁר לִי וְהוֹרַדְתֶּם אוֹתוֹ אֶל גִּיחוֹן וּמָשַׁח אוֹתוֹ שָׁם צָדוֹק הַכֹּהֵן וְנָתָן הַנָּבִיא לְמֶלֶךְ עַל יִשְׂרָאֵל". אֵין ה) מוֹשְׁחִין מֶלֶךְ בֶּן מֶלֶךְ אֶלָּא [ה] מִפְּנֵי הַמַּחֲלוֹקֶת. מִפְּנֵי מָה נִמְשַׁח שְׁלֹמֹה — מִפְּנֵי מַחֲלוֹקְתּוֹ שֶׁל אֲדוֹנִיָּהוּ, יוֹאָשׁ — מִפְּנֵי עֲתַלְיָהוּ, יְהוֹאָחָז — מִפְּנֵי יְהוֹיָקִים אָחִיו שֶׁהָיָה גָּדוֹל מִמֶּנּוּ ב' שָׁנִים, יֵהוּא מִפְּנֵי יוֹרָם. לֹא כֵּן כְּתִיב "קוּם מְשָׁחֵהוּ כִּי זֶה הוּא" זֶה טָעוּן מְשִׁיחָה וְאֵין מַלְכֵי יִשְׂרָאֵל טְעוּנִין מְשִׁיחָה! [ו] אֶלָּא, יְהוֹאָחָז מִפְּנֵי יְהוֹיָקִים אָחִיו שֶׁהָיָה גָּדוֹל מִמֶּנּוּ שְׁתֵּי שָׁנִים. וְלֹא יֹאשִׁיָּהוּ גְּנָזוֹ? הָדָא אָמְרָה: יבַּאֲפַרְסְמוֹן נִמְשַׁח.§ אֵין מוֹשְׁחִין הַמְּלָכִים אֶלָּא מִן הַקֶּרֶן. שָׁאוּל ו) וְיֵהוּא נִמְשְׁחוּ מִן הַפַּךְ — הָיְתָה מַלְכוּתָן מַלְכוּת עוֹבֶרֶת, דָּוִד וּשְׁלֹמֹה נִמְשְׁחוּ מִן הַקֶּרֶן — הָיְתָה מַלְכוּתָן מַלְכוּת קַיֶּימֶת.§ [ז] אֵין מוֹשְׁחִין כֹּהֲנִים מְלָכִים. אָמַר רַבִּי (יוֹנָה אָמַר ר' אֲבִי) יוּדָה עֲנְתוֹנְדְרָיָא: עַל שֵׁם "לֹא יָסוּר שֵׁבֶט מִיהוּדָה". אָמַר ר' חִיָּיא בַּר אַדָּא "לְמַעַן יַאֲרִיךְ יָמִים עַל מַמְלַכְתּוֹ הוּא וּבָנָיו בְּקֶרֶב יִשְׂרָאֵל" מַה כְּתִיב בַּתְרֵיהּ — "לֹא יִהְיֶה לַכֹּהֲנִים הַלְוִיִּם". א"ר ז) יוֹחָנָן: הוּא יוֹחָנָן הוּא יְהוֹאָחָז. וְהָא כְּתִיב "הַבְּכוֹר יוֹחָנָן"? בְּכוֹר לְמַלְכוּת. א"ר יוֹחָנָן: הוּא שַׁלּוּם הוּא צִדְקִיָּהוּ. וְהָכְתִיב הַג' צִדְקִיָּהוּ וְהָרְבִיעִי שַׁלּוּם"! ג' לְתוֹלְדוֹת ד' לְמַלְכוּת. צִדְקִיָּהוּ — שֶׁצִּידֵּק עָלָיו מִדַּת הַדִּין, שַׁלּוּם — שֶׁבְּיָמָיו שָׁלְמָה מַלְכוּת בֵּית דָּוִד. (רֵישׁ לָקִישׁ אָמַר) לֹא שַׁלּוּם הֲוָה שְׁמֵיהּ וְלֹא צִדְקִיָּהוּ הֲוָה שְׁמֵיהּ, אֶלָּא מַתַּנְיָה, הָדָא הוּא דִכְתִיב "וַיַּמְלֵךְ מֶלֶךְ בָּבֶל אֶת מַתַּנְיָה דוֹדוֹ תַּחְתָּיו וַיַּסֵּב אֶת שְׁמוֹ צִדְקִיָּהוּ".§ א"ר ח) יוֹחָנָן: [ג] בְּאַמָּה שֶׁל שִׁשָּׁה טְפָחִים הָיָה הָאָרוֹן עָשׂוּי. מַאן תַּנָּא בְּאַמָּה שֶׁל שִׁשָּׁה טְפָחִים — ר' מֵאִיר הִיא. דִּתְנַן, ט) ר' מֵאִיר אוֹמֵר: יכָּל הָאַמּוֹת הָיוּ בְּבֵינוֹנִית. ר' יְהוּדָה אוֹמֵר: אַמּוֹת הַבִּנְיָן שִׁשָּׁה, שֶׁל כֵּלִים חֲמִשָּׁה. עַל י) דַּעְתֵּיהּ דר"מ דּוּ אָמַר בְּאַמָּה שֶׁל ו' טְפָחִים הָיָה הָאָרוֹן עָשׂוּי, אוֹרְכּוֹ שֶׁל אָרוֹן ט"ו טְפָחִים, דִּכְתִיב "אַמָּתַיִם וָחֵצִי אָרְכּוֹ" אַמְּתָא אֲשִׁיתָא, וְאַמְּתָא אֲשִׁיתָא, וּפַלְגוּת אַמְּתָא תְּלָתָא. וְאַרְבָּעָה כ) לוּחוֹת הָיוּ בּוֹ, שְׁנַיִם שְׁלֵמִים וּשְׁנַיִם שְׁבוּרִים, דִּכְתִיב *) "אֲשֶׁר שִׁבַּרְתָּ וְשַׂמְתָּם בָּאָרוֹן". הַלּוּחוֹת הָיוּ כָּל אֶחָד וא' אָרְכּוֹ ו' טְפָחִים [ד] רָחְבּוֹ [ו] (שְׁלֹשָׁה) שִׁשָּׁה. וְתֵן אָרְכָּן שֶׁל לוּחוֹת לְאוֹרְכּוֹ שֶׁל אָרוֹן — נִשְׁתַּיֵּיר שָׁם שְׁלֹשָׁה טְפָחִים תֵּן

*) דברים י

מסורת הש"ס

א) יומא עב: ב) מדרש חזית פ' תורי זהב: ג) מדרש חזית פ' ידיו גלילי זהב: ד) שם פ' ראשו כתם פז: ה) מדות פ"ב מ"ו:

נוסחאות ישנות

תֵּן מֵהֶם חֲצִי טֶפַח לְכָל כּוֹתֶל — נִשְׁתַּיֵּיר שְׁנֵי טְפָחִים לְסֵפֶר תּוֹרָה. רָחְבּוֹ שֶׁל אָרוֹן תִּשְׁעָה טְפָחִים, דִּכְתִיב "אַמָּה וָחֵצִי רָחְבּוֹ" אַמְתָא אַשִׁיתָא, וּפַלְגּוּת אַמְתָא תְּלָתָא. [א] וְאַרְבָּעָה לוּחוֹת הָיוּ בוֹ, שְׁנַיִם שְׁלֵימִים וּשְׁנַיִם שְׁבוּרִים, דִּכְתִיב "אֲשֶׁר שִׁבַּרְתָּ וְשַׂמְתָּם בָּאָרוֹן". הַלּוּחוֹת הָיוּ כָּל אֶחָד וְאֶחָד אָרְכָּן שִׁשָּׁה טְפָחִים וְרָחְבָּן שִׁשָּׁה טְפָחִים, [ב] תֵּן רָחְבָּן שֶׁל לוּחוֹת לְרוֹחְבּוֹ שֶׁל אָרוֹן — נִשְׁתַּיֵּיר שָׁם שְׁלֹשָׁה טְפָחִים, חֲצִי טֶפַח מִכָּאן לְכוֹתֶל זֶה, וַחֲצִי טֶפַח מִכָּאן לְכוֹתֶל זֶה, וּטְפָחַיִים לְשִׁילוּט מָקוֹם שֶׁסֵּפֶר תּוֹרָה (א) מוּנָּח. ר"ש בֶּן לָקִישׁ אָמַר: בְּאַמָּה בַּת חֲמִשָּׁה טְפָחִים הָיָה הָאָרוֹן עָשׂוּי. מַאן תָּנָא בְּאַמָּה בַּת חֲמִשָּׁה טְפָחִים ר' יְהוּדָה. דְּתָנִינָן תַּמָּן: ר' יְהוּדָה אוֹמֵר: אַמַּת הַבִּנְיָן שִׁשָּׁה,* שֶׁל הַכֵּלִים חֲמִשָּׁה. וְהָהֵן אָרוֹן — כְּלִי הוּא. עַל דַּעֲתֵיהּ דְּרַבִּי יְהוּדָה דוּ אָמַר בְּאַמָּה שֶׁל חֲמִשָּׁה טְפָחִים — הָיָה אוֹרְכּוֹ* עָשׂוּי שְׁנֵים עָשָׂר טֶפַח וּמֶחֱצָה, דִּכְתִיב "אַמָּתַיִם וָחֵצִי אָרְכּוֹ" אַמְתָא חַמְשָׁא וְאַמְתָא ה' וּפַלְגּוּת אַמְתָא תְּרֵי וּפָלֵיג. וד' לוּחוֹת הָיוּ בוֹ שְׁנַיִם שְׁלֵימִים וּשְׁנַיִם שְׁבוּרִים, דִּכְתִיב "אֲשֶׁר שִׁבַּרְתָּ וְשַׂמְתָּם בָּאָרוֹן" וְהַלּוּחוֹת הָיָה כָּל אֶחָד וְאֶחָד אָרְכָּן שִׁשָּׁה טְפָחִים וְרָחְבָּן [ג] שִׁשָּׁה טְפָחִים, תֵּן (רָחְבָּן) אָרְכָּן שֶׁל לוּחוֹת לְאָרְכּוֹ שֶׁל אָרוֹן וְנִשְׁתַּיֵּיר שָׁם חֲצִי טֶפַח. אֶצְבַּע לְכוֹתֶל מִכָּאן, וְאֶצְבַּע לְכוֹתֶל מִכָּאן. רוֹחְבּוֹ שֶׁל אָרוֹן שִׁבְעָה טְפָחִים וּמֶחֱצָה, דִּכְתִיב "אַמָּה וָחֵצִי רָחְבּוֹ" אַמְתָא חֲמִשָּׁה וּפַלְגּוּת אַמְתָא תְּרֵי וּפָלֵיג, [ד] וד' לוּחוֹת הָיוּ בוֹ שְׁנַיִם שְׁלֵימִים וּשְׁנַיִם שְׁבוּרִים, דִּכְתִיב "אֲשֶׁר שִׁבַּרְתָּ וְשַׂמְתָּם בָּאָרוֹן". הַלּוּחוֹת הָיָה כָּל אֶחָד וְאֶחָד אָרְכָּן שִׁשָּׁה טְפָחִים וְרָחְבָּן שִׁשָּׁה טְפָחִים. תֵּן רָחְבָּן (אָרְכָּן) לְרוֹחְבּוֹ שֶׁל אָרוֹן וְנִשְׁתַּיֵּיר שָׁם טֶפַח וּמֶחֱצָה, אֶצְבַּע לְכוֹתֶל מִכָּאן וְאֶצְבַּע לְכוֹתֶל מִכָּאן, חֲצִי טֶפַח מִכָּאן וַחֲצִי טֶפַח מִכָּאן לְשִׁילוּט. כֵּיצַד א) עָשָׂה בְּצַלְאֵל אֶת הָאָרוֹן? [ה] ר"ח (בֶּן גַּמְלִיאֵל) אָמַר: שָׁלֹשׁ תֵּיבוֹת עֲשָׂאוֹ, שְׁתַּיִם שֶׁל זָהָב וְאַחַת שֶׁל עֵץ. נָתַן שֶׁל זָהָב בְּשֶׁל עֵץ, וְשֶׁל עֵץ בְּשֶׁל זָהָב, וְצִיפָּהוּ, דִּכְתִיב "וְצִפִּיתָ אוֹתוֹ זָהָב טָהוֹר מִבַּיִת וּמִחוּץ". מַת"ל "תְּצַפֶּנּוּ" — לְהָבִיא שְׂפָתוֹ הָעֶלְיוֹנָה. רשב"ל ב) אָמַר: תֵּיבָה אַחַת עֲשָׂאוֹ וְצִיפָּהוּ, דִּכְתִיב "וְצִפִּיתָ אוֹתוֹ זָהָב טָהוֹר מִבַּיִת וּמִחוּץ". מַת"ל "תְּצַפֶּנּוּ"? א"ר פִּנְחָס לְהָבִיא בֵּין נֶסֶר לְנֶסֶר. [א] כֵּיצַד הָיוּ הַלּוּחוֹת כְּתוּבִים? [ו] ר' ג) (ב) חֲנִינָה (בֶּן אֲחִיהּ ר' יְהוּדָה) בֶּן גַּמְלִיאֵל אוֹמֵר: חֲמִשָּׁה עַל לוּחַ זֶה וַחֲמִשָּׁה עַל לוּחַ זֶה, הה"ד [ז] "וַיִּכְתְּבֵם עַל שְׁנֵי לוּחוֹת אֲבָנִים", חֲמִשָּׁה עַל לוּחַ זֶה וַחֲמִשָּׁה עַל לוּחַ זֶה. וְרַבָּנַן אָמְרֵי: עֲשָׂרָה עַל לוּחַ זֶה וַעֲשָׂרָה עַל לוּחַ זֶה, [ח] הה"ד "וַיַּגֵּד לָכֶם אֶת בְּרִיתוֹ אֲשֶׁר צִוָּה אֶתְכֶם לַעֲשׂוֹת עֲשֶׂרֶת הַדְּבָרִים" — עֲשָׂרָה עַל לוּחַ זֶה וַעֲשָׂרָה עַל לוּחַ זֶה. ר"ש בֶּן יוֹחַאי אוֹמֵר: עֶשְׂרִים עַל לוּחַ זֶה וְעֶשְׂרִים עַל לוּחַ זֶה, [ט] דִּכְתִיב "וַיִּכְתְּבֵם עַל שְׁנֵי לוּחוֹת אֲבָנִים" עֶשְׂרִים עַל לוּחַ זֶה, וְעֶשְׂרִים עַל לוּחַ זֶה. רַבִּי סִימַאי אָמַר: אַרְבָּעִים עַל לוּחַ זֶה, וְאַרְבָּעִים עַל לוּחַ זֶה, דִּכְתִיב "מִזֶּה וּמִזֶּה הֵם כְּתוּבִים" — טַטְרוֹגָה. חֲנַנְיָה בֶּן אֲחִי רַבִּי יְהוֹשֻׁעַ אוֹמֵר: בֵּין כָּל דִּבּוּר וְדִבּוּר דִּקְדּוּקֶיהָ וְאוֹתִיּוֹתֶיהָ שֶׁל תּוֹרָה, דִּכְתִיב "מְמוּלָּאִים בַּתַּרְשִׁישׁ" — כְּיַמָּא רַבָּא. ר"ש בֶּן לָקִישׁ כַּד הֲוָה מָטֵי הָדֵין קְרָיֵיהּ הֲוָה אָמַר: יָפֶה לִמְּדַנִי חֲנַנְיָה בֶּן אֲחִי רַבִּי יְהוֹשֻׁעַ, מַה הַיָּם הַזֶּה בֵּין גַּל גָּדוֹל לְגַל גָּדוֹל גַּלִּים קְטַנִּים — כָּךְ בֵּין כָּל דִּבּוּר וְדִבּוּר דִּקְדּוּקֶיהָ וְאוֹתִיּוֹתֶיהָ שֶׁל תּוֹרָה, אָמַר ר' תַּנְחוּמָא [י] אִיתְקַשְׁיַית קוֹמֵי רַבִּי פִּנְחָס: אַתְיָא כְּר' יְהוּדָה וְלָא אַתְיָא כר"מ מ"ט דר' יְהוּדָה — דִּכְתִיב "לָקוֹחַ אֵת סֵפֶר הַתּוֹרָה הַזֶּה וְשַׂמְתֶּם אוֹתוֹ מִצַּד אֲרוֹן בְּרִית ה' וְגוֹ' [כ] עַל דַּעֲתֵיהּ דר' יְהוּדָה דוּ אֲמַר הֵיכָן הָיָה סֵפֶר תּוֹרָה נָתוּן — כְּמִין גְּלוּסְקְמָא עָשׂוּי לוֹ מִבַּחוּץ, וְהָיָה סֵפֶר תּוֹרָה נָתוּן בְּתוֹכוֹ. מ"ט דר"מ דִּכְתִיב "וְנָתַתָּ אֶת הַכַּפּוֹרֶת עַל הָאָרוֹן מִלְמָעְלָה וְאֶל הָאָרוֹן תִּתֵּן אֶת הָעֵדוּת אֲשֶׁר אֶתֵּן אֵלֶיךָ". עַל דַּעֲתֵיהּ [ל] דר"מ דוּ אֲמַר אֵין מוּקְדָּם וּמְאוּחָר בַּתּוֹרָה אֶלָּא "וְאֶל הָאָרוֹן תִּתֵּן אֶת הָעֵדוּת אֲשֶׁר אֶתֵּן אֵלֶיךָ" וְאח"כ "וְנָתַתָּ אֶת הַכַּפּוֹרֶת עַל הָאָרוֹן מִלְמָעְלָה". רַבִּי פִּנְחָס (ג) בְּשֵׁם רשב"ל [מ] הַתּוֹרָה ז) שֶׁנָּתַן לוֹ הקב"ה לְמֹשֶׁה נְתָנָהּ לוֹ אֵשׁ לְבָנָה חֲרוּתָה בְּאֵשׁ שְׁחוֹרָה, הִיא אֵשׁ מוּבְלֶלֶת בָּאֵשׁ, חֲצוּבָה מֵאֵשׁ, וּנְתוּנָה מֵאֵשׁ, *דִּכְתִיב "מִימִינוֹ אֵשׁ דָּת לָמוֹ".§

(Margin references: שמות כה; דברים י; טפחים; של ארון; שמות כה; דברים י; שם; שמות כה; דברים ד; שם; שמות לב; שיר ה; דברים לא; שמות כה; הדא הוא דברים לג)

הלכה ב מתני'

(ד) הֵיכָן הָיוּ הַשְׁתַּחֲוָיוֹת הָאֵלּוּ? אַרְבַּע בַּצָּפוֹן, וְאַרְבַּע בַּדָּרוֹם, שָׁלֹשׁ בַּמִּזְרָח וּב' בַּמַּעֲרָב, כְּנֶגֶד ה) שְׁלֹשָׁה עָשָׂר שְׁעָרִים, דְּרוֹמִיִּים סְמוּכִים לַמַּעֲרָב — שַׁעַר הָעֶלְיוֹן, שַׁעַר הַדֶּלֶק, שַׁעַר הַבְּכוֹרוֹת, שַׁעַר הַמַּיִם. וְלָמָּה נִקְרָא שְׁמוֹ שַׁעַר הַמַּיִם — שֶׁבּוֹ מַכְנִיסִין צְלוֹחִית שֶׁל

קרבן העדה

תן מהם חצי טפח לכל כותל. שהרי מבחוץ נמדד אמתיים ומחצה ארכו: ה"ג: תן רחבן של לוחות לרחבו של ארון: ה"ג: חצי טפח מכאן וחצי טפח מכאן לכותל, נשתיירו שני טפחים לשילוט. וה"פ: לשילוט — שתהא ס"ת נכנסת ויוצאת בריוח, לפי שהיתה מונחת אורכה לרוחב הארון. דהיינו באותן שני טפחים שנשתיירו באורך הארון, וס"ת עביה שני טפחים וארכה ששה טפחים, והיתה מונחת בדוחק באותן שני טפחים שבאורך. לכך היה הארון רוחב יותר ב"ט, לשילוט וליטלה כרצונו: והחן ארון. והאי ארון נמי כלי הוא, שהרי מיטלטל בשעת הנסיעה: ה"ג: ורחבן שלשה, תן ארכן של לוחות לארכו של ארון: אצבע לכתלים מכאן. שהטפח ד' אצבעות: חצי טפח מכאן וכו' לשילוט. ליטול הלוחות מן הארון לעת הצורך: נתן של זהב הפנימית בשל עץ האמצעי, ושל עץ נתן בשל זהב החיצון: להביא שפתו העליונה. של העץ שיחפנו בזהב: להביא בין נסר לנסר, נמי יצפה זהב. דקמ"ל קרא בכל היכא דאפשר לצפותו זהב יצפה. אבל ציפוי העליון לרשב"ל א"צ ריבוי, דלא גרע משאר מקומות: ויכתבם על שני לוחות אבנים. מיעוט "לוחות" שנים. מה ת"ל "שני" — שיהיו שניהם שוים, חמשה על לוח זה וחמשה על לוח זה: "עשרת הדברים, ויכתבם על שני לוחות אבנים". משמע דעשרה על כל אבן כתב, דאל"כ "עשרת הדברים" ל"ל: דכתיב "ויכתבם". משמע שיהו כתובים שני פעמים על כל לוח: מזה ומזה הם כתובים. היינו ב' בארכו, וב' פעמים על שני צידי רחבו. ועל שטח שלמעלה ושלמטה לא היו נכתבים. שכל לוח ארכו ו' ורחבו ג' ועביו ג', א"כ השטחיים שלמעלה ושלמטה לא היו כ"א שלשה על שלשה, ולא היו ראויין לעשרת הדברים. ולכתוב חמשה מכאן וחמשה מכאן — אין זה דרך כבוד לחלקם, למ"ד שכולן היו נכתבין באורך (ועיין ביפה מראה): טטרוגא. מרובע, בלשון יון: בין כל דבור ודבור. היו כתובים דקדוקי התורה: כימא רבא. ששמו "תרשיש", והוא הים הגדול, והוא מלא מיני דגים הרבה: אתקשית וכו'. הקשיתי לפני ר"פ, דקראי כר"י דייקי ולא כר"מ: מצד ארון ברית ה'. מצד הוא מונח, ולא בתוכו: ע"ד דר"י. דהוא אמר שמצד היתה מונחת, היכן היתה מונחת?: כמין. תיבה עשה לארון מבחוץ, ועלי' היתה ס"ת מונחת: "ונתת את הכפרת על הארון ואל הארון תתן את העדות אשר אתן אליך". וה"ל למיכתב תחלה "ואל הארון תתן את העדות", ואח"כ "ונתת את הכפורת"! אלא ודאי ד"עדות" דקרא היינו ס"ת, והיא נתונה לתוך הארון, בסוף מ' שנה שכבר היה הכפורת נתון על הארון: ה"ג: ע"ד דר"י דו אמר אין מוקדם ומאוחר בתורה. וה"פ: לר"י ל"ק הך קרא, דאיכא לשנויי: אין מוקדם ומאוחר בתורה אפי' בחד ענינא. והיינו דקשיא ליה לר' תנחומא קרא דר"י לר"מ, דקרא דר"מ לר"י ל"ק, כדשנינן. (ומה מאוד נתלבטו המפרשים בפי' סוגיא זו, ועיין בי"מ. והנראה לי כתבתי): אש לבנה. הם האותיות חקוקים ע"ג אש שחורה, והיינו כתב ליבונאה. א"נ: בהיפך, והוא ככתב שלנו: היא אש. התורה עצמה אש ובלולה באש: חצובה. אותיותיה באש: ונתונה. מהקב"ה למשה מאש שלמעלה:

הלכה ב מתני' והיכן היו משתחוין. שלש עשרה השתחויות דתנן לעיל: שער העליון. הר הבית היה משופע ועולה ממזרח למערב. והשער הסמוך למערב הוא שער העליון, ואחריו שער הדלק, הוא שער של לשכת העצים שהיתה בעזרה, ודרך שם מכניסין עצי המערכה שדולקין על המזבח: שער הבכורות. שמכניסין שם הבכורות הנשחטים בדרום:

משנת אליהו

ריבב"ן

מתני' *)(עד ד') צלוחית. שלימה שהיתה מחזקת ג' לוגין כדאמר בסוכה בפ' בתרא שהיו מנסכין בתמיד של שחר בחג בשעת ניסוך היין שהוא רביעית ההין דהיינו ג'

תקלין חדתין

טפחים: חצי טפח לכל כותל. לעובי הכתלים, שהרי מבחוץ נמדד אמתים וחצי ארכו: לס"ת. שכתב משה, כמ"ש "ויכתוב משה את התורה" וגו': חצי טפח. דד' לוחות רחבן י"ב: לשילוט. היינו שיהיה ריוח קצת ללוחות, דיתבי י"ב בי"ב. וכמו דפריך בבבלי: תרי בתרי היכא יתיב: כיצד כו'. איידי דמביא סדר הלוחות בארון, מפרש למעשה הארון: ה"ג: ר"ח. ול"ג "בן גמליאל". ונשתבש מסוגיא דלקמן. והכא הוא בר פלוגתיה דר"ל, והוא סתם ר"ח: שלש תיבות כו'. שנאמר "מבית ומחוץ תצפנו". ושל עץ באמצע, והושיבו בתוך של זהב. וחזר ונתן של זהב שני בתוך של עץ, וחיפה שפתו העליונה בזהב, נמצא מחופה מבית ומבחוץ: של זהב. ראשון: בשל עץ. ושל עץ הוא אמצעי: שפתו העליונה ליפה זהב, שלא יהא העץ ניכר: בין נסר לנסר. שיהיה כאחת: כיצד היו הלוחות. אחר שפירש מדת הלוחות והארון ומעשיהם, מפרש כתיבת הלוחות כילד: "ר"ח ב"ג" גרים. דהא כאן בר פלוגתיה רשב"י. ורמב"ג מלינו בנדה פ"ג א' שהיה בימי ר"מ. ואילו חנניה אחי ר"י היה בימי ר"ג, כמ"ש בנדה כ"ד ב', וגם דמייתי ליה על מילתא אחריתא: ה"ג: ויכתוב על הלוחות עשרת הדברים. ודריש עשרה על שתיהן יחד, ה' על זה וה' על זה. ופסוק הכתוב בספרים שיבוש הוא: ה"ג: דכתיב ויגד וגו' לעשות עשרת הדברים ויכתבם על שני לוחות אבנים. דריש "ויכתבם" לעשרת הדברים על זה: רשב"י אומר כ' שנאמר כתובים מב' עבריהם. וס"ל כרבנן דעל עבר א' היה כתוב עשרה, וכן על עבר הב', וכן בשני: מ' על לוח זה. ס"ל כרשב"י שהיו כתובים מב' עבריהם. אך דדריש "מזה ומזה" שבכל עבר היו כתובים עשר מול עשר: טטרגא. מרובעים: בין כל דיבור כו' שבעשרת הדברות נכלל כל התורה. ובינים היו כל דקדוקיה ואותיותיה. וכמ"ש במדרש ע"פ "תורי זהב נעשה לך עם נקודות הכסף": כימא רבא. כדמפרש ר"ל, וכמ"ש "ומלאה הארץ דעה כמים לים מכסים": בין גל גדול לגל גדול גלים קטנים. עשרת הדברות היו כלליות ונקרא גל גדול, ובינים דקדוקי תורה ודברי סופרים והן גלים קטנים. וז"ש יפה לימדני כו': ה"ג: א"ר תנחומא כו' דרבי פנחס כרבי מאיר ניחא לרבי יהודה קשיא ס"ת היכן מנח. דלר"מ היה מקום לס"ת, כדלעיל, אבל לרבי יהודה היכן היה הס"ת מונח? ומשני: כמין גלוסקום. = דפא. ובבבלי שם: ארגז ששיגרו פלשתים, עליו היה ס"ת מונח: מאי טעמא דרבי יהודה. דסבירא ליה שלא היה ס"ת בארון: מצד ארון ולא בתוכו. ולר' מאיר לא קשיא, האי קרא מתרץ בבבלי בבא בתרא (יד, ב): מאי טעמא דרבי מאיר. ולמה לא ס"ל כרבי יהודה וכפשטיה דקרא?: "ונתת את הכפרת על הארון מלמעלה ואל הארון תתן את העדות אשר אתן אליך". ר"מ הכי דייק: דלעיל מניה כתיב "ונתת אל הארון את העדות אשר אתן אליך", והאי קרא תנינא למה ליה? אע"כ דקרא קמא איירי בלוחות שנקראו "לוחות העדות". ואחר כך כתיב "ונתת את הכפורת על הארון" וגו' לאורויי: דתחילה יתן את הלחות ואח"כ את הכפורת. ואח"כ כתיב "ואל הארון תתן את העדות אשר אתן אליך" — קאי אס"ת שנקראת גם כן 'עדות', וגם כן היתה מונחת בתוך הארון. אך דס"ת עדיין לא ניתנה בתוכו עד סוף מ' שנה, כמ"ש "לקוח את ספר התורה גו' ושמתם מצד ארון" גו'. ולכן כתב לווי נתינתה אחר נתינת הכפורת על הארון. והכי כתיבה בסדר העשיה בהקמת המשכן בפרשת פקודי: תחלה נתינת העדות, היינו הלוחות, דהס"ת עדיין לא היתה כתובה. ואחר כך נתינת הכפרת. אבל לרבי יהודה דס"ל דהס"ת לא היתה מקומה בתוך הארון, א"כ הני קראי ל"ל הכל בלוחות, ותרי קראי ל"ל? וצריך לפרש דקרא בתרא לאורויי סדר נתינתן, שיהיה תחלה נתינת הלוחות, ואח"כ נתינת הכפרת, א"כ הכי הל"ל: "ואל הארון תתן את העדות", אח"כ "ונתת את הכפורת"! וזהו דאמר: על דעתיה דר' יהודה אין מוקדם ומאוחר בתורה אף בחד ענינא, וה"ל כאילו כתיבה "ואל הארון" וגו' ואח"כ "ונתת" וגו'. וכמ"ש בקדושין ע"ח דאורחיה דקרא הכי הוא, כמו דכתיב "ונר אלהים טרם יכבה גו' ושמואל שוכב בהיכל ה'" וגו'. והמפרשים נתלבטו בזה באין מבין: רבי פנחס. איידי דאיירי בענינא דס"ת, מפרש נתינתה איך היה: ה"ג: אש לבנה. הן רזין דאורייתא, כענין לבנת הספיר: מובללת מאש. כמ"ש ז"ל ע"פ "לדבקה בו": וכי אפשר לדבק בהקב"ה? והלא אש אוכלה! אלא לדבק בתורתו ולומדיה כו'. והן חלק ההלכות, ריתחא דאורייתא. כמ"ש "הלא כה דברי כאש" גו'. וזהו מובללת, דאיהי כלולה מאש: חצובה באש. מלובשת בשרשי נשמות ישראל שהן לבושין למחצב התורה. שהנשמה חלק אלהי ממעל, שהן ג' חלקי התורה כידוע: ונתונה באש. בשעת מתן תורה עיקר נתינתה באש היתה: שנאמר. "מימינו" — זו אש לבנה, ימין — חסד, "אש" — נגד אש שחורה: דת למו. הן אותיות תלמו"ד, כדכתב רבינו הגאון נ"ע. ו"למו" — היינו שניתנה לנו. וגם כן שמחוברת לנשמתינו. וזהו "למו", וגם קאי על "מימינו", שמחוברת לו ית"ש, ומהכא דריש כל הנ"ל: **מתני'** היכן היו משתחוים. י"ג השתחויות דלעיל: שער העליון. הוא שער הסמוך למערב, שהוא שער העליון. ואחריו שער הדלק שהוא שער של לשכת העצים שהיתה בעזרה, ודרך שם היו מכניסים עצי המערכה שדולקים ע"ג המזבח: שער הבכורות. שמכניסים שם הבכורות הנשחטים

*) נראה דצ"ל עד שער המים שבו מכניסין צלוחית וכו'.

נוסחת הבבלי

(א) שס"ת מונח בתוכה ריש לקיש כו' אצבע (ומחצה) לכתלים כו' ואצבע (ומחצה) לכתלי' כו' אצבע לכל כותל נשתייר חצי טפח מיכן וחצי טפח מיכן לשלוט מקום שס"ת מונח: (ב) חנניה בן אחי ר' יהושע אומר כו': (ג) ר"פ אמר בשם ר"ש תורה שנתן הקב"ה לו למשה אש לבנה כו' היא מאש חצובה נולדת מאש מובללת מאש נתונה מימינו של הקב"ה שנאמר מימינו אש דת למו: (ד) והיכן היו משתחוים כו' י"ג שערי' דרומיים כו':

הגהות הגר"א

[א] מן וארבעה לוחו' עד תן רוחבן נמחק: [ב] צ"ל תן אורכן של לוחות לרוחבו של ארון וכו': [ג] צ"ל ורחבן שלשה טפחים וכ"כ גירסת הק"ע: [ד] מכאן עד תן רחבן כו' נמחק: [ה] ר"ח בן גמליאל ל"ג. ונשתבש מסוגיא דלקמן והכא בר פלוגתיה ר"ש ב"ל והוא סתם ר"ח: [ו] ר"ח בן גמליאל גרסינן דהא כאן בר פלוגתיה רשב"י: [ז] ה"ג ויכתוב על הלוחות את דברי הברית עשרת הדברי' כו'. ודריש עשרת על שתיהן יחד ה' על זה וה' על זה. ופסוק הכתוב בספרי' שבוש הוא: [ח] ה"ג שנאמר ויגד לכם את בריתו וכו' ויכתבם על שני לוחות האבנים. כי ממלת ויכתבם קא דריש י' על לוח זה וי' על לוח זה לכן ראוי לכתוב גם סיפי' דקרא: [ט] צ"ל שנא' כתובים משני עבריה' כתב על לוח זה וכתב על לוח זה: [י] ה"ג אמר ר' תנחומא אתקשיתא קומי דר' פינחס כר"מ ניחא לר"י קשיא ס"ת היכן מונח על דעתיה דר' יהודה כמין גלוסקי' עשו לו מבחוץ והיה ס"ת מונח בתוכו כצ"ל וה"פ דלר"מ יהיה מקום לס"ת כדלעיל אבל לר"י היכן היה הס"ת מונח ומשני כמין גלוסקי' כו'. ובבבלי שם איתא ארגז ששיגרו פלשתי' עליו הי' הס"ת מונח: [כ] מן על דעתי' דר"י עד מ"ט דר"מ ל"ג. כי כבר גרסינן לה לעיל קודם מ"ט דר"י: [ל] צ"ל ע"ד דר' יהודה. ועי' בספר תקלין חדתין ותמלא טעם לשבח לכל הגרסאות הנ"ל: [מ] ה"ג תורה שנתן הקב"ה למשה אש לבנה חרותה באש שחורה מובללת מאש חצובה באש נתונה באש שנאמר מימינו וכו':

גליון הש"ס

[א] ע' שו"ת הרדב"ז ח"ג סימן תקמ"ט:

המים מפכים. מפרש בגמ': שער הקרבן. שם מכניסין קדשי קדשים ששחיטתן בצפון: שער הנשים. שבו הנשים נכנסות לסמוך על קרבנן, א"נ: לעמוד על קרבנן: שער השיר. דרך שם היו מכניסין כלי שיר: שבו יצא יכניה בגלותו. שנכנס לבית המקדש להשתחות וליטול רשות כשהלך לגולה לבבל, ויצא דרך אותו השער: שער נקנור. מפרש בפרק "א"ל הממונה": פשפשין. שערים קטנים בתוך שערים גדולים. ואף הם ממנין שלשה עשר שערים. ואע"ג דגם לשער בית המוקד היה לו פשפש — לא חשיב ליה, לפי שהיה קטן ביותר: גמ' מתני'. אתיא כאבא יוסי בן יוחנן דאמר י"ג שערים היו במקדש. אבל לרבנן דאמרי שבעה שערים היו במקדש, קשיא: היכן היו משתחוים. דקים להו שהיו משתחוים י"ג השתחוות:

תורה אור

שֶׁל נִיסּוּךְ הַמַּיִם בֶּחָג. רַבִּי אֱלִיעֶזֶר בֶּן יַעֲקֹב אוֹמֵר:
בּוֹ הַמַּיִם מְפַכִּים וַעֲתִידִין לִהְיוֹת יוֹצְאִין מִתַּחַת מִפְתַּן
הַבַּיִת. לְעוּמָּתָן א) בַּצָּפוֹן סְמוּכִים בַּמַּעֲרָב: שַׁעַר יְכָנְיָה,
שַׁעַר הַקָּרְבָּן, שַׁעַר הַנָּשִׁים, שַׁעַר הַשִּׁיר. וְלָמָּה ב) נִקְרָא
שְׁמוֹ שַׁעַר יְכָנְיָה — שֶׁבּוֹ יָצָא יְכָנְיָה בְּגָלוּתוֹ. שֶׁבַּמִּזְרָח
שַׁעַר נִקָּנוֹר, וּשְׁנֵי פִשְׁפְּשִׁין הָיוּ לוֹ אֶחָד מִימִינוֹ וְאֶחָד
מִשְּׂמֹאלוֹ, וּשְׁנַיִם בַּמַּעֲרָב וְלֹא הָיָה לָהֶן שֵׁם.§
גמ' מַתְנִיתִין אַבָּא יוֹסֵה בֶּן (חָנָן) יוֹחָנָן הִיא, דְּאָמַר
כְּנֶגֶד י"ג שְׁעָרִים. בְּרַם כְּרַבָּנַן א שִׁבְעָה שְׁעָרִים הָיוּ
בָּעֲזָרָה. ע"ד דְּרַבָּנַן הֵיכָן ג) הָיוּ הִשְׁתַּחֲוָואוֹת הַלָּלוּ?
כִּי הַהִיא דְּתָנֵינַן תַּמָּן: י"ג פְּרָצוֹת הָיוּ בּוֹ שֶׁפְּרָצוּם
מַלְכֵי יָוָן (א) וְחָזְרוּ וּגְדָרוּם בְּנֵי חַשְׁמוֹנַאי, וְגָזְרוּ כְּנֶגְדָּן
זכריה יד י"ג (ב) הִשְׁתַּחֲוָואוֹת. כְּתִיב "וְהָיָה בַּיּוֹם הַהוּא יֵצְאוּ מַיִם
חַיִּים מִירוּשָׁלַיִם" וְגו'. תָּנֵי: ד) מִבֵּית ק"ק עַד הַפָּרוֹכֶת
— כְּקַרְנֵי סִילֵּי וְכִילַּיי, מִן פָּרוֹכֶת עַד מִזְבַּח הַזָּהָב — כְּקַרְנֵי
חֲגָבִים. [א] מִמִּזְבַּח הַזָּהָב עַד עֲזָרוֹת — כְּחוּט שֶׁל שְׁתִי,
מִן הָעֲזָרוֹת עַד מִפְתַּן הַבַּיִת — כְּחוּט שֶׁל עֵרֶב. מִיכָּן
יחזקאל מז וְאֵילָךְ כְּמִפִּי הַפַּךְ. כְּתִיב "וְהִנֵּה מַיִם מְפַכִּים מִן הַכָּתֵף
הַיְמָנִית בְּצֵאת הָאִישׁ קָדִים וְקָו בְּיָדוֹ וַיָּמָד אֶלֶף
שם בָּאַמָּה וַיַּעֲבִרֵנִי בַמַּיִם מֵי אָפְסָיִם" — עַד קַרְסוּלָה. "וַיָּמָד
אֶלֶף וַיַּעֲבִירֵנִי בַמַּיִם מֵי בִּרְכָּיִם" — עַד בִּרְכַּיָּיה, "וַיָּמָד
אֶלֶף וַיַּעֲבִירֵנִי מֵי מָתְנָיִם" — עַד מָתְנַיָּיא, מִכָּאן וְאֵילָךְ
"וַיָּמָד אֶלֶף נַחַל אֲשֶׁר לֹא אוּכַל לַעֲבוֹר" אֲפִי' לַבִּירָנִין
ישעיה לג גְּדוֹלָה אֵינָהּ יְכוֹלָה לַעֲבוֹר בּוֹ. מ"ט "וְצִי אַדִּיר לֹא
יַעַבְרֶנּוּ". מִפְּנֵי מָה "כִּי גָאוּ הַמַּיִם מֵי שָׂחוּ" מַהוּ מֵי שָׂחוּ —
מִלְּשׁוּט. (ג) אָמַר רַב חוּנָה (הוּנָא) בְּאַתְרִין קָרוּ
שם כה לְשַׁיְיטָא שָׁחוּנָא [ב] "וּפֵרַשׂ יָדָיו בְּקִרְבּוֹ כַּאֲשֶׁר יְפָרֵשׂ
הַשּׂוֹחֶה לִשְׂחוֹת". מַהוּ [ג] "לִשְׂחוֹת"? אָמַר רַבִּי יוֹסֵי בֵּי ר'
זכריה יג בּוּן (בֵּיבָן) מַיִין דְּמִתְמַלְּלִין בְּעָלְמָא. כְּתִיב "בַּיּוֹם
הַהוּא יִהְיֶה מָקוֹר נִפְתָּח לְבֵית דָּוִיד וּלְיוֹשְׁבֵי יְרוּשָׁלַם
לְחַטַּאת וּלְנִידָּה". ר' שְׁמוּאֵל בַּר נַחְמָן בְּשֵׁם ר' (נָתָן)
יוֹנָתָן: מִבֵּית דָּוִד וְעַד יוֹשְׁבֵי יְרוּשָׁלַם — כְּשֵׁרִים לְנִדָּה
וּלְחַטָּאת, מִכָּאן וְאֵילָךְ מֵי תַעֲרוּבוֹת הֵם, כְּשֵׁרִים לְנִדָּה
ב וּפְסוּלִים לְמֵי חַטָּאת. אר"א (ר"מ אוֹמֵר) מִבֵּית דָּוִד
וְעַד יוֹשְׁבֵי יְרוּשָׁלַם כְּשֵׁרִים לְנִידָּה וּלְחַטָּאת, מִכָּאן
וְאֵילָךְ [א] — מֵי קַטַפְרִיסוֹת הֵן, ג פְּסוּלִין לְנִדָּה וּלְחַטָּאת.
יחזקאל מז כְּתִיב ה) "וַיֹּאמֶר אֵלַי הַמַּיִם הָאֵלֶּה יוֹצְאִים אֶל
הַגְּלִילָה הַקַּדְמוֹנָה" — זֶה ו) יָם שֶׁל סַמְכוּ, (סִיבוּכָא) "וְיָרְדוּ
אֶל הָעֲרָבָה" — זֶה יָם שֶׁל טִבֶּרְיָא, "וּבָאוּ הַיָּמָּה" — זֶה יַם
הַמֶּלַח, "אֶל הַיָּמָּה הַמּוּצָאִים" — זֶה הַיָּם הַגָּדוֹל, וְלָמָּה
נִקְרָא שְׁמוֹ "מוּצָאִים" — כְּנֶגֶד שְׁתֵּי פְעָמִים שֶׁיָּצָא, אֶחָד
בְּדוֹר אֱנוֹשׁ וְאֶחָד בְּדוֹר הַפְּלָגָה. רַבִּי ז) לְעָזָר בְּשֵׁם
רַבִּי חֲנִינָה: בָּרִאשׁוֹנָה יָצָא עַד קַלַבְּרִיאָה וּבַשְּׁנִיָּה
יָצָא עַד כֵּיפֵי בַּרְבַּרִיאָה, רַבִּי אַחָא בְּשֵׁם ר' חֲנִינָה:
בָּרִאשׁוֹנָה יָצָא עַד כֵּיפֵי בַּרְבַּרִיאָה, וּבַשְּׁנִיָּה יָצָא עַד
איוב לח עַכּוֹ וְעַד יָפוֹ. "עַד פֹּה תָבֹא וְלֹא תוֹסִיף" — עַד עַכּוֹ תָּבֹא
וְלֹא תוֹסִיף. "וּפֹה יָשִׁית בִּגְאוֹן גַּלֶּיךָ" — עַד יָפוֹ אָשִׁית
גְּאוֹן גַּלֶּיךָ. נִיחָא, יַמָּא רָבָא וְיַמָּא דְמִילְחָא — בִּשְׁבִיל
לְמִיתְקָן. יַמָּא דְטִבֶּרְיָא יַמָּא [ד] דְסָמְכוּ — לְרַבּוֹת דְּגָתָם,
יחזקאל מז דִּכְתִיב בֵּיהּ "לְמִינָהּ תִּהְיֶה דְגָתָם" — לְמִינֵי מִינִים תִּהְיֶה
דְּגָתָם. תָּנֵי, אָמַר רשב"ג מַעֲשֶׂה שֶׁהָלַכְתִּי לְצַיְידָן
וְהֵבִיאוּ לְפָנַי יוֹתֵר מִשְּׁלֹשׁ מֵאוֹת מִינֵי דָּגִים בְּתַמְחוּי
שם א' "וְנִרְפְּאוּ הַמַּיִם בִּצָּאתָיו וּגְבָאָיו וְלֹא יֵרָפְאוּ לְמֶלַח
נִיתָּנוּ", כְּתִיב "וְנִרְפְּאוּ הַמַּיִם" וְאַתְּ אָמַרְתְּ וְלֹא (ד) יֵרָפְאוּ
שם הַמַּיִם? מָקוֹם הוּא וּשְׁמוֹ "וְלֹא יֵרָפְאוּ". כְּתִיב "וְעַל הַנַּחַל
יַעֲלֶה עַל שְׂפָתוֹ מִזֶּה וּמִזֶּה כָּל עֵץ מַאֲכָל לֹא יִבּוֹל
עָלֵהוּ וְלֹא יִתֹּם פִּרְיוֹ לָחֳדָשָׁיו יְבַכֵּר". תָּנֵי: ח) אָמַר רַבִּי
יְהוּדָה: לְפִי שֶׁבָּעוֹלָם הַזֶּה תְּבוּאָה עוֹשָׂה לְשִׁשָּׁה
חֳדָשִׁים וְאִילָן עוֹשֶׂה לִשְׁנֵים עָשָׂר חוֹדֶשׁ, אֲבָל לֶעָתִיד לָבֹא הַתְּבוּאָה עוֹשָׂה לְחֹדֶשׁ אֶחָד
וְאִילָן עוֹשֶׂה לִשְׁנֵי חֲדָשִׁים. מ"ט "לָחֳדָשָׁיו יְבַכֵּר". אָמַר ט) רַבִּי יוֹסֵי: לְפִי שֶׁבָּעוֹלָם הַזֶּה הַתְּבוּאָה
עוֹשָׂה לְשִׁשָּׁה חֳדָשִׁים וְאִילָן עוֹשֶׂה לְי"ב חֹדֶשׁ, אֲבָל לֶעָתִיד לָבֹא הַתְּבוּאָה עוֹשָׂה לְט"ו יוֹם
וְאִילָן עוֹשֶׂה לְחֹדֶשׁ אֶחָד. שֶׁכֵּן י) מָצִינוּ שֶׁעָשְׂתָה הַתְּבוּאָה בִּימֵי יוֹאֵל לַחֲמִשָּׁה עָשָׂר יוֹם וְקָרַב
יואל ב מִמֶּנָּה הָעוֹמֶר, מ"ט "וּבְנֵי צִיּוֹן גִּילוּ וְשִׂמְחוּ בַּה' אֱלֹהֵיכֶם כִּי נָתַן לָכֶם אֶת הַמּוֹרֶה לִצְדָקָה וַיּוֹרֶד
לָכֶם גֶּשֶׁם מוֹרֶה וּמַלְקוֹשׁ בָּרִאשׁוֹן". וּמָה מְקַיֵּים רַבִּי יוֹסֵי "לָחֳדָשָׁיו יְבַכֵּר" — בְּכָל חוֹדֶשׁ וְחוֹדֶשׁ יִהְיֶה
יחזקאל שם מְבַכֵּר. "וְעָלֵהוּ לִתְרוּפָה" רַבִּי יוֹחָנָן אָמַר: תַּרְפֵּיהּ, מֵצִיץ עָלֶיהָ וְתָרַף מְזוֹנֵהּ. רַב כ) וּשְׁמוּאֵל חַד
אָמַר: לְהַתִּיר פֶּה שֶׁלְּמַעְלָן, וְחַד [א] אָמַר: לְהַתִּיר פֶּה שֶׁלְּמַטָּן. ר' חֲנִינָה ור' יְהוֹשֻׁעַ בֶּן לֵוִי, ח"א
לְהַתִּיר פֶּה עֲקָרוֹת, וח"א [ב] לְהַתִּיר פֶּה אִלְּמִים. "וּלְעוּמָּתָן בַּצָּפוֹן" וכו'. אַתְּ ל) מוֹצֵא בְּשָׁעָה שֶׁעָלָה
נְבוּכַדְנֶאצַּר לְכָאן בָּא וְיָשַׁב לוֹ בְּדוֹפְנֵי שֶׁל אַנְטוֹכְיָא, וְיָצְאָה סַנְהֶדְרִין גְּדוֹלָה לִקְרָאתוֹ, וְאָמְרָה לוֹ:
הִגִּיעַ זְמַן הַבַּיִת הַזֶּה לֵיחָרֵב? אָמַר לָהֶן: אוֹתוֹ (ה) שֶׁהִמְלַכְתִּי עֲלֵיכֶם תְּנוּהוּ לִי וַאֲנִי הוֹלֵךְ". בָּאוּ וְאָמְרוּ
לִיהוֹיָכִין מֶלֶךְ יְהוּדָה: נְבוּכַדְנֶאצַּר בָּעֵי לָךְ. כֵּיוָן שֶׁשָּׁמַע מֵהֶן כָּךְ נָטַל מ) מַפְתְּחוֹת שֶׁל בה"מ עָלָה
לְגַגּוֹ שֶׁל הֵיכָל, אָמַר לְפָנָיו: רבש"ע לְשֶׁעָבַר הָיִינוּ נֶאֱמָנִים לְךָ וְהָיוּ מַפְתְּחוֹתֶיךָ מְסוּרִין לָנוּ, עַכְשָׁיו
שֶׁאֵין אָנוּ נֶאֱמָנִים — הֲרֵי מַפְתְּחוֹתֶיךָ מְסוּרִין לָךְ. תְּרֵין אֲמוֹרָאִין, חַד אָמַר: זָרְקָן וְעוֹד לֹא יָרְדוּ, וח"א [ג] בָּאָה כְּמִין יָד וּנְטָלָתַן מִיָּדוֹ. כֵּיוָן שֶׁרָאוּ כָּל
חוֹרֵי

נוסחאות ישנות א] וחורנא. ב] וחורנא אמר. ג] וחורנא אמר ראה.

קרבן העדה

ומשני: בהאי דתנינן תמן. במסכת מדות: בקרני ביילי וסיילי. מיני שבלול הם, וקרניהם דקים מאוד, וקרני חגבים עבים מהם, וחוט של שתי עב מהם, וחוט של ערב עב ממנו: מכאן ואילך. מתגבר והולך כמפי הפך: "מן הכתף הימנית". מצד דרום: "וימד אלף באמה". המלאך הראה ליחזקאל נחל היוצא מבית קדשי קדשים, תחלתו דק מאד והולך וגדל מאד. וכל אלף אמה אורך משילא חוץ לירושלים לא היה עמוק: "מי אפסים". שהגיעו עד קרסולים: "וימד אלף" — באמה שנית והעמיקו עד הברכים. מכאן ואילך — וימד אלף אשר לא יוכל לעבור בו, שהיו מימיו רדופים: לבירנין גדולה. לספינה גדולה: מלשוט. דאפי' בדרך שייטא לא יכול לעבור בו, דרדיפו מיא: באתרין. במקומנו קורין לשייט 'שחונא': ופרש ידיו וכו'. מייתי ראיה ד'לשחות' היינו לשוט: מיין דמתמללין בעלמא. שידברו העולם בו ויראו אותו. ל"א: שידברו העולם בהן מחמת גדולתן: מבית דוד ועד יושבי ירושלים. קשיא ליה: אטו לשאר ישראל אינן כשרים? הלכך קאמר מה שהמקור הולך מבית דוד ועד יושבי ירושלים — הוא דכשר לאפר פרה ולטבול בהן נדות. אבל משם ואילך — פסול למי חטאת, דמי תערובות הם ממי גשמים ולחטאת בעינן מים חיים: מי קטפריסות הן. הר משופע שמדרונו מחודד מאד, והעבירו המים דרך דף הנתון במדרון. ופסולין גם לנדה לטבול בהן. א"נ: "לנדה" — היינו זבה: זה ים של סמכו. דשבע ימים סובבים לא"י, וד' מהם: ים של סמכו ושל טבריא וים המלח וים הגדול. ומפרש ד"גלילה הקדמונה" — הוא ים של סמכו: ים הגדול. הוא הים ההולך מא"י למדינת אספניא: בראשונה. בדור אנוש, יצא עד מדינה ששמה קלבריאה והיא במדינת צרפת. ובדור הפלגה יצא עד הסלעים שבמדינת ברבריאה: עד עכו תבוא. דריש "פה" כמו כה: ניחא ימא רבא וימא דמלחא. שהולך המעין לבא לשם כדי למתקן, שמימיהם מלוחים וסרוחים. אלא ימא דטבריא וימא דסמכו למה באו לשם: ומשני: לרבות דגתם. שע"י מים אלו יתברכו מימיהם לגדל דגים הרבה: למינה תהיה דגתם. קרא יתירא הוא. דפשיטא דלמינה תהיה אלא ללמד דמיני מינים משונים שלא היו בתוכם מקדם יגדלו בהם: מקום הוא ששמו "ולא ירפאו". וה"פ: ביצאתיו וגבאיו ומקום ששמו "ולא ירפאו" — למלח ניתנו, ולא יבואו לשם המים הקדושים: תבואה עושה. פי': תבואה גדילה לששה חדשים: "לחדשיו יבכר". האילן יוציא פירותיו לשני חדשים. וכיון דמשנים עשר חדשים נעשו שני חדשים — ה"ה מה שנעשה בתבואה בעוה"ז בששה חדשים, נעשה לעתיד בחודש א': שהתבואה עשתה בימי יואל לט"ו יום. א"כ אילנות לשלשים יום כפל מהתבואה: בראשון. היינו בר"ח ניסן ירדו הגשמים. וכתיב "ובני ציון גילו ושמחו בה' אלהיכם" — היינו הקרבת העומר: ומשני: בכל חדש וחדש יהא מבכר. האילן, "ולחדשיו" — היינו חדשים דעלמא: תרפיה מציץ עליה. הפירות נראים יותר מן העלין שבאילנות: ופריך: "ותרף" מזונה? וכי "תרף" מזון הוא, דקאמרת הפירות נראים יותר מן העלין. ל"א: דרש "תרפיה" כמו טרף בטי"ת, מלשון מזון. וה"ק: משעה שפורח עליה — מיד נותן מזונו, שלא כדרך הטבע שהפרח מתאחר לגוף אחר יציאת העלים ימים רבים. והראשון נ"ל: להתיר פה שלמעלן. היינו פה אלמים: פה שלמטן. היינו פה עקרות: את מוצא בשעה שעלה נ"נ. לא"י כדי ליקח את יהויכין אחר שהמליכוהו במקום יהויקים אביו, ויעצוהו שרי בבל לסלקו: זרקן. כלפי מעלה, ועוד לא ירד, ולהראות להם שאינו חפץ בעבודתם: כיון שראו כל חורי יהודה כן. שאין רצון המקום בעבודתם, ושנמס לב המלך בקרבו:

ריבב"ן

לוגין: מים מפכין עתידין להיות יוצאין מבית קדש הקדשים. כדאיתא ביומא פרק בתרא אמר ר' מנחם משום ר' חנא ליפוראה מעין היוצא מבית קדש הקדשים בתחלה דומה לקרני סלעם עד שמגיע לפתח ההיכל כיון שמגיע לפתח ההיכל נעשה כחוט של שתי עד שמגיע לפתח האולם נעשה כחוט של ערב עד שמגיע לפתח העזרה כפי פך קטן היינו דתנן ר' אליעזר בן יעקב אומר מים מפכין עתידין להיות יוצאין מתחת מפתן הבית מפכים לשון פך: מתני' שער נקנור. על שם נקנור שנעשו נסים לדלתותיו

תקלין חדתין

הנשחטים בדרום: המים מפכים. בגמ' מפרש: שער הקרבן. שם מכניסים ק"ק ששחיטתן בצפון: שער הנשים. שבו נכנסות לסמוך על קרבנן: שער השיר. דרך שם היו מכניסין כלי שיר: שבו יצא יכניה בגלותו. שנכנס לבהמ"ק שם להפטר מלפני המלך מלכי המלכים וליטול רשות, כשהלך בגולה ויצא דרך אותו השער: שער נקנור. מפורש ביומא: פשפשים. שערים קטנים בתוך שערים גדולים, וגם הם ממנין י"ג שערים, ואע"ג דגם לשער בית המוקד היה לו פשפש — לא חשיב לה, לפי שהיה קטן ביותר: גמ' מתני' דקתני כנגד י"ג שערים. אתיא כאבא יוסא דס"ל הכי, בספ"ב דמדות, דהדיא: ברם כרבנן. דמדקאמר אבא יוסי כו' כנגד י"ג שערים, ע"כ רבנן פליגי עליה. וסתמא דמתני' דפ"ק דמדות ז' שערים היו סתמא כרבנן: היכן היו ההשתחויות. שהיו י"ג מכוונות: בקרני ביילי וסיילי. מיני שבלול שקרניהם דקים, ושל חגב עבים מהם, וחוט של שתי עב מהם, וחוט של ערב עב מהם: ה"ג: ממזבח הזהב למפתן הבית כו' ממפתן הבית לעזרה כו'. דהכי כתיב בקראי "והנה מים יוצאים מתחת מפתן הבית" ולשם באו מן המזבח, כמ"ש שם, ומפתן הבית קדים לעזרה: כמפי הפך. מתגבר והולך: הימנית. מצד דרום: מי אפסים. שהגיעו המים עד קרסולים: לבירני גדולה. שיוכל לילך שם ספינה גדולה: מי שחו מלשוט. דרדיפי מיא ולא יוכל לשוט שם: באתרין. במקומינו קורין לשייטא 'שחונא': ופרש ידיו כו'. מראה בכתוב סמך לדרשתו: דמתמללין בעלמא. מרוב פרסום גדולתן. א"נ: כמ"ש לקמן להתיר פה אלמין — שעל ידם יהיו יכולים לדבר. וכן יהיה בהם רוחניות יותר, כמ"ש במדרש: מתחלה לא היו קילוסו עולה אלא מן המים, כמ"ש "נשאו נהרות קולם" ומים אלו יהיה קדושתם יותר מכולם, וזהו דמתמללין בעלמא: מבית דוד כו'. דכפשטיה קשיא, וכי לשאר ישראל אינם כשרים? אלא דסימנא נקט קרא: המקור שהולך מבית דוד ועד יושבי ירושלים כשר לפרה ולטבילת נדות, אבל מכאן ואיך מי תערובו' הן. ולמי חטאת בעינן מים חיים: מי קטפרסאות. הוא שיפוע הר שמדרונו מחודד הרבה, והעברת המים דרך דף הנתון במדרון, ופסולין גם לנדה. ודריש דמכאן ולהלן לשניהם פסולין, ועיין תוספות (גיטין טז, א) ד"ה "הנצוק והקטפרס" כו': כתיב ויאמר כו'. דריש קראי דיחזקאל שהביא, ועניני המים והימים דסביבות ארץ ישראל: אל הגלילה הקדמונה זה ימה של סבכי כ"ה גירסת הילקוט. דשבע ימים הן סובבים לא"י. ודריש "הגלילה הקדמונה" — הוא ימה של סבכי, שהוא קרוב לגליל: ים הגדול. הוא הים שעוברין בו לא"י מהמדינות: בראשונה. בדור אנוש יצא עד מדינה ששמה קלבריאה, ובדור הפלגה עד מדינת ברבריאה: עד פה תבוא עד עכו תבוא. לפי שהוא הגבול של א"י, וכן יפו: ניחא ימא רבא וימא דמילחא. שהיה צריך לבוא המים לשם כדי למתקן, שמימן מלוחים וסרוחין. אבל ימה של טבריא וימה דסבכי למה צריך למים הסם: להרבות דגתן. שעל ידי המים ירבו הדגים. והכי דריש לה בקרא: למינה תהיה דגתם — כדגת ים הגדול רבה מאוד. ו"למינה" יתירה הוא, אלא דלמיני מינים יתרבו דגתם: ששמו ולא ירפאו. שם למלח ניתנו, שלא יבואו שמה מים הקדושים הנ"ל: לחדשיו יבכר. לב' חדשים. ולתבואה חצי מפירות, כמו בעוה"ז: לט"ו יום. ואילן כפל מהתבואה: בראשון. ר"ח ניסן ירדו הגשמים. ושמחו בה' היינו בהבאת העומר, והן ט"ו יום: לחדשיו. בכל חדש וחדש דעלמא: ועלהו לתרופה. טרפיה הוא פירושא ד"תרופה". שהוא כמו טרף, לשון מזון, כמו "הטריפני לחם חוקי". ודרש "לתרופה" — לטרפיה. ואחר כך מפרש היאך יהיה המזון וקאמר מייצץ עלה — שימוץ העלה: ותרף מזוניה. הוא לשון מזון, לפרושי מלת "תרופה" קאתי: פה של מעלה. פי' הערוך: לתאות המאכל, ושל מטן — לשלשל. ואם כן פלוגתא דר"ח וריב"ל פירושא אחרינא הוא: את מוצא כו'. הואיל והזכיר י"ג פרצות שפרצו מלכי יון, מביא לדרשא דחורבן. ולפי דמתני' כאבא יוסא די"ג השתחויות כנגד י"ג שערים שבמקדש מייתי לה תחלה אגדתא דאמרי במקדש. ולרבנן דכנגד י"ג פרצות, מפרש באחרונה מילי דחורבן: בשעה שעלה נ"נ. ליקח את יהויכין שהמליכוהו במקום יהויקים אביו. ויעצוהו שריו לסלקו: זרקן ועוד לא ירדו. להראות שמן השמים מסכימים על זה: ונטלתן מידו. כמו שאין חפץ בשימושו: כיון שראו

מסורת הש"ס

א) מדות פ"ב מ"ו: ב) שם: ג) שם מ"ג: ד) עי' יומא עז ב: ה) עי' תוספתא סוכה פ"ג: ו) עי' ב"ב עד ב: ז) ב"ר פ' כג: ח) ירוש' תענית פ"א הל"ב: ט) עיין תוספתא שם פ"א: י) עי' תענית הל"א: כ) סנהדרין קא א ע"ש מנחות לח א: ל) ויקרא רבה פי"ט: מ) עי' תענית כט א:

עין משפט נר מצוה

יא א מיי' פרק ה מבית הבחירה הלכה ד:

יב ב מיי' פרק ו מפרה הלכה יג:

יג ג מיי' פרק ט ממקואות הלט"ז:

נוסחת הבבלי

(א) וחזרו וגדרום וחזרו כו': (ב) השתחואות תני כו': (ג) א"ר הונא כו' מאי מי שחו אר"י בר ביבין מיא כו' ר"ש בר נחמני בשם ר' נתן מבית דוד ויושבי כו' רמ"א כו' זה ימא סיבוכא כו': (ד) ירפאו אלא מקו' היה ושמו לא כו' לחדש ואילן כו' שנאמר לחדשיו כו' יבכר אר"י בכל כו': (ה) שהמלכתי תנו אותו לי ואני אלך לי מכאן אתון ואמרין ליה ליהויכין כו' וח"א יצתה כמין פיסת יד כו' כיון (ששמעו) חורי יהודה כן אף הן עלו כו':

הגהות הגר"א

[א] ה"ג ממזבח הזהב למפתן הבית כחוט של שתי ממפתן הבית לעזרה כחוט של ערב מיכן ואילך כו' כצ"ל. דהכי כתיב בקרא והנה מים יוצאים מתחת מפתן הבית ולשם באו מן המזבח כמ"ש שם ומפתן הבית קדי' לעזרה: [ב] צ"ל שנא' ופרש ידיו כו': [ג] צ"ל מאי מי שחו מיא דמתמללין בעלמא כצ"ל: [ד] צ"ל ימא של סיבוכה:

ציון ירושלים

מכאן ואילך מי קטפריסות הן. עיין מהר"א פולדא שמיישב הדברים בין לפירוש ר"ת ובין לפירוש ר"י ובס' נדפס מחדש על הלכות מקוואות מהגאון מוה' מענדיל ס"ב ס"ק ה לא ראה זאת:

גליון הש"ס

[א] עי' ק"ע שכתב א"נ לנדה היינו זבה ועי' בתוס' שבת דף סה ע"ב ד"ה שמא דאין חילוק בין נדה לזבה וכו' קי"ל ועי' ברמב"ם פ"א ממקוואות הל"ט:

הלכה ג מתני' על של שיש מניחין את האברים. אחר הנתוח מסדרין אותן על השלחן עד שיעלום הכהנים. ובגמרא מפרש למה לא עשאו של כסף או של זהב: ועל של כסף. כלי שרת שמוליאין בכל בוקר שלשה ותשעים כלי שרת, כדתנן בתמיד: נותנין לחם הפנים בבניסתו. אחר שנאפה, עד שיסדרוהו על השלחן: ועל של זהב ביציאתו. והיה מונח שם עד זמן סילוק: שמעלין בקדש ולא מורידין. דכיון שסלקוהו מעל השלחן של זהב אין מורידין אותו להניחו בשל כסף: גמ' תני: על של כסף. אותן של אולם, אחד היה של כסף, ואחד של זהב. על של כסף היו נותנין בכניסתו, דאין עניות במקום עשירות: לית כאן של כסף. לא היה באולם של כסף. אלא כדתנן במתני' דשל כסף מרתיח ומתחמם הלחם, ויש לחוש שיתעפש: ופריך: לא כן תני זה אחד מן הנסים וכו', שהיה נשמר חום הלחם עד שעת סילוקו בשבת הבא, א"כ לא היה מתעפש אפי' היו מניחין אותו על שלחן של כסף: אין מזכירין מעשה נסים. כלומר, אין סומכין על הנס, ועושין הכל שלא יתעפש בדרך הטבע: לא היה שם לחם לסדר בשבת, ובתוך ימי השבוע נזדמן להם, מהו להניחם מלסדר עד שבת הבאה? או דלמא: אע"ג שהוא פסול, דכל שלא עברה עליו שבעה ימים על השלחן — פסול הוא, מ"מ לקיים מצות "לחם הפנים לפני תמיד" אין להניחו בלא לחם. א"נ: לא היה שם לחם לערוך ביום השבת, מהו להניח הלחם הראשון על השלחן? שהרי לא יתקלקל גם בשבת הבאה. מיהו, פסול הוא משום לינה: "לפני תמיד". שיהו תמיד לפני ה' אע"פ שהן פסולין: עשרה שולחנות עשה שלמה. דכתיב "ויעש שולחנות עשרה" וגו': אין תימר חמשה בדרום וכו'. ו"מימין" — היינו מימין הפתח, ו"משמאל" — היינו משמאלו של פתח. שהפתח היתה באמצע ההיכל בכותל מזרחי. א"נ: "מימין" — היינו דרום שנקרא "ימין", ומדרום נקרא "ימין" — לפון נקרא "שמאל": אלא. של משה באמצע, וה' מימינו וחמשה משמאלו, וכולן בצפון ההיכל: את השלחן. לשון יחיד: על כלם היה מסדר. פעמים בזה ופעמים בזה: מזרח ומערב היו נתונין. השולחנות, ראשו אחד למזרח ואחד למערב. דהיינו ארכו לאורך הבית: כולהון ראוין לשירות. ואיכא למימר על כולם היה מסדר: נמצא שלחן בדרום. וה"פ: שלחן ארכו ב' אמו' (ומחצה), הרי הוא (שלשים) עשרים אמה לעשרה שלחנו', וההיכל כולו אינו אלא עשרים, אם כן חמשה שלחנות

תורה אור

חוֹרֵי יְהוּדָה כֵּן — עָלוּ לְרֹאשׁ גַּגּוֹתֵיהֶן וְנָפְלוּ וּמֵתוּ. הָדָא הוּא דִכְתִיב "מַשָּׂא גֵּיא חִזָּיוֹן מַה לָּךְ אֵפוֹא כִּי עָלִית כּוּלָּךְ לַגַּגּוֹת תְּשֻׁאוֹת מְלֵאָה עִיר הוֹמִיָּה" וְגוֹ'.§ ישעיה כב

הלכה ג מתני' א) י"ג שׁוּלְחָנוֹת הָיוּ בַּמִּקְדָּשׁ. אח' שֶׁל שַׁיִשׁ בְּבֵית הַמִּטְבָּחַיִם, שֶׁעֲלֵיהֶם מְדִיחִין אֶת הַקְּרָבַיִם. בוב' בְּמַעֲרַב הַכֶּבֶשׁ, אֶחָד שֶׁל שַׁיִשׁ וְאֶחָד שֶׁל כֶּסֶף. עַל שֶׁל שַׁיִשׁ נוֹתְנִין אֶת הָאֵבָרִים, וְעַל שֶׁל כֶּסֶף כְּלֵי שָׁרֵת. גוב' בָּאוּלָם (מִבַּחוּץ) מִבִּפְנִים עַל פֶּתַח הַבַּיִת, א' שֶׁל שַׁיִשׁ וא' שֶׁל זָהָב. עַל שֶׁל שַׁיִשׁ נוֹתְנִין לֶחֶם הַפָּנִים בִּכְנִיסָתוֹ, דוְעַל שֶׁל זָהָב בִּיצִיאָתוֹ, שֶׁמַּעֲלִין בַּקּוֹדֶשׁ וְלֹא מוֹרִידִין. אֶחָד שֶׁל זָהָב מִבִּפְנִים שֶׁעָלָיו לֶחֶם הַפָּנִים תָּמִיד.§

גמ' תָּנֵי: עַל שֶׁל (א) כֶּסֶף (ר' אַחַי ור' מְיָישָׁא וּמָטוּ בְּשֵׁם רַב שְׁמוּאֵל בַּר רַב יִצְחָק) ר' יוֹסֵי בְּשֵׁם ר' שְׁמוּאֵל בַּר רַב יִצְחָק ר' חֲנַנְיָה מָטֵי בָהּ בְּשֵׁם ר' יוֹחָנָן: [א] לֵית ב) כָּאן שֶׁל כֶּסֶף מִפְּנֵי שֶׁהוּא [א] מַרְתִּיחַ. לֹא כֵן תָּנֵי: זֶה ג) אֶחָד מִן הַנִּסִּים שֶׁנַּעֲשׂוּ בְּבֵית הַמִּקְדָּשׁ, שֶׁכְּשֵׁם שֶׁהָיוּ מַנִּיחִין אוֹתוֹ חוֹם כָּךְ הָיוּ מוֹצִיאִין אוֹתוֹ חוֹם, שֶׁנֶּאֱמַר "לָשׂוּם לֶחֶם חֹם בְּיוֹם הִלָּקְחוֹ". שמואל א כא רַבִּי יְהוֹשֻׁעַ בֶּן לֵוִי אָמַר: אֵין ד) מַזְכִּירִין מַעֲשֵׂה נִסִּים. בְּעוֹן קוֹמֵי רַבִּי (לֵוִי) אִילָא: לֹא הָיָה שָׁם לֶחֶם הַמַהוּ לְהָנִיחוֹ לְשַׁבָּת הַבָּאָה? אֲמַר לוֹן: כְּתִיב "וְנָתַתָּ עַל הַשּׁוּלְחָן לֶחֶם פָּנִים לְפָנַי תָּמִיד" — לֶחֶם פָּנִים [ב] אֲפִילוּ פָּסוּל. שמות כה עֲשָׂרָה ה) שֻׁלְחָנוֹת עָשָׂה שְׁלֹמֹה, דִּכְתִיב "וַיַּעַשׂ שׁוּלְחָנוֹת עֲשָׂרָה וַיַּנַּח בַּהֵיכָל חֲמִשָּׁה מִיָּמִין וה' מִשְּׂמֹאל". דה"ב ד אִין תֵּימַר חֲמִשָּׁה בַּדָּרוֹם וה' בַּצָּפוֹן — וַהֲלֹא אֵין הַשֻּׁלְחָן כָּשֵׁר אֶלָּא בַּצָּפוֹן, שֶׁנֶּאֱמַר "וְאֶת הַשֻּׁלְחָן תִּתֵּן עַל צֶלַע צָפוֹן", שמות כו מַה ת"ל "חֲמִשָּׁה מִיָּמִין וַחֲמִשָּׁה מִשְּׂמֹאל" אֶלָּא, חֲמִשָּׁה מִימִין שֻׁלְחָנוֹ שֶׁל מֹשֶׁה וַחֲמִשָּׁה מִשְּׂמֹאלוֹ. אעפ"כ ו) לֹא הָיָה מְסַדֵּר אֶלָּא בְּשֶׁל מֹשֶׁה בִּלְבָד, שֶׁנֶּאֱמַר "אֶת הַשֻּׁלְחָן אֲשֶׁר עָלָיו לֶחֶם הַפָּנִים", מ"א ז (ב) רַבִּי יוֹסֵי בֵּי רַבִּי יְהוּדָה אוֹמֵר: עַל כּוּלָּן הָיָה מְסַדֵּר, שֶׁנֶּאֱמַר "אֶת הַשּׁוּלְחָנוֹת וַעֲלֵיהֶם לֶחֶם הַפָּנִים". דה"ב ד § תָּנֵי: ז) [ב] מִזְרָח וּמַעֲרָב הָיוּ נְתוּנִין דִּבְרֵי רַבִּי, ר"א בֵּי רַבִּי שִׁמְעוֹן אוֹמֵר: צָפוֹן וְדָרוֹם הָיוּ נְתוּנִין. מ"ד מִזְרָח וּמַעֲרָב — נִיחָא, [ג] כּוּלְּהֶן רְאוּיִן לְשֵׁירוּת. מ"ד צָפוֹן וְדָרוֹם — נִמְצָא שֻׁלְחָן בַּדָּרוֹם וּמְנוֹרָה

ריבב"ן

כדאי' ביומא פ"ג (דף לו.) נקנור שם אדם ומזכירין אותו לשבח. פשפשין שערים קטנים שלא היו גבוהין ורחבין כשאר שערי הבית: לא היה להם שם. מה היה משמש: מתני' י"ג שולחנות. אינו מונה י' שוחנות שעשה שלמה כדכתיב במשכן דשלמה במלכים וסדר הנתתן מביא בפ' שתי הלחם במנחות אלא בבית שני עסקינן שלא היו שם אותן שלחנות: אחד של שיש. שמניחין שם האברים: ירושלמי ר' יוסי בשם ר' שמואל בר יצחק בשם ר' יוחנן לית כאן של כסף מפני שהוא מרתיח יתחממו האברים ויסריחו ולפי שבקרבנות יחיד כהן א' יכול להוליך כל האברים ומניחן שם כדי לנוח והא דתנן בפ"ב דיומא תמיד קרב בא' עשר וכו' ומונה שם דכך הולכת אברין למזבח הא אמרינן התם (דכ"ו:) בד"א בקרבנות לבור אבל בקרבנו' יחיד כל שרולה להקריב מקריב אפילו אחד: על של שיש נותנין לחם הפנים בבניסתו. כדי לנוח: ועל של זהב ביציאתו. עד שיוקטרו בזיכי לבונה הבאין עם הלחם כך פירש רבינו שלמה בפ' שתי הלחם הכא תנן אחד של שיש ובפ' שתי הלחם (דל"ט.) תניא ר' יוסי בר יהודה אומר שנים שהיו באולם אחד של כסף ואחד של זהב ופירש רבינו שלמה אותו של כסף על שהוא לבן כשיש נקרא של שיש ולי נראה דתנאי היא דההיא ר' יוסי היא*): שמעלין בקודש. מנלן בפרק שתי הלחם אמר רב אחא בר יעקב אמר קרא את מחתות החטאים האלה בנפשותם ועשו אותם רקועי פחים לפוי למזבח בתחלה תשמישי מזבח ולבסוף גופו של מזבח: ולא מורידין. מנלן אמר ר' אחי דאמר קרא ויקם משה את המשכן ויתן את אדניו וישם את קרשיו ויתן את בריחיו ויקם את עמודיו רישיה וסיפיה לשון הקמה ולא כתיב ירידה ועוד שלא סייעו אחר אלא הוא עשהו שהוא גדול כך פירש רבינו שלמה:

תקלין חדתין

כו'. שמן השמים הסכימו: מתני' שעליהן מדיחין את הקרבים. לשון רבינו הגאון: וכן הפשט וניתוח היה שם, אלא שלזה משמש יותר בקבע. שהיו מדיחין עליו, ומונח עד הקרבה. ועי' תוי"ט פ"ה דמדות (מתני' ג'): על של שיש. אחר הניתוח מסדרין שם האיברים עד שיעלום הכהנים: ועל של כסף כלי שרת. שהיו מוליאין בכל בקר, כדתנן בתמיד: על של שיש נותנין לחם הפנים בבניסתו כו' שמעלין בקדש. לכן ביליאתו של זהב, ותחלה על של שיש: גמ' תני על של כסף. הא דתני במתני' על של שיש בכניסתו, תני בברייתא על של כסף. ומכל מקום שפיר הוי מעלין בקדש, מכסף לזהב: ה"ג: לית כאן של שיש מפני שהוא מקרר. כלומר, דמפרש למה לא תני בברייתא של שיש כמו במתני'. והיינו לפי שהשיש מקרר כמו בסוף פרק קמא דיומא: עמוד והפג אחת על הרלפה. ולחם הפנים לריך שיהיה חם, כמ"ש "לשום לחם חום" וגו': ופריך: לא כן תני זה א' מן הנסים כו'. ואם כן, כיון שדרך גם היה חם כל השבוע, אם כן ליכא למיחש לשיתקרר: אין מזכירין מעשה נסים. דתחלת סידורו לריך שלא יתקרר, ולא לסמוך על הנס. ומתניתין דסבירא ליה על של שיש — מפרש בבבלי תמיד (לא, ב): מפני שכל כסף מרתיח, ואיכא למיחש שלא יתעפש: לא היה שם לחם מהו להניחו לשבת הבאה. בלחם כשר איירי, אי רשאי להניחו לשבת הבאה ולא מיפסל בלינה אף בנסדר כהלכתו, או דמיפסיל בלינה בנסדר כהלכתו: ה"ג: א"ק "ונתת על השלחן לחם פנים לפני תמיד". ואפילו הוא כמה ימים. וגם לכתחלה יכול להניחו על כמה ימים, דקרא ודאי איירי בנסדר כהלכתו, דכתיב "ונתת לחם" וגו' — והיינו לחם כשר, ואפילו הכי כתיב "תמיד" — להורות דרשאי להניחו לכתחלה, ולא מיפסל בלינה: עשרה שולחנות כו'. סוגיא זו במנחות (צ,ח ב - צט, א), ומסקנא דהכא כמ"ד דהתם מיתוקמא: וא"ת ה' בדרום כו'. והאי "מימין" — מימין דפתח, וכן משמאל דפתח קאמר. ובבבלי שם קאמר בהדיא: וא"ת מימין דפתח כו': והלא אין שלחן כו'. הפתח היה באמצע ההיכל בכותל מזרחי, ונמצאו ה' שלחנות שבשמאל דרך כניסה כולם בדרום: אלא כו' ה' מימין שלחנו של משה כו'. וכולן בצפון ההיכל. וכדמפרש לקמן: רבי יוסי בר"י אומר על כולן כו'. ובבבלי נקט לה בדר"א בן שמוע. ורבי יוסי בר"י ס"ל דאין מסדר אלא על של משה כו', ע"ש: ה"ג: מזרח ומערב כו' דברי רבי. וכן הוא בכולא תלמודא פלוגתייהו: ה"ג: מ"ד מזרח ומערב ניחא. דסוגיא זו ס"ל למסקנא כסלקא דעתא דבבלי שם, שהיו מסודרים ראשו של זה בלד ראשו של זה. ואם כן, למאן דאמר מזרח ומערב מונחים — שפיר היו עומדים בלד לפון עשרה שלחנות ראשו של זה בלד ראשו של זה. אע"ג דאי אפשר שישבו י' שלחנות של עשרים אמה בעשרים אמה מלומלמות שלא יצאו קצת חוץ לעשרים אמה הפנימיות — איכא למימר לא דק כולי האי הא דנקט בסוגיין וכולן היו נתונין משליש הבית ולפנים: ה"ג: מאן דאמר צפון ודרום נמצא שלחן בדרום. שאורך העשרה שולחנות עשרים, וההיכל מלפונו לדרומו לא היה אלא עשרים מלומלמות, ואם כן ה' שלחנות ע"כ יהיו בדרום. ובקרא קפיד שיהיו השולחנות דוקא בלפון, ונשאר בקושיא. ולא חש להאריך בקושיות האחרות שבבבלי וליישבם אליביה דמ"ד לפון ודרום מונחים, משום דלית הלכתא כוותיה דראב"ש, דהלכה כרבי מחבירו, וגם

משנת אליהו

ה"ג לית כאן של שיש מפני שהוא מקרר כו'. ובבבלי בתמיד (ל"א ב') הגי' במתני' דידן שהביא שם גבי ב' דבאולם א' של כסף ואחד של זהב ופריך שם מכדי אין עניות כו' אמרי עבדי דשיש ליעבדו דכסף ליעבדו דזהב ומשני בשם ר"ש בר"י מפני שמרתיח ועיין תוס' במנחות (ל"ט ב') ד"ה אחד של כסף שהביאו סוגיא דירושלמי כגי' הספרים ולית כאן של כסף לדידהו אמתני' קאי ומפני שמרתיח ע"ש ומשמע שם דדעתם דגרסינן של כסף כמו שכתבו ומיהא בכל הספרים כו' של כסף כו' אך דבשם רש"י כתבו דגרס של שיש כמש"ש במתני' ד"ה על פתח כו' דעכשיו מניחו על של שיש כו' ובברייתא שם במנחות דתני של כסף היא ברייתא דירושלמי דתני של כסף. ובתמיד שם אכולהו פריך ומשני מפני שמרתיח ולשיטתו אזיל בירושלמי. ומה שכתב שם ברש"י ד"ה שנים דהא דקרי כסף בברייתא משום דשיש לבן ככסף ליתא ולאו דברי רש"י הוא כמו שהביאו התוס' בשמו דפלוגתא דתנאי הוא ובמתניתין דמנחות פירש רש"י פשטא דמתני' [illegible]

א) תמיד לא מנחות לט ב: ב) עי' תמיד לא ב: ג) יומא כא א: ד) עי' פסחים סד ב: ה) מנחות לח ב: ו) שם לט א: ז) שם לח ב:

עין משפט נר מצוה

יד א מיי' פ"ה מבית הבחירה הלי"ד:
טו ב מיי' שם פ"ג הלכה טו:
טז ג מיי' שם פ"ג הלכה טז:
יז ד מיי' שם הלכה יב:
יח ה מיי' פרק ה מתמידין הלי"ג:

נוסחת הבבלי

(א) כסף והיו ר"א כו' לית כו': (ב) ר"י בר' יהודה כו' ד"ר (אלעזר) ר"א בר"ש כו' ודרום מ"ד כו':

הגהות הגר"א

[א] ה"ג לית כאן של שיש מפני שהוא מקרר וה"פ שהוא מפרש למה לא תני בברייתא של שיש כמו במתני' והיינו לפי שהשיש מקרר כמו בספ"ק דיומא עמוד והפג אחת על הרלפה ולחם הפנים לריך שיהיה חם כמ"ש לשו' לחם חום וגו'. ועי' בס' ת"ח שמאריך בפלפולו: [ב] ה"ג ואפי' הוא כמה ימים וז"ל של הרב בעל תקלין חדתין ול"ל לפי גי' רבינו דהכא איירי בלחם הפנים דנסדר כהלכתו בשבת וקמבעיא לן שאם אין לחם הפנים לשבת הבאה אי רשאי להניחה משבת זה לשבת הבאה אי אמרינן משום שנסדר כהלכתו מפסיל בלינה או לא מפסיל ופשיט ליה ר' לוי. דבנסדר כהלכתו רשאי להניחו לכתחלה דהא קרא דונתת על השלחן ודאי בנסדר כהלכתו משתעי וכתיב תמיד ואפילו כמה ימים ומש"ה מחק רבינו תיבת פסול דקרא לא איירי אלא בכשרי וע' בספר תקלין חדתין ובמשנת אליהו כי מאריך בפלפולו וכמה הלכתא גברוותא איכא למשמע מהאי גי': [ג] צ"ל כולהן לצפון וצ"ג ראוים לשירות:

גליון הש"ס

[א] עי' הגהות הגר"א אבל במפרש בתמיד שם לא נראה כגירסתו וגם התוס' במנחות דף לט ע"ב ד"ה אחד היה לחם הגי' שלפנינו: [ב] עי' בתוס' מנחות דף לט ע"א ד"ה תרי שהיה לחם נגירסא לאחרת:

בדרום: ומנורה בצפון. ל"ג: משוך מן הכותל בשתי אמות כלפי צפון. שיהיו שני כהנים הנושאים ב' סדרים הולכין זה בצד זה. ותוס' גורסין "משוך ב' אמות ומחצה": באמצע הבית. היינו באמצע ההיכל, כשלא נחשב בית קדשי קדשים עמו. ההיכל ארכו ארבעים, ובית קדשי קדשים ארכו עשרים אמה, והמזבח היה עומד בתחלת עשרים אמה של היכל המערביים: משליש הבית. של צד מזרח: ולפנים. לצד מערב. והיינו כשנחשב בית קדשי קדשים עמו: הוא "מכלות הזהב". פסוק הוא בד"ה, וקמפרש מהו "מכלות זהב", וקאמר שהן כולו של זהב סגור שהיה לשלמה. שהרי עשר מנורות עשה, ולכל אחת היה צריך אלף ככר, כדמסיק: לקיים מה שנאמר במנורת משה "ככר זהב טהור וגו'": ה"ג: מעשה במנורת המקדש שהיתה יתירה על מנורה שעשה משה במדבר דינר זהב, והכניסוהו לכור פ' פעמים, ולא חסר האש ממשקלה: ופריך: ויאות. בתמיה: וכי כך הוא? והלא עינינו רואות כשנותנין זהב בכור באש הוא נחסר! ומשני: עד דלא יקום וכו'. כשעדיין לא קם הזהב על בירורותיה, שלא נצרף כל צרכו — נחסר ממנו. אבל בשכבר נצרף כל צרכו — לא נחסר ממנו כלום, אפי' מכניסין אותה לאש כמה פעמים:

תורה אור

וּמְנוֹרָה בַּצָּפוֹן. וְהָא תָּנֵי: הַשֻּׁלְחָן א) הָיָה נָתוּן מֵחֲצִי הַבַּיִת וְלִפְנִים. מָשׁוּךְ (א) מִן הַכּוֹתֶל ב' אַמּוֹת וּמֶחֱצָה כְּלַפֵּי הַצָּפוֹן, וּמְנוֹרָה כְּנֶגְדוֹ בַּדָּרוֹם. מִזְבַּח הַזָּהָב הָיָה נָתוּן [א] בְּאֶמְצַע הַבַּיִת, חוֹלֵק אֶת הַבַּיִת מֵחֶצְיוֹ וְלִפְנִים, [א] מָשׁוּךְ אִקִימְעָא כְּלַפֵּי (צָפוֹן) חוּץ, וְכוּלְּהֶן הָיָה ב) נָתוּן מִשְּׁלִישׁ הַבַּיִת וְלִפְנִים עֶשֶׂר מְנוֹרוֹת עָשָׂה

דה"ב ד שְׁלֹמֹה, שֶׁנֶּאֱמַר "וַיַּעַשׂ אֶת מְנֹרוֹת הַזָּהָב עֶשֶׂר כְּמִשְׁפָּטָם וַיִּתֵּן בַּהֵיכָל ה' מִיָּמִין וה' מִשְּׂמֹאל". אִין תֵּימַר חָמֵשׁ בַּצָּפוֹן וְחָמֵשׁ בַּדָּרוֹם — וַהֲלֹא אֵין הַמְּנוֹרָה

שמות כו כְּשֵׁירָה אֶלָּא בַּדָּרוֹם, שֶׁנֶּאֱמַר "וְאֶת הַמְּנֹרָה נֹכַח הַשֻּׁלְחָן עַל צֶלַע הַמִּשְׁכָּן תֵּימָנָה". מַה ת"ל חָמֵשׁ מִיָּמִין וְחָמֵשׁ מִשְּׂמֹאל, אֶלָּא חָמֵשׁ מִימִין מְנוֹרָתוֹ שֶׁל מֹשֶׁה וְחָמֵשׁ מִשְּׂמֹאלָהּ. אעפ"כ ג) לֹא הָיָה מַבְעִיר אֶלָּא שֶׁל

דה"ב יג מֹשֶׁה בִּלְבָד, שֶׁנֶּאֱמַר "וּמְנוֹרַת הַזָּהָב וְנֵרֹתֶיהָ לְבָעֵר בָּעֶרֶב בָּעָרֶב". ר' יוֹסֵה בֵּי ר' יְהוּדָה אוֹמֵר: עַל כּוּלָּן

שם ד הָיָה מַבְעִיר, שנא' "וְאֶת הַמְּנֹרוֹת וְנֵרֹתֵיהֶם לְבַעֲרָם כַּמִּשְׁפָּט לִפְנֵי הַדְּבִיר זָהָב סָגוּר. וְהַפֶּרַח וְהַנֵּרוֹת וְהַמֶּלְקָחַיִם זָהָב הוּא מִכְלוֹת זָהָב" — הֵן ד) כִּילּוּ זְהָבוֹ שֶׁל מֹשֶׁה. תָּנֵי רַב יְהוּדָה בְּשֵׁם אַסִּי הָיָה שְׁלֹמֹה נוֹטֵל אֶלֶף כִּכְּרֵי זָהָב וּמַכְנִיסָן לַכּוּר וּמוֹצִיאָן, עַד שֶׁהוּא

שמות כה מַעֲמִידָן עַל א' לְקַיֵּים מַה שֶּׁנֶּאֱמַר "כִּכַּר זָהָב טָהוֹר עָשָׂה אוֹתָהּ" וְגו'. תַּנְיָא: ה) אָמַר רַבִּי יוֹסֵי בֵּי רַבִּי יְהוּדָה: מַעֲשֶׂה בִּמְנוֹרַת זָהָב שֶׁעָשָׂה מֹשֶׁה בַּמִּדְבָּר וְהָיְתָה יְתֵירָה דִּינַר זָהָב, וְהִכְנִיסוּהָ לַכּוּר שְׁמוֹנִים פַּעַם [ב] וְלֹא חָסְרָה כְּלוּם. וְיָאוּת, עַד דְּלָא יָקוּם עַל בְּרָרֵיהּ — הֲוָה חָסַר סַגִּין, מִן דּוּ קַיֵּים עַל בְּרָרֵיהּ — לָא חָסַר כְּלוּם.§

הלכה ד מתני'

בשְׁלֹשָׁה ו) עָשָׂר שׁוֹפָרוֹת הָיוּ בַּמִּקְדָּשׁ, וְכָתוּב עֲלֵיהֶן: תִּקְלִין חֲדַתִּין, וְתִקְלִין עַתִּיקִין, קִנִּין, וְגוֹזְלֵי עוֹלָה, עֵצִים, לְבוֹנָה, זָהָב לְכַפּוֹרֶת, שִׁשָּׁה ז) לִנְדָבָה. תִּקְלִין חֲדַתִּין — שֶׁבְּכָל שָׁנָה וְשָׁנָה, וְעַתִּיקִין — מִי (ב) שֶׁלֹּא הֵבִיא אֶשְׁתַּקַּד שׁוֹקֵל לְשָׁנָה הַבָּאָה. קִנִּין הֵן תּוֹרִין, וְגוֹזְלֵי עוֹלָה הֵן בְּנֵי יוֹנָה, כּוּלָּן עוֹלוֹת, דִּבְרֵי ר' יְהוּדָה. וחכ"א קִנִּין — אֶחָד חַטָּאת וא' עוֹלָה, גּוֹזְלֵי עוֹלָה — כּוּלָּן עוֹלוֹת. הָאוֹמֵר ח) ג"הֲרֵי עָלַי עֵצִים" — לֹא יִפְחוֹת מִשְּׁנֵי גְּזִירִין, לְבוֹנָה — לֹא יִפְחוֹת מִקּוֹמֶץ, רזָהָב — לֹא יִפְחוֹת מִדִּינַר זָהָב. שִׁשָּׁה לִנְדָבָה. נְדָבָה מֶה הָיוּ עוֹשִׂין בָּהּ? הלוֹקְחִים בָּהּ עוֹלוֹת, הַבָּשָׂר לַשֵּׁם וְעוֹרוֹת לַכֹּהֲנִים. זֶה ט) מִדְרָשׁ דָּרַשׁ יְהוֹיָדָע כֹּהֵן גָּדוֹל:

ויקרא ה "אָשָׁם הוּא אָשׁוֹם אָשַׁם לַה'" זֶה הַכְּלָל: כָּל שֶׁהוּא בָּא מִשּׁוּם חַטָּאת וּמִשּׁוּם אַשְׁמָה — יִלָּקַח בָּהֶן עוֹלוֹת, הַבָּשָׂר לַשֵּׁם וְהָעוֹרוֹת לַכֹּהֲנִים. נִמְצְאוּ שְׁנֵי כְתוּבִין

מ"ב יב קַיָּימִין אָשָׁם לַה' וְאָשָׁם לַכֹּהֵן. וְאוֹמֵר "כֶּסֶף אָשָׁם וְכֶסֶף חַטָּאוֹת לֹא יוּבָא בֵּית ה' לַכֹּהֲנִים יִהְיוּ".§ גמ' תַּנְיָא, י) אָמַר ר' יְהוּדָה: לֹא הָיָה שׁוֹפָר שֶׁל קִינִּין בִּירוּשָׁלַיִם מִפְּנֵי הַתַּעֲרוֹבוֹת שֶׁמָּא תָּמוּת אַחַת,* וְנִמְצְאוּ דְּמֵי חַטָּאוֹת מֵיתוֹת מְעוֹרָבוֹת בָּהֶן. וְהָתַנְיָא: כ) הָאִשָּׁה שֶׁאָמְרָה "הֲרֵי עָלַי קֵן" — (ג) מְבִיאָה דְּמֵי קֵן וְנוֹתַנְתּוֹ בַּשּׁוֹפָר, וְאוֹכֶלֶת

ריבב"ן

מתני' י"ג שופרות היו במקדש. וכולן פיהן צר כדי שלא יוכל אדם להכניס ידו בפניס ולגנוב מן הכסף וכולהו מפרש למאי אצטריכו. עצים ולבונה גרסי' וברוב ספרים כתוב ללבונה וטעות הוא דהא כל אחד ואחד יש לו שופר בפני עצמו ולבונה לבד ועצים לבד כדתני וזהב. והב לכפורת לשון כפורי זהב פי' מזרקים ולמה נקרא שמם כפורי ע"ש שמקנחין ידיהם מן הדם כדאמרי' בגיטין [דף נו] בענין*) נבוזראדן בעי לכפורי ידיה בההוא גברא. ששה לנדבה לקיץ המזבח: מתני' קינין. הן תורין גוזלי עולה הן בני יונה אבל שופר לקיני חובה לא בעי ר' יהודה והטעם כדאיתא בפ' הוציאו לו (דף נה) דשמא ימות א' מהן נמצאו כל המעות שבשופר הולכות ליס המלח כי היכי דאמרינן בחטאת שמתו בעליה דאזלא למיתה הכי נמי מעות שהופרשו לחטאת ומתו בעליהן הולכות ליס המלח ופריך התם ונברור ד' זוזי ונשדי במיא והכא ליסתרו ר' יהודה לטעמיה דלית ליה ברירה כדאמר בעירובין [דף לז] מדתני איו: וחכ"א קינין הן קיני חובה אחד לעולה ואחד לחטאת ורבנן לא חיישי למיתה. גוזלי עולה בין תורין בין בני יונה כולן עולות נדבה: שני גזירין. מפורש ביומא פ"ב (דף כו) תניא ר"ש בן יוחאי אומר מנין לתמיד של בין הערבים שטעון שני גזרי עצים בשני כהנים שנאמר וערכו עצים על האש וערכו שנים אם אינו ענין לתמיד של שחר שהרי כבר נאמר ובער עליה הכהן עצים בבקר תנהו ענין לתמיד של בין הערבים ואמרינן בפרק בתרא דמנחות (דף קו) ת"ר קרבן מלמד שמתנדב עצים וכמה שני גזירין וכן הוא אומר והגורלות הפלנו על קרבן העצים ותניא בתוספתא בפרק [ג' דמכילתין] האומר הרי עלי עצים מביא דמי שני גזרין ונותן לשופר והכהנים מקבלין אותן ולוקחין בהן עצים ומקריבין אותן ע"ג המזבח ונאותין בהן ואין מועלין ואם הקריבן בחוץ פטור אבל אם אומר שני גזירין של עצים אלו לגבי מזבח הכהנים מקבלין אותן ממנו ומקריבין אותן ע"ג המזבח ואין נאותין בהן ומועלין בהן ואם הקריבן בחוץ חייב דברי ר' וחכ"א אם הקריבן בחוץ פטור ואלו ואלו הולכין ללשכת העצים: קומץ לבונה. כדתנן בפרק בתרא דמנחות ה' קמלין הן: האומר הרי עלי לבונה לא יפחות מקומץ. המתנדב מנחה יביא עמה קומץ לבונה. המעלה את הקומץ בחוץ חייב שני מיני לבונה טעונין שני קומצין: זהב לא יפחות מדינר זהב. ופריך בפרק בתרא למנחות ודלמא נסכא א"ר אלעזר דאמר מטבע ודלמא פריטי דדהבא לא עבדי אינשי. תניא בתוספתא בפ' בתרא [דמכילתין] האומר הרי עלי לבונה מביא דמי מלא קומץ לבונה ונותן לשופר והכהנים מקבלין אותו ולוקחין מהן לבונה ומקריבין אותו ע"ג המזבח. האומר הרי עלי זהב מביא דמי דינר זהב ונותן לשופר והכהנים מקבלין אותו ולוקחין בהן זהב ועושין אותן רקועי פחים לפוי למזבח: ששה לנדבה. מפרש בפרק בתרא דמנחות ששה כנגד מי אמר ר' חזקיה כנגד ששה בתי אבות הכהנים שיהא להם שלום זה עם זה ר' יוחנן אמר מתוך שהנדבה מרובה תקנו להם שופרות מרובין כדי שלא יתעפשו המעות זעירי אמר כנגד פר ועגל ואיל וכבש וגדי כולן הן נדבה ודמיהן יודעין פר מביא מנה עגל מביא חמשה סלעים איל מביא ב' סלעים כבש מביא סלע הכי איתא בפרק בתרא דמנחות אבל לגדי ושעיר לא מצינו דמיהן ושמא דמיהן כאיל וכבש ור' היא דאמר קטן והביא גדול לא יצא אם נדר להביא עגל והביא פר לא יצא להכי אצטריך לכל אחד ואחד שופר בפני עצמו שאם מערבן והביא פרים מכל המעות לא יצא ידי נדרו מי שנדר עגל בר פדא אמר כנגד פרים אילים וכבשים ושעירים ומותרות והמעה דהיינו קולבון פרים פר חטאת של צבור שאבדו והפריש אחרים תחתיהן ירעו עד שיסתאבו וימכרו ויפלו דמיו לאותו שופר אילים אשם גזלות ומעילות שעירים שעיר הרגלים כבשים אשם נזיר ואשם מצורע ואהכי לא מערבו עם מותר גזילות ומעילות דאלו בני שנה ואלו בני שתים ואלו באים לכפר ואלו באין להכשיר וכולן אם אבדו והפריש אחרים תחתיהן ירעו עד שיסתאבו וימכרו ויפלו דמיהן כל א' א' לשופרו. והמותרות כגון הפריש מעות לכל אלו ונותרו כגון שהוזלו הבהמות ושמואל אמר כנגד מותר חטאת ומותר אשם ומותר אשם נזיר ומותר

*) לפנינו שם איתא לשון זה גבי נירון דשדריה טיטוס לגור את ירושלים ועי' רש"י במנחות ד' ז' ע"ב ובהגהות מהרי"ב ז"ל שם.

נוסחאות ישנות

הלכה ד מתני'

"תקלין חדתין". שבו נותנין שקלי שנה זו. וכשמגיע זמן התרומה, הגזבר מוליא כל שקלים שבשופר ונותנן ללשכה, כדי שיתרמו מהם. והשני כתוב עליו "תקלין עתיקין", ומי שלא הביא שקלו בשנה זו — מביא בשנה שאח"כ, ונותנו לשופר. והגזבר נוטלם ונותנם בשירי הלשכה. והג' כתוב עליו "קינין", והן תורין גדולים. והד' — "גוזלי עולה", והן בני יונה הקטנים. וכולן עולות, אבל לקני חובה לא היה שופר, כדמפרש בגמרא: "עצים". המתנדב עלים למערכה נותן דמיהן לתוכו: "לבונה". המתנדב לבונה נותן דמיו לתוכו: "וזהב". המתנדב זהב נותנו שם או דמי שויו, והוא לכפורת. כלומר, לכלי שרת, שהמזרקות נקראים "כפורי זהב" בעזרא ובד"ה. לפי שהכהן מקנח בהן אלבעו בין הזאה להזאה, שהשיריים שבאלבעו פסולים: ששה. שופרות הנותרות הן לנדבה, ובגמרא מפרש: האומר "הרי עלי עצים" סתם: לא יפחות משני גזירין. כאותן שמסדרין על המערכה, ושיעורן מפורש בגמ': לא יפחות מן קומץ. שזהו שיעור הלבונה הבאה עם המנחה. ובגמרא מפרש מנ"ל ודוקא המתנדב סתם, אבל אם רלה להביא אפי' קורט של לבונה — מביא: זהב. המתנדב זהב סתם, לא יפחות מדינר זהב: "אשם הוא אשום אשם לה'". וקשיא רישא לסיפא, ד"אשם הוא" — משמע בהווייתו יהא, כהלכתו, שהוא נאכל לכהנים. ו"אשם לה'" — משמע שכולו לה'. ודרש יהוידע הכהן: כל שהוא מותר חטאת ואשם — ילקח באותו המותר עולות. נמלא ב' הכתובים קיימים, "אשם לה'" — הבשר, ו"אשם לכהנים" — העורות. והיכן מלינו מדרש זה ביהוידע? — "כסף אשם וכסף חטאת לא יובא בית ה' לכהנים יהיו". וא"א לומר דכסף שקדש לשם חטאת ולשם אשם יהנו בו הכהנים. אלא ה"ק: יעשו ממנו דבר שיהנו בו הכהנים, והיינו עולות, שהעורות לכהנים: גמ' לא היה שופר של קיני. חובה, כגון זב וזבה ויולדת. שיתנו לתוכו מעות, כשם שהיו שופרות לקן נדבה, כדתנן במתני': מפני התערובות. שמא תמות אחת מאותן שנתנו מעות בשופר, וה"ל מעות חטאת שמתו בעליה מעורבין עם הכשרות, והכל פסולין והולכין ליס המלח: ה"ג: והתני: האשה שיש עליה לידה או זיבה מביאה דמי קן וכו'. כ"ה ברמב"ם פ"ק מהל' מחוסרי כפרה: אבל באומרת "הרי עלי קן". שניהם עולות. והרא"פ לא הרגיש בזה: ונותנתו בשופר. שכתבו עליו "קנין", ודמי

משנת אליהו

הסוגיות ועי' תוס' שם (ל"ו א') ד"ה כל ול"ח ב' ד"ה מזרח כו' עי' רמב"ם פ"ג מהל' בית הבחירה הלכה י"ב:

מהן **ה"ג** ומזבח הזהב באמצע משוך כלפי חוץ. ולא גרס רבינו כלפי חוץ קימעה שכן הוא בתוספתא פ"ב דיומא והכי דייקא הסוגיא דקאמר דכולן היו נתונין משליש הבית ולפנים א"כ לא היה משוך לחוץ וכ"ה לשון הרמב"ם פ"ג מהל' ב"ה הלכה י"ז ומשוך לחוץ ר"ל כלפי חוץ וכ"מ בתוספתא שם וכ"מ ברש"י ביומא שם שלא הזכיר קימעה וגם לחוץ משמע חוץ דשלחן דמשה דנקט שלחן ומנורה ומאלו היה יכול לימשך יותר אבל לא הי' משוך משאר השלחנות וגי' הספרים חולק את הבית כו' שיבוש הוא: **ולא** חסר כלום. מרן הגאון כתב בגליון ובגמ' דידן הגי' והעמידו על ככר והיינו דפריך שם ומי חסר כולי האי ככר בכל פעם והא מעובדא דמנורת בית המקדש משמע דלא חסר כולי האי אבל כ"ש מיהא חסר והיינו ההוא דינר והכא בסוגין דקאמר יאות עד דלא קאים כו' אבל כשנתברר הרבה לא חסרה כלום ונשאר גם הדינר ולכן לא הגיה רבינו בסוגין כגי' הבבלי דמשמע דמילק

תקלין חדתין

וגם שם מתניתין מנחות (לו, א) כוותיה דרבי, ולאו אורחא דירושלמי להאריך בפלפולא שלא איתא דהלכתא: ה"ג: תני השלחן היה נתון מחצי הבית ולפנים משוך מן הכותל ב' אמות ומחצה. שההיכל היה ארכו ס' אמה, כדכתיב "והבית אשר בנה שלמה" וגו', ומאותן ס' היה עשרים בדביר, כדכתיב "ולפני הדביר עשרים אמה" וגו'. וההיכל ארבעים, כדכתיב "ארבעים באמה היה הבית הוא ההיכל לפניס". והשולחנות היו נתונין בעשרים אמה של היכל של לד הדביר והוא מחציו ולפנים, חציו דהיכל שהוא מ': משוך כו'. מן הכותל לפוני: ב' אמות ומחצה. כדי שיהיו הכהנים הנושאים ב' סדרים יכולין להלך זה בצד זה, כדאמרי' במתני' דמנחות שהיו מסדרין בב"א ולהילוך ב' ב"א בעינן ב' אמות ומחצה, כדמצינו גבי בדי ארון, במנחות שם: ומנורה כנגדו בדרום. כדכתיב "את המנורה נכח השלחן". וגם כן היתה משוכה מן הכותל דרומית ב"א ומחצה. כ"ה ביומא שם: ומזבח הזהב באמצע משוך כלפי חוץ. לצד חוץ. וברייתא זו למ"ד מזרח ומערב מונחים, וכדכתבו התוס' במנחות שם: וכולן היו נתונין משליש הבית ולפנים. כשנחשב כ' דדביר גם כן — או הוו שלחנות כולן משליש הבית, וכדמוקי בבבלי שם: כילו זהבו של שלמה. במנחות (כט, א) פריך התם: והכתיב "וכל כלי" כו' אין כסף נחשב בימי שלמה למאומה"! ומשני: זהב סגור קאמרינן: מכניסן לכור כו' על א'. לכל מנורה עשה כן. וכ"ה במנחות שם. והכי דייקא קרא זהב טהור אותה: ה"ג: במנורת מקדש. וכ"ה במנחות שם. וגי' הספרים שיבוש ניכר: ולא חסרה כלום. וקאמר שלא תקשי ממה שאמרו שהיה חסר בכל פעם הרבה, דזהו עד דלא קאים על בירורו. אבל כשקאים על בירורו — לא חסר כלום: מתני' חדתין. שקלי שנה זו היו מטילין לשם. וכשמגיע זמן התרומה הגזבר מוליא כל השקלים שבשופר ונותנן ללשכה, כדי שיתרמו מהם: עתיקין. של אשתקד, ומהן ניתנין לשירי לשכה: תורים. גדולים: בני יונה. קטנים: קינין. כולן עולות. אבל לקיני חובה לא היה שופר. ובגמרא מפרש טעמא דר"י: עצים לא יפחות. עלים סתם ב' גזירין, כמו שהיו במערכה, וכדמפרש בגמרא: לא יפחות מקומץ. שזהו שיעור לבונה שבאה עם המנחה. ובגמרא יליף ליה מנ"ל: זה מדרש דרש כו'. לשון רבינו הגאון: שיהוידע חידש שהעורות לכהנים, דסד"א דנדבה הוא כולו לגבוה, כמו הקדש בד"ה. וז"ש: ואומר "כסף אשם וכסף חטאות". דסד"א שיובאו בית ה' ולא למזבח משום העור. אבל זה לא היה בס"ד כלל שיביא קרבן אחר חטאת ואשם, שיאכלו הכהנים מנדבה, דאף עולות מידוש הוא: גמ' תניא א"ר יהודה לא היה שופר של קינין כו'. לקיני חובות, כמו זב וזבה ויולדת, שיתנו לתוכו, כמו שהיה לקן נדבה: שמא תמות. א' מבעלי הקינין שנתנו בשופר: מתות. שמתו בעליהן. וה"ל מעות אותן שמתו בעליהן מעורבות עם הכשרות, וכולן ילכו ליס המלח: והתניא האשה כו'. הוא תוספתא פרק ג' דשקלים, והובאה בעירובין (לב, א) ושם בגמרא הגירסא: "האשה שיש עליה לידה או זיבה מביאה מעות ונותנת בשופר, וטובלת ואוכלת בקדשים לערב". וה"נ הכי פירושו: שאמרה היינו ששואלת הרי עלי חיוב קן מלידה או מזיבה, ושואלת מה תעשה, אי תביא דמיהן? וכן באיסור אכילת קדשים: מביאה דמיהן.

א) יומא לג ב: ב) מנחות לח ב: ג) שם לט א: ד) שם כט א: ה) עיין מנחות כט א וירושל' יומא פ"ד הלכה ד ומדרש חזית פ' עמודיו עשה כסף: ו) יומא נה ב תמורה כג ב: ז) מנחות קד א קז ב תמורה כג א: ח) מנחות קו ב: ט) זבחים קג א [תמורה כג ב]: י) עי' יומא נה א: כ) עי' עירובין לב א:

עין משפט נר מצוה

יט א מיי' פ"א מבית הבחירה הל"ז:

כ ב מיי' פרק ב משקלים הל"ב:

כא ג מיי' פט"ז ממעשה"ק הל"ג:

כב ד מיי' פרק ב מערכין הל"ט וכס"מ:

כג ה מיי' פרק ה מפסה"ק הל"ט:

נוסחת הבבלי

(א) מן הקרן ב' כו' היה באמצע כו' על צלע המשכן כו' לבער בערב ר"י בר"י כו' כילו זהבו של שלמה כו' ר"י בשם איסי כו' במנורת [מקדש שהיתה יתירה על מנורה שעשה משה במדבר דינר זהב] והכניסוה כו': (ב) שלא אישתקד כו': (ג) מביאה דמיהן ונותנת כו' ר' יוסי בר בִיבין א"ר ביבי ב"מ כו' א"ר אליעזר מתני' כו' באמה גרומה ר"ח אמר כמין כו':

הגהות הגר"א

[א] ה"ג ומזבח הזהב היה נתון באמצע מושך כלפי חוץ וכולן היו נתונים משליש הבית ולפנים כצ"ל והשאר שבינתים נמחק. וכ"ה בתוספ' פ"ב דיומא והכי דייקא הסוגיא שם ע"ש וכ"ה ברמב"ם פ"ג מהלכות ב"ה הלי"ז ע"ש. וכ"מ ברש"י ביומא שם שלא הזכיר קמעה וגם לחוץ משמע חוץ דשלחן דמשה דנקט שלחן ומנורה ומאלו היה יכול למשוך יותר אבל לא היה משוך משאר השלחנות וגי' הספרים חולק את הבית שבוש הוא: [ב] בגמ' דידן הגי' והעמידו על ככר ועי' בס' ת"ח טעם הגון על שלא הגיה הגאון בתוך הסוגיא כגי' הבבלי כדרכו בקדש:

גליון הש"ם

[א] היינו ממנורה של משה אבל שאר המנורו' משוכות חוץ מן המזבח ולכך אמרו ביומא דמזבח פגע ברישא דלא היה מבעיר אלא בשל משה וכזה אפשר ליישב דברי הרמב"ם פ"ה ממעשה"ק הלי"ד ופ"ד מעיוה"כ מקושית הרשב"א עי' בכ"מ ולח"מ ודו"ק:

נוסחאות ישנות | תורה אור

וְאוֹכֶלֶת בַּקֳּדָשִׁים. אוְאֵינָהּ חוֹשֶׁשֶׁת שֶׁמָּא נִתְעַצֵּל בָּהֶן. [א] וְאֵין הַכֹּהֵן חוֹשֵׁשׁ שֶׁמָּא דְּמֵי חַטָּאוֹת מֵיתוֹת מְעוֹרָבוֹת בָּהֶן. כִּי א) קָאָמְרִינַן בְּחַטָּאוֹת שֶׁמֵּתוּ בַּעֲלֵיהֶן וַדַּאי. וְאִי אָמְרִינַן [ב] נִבְרוֹר ד' זוּזֵי וְנִישְׁדֵי בְּנַהֲרָא וְאִידָךְ לִישְׁתְּרוּ — הָא אָמְרִינַן בְּעָלְמָא: ר' יְהוּדָה לֵית לֵיהּ בְּרֵירָה.§ רַבִּי ב) יוֹסֵה בֵּי ר' בּוּן (בִּיבָא) א"ר בָּא בַּר מָמָל בָּעֵי: אָמַר [א] "הֲרֵי עָלַי עֵץ" — בּמֵבִיא גֵּיזֶר אֶחָד. א"ר לְעָזָר: מַתְנִיתָא אֲמָרָה כֵּן, שֶׁזֶּה קָרְבָּן בִּפְנֵי עַצְמוֹ וְזֶה קָרְבָּן בִּפְנֵי עַצְמוֹ. כְּהָאי דְּתָנֵינַן ג) תַּמָּן: שְׁנַיִם בְּיָדָם שְׁנֵי גִּזְרֵי עֵצִים. [ג] "קָרְבָּן" ד) — לְרַבּוֹת אֶת הָעֵצִים. ריב"ל אָמַר: עוֹבְיָין ה) אַמָּה גבְּאַמָּה שׁוֹחֶקֶת, וְאָרְכָּן בְּאַמָּה גְּדוּמָה. ר' חוּנִי בְּשֵׁם ר' אַמִּי: כְּמִין טוּרְטָנֵי. א"ר שְׁמוּאֵל בַּר רַב יִצְחָק: לְפִי ו) דשֶׁלֹּא הָיָה מְקוֹם הַמַּעֲרָכָה אֶלָּא אַמָּה עַל אַמָּה, לְפִיכָךְ לֹא הָיָה בּוֹ אֶלָּא אַמָּה גְּדוּמָה. וְתָנֵי כֵן: [ד] אַמָּה הַיְסוֹד, אַמָּה סוֹבֵב, אַמָּה כַּרְכּוֹב, וְאַמָּה קְרָנוֹת, וְאַמָּה מַעֲרָכָה.§ לְבוֹנָה לֹא יִפְחוֹת מִקּוֹמֶץ. [ג] נֶאֱמַר ז) כָּאן "אַזְכָּרָה" וְנֶאֱמַר לְהַלָּן "אַזְכָּרָה", מָה "אַזְכָּרָה" הָאָמוּר לְהַלָּן מְלֹא קוֹמֶץ — אַף "אַזְכָּרָה" הָאָמוּר כָּאן מְלֹא קוֹמֶץ. אִי מָה "אַזְכָּרָה" הָאֲמוּרָה לְהַלָּן ה — שְׁנֵי קוֹמְצִין, אַף "אַזְכָּרָה" הָאֲמוּרָה כָּאן שְׁנֵי קוֹמְצִין! [ה] אָמַר רַבִּי אִילָא: כְּלוּם לָמְדוּ לַקּוֹמֶץ (א) אֶלָּא (מִלֶּחֶם הַפָּנִים) מִמִּנְחַת חוֹטֵא, מַה לְּהַלָּן קוֹמֶץ הֶחָסֵר פָּסוּל — אַף כָּאן קוֹמֶץ הֶחָסֵר [ג] פָּסוּל. אָמַר רַבִּי יוֹסֵה מִילְּתָא דְּרַבִּי אִילָא אָמְרָה: הַמִּתְנַדֵּב (מִנְחָה) לְבוֹנָה, מְבִיאָהּ בְּקוֹמְצוֹ [ד] שֶׁל [ו] כֹּהֵן (גָּדוֹל) (ר' אֶלְעַי בְּשֵׁם ר"א) רַבִּי חִזְקִיָּה בְּשֵׁם רַבִּי יִרְמְיָה: וַאֲפִילוּ בַּקּוֹמֶץ הַבְּעָלִים.§ זָהָב לֹא יִפְחוֹת כו'.§ אָמַר ח) יר"א וְהוּא שֶׁהִזְכִּיר צוּרָה, אֲבָל אִם לֹא הִזְכִּיר צוּרָה — מֵבִיא אפי' צִינּוֹרָה.§ שִׁשָּׁה לִנְדָבָה. (ב) (רַב אָמַר) חִזְקִיָּה ט) אָמַר: כְּנֶגֶד שִׁשָּׁה בָּתֵּי אָבוֹת. בַּר פְּדָיָה אָמַר: כְּנֶגֶד שֵׁשׁ בְּהֵמוֹת: פָּר, וְעֵגֶל, וְשָׂעִיר, אַיִל, גְּדִי, וְטָלֶה. שְׁמוּאֵל י) אָמַר: כְּנֶגֶד שִׁשָּׁה קָרְבָּנוֹת (קִנֵּי זָבִים וְקִנֵּי זָבוֹת קִנֵּי יוֹלְדוֹת) [ז] חַטָּאוֹת, וַאֲשָׁמוֹת, הַמְּנָחוֹת, וַעֲשִׂירִית הָאֵיפָה. א"ר יוֹחָנָן: ע"י שֶׁהַנָּדָב' מְרוּבָּה רִיבּוּ לָהּ שׁוֹפָרוֹת הַרְבֵּה. [ח] *כְּתִיב: כ) "וּכְכַלּוֹתָם הֵבִיאוּ לִפְנֵי הַמֶּלֶךְ וִיהוֹיָדָע" וְגו' (ג) ר"ש ד"ה ב כד בַּר נַחְמָן בְּשֵׁם רַבִּי יוֹנָתָן אָמַר: שְׁתֵּי נְדָבוֹת עָשָׂה, תָּנֵי

קרבן העדה

הקנין קלובין היו: ואוכלת בקדשים. לערב: ואינה חוששת שמא נתעצל בהן. דמוקה על ב"ד של כהנים שאינן עומדים משם עד שיכלו כל מעות של אותו שופר, כדי שלא יאכלו מחוסרי כפרה בקדשים: ואין הכהן חושש וכו'. ולא פליג ר"י. משמע דכ"ע מודים דלא חיישינן שמא מתה אחת מהן: ומשני: כי קאמרינן לר"י דחייש לתערובת — היינו שיודע לן שבודאי מת א' מהנותנין לתוך השופר, נמצא שהן מעורבות: ופריך: ואי אמרי' כו'. כלומר, אמאי? ונברור ד' זוזי דמי החטאת ונאמר דאלו הן דמי החטאת שמתו בעליהן, והשאר יקרבו! ודקאמר ד' זוזי — היינו זוזי פשיטי שא' מהן הוא דינר צורי, והן דמי פרידה אחת. דתנן: בו ביום עמדו קינין ברבעתים. פי': פרידה אחת. והרובע הוא חצי דינר צורי, שהוא ד' זוזי מדינה. א"נ: אורחיה דש"ס למתני ד': לית ליה ברירה. לא סמכינן אברירה למשרי איסורא: בעי אם אמר "הרי עלי עץ" ולא אמר "עצים", שלא נתכוין אלא לעץ אחד, מהו שיביא א' או שנים?: מתניתא אמרה כן. שאף גיזר א' הוה קרבן, ונדרו נדר: כהאי דתנינן תמן. ביומא פ"ב: ושנים שני כהנים בידם שני גזרי עצים. ביד כל א' גיזר א', ש"מ: שכל א' קרבן בפני עצמו: ה"ג: "קרבן" — לרבות את העצים. וה"פ: כתיב "כי תקריב קרבן מנחה", ומלינו לעצים שנקראו "קרבן", דכתיב "והגורלות הפלנו על קרבן העצים": באמה שוחקת. פי': באמה גדולה: גדומה. פחותה: כמין טורטני. קנה מאזנים. ול"נ דאעוביו קאי, שלא היתה עוביו אלא כטורטני, והוא כמחק גודש סאה השנוי בבבלי: אלא אמה על אמה. ואמתא באמתא היכי יתיב? וכתיב "על העצים אשר על המזבח" — שלא יהו העצים יוצאין מן המזבח. לפיכך לא היו העצים אלא אמה גדומה: ותני כן. ותניא נמי הכי שמקום המערכה לא היה אלא אמה על אמה: נאמר כאן. גבי לבונה דלחם הפנים "אזכרה", דכתיב "ונתת על המערכה לבונה זכה והיתה ללחם לאזכרה": ונאמר להלן. גבי מנחה "וקמץ משם מלא קמצו מסלתה ומשמנה על כל לבונתה והקטיר הכהן את אזכרתה": אף כאן קומץ. לכל מערכה. וכי היכי דסתם מנחה מלא קומץ — אף סתם נדבת לבונה מלא קומץ: ה"ג: אי מה להלן שני קומצין. וה"פ: אי מה להלן בלחם הפנים ב' קומצין, כדאמרינן לעיל על כל מערכה קומץ — אף סתם נדבת לבונה ב' קומצין: כלום למדו לקומץ. לבונה אלא מלחם הפנים. והתם בעינן שיהא כל קומץ בפני עצמו מלא. ואם חסר ממנה — פסול. ש"מ, אע"ג דבהצטרפות יש שני קומצין, כגון שהשני יתר — אפ"ה פסול. כדילפי' ממנחת חוטא, ש"מ דכל קומץ קרבן בפני עצמו: מילתא דרבי אילא אמרה. מדברי ר' אילא שמעינן: ה"ג: המתנדב לבונה — מביאה בקומצו של כה"ג. וה"פ: מדיליף לה מלחם הפנים ובפיים נעשה, ולא ידעינן הי כהן דמתרמי, וצריך שיהיה הרבה, שיקמוץ ממנו גדול שבכהנים: ואפי' בקומץ הבעלים. ממנחה ילפינן, ויכול ליתן אותה לכל כהן שירצה שבאותו משמר: והוא שהזכיר צורה. דאמר מטבע: צינורא. שיעורו מזלג קטן: כנגד ששה בתי אבות. הכהנים, שתקנו להם חכמים שיהא כל משמר חלוק לששה בתי אבות כנגד ששת ימי השבוע, שיעבוד כל אחד ביומו, ובשבת כולן שוין, שיהא שלום ביניהן. שעורות של בהמות הנקחות מן השופרות — היו לכהנים שמקריבין העולות. וכל זמן שאין המזבח בטל — לא היו לוקחין מן השופרות. ואם לא היה להם אלא שופר אחד — אתי לאנצויי. דשמא באותו יום של בית אב הראשון או השני יביאו נדרים ונדבות הרבה, ולא יטול הבית אב מן השופר כלום, ובשאר ימות השבוע לא יבואו נדרים ונדבות הרבה, נמצא אותן בתי אבות מקריבין מן השופר שלא יהא המזבח בטל, והוו עורות שלהם, ומגלו הנך קמאי בהדי הנך, ואמרי: יש לכם עורות ואנו אין לנו כלום. ואי משום הנך עולות שהביאו יחידים במשמרות שלנו — מזלנו גרם. א"נ: פעמים שמקריבים שלמים והעורות לבעלים. הלכך תקינו ששה שופרות, שלא יטול זה משופרו של זה. וכשהמעו' באות — נותנין אותו לו' שופרות: כנגד פר וכו'. שהמתנדב פר ועולה מביא ונותן לשופר שכתוב עליו "פר" מנה, כדאמרי' יביא במנה. והמתנדב עגל — מביא ה' סלעי' ונותן לשופר שכתוב עליו "עגל". וכן כולם. והכהנים מקריבין מכל שופר קרבן הכתוב עליו. ומתני' רבי היא, דאמר: קטן והביא גדול — לא יצא: קני זבים וקני זבות. בחד ניתנו, דשם זב אחד הוא: וחטאת ואשמות. בתרין הוו: המנחות. היינו מותר מנחת חוטא דלנדבה אזיל. דאילו מותר מנחת יחיד — הוסיף משלו, ומביא מנחה אחרת: ועשירית האיפה שכה"ג מקריב בכל יום. ואם הפריש לעשירית האיפה של יום וניתותרו — שוב אין יכול להקריבו לשם מחר, אלא תפול לנדבת צבור, וכדר"א לעיל בפ"ב דף ח'. ורש"י במנחות פרק "האומר עלי" יש לו גירסא אחרת, ע"ש: ריבו לה שופרות הרבה. כדי שלא יתעפשו המעות: ה"ג: כתיב "וככלותם" וכו': שתי נדבות עשה. דבמלכים כתיב "ויקח יהוידע הכהן ארון אחד ויקוב חור בדלתו ויתן אותו אצל המזבח בימין" וגו', ובד"ה כתיב "ויאמר המלך ויעשו ארון ויתנהו בשער בית ה' החוצה", משמע דב' ארונות עשה, א' בפנים וא' בחוץ,

ריבב"ן

אשם מצורע ומותר מנחת חוטא ומותר עשירית האיפה של כ"ג שגם היא נקראת חטאת שנאמר יביא חטאתו זו עשירית האיפה. ר' אושעיא אמר כנגד מותר חטאת ומותר אשם ומותר אשם נזיר ומותר אשם מצורע ומותר קינין אלו קיני חובה ומותר מנחת חוטא מכל אלו לוקחין עולות הבשר לשם והעורות לכהנים כשאר עולות שנאמר עור העולה אשר הקריב לכהן לו יהיה. כתוב אחד אומר אשם הוא אשום אשם לה' וכתיב בפרשת נשא האשם המושב לה' לכהן הא כיצד כל שהוא בא משום חטא ומשום אשמה שהיה חייב אשם כגון אשם גזלות אשם מעילות אשם תלוי אשם שפחה חרופה אשם נזיר אשם מצורע אם הפריש אשמו ונאבד והביא אחר תחתיו ונמצא הראשון ירעה עד שיסתאב וימכר ויפלו דמיו לנדבה. מותר חטאת מי שהפריש חטאתו ואבדה והביא אחרת תחתיה ונמצאת הראשונה לרבנן דפליגי עליה דר' בתמורה פ"ד תרעה עד שתסתאב ויפלו דמיה לנדבה דלא אזלא למיתה אלא אם נמצאת לאחר כפרה ולר' דאמר אפילו נמצאת לאחר הפרשה אזלא למיתה משכחת לה כגון שהפריש שתי בהמות לאחריות ואחת תרעה. ולר' שמעון דאמר כל אבודין מתין אפילו הפרישן לאחריות לא משכחת לה אלא כדאמר ר' אמי הפריש שני לבורי מעות מתכפר באחד מהן והשני יפלו לנדבה ומוקי לה בתמורה פ"ד אליבא דר' שמעון. א"נ הפריש מעות לכל אלו ונותרו מותרן נדבה:

תקלין חדתין

כך הוא דינה שתביא דמיהן של שני התורים, ונותנת בשופר שכתוב עליה "קינין", ששם נותנין מעות קיני חובה: ואוכלת בקדשים. שם גרס "וטובלת", כדתנן חגיגה (כ"א): האונן והמחוסר כיפורים צריכים טבילה לקודש: שמא יתעצל בהן. דמוקה כהנים עושין שליחותן, כדאמרינן במנחות (כו, ב): ה"ג: ואינו חושש שמא דמי חטאות מתות מעורבות. בהן, מדאמרי' שתטיל בשופר זה. ולא פליג עליה רבי יהודה: כי קאמרינן בחטאת שמתו בעליה ודאי. דחיישינן שמא יתוודע בבירור שמתה א', ונמצא כולן אזלי לאיבוד. אבל למיחש שמא תמות — לא חיישינן: ואי אמרינן ברירה כו' ד' זוזי. שיעור דמי פרידה אחת. כדתנן בקינין: עמדו קינין ברבעתים: ר"י ל"ל ברירה. ואנן לר"י קיימינן: בעי. שאל מה שאמר אם יסכימו כן, כדפרישית בפרק קמא: מביא גזיר א'. דחשיב קרבן בפ"ע, שזה קרבן בפ"ע כ"א מהגיזרין: בידם. ביד כל אחד גזיר א'. ש"מ: דכל אחד קרבן בפ"ע, ולכן היה כהן לכל אחד: שוחקת. רווחת וגדולה. ועוביין של כל אחד וא', כדאמר שכל א' קרבן בפ"ע. ולכן קאי אכ"א בפ"ע דלא כרא"פ: גדומה. פחותה: טורטני. קנה מאזנים, ואפי' כ"ש בעוביה. א"נ: שיהיו שוין בהיקף, אורכן כעוביין, כקנה מאזנים שוין. כך למדתי ממשמעות פי' הרמב"ם במתני'. א"נ: כמחק גודש סאה, כמ"ש בבבלי זבחים (ס"ב ב'): לפי שלא היה כו'. דבעינן "עצים ע"ג המזבח" — שלא יצאו העצים מן המזבח, לפיכך לא היו העצים אלא אמה גדומה: ותני כן. שלא היה מקום המערכה אלא אמה: ה"ג: אמה כרכוב אמה קרנות אמה מערכה. דאמה שבין הקרנות ומקום הילוך ממעטין בו אמתים לכל צד, פש ליה אמה על אמה. וזה הביא ראיה: דאמה כרכוב ואמה קרנות, א"כ לא נשאר רק אמה מערכה: לבונה לא יפחות מקומץ נאמר כאן כו'. הכא במתני' בלבונה הבאה בפני עצמה איירי. ולא אשכחן קומץ אחד רק בלבונה הבאה עם המנחה. ונכלל עמה לבונה דבפני עצמה בשיעורן. ומפני שרוצה לפרש משנתינו התחיל לפרש לבונה הבאה עם המנחה, שממנה יתפרש לבונה בפ"ע דמתני': נאמר כאן. היינו בלבונה הבאה עם המנחה כתיב "ואת כל הלבונה וגו' אזכרתה לה'" ומשמע להו ד"את כל הלבונה" דקאמר — היינו כל שם הקטרת לבונה אף הבאה בפני עצמו וכדמשמע בבבלי מנחות (קו, ב): ונאמר להלן. בלחם הפנים "ונתת על המערכת לבונה זכה" וגו' לאזכרה": מה להלן מלא קומץ. למערכה, וכדתנן במתני' דמנחות (קו, ב), ואם חסר ממלא קומץ — פסול, כדאמר שם בהדיא: אף כאן מלא קומץ. וחסר פסול: ה"ג: אי מה להלן ב' קמצים. בלחם הפנים. כמ"ש במתני' ב' בזיכין ב' קומצין, לכל מערכה קומץ א', ה"ג הכא: כלום למדו לקומץ מלחם הפנים אלא ממנחה למדו. ר' אילא בא לסתור מה דהתחיל ללמוד מלחם הפנים. ואמר: כלום למדו לקומץ מלחם הפנים? וכי שיעורא דקומץ לבונה הן הבאה עם המנחה הן בפני עצמה למדו מלחם הפנים? אלא ממנחה למדו. כדאמרינן במנחות (קו, ב), דכתיב "והרים ממנו בקומצו מסלת המנחה ומשמנה ואת כל הלבונה" — מקיש לבונה להרמה דמנחה, מה הרמה דמנחה קומץ — אף לבונה ג"כ קומץ. ומינה, מה להלן קימוץ החסר כשר — אף כאן קימוץ החסר כשר. להאי סוגיא צ"ל דרב אילא ס"ל בלבונה הבאה עם המנחה כר"ש ור"י דאפליגו במנחות (יא, ב) גבי חיסר לבונתה, וס"ל דכשר. וגם ס"ל כחד מהני אמוראי, ר' אמי ור"י נפחא, דס"ל כמחלוקת בלבונה הבאה עם המנחה, הכי נמי בלבונה בפני עצמו ס"ל לר"ש ור"י דקומץ החסר כשר. משא"כ בקמצין דבזיכין דלחם הפנים, לדברי הכל חסר פסול, כדאמר התם: מילתיה דר"א אמרה. מדבריו מוכח: ה"ג: המתנדב לבונה מביאה בקומצו של כהן. דהואיל דלמד ממנחה. ודינו כלבונה הבאה עם המנחה, אף לקולא, אם כן לכולא מילתא נשוויה דמשערינן בשיעור קומצו של יד הכהן: אפילו בקומץ בעלים. דמ"מ נדבה בפני עצמו היא: צורה. מטבע. כמ"ש בגמרא "אלורתא דזוזי": צינורא. מזלג קטן: כנגד ו' בתי כו'. שכל משמר חלוק לו' בתי אבות כנגד ו' ימי השבוע, זה עובד יומו וזה יומו, ובשבת כולן שוין. ולכן תקנו ו' שופרות שלא יטול זה משופרו של זה ולא אתי לאינצויי, כדאיתא בבבלי מנחות (ק"ו) וע"ש: ששה בהמות פר. שהמתנדב פר לעולה מביא ונותן לשופר ששמו "פר" במנה אחד, דפר במנה אחד: ועגל. המתנדבו מביא ה' סלעים ונותן לשופר ששמו "עגל". וכן כולם. והכהנים לוקחים משופר ששמו "פר" ומקריבים פר, ויקרבו מאותו שופר פרים עד שיכלו המעות. ולהכי נקט ששה בהמות — שאין עולה באה אלא מששה בהמות אלו: בנגד ששה קרבנות. המנויין בפ"ב מתני' ה': שופרות הרבה. כדי שלא יתעפשו המעות. והתם מפרש מ"ע דמר, דלא אמר כמר: ה"ג: "וככלותם" גו' כמ"ש בפנים. ואגב דמזכיר במתניתין מדרש יהוידע לא יוצא בית ה', דריש להני קראי ורמי קראי אהדדי, הכי גרסי' בבבלי כתובות (קו, ב), ומשני

עין משפט נר מצוה

כד א מיי' פרק א ממחוסרי כפרה הלכה יב:

כה ב מיי' פרק ט"ז ממעה"ק הל"ג:

כו ג מיי' פרק ז מאיסורי מזבח הלכה ג:

כז ד מיי' פרק ב מבית הבחירה הלכה יז:

כח ה מיי' פרק ה מתמידין הל"ב:

כט ו מיי' פרק ג מערכין הל"ט י:

מסורת הש"ס

א) יומא נה ב: ב) ירושלמי שבועות פ"ט הלכה ה: ג) שם כו ב: ד) עי' מנחות קו ב: ה) זבחים סב ב: ו) ע"ש ע"א: ז) תורת כהנים פ' אמור פי"ג ועיין תוספתא מנחות פי"א וש"ס מנחות קו ב: ח) מנחות קז א: ט) שם ע"ב: י) ע"ש קח א: כ) עי' כתובות קו ב:

נוסחת הבבלי

(א) אלא ממנחת חוטא כו' אמרה (הא דתני) המתנדב מנחה מביאה כו' ר' אלעי בשם ר"א בשם ר"י כו': (ב) רב אמר כנגד כו' ור' חזקיה אמר כנגד כו' מרובה לפיכך הרבו לה כו': (ג) ר"ש בר' נחמני בשם ר' נתן כו' ויתנהו בשער בית ה' כו' רב הונא אמר מפני כו' רב הונא בשם ר' יוסי כו':

הגהות הגר"א

[א] צ"ל ואין חושש ומלת כהן נמחק: [ב] ואי אמרי' ברירה נברור ד' זוזי וכו'. כצ"ל: [ג] מלות קרבן לרבות את העצי' צ"ג: [ד] ה"ג אמה כרכוב אמה קרנות אמה מערכה כצ"ל. וז"ל בעל ת"ח מרן לא גרס אמה יסוד ואמה סובב וטעמו מסוגיא דזבחים (סב.) וע"ש ובפרש"י וז"ש להביא ראי' שמקום המערכה אמה על אמה דאמה היה כרכוב ואמה קרנות וממילא רק אמה מערכה ועיין במנחו' (לז:) בסוגיא: [ה] ה"ג א"ר אילא כלום למדו לקומץ מלחם הפנים אלא ממנחה למדו מה להלן קימוץ החסר כשר אף כאן קימוץ החסר כשר כצ"ל. וה"פ אילא בא לסתור מה דהתחיל ללמוד מלחם הפנים ואמר כלום למדו לקומץ מלחם הפנים וכי שיעורא דקומץ לבונה הן הבאה עם המנחה הן בפ"ע למדו מלה"פ אלא ממנחה למדו כדאמרינן במנחות (קז:) דכתיב והרים ממנו בקומצו מסלת המנחה ומשמנה ואת כל הלבונה מקיש לבונה להרמה דמנחה מה הרמה דמנחה קומץ אף לבונה ג"כ קומץ ומינה מה להלן קימוץ החסר כשר אף כאן קימוץ החסר כשר להאי סוגיא צ"ל דר' אילא ס"ל בלבונה הבאה עם המנחה כר"ש ור"י דאיפלגו במנחות (יא:) גבי חיסר לבונתה וס"ל דכשר וגם ס"ל כחד מהני אמוראי ר' חמי ור"י נפחא דס"ל כמחלוקת בלבונה הבאה עם המנחה ה"נ בלבונה בפ"ע ס"ל לר"ש ור"י דקומץ החסר כשר משא"כ בקמצין דזיכין דלחה"פ לד"ה חסר פסול כדאמר התם כנ"ל הפירוש בסוגיא זו וגי' הספרים ופירושי המפרשים אין הדעת סובלתן. כ"ז הועתק מס' ת"ח ע"ש: [ו] צ"ל מביאה בקומצו של כהן ול"ג כ"ג. ועי' תוספות מנחות (קו:) ד"ה לא יפחות וכו'. והבק"ע לא ראה דברי תוס' ונדחק מאוד לפרש כהן גדול שבכהנים ועי' בספר ת"ח: [ז] ה"ג חטאות ואשמות ועשירית האיפה כצ"ל: [ח] ה"ג כתיב וככלותם הביאו לפני המלך ויהוידע את שאר הכסף ויעשהו כלים לבית ה' כלי שרת וכתיב אך לא יעשה בבית ה' וכו'. ר"ש

משנת אליהו

גירסאות להתלמודים בהא דתני ר"י ב"ר: **תני** בן אמה ברכוב כו'. מרן לא גרס אמה יסוד ואמה סובב וטעמו מסוגיא דזבחים (ס"ב א') וע"ש ובפי' רש"י וז"ש כאן להביא ראיה שמקום המערכה אמה על אמה דאמה היה כרכוב ואמה קרנות וממילא רק אמה מערכה ועי' מנחות (ל"ז ב') בסוגיא: **נאמר** כאן כו'. עי' רש"י במנחות (ק"ו ב') ד"ה מנ"ל דסתם כו' ושם (י"א ב') ד"ה לבונה כו' הבאה בפ"ע כגון האומר הרי עלי כו'. וכדפרישית לגירסת רבינו דרלה לאוכוחי דלבונה הבאה בפ"ע קומץ א' ומתחיל בלימוד לבונה הבאה עם מנחה דקומץ א' ג"כ אינו מפורש בהדיא ולמד מלחה"פ לאומרא רק דמשם הקשה דלימא ב' קומצין ודחה כלום למדו קומץ כל עיקרא דקומץ ממנחה למדו וגדולה מזו אף קומץ דלחה"פ למד בספרא ג"כ ממנחה בספרא פ' אמור פרשה י"ג הלכה ז' לאזכרה ר"ש אומר נאמרה כאן אזכרה ונאמרה להלן (במנחה) אזכרה מה אזכרה האמור להלן מלא הקומץ אף כאן מלא קומץ מלמד שהיא טעונה ב' קמצין מלא הקומץ לסדר זה ומלא הקומץ לסדר זה עכ"ל ועי' תוס' דמנחות (י"א ב') ד"ה קומץ כו' וגיר' הספרים ופירושי המפרשים אין הדעת סובלתן: **ה"ג** מביאה בקומצו של כהן. עי' תוס' דמנחות (ק"ו ב') ד"ה לא יפחות כו' והבק"ע לא ראה דברי התוס' ונדחק מאד לפרש כהן גדול הגדול שבכהנים ושגה מאוד:

הדרן עלך שלשה עשר שופרות

גליון הש"ס

[א] עי' תוספות מנחות דף קו ע"ב ד"ה לא: [ב] עי' תוספות מנחות דף יא ע"ב ד"ה קומץ: [ג] הגר"א הגיה כשר ועי' ברמב"ם פי"א מפהמ"ק הלכה ה פסק דחיסר לבונתה כשר ועי' בכ"מ שם ואפשר שסמך על הירושלמי לפי גירסת הגר"א: [ד] עי' תוס' מנחות דף קו ע"ב ד"ה לא:

ציון ירושלים

חזקיה אמר כנגד ששה בתי אבות. עי' רש"י פסחים דף נ"ז ד"ה לערב שכתב שמשמר נתחלק לששה בתים אבל בתענית דף ט"ו ע"ב ד"ה אנשי כתב לשבעה וכ"כ הריטב"א בתענית וברטנורא פ"א ממדות ופ"א מתמיד כתב לשבעה וכ"כ הברטנורא פ"ב דתענית מ"ו והארכתי בזה הרבה והראיתי כמה מקומות בש"ס שגם בשבת היו משמרות

ומסתמא לשני מינין נדבות עשה אותן: **מפני הטמאין.** לעולם נדבה א' היתה, אלא שיהוידע נתנו בפנים, אבל המלך אמר שיתנהו בחוץ כדי שיוכלו גם הטמאים, דהיינו טמאי מת ושרץ, ליתן לתוכו, שהם מותרים לבא במחנה לויה: **על שם וכו'.** כלומר, ע"כ לומר דשתי נדבות היו, דבמלכים כתיב "אך לא יעשה בית ה' ספות מזמרות וכו' מן הכסף המובא בית ה'". ובד"ה כתיב "וככלותם וגו' את שאר הכסף ויעשוהו כלי שרת". אלא ודאי דשתי נדבות היו, ומן הכסף המובא בית ה', והיינו הנדבה הכתובה במלכים, לא נעשו כלי שרת, אבל מנדבה הכתובה בד"ה, והיא ניתנה חוץ לבית ה', ממנה עשו כלי שרת: ה"ג: **ספות כסף וכו'.** מן כסף המובא בית ה': הדרן עלך פרק שלשה עשר שופרות

תורה אור

מ"ב יב תָּנֵי דְּבֵי ר' יִשְׁמָעֵאל: נְדָבָה אַחַת. דִּכְתִיב "וַיֹּאמֶר (א)
הַמֶּלֶךְ וַיַּעֲשׂוּ אֲרוֹן אֶחָד וַיִּתְּנֻהוּ בְּהֵיכַל בֵּית ה' וַיִּקֹּב
ד"ה ב כד חוֹר בְּדַלְתוֹ". וְהָא דִּכְתִיב "וַיֹּאמֶר הַמֶּלֶךְ וַיַּעֲשׂוּ אֲרוֹן
אֶחָד וַיִּתְּנֻהוּ בְּשַׁעַר בֵּית ה' חוּצָה"! אָמַר רַב חוּנָא:
מ"ב יב מִפְּנֵי הַטְּמֵאִים. ר"ח בְּשֵׁם ר' יוֹסֵף (עַל שֵׁם) "אַךְ לֹא
יֵעָשֶׂה בֵּית ה' סִפּוֹת כֶּסֶף מְזַמְּרוֹת" וְגו'.§

הדרן עלך פרק י"ג שופרות

הלכה א מתני'

אמָעוֹת שֶׁנִּמְצְאוּ בֵּין הַשְּׁקָלִים לִנְדָבָה, קָרוֹב לַשְּׁקָלִים — יִפְּלוּ לַשְּׁקָלִים, לַנְּדָבָה — יִפְּלוּ לַנְּדָבָה, מֶחֱצָה לְמֶחֱצָה — יִפְּלוּ לַנְּדָבָה. בבֵּין עֵצִים לִלְבוֹנָה, קָרוֹב לָעֵצִים — יִפְּלוּ לָעֵצִים, לַלְּבוֹנָה — יִפְּלוּ לַלְּבוֹנָה, מֶחֱצָה לְמֶחֱצָה — יִפְּלוּ לַלְּבוֹנָה. בֵּין קִינִּין לְגוֹזְלֵי עוֹלָה, קָרוֹב לַקִּינִּין — יִפְּלוּ (א) לַקִּינִּין, קָרוֹב לְגוֹזְלֵי עוֹלָה — יִפְּלוּ לְגוֹזְלֵי עוֹלָה, מֶחֱצָה לְמֶחֱצָה — יִפְּלוּ לְגוֹזְלֵי עוֹלָה. גבֵּין חוּלִּין לְמַעֲשֵׂר שֵׁנִי, קָרוֹב לַחוּלִּין — יִפְּלוּ לַחוּלִּין, לְמַעֲשֵׂר שֵׁנִי — יִפְּלוּ לְמַעֲשֵׂר שֵׁנִי, מֶחֱצָה לְמֶחֱצָה — יִפְּלוּ לְמַעֲשֵׂר שֵׁנִי. זֶה הַכְּלָל: הוֹלְכִין אַחַר הַקָּרוֹב לְהָקֵל, מֶחֱצָה לְמֶחֱצָה לְהַחְמִיר.§ **גמ'** לֹא הוּצְרְכָה דְּלָא בֵּין שְׁקָלִים לְקִינִּים? ר' אָבוּן בְּשֵׁם ר' פִּנְחָם: (ב) כְּמִין בּוּכְלַיָּאר הָיוּ עֲשׂוּיִן. מֶחֱצָה לְמֶחֱצָה יִפְּלוּ לִנְדָבָה [א] (לָא צוֹרְכָה דְּלָא מֶחֱצָה לְמֶחֱצָה יִפְּלוּ לַשְּׁקָלִים) אִית דְּבָעֵי מֵימַר: שֶׁמָּא יִפְּלוּ לִשְׁיָרֵי הַלִּשְׁכָּה, אִית דְּבָעֵי מֵימַר: מֶחֱצָה לְמֶחֱצָה כְּמִי שֶׁמֵּת. א"ר ג) יֹסָא: עַד דַּאֲנָא תַּמָּן שְׁמָעִית קַל רַב יְהוּדָה שְׁאַל לִשְׁמוּאֵל: דהִפְרִישׁ שִׁקְלוֹ וָמֵת? אֲמַר לֵיהּ: יִפְּלוּ לִנְדָבָה (מוּתָּר) עֲשִׂירִית הָאֵיפָה שֶׁלּוֹ, רַבִּי יוֹחָנָן אָמַר: היוֹלִיכֵם לְיָם הַמֶּלַח, רַבִּי לְעָזָר אָמַר: יִפְּלוּ לִנְדָבָה. וְקַשְׁיָא: וְיֵשׁ חַטָּאת קְרֵיבָה עוֹלָה! *חִזְקִיָּה (אֲחִי) בְּשֵׁם רַבִּי רַבִּי שִׁמְעוֹן בֶּן לָקִישׁ: תְּנַאי בֵּית דִּין הוּא עַל הַמּוֹתָרוֹת שֶׁיִּקְרְבוּ עוֹלוֹת. הָאִשָּׁה הַזֹּאת בַּמָּה הִיא מִתְכַּפֶּרֶת? אָמַר ג) ר' יִצְחָק: [א] תְּנַאי ב"ד הוּא והַמְסַפֵּק אֶת הַקִּינִּין — הוּא מְסַפֵּק אֶת [ב] הַפְּסוּלוֹת. לָא צוֹרְכָה [ג] דְּלָא בֵּין קְטוֹרֶת לָעֵצִים, לִלְבוֹנָה, לְזָהָב לְכַפּוֹרֶת? וּתְנִיתָהּ בְּסוֹפָהּ: זֶה הַכְּלָל, הוֹלְכִין אַחַר הַקָּרוֹב, מֶחֱצָה לְמֶחֱצָה לְהַחְמִיר.§

הלכה ב מתני'

זמָעוֹת ד) שֶׁנִּמְצְאוּ לִפְנֵי סוֹחֲרֵי בְהֵמָה — לְעוֹלָם מַעֲשֵׂר, וּבְהַר הַבַּיִת — חוּלִּין. (ג) חוּבִירוּשָׁלַם, בִּשְׁאָר כָּל יְמוֹת הַשָּׁנָה — חוּלִּין. וּבִשְׁעַת הָרֶגֶל — הַכֹּל מַעֲשֵׂר. טבָּשָׂר שֶׁנִּמְצָא בָּעֲזָרָה, אֵיבָרִים — עוֹלוֹת, וַחֲתִיכוֹת — חַטָּאוֹת. וּבִירוּשָׁלַם — זִבְחֵי שְׁלָמִים. זֶה וָזֶה תְּעוּבַּר צוּרָתוֹ וְיֵצֵא לְבֵית הַשְּׂרֵפָה. נִמְצָא ה) בַּגְּבוּלִין, אֵבָרִים — נְבֵילוֹת, וַחֲתִיכוֹת — מוּתָּרוֹת. וּבִשְׁעַת

ריבב"ן

מתני' מעות שנמצאו בין שופר שקלים לשופר נדבה. הולכין אחר הקרוב בין להקל בין להחמיר: מחצה על מחצה יפלו לנדבה. דנדבה חמורה דכולה עולה אבל שקלים שיריהן קילי קדושתייהו דניתנין לחומת העיר ומגדלותיה: לבונה. חמירא דלבונה היא עצמה קריבה אבל עצים הן מכשירי קרבן: בין קינין לגוזלי עולה יפלו לגוזלי עולה. סתמן כרבנן דקיני חובה הן ואחד לעולה וא' לחטאת וחטאת הבשר נאכל לכהנים ומיד שיש לו שעת היתר לכהנים אין בו מעילה והעולה כליל ומחמרא טפי: בין חולין למעשר שני. לאו במקדש עסקינן אלא אם היו שני צבורי מעות בתיבתו מחצה למחצה יפלו למע"ש ויאכלם בירושלים כגון שנשתמש בהן כאחד דאי לא הוה אזלינן בתר בתרא כדמוכח בפסחים בפ"ק (דף ז.): מתני' מעות שנמצאו לפני סוחרי בהמה בירושלים לעולם מעשר שני. לפי שרוב מעות מעשר שני שלמים אזלא דאתיא שם שם כתיב הכא ואכלת לפני ה' אלהיך מעשר דגנך ותירושך וגו' ואכלת שם וגו' והתם [כתיב] וזבחת שלמים ואכלת שם [דברים כז] לא שאינו רשאי לאוכלן בתורת חולין כלל אפילו בירושלים דאפילו בהתפסה לשלמים לא תפסי דאמרינן בפרק התודה א"ר אמי המתפיס מעות מעשר לשלמים לא קנו שלמים ואם רצה ליקח בהן חטין או דבר אחר רשאי ותניא התם הלוקח חיה לזבחי שלמים ובהמה לבשר תאוה לא יצא העור לחולין כגון שלקחה ממעות מעשר שני ומפרש דאפילו העור אינו בתורת לצאת העור לחולין כשאר שלמים שהעור לחולין ואפילו של מע"ש דאמרינן בעירובין פ"ג בבקר מלמד שלוקחין בקר אגב עורו דפשיטא שהעור חולין גמור: ובהר הבית חולין. ירושלמי אמר רבא בר חייא בשם ר' יוחנן מוקה שאין כהן מוליא מעות מן הלשכה עד שמתחללת על הבהמה: [ובירושלים] **בשאר כל ימות** השנה חולין ובשעת הרגל מעשר. מפרש בפסחים פ"ק אמר רב שמעיה בר זירא מ"ט הואיל ושוקי ירושלים עשוין להתכבד בכל יום וקמאי קמאי אזלו להו: מתני' דלא כר' יוסי דתניא [תוספתא פ"ג] א"ר יוסי אלו דברי בית שמאי אבל ב"ה אומרים לעולם מעשר חוץ מהנמצאין בהר הבית בשאר ימות השנה שהן חולין: מתני' אברין עולות. ודווקא שמנותחין כמפורש במס' יומא פ"ב וחתיכות חטאות וה"ה דאיכא לספוקי באשם אבל חטאת שכיחא טפי מ"מ אכילתן ליום ולילה ודוקא בעזרה איכא לספוקי אבל בירושלים לא דאינה נאכלת חוץ לעזרה בירושלים בין אברין בין חתיכות זבחי שלמים וה"ה דאיכא לספוקי בתודה ובמעשר בהמה ומידי דשכיחא נקט: זה וזה תעובר **צורתו ויצא** לבית השרפה. ירושלמי אמר ר' יוסי יאות לאוכלו אי את יכול שמא נתקלקלה צורתו פי' שמא נותר לשורפו אי את יכול שמא לא נתקלקלה צורתו. כלומר, שמא עדיין לא בא לידי נותר לפוס כן צריך מימר תעובר למחר וילא לבית השרפה ולזבחי שלמים צריך אתה לפרש תעובר צורתו עד יום ג' שמא היום נשחט ואינו נותר עד יום ג' לשלישיתו: מתני' אברין נבלות. והאוכלן לוקה לפי שנתנבלה השליכוה אברין. חתיכות מותרות ירושלמי חתיכות מותרות לא ממש מותרות אלא מותרות משום נבילה

קרבן העדה

הלכה א מתני' יפלו לשקלים. דבתר קרוב אזלינן. כדכתיב "והיתה העיר הקרובה אל החלל": **מחצה על מחצה יפלו לנדבה.** בגמ' מפרש טעמא: **מחצה על מחצה יפלו ללבונה.** דלבונה היא עצמה קרבן, ועלים מכשירי קרבן: **מחצה על מחצה יפלו לגוזלי עולה.** מפרש בגמ': **גמ'** ופריך **לא צורכה.** לא היה לו לתנא לשנות אלא מעות שנמצאו בין שקלים לקיני', שהרי שופר של שקלים היה סמוך לקינים, כפי סדר השנוי בפ' דלעיל. ולא לנדבה, שהנדבה בסוף ושקלים בראש: ומשני **כמין כובליים.** פי' בעיגול סביב היו עומדין, והיו השקלים סמוך לנדבה מצד א': ופריך: **לא צורכה.** לא הל"ל אלא מחצה למחצה יפלו לשקלים, שמביאין מהן קרבנות צבור הקבועים. משא"כ נדבה, שאינן אלא לקיץ המזבח: ומשני: **אית דבעי וכו'.** יש שרצו לתרץ דהיינו טעמא דלא יפלו לשקלים, דלפעמים יותרו השקלים, ושירי שקלים לחומת העיר ולא לקרבנות באין, נמצא שהנדבה חמורה ממנה: **מחצה למחצה.** שקלים שנמצאו במחצה למחצה ה"ל כשקל שמתו בעליו, שנופל לנדבה, כדמסיק: **עד דאנא תמן.** כשהייתי בבבל שמעתי ששאל ר"י לשמואל: הפריש שקלו ומת מה יעשה בו?: **מותר עשירית האיפה שלו.** של כה"ג מה יעשה בו: **יוליכם לים המלח לא נהנין ולא מועלין בו.** וקשיא: **ויש חטאת וכו'.** אמתני' פריך, דתני: בין קינין וכו' מחצה למחצה — יפלו לגוזל עולה. בשלמא קרוב לגוזלי עולה, כיון דמדאורייתא אזלינן בתר קורבה, הוה כאילו הן ודאי גוזלי עולה. אלא מחצה על מחצה, דמספיקא שדינן להו לגוזלי עולה, קשיא: וכי חטאת יכול להקריב עולה מספק? ומשני: **תנאי ב"ד הוא על המותרות שיקרבו עולות.** אע"ג דמותרות חטאת הן. ה"נ תנאי בית דין הוא שיקרבו עולות: ופריך: **האשה הזאת שהביאה המעות הללו במה תתכפר.** כלומר, שמא מקיני חובה נפלו, ובמה תתכפר? שהרי לא הקריבה חטאתה: ומשני: **תנאי ב"ד הוא: המספק את הקינין מספק את הפסולות.** ואף זו מן הפסולות היא, וצריך המספק קינין ליתן קינין כפי המעות הנמצאים. ושוחטן חטאת על הספק, דחטאת העוף באה על הספק, ואינה נאכלת: ופריך: **לא צורכה.** וכי לא היה צריך לתנא לשנות נמי בין קטורת לעצים ובין לבונה לזהב לכפורת, מה דינם: ומשני: **ותניתה בסיפא.** כבר תנא בסיפא: זה הכלל הולכין אחר הקרוב וכו'. ומרבינן הכל ב"זה הכלל". ומיהו, הנך דתני איצטריך לאשמעי' שום חידוש, כדשנינן:

הלכה ב מתני' לעולם מעשר. אפי' כל השנה כולה. לפי שעולי רגלים אינן מספיקין להוציא כל מעשר שני שלהם ברגלים, ומניחין אותן לקרוביהם או לאוהביהן בטובת הנאה, והן אוכלין אותן בקדושתן. ועיקר אכילת מעות מעשר — שלמים היו מביאין מהן, הלכך לוקחין מהן בהמות. ואע"ג דאיכא למימר שמא מן המוכרין נפלו ונתחללו כבר, כיון דלוקחין הוי רובא, שהרי כמה אנשים לוקחים מתגר א' — אמרי דלוקחין הן ולא נתחללו, והרי הן מעשר: **בהר הבית חולין.** ואפילו ברגל, שרוב מעות שביד בני אדם אז הן של מעשר. אפ"ה הוי חולין, דאזלינן בתר רובא דשתא, ואימור מקמי רגל נפיל: **בירושלם.** שלא בשוק הבהמות: **בשעת הרגל הכל מעשר.**

מסורת הש"ם

א) א"ה ערבוב מקראות יש כאן כי רישא דקרא ויאמר המלך ויעשו ארון א' וגו' הוא בד"ה ב' כ"ד וסיפא דקרא ויקב חור בדלתו הוא במלכים ב יב: ב) לעיל פ"ב הל"ד וש"נ: ג) לקמן הל"ג: ד) ב"מ כו א פסחים ז א: ה) חולין לה א:

עין משפט נר מצוה

א א מיי' פרק ג משקלים הל"ד:
ב ב מיי' שם הלט"ו:
ג ג מיי' פ"ו ממעשר שני הלכה יב:
ד ד מיי' פרק ג משקלים הל"ב:
ה ה מיי' פרק ה מפסמ"ק הל"ח:
ו ו מיי' פ"ז מהלי המקדש הל"ט:
ז ז מיי' פ"ו ממעשר שני הלכה י:
ח ח מיי' שם הל"ט:
ט ט מיי' פרק י"ט מפסמ"ק הל"ד:

נוסחת הבבלי

(א) לקינין לגוזלי כו': (ב) כמין קובליים כו' יפלו לשקלים אית כו' שמת (אביה) א"ר אסי כו' ומת מהו א"ל כו' עולה רבי חזקי' אמר בשם ר"ל תנאי ב"ד כו' עולות אם כן האשה כו': (ג) בירושלם בשעת הרגל מעשר ובשאר כל ימו' השנה חולין:

הגהות הגר"א

בר נחמני בשם ר' נתן אמר ב' נדבות עשה ותנא דבי ר"י נדבה אחת מאי ככלותם לאחר שהותירו וקשיא על דר"י כתיב ויקח יהוידע הכהן ארון א' ויקב חור בדלתו ויתן אותו אצל המזבח וגו' וכתיב ויאמר המלך יעשו ארון א' ויתנהו בשער בית ה' חולה רב הונא אמר מפני הטמאי' כל"ל. והשאר שבינתים עד סוף הפ' נמחק.

א) עי' פסחים לד א:
ב) תוספתא פ"ג:
ג) פסחים ט ב וש"נ:
ד) עי' חולין לה א:

לחתיכות קטנות אלא הכשרות למכרן, או לתת אותן לקדרה: שהבשר מרובה. ואין חותכין הבשר לחתיכות קטנות, אלא מבשלים אותו איברים איברים: גמ' ופריך: לא צורכה. לא ה"ל לתנא למתני אלא בהר הבית קדש. דודאי מתרומת הלשכה נפל, שהרי אין אדם רשאי לכנוס לשם במעות צרורין בסדינו: חזקה שאין הכהן. הגזבר אין מוציא מעות מן הלשכה אלא אם כן נתחלל. הלכך, כל הנמצא בהר הבית חולין: הסיע דעת. היסח הדעת מן הקדשים, אע"ג דפסולין — טעונין עיבור צורה קודם שריפתו: מתניתא אמרה כן. כלומר, מתני' נמי דייקי: ויאות. בתמיה: וכי שפיר קאמרת? דלמא במתני' אין הטעם משום היסח הדעת, דכל שהוא בעזרה לא מיקרי היסח הדעת, דליכא למיחש לשום טומאה. והכא היינו טעמא דפסול — שמא כבר נתעברה צורתו, לפיכך טעון עיבור צורה ודאי. אבל כל שנפסל בהיסח הדעת בודאי — אפי' עיבור צורה אין צריך: לוקין עליה משום נבלה. דודאי נבלה היא: חתיכות מותרות לא ממש דמותרות לאכול, ה"נ איברים נבלות — נבלות ממש, דלוקין עלייהו: אם היו מחרוזות. קשורות זו בזו — מותרות. דודאי נפלו מיד אדם בשוגג: נתחלפו לו. אינו יודע איזו היא: חושש. ומספיקא אסורות כולן. אבל אין לוקין עליו, דכל קבוע כמחצה על מחצה דמי: ולנמצאת הולכין אחר הרוב. דכל דפריש מרובא פריש, וכודאי טריפה הוא, ולוקין עליו. וכן אם הרוב כשירות, אם פריש — מותר אפילו באכילה: הנמצא ביד נכרי. בשר הנמצא ביד נכרי, כאילו נמצא ברה"ר. אם רוב טבחי ישראל — מותר: הוה מסמך. היה סמוך על רבי מנא, וראה נכרי א' חותך בשר מן הסוס ויוצא לחוץ: א"ל: הא דאר"י הנמצא ביד נכרי כנמצא ברה"ר ומותר, אמאי ניחוש דלמא מן בהמתו חתך? ואפי' מקולין וטבחי ישראל נינהו — יש לאוסרו: א"ל. הכי אר"י (רבי): והוא שראו הנכרי יוצא מן המקולין של ישראל, אז סמכינן להתירו: חד בר נש וכו'. אדם אחד בציפורי הלך ליקח בשר מן הטבח ולא נתן לו: א"ל. לחד נכרי שיקח לו, והביא לו: א"ל. הרי בר נש לטבח: לא לקחתי בע"כ ממך, שהנכרי הביא לי: אמר. הטבח ולאו בשר נבילה מכרתי לנכרי: מעשה זה בא לפני רבי. ושאל לו אם נאמן הטבח לאסרו: ואמר. רבי: לאו כל כמיניה לאסור מקולין דציפורי. וכיון שלא הכריזו טריפה בו ביום — הבשר מותר: רב ירד לבבל, ראה אותן שהן מקילין באיסור בשר להניחו ביד נכרי, והחמיר עלייהו ואסר כל בשר שנתעלם מן העין, וכדמסיק:

ובשעת הרגל, שהבשר מרובה — אף איברים מותרות.§ גמ' לא צורכה דלא בהר הבית קודש? (א) רבי בא ר' חייה בשם רבי יוחנן: חזקה שאין הכהן מוציא מן הלשכה מעות עד שהוא מחללן על הבהמה.§ בשר שנמצא כו'.§ רבי א) לעזר בשם ר' הושעיא [א] הסיע דעת טעון עיבור צורה. א"ר הושעיה: [א] מתני' אמרה כן: תעובר צורתו ויצא לבית השריפה. א"ר [ב] יוסי: ויאות, לאכלו אין את יכול — שמא נתקלקל צורתו, לפום כן צריך מימר — תעובר צורתו ויצא לבית השריפה.§ נמצא בגבולין וכו'.§ רבי קריספא בשם (ב) רבי יוסי ברבי חנינה: איברים נבילות, לוקין עליהן משום נבילה. מתניתא אמרה כן: איברי נבילות, וחתיכות מותרות. חתיכות מותרות [ג] לא ממש? ודכוותה איברים נבילות — לוקין עליהן משום נבילה. רבי קריספא בשם רבי יוסי ברבי חנינה: אם ב) היו מחרוזות — מותרות. תשע חנויות [ג] מוכרות בשר נבילה ואחת מוכרת בשר שחוטה, נתחלפו לו, חושש. ולנמצאת הולכין אחר הרוב. אתשע ג) חנויות מוכרות בשר שחוטה ואחת מוכרת בשר נבילה, נתחלפו לו — חושש, ולנמצאת הולכין אחר הרוב. א"ר יוחנן: הנמצא ביד נכרי כנמצא בפלטיא. (ג) רבי לעזר בי רבי חגיי הוה מסמך לר' מנא. חמא לחד ארמאי מקטע מן סוסיה ומפיק לברא, א"ל [ג] הדא היא דאמר רבי יוחנן: הנמצאה ביד נכרי כנמצא בפלטיא. א"ל כן א"ר יוסי [ד] ר' בוהן שראו אותו יוצא ממקולין של ישראל. חד בר נש בציפורין אזיל בעי מיזבון קופד מן טבחא ולא יהב ליה. אמר ליה לחד רומיי, ואייתי ליה. א"ל לא נסבית על כרחיה? א"ל ולאו בשר דנבילה יהבית ליה? רבי ירמיה בשם ר' חנינה: מעשה ד) בא לפני ר' ואמר: לא כולא מיניה מיסר מקולין דציפורין. רב נחת לתמן חמתון מקילין, וחמר עליהן. חד בר נש אזיל בעי

ריבב"ן

שאין לוקין עליהן אבל אסור באכילה אברין נבילות ולוקין עליהן משום נבילות: ובשעת הרגל שהבשר מרובה אפילו אברין מותרין. ודוקא מותר משום נבילה אבל באכילה אסור ואע"ג דאמרינן ט' חנויות כולן מוכרות בשר שחוטה וא' בשר נבילה ולקח מאחד מהן ואינו יודע איזו לקח ספיקו אסור ובנמצא הלך אחר הרוב ומותר באכילה התם חתיכות ולא הרגיש כשנפל אבל אברין שמא נתנבלה והשליכוה ולא נפלה מידו דמתוך כובדה היה מרגיש לפיכך השליכוה לאברין: בהמה שנמצאת וכו'. בפ"ב דקדושין מייתי להא זכרים עולות ופריך זכרים עולות הוא דהוו ושלמים לא הוו אמר ר' הושעיא בבא לחוב בדמיה עסקינן וה"ק חיישינן שמא עולות נינהו ור"מ היא דאמר הקדש במזיד

תקלין חדתין

מה טעם בשעת הרגל מעשר ולא אמרינן קודם הרגל נפלו כדאמרינן בנמצאין בהר הבית — הואיל ושווקי ירושלים עשויין להתכבד בכל יום מפני הטיט, ואי נפול קודם הרגל הוי משתכחי בשעת כיבוד. אבל הר הבית, מתוך שהוא משופע והרוח מכבדתו מעפרו, ועוד, שאין אדם נכנס באבק שעל גבי רגליו ואינו עשוי להתכבד: גמ' לא צריכא כו'. פריך על מ"ש בהר הבית לעולם חולין: וכי לא צריכא שלא יהיה בהר הבית אלא קודש, דמתרומת הלשכה נקחין שם המעות והן קודש, דמחוץ אסור להביא שם מעות, כדתנינא בתוספתא פ"ו דברכות: ולא יכנס במעות הצרורין לו בסדינו. א"נ: אע"ג דנימא דדוקא דרך בזיון אסור להביא לשם מעות בפרהסיא, כמו בסדינו שנראה שהוא דרך גנאי כהולך לסחורה, אבל בצנעה שרי, מ"מ למה לעולם חולין? והלא שם מעות קדש מצויין! ומשני: חזקה שאין כו' עד שהוא מחללן על הבהמה תחלה. וכל המעות הנמצאים שם חולין. ולפי' השני צ"ל: אף על גב דברגל אפשר שיובא לשם מעות מעשר גם כן, מכל מקום כיון דמעות דמקומן רק חולין וממחולה לה בפרהסיא אסור רק בצנעא, ה"ל חולין רובא, ולכן הכל חולין: מתני' איברים עולות. שכן דרך העולות שכולן כליל ואין חותכין אותן חתיכות, ודי להן לעשותן איברים איברים. מה שאין כן חטאות שנאכלין — חותכין אותן לחתיכות:

בירושלים וזבחי שלמים. כי שלמים נאכלים בכל ירושלים, ולפיכך חוששין בבשר הנמצא שם שמא הוא שלמים. ולכן דינן כשלמים: זה וזה. בין שנמצא בעזרה בין שנמצא בירושלים: תעובר צורתן. שיפסלו ודאי בנותר. וכדמפרש בגמרא. ומה שיש תועלת בין אם יהיה הבשר עולה או שלמים. היינו אם עבר אדם ואכלו חתיכות הנמצאות בירושלים, או כהן לחתיכות הנמצאות בעזרה — אינם חייבים כלום, שהן שלמים. משא"כ איברים הנמצאים בעזרה אם אכלן — חייב, שהן עולה, שכולה כליל: בגבולין. בשאר מקומות: איברים נבלות. דחיישינן שמא נבילה הוא, ותתכו להאכיל לחיות או למכור. ואם הוא חתיכות — לא חיישינן להכי, דאין דרך לחתוך חתיכות אלא מה שאוכלין אותו בני אדם. ואם כן בשר שחוטה הוא, ומותר באכילה, והיינו דוקא בעיר שכולה ישראל. אבל בעיר נכרים — אסור, מחמת בשר שנתעלם מן העין: בשעת הרגל שהבשר מרובה. אבל בני אדם. אין צריכין לחתכן חתיכות אלא שמבשלין אותן איברים, ולפיכך אף איברים מותרים: גמ' ה"ג: ר"א בשם רבי הושעיא היסח הדעת פסול וטעון עיבור צורה. כלומר, דאיכא למ"ד דס"ל היסח הדעת פסול הגוף הוי, שהוא מעלה בקדשים שנפסלין בכך. ואפי' יבוא אליהו ויאמר שלא נטמאו כל אותן הימים שהסיח דעתו מהן — אין שומעין לו. ולהך מ"ד לא בעי עיבור צורה בפסול דהיסח הדעת. ורבי הושעיא ס"ל כאידך מ"ד דהיסח הדעת פסול טומאה הוי, מחשש שמא נטמא. וכיון דלא חזינא ליה שנטמא, אלא חששא בעלמא — לכן א"א לשרפו בלא עיבור צורה, שמא לא נטמא. וזהו דאמר: פסול וטעון עיבור צורה: מתני' אמרה בן תעובר צורתו ויצא לבית השריפה. ואי ס"ד פסול הגוף הוא, ל"ל עיבור צורה?: ויאות. מפרש טעמא דמתניתין דמצריך עיבור צורה לשרוף. והא בנידון דידן דליכא בהא מילתא אלא ספק טומאה. ומתני' איירי בעזרה. וקי"ל בפסחים (יט, ב) דעזרה רה"ר לטומאה. וכן ירושלים ג"כ, קי"ל דהוי רה"ר, כדאמרינן בעירובין (קא, א). וקי"ל דכל ספק ברה"ר טהור, ולמה יצטרך עיבור צורה ולשרפו? לדידיה דס"ל דפסול טומאה הוי: דלאכלו אי אפשר. גם דמחשש טומאה הוי טהור בכה"ג, אבל יש לחוש שמא הוא נותר. דהא בנמצא איירי מתני', וזהו שמא נתקלקלה צורתו. לשרפו אי את יכול — שמא לא נתקלקלה צורתו, ולכן אי אפשר כי אם שתעובר צורתו ויצא לבית השריפה: נמצא בגבולין כו' רבי קריספא כו' איברי נבלות לוקין כו'. דלאו לאיסור אכילה בלחוד משום חששא, אלא דודאי נבילה, ולוקין על אכילתה. דאיברין מוכיחים דודאי נבילה היא, ותתכה להאכילן לחיות או למכרן לנכרים, או לזרקן לאשפה: חתיכות מותרות. וכי לא ממש מותרות משום שאין דרך נבילות לחתכן לחתיכות, רק לבשר שחוטה. ה"נ באיברים נבילות ממש: מחרוזות מותרות. קשורות בחוט. לפי שאין דרך לחרוז נבילות, ולכן אף איברים מותרים בגבולין. ולי נראה דגם ארישא קאי, בנמצא בעזרה וכדתנינא בתוספתא פרק בתרא דמכילתין: בשר שנמצא בעזרה — מחרוזות מותרות, שאין עושין בשר הקודש מחרוזות. שע"ג אשפה, בכל מקום — אסור: נתחלפו לו. היינו שלקח ואינו יודע מאיזה מהן לקח, ספיקו אסור. דכל קבוע כמחצה על מחצה דמי, וספק איסורא לחומרא: ובנמצא. בשר הנמצא בקרקע בין החנויות: אחר הרוב. דכל דפריש מרובא פריש, דכיון דפריש — אין כאן קבוע: הנמצא ביד נכרי כנמצא בפלטיא. והולכין אחר הרוב. וקמ"ל דאף בידי נכרי מותר, והוא שרוב טבחי העיר ישראל: מסמיך לרבי מנא. שר' מנא היה נשען עליו: מקטע מן סוסיה. מחתך מן סוס שלו ונשאו לחוץ: ה"ג: לית הדא כו'. כלומר, שנדחה דברי רבי יוחנן שהתיר נמצא ביד נכרי דהא ראינו שנכרי מוליא בשר נבילה: והוא שראהו יוצא. שם התיר ר"י ובההיא עובדא שראינו לא יצא הנכרי ממקולין של ישראל: קופד. בשר: ולא מיתן ליה. שהיו שונאים זה לזה: לחד ארמאי. לנכרי אחד, שלקח מהטבח הזה בשר כמו שהיו רגילין הטבחי ישראל ליתן לנכרי בשר שימכור במקולין להשתכר בו ולטריפה ליכא למיחש דבתר רוב טבחי העיר שהם ישראל אזלינן: ולא נסבית ע"כ. שלא ברצונך לקחתי מבשר שלך: לא בשר נבילה כו'. שנתתי לנכרי: לא כולא מינה כו'. אינו נאמן זה הטבח לאסור מקולין של העיר. וכי בשביל שזה הטבח הטעה את חבירו ומכר טרפה לנכרי למכרה במקולין, ותבירו לקח מהנכרי נאסור בשביל זה ליקח בשר היום מן הנכרי במקולין, הואיל ורוב טבחי העיר ישראל. והכי איתא הסוגיא בפרק "גיד הנשה" בבבלי (צה, א): נחת לתמן. לבבל, וראה אותן מקילין

משנת אליהו

לא צריכא דלא בהר הבית קדש. בפסחים ז' א' בתוס' ד"ה בהר הבית הקשו בשם ר"י היאך נמצאו שם הא אמר פ' הרואה לא יכנס בהר הבית במעות הצרורין בסדינו ותירצו דדוקא בסדינו בפרהסיא דגנאי הוא כמו הולך לסחורה אבל בצנעה שרי והתוי"ט הביא הקושי' זו דוקא לפי' הא' של הרע"ב בפ' בתרא דברכות דאפונדתו הוא אזור חלול ששמים בו מעות ודבריו מוכיחים דלפי' הב' שהוא פי' הרמב"ם שהוא בגד הזיעה א"כ ל"ק דשרי לילך במעות כיון דבמתני' לא איירי באיסור לילך שם עם מעות ושגגה היא דהא הרמב"ם גופי' בחבורו פ"ז מהל' ב"ה הלכה ב' פוסק דאסור ליכנס במעות צרורין בסדינו ולא באפונדתו ומולאו נראה שהוא משום דתוספתא ערוכה היא בפ"ו דברכות לא יכנס להר הבית במעות צרורין בסדינו כו' ולא באפונדתו המגורה לו מבחוץ משום שנאמר שמור רגליך כו' שלא ככ"מ שליין למתני' ולשון התוס' מעות שבסדינו כו' וכ"ה בתוס' ב"מ כ"ו א' ואפשר דבאפונדתו ס"ל כפי' הרמב"ם מדלא הקשו ממתני' דעדיפא לאקשויי מינה אם לא משום דבתוספתא מפורש מעות הקשו ממנה ואפשר דלשון התוספתא משמע דאפונדתו המגורה מבחוץ בלא מעות ג"כ אסור משום בזיון כדקאמר משום שנאמר כו' וכה"ג פי' מ"ש במתני' אפונדתו ושיטת רש"י דמתוספת' משמע דשניהם במעות איירי אלא דזה בסדינו וזה באפונדתו המגורה מבחוץ ורגילין לשום בה מעות ולכן פירש גם במתני' כן ולדעת הרמב"ם אי הוי גירסתו ג"כ מבחוץ בתוספתא צ"ל דבמתני' חשיב לה למילתא אחריתא דהא פירושו בגד הזיעה מלבוש שנותן תחת בגדיו לקבל הזיעה ואין רגילין לילך בו כ"א בבגד עליון עליו וא"כ לא שייך המגורה מבחוץ אלא דמילתא אחריתי הוא ותרוייהו אסירי משום בזיון ומזה הפירוש דפליגי רש"י ותוס' עם הרמב"ם נראה דנתחלקו ונפרדו שיטתם בסוגי' דפסחים במעות הנמצאות כו' דרש"י פי' דעיקר טעמא דהואיל ושוקי ירושלים עשויין להתכבד לא קאי רק להסביר דלמה בירושלים בשעת הרגל מעשר ולא חולין כמו בהר הבית דשם לעולם חולין אע"ג דיש לתלות בירושלים ממעות שקודם הרגל נפול כמו בהר הבית והיינו מטעם דשוקי ירושלים עשויין להתכבד אבל לא הר הבית דמשופע והיינו משום דלחילוקם בהר הבית היו יכולים לבוא עם מעות שלא כדרך בזיון וא"כ הא דבהר הבית אף בשעת הרגל חולין ע"כ משום דאמרינן קודם הרגל נפול ממה שהביאו לשם מעות חולין דבשעת הרגל גם מה שהביאו הוא מעשר וא"כ למה לא נימא הכי גבי ירושלים דקודם הרגל נפול אע"כ משום דעשויין להתכבד כו'. אבל הרמב"ם דשיטתו דלהר הבית אסור לבוא עם מעות בכל ענין כדפסק בחבורו בר"פ מהל' ב"ה. וטעמא דבהר הבית חולין מפרש הרמב"ם במתני' כמו דמשני בירושלמי שהגזברין מחללין המעות על הבהמה והמעות נעשו חולין ולא ימצא בהר הבית רק חולין לכן שיטתו בסוגי' דפסחים שם דטעמא דהואיל ושוקי ירושלים לא קאי אשינוי דהר הבית מירושלים בדינא דשעת הרגל. כדפירש במתני' טעמא דשעת הרגל משום שכל ישראל יש להם אז מעות מעשר בבואם לעלות לרגל וכן בהר הבית ג"כ מטעמא דירושל' שאין שם רק חולין אלא מפרש דקאי אירושלים ובשאר ימות השנה ולכן סתם הרמב"ם ז"ל בהלכות מ"ש וג"ר פרק ו' הלכה ט' י' מעות הנמצאות בירושלים כו' הרי אלו חולין הואיל ושוקי ירושלים מתכבדין בכל יום כו' בד"א בשאר ימות השנה אבל ברגל הכל מעשר מעות הנמצאות לפני סוחרי כו' והנמצאות בהר הבית לעולם חולין שמוקמן מתרומת הלשכה שמללום הגזברין על הבהמה. נראין דבריו להדיא דטעמא דהואיל לא קאי רק אשאר ימות השנה. רק שצ"ע למה לן טעמא על שאר ימות השנה בירושלים שרוב העיר חולין א"ל משום סמוך לרגל מאחריו ועי' בשיטה מקובצת לר' בצלאל בב"מ שם שכתב בשם הראב"ד דהטעם קאי על שאר ימות השנה בלבד דנימא משעת הרגל נשארו שם וגם צ"ע למה השמיט הרי"ף והרמב"ם כל סוגי' דפת שעיפשה וכן אוקימתות דאוקמוהו אמוראי במיבה של חולין כו' ופסק הרמב"ם שם הלכה י"א כסתמא דברייתא תיבה של חולין כו' דאזלינן בתר רובא וצ"ע ולשון התוס' שהקשו היאך נמצאו שם בהר הבית חולין תמוה שהוא נגד סוגי' דירושלמי שהגזברין היו מחללין ולשיטתם הי' להם להקשות אמאי בהר הבית אף ברגל חולין הא מביאין שם מעות מעשר ג"כ לשיטתם שאינו אסור להביא מעות לשם רק דרך בזיון וכ"ה שיטת רש"י וכרש"י שברי"ף מפורש משום בזיון ע"ש וצ"ע בדעת הרמב"ם הנ"ל: ה"ג היסח הדעת פסול וטעון עיבור צורה כו' כמ"ש בפנים. ועי' מה שפי' בקונטרס וכן נראה לי ברור שזהו טעם דרבינו הגדול משום דבפסחים (ל"ה א') פליגי בזה ר"ל ור"י ורבי יוחנן ס"ל דפסול טומאה הוי ור"י ורבי הושעיא דהכא בשיטתא חדא קיימין דר"י תלמידיה הוא וטעם סברת רבינו כדפרישית בקונטרס דבעזרה מספיקא דטומאה טהור כדאמרינן בפסחים (י"ט ב') עזרה רה"ר היא וספק ברה"ר טהור וכן הנמצא בירושלים ג"כ טהור מספק טומאה דמסקינן בעירובין (ק"א א') דירושלים רה"ר היא אמר שפרצו בה פרצות וכן מוכח סוגיא דפסחים (ס"ו א') ועי' תוס' שם ד"ה תוחב כו' דיש איסור רה"ר בירושלים כו' לאחר שנפרצו בה פרצות ועיין שם בי' דאיסורא דאורייתא כו' וכ"פ הרמב"ם בפ"ח מהל' ק"פ הל' י"ח ואף את"ל דירושלים כרמלית היא בחילוק הסוגיות והמסקנות אינו ענין לדינא דידן דהא פסק הרמב"ם בפרק כ' מהל' אבות הטומאה הל' ב' דכל שהוא כרמלית לענין שבת הוי רה"ר לענין טומאה והוא בפ"ו דטהרות וא"כ אף דאיכא למיחש לטומאה ספק טומאה טהור

עין משפט נר מצוה

י א מיי' פרק י"ח ממ"א הלי"א טור שו"ע יו"ד סימן קי סעיף ג:

יא ב מיי' שם הלכה יב טור שו"ע שם סימן סג:

נוסחת הבבלי

(א) א"ר חייא בשם ר"י כו': (ב) ר"י בר חנינא כו' ר"י בר חנינא כו': (ג) ר"א בר' חנינא כו' ומפיק לשוקיה א"ל כו' מזבין קופר גבי טבחא כו' בר נש נחית משוני בשר איסקופתיה גו נהרא אינשיתא וסליק לי' כו' בשוקא מעין קופר כו':

הגהות הגר"א

[א] ה"ג היסח הדעת פסול וטעון עיבור צורה. וה"פ דהא איכא למ"ד דס"ל היסח הדעת פסול הגוף הוי שהוא מעלה בקדשים שנפסלין בכך ואפילו יבוא אליהו ויאמר שלא נטמא כל אותן הימים שהסיח דעתו מהן אין שומעין לו ולהך מ"ד לא בעי עיבור צורה בפסול דהיסח הדעת ור' הושעיא ס"ל כאידך מ"ד דהיסח הדעת פסול טומאה הוי מחשש שמא נטמא וכיון דלא חזינא ליה שנטמא אלא חששא בעלמא לכן א"א לשרפו בלא עיבור צורה שמא לא נטמא וזהו דאמר פסול וטעון עיבור צורה: [ב] א"ר יוסי ויאות לאכלו אין את יכול כו' לשריפה אין

ציון ירושלים

גליון הש"ס

חד בר נש. אדם אחד הלך לרחוץ בשר בנהר, ונפל מידו, והלך לו. חזר ורצה ללקחו מתוך הנהר. א"ל רב: אסור לך בשר זה, שאני אומר: הראשון שטפו נהר, והביא בשר אחר של נבלה במקומו: חד בר נש. אדם אחד הוה מהלך בשוק טעון בשר, בא עוף ששמו 'דיה' וחטפו ממנו והשליכו במקום אחר, ורצה האדם ההוא לחזור ללקחו. א"ל רב: אסור לך הא, שאני אומר נבילה היתה נושאת וזרקתו, והאי שלקחו ממנו אכלה: גינאי. נהר ששמו 'גינאי' שטף נודות של יין של ישראל, ומצאוהו אח"כ: יחכמון וכו'. יראו שופכי יין, אם מכירין קשריהן שקושרין הנודות יחד, ויש להן סימן בקשרים — מותרים: נקוניקה. מין קנקן נמצא בבית הכנסת של עיר ששמה 'בולי', והיה מלא יין: אמר יחכמון וכו'.

ריבב"ן

חילל. תהי בה ר' יוחנן וכי אומרים לו לאדם חטא בשביל שתזכה בהקרבתה אלא אמר ר' יוחנן ממתין לה עד שתומס ומייתי שתי בהמות אחת לעולה ואחד לשלמים ומסיק דבכל מידי *)דאיכא לספוקה: ירושלמי אמר ר' יוחנן אומר לאדם צא ומעול בקדשים אלא אם רוב זכרים עולות ואם רוב נקבות זבחי שלמים ואין השלמים באין מן הזכרים ומן הנקבות כיצד עושה מוליאן לחולין ע"י מום וחוזר ועושה אותן עולות ר' זעירא אמר כמו דאתמר תמן תניי ב"ד על המותרות שיקרבו עולות כן אומר הכא תניי בית דין על האובדות שיקרבו עולות אמר ר' יוסי בר' יעקב אין זה מזיד בתמיה א"ל מכיון שהוא תנויי ב"ד אין זה מזיד: הראוי לפסח. כגון זכר ובן שנה ויש לספק שמא פסח הוא הנמצא וסמוך לפסח שלשים יום ושמא קנאו לצורך פסח ועדיין איכא לספוקי באשם נזיר ובאשם מצורע שהן בני שנה אבל לא שכיחן: ממשכנין את מוצאיה. שיביא נסכיה משלו בעל כרחו: מתני' נכרי ששלח עולתו. דגרסינן בחולין פ"ק איש מה ת"ל איש איש מלמד שהנכרים נודרים נדרים ונדבות כישראל: על כהן גדול שמת שתהא מנחתו. דהיינו עשירית האיפה שלו קריבה משל צבור. ואמרינן בפרק התכלת [דף נב] א"ר אבהו ב' תקנות הוו דאורייתא משל צבור כיון דחזו דמידחקא לשכה תקינו דליגבו מיורשין כיון דחזו דקא פשעי בה אוקמוה אדאורייתא: ר' יהודה אומר משל יורשין באה ושלימה היתה קריבה. ותניא בפ' התכלת שלימה שחרית ושלימה בין הערבים וקומץ לבונה הבא עם המבית ין**) [פליגי אמוראי התם] ועוד תניא התם כה"ג שמת ולא מינו כה"ג אחר תחתיו מנין שתהא מנחתו קריבה משל יורשין ת"ל והכהן המשיח תחתיו מבניו יעשה אותה יכול יקריבנה חציים ת"ל אותה אותה שלמה ולא חסרה דברי ר' יהודה ר' שמעון אומר חק עולם חקה משל עולם תהא, כלומר, משל צבור: מתני' על המלח ועל העצים שיהו הכהנים נאותין בהן. אמרי' בזבחים [דף כא] אמר שמואל ל"ש אלא לקרבן אבל לאכילה לא ואסיק [לקרבן] לאכילת קרבנן ומאי אכילה אכילה דחולין ואע"ג דאמר מר מלחו אותה שיאכלו עמה חולין ותרומה כדי שתהא המנחה נאכלת על השובע ויהא טעם קדשים בפיו ויאכל חוץ לעזרה חולין ותרומה

תקלין חדתין

כבשר שנתעלם מן העין, והחמיר עליהן: משזגי בשר אסקופתיה. רחץ בשר בנהר ונפל לנהר, ואזל ואחר כך רצה ליקחה מהנהר: ההיא שטף כו'. אסיר לו משום חומרא, שבשר ההוא שטף הנהר והביא אחר דנבילה: דייתא. חיה ששמה 'דיה': וטלקתא. והשליכה: מסביניה. רצה האדם ליקח הבשר שהשליכה: בשר דנבילה כו'. שהחיה היתה טעונה אפשר בשר דנבילה והשליכה, ולקחה זה הבשר, וכל כך החמיר במקום שרצה מקילים: גינאי. שם נהר המוזכר בפ"ק דחולין: זיקין. נודות של יין: יחכמו כו'. יכירו בעליהן קשרי הנודות אם שלהן הוא, והביא אהנהו עובדי אבג דמיירי בבשר שנמצא בנהר: דבולי = שם מקום: סיקוריא. אותן שסקרו בסיקרא לרשום הסביות: באסטרטיא. בשוק: דגופתא = שם מקום: משום מציאה. שכבר נתייאשו בעליהן: משונת הים. הן כיפין הסמוכין לגמל הים: משום שחיטת הנכרים. דרוב מהלכי דרכים שם היו ישראל: דבית רבי. מבית רבי היה הגדי: דגובנא. גבינה: בפונדקא דלוי. שהיו שם רוב ישראל: מכריזין. אפי' בנמצא בסרטיא: את כו'. אילו היית מוצא, לא היית לוקח בלא הכרזה: הפיוסא ולפנים. מקום שרבים שם: אפילו כן אשתכח. אפילו הכי שהיה רגיל לומר הכי, מ"מ פ"א מצא בכה"ג ולא נסיב. א"נ: דקאי ארבי מנא, אע"פ שאמרו לו בשם אביו שהיה מיקל בדבר, אפילו הכי פעם אחת מצא ולא עשה הלכה למעשה להקל לעצמו: מתני' זכרים עולות. דתלינן שמירושלים באו לשם. ובגמרא מפרש טעמא: הראוי לפסחים. זכר בן שנה מן הכבשים או מן העזים, והמוצאו מותר להקריבו לפסחו: ל' יום. ששואלין ודורשין בהלכות פסח: ממשכנין את מוצאיה. בהמות שמצאו מירושלים למגדל עדר, שיביאו משלהן נסכיהן: עולתו. שמקבלין מהן נדרים ונדבות, דדרשינן "איש איש" — להביא את הנכרים: ר"י אומר: משל יורשים. מפרש בגמרא: על המלח כו' שלא יהיו מועלין באפרה. בגמ' מפרש: הפסולות. אם נפסלו הקינין שלקחו בדמים שנתנו בעליהם לשופר, תנאי ב"ד שיקח אותן משל צבור. ומקנין אותם לבעלים שיצאו י"ח בהם: המספק את הקינין. שקבל על עצמו לספק בכל עת שיצטרך קינין, וכל האחריות עליו, ולכן אם נפסלו עליו לספק: גמ' ה"ג: ואין השלמים כו'. וכי זכרים עולות אינם ולא שלמים? דלמא שלמים הוי, והיכי מקריב לה עולה? לבא בדמיהן שנו. הן בעצמם אינם קרבים כלל, אלא דמיירי: אם בא אדם לזה מצוא תקנה לבהמות אלו, ובא לקבל על עצמו טוב כל דמיה שהן בספק ולהוציאן לחולין ולהקדיש את דמיהן, אם זכרים הן — נתחייב אף בדמי עולה, דחיישינן שמא עולות הן: כיצד הוא עושה — מוציא לחולין כו'. כלומר, אע"ג דקדושת הגוף לא מתחלל בלא מום, כדתנן (מעילה יט) "אין מועל אחר מועל במוקדשין", דהיינו קרבן אחד של הקדש אי אפשר להיות ב' מעילות זו אחר זו, דכיון שמעל הראשון יצא לחולין, אלא בבהמה, וכ"ש בלבד דבהמה של קדשי מזבח הראויה לקרבן אינה יוצאה לחולין כשהיא תמימה — שאני התם דלא מכוין לאפוקינהו לחולין, הלכך קדושת הגוף לא מיתחיל. אבל הכא ועושה אותן עולות": ואין זה מזיד. דהא מכוין לאפוקינהו לחולין. ור"מ הוא דס"ל הכי בלחוד, ו[...] לקמיה כיחידאה ודלא כהלכתא: ומשני: מכיון שתנאי ב"ד כו'. דבתחלה נתקדש לשלמים על תנ[...] ואינו מזיד הוא: אומרים לו לאדם צא ומעל כו'. דכל בהמות מזבח אסור לחללן תמימין, [...] מדבר, וזה שבא ליטלן לחוב בדמים נאמר לו שימעול לחללה מיד, בשביל שתזכה לתקן הקרבנ[...] דלשלמים כשרים גם נקבות, ואי חזינן רובא זכרים, אמרינן מסתמא לא הוקדשו אלא לעולות [...]

בעי משיזגה אסקיפתיה בגו נהרא ואינשתה, ואזיל ליה. חזר בעי מיסבינא אמר ליה רב: אסור לך, דנא אמר: ההיא שטף נהרא [א] ואייתי חורי דנבילה תחתוי חד א) בר נש הוה מהלך בשוקא טעין קופד, (א) אתא דייתא וחטפתיה מיניה, וטלקתיה. חזר בעי מיסבינא. [ב] א"ל רב: אסור לך, דנא אמר בשר דנבילה הוות טעינא, וטלקתיה ונסבא ההוא אוחרנא. גינאי שטף זיקין, אתא עובדא קומי ר' יצחק בר"א ואמר: יחכמון שפייא קיטרהון. נקוניקה אשתכח בכנישתא דבולי, אתא עובדא קומי רבי ירמיה, אמר: יתחכמון סקוריי' עבידתהון. גדי ב) צלי אשתכח באסרטי דגופתא והתירוהו משום שני דברים, משום מציאה ומשום רוב מהלכי דרכים. משום מציאה — דתני: ג) אהמציל מיד הארי, מיד הגיים, משונת הים, ומשונת הנהר, ומאיסרטיא גדולה, ומפלטיא גדולה — הרי אלו שלו, מפני שהבעלים מתייאשין מהן. משום רוב מהלכי דרכים — משום שחיטת נכרי ואישתכח מן דבית רבי. עיגול דגובנא אישתכח בפונדקא דלוי והתירוהו משום שני דברים משום מציאה בומשום רוב מהלכי דרכים. משום מציאה — דתני: המציל מיד הגיים, מיד הארי, משונת הים, ומשונת הנהר, מאיסרטיא גדולה, ומפלטיא גדולה — הרי אלו שלו, מפני שהבעלים מתייאשין מהן. משום רוב מהלכי דרכים — משום גבינת נכרי ואישתכח מן דר"א בר' יוסי. א"ר מנא קומי ר' יוסי: ואנן חמיין רבנן מכריזין. א"ל את אין הוויתה משכח לא נסבת רבי יונה אבוך לא אמר כן, אלא אמר: הלואי כד נשכח נשכח מן פיוסא ולגוא אפילו כן אשכח ולא נסיב.§

הלכה ג מתני'

גבהמה ד) שנמצאת מירושלם ועד מגדל עדר, וכמדתה לכל רוח, זכרים — עולות, נקבות — זבחי שלמים. רבי יהודה אומר: הראוי לפסחים [ג] לפסחים, קודם לרגל ל' יום. בראשונה היו ממשכנין את מוצאיה עד שהוא (ב) מביא (עמה) נסכיה. חזרו להיות מניחין אותה ובורחין. התקינו ב"ד שיהו נסכיה באין משל צבור. אר"ש ה) ז' דברים התקינו ב"ד וזה אחד מהן: ינכרי ששלח עולתו ממדינת הים ושלח עמה נסכים — קריבין משלו, ואם לאו — קריבין משל צבור. וכן הגר שמת והניח זבחים, אם יש לו נסכים — קריבין משלו, ואם לאו — קריבין משל צבור. ותנאי ב"ד הוא על כה"ג שמת שתהא מנחתו קריבה משל צבור. רבי יהודה אומר: ימשל יורשין, ושלימה היתה קריבה. יעל המלח ועל העצים שיהו הכהנים נאותין בהן. חועל הפרה שלא יהו מועלין באפרה. ועל הקינין הפסולות שיהו באות משל צבור. טר' יוסי אומר: המספק את הקינין הוא מספק את הפסולות.§ גמ' [א] ר' הושעיא רבה אמר: לבא ו) בדמיהן שנו. א"ל רבי יוחנן: אומרים לו לאדם צא ומעול בקדשים? אלא, הילכו בהן אחר הרוב, אם רוב זכרים — עולות, אם רוב נקבות — זבחי שלמים. ואין השלמים באין מן הזכרים ומן הנקבות?! כיצד הוא עושה? מוציאן לחולין, וחוזר ועושה אותן עולות.

קרבן העדה

יראו רושמי החביות בסיקרי, אם יכירו שהוא מרושם שלהם — ה"ל סימן, ומותר: באסרטיא דגופתא. ברחוב של עיר ששמה 'גופתא': משונת הים. מקום שהים מגיע לשם בשעה שהוא סוער: משום שחיטת הנכרי. דאזלינן בתר רוב מהלכי דרכים, ובדרך ההוא היו הרוב ישראל: ואשתכח דבית ר'. ונתברר אח"כ שהיה הגדי משל בית ר', וכדין התירוהו: עיגול דגובנא. עיגול של גבינה מצאו בפונדק של לוי, והיו שם רוב ישראל: ומשום רוב מהלכי דרכים. ולא אסרו משום גבינות הנכרים: ואשתכח מן דר' אלעזר בר' יוסי. ומצאו שהיה הגבינה של ראב"י וכדין התירוהו (והר"א פולדא לא דק): א"ר מנא. לפני ר' יוסי: ואנו רואין שחכמים מכריזין אפילו מוצאין בפלטיא הגדולה ושאר מקומות כיוצא בהן: א"ל. אתה אם היית מוצא דבר לא היית נוטלו לעצמך? ורבי יונה אביך לא אמר כן, אלא אמר: הלואי שאמצא מציאה לפנים מן פיוסרום, והוא מקום שרבים מצויין שם, ולא אכריזנה: אפילו כן. שמא דס"ם קאמר, אפ"ה פעם אחרת מצא ר' יונה לפנים מן פיוסרום, והחמיר על עצמו, והכריזו:

הלכה ג מתני' זכרים עולות. שאנו תולין שיצאו מירושלים, ורוב זכרים שבירושלים הן עולות, ורוב נקבות זבחי שלמים: הראוי לפסחים. זכר בן שנה מן הכבשים או מן העזים — פסחים. והמוצאו מותר להקריבו לפסחו: קודם לרגל שלשים יום. משעה שמתחילין לדרוש בהל' פסח, ואדם מפריש את פסחו: ממשכנין את מוצאיה. המוצא עולות או שלמים, היו ממשכנין אותו עד שיביא נסכיה משלו: שלשה עשרונים לפר, ושני עשרונים לאיל, ועשרון לכבש: מניחין אותה ובורחין. כדי שלא להתחייב בנסכיה: שבעה דברים קחשיב להו ואזיל: נכרי ששלח עולתו. דדרשינן "איש איש" — שנכרים נודרים נדרים ונדבות כישראל: שתהא מנחתו. עשירית האיפה שכהן גדול מקריב בכל יום מחציתה בבוקר ומחציתה בערב: קריבה משל צבור. בגמ' מפרש טעמייהו דר"ש ור' יהודה: ושלימה היתה קריבה. כשהיא באה משל צבור לר"ש, או משל יורשים לר"י — עשרון שלם היתה קריבה ולא חצי עשרון. ובגמרא מפרש מנ"ל: שיהיו הכהנים נאותים בהן. דוקא לאכילת קרבנות, אבל לאכילת חולין, אפילו אותן הנאכלין בעזרה כדי שיאכלו הקרבנות על השובע — אין נאותין בהן: שלא יהיו מועלין באפרה. בגמ' מפרש לה: ועל הקינין הפסולות. המחוייבין קינין מביאין מעות ונותנין לשופר, וב"ד לוקחין המעות וקונין בהן קינין, והבעלים הולכים להם, וסומכין על הב"ד שיקריבו קיניהן. ואם פרחו הקינים או נמצאו פסולים — תנאי ב"ד הוא שיקחו אחרים מתרומת הלשכה, ומקנים אותן לבעלים, ויוצאים בהן ידי חובתן: המספק את הקינים. אותן שפסקו עם הגזברים למכור להם כל הקינין הצריכין — הוא חייב להחליף כל שימצא בו פסול: גמ' לבא בדמיהן שנו. כלומר, היכי ודאי לא קרבה. וה"ק: אם בא אדם זה המוצאה לעשות לה תקנה, ובא לקבל על עצמו חוב כל דמים שהוא (שהוא) בספק ולהוציאה לחולין, ולהקדיש את דמיה. אם זכר הוא — נתחייב אף בדמי עולה, דחיישינן שמא עולות הן: אומרים לאדם וכו'. דכל בהמות הקדש הראויה למזבח אסור לחללן, דכתיב "אם בהמה טמאה ופדה בערכך", ואמר מר: בבעלי מומין שיפדו הכתוב מדבר, אבל תמימים — לא. וזה שבא לימלך ולחוב בדמיה, וכי נאמר לו עמוד וחטא לחללה מזיד בשביל שתזכה לתקן הקרבתה של בהמה זו?: אם רוב זכרים עולות. וה"פ דמתני': אם רוב בהמות שנמצאו זכרים — כולן עולות, ואם רובן נקבות — אף זכרים שבהן שלמים: ופריך: ואין השלמים באין מן הזכרים. נמי? וא"כ, אף זכרים ניחוש שמא שלמים הן: ומשני: כיצד הוא עושה מוציאן לחולין. ע"מ שיחזרו להיות עולות. ואין זה חטא, דהא עכ"פ מקריבה ע"ג המזבח. ויותר נ"ל דאף זה מן הקושיא: אף לר"י קשיא, כילד הוא עושה וכו' אלא שמוציאן לחולין. א"כ אף לר' הושעיא ל"ק. ומשני: דתנאי ב"ד

משנת אליהו

[illegible]

*) דברי רבינו המחבר מעורבבין וכצ"ל ומסיק דבכל מידי דאיכא לספוקה מספקינן כגון אם הוא זכר וב[...] ב"ד אין זה מזיד וא"כ צריך לציין על המשנה ממשכנין את מוצאיה וכו'. **) נ"ל אם צריכה שני קמצים [...]

א) ירושלמי ע"ז פ"ב הל"ח: ב) עי' ב"מ כד ב: ג) שם ע"א בשם רשב"א ובשקלים הנספח לבבלי רשב"י: ד) קדושין נה א: ה) מנחות נא ב נא ב וע"ש: ו) עי' קדושין נה א ב:

עין משפט נר מצוה

יב א מיי' פרק ו מגזילה הלכה ג טוש"ע חו"מ סימן רנט סעיף ז:

יג ב מיי' פרק ד משחיטה הל"ח טוש"ע יו"ד סימן א סעיף ד:

יד ג מיי' פרק ו מפסה"ק הל"ח:

טו ד מיי' פרק ג ממעשה"ק הל"ה ופ"ד משקלים הל"ג:

טז ה מיי' פרק ד משקלים הל"ד:

יז ו מיי' פרק ג מתמידין הלכ"ב:

יח ז מיי' פרק ח ממעילה הל"ו:

יט ח מיי' שם פ"ב הלכה ה:

כ ט מיי' פ"ז מכלי המקדש הל"ט:

נוסחת הבבלי

(א) וחטפתה נמייה וטלקתא חזר אזל בעי מסבינה כו' ההוא תחותיה גינזי שטף כו' נקוניא (כי קא) אישתכח בבנישתא דבולי כו' דתני ר"ש ב"א כו' א"ר מונא קומי דר' ואנא חמוי כו': (ב) מביא נסכים כו':

הגהות הגר"א

[א] כל הפסקא נדפסת בחלוף גרסאו' ומבולבלת מאוד וה"ג ואין השלמים באין מן הזכרים ומן הנקבות ר' הושעיא רבה אמר לבא בדמיהן שנו כילד הוא עושה מוליא לחולין וחוזר ועושה אותן עולות א"ר אסי לר' יעקב בר אחא ואין זה מזיד א"ל מכיון שתנאי ב"ד הוא אין זה מזיד א"ל ר' יוחנן אומרין לאדם צא ומעל בקדשים אלא הולכין בהן אחר הרוב אם רוב זכרים עולות אם רוב נקבות זבחי שלמים א"ר זעירא כמה דאת אמר תמן תנאי ב"ד על האובדו' שיקרבו עולות כן את אמר אוף הכא תנאי ב"ד על האובדות שיקרבו עולות כצ"ל. ועי' בת"ח כי הוא מפ' ג' הגאון ז"ל:

ציון ירושלים

ועל הקינן הפסולו' עי' תוי"ט ותוספות שם ובמחכ"ת אישתמיטתיה ש"ס ערוך סוטה דף ח ואמרי דאתון וקיימין אקורבניא וכ"כ

גליון הש"ס

קבוע כמע"מ אף לקולא. ועי' בש"ך ביו"ד סי' קי ס"ק טו: [א] עי' תוספות חולין דף לה ע"ב ד"ה אסיק ול"ע: [ב] עי' תוס' ב"מ דף כד: ד"ה אתא ועי' ברשב"א בתה"א בית ד' שער ב': [ג] עי' ק"ע והמוצאו מותר להקריבו לפסחו כן הוא לשון הרע"ב והיינו שמוכרו לעצמו ועי' בתוי"ט ול"ע דהא אין מכר אלא הוצאת הדבר מרשות לרשות עי' בטור חו"מ סי' קפה ושו"ת מהרי"ט ח"א סי' לג נתעורר בזה. ונראה כיון דבשעת קנין קונה אותה להיות הקדש לפסח לא נכנס לרשותו והוי כקונ' בשביל אחר ומשיכתו כמשיכת ההקדש ודוק:

הוא, וכו' ול"ק לר"י: כמה דאת אמר תמן. בריש פרקין: תנאי ב"ד הוא על האובדות שיקריבו עולות. הלכך לא חיישינן דלמא שלמים הן: אין זה מזיד. בתמיה, וכי אין זה כמחלל מזיד שלמים על עולות: מכיון שתנאי ב"ד הוא. עקרו לשם שלמים מינייה וכאילו לא נתקדש מעולם לשם שלמים, ואין זה מחלל במזיד: עד דאנא תמן. כשהייתי בבבל שמעתי ששאל ר"י לשמואל הפריש שקלו ומת מה יעשה בו: מותר עשירית האיפה של כה"ג. כגון שהפריש מעות לעשירית האיפה של היום, וניתותר שאינו ראוי למחר, מה יעשה בו: יוליכם לים המלח. לא נהנין ולא מועלין בו: חוצה אותה ואח"כ מקדשה. אבל הכלי שמודדין בו העשרון לא היה קודש: מקדשה. כל העשרון בעשרון: ה"ג: מקריב מחצה ומחצה אבד. כ"ה במנחות פרק "התכלת": ואיירי כגון שנטמא מחצה של בין הערבים, שמביא עשרון שלם וחוצהו ומקריב מחצה ומחצה אבד, שמעינן דאינה קדושה לחצאין, אלא כולו בבת אחת, וכיון דלא צריך למחצה השני בכבר נתקדש — הרי הוא אבד, וקשיא לר"י: שכן אפי' מעות שנתותר מעשירית האיפה סובר ר"י ילכו לים המלח, דס"ל מותר עשירית האיפה, וכדאמר ר"י בסמוך, וכ"ש הסולת שניתותר: ה"ג: מתניתא פליגא על ר"י נמצאו וכו': נמצאו ב' חציין וכו'. קאי אכה"ג שהקריב מחצה שחרית ומינו אחר תחתיו, מביא עשרון שלם, וחוצהו, ומקריב, ומחצה אבד. נמצאו ב' חצאין אובדין וב' חצאים קריבין: תעובר צורתו ויפסול בלינה. וקשיא לר"י: למה ליה עיבור צורה, ולמה יוצא לבית השריפה, הא לא נתקדש מעולם! ואי משום מותר עשירית האיפה — יוליכם לים המלח, אבל שריפה לא צריך: פתר לה. למתני' כר"י, דאמר: עשרון מקדש, וכיון שצריך ליתנו לתוך העשרון כדי לחצותו, דלכ"ע למצוה צריך להביא עשרון שלם מביתו כדי לחצותו, א"כ כבר נתקדש ויוצא לבית השריפה: כשהכהן מתקרב תחלה לעבודה. והיינו יום חנוכו, צריך להביא עשירית האיפה משלו. שנאמר "זה קרבן אהרן ובניו אשר יקריבו לה' ביום המשח אותו עשירית האיפה וגו'" ו"בניו" היינו כהנים הדיוטים: ועובד בידו. הוא עצמו מקריבה: בו ביום נתקרב בתחלה לעבודה. כהן שלא עבד כל ימיו ונתמנה להיות כהן גדול: מביא שתים. שתי מנחות מעשירית האיפה: אחת לחנוכו. ככהן הדיוט: ואחת לחובת היום. שהוא חביתי כ"ג שמקריב בכל יום: תופיני. כתיב "מרבכת תביאנה תופיני", וקדריש: בשעת הבאה אז תאפנה, אבל לא בלילה שלפניו: ואין בשחרית תופיני. היינו קודם עלות השחר לא יאפו אותן: ופריך: והא תנינן. בתמיד פ"ק: העמידו עושי חביתין בשחרית קודם עלות השחר לעשות חביתין. ושמעינן שבלילה היתה נאפית: ומשני: לעשות חמין לרבכם העמידוהו אז, אבל לאפות לא היו אופין עד עלות השחר (ודברי הר' אליהו פולדה בסוגיא זו אינן מחוורים): מטגנה בתחלה, ואח"כ אופה אותה בתנור: תאפנה נא. בשעת אפייתה בתנור תהא נא, כמו "אל תאכלו ממנו נא", כלומר, תהא מבושלת קצת ולא כל צרכה, והיינו טגון. דהא מודו כ"ע דתרווייהו בעינן, דכתיב "על מחבת בשמן" וכתב "תופיני": תיאפנה רבה. אפיות הרבה אופה ומטגנה ואופה:

נוסחאות ישנות

תורה אור

עולות א"ר זְעֵירָא: כְּמָה דְּאַתְּ אָמַר תַּמָּן (א) תְּנַאי ב"ד הוּא עַל הַמּוּתָרוֹת (הָאוֹבְדוֹת) שֶׁיִּקָּרְבוּ עוֹלוֹת, כֵּן אַתְּ מַר אוּף הָכָא: תְּנַאי ב"ד הוּא עַל הָאוֹבְדוֹת שֶׁיִּקָּרְבוּ עוֹלוֹת. א"ר יוֹסֵי לְרַבִּי יַעֲקֹב בַּר אַחָא: אֵין זֶה מֵזִיד? א"ל מִכֵּיוָן שֶׁהוּא תְּנַאי ב"ד אֵין זֶה מֵזִיד.§ א"ר א) יֵסָא: עַד דַּאֲנָא תַּמָּן שְׁמָעִית קָל רַב יְהוּדָה שָׁאַל לִשְׁמוּאֵל: הִפְרִישׁ שִׁקְלוֹ וּמֵת? א"ל יִפְּלוּ לִנְדָבָה. וּמוֹתַר עֲשִׂירִית הָאֵיפָה שֶׁלּוֹ, רַבִּי יוֹחָנָן אָמַר: ביוֹלִיכֵם לְיָם הַמֶּלַח. ר"א אָמַר: יִפְּלוּ לִנְדָבָה. עֲשִׂירִית ג) הָאֵיפָה שֶׁל כ"ג רַבִּי יוֹחָנָן אָמַר: חוֹצֶה אוֹתָהּ ואח"כ מְקַדְּשָׁהּ. רשב"ל אָמַר: גמְקַדְּשָׁהּ ואח"כ חוֹצֶה אוֹתָהּ. מַתְנִיתָא פְּלִיגִי עַל רַבִּי יוֹחָנָן: מַקְרִיב ג) מֶחֱצָה וּמֶחֱצָה אָבֵד. — פָּתַר לָהּ שֶׁכֵּן אפי' מָעוֹת יֵלְכוּ לְיָם הַמֶּלַח. מַתְנִיתָא פְּלִיגִי עַל [א] ר"ש בֶּן לָקִישׁ: נִמְצְאוּ שְׁנֵי חֲצָאִין קְרֵיבִין וּשְׁנֵי חֲצָאִין אֲבוּדִין, וְתָנֵי עֲלָהּ: מֶחֱצָה רִאשׁוֹן דוּמֶחֱצָה שֵׁנִי — תְּעוּבַּר צוּרָתָן וְיֵצְאוּ לְבֵית הַשְּׂרֵיפָה. — פָּתַר לָהּ [ב] [א] (ב) כר' יִשְׁמָעֵאל, דְּאָמַר: הָעִשָּׂרוֹן מְקַדֵּשׁ. כְּשֶׁהַכֹּהֵן ד) מִתְקָרֵב תְּחִילָּה לַעֲבוֹדָה מֵבִיא עֲשִׂירִית (ג) הָאֵיפָה שֶׁלּוֹ [ג] וְעוֹבְדָהּ בְּיָדוֹ. יא' כה"ג וְאֶחָד כֹּהֵן הֶדְיוֹט שֶׁעָבְדוּ עַד שֶׁלֹּא הֵבִיאוּ עֲשִׂירִית הָאֵיפָה שֶׁלָּהֶם — [ד] עֲבוֹדָתָן כְּשֵׁירָה. רַבִּי ה) מָנָא בָּעֵי מֵימַר: יָבוֹ בַּיּוֹם שֶׁנִּתְקָרֵב תְּחִילָּה לַעֲבוֹדָה בּוֹ בַּיּוֹם נִתְמַנָּה לִהְיוֹת כֹּהֵן גָּדוֹל — מֵבִיא שְׁתַּיִם, אַחַת לְחִינּוּכוֹ וְאַחַת לְחוֹבַת הַיּוֹם. "תּוּפִינֵי" — [ג] בִּשְׁעַת הֲבָאָה תּוּפִינֵי, וְאֵין בְּשַׁחֲרִית תּוּפִינֵי. וְהָא תְּנִינַן: ו) חהֶעֱמִידוּ עוֹשֵׂה חֲבִיתִּין לַעֲשׂוֹת חֲבִיתִּין! א"ר חִיָּיא בַּר *אַחָא: לַעֲשׂוֹת חַמִּין *לִרְבוּכָה. "תּוּפִינֵי", רַבִּי ז) יֵסָא בְּשֵׁם ר' חֲנִינָה: מְטַגְּנָהּ ואח"כ אוֹפֶה אוֹתָהּ, רַבִּי אַחָא בְּשֵׁם ר' חֲנִינָה: טאוֹפֶה אוֹתָהּ ואח"כ מְטַגְּנָהּ. [ה] "תּוּפִינֵי" — תֵּאָפֶינָה נָא. רַבִּי אוֹמֵר: יתֵּאָפֶינָה *נָאָה. רַבִּי דּוֹסָא אוֹמֵר: תֵּאָפֶינָה *רִיבָּה. אָתְיָין אִלֵּין פַּלְגְּוָותָא כְּהִינֵין פַּלְגְּוָותָא. מ"ד תֵּאָפֶינָה נָאָה — כמ"ד *אוֹפָהּ ואח"כ מטגנ' ומ"ד תאפינ' נָא כמ"ד* מְטַגְּנָהּ. ואח"כ אוֹפָהּ. [ו] לֹא סוֹף דָּבָר שֶׁמֵּת, אֶלָּא כאֲפִילוּ נִטְמָא, וַאֲפִילוּ נִדְחָה מִמּוּם. תָּנֵי (ד) (ר' יוֹסֵי בֶּן עֲזַי) ר' יְהוּדָה בַּר פַּזִּי דְּבַר דְּלָיָה: וַאֲפִילוּ נִדְחָה מִמּוּם. מִנַּיִן ח) לְכֹהֵן גָּדוֹל שֶׁמֵּת וְלֹא מִינּוּ *אַחֵר תַּחְתָּיו שֶׁתְּהֵא מִנְחָתוֹ קְרֵיבָה מִשֶּׁל יוֹרְשִׁים? ת"ל "מִבָּנָיו יַעֲשֶׂה אוֹתָהּ". יָכוֹל יְבִיאֶנָּה לַחֲצָיִים — ת"ל "אוֹתָהּ" — כּוּלָּהּ אָמַרְתִּי, דִּבְרֵי רַבִּי יְהוּדָה. ר"ש אוֹמֵר: אֵינָהּ בָּאָה אֶלָּא מִשֶּׁל צִבּוּר, [ז] שֶׁנֶּאֱמַר "חֹק עוֹלָם" (מִמִּי שֶׁהַבְּרִיּוֹת שֶׁלּוֹ) מִי שֶׁהַבְּרִית כְּרוּתָה לוֹ, "כָּלִיל תָּקְטָר" — כָּלִיל לְהַקְטָרָה.§ "כֹּהֵן גָּדוֹל שֶׁמֵּת" וכו'.§ רַבִּי בָּא בַּר מָמָל בָּעֵי: מְחַלְּפָה ט) שִׁיטָּתֵיהּ דר"ש [ח] תַּמָּן אָמַר: מִשֶּׁל יוֹרְשִׁין, וְהָכָא אָמַר: מִשֶּׁל צִבּוּר! (ה) ,א"ר חִיָּיה בַּר

(margin: ויקרא ו; ארא; לרככה; רכה; נויי; כהן; שם; מטגנה ואח"כ אופה / אופה אותה ואח"כ מטגנה)

ריבב"ן

דבעזרה אסור דאין יכול להביא חולין בעזרה ואעפ"י שבאכילת חולין לצורך אכילת קדשים הן מלח של הקדש לא יאכל עמהן: ועל הפרה שלא יהיו מועלין באפרה. בפ' התכלת פריך וכי תקנה דרבנן היא מדאורייתא היא דכתיב חטאת היא מלמד שמועלין בה. בה מועלין ולא באפרה אמר רב אשי שתי תקנות הוו דאורייתא בה מועלין באפרה אין מועלין כיון דחזו דקא מזלזלין וקא עבדי מינה למכתן גזרו בה מעילה כיון דקא חזו דקא פרשו מספק הזאה אוקמוה אדאורייתא: ועל הקינין הפסולות. קיני חובה שנפסלו והיא אינה יודעת ואוכלת בקדשים

תקלין חדתין

הוקדשו לשלמים שנקבות ג"כ כשרין ולא לעולות, וכולן זבחי שלמים: אמר רבי זעירא כמה דאת אמר כו'. רבי זעירא פריק לה לקושיא קמא, דאימא זכרים הוי לשלמים והיאך מקריב עולות. דלא קשיא כלל, דהא לעיל גבי קינין וגוזלי עולה, דפריך: ויש חטאת קריבה עולה?! ואמרי': תנאי ב"ד הוא על האובדות שיקריבו עולות, ה"נ תנאי ב"ד הוא

מסורת הש"ס

א) לעיל פ"ב הל"ד וש"נ: ב) עי' מנחות ח א: ג) שם כ ב: ד) תו"כ פ' צו פ"ג: ה) עי' מנחות עח א: ו) תמיד כח א: ז) מנחות כ ב: ח) שם נא ב: ט) ע"ש:

עין משפט נר מצוה

כא א מיי' פרק ג משקלים הל"ב:

כב ב מיי' פרק ה מפסמ"ק הל"ח:

כג ג מיי' פרק י"ג ממעס"ק הל"ב:

כד ד מיי' פרק ג מתמידין הלכ"א:

כה ה מיי' פרק א מכלי המקדש הלכה יט:

כו ו מיי' שם פ"ה הלכה טז:

כז ז מיי' שם הלי"ז:

כח ח מיי' פרק ה מבית הבחירה הלכה יא:

כט ט מיי' פרק י"ג ממעס"ק הל"ג:

ל י מיי' פרק ג' מתמידין הלי"ח:

לא כ מיי' פרק ג מתמידין הל"ב:

נוסחת הבבלי

(א) תנאי ב"ד על האובדות כו' א"ר אסי כו' א"ר אסי כו': (ב) כר"ש דאמר ר"ש עשרון כו': (ג) האיפה

בַּר בָּא: וְלֹא יָאוּת הוּא מַקְשֶׁה? אֲתָא רַבִּי יַעֲקֹב בַּר אַחָא רַבִּי אַבָּהוּ בְּשֵׁם רַבִּי יוֹחָנָן: דְּבַר תּוֹרָה הוּא שֶׁתְּהֵא בָּאָה מִן הַצִּבּוּר. (כֵּיוָן דְּחָזֵי דְּקָא מִידְּחֲקָא לִשְׁכָּה) הָיִיתִי אוֹמֵר יִגְבּוּ לָהּ (מִן הַיּוֹרְשִׁין) (כֵּיוָן דְּחָזֵי דְּפָשְׁעֵי בָּהּ) — הִתְקִינוּ שֶׁתְּהֵא בָּאָה מִתְּרוּמַת הַלִּשְׁכָּה. [א] רַבִּי יוֹסֵה אָמַר ר' יוֹחָנָן בָּעֵי: מַהוּ א) אשְׁלֵימָה בְּשַׁחֲרִית וּשְׁלֵימָה בֵּין הָעַרְבַּיִם? אוֹ ב) שְׁלֵימָה בְּשַׁחֲרִית וּבְטֵילָה בֵּין הָעַרְבַּיִם? כַּד תְּהֵא פְּשִׁיטָא לֵיהּ, דִּכְתִיב "מִנְחַת תָּמִיד שְׁלֹשֶׁת לוּגִּין" מַה הֵין, שְׁלֹשֶׁת לוּגִּין שַׁחֲרִית וּשְׁלֹשֶׁת לוּגִּין בֵּין הָעַרְבַּיִם, אוֹ בלוֹג וּמֶחֱצָה שַׁחֲרִית וְלוֹג וּמֶחֱצָה בֵּין הָעַרְבַּיִם? אָמַר רַבִּי חִזְקִיָּה: אוּף הָדָא צְרִיכָה לֵיהּ: שְׁנֵי ג) קוֹמְצִין מַה הֵין, שְׁנֵי קוֹמְצִין בְּשַׁחֲרִית וּשְׁנֵי קוֹמְצִין בֵּין הָעַרְבַּיִם, אוֹ קוֹמֶץ אַחַת בְּשַׁחֲרִית וְקוֹמֶץ אַחַת בֵּין הָעַרְבַּיִם. א"ר יוֹסֵה: כְּלוּם לָמְדוּ לַקּוֹמֶץ — לֹא מִמִּנְחַת חוֹטֵא, מַה לְּהַלָּן שְׁנֵי (א) קוֹמְצִין — אַף כָּאן שְׁנֵי קוֹמְצִין (מַה תַּמָּן צְרִיכָה לֵיהּ אַף הָכָא צְרִיכָה לֵיהּ) אָמַר רַבִּי חִזְקִיָּה: כְּלוּם לָמְדוּ שְׁלֹשֶׁת לוּגִּין לֹא מִתָּמִיד שֶׁל בֵּין הָעַרְבַּיִם, מַה לְּהַלָּן שְׁלֹשֶׁת לוּגִּין — אַף כָּאן שְׁלֹשֶׁת לוּגִּין. וּמַה תַּמָּן צְרִיכָה לֵיהּ — אַף כָּאן צְרִיכָה לֵיהּ.§ "שֶׁלֹּא יְהֵיֶה" כו'.§ (ב) ר"ש בַּר נַחְמָן בְּשֵׁם ר' יוֹנָתָן: בְּדִין הָיָה שֶׁיִּמְעֲלוּ בָהּ, וְהֵן גָּזְרוּ שֶׁלֹּא יִמְעֲלוּ בָהּ. וְהָא ד) תָּנֵי: "חַטָּאת" — מְלַמֵּד שֶׁמּוֹעֲלִין בָּהּ! בָּהּ מוֹעֲלִין וְאֵין מוֹעֲלִין בְּאֶפְרָהּ. אָמַר רַבִּי אַבָּהוּ: בָּרִאשׁוֹנָה הָיוּ מִשְׁתַּקְשְׁקִין בָּהּ וְנוֹתְנִין אוֹתָהּ ע"ג מַכּוֹתֵיהֶן, וְגָזְרוּ שֶׁיִּמְעֲלוּ בָהּ. כֵּיוָן שֶׁנִּגְדְּרוּ — גָּזְרוּ שֶׁלֹּא יִמְעֲלוּ בָהּ.§ "וְעַל הַקִּינִּין" כו'.§ [ב] הָאִשָּׁה ה) הַזֹּאת בַּמֶּה הִיא מִתְכַּפֶּרֶת? אָמַר רַבִּי יִצְחָק: תְּנַאי ב"ד הוּא: הַמְסַפֵּק אֶת הַקִּינִּין הוּא מְסַפֵּק אֶת הַפְּסוּלוֹת וְאֶת הָאוֹבְדוֹת.§

הדרן עלך פרק מעות שנמצאו

הלכה א מתני' כָּל הָרוּקִּין ו) הַנִּמְצָאִין בִּירוּשָׁלַיִם טְהוֹרִין, חוּץ

מִשֶּׁל שׁוּק הָעֶלְיוֹן, דִּבְרֵי ר"מ (ג) רַבִּי יוֹסֵי אוֹמֵר: גבִּשְׁאָר כָּל יְמוֹת הַשָּׁנָה, שֶׁבָּאֶמְצַע — טְמֵאִין, שֶׁבַּצְּדָדִין — טְהוֹרִין. וּבִשְׁעַת הָרֶגֶל — שֶׁבָּאֶמְצַע טְהוֹרִין שֶׁבַּצְּדָדִין — טְמֵאִין, מִפְּנֵי שֶׁהַמּוּעָטִין מִסְתַּלְּקִין לַצְּדָדִין. כָּל ז) הַכֵּלִים הַנִּמְצָאִין בִּירוּשָׁלַיִם דֶּרֶךְ יְרִידָה לְבֵית הַטְּבִילָה — טְמֵאִין, וְדֶרֶךְ עֲלִיָּה — טְהוֹרִין, שֶׁלֹּא כִּירִידָתָן עֲלִיָּיתָן, דִּבְרֵי ר"מ ר' יוֹסֵי אוֹמֵר: דכּוּלָּן טְהוֹרִין, חוּץ מִן הַסַּל וְהַמַּגְרֵיפָה וְהַמְּרִיצָה הַמְיוּחָדִין לַקְּבָרוֹת. סַכִּין ח) השֶׁנִּמְצֵאת בי"ד שׁוֹחֵט בָּהּ מִיָּד. ובִּשְׁלֹשָׁה עָשָׂר — שׁוֹנֶה וּמַטְבִּיל. (ד) קוֹפִיץ — [א] בָּזֶה וּבָזֶה שׁוֹנֶה וּמַטְבִּיל. חָל אַרְבָּעָה עָשָׂר לִהְיוֹת בַּשַּׁבָּת — שׁוֹחֵט בָּהּ מִיָּד, בט"ו

קרבן העדה

בברייתא דריש מקרא דמשל צבור: ולא יאות הוא מקשה. בתמיה, דודאי שפיר קא מקשי. א"נ בניחותא, דלאו שפיר מקשה, דידע ר"ח בר בא דשני תקנות הוו: הייתי אומר. שיגבו מכל ישראל לצורך עשירית האיפה ותנאי ב"ד הוא שתבא מתרומת הלשכה, אבל לעולם מן התורה משל צבור: בעי. הא דתני במתני' "ושלימה היתה קריבה", מי אמרינן שלימה שחרית ושלימה בין הערבים: ה"ג: ושלימה בין הערבים, או שלימה שחרית ובטילה בין הערבים. וכ"ה ב"הכלכת": כד תהא פשיטא ליה. כלומר, את"ל דשלימה שחרית ושלימה בין הערבים: ג' לוגין מה הן. דלעשירית האיפה היה הכה"ג מביא ג' לוגין. וקמבעיא ליה: כשמת כה"ג והיתה המנחה כפולה בסולת, אם היתה כפולה גם בשמן, או לא: אוף הדא צריכה ליה. גם זה מבעיא ליה: ב' קמצין מה הן. דס"ל לחזקיה כאבא יוסי בן דוסתאי שסובר ב"הכלכת" דבכל יום היה כה"ג מביא ב' קמצין לבונה ומקריב אחד מהן בשחרית וא' בין הערבים, ואמר רבי יוחנן התם דהלכתא כאבא יוסי, וקמיבעיא ליה: כשהוא מביאה שלימה בשחרית ושלימה בין הערבים, אם מביא כל פעם ב' קומצין, או דלמא בקומץ אחד סגי: כלום למדו לקומץ. כלומר, דלבונה בעי קומץ למדו ממנחת חוטא, כדתניא בפרק דלעיל: מה להלן ב' קמצין לכל עשרון קומץ לבונה, דס"ל כי היכי דבעינן שעור שמן לכל עשרון אפי' נעשו הרבה עשרונות בכלי אחד, כדתנן בפ' "שתי מדות", ה"נ בעינן קומץ לבונה לכל עשרון, ה"ה כאן דכופל הסולת — כופל נמי הקומצין: ומשני: מה תמן צריכה ליה. כי היכי דמיבעיא ליה גבי חביתי כה"ג אם כופל הקומצין, ה"נ מיבעיא ליה במביא מנחות הרבה בכלי אחד אם צריך קומץ לבונה לכל אחד, או סגי ליה בקומץ אחד, יהיו המנחות ששים או אחד. ובגיר' הירושלמי שבבבלי לא גרסי' כאן "מה תמן צריכא ליה": כלום למדו שלשה לוגין דחביתין בעינן ג' לוגין אלא מתמיד, שנאמר גבי חביתין "מנחת תמיד" — הרי היא לו כמנחת תמיד, מה להלן שלשה לוגין לעשרון — אף כאן ג' לוגין לעשרון: ומשני: מה תמן צריכה ליה. כי היכא דקמבעיא ליה בחביתין, ה"נ מבעיא ליה בתמיד, כגון שלא הקריב מנחה בבקר שהביאה אפילו בערב, דכתיב "ומנחתם ונסכיהם" בלילה או למחר אם צריך ג' לוגין לכל אחת, או דסגי להו בג' לוגין. א"נ: "ומה תמן כו'" מדברי רבי חזקיה הוא, דקאמר לרבי יוסה שהשיב על דבריו, דקאמר דלא קמבעיא ליה לר' יוחנן אקומץ דדומיא דמנחת חוטא הוא, וקאר"ח: א"כ מאי קמבעיא ליה לר"י מג' לוגין, נילף מתמיד! אלא ודאי מאי דגלי — גלי, מאי דלא גלי — לא גלי, א"כ ה"ה לענין קמצין. והראשון נ"ל עיקר: בדין היה שימעלו באפר פרה, אלא שתנאי ב"ד הוא שאין מועלין באפרה: ופריך: והא תני "חטאת היא" דכתיב בפרה, ללמדך שמועלין בה כשאר חטאות עד שלא היתה להן שעת היתר לכהנים: ה"ג: "היא" — בה מועלין, ואין מועלין באפרה: משתקשקין בה. באפרה היו מתרפאין, ונותנים אותה ע"ג מכותיהן, דאפר מרפא מכה: כיון שנגדרו. ופרשו: מספק הזאות אם נטמאו בספק טמאת המת לא היו מזין עליו שלא ימעלו בה: האשה הזאת במה היא מתכפרת. ל"ג ליה הכא. ואגב גררא דר"פ מייתי ליה לכאן: ואת האובדות. שנאבד המעות בין שקלים לנדבה, וכדאמרי' לעיל בר"פ, דאל"כ האשה הזאת במה מתכפרת:

הדרן עלך פרק מעות שנמצאו

הלכה א מתני' כל הרוקין הנמצאין בירושלים טהורין. ולא מחזקינן להו ברוקו של זב וזבה שהן מטמאין אדם וכלים, משום דאזלינן בתר רובא: חוץ משל שוק העליון. בגמרא מפרש טעמא: שבאמצע טמאים. משום דזבין וזבות שכיחי ומהלכים באמצע הדרכים, והטהורים מסתלקין לצידי הדרכים מקום שאין דריסת הרגל מצוי', ומזהירין לכל טמא שלא יגע בהן. אבל בשעת הרגל שרוב ישראל טהורין, הטמאים מסתלקין לצדדים שלא יטמא את העם, והטהורים הולכין באמצע הדרכים. הלכך בשעת הרגל רוקין הנמצאים באמצע טהורין ושבצדדין טמאין: דרך ירידה לבית הטבילה. ב' דרכים היו למקוה, בא' יורדים ובאחד עולים שלא יגעו הטמאין בטהורין. ושל דרך ירידה ודאי טמאין, לפי שנפלו מיד המביאין לטבילה: שלא כירידתן עלייתן. דבירידתן ודאי טמאין היו, לכך היו מורידין לבית הטבילה, ובעלייתן טהרו לאחר שהטבילן: ר' יוסי אומר כולן טהורין. דלא גזרו על ספק כלים בירושלים: מגריפה. כלי שגורפין וכונסים בו עצמות המתים כשהם מפוזרין: מריצה. מפרש בגמרא: שוחט בו מיד. דודאי הטבילוה בעלים מאתמול כדי שיהיה לה הערב שמש ותהא ראויה לשחוט בה היום בערב פסח: בי"ג שונה ומטביל. כלומר, אע"ג דאיכא למימר כבר הטבילוה בעלים — צריך המוצאה להטבילה שנית, דשמא לא הטבילוה בעלים, דהוה לה שהות להמתין עד סמוך לחשיכה. ואע"פ שלא גזרו על ספק כלים, אפ"ה גבי קדשים הצריכוה טבילה: קופיץ = סכין גדול. רוצן עשויין לחתוך בשר ולשבר בו עצמות: בזה ובזה. בי"ג ובי"ד שונה ומטביל, לפי שעיקרה לחגיגה ששבירת העצם מותר בה. ואיירי כגון שהיו הכהנים טמאי מתים בספק וחל שביעי שלהן בע"פ, דאין מביאין עמו חגיגה, דהוה ליה כפסח הבאה בטומאה. וחגיגת ט"ו יעשו בטהרה, ואין הכהנים שהן טבולי יום מטמאין הסכין שאין טבול יום אפי' דמת מטמא כלים: חל י"ד להיות בשבת שוחט בה מיד. ולא אמרינן כיון דשבת הוא לא נשחט בה מספיקא שמא טמאה היא ונמצא הפסח טמא ומחלל את השבת שלא במקום מצוה. וי"מ: שוחט בה מיד — בקופיץ קאמר. דאף על גב דאין חגיגה בשבת, מ"מ חזקה שהטבילוהו מערב שבת לצורך חגיגת י"ד:

ריבב"ן

לערב וסיא מחוסרת כפרה ובכרת היא תיקנו ב"ד שיהו באות משל צבור: המספק את הקינין. שהגזבר לוקח את הקינין מאחד בדמים קצובין וקצבה שלהן כדמפורש בסוף פרק קמא דכריתות אמר רשב"ג המעון הזה אם אלין בלילה עד שיהו בדינרין נכנס ודרש ולימד האשה שיש עליה חמש לידות ודאות מביאה קרבן ואוכלת בזבחים ואין השאר עליהן חובה ועמדו קינין בו ביום ברבעתים ומייתי לה נמי בב"ב פרק בתרא (דקס"ו) וה"נ אמרינן בכריתות בפ' ב' נכרי שנתגייר בזמן הזה צריך שיפרים רובע *)שקל לקינו דהיינו דינר:

מתני' כל הרוקין הנמצאין בירושלים טהורין. ומוקי בפסחים פ"ק ואע"ג דאתחזק זב התם משום דלא גזרו על ספק הרוקין בירושלים חוץ משל שוק העליון שכל זב נפנה לשם: בשאר כל ימות השנה שבאמצע טמאין. ירושלמי ר' אבין בשם ר' יהושע בן לוי קלרן של נכרים היה שם בשאר ימות השנה הטמאין מהלכין שיבולת פי' באמצע הדרך לשון שביל והטהורין הולכין מן הצד והטהורין הולכין סתם והטמאין אומרים להם פרושו בשעת הרגל הטהורים הולכין שיבולת והטמאין הולכין מן הצד והטמאין הולכין סתם והטהורין אומרים להם פרושו: מתני' כל הכלים הנמצאים בירושלים דרך ירידה לבית הטבילה טמאין. בפסחים בסוף פ"ק פריך רישא לסיפא דרך ירידה לבית הטבילה טמאין הא דעלמא טהורין אימא סיפא דרך עליה טהורין הא דעלמא טמאין אלא רישא דוקא הא בעלמא טהורין לפי שלא גזרו על ספק כלים וסיפא לאפוקי גזייתא ופרש"י ז"ל מבואות קטנים שהיו סמוכין לדרך הירידה ועליה ופעמים שהיו יורדין דרך אותן מבואות ופעמים היו עולין בהנהו מבואות טמאים מספק שהרי תחלתן טמאין היו ספק נפלו בירידה ספק נפלו בעליה ומספיקא לא נפקי מטומאתן אבל שאר כלים דספק נטמאו ספק לא נטמאו לא גזרו עליהן מספק: שלא כירידתן עלייתן. שבדרך אחד היו יורדין לבית הטבילה ובדרך אחר היו עולין: והמריצה המיוחדין לקברות. פי' כלי ברזל שבראשו חד וראוי לחפור בו ארץ קשה ובלע"ז סובולוצ"י ובירושלמי קורא אותה צפורן שדומה לצפורן מאן דאמר מרילה שהיא מרילה את האבן: מתני' סכין שנמצאת בי"ד בניסן שוחט בה מיד. הפסח שהטבילוהו בעלים בי"ג שיהא לה הערב שמש בי"ג שונה ומטביל שמא לא הטבילה בעלים עדיין. קופיץ בין בזה ובין בזה בין בי"ג ובין בי"ד שונה ומטביל שמא עדיין לא הטבילוה בעלים אפילו מצאה בי"ד שמא אין דעתו לעשות חגיגה בי"ד שלא במרובה ואפי' בחול וכ"ש בשבת ובטומאה דלא עבדינן חגיגה כלל: חל י"ד להיות בשבת. אפי' קופיץ שוחט בה מיד. לפי שהטבילה בי"ג שאין מטבילים כלים בשבת כדאיתא בבילה פ"ב לפי שנראה כמתקן כלי א"נ גזרה שמא ישהה ועל כרחו הטבילה בע"ש שצריך לו לטבילת ט"ו שהוא יו"ט: נמצאת קשורה.

תקלין חדתין

במתני' דמנחות, כדקאמר מ"חק עולם", והכא במתניתין דידן אמר מתנאי ב"ד: ד"ת משל צבור הייתי אומר יגבו לה. כלומר, הא ודאי פשיטא דמשל צבור דבר תורה, מקרא ד"חק עולם", אבל הייתי אומר שלא ליקחה מתרומת הלשכה, אלא לגבות מכל יחיד ויחיד, דהכי משמע קרא ד"חק עולם" — משל עולם. והתנו ב"ד שיהא באה מתרומת הלשכה, ואיזה תלמיד טועה נסתבך בתירוצא דבבלי שם והרכיב לה בתירוצא דהכא דירושלמי. ולא נהיר ולא בהיר, דסוגיא דירושלמי ס"ל דלא הוה אלא חדא תקנה וכדפרישית, ובבבלי משני ב' תקנות הוו: ר"י בעי שלימה בשחרית כו'. אמתניתין קאי, דקתני בר"י: "ושלימה היתה קריבה", ומבעיא ליה: או שלימה בין הערבים ג"כ, או דילמא בין הערבים בטילה: ודא צריכא ליה. הא מבעיא ליה: ג' לוגין מהו. כלומר, אלו הג' לוגין שהיה מביא הכהן גדול וחולהו, לוג ומחצה בבוקר ולוג ומחצה בין הערבים, ועכשיו כשמת והוכפלה הסולת כדקתני לה בברייתא דלעיל שלמה בבוקר כו', ומספקא ליה: אם הוכפל גם כן השמן, או דילמא סולת דגלי קרא דאותה לר"י ולר"ש מתקטר — גלי, אבל בשמן לא גלי קרא: קומץ בשחרית. אי אמרי' הואיל והוכפלה סולתה — הוכפלה לבונתו, או דילמא מאי דגלי — גלי: אמר רבי יוסי. מהדר למפשט בעיא שניה: כלום למדו לקומץ דלבונה לא מלחם הפנים. דהא גבי חביתין לא כתיב קומץ כלל, ועל כרחך מלחם הפנים למדו לקומץ דחביתין, או מגזרה שוה ד"חק עולם" דבתרווייהו כתיב. או דס"ל כסוגיא דלעיל פרק ו' דלמד לשיעורא דקומץ מלחם הפנים לכל המנחות: מה להלן ב' קמצים אף כאן ב' קמצים. ותיבת "בחסר" ליתא בנוסח הירושל'. ואי גרסי' לה, נ"ל דה"ק: בהפחות — אינו פחות מב' קומצין, דבלחם הפנים חסר לבונתה פסול, כדאמרינן מנחות (יא, ב), הכא נמי ב' קומצין, קומץ אחד בבוקר וכו'. והוא אליבא דרבנן דפליגי אאבא יוסי בן דוסתאי בבבלי מנחות (נב): אר"ח. מהדר למפשט קמייתא: כלום למדו לג' לוגין לא מתמיד. הכי מפורש בספרא פרשה "צו" פרשה ד' פסקא ה', וכ"ה במנחות (נא, א), ר"י בנו של רבי יוחנן בן ברוקא אומר: "סלת מנחה תמיד" — ה"ה כמנחת תמידין, מה תמידין ג' לוגין וכו'. וגי' הספרים והמפרשים נשתבשו מאד: בדין הוא שימעלו. באפר פרה, אלא שתנאי כו': והתני חטאת מלמד כו' בה מועלין ואין מועלין באפרה. הכי פריך: דאמר תנאי ב"ד דאין מועלין, הא בברייתא תני דמדאורייתא אין מועלין באפרה! והכי פריך בבבלי במנחות שם: ומשני: בתחלה היו מקשקשין. לשון זילותא, ד'קשקוש' לשון זילותא הוא. ונותנין אותה על גבי מכותיהן, וגזרו שימעלו בה. וכיון שנגדרו, גזרו שלא ימעלו בה. וניחא מה שאמר שהוא תנאי ב"ד. ובבבלי קאמר: כיון דחזו דפרשי מספק הזאות, אוקמוה אדאורייתא, ודלא כהמפרשים: האשה הזאת במה מתכפרת. ומשני: תנאי ב"ד כו', וכדפרישית בריש פרקין: סליק פרק שביעי

כל הרוקין כו' טהורין. ולא גזרינן שמא של טמאים הם שהן מטמאין אדם וכלים, משום דאזלינן בתר רובא: של שוק העליון. בגמרא מפרש: שבאמצע שבצדדין. בגמרא מפרש טעמא מאי: כל הכלים כו' דרך ירידה כו'. שהיו ב' דרכים, אחד — שהיו נושאין הכלים לטובלן, והוא דרך ירידה, והב' — דרך עלייתן מהטבילה: שלא כבדרך ירידתן. דבירידתן ודאי טמאים הוו, משא"כ בעלייתן: טהורים. דלא גזרו על ספק הכלים שבירושלים: מגריפה. כלי שמקבצים בו עצמות המתים: שוחט בה מיד. פסחו. וא"צ להטבילה זה המוצאה, דמסתמא הטבילה בעלה, אם טמאה היתה — הטבילוה בי"ג כדי שיהא הערב שמש ותהא טהורה בי"ד: בי"ג שונה ומטביל. כלומר, אע"פ שספק שמא הטבילוה הבעלים, זה שונה ומטבילה מספק, שמא עדיין לא הטבילוה, שהיה להן שהות ביום להטבילה ולהעריב שמשה: קופיץ. סכין גדול הוא, ורובן אין לשחיטה אלא לחיתוך בשר ולשבירת עצמות: בין בזה כו'. אפילו נמצאת בי"ד: שונה כו'. דמחתך שאין שבירת העצם בפסח, הבעלים אין צריכים לה כל י"ד עד למחר, וי"ל: לא הטבילה, שהיה לו שהות ביום להטבילה סמוך לבין השמשות: חל י"ד בשבת שוחט. בקופיץ זה מיד, וא"ל

*) [נראה דכן היה גורס שם בגמ' רובע שקל אבל לפנינו הגיר' שם רובע סתמא ופירש"י רבע הדינר ועי' היטב בתוס' ב"ב ד' קסו: ד"ה ריבעתים:]

משנת אליהו

ממום ונטמא נשאר בבעי' והרמב"ם דפסק בפ"ג מהל' תמידין הל' כ' כהן שהקריב מחצה ומת או נטמא או טלד בו מום כו' פשט הבעי' לחומרא ודלא כמ"ש בק"ע:

גליון הש"ס [א] עי' ק"ע וש"ק רלה לפרש פי' חדש והוא פלוגי דא"כ בחל י"ד בשבת אמאי שוחט בה מיד הא כיון דאין הזאה דוחה שבת ואף בספק טומאה אין מזין בשבת עי' יומא דף ח ע"ב וא"כ בא הפסח בטומאה וא"כ

מסורת הש"ס

א) מנחות נב א: ב) בס"א או מחצה בשחרית ומחצה בין הערבים: ג) מנחות נא ב: ד) שם נא ב: ה) לעיל הל"א: ו) פסחים יט ב: ז) שם: ח) שם ע א:

עין משפט נר מצוה

לב א מיי' פ"ג מתמידין הל' כב:
לג ב מיי' שם:
א ג מיי' פרק י"ג מאה"ט הל"ח:
ב ד מיי' שם הל"ט:
ג ה מיי' שם ובהשגו':
ד ו מיי' שם הל"ו:

נוסחת הבבלי

(א) קומצין (בחסר) כו' קומצין בחסר כו' אר"ח כו': (ב) ר"ש בר נחמן בשם ר' יוחנן כו' היו מקשטין בה כו': (ג) וחכ"א בשאר ימות כו': (ד) וקופיץ בין בזה ובין בזה כו':

הגהות הגר"א

חייא בר אבא יאות הוא מקשה אתא ר' יעקב ב"א ר' אבהו בשם ר"י ד"ת הוא שתהא באה משל צבור הייתי אומר יגבו לה התקינו שתהא באה מתרומת הלשכה כצ"ל. וה"פ תמן הייתי במתני' דמנחות אמר משל צבור כדקאמר מחק עולם והכא במתני' דידן אמר מתנאי ב"ד דבר תורה משל צבור הייתי אומר יגבו לה כלומר הא ודאי פשיטא דמש"צ ד"ת מקרא דחק עולם אבל הייתי אומר שלא ליקח אותה מתרומת הלשכ' אלא לגבות מכל יחיד ויחיד דהכי משמע קרא דחק עולם משל עול' והתנו ב"ד שיהא בא מתרומת הלשכה ואיזה תלמיד טועה נסתבך בתירוצא דבבלי שם והרכיב לה בתירוצא דהכא דירו' ולא נהיר ולא בהיר דסוגיא דירושל' ס"ל דלא הוה אלא חדא תקנה ובבבלי משני ב' תקנות הוו: [א] מכאן עד הפסק ר"ש בר נחמן וכו' מבולבלת מאוד וגי' הגאון ז"ל מלובנת ומחוורת. וה"ג ר' אסי א"ר יוחנן בעי מה שלימה שלימה בשחרית ושלימה בין הערבים או שלימה שחרית ובטלה בין הערבים הדר פשיטא ליה שלימה בשחרית שלימה בין הערבים ודא צריכא ליה שלשת לוגין מהו שלשת לוגין בשחרית ושלשת לוגין בין הערבים או לוג ומחצה שחרי' ולוג ומחצה בין הערבים א"ר חזקיה אף הדא צריכה ליה קומץ בשחרית וקומץ בין הערבים או חצי קומץ בשחרית וחצי קומץ בין הערבים א"ר יוסי כלום למדו לקומץ לא מלחם הפנים מה להלן שני קמצים בחסר אף כאן שני קמצים בחסר א"ר חזקיה וכלום למדו לג' לוגין לא מתמיד מה להלן שלשת לוגין אף כאן ג' לוגין כצ"ל. ותיבו' מה תמן צריכא ליה אף כאן צריכא ליה שלא יהי' וכו'. נמחקו: [ב] חסר כאן תמן תנינן מחצה למחצה יפלו לנוזלי עולה האשה הזאת וכו':

בט"ו שוחט בה מיד. לפי שכל העם יודעין שהזאה וטבילה אסורה ביו"ט ומטבילין את הכל מעיו"ט: נמצאה קשורה לסכין. בגמ' מפרש: גמ' קצרן של נכרים. כובס של נכרים היה שם בשוק העליון, וחכמים גזרו על הנכרים שיהו כזבים לכל דבריהם ורוקו טמא: ערודות. ערודי היער היו נוחרין לצורך אריות של מלך: ר"ש בר אבא בשם ר"ח: קצרן של נכרים היה שם. ל"ג ליה הכא: וטהרו את דמיה משום נבילה. כל הסוגיא פירשתי לעיל פ"ג הל"ב: לא כן וכו'. אמתני' פריך: "לא גזרו על הרוקין שבירושלים", ולמה גזרו על הרוקין שבשוק העליון? שיבולת. היינו באמצע: ופריך: לא כן וכו'. ובמתני' תנן "חוץ מדרך ירידתן לבית הטבילה": ומשני: מכיון וכו' נעשו הוכיח. יש הוכחה שהן טמאין ודאי ולא משום גזרה: שהיא דומה לצפורן. שעשויה כדמות צפורן של אדם: תני: הסכין קשורה לו. אם נמצא הסכין קשור בקופיץ — הרי זה כקופיץ, ובזה ובזה שוחט ומטביל, ופליג אמתני'. ויותר נ"ל דברייתא לפרושי למתני' קאתי. דה"ק: נמצאת סכין סתמא קשורה עם סכין אחרת ידועה — הריהוא כסכין ידועה, אם טמאה — טמאה, ואם טהורה — טהורה. וכן פי' הרמב"ם בפי' המשנה:

הלכה ב מתני' פרוכת שנטמאה בולד הטומאה. שנגעה במשקין טמאין, שחכמים גזרו על המשקין שמטמאין כלים, גזרה משום משקה דזב וזבה: מטבילין אותה בפנים. ואינה טעונה שילוח חוץ למחנה שכינה, כיון שלא נטמאת אלא בולד הטומאה. ומכניסין אותה מיד, שאינה טעונה הערב שמש: מטבילין אותה בחוץ. דטעונה שילוח: ושוטחין אותה בחיל. חוץ לעזרה: נימין. ליל"ס בלע"ז: כ"ד חוטין. מפרש בגמ': ארכה ארבעים ורחבה עשרים. כמדת פתח האולם, שהיה גובהו ארבעים ורחבו עשרים: פ"ב רבוא. דינרי זהב נעשית: גמ' אילו אמר "חוט" גבי מלאכת הפרוכת, הייתי אומר שיהא כל חוט כפול לשנים: שזור. אילו נאמר "חוט שזור" הייתי אומר שיהא חוטין כפול לשלשה, השתא דכתיב "משזר" ילפי' מיניה דבעינן חוטין כפול ששה, דהיינו כפל משזר: ארבעה. כלומר, וארבעה מינין היו בו: תכלת, וארגמן, ותולעת שני, ושש משזר, כל אחד חוטין כפול שש, מכאן שהיה כפול כ"ד: "מעשה רוקם". גבי מסך הפתח כתיב, וגבי פרכת כתיב "מעשה חושב", מאי בינייהו: ר"י ור' נחמיה פליגי. איך היו 'מעשה חושב' ו'מעשה רוקם', והיאך היו שני פרצופין: גוזמא. מילתא בעלמא, ולאו דוקא: תמן תנינן. במסכת תמיד פ"ב: החלו מעלין באפר ע"ג תפוח. ותפוח היה באמצע המזבח, ולפעמים עליו כשלש מאות כור אפר:

הלכה ג מתני' הכל ישרף בפנים. בבית הדשן הגדול שבעזרה, ששם שורפין פסולי קדשים, שכל שפסולו בקדש שורפין אותו בקודש: חוץ משנטמא בולד הטומאה בפנים.

תורה אור

בט"ו שוחט בה מיד. אנמצאה קשורה לסכין — הרי היא כסכין.§ גמ' ר' אבין בשם ר' יהושע בן לוי: (א) קצרן (זבין) של נכרים היה שם. אמר ר' חנינה: ערודות א) [א] היו נוחרין בירושלים, והיו עולי רגלים משתקעין בדם עד ארכובותיהן. ובאו לפני חכמים ולא אמרו להן דבר. (ר"ש בר אבא (ב) בשם ר"ח קצרן של נכרים היה שם) רבי סימון בשם רבי יהושע בן לוי: מעשה ב) בפרדה משל בית רבי שמתה, וטהרו את דמיה משום נבילה. ר"א שאיל לרבי סימון: עד כמה? ולא אגיביה. שאיל לרבי יהושע בן לוי: א"ל עד רביעית — טהור, יותר מיכן — טמא. ובאש לרבי לעזר דלא חזר ליה ר' סימון שמועתא. רב ביבי הוה יתיב מתני הדין עובדא. א"ל רבי יצחק בר ביסנא: עד כמה? א"ל עד רביעית — טהור, יותר מיכן — טמא. ובעט ביה. א"ל ר' זריקא: בגין דההוה שאיל לך את בעיט ביה? א"ל בגין דלא הוות דעתי בי, דאמר ר' חנין: דברים כד "והיו חייך תלואים לך מנגד" — זה שהוא לוקח לו חטין לשנה, שם "ופחדת לילה ויומם" — זה שהוא לוקח מן הסדקי, שם "ולא תאמין בחייך" — זה שהוא לוקח מן הפלטור. ואנא סמיך אפלטירא. מאי כדון, ג) העיד רבי יהושע בן פתורה בעל דם נבילות שהוא טהור. מהו טהור — טהור מלהכשיר, הא ליטמאות — מטמא. תמן ד) תנינן: גדם השרץ מטמא כבשרו, מטמא ואינו מכשיר, ואין לנו כיוצא בו. ואין לנו כיוצא בו כשיעור טומאתו, אבל דמו מטמא כבשרו. א"ר יוסי: פליגי בה תרין אמוראין, חד אמר: טמא, וחד אמר: טהור. מ"ד טמא — כר' יהודה, ומ"ד טהור — כר' יהושע בן פתורה. א"ל רב אבדומה דמן נחותה: ויאות, דרבי יהודה מוריינה דבי נשיאה הוה.§ "כל הרוקין" וכו'.§ לא כן אמר רבי אבהו בשם ר' יוסי בן חנינה: לא ה) גזרו על הרוקין שבירושלים! הא איתמר עליה, רבי אבין בשם ריב"ל קצרן של נכרים היה שם.§ דבשאר ימות השנה הטמאין מהלכין שיבולת והטהורין מהלכין מן הצד, [ב] והטהורין מהלכין סתם, והטמאים אומרין להן "פרושו". בשעת הרגל הטהורים מהלכין שיבולת, והטמאין מהלכין מן הצד, הטמאין מהלכין סתם, והטהורין אומרים להן "פרושו".§ "וכל הכלים הנמצאים" כו'.§ לא כן א"ר אבהו בשם ר' יוחנן לא ו) גזרו על הכלים שבירושלם? מכיון שנמצאו דרך ירידה לבית הטבילה — נעשו הוכיח, אבא שאול היה קורא אותן ציפורין. מ"ד ציפורין — שהיה דומה לציפורין, מ"ד מריצה — שמריצה את האבן לבית הקברות.§ קופיץ וכו'.§ תני: הסכין קשורה לה — הרי זו כמותה.§

הלכה ב מתני' הפרוכת שנטמאת בולד הטומאה — מטבילין אותה בפנים, ומכניסין אותה מיד. ושנטמאת באב הטומאה — מטבילין אותה בחוץ, ושוטחין אותה (ג) בחיל, מפני שהיא צריכה הערב שמש. אם היתה חדשה — שוטחין אותה על גג האיצטבא, כדי שיראה העם את מלאכתה שהיא נאה. רשב"ג ז) אומר משום ר"ש בן הסגן: ופרוכת עוביה טפח על שבעים ושתים נימים נארגת על כל נימה ונימה כ"ד חוטין. ארכה מ' אמה ורחבה כ' ומשמונים ושתים רבוא היתה נעשית, ושתים עושין בכל שנה, ושלש מאות כהנים מטבילין אותה.§ גמ' אילו אמר חוט — א' כפול — לשנים, שזור — לשלשה, משזר — לששה. ארבע מכאן — הא ח) עשרים וארבעה. תני: שלשים ושתים, אילו אמר חוט — א' כפול — לשנים, שזור — לארבע, משזר — לשמונה, ארבע מכאן — הא תלתין ותרין. תנא ארבעים ושמונה, אילו אמר חוט — אחד, כפול — לשנים, קליעה — לשלשה, שזור — לששה, משזר — לשנים עשר, ארבעה מיכן — הא ארבעים ותמניא. שמות כח כתוב אחד אומר "מעשה רוקב" וכתוב א' אומר "מעשה חושב". "מעשה ט) רוקם" — שם פרצוף אחד, "מעשה חושב" — שני פרצופות. רבי יהודה ורבי נחמיה, [ג] חד אמר: "מעשה רוקם" — [א] ארי מכאן וארי מכאן, "מעשה רושב" — ארי מכאן וחלק מכאן. וחרנה אמר: "מעשה רוקם" — ארי מכאן וחלק מכאן, "מעשה חושב" — ארי מכאן ונשר מכאן.§ בשמונים ושתים רבוא היתה נעשית וכו'.§ ר' י) יצחק בר ביזנא בשם שמואל: גוזמא. תמן (ד) תנינן: פעמים היה עליה כשלש מאות כור. רבי יוסי בי רבי בון בשם שמואל: גוזמא.§

הלכה ג מתני' בשר קדשים שנטמא, בין באב הטומאה בין בולד הטומאה, בין בפנים בין בחוץ, בש"א הכל ישרף בפנים, חוץ משנטמא באב הטומאה בחוץ. בית הלל אומרים: הכל ישרף בחוץ, חוץ משנטמא בולד הטומאה בפנים.

ר"א

משנת אליהו

קצרין של נכרים היו שם. עיין רש"י בפסחים (י"ט ע"ב) ד"ה של שוק העליון שם היו מתקבצים טמאים שלא לטמא את חבריהם ותמוה למה לא פירש טעמא דגמרא דכולה סוגיא ס"ל כן: סליקא לה מסכת שקלים

ריבב"ן

הקופיץ נסכין אפילו נמצאת בחול בי"ד אינו צריך להטבילה הואיל דהיא קשורה עמו הטבילן יחד והסכין צריך לו בי"ד לשחוט הפסח והטבילה בי"ג שיהא להם הערב שמש: מתני' בולד הטומאה. לאשון לטומאה: [מטבילין אותה] אפילו בפנים. לפי שאין טומאתה מדאורי' שאין אדם וכלים מקבלין טומאה אלא מאב הטומאה ואם הטבילוה בחוץ מכניסין אותה מיד שאינה צריכה הערב שמש דטומאתן מדרבנן ושנטמאת באב הטומאה מטבילין אותה בחוץ לפי שאסור להשהותה בפנים וחייב להוציאה בחוץ הואיל דטומאתה מדאורייתא דאמרינן בעירובין בפרק בתרא מזכר עד נקבה תשלחו פרט לכלי חרס דברי ר' יוסי הגלילי ומפרש טעמא לפי שאין לו טהרה במקוה א"נ לפי שאינו נעשה אב הטומאה אבל הפרכת יש לה טהרה במקוה ונעשית אב הטומאה חייב לשלחה ולהוציאה בחוץ ושוטחין אותה בחיל במקום שנקרא חיל לפנים מהר הבית ומקודש ממנו כדאיתא בריש מסכת כלים אם היתה חדשה ונטמאת מטבילין אותה בחיל ושוטחין אותה שם כדי לנוגבה ובין כך ובין כך יראו העם מלאכה שהיא נאה: מתני' על כל נימא ונימה כ"ד חוטין. כדאיתא ביומא פרק בא לו הפרכת כ"ד חוטין: ארכה מ' ורחבה כ'. כנגד פתח האולם כדאיתא במסכת מדות ומשמונים ושתים ריבוא חוטין נארגת ויש גורסין ריבות פירוש נערות האורגות בפרוכת ושלש מאות כהנים מטבילין אותה. אמרינן בחולין פרק גיד הנשה אמר רבא גוזמא דלא צריכי כ"כ כהנים להטבילה ואמרינן התם בג' מקומות דברו חכמים בלשון הבאי גפן תפוח ופרוכת ומפורשים התם: מתני' בשר שנטמא בין באב הטומאה וכו' ב"ש אומר ישרף בפנים הכל. [ואינו] חייב להוציאו מיד לחוץ (ליכא) כדפרישית לעיל דכל שאין לו טהרה במקוה ואינו נעשה אב הטומאה אין חייבין עליו ואוכלין ומשקין לא מצינו להם טהרה במקוה כלל אלא למים דרך זריעה וגם אינן נעשין אב הטומאה דכתיב וכל אשר יגע בו הטמא יטמא וכתיב לעיל מיניה

תקלין חדתין

להטביל. דאע"ג דשמא בעלים היה להן סכין לשחוט ולא היתה קופיץ זו להן אלא לשבירת עצמות והיום אין שבירת העצם בשבת, אפילו הכי כיון דצריכה להם ביו"ט אחר שבת, כבר הטבילה מערב שבת, דהא בשבת לא מצו להטבילה. כמ"ש במסכת ביצה (יז, ב): חל יו"ט אחר השבת כו' מלפני השבת: ובט"ו. אם מצאה ביו"ט עצמו: שוחט בה. שלמים מיד, דודאי הטבילוה בעלים מאתמול: הרי היא כסכין. ואפילו נמצאת בי"ד שחל להיות בחול, שוחט בה מיד, דודאי הוטבלה עם הסכין בי"ג, הואיל וקשורה עמו. לשון רש"י. וכן פי' רבינו הגאון, דקאי הכל אקופיץ: גמ' קצרין של נכרים. להכי בשוק העליון טמאים, לפי שהיה שם כובסים של נכרים, והן כזבים לכל דבריהם, ולכן הרוקין דשם טמאים: ערודות. חיות ששמן 'ערוד'. ולהכי טמאין הרוקין דשם, ששם היו נכרים נוחרין הערודות: אריב"ל: מעשה כו'. מייתי לה כל הסוגיא אגב שאמר "ערודות היו כו'". וכל הסוגיא פירשתי בפ' ג': לא כן א"ר אבהו כו' לא גזרו על הרוקין שבירושלים. אשוק העליון פריך, ולא שמיעא להו סוגיא דרבי אבין. ומשני: הא אתמר עלה כו': שיבולת כו'. מפרש טעמא דרבי יוסי. ו"שיבולת" הוא באמצע. והטהורים מהלכים מן הצד, שהיו מרחיקין עצמן לצדדין, והטמאים מהלכים סתם, שאינם מוזהרים לפרוש מהם: והטהורים אומרים להם פרושו. שהיו מזהירין להטמאים שיפרשו מלטמאן, לכן הרוק הנמצא בצדדין טהורין ובאמצע טמא: ובשעת הרגל. כי כל ישראל חברים ברגל, שנאמר (שופטים כ): "ויאסף כל איש ישראל אל העיר כאיש אחד חברים". וכולם טהורים, כי החיוב על כל ישראל לטהר עצמם ברגל. וכל טמא שאינו יכול ליטהר, יפריש עצמו לצדדים, ויתרחקו בני אדם ממנו, כדי שלא יטמאו, כי כל העדה כולם טהורים. וזהו דאמר: וטהורין מהלכים סתם וטמאים מוזהירים להן שיפרשו, לעולם המועטים הולכין בצדדין והן המוזהירין. וגירסא זו כגירסת הרמב"ם בפירושו: לא כן אמר ר"י. ואמאי אמר במתני' דרך ירידה טמאים: נעשו הוכיח. שמוכח שבירידתן לטבילה נפלו והן טמאים: אבא שאול. שהיה קורא אותם "לפורן" למגריפה דמתני': מריצה. שהיא מרילה את האבן לבית הקברות, כשחופרין ומזדמן אבן — מרילה. וגירסת הרמב"ם שהיא "מרילה את העצם". ופי' דהכי קאמר: שהיה כלי שהיו מכתתין ומרצצים בו העצמות, כדי שיכנסו בסל להוליך אותו ממקום למקום, וזה השם מגזרת "ותרץ את גלגלתו", ולמוק טומאתן היו במוקת טומאה: תני הסכין קשורה לו ה"ז כמותה. ברייתא פליגא אמתני', וס"ל דאם נמצא הסכין קשור בקופיץ הרי זה כקופיץ, ובזה ובזה שוחט ומטביל: מתני' פרכת. בולד הטומאה. שנגעה במשקים טמאים. דרבנן גזרו על המשקים שמטמאים כלים, גזירה משום משקה זב וזבה, כגון רוקו וש"ז שהן אבות הטומאה ומטמאים אדם וכלים מדאורייתא. ופרכת הוי כלי, דכשעושאין אותו ממקום למקום נותן הכלים לתוכה, ויש תורת כלי עליה לקבל טומאה: בפנים. ואינה טעונה שילוח חוץ למחנה שכינה, כיון שלא נטמא אלא בולד הטומאה: מיד. לשון הגאון: בולד הטומאה, דאין צריך הערב שמש בד"ס, כמ"ש בפ"א דטהרות. ועי' ר"ש שם: באה"ט. בשרץ או נבילה: בחוץ. דטעונה שילוח, כמ"ש בסוף עירובין: בחיל. חוץ לעזרה: כ"ד חוטין. מפרש בגמ': ארכה מ' כו'. כפתח האולם שהיה גבוה מ' ורחבו כ': ומשמונים ושתים רבוא. לשון הגאון. ר"ל: דינרים. דאי אפשר לומר על הנימין, דאם כן הל"ל קודם שאמר ארכה מ' כו': היו מטבילין. דכלים הנגמרים, אע"פ שנגמרים בטהרה, צריכים טבילה לקדש, כמ"ש בחגיגה: גמ' אילו נאמר חוט אחד. כלומר, אילו היה נאמר "חוט" הייתי מפרש אחד כלישנא דחוט יחידי. ואילו היה נאמר כפול הייתי אומר לשנים כלישנא דכפל: שזור לשלשה. משזר לששה. ד', שהיה ד' מינין: תכלת וארגמן תולעת שני ושש. הרי ד' פעמים ו', הא כ"ד: תני. בברייתא: ל"ב, שהיו החוטין כולן ל"ב: משזר לח'. ד"משזר" משמע כפול, דשזור וד' פעמים ח' הא ל"ב: קליע. הוא קלוע ג' יחד: שזור כפול דקליע. ו"משזר" י"ב, וד' פעמים י"ב, הא מ"ח: מעשה רוקם כו'. איידי דנקט דרשא ד"פרכת", נקט נמי הכי דרשא ד"מעשה חשב" ו"מעשה רקם" דכתיבי בפרכת: ה"ג: חד אמר ארי מכאן וארי מכאן וחלק כו'. מעשה חושב כו' וארי מכאן, דהיינו ב' פרצופות: ואוחרנא כו'. מעשה רוקם ב' פרצופות שוות. לשון "רוקם" — שנרקם צורה בב' הצדדין: גוזמא. קאי על הא דתני במתניתין שלש מאות כהנים, דהוא גוזמא בעלמא. ומביא מתני' דתמיד ג"כ ג' מאות, ואמר עלה דהוא גוזמא: מתני' ישרף בפנים. בבית הדשן הגדול שהיה בעזרה ששם שורפין פסולי קדשי קדשים, שכל שפסולו בקודש שורפין אותו בקדש [לשון הגאון], דמותרין להיות במקדש משום שאין לו טהרה במקוה, או משום שאינו נעשה אב הטומאה, כמ"ש בסוף עירובין: באה"ט בחוץ. כיון דחמירא טומאתו ונפסל בחוץ, אף להכניסן לעזרה, הואיל ולא היה פסולו בקדש: בולד הטומאה בפנים. דלית בה תרתי: טומאתו בפנים וקילא טומאתו, אבל נטמא

מסורת הש"ס

א) מנחות קג ב: ב) לעיל פ"ג הל"ב וירושלמי שבת פ"ח הל"א ועי' מנחות קג ב: ג) עדיות פ"ח מ"א: ד) מכשירין פ"ו מ"ה: ה) פסחים יט ב: ו) שם יט ב: ז) תמיד כט א חולין צ ב: ח) יומא עא ב: ט) שם עב ב: י) תמיד כט א חולין צ ב:

עין משפט נר מצוה

ה א מיי' פי"ג מהלכ' מאה"ט הל"ז:

ו ב מיי' פרק א מאה"ט הל"ד:

ז ג מיי' פרק י מטומאת אוכלין הלכה ג:

ח ד מיי' פרק י"ג מאה"ט הל"ח:

ט ה מיי' פ"ז מכלי המקדש הל"ח:

י ו מיי' שם הלט"ז:

יא ז מיי' שם פ"ח הלכה טו:

נוסחת הבבלי

(א) קצירן של זבין היו שם כו' נוחרין לאריות בירושלם כו': (ב) בשם דר' יוסי קצרין כו' ולא אניביה כו' ר' ביבין כו' יצחק עד כו' דעתי כי משום דאית לי חטין למיזבן דא"ר חנינה והיו כו' ר"י בן בתירה על כו' א"ר יוסף פליגי כו' כר"י בן בתירה כו' לא כן א"ר יעקב בר' אחא בשם ר"י בר' חנינא כו' קצרין של זבין היו שם כו' מן הצד וטהורי' מהלכין מן סתם וטמאים וכו' לא כן א"ר יוחנן כו' הוכיח ר"י אומר כולן טהורין אבא שאול היה קורא כו': (ג) בחיל ואם היתה כו': (ד) תנינן החלו מעלים באפר ע"ג תפוח ותפוח היה באמצעיתו של מזבח פעמים עולה

הגהות הגר"א

[א] ה"ג א"ר חנינא ערודות היו נוחרין שם אריב"ל מעשה היו נוחרין ערודות באסטרטיא של מלך והיו עולי רגלים משתקעין בדם עד וכו'. כצ"ל: [ב] ה"ג הטמאים מהלכין מן סתם והטהורים אומרים להן פרושו ובשעת הרגל טהורין מהלכין שבולת והטמאין מהלכין מן הצד וטהורין מהלכין מן סתם והטמאים אומרים להם פרושו כצ"ל וה"פ דסתם גמ' בא לפרש טעמא דר' יוסי ושבולת הוא הוא באמצע והטהורי' מהלכים מן הצד שהיו מרחיקין עצמן לצדדין והטמאים מהלכין סתם שאינם מזהירי' לפרוש מהם והטהורי' אומרים להם פרושו שהיו מזהירין להטמאים שיפרשו מלטמאן ולכן הרוק הנמצא בצדדין טהורין ובאמצע טמא. ובשעת הרגל שכל ישראל חברים שנא' (שופטי' כ) ויאסף כל איש ישראל אל העיר כאיש אחד חברים וכולם טהורים כי החיוב על כל ישראל לטהר עצמם ברגל וכל טמא שאינו יכול ליטהר יפרים עצמו לצדדים ויתרחקו ב"א ממנו כדי שלא יטמאו כי כל העדה כל העדה כולם טהורים וזהו דאמר וטהורין מהלכין סתם וכמאן מזהירין להן שיפרשו לעולם המועטין הולכין בצדדין והן המזהירין וגירסא זו כגירסת הרמב"ם בפירושו: [ג] ה"ג חד אמר מעשה רוקם ארי

גליון הש"ס לא הטבילו הבעלים הסכין מאתמול ואין לדון על הסכין והקופיץ כלל ועי' ש"ס פסחים שם: [א] עי' בהגר"א שהגיה ועי' מלמ"ל פ"ח מכלי המקדש הלכה טו:

דאית ביה תרתי: טומאתו בפנים, וקילא טומאתו. אבל נטמא באב הטומאה — אין להשהותו עד שתשרף, אלא יוציאנה מיד וישרפנה בחוץ: ישרף בפנים. דכיון דטהור מדאורייתא, אפי' נטמא בחוץ יש לקיים בו שריפתו בקדש: גמ' ולד הטומאה. היינו שנטמא בטומאה דרבנן: זה וזה לא דבר תורה. בתמיה. וכיון דמדאורייתא טמא — אין להכניסו לעזרה, הואיל ולא היה פסולו בקודש: לא הוו רבנן. לא פלפלו חכמים בדברי ר' יוחנן, דלר' יוחנן ל"ק, דאב הטומאה חמירא. אבל מולד הטומאה הקילו בה. א"נ: לא פלפלו חכמים בדברי ר"י, דודאי קשיא. אלא בדברי בר קפרא דקדקו: ומשני: בגין דר"ע. בשביל טעמו של ר"ע, דקאמר: מקום טומאתו שם שריפתו, ה"נ קאמרי ב"ש באב הטומאה: ישרף בחוץ, אבל בולד הטומאה — ישרף בפנים, כיון דמדבריהם הוא — ישרף בפנים, ששריפתו בקדש: בגין דר"ש וכו'. בשביל הא דאמר ר' שמעון דמשלחין אפי' אוכלין טמאין לחוץ, הלכך כל מה שנטמא בחוץ אין מביאין אותו לפנים:

הלכה ד מתני' מחצי הכבש ולמטה במערב. כהנים הזוכים בפייס באברי התמיד להעלותם, לא היו מעלים אותם בפעם אחת, אלא נותנים אותם על הכבש, והולכים ללשכת הגזית לקרות את "שמע", ואחר כך חוזרין ומקריבין האברים ע"ג המזבח. הכבש ארוך ל"ב אמה, ומחציו ולמטה נותנין אותן, ורוחב הכבש ט"ז אמה, ובחציו של צד מערב היו נותנים אותן: ושל ראש חדש על כרכוב המזבח. בגמרא מפרש: אינן נוהגין אלא בפני הבית. שקלים — משום דלורך קרבן נינהו, וכיון שאין קרבן — אין שקלים. ובכורים — דכתיב "ראשית בכורי אדמתך תביא בית ה' אלהיך" — בזמן שיש בית — יש ביכורים, אין בית — אין ביכורים: אבל מעשר דגן וכו'. נוהגין בפני הבית, דקדושת הארץ לא בטלה: מעשר בהמה. צריך להפריש העשירי: המקדיש שקלים וביכורים. בזמן הזה: ביכורים אינן קדש. דכתיב בהו בהדיא "תביא בית ה'" — אין שם ביכורים חל עליהן שלא בפני הבית: גמ' מי קודם בהקרבתן, אם שתיהן לפניו: חייליה דרבי ירמיה. כלומר, כוחו וראייתו דר"י מהא: שירו של ר"ח קודם. וסבר ר"י דה"ה קרבן ר"ח קודם: א"ר יוסי. שאני התם דלכך שיר של ר"ח קודם כדי לפרסם שהוא ר"ח, אבל קרבן שבת קודם לר"ח: הא שקלים קדשי. מודה ר"ש אם אומר "ביכורים קדש" שהן קדש: הגר בזמן הזה. אע"ג דליכא מקדש — צריך שיפריש רובע דינר לקינו, דלכשיבנה ב"ה יביא קן. דגר צריך קרבן, ובפחות מרובע לא מצי להפריש, דאין מצוי קן בפחות מרובע: מפני התקלה. שמא יהנה ממנו: ואין מחרימין. דחרם הוא ק"ק, דכתיב "כל חרם קדש וגו'": הבהמה תעקר. דלא ליתי בה לידי תקלה: והיא מתה מאיליה. ברעב: עבר והקדיש. מהו שיהיה קדש? הכא. גבי קן של גר את אמר אם עבר וקדשו קדש, והכא גבי שקלים

ר"א אוֹמֵר: שֶׁנִּטְמָא בְּאַב הַטּוּמְאָה, בֵּין בִּפְנִים בֵּין בַּחוּץ — יִשָּׂרֵף בַּחוּץ, שֶׁנִּטְמָא בִּוְלַד הַטּוּמְאָה בֵּין בַּחוּץ בֵּין בִּפְנִים — יִשָּׂרֵף בִּפְנִים. ר"ע אוֹמֵר: אמְקוֹם טוּמְאָתוֹ שָׁם שְׂרֵיפָתוֹ.§ **גמ'** בַּר א) קַפָּרָא אָמַר: אַב הַטּוּמְאָה — דְּבַר תּוֹרָה, וְלַד הַטּוּמְאָה — מִדִּבְרֵיהֶם. ר' יוֹחָנָן אָמַר: בֵּין זֶה בֵּין זֶה דְּבַר תּוֹרָה. וְקַשְׁיָא דר' יוֹחָנָן עַל דְּבֵית שַׁמַּאי, דְּבֵית שַׁמַּאי אוֹמְרִים: הַכֹּל יִשָּׂרֵף בִּפְנִים, חוּץ מִשֶּׁנִּטְמָא בְּאַב הַטּוּמְאָה בַּחוּץ. מַה בֵּין אַב הַטּוּמְאָה בַּחוּץ מַה בֵּין וְלַד הַטּוּמְאָה בַּחוּץ, זֶה וְזֶה לֹא דְּבַר תּוֹרָה הוּא? וַאֲפִילוּ עַל דְּבֵית הִלֵּל לָא מִקַּשְׁיָא, דב"ה אָמַר: הַכֹּל יִשָּׂרֵף בַּחוּץ — חוּץ מַה שֶּׁנִּטְמָא בִּוְלַד הַטּוּמְאָה בִּפְנִים. מַה בֵּין וְלַד הַטּוּמְאָה בִּפְנִים מַה בֵּין אַב הַטּוּמְאָה בִּפְנִים, זֶה וְזֶה לֹא דְּבַר תּוֹרָה הוּא? לָא הָווּ בָהּ רַבָּנַן אֶלָּא עַל דְּבַר קַפָּרָא. וְקַשְׁיָא דְּבַר קַפָּרָא עַל דְּבֵית שַׁמַּאי. דְּבֵית שַׁמַּאי אוֹמְרִים: הַכֹּל יִשָּׂרֵף בִּפְנִים חוּץ מִשֶּׁנִּטְמָא בְּאַב הַטּוּמְאָה בַּחוּץ, מַה בֵּין אַב הַטּוּמְאָה בֵּין בַּחוּץ בֵּין בִּפְנִים, זֶה וְזֶה לֹא ד"ת הוּא? (א) בְּגִין דר"ע אָמַר מְקוֹם טוּמְאָתוֹ שָׁם תְּהֵא שְׂרֵיפָתוֹ. וַאֲפִילוּ עַל דְּבֵית הִילֵּל לָא מִקַּשְׁיָא. דב"ה אָמַר: הַכֹּל יִשָּׂרֵף בַּחוּץ חוּץ מִשֶּׁנִּטְמָא בִּוְלַד הַטּוּמְאָה בִּפְנִים, מַה בֵּין וְלַד הַטּוּמְאָה בֵּין בִּפְנִים בֵּין בַּחוּץ זֶה וְזֶה לֹא מִדִּבְרֵיהֶם הוּא? בְּגִין דר"ש אָמַר: [א] מַאֲכָלוֹ וּמַשְׁקוֹ שֶׁל מְצוֹרָע מִשְׁתַּלְּחִין חוּץ לְשָׁלֹשׁ מַחֲנוֹת.§

הלכה ד מתני' באֵיבְרֵי ב) הַתָּמִיד נִיתָּנִין מֵחֲצִי כֶּבֶשׁ וּלְמַטָּה (ב) (בַּמִּזְרָח) בַּמַּעֲרָב. שֶׁל מוּסָפִין — נִיתָּנִין מֵחֲצִי כֶּבֶשׁ וּלְמַטָּה (בַּמַּעֲרָב) בַּמִּזְרָח. שֶׁל רָאשֵׁי חֳדָשִׁים נִיתָּנִין עַל כַּרְכּוֹב הַמִּזְבֵּחַ (לְמַטָּה) מִלְמַעְלָן. גהַשְּׁקָלִים דוְהַבִּיכּוּרִים אֵינָן נוֹהֲגִין אֶלָּא בִּפְנֵי הַבַּיִת, אֲבָל ג) המַעֲשֵׂר דָּגָן ווּמַעֲשַׂר בְּהֵמָה זוּבְכוֹרוֹת — נוֹהֲגִין בֵּין בִּפְנֵי הַבַּיִת וּבֵין שֶׁלֹּא בִּפְנֵי הַבַּיִת. הַמַּקְדִּישׁ שְׁקָלִים וּבִיכּוּרִים — הֲרֵי זֶה קוֹדֶשׁ. ר"ש אוֹמֵר: הָאוֹמֵר בִּיכּוּרִים קוֹדֶשׁ — אֵינָן קוֹדֶשׁ.§

גמ' [א] אֵיזֶהוּ ד) כַּרְכּוֹב הַמִּזְבֵּחַ — חאַמָּה בֵּין קֶרֶן לְקֶרֶן, מְקוֹם הִילּוּךְ רַגְלֵי כֹהֲנִים. מוּסְפֵי ה) שַׁבָּת מוּסְפֵי ר"ח מִי קוֹדֵם? ר' יִרְמְיָה סָבַר (ג) מֵימַר: מוּסְפֵי שַׁבָּת וּמוּסְפֵי ר"ח — מוּסְפֵי ר"ח קוֹדְמִין. חַיְילֵיהּ דר' יִרְמְיָה מִן הָדָא: שִׁירוֹ ו) שֶׁל שַׁבָּת וְשִׁירוֹ שֶׁל ר"ח טשִׁירוֹ שֶׁל ר"ח קוֹדֵם. א"ר יוֹסֵה: שַׁנְיָיא הִיא תַּמָּן, דְּאָמַר ר' חִיָּיא בְּשֵׁם רַבִּי יוֹחָנָן: כְּדֵי לְפַרְסְמוֹ וּלְהוֹדִיעַ שֶׁהוּא ר"ח [ב] כֵּיצַד הָיָה עוֹשֶׂה? שׁוֹחֵט מוּסְפֵי שַׁבָּת וְאוֹמֵר עֲלֵיהֶן שִׁירוֹ שֶׁל ר"ח בְּרַם הָכָא — מוּסְפֵי שַׁבָּת וּמוּסְפֵי ר"ח — ימוּסְפֵי שַׁבָּת קוֹדְמִין, עַל שֵׁם כָּל הַתָּדִיר מֵחֲבֵירוֹ קוֹדֵם אֶת חֲבֵירוֹ.§ [ג] "שְׁקָלִים וּבִיכּוּרִים" וְכוּ'.§ הָא שְׁקָלִים קָדְשׁוּ. רַבִּי שִׁמְעוֹן בֶּן יְהוּדָה מִשּׁוּם רַבִּי שִׁמְעוֹן: בֵּין אֵלּוּ וּבֵין אֵלּוּ לֹא קָדְשׁוּ. תָּנֵי: ז) כגֵּר בִּזְמַן הַזֶּה צָרִיךְ לְהָבִיא קִינּוֹ רִיבְעִית כֶּסֶף. אר"ש בִּיטְּלָהּ ר' יוֹחָנָן בֶּן זַכַּאי מִפְּנֵי הַתַּקָּלָה. מַהוּ מִפְּנֵי הַתַּקָּלָה — כְּהָדָה דְּתָנֵי: ח) אֵין מַקְדִּישִׁין וְלֹא מַעֲרִיכִין וְלֹא מַחֲרִימִין [ד] וְלֹא מַגְבִּיהִין תְּרוּמוֹת וּמַעַשְׂרוֹת בַּזְּמַן הַזֶּה, וְאִם הִקְדִּישׁ אוֹ הֶעֱרִיךְ אוֹ הֶחֱרִים [ה] אוֹ הִגְבִּיהַּ — הַכְּסוּת תִּשָּׂרֵף, הַבְּהֵמָה — תֵּיעָקֵר. כֵּיצַד? נוֹעֵל בְּפָנֶיהָ הַדֶּלֶת וְהִיא מֵתָה מֵאֵילֶיהָ. וְהַמָּעוֹת יֵלְכוּ לְיָם הַמֶּלַח.§ עָבַר וְהִקְדִּישׁ, מִן מַה דְּאָמַר ר"ש בִּיטְּלָהּ רַבָּן יוֹחָנָן בֶּן זַכַּאי מִפְּנֵי הַתַּקָּלָה — הָדָא (ד) אֲמָרָה עָבַר וְהִקְדִּישׁ קָדְשׁוּ. רַבִּי יוֹדֶה עֲנְתוֹדְרַיָּיא בָּעֵי קוֹמֵי רַבִּי יוֹסֵי: הָכָא אַתְּ אָמַר

ריבב"ן

ומטאו ביום השביעי כל היכא דקרינא ביה ומטאו דראוי לחיטוי (מי שראוי לחיטוי ראוי *)לטבילה וקרינן ביה והנפש הנוגעת בו תטמא וכל היכא דלא קרינן ביה ומטאו לא קרינן ביה והנפש הנוגעת יטמא לאפוקי כלי חרס ואוכלין ומשקין הואיל ואין להם טהרה במקוה אינן נעשין אב הטומאה כפירש"י בסוף עירובין: ישרף בפנים. במקום ששורפין שאר פסולי ק"ק דתניא בפסחים פ"ג [דף כד] ר"ש אומר בקדש באש תשרף לימד על חטאת ששריפתה בקדש אין לי אלא זו בלבד שאר פסולי ק"ק ואימורי קדשים קלים מנין ת"ל כל בקדש באש תשרף ואמרינן בפרק טבול יום ת"ר ג' בית הדשנין הן א' בעזרה ששם שורפין פסולי ק"ק ואימורי קדשים קלים וכו': חוץ משנטמאת באב הטומאה בחוץ. שלא ישרפום בפנים דהואיל ויצא יצא: ב"ה אומרים ישרף הכל בחוץ. והא דתניא לעיל פסולי קדשי קדשים נשרפין בפנים בשאר פסולין כגון הלן והיוצא והנשחט חוץ לזמנו וחוץ למקומו וכיוצא בו אבל פסול טומאה לא ובירושלמי מקשה בין לב"ש בין לב"ה אידי ואידי לאו דבר תורה הוא פי' בין שנטמאה באב בטומאה בין שנטמאה בולד הטומאה טומאתו לאו דאורייתא ואמאי מחלקין בין נטמא באב הטומאה לנטמא בולד הטומאה: מתני' ר' **אליעזר אומר באב הטומאה.** דחמירא טומאתו ישרף בחוץ בולד הטומאה דקילא טומאתו מכניסה בפנים ושורפה ור' עקיבא סבר מקום טומאתו שם תהא שריפתו בין שנטמא באב הטומאה בין שנטמא בולד הטומאה ישרף בפנים: מתני' אברי **תמיד** נתנין **מחצי כבש ולמטה במערב.** כשמוליכין אברים מבית המטבחיים מניחין האברים בכבש כדתנן בפ"ב דיומא הפיים השני מי שוחט מי זורק מי מעלה אברים לכבש ותניא בסיפא הפיים הרביעי מי מעלה אברים מן הכבש למזבח ושל מוספין ניתנין מחצי כבש ולמטה במזרח להיכרא בעלמא ושל ראשי חדשים ניתנין על כרכוב המזבח ומפרש במסכת סוכה [דף נה] א"ר יוחנן לידע שהוקבע ר"ח בזמנו: השקלים והבכורים אין נוהגין **אלא בפני הבית.** לפי שהשקלין נעשין לצורך תמידין ומוספין ובכורין בעו הנחה לפני המזבח כדכתיב והניחו לפני מזבח ה' ועכשיו אין מזבח מעשר דגן דהיינו מעשר שני נוהגין אפילו בזמן הזה וצריך להעלות לירושלים כדאיתא בבילה פ"ק במעשה דר' אליעזר שהיה [לו] כרם רבעי והפקירו לעניים מפני שלא היה יכול לעלות הוא ונתנו לעניים כדי שיוליכוהו שם וכרם רבעי ומעשר שני דינן שוה דילפינן קודש קודש ממעשר ומתני' דלא כר' ישמעאל דתניא בתמורה בפ"ג ר' ישמעאל אומר יכול יעלה אדם מעשר שני בזמן הזה לירושלים ודין הוא בכור טעון הבאת מקום וכו' ומעשר בהמה ובכורות ימתין עד שיוממו ובכורות נותנין לכהנים ויאכלום במומן והמעשר יאכלוהו בעלים: **המקדיש שקלים** ובכורים הרי זה קודש. בכורים ירקבו ושקלים יגנזו **ר"ש אומר האומר בבורים** קודש **אינם** קודש. ירושלמי הא שקלים קדש ר"ש בן יהודה אומר משום ר"ש בין אלו ובין אלו לא קדשו. תניא בתוספתא בפ' בתרא קינו של גר אינה נוהגת אלא בפני הבית ר' שמעון אומר אינו צריך להביא מפני התקלה מפני מה אמרו שקלים אינם נוהגים אלא בפני הבית לפי שאין תורמין מן הישנה מפני מה אמרו ביכורין אינן נוהגין אלא בפני הבית משום שנאמר ראשית בכורי אדמתך תביא בית ה' אלהיך כל זמן שיש לך בית יש לך בכורין אין בית אין בכורים: ירושלמי תני הגר בזמן הזה צריך להביא קינו ריבעת כסף אמר ר' שמעון ריב"ז בטלה מפני התקלה פי' הגר שנתגייר בזמן הבית היה צריך להביא קרבן דוקא קינין ושתיהן עולות ותניא בפ"ב דכריתות ר' אומר ככם כגר כאבותיכם מה אבותיכם לא נכנסו לברית אלא במילה וטבילה והרצאת דמים כך הם לא יכנסו לברית אלא במילה וטבילה והרצאת דמים והאי דאמר רובע שקל היינו דינר כדפרישית לעיל עמדו בו ביום

*) נ"ל והיינו שיש לו טהרה בטבילה קרינן ביה והנפש וכו' וכ"ה בפירש"י ז"ל שם.

תקלין חדתין

באה"ט אין להשהות הטומאה בפנים עד שתשרף, אלא יוציאנה מיד וישרפנו בחוץ: ישרף בפנים. דכיון דטהור מדאורייתא, אפי' נטמא בחוץ יש לקיים שריפתו בקדש: **גמ'** בר קפרא אומר: ד"ת אב הטומאה ולד הטומאה מדבריהם. דמוקי מה דאמר במתני' אה"ט ודאי דאורייתא, אבל ולד הטומאה — היינו בדרבנן, כגון שנגע במשקין דמדאורייתא, אין אוכלין ומשקין מטמאין כלי, שאין אוכל נעשה אב הטומאה. ורבנן גזרו שיהא משקין מטמאין כלי משום משקה זב וזבה שהן אב הטומאה, כגון רוקו ומימי רגליו. וזה הבשר נגע בולד הטומאה דרבנן זה, דמדאורייתא לא הוי אפילו ולד הטומאה, דאין כלי נטמא ממשקין הנ"ל. והא דנקט אב הטומאה דאורייתא — היינו דכל אב הטומאה דאורייתא. א"נ: משום דאיכא אב הטומאה דרבנן, כגון מעת לעת שבנדה ובית הפרס וארץ העמים: בין בזה כו'. דולד הטומאה היינו שנגע הבשר בכלי שנגע במשקה זב וזבה שהוא ולד הטומאה דאורייתא, והוי הבשר שני, שהכלי שהוא ראשון לטומאה אם נגע באוכל עשהו שני: זה וזה לא ד"ת הוא. בתמיה. הא לר"י גם ולד הטומאה ד"ת היא, ומ"ש לב"ש אה"ט מולד הטומאה: ופריך: ואפילו על דבית הלל. מי לא קשיא לר"י: לא הוו בה רבנן. לא שקלי וטרי רבנן, אלא לפרושי מתני' אליבא דבר קפרא: מה בין אה"ט בין בחוץ כו'. וקשיא לבר קפרא: בגין דר"ע. דר"א קושטא דקאמר בסיפא בין בפנים כי קושין, אבל ר"ע ס"ל מקום טומאתו שם שריפתו. וטעמיה: דולד הטומאה משום דהוי טהור מדאורייתא, דולד הטומאה דרבנן איירי כאן, ולכך ישרף בפנים מקום טומאתו: בגין דר"ש ה"נ דר"ש **אמר אוכלין** ומשקין של **מצורע אין מביאין** לג' מחנות. ולהכי מה שנטמא בחוץ אף בולד הטומאה דרבנן אין מביאין לפנים. ור"ש זה לא מצאתי מקומו. ונראה דר"ש לטעמיה אזיל, דבספ"ק דכלים בתוספתא ר"ש אומר: כשם שאין זבות ונדות ויולדות נכנסין להר הבית, כך משכבן ומושבן כיוצא בהן. והכי נמי במצורע אוכלין ומשקין שלו, שנטמאו ממנו. וגירסת הספרים "משתלחין" שיבושא. דאם כן, אף בולד הטומאה בפנים ישרף בחוץ מה"ט! ועוד, שילוח אוכלין ומשקין מאן שמעת ליה? **מתני'** מחצי כבש ולמטה במערב. כהנים הזוכים בפייס באיברי התמיד להעלותם לא היו מעלים אותן בפעם אחת, אלא נותנים אותן על הכבש, ומחציו ולמטה נותנין אותו. שרוחב הכבש ט"ז אמה, ובחציו שלצד מערב היו נותנין אותן: ושל ר"ח על כרכוב המזבח. בגמ' מפרש: השקלים כו' בפני הבית. שקלים — משום דלורך קרבן נינהו, וכשאין קרבן אין שקלים: וביכורים. דכתיב "ראשית בכורי אדמתך תביא בית ה' אלהיך" — בזמן שיש לך בית, יש לך ביכורים כו': מעשר דגן כו'. דקדושת הארץ לא בטלה: מעשר בהמה. בריש פרק בתרא דבכורות אמרו שביטלוהו מפני התקלה: המקדיש שקלים וביכורים דאינם נוהגים אלא בפני הבית, אם הפרישן שלא בפני הבית — קדשי. לשון רבינו הגאון נראה כפירוש ראשון של הרע"ב דמפריש קאמר, מדלא נקט אלא הני תרתי: "ביכורים קדש" אינן קדש. כיון דבהדיא כתיב בהו "תביא בית ה' אלהיך", אפי' הפרישן בדיעבד — לא קדשי, ואין שם ביכורים חל עליהן שלא בפני הבית: **גמ'** איזהו כרכוב המזבח. פרישית לעיל פרק ו' הלכה ה': מוספי שבת כו'. קאי אמתני' שהזכיר מוספי שבת ור"ח. ושואל: איזה מהן קודם להקרבה כשחל ר"ח בשבת: חיליה דר"י. ראייתו: כדי לפרסמו כו'. הכי מתרץ לה ר"י בבבלי סוכה: דהאי תשיותא עבדינן להיכרא, שיכירו הכל דפשיטא להו לב"ד שקדשוהו כהלכתו, ולא יגמגם לב אדם עליו, דרוב בני אדם לא ראו חידוש הלבנה. וזהו דוקא בשיר, משא"כ לענין הקרבה כו' "כל התדיר כו'". כילד הוא עושה כו' — שיר ראש חודש קודם שיר שבת. וגירסת הספרים שיבוש דמוכח: הא שקלים קדשי רשב"י **אומר משום** ר"ש כו'. פליג אתנא דמתני' בשם ר"ש: תני. במסכת כריתות (ט, א): רביעית כסף. רובע דינר. דלכשיבנה בהמ"ק יביא קן. דאמרינן דצריך קרבן, וקרבן בפחות מרובע לא אפשר להפריש, דאין מצוי קן בפחות מרובע, כדאמרינן במתניתין "ועמדו קינין ברבעתים", אבל פחות אי אפשר: מפני התקלה. שלא יהנה ממנו: אין מקדישין ואין מחרימין. דחרם הוי קדש כהקדש, דכתיב "כל חרם קדש קדשים": תעקר. דלא ליתו בה לידי תקלה: לים המלח. משום דבעי שחיקה בשאר נהרות, ובים המלח מטיל בעיניה לכן אמר ים המלח: עבר והקדיש. גבי רביעית כסף דגר, אם עבר והקדיש לאחר שבטלה ריב"ז: מאי. אם קדש בדיעבד ודינו כדין הקדש וחרם דתנן המעות יוליכו לים המלח, או לא חל שם הקדש עלייהו: מן מה **דאמר מפני התקלה.** משמע דלא בטלה אלא מפני התקלה, אבל בדיעבד קדשה: **ענתודריא**= שם מקומו: **הכא את**

...שקלים וביכורים וכו': [ג] כאן גרסי' כילד הוא עשה שוחט מוספי שבת ואומר עליהן שיר ר"ח וגי' הספרי' שבוש דמוכח: [ד] ולא מגביהין תרומות ומעשרות לא גרסינן: [ה] או הגביה ליג:

מסורת הש"ס

א) ירושלמי מע"ש פ"ג הל"ט ועי' פסחים פ"א ה"ו ב) סוכה נה: ג) בכורות נג: ד) ירושלמי סוכה פ"ה ה"ו ה) תוספתא פרק ב ו) סוכה נד ב: ז) כריתות ט א: ח) יומא סו א וש"נ:

עין משפט נר מצוה

יב א מיי' פרק י"ט מפסולי המוקדשין הל"ט
יג ב מיי' פרק ו מתמידין הל"ב
יד ג מיי' פרק א משקלים הל"ח
טו ד מיי' פרק ב מבכורים הל"ב
טז ה מיי' פרק א מתרומות הל"א
יז ו מיי' פרק ו מבכורות הל"ב
יח ז מיי' שם פ"א הלכה ה
יט ח מיי' פרק ו מתמידין הל"ב
כ ט מיי' שם הל"ו
כא י מיי' שם פ"ט הלכה ב
כב כ מיי' פרק ו מאיסורי ביאה הלכה ג

נוסחת הבבלי

עליו ג' מאות כו' ר"י בר אבין בשם שמואל נחמא: (א) בגין דר"ע אמר כו' בגין דר"ש אמר כו': (ב) במזרח של מוספין כו' במערב ושל ר"ח כו' ניתנין מתחת כרכוב כו' מלמטה כו': (ג) מימר מוספי ר"ח קודם כו': (ד) אמורה הקדש עבר כו' בבן הבא כו' שנה היא אבל לגבי כו' הל' כר"ש:

הגהות הגר"א

[א] ה"ג מאכלו ומשקו של מצורע אין מביאין לג' מחנות...

גליון הש"ס [א] עי' במלמ"ל פ"ו ממעה"ק הלכה ד':

ציון ירושלים דר"ש אמר מאכלו ומשקו של מצורע משתלחין חוץ לשלש מחנות. לא ראיתי מוזכר זאת אבל בהגהת הגאון מהרא"י הגיה בזה ע"ש: **סליק**

עין משפט נר מצוה

כג א מיי' פרק ח מערכין הל"ח ט:

כד ב מיי' שם פ"ו הלכה טז:

הגהות הגר"א

[א] ה"ג א"ל תמן אין מקדש ויניח עד שיבנה בה"מ שמא יבנה הבית בראשון ותתרם תרומת הלשכ' מן החדש בזמנה בא' בניסן והכא מאי אית לך רב המנונא ורב אדא בר אהבה בשם רב הלכה כר' שמעון כל"ל והשאר שבינתי' נמחק וה"פ תמן אין מקדש ולהכי בשקלים לא קדשי דעיקר טעם דאין להקדיש שקלים בזמן הזה משום שאין מקדש ולא חל שם הקדש עליו כלל דאף אם יבנה בהמ"ק חיישינן שלא יבואו להקדש וזהו דקאמר ויניח עד וכו' שמא יבנה הבית בראשון היינו בחדש ניסן בתחלתה כמ"ש ויהי בחדש הראשון וכו' הוקם המשכן ותתרם תרומת הלשכה מן החדש ולא יהיה ראוי שקליו שהקדיש כלל דהוי לה ישנה ולא משום תקלה דאף אם יבנה בהמ"ק בכה"ג לא יקדש ולכן לא חל והכי איתא בתוספתא פ' בתרא דמכילתין טעמא דאין שקלים נוהגים בזמן הזה משום תרומה ישנה משא"כ הכא ברביעית כסף דגר דהקדש חל עליה דכשיבנה בהמ"ק ראוי רובע דינר שלו לקרבן רק דבטלה ריב"ז מפני תקלה להקדישו לכתחלה ולא אתי טעמא דתקלה ומפקיע לשם הקדש ממנו. וגירסת הספרים משובשים והקדשות אחרים מאן דכר שמייהו הכא: סליק

קרבן העדה

שקלים את אמר לא קדשו! ולר"ש בן יהודה דלעיל פריך: **א"ל: תמן גבי שקלים** — אין מקדישין לכתחלה, דה"ל מתרומה ישנה, שמא יעבור השנה, ומתקנת חכמים דאפי' בדיעבד לא קדשי: ה"ג: **האי ישנה היא לגבי הקדשות אחרים, וקינו של גר א"צ שיהיה** מן החדש. הלכך: אם הקדיש — קדוש בדיעבד: ופריך: **ויניח עד שיבנה בהמ"ק.** גם בשקלים יניח עד בנין בהמ"ק ותהיה חדשה: ומשני: **שמא יבנה הבית כבראשונה. בניסן ותתרם** התרומה אז, ומה שנדר כבר — ה"ל ישנה: **והכא.** גבי קינו של גר מה אית לך למיחש? הלכך קדוש:

הדרן עלך פרק כל הרוקין
וסליקא לה מסכת שקלים

אָמַר קָדְשׁוּ! וְהָכָא אַתְּ אֲמַר לֹא קָדְשׁוּ א"ל [א] תַּמָּן לְכָךְ אֵין אמַקְדִּישִׁין לְכַתְּחִלָּה — לְפִי שֶׁמִּצְוָה לְהַקְרִיב מִתְּרוּמָה חֲדָשָׁה, וְהֵיאַךְ ה"ל יְשָׁנָה. וְהָכָא מַאי אִית לָךְ לְמֵימַר הַאי יְשָׁנָה הִיא *לְגַבֵּי הֶקְדֵּשׁוֹת אֲחֵרִים. וְקִינּוֹ שֶׁל גֵּר אֵינוֹ צָרִיךְ חֲדָשָׁה, וְאִם הִקְדִּישׁ — קָדוֹשׁ, וְיַנִּיחֶנָּה עַד שֶׁיִּבָּנֶה בֵּית הַמִּקְדָּשׁ. שֶׁמָּא יִבָּנֶה הַבַּיִת כְּבָרִאשׁוֹנָה, וְתִתָּרֵם תְּרוּמַת הַלִּשְׁכָּה מִן הַחֲדָשָׁה בִּזְמַנָּהּ בְּאֶחָד בְּנִיסָן. וְהָכָא מַאי אִית לָךְ? רַב הַמְנוּנָא וְרַב אַדָּא בַּר אַהֲבָה בְּשֵׁם רַב: בהֲלָכָה כר"ש (רַב אַדָּא וְרַב הַמְנוּנָא רַב אַדָּא בַּר אַחֲוָה בְּשֵׁם רַב הֲלָכָה כר"ש).§

הדרן עלך פרק כל הרוקין וסליקא לה מסכת שקלים

ריבב"ן

ברבעתים ושקל היינו סלע וסלע ד' דינרין. פי' אמר רובע דינר כדאמרינן לעיל. ירושלמי עבר והקדיש מן מה דאמר ר' שמעון ריב"ז בטלה הדא אמרה עבר והקדיש קדשו ר' יודן בעא קומי ר' יוסי הכא אתמר קדשו פי' ברובע שקל של גר והכא אתמר לא קדשו פי' בשקלים ובכורים אמר ליה תמן שמא יבנה בית המקדש ותתרם תרומת הלשכה בזמנה באחד בניסן והכא מה אית לך רב אדא ורב המנונא בשם רב אמרי הלכה כר' שמעון:

סליקא לה מסכת שקלים בס"ד

נוסחאות ישנות

אבל

תקלין חדתין

אמר קדשו. היינו ברביעית כסף דגר, כדאמר הכא: **והכא את אמר לא קדשו.** היינו בשקלים לר"ש בן יהודה אליבא דר"ש, דגם בשקלי' ס"ל דלא קדשו אף בדיעבד. ומביכורים לא קשיא, משום דאימעיטא לה מקרא דלא חל עליה שם "ביכורים" כלל. אבל שקלים ס"ד דמשום תקלה גם כן דומיא דרביעית של גר, ואם כן אמאי לא קדשו בדיעבד כמו רביעית של גר: ה"ג: **תמן אין מקדש.** להכי בשקלים לא קדשי, דעיקר טעם דאין להקדיש שקלים בזמן הזה, משום שאין מקדש ולא חל שם הקדש עליה כלל, דאף אם יבנה בית המקדש חיישינן שלא יבואו להקדש. וזהו דקאמר "ויניח עד כו' שמא יבנה הבית בראשון", היינו במודש ניסן כתחלתה, כמ"ש "ויהי בחדש הראשון כו' הוקם המשכן", ותתרם תרומת הלשכה מן החדש ולא יהיה ראוי שקליו שהקדיש כלל, דהוי לה ישנה. ולא משום תקלה, דאף אם יבנה בית המקדש בכה"ג לא יקדש, ולכן לא חל. והכי איתא בתוספתא פרק בתרא דמכילתין: טעמא דאין שקלים נוהגים בזמן הזה — משום תרומה ישנה. משא"כ הכא ברביעית כסף דגר דהקדש חל עליה, דכשיבנה בית המקדש ראוי רובע דינר שלו לקרבן, רק דבטלה רבי יוחנן בן זכאי מפני תקלה להקדישו לכתחלה, ולא אתי טעמא דתקלה ומפקיע לשם הקדש ממנו. וגירסת הספרים משובשים, יהקדשות אחרים מאן דכר שמייהו הכא: הלכה כרבי שמעון. דמתני', דביכורים לא קדשי, ושקלים קדשי, וכן קינו של גר קדשו:

סליק לה מסכת שקלים בעזר המרחם על אומללים:

The following paragraph is recited three times:

הַדְרָן עֲלָךְ מַסֶּכֶת שְׁקָלִים וְהַדְרָךְ עֲלָן, דַּעְתָּן עֲלָךְ מַסֶּכֶת שְׁקָלִים וְדַעְתָּךְ עֲלָן, לָא נִתְנְשֵׁי מִנָּךְ מַסֶּכֶת שְׁקָלִים וְלָא תִתְנְשֵׁי מִנָּן, לָא בְּעָלְמָא הָדֵין וְלָא בְּעָלְמָא דְאָתֵי.

יְהִי רָצוֹן מִלְּפָנֶיךָ יהוה אֱלֹהֵינוּ וֵאלֹהֵי אֲבוֹתֵינוּ, שֶׁתְּהֵא תוֹרָתְךָ אֻמָּנוּתֵנוּ בָּעוֹלָם הַזֶּה, וּתְהֵא עִמָּנוּ לָעוֹלָם הַבָּא. חֲנִינָא בַּר פַּפָּא, רָמֵי בַּר פַּפָּא, נַחְמָן בַּר פַּפָּא, אֲחַאי בַּר פַּפָּא, אַבָּא מָרִי בַּר פַּפָּא, רַפְרָם בַּר פַּפָּא, רָכִישׁ בַּר פַּפָּא, סוּרְחַב בַּר פַּפָּא, אַדָּא בַּר פַּפָּא, דָּרוּ בַּר פַּפָּא.

הַעֲרֶב נָא יהוה אֱלֹהֵינוּ אֶת דִּבְרֵי תוֹרָתְךָ בְּפִינוּ וּבְפִי
עַמְּךָ בֵּית יִשְׂרָאֵל, וְנִהְיֶה אֲנַחְנוּ וְצֶאֱצָאֵינוּ (וְצֶאֱצָאֵי
צֶאֱצָאֵינוּ) וְצֶאֱצָאֵי עַמְּךָ בֵּית יִשְׂרָאֵל, כֻּלָּנוּ יוֹדְעֵי
שְׁמֶךָ וְלוֹמְדֵי תוֹרָתְךָ לִשְׁמָהּ. מֵאֹיְבַי תְּחַכְּמֵנִי מִצְוֹתֶךָ תהלים קיט
כִּי לְעוֹלָם הִיא־לִי: יְהִי־לִבִּי תָמִים בְּחֻקֶּיךָ לְמַעַן לֹא
אֵבוֹשׁ: לְעוֹלָם לֹא־אֶשְׁכַּח פִּקּוּדֶיךָ כִּי־בָם חִיִּיתָנִי:
בָּרוּךְ אַתָּה יהוה לַמְּדֵנִי חֻקֶּיךָ: אָמֵן אָמֵן אָמֵן סֶלָה
וָעֶד.

מוֹדִים אֲנַחְנוּ לְפָנֶיךָ יהוה אֱלֹהֵינוּ וֵאלֹהֵי אֲבוֹתֵינוּ
שֶׁשַּׂמְתָּ חֶלְקֵנוּ מִיּוֹשְׁבֵי בֵּית הַמִּדְרָשׁ, וְלֹא שַׂמְתָּ חֶלְקֵנוּ
מִיּוֹשְׁבֵי קְרָנוֹת. שֶׁאָנוּ מַשְׁכִּימִים וְהֵם מַשְׁכִּימִים,
אָנוּ מַשְׁכִּימִים לְדִבְרֵי תוֹרָה, וְהֵם מַשְׁכִּימִים לִדְבָרִים
בְּטֵלִים. אָנוּ עֲמֵלִים וְהֵם עֲמֵלִים, אָנוּ עֲמֵלִים וּמְקַבְּלִים
שָׂכָר, וְהֵם עֲמֵלִים וְאֵינָם מְקַבְּלִים שָׂכָר. אָנוּ רָצִים וְהֵם
רָצִים, אָנוּ רָצִים לְחַיֵּי הָעוֹלָם הַבָּא, וְהֵם רָצִים לִבְאֵר
שַׁחַת, שֶׁנֶּאֱמַר: וְאַתָּה אֱלֹהִים תּוֹרִדֵם לִבְאֵר שַׁחַת תהלים נה
אַנְשֵׁי דָמִים וּמִרְמָה לֹא־יֶחֱצוּ יְמֵיהֶם וַאֲנִי אֶבְטַח־בָּךְ:

יְהִי רָצוֹן מִלְּפָנֶיךָ יהוה אֱלֹהַי, כְּשֵׁם שֶׁעֲזַרְתַּנִי לְסַיֵּם
מַסֶּכֶת שְׁקָלִים כֵּן תַּעַזְרֵנִי לְהַתְחִיל מַסֶּכְתּוֹת וּסְפָרִים
אֲחֵרִים וּלְסַיְּמָם, לִלְמֹד וּלְלַמֵּד לִשְׁמֹר וְלַעֲשׂוֹת וּלְקַיֵּם
אֶת כָּל דִּבְרֵי תַלְמוּד תּוֹרָתְךָ בְּאַהֲבָה, וּזְכוּת כָּל
הַתַּנָּאִים וְאָמוֹרָאִים וְתַלְמִידֵי חֲכָמִים יַעֲמֹד לִי וּלְזַרְעִי
שֶׁלֹּא תָמוּשׁ הַתּוֹרָה מִפִּי וּמִפִּי זַרְעִי וְזֶרַע זַרְעִי עַד
עוֹלָם, וְיִתְקַיֵּם בִּי: בְּהִתְהַלֶּכְךָ תַּנְחֶה אֹתָךְ בְּשָׁכְבְּךָ משלי ו
תִּשְׁמֹר עָלֶיךָ וַהֲקִיצוֹתָ הִיא תְשִׂיחֶךָ: כִּי־בִי יִרְבּוּ יָמֶיךָ משלי ט
וְיוֹסִיפוּ לְךָ שְׁנוֹת חַיִּים: אֹרֶךְ יָמִים בִּימִינָהּ בִּשְׂמֹאולָהּ משלי ג
עֹשֶׁר וְכָבוֹד: יהוה עֹז לְעַמּוֹ יִתֵּן יהוה יְבָרֵךְ אֶת־עַמּוֹ תהלים כט
בַשָּׁלוֹם:

The following paragraph is recited three times:

הַדְרָן We shall return to you, tractate *Shekalim,* and your glory is upon us. Our thoughts are upon you, tractate *Shekalim,* and your thoughts are upon us. We will not be forgotten from you, tractate *Shekalim,* and you will not be forgotten from us; neither in this world nor in the World-to-Come.

יְהִי רָצוֹן May it be Your will, Lord our God and God of our ancestors, that Your Torah will be our avocation in this world and will accompany us to the World-to-Come. Ḥanina bar Pappa, Ramei bar Pappa, Naḥman bar Pappa, Aḥai bar Pappa, Abba Mari bar Pappa, Rafram bar Pappa, Rakhish bar Pappa, Surḥav bar Pappa, Adda bar Pappa, Daru bar Pappa.

הַעֲרֶב נָא Please, Lord our God, make the words of Your
Torah sweet in our mouths and in the mouths of Your
people, the house of Israel, so that we, our descendants
(and their descendants), and the descendants of Your
people, the house of Israel, may all know Your name and
study Your Torah for its own sake. Your commandments *Psalms 119*
make me wiser than my enemies, for they are ever with
me. Let my heart be undivided in Your statutes, in order
that I may not be put to shame. I will never forget Your
precepts, for with them You have quickened me. Blessed
are You, O Lord; teach me Your statutes. Amen, Amen,
Amen, Selah, Forever.

מוֹדִים We give thanks before You, Lord Our God and
God of our ancestors, that You have placed our lot
among those who sit in the study hall and that you have
not given us our portion among those who sit idly on
street corners. We rise early and they rise early. We rise
early to pursue matters of Torah and they rise early to
pursue frivolous matters. We toil and they toil. We toil
and receive a reward and they toil and do not receive a
reward. We run and they run. We run to the life of the
World-to-Come and they run to the pit of destruction,
as it is stated: But You, God, will bring them down into *Psalms 55*
the pit of destruction; men of blood and deceit shall not
live out half their days; but as for me, I will trust in You.

יְהִי רָצוֹן May it be Your will, Lord my God, just as you
have assisted me in completing tractate *Shekalim* so assist
me to begin other tractates and books and conclude
them to learn and to teach, to observe and to perform,
and to fulfill all the teachings of Your Torah with love.
And may the merit of all the *tanna'im* and *amora'im* and
Torah scholars stand for me and my descendants so that
the Torah will not move from my mouth and from the
mouths of my descendants and the descendants of my
descendants forever. And may the verse: When you *Proverbs 6*
walk, it shall lead you, when you lie down, it shall watch
over you; and when you awaken, it shall talk with you
be fulfilled in me. For in the Torah your days shall be *Proverbs 9*
multiplied, and the years of your life shall be increased.
Length of days is in her right hand; in her left hand are *Proverbs 3*
riches and honor. May the Lord give strength to His *Psalms 29*
people; the Lord will bless His people with peace.

The following קדיש *requires the presence of a* מנין.

יִתְגַּדַּל וְיִתְקַדַּשׁ שְׁמֵהּ רַבָּא
בְּעָלְמָא דְּהוּא עָתִיד לְאִתְחַדָּתָא
וּלְאַחֲיָאָה מֵתַיָּא, וּלְאַסָּקָא יָתְהוֹן לְחַיֵּי עָלְמָא
וּלְמִבְנֵא קַרְתָּא דִירוּשְׁלֵם, וּלְשַׁכְלָלָא הֵיכְלֵהּ בְּגַוַּהּ
וּלְמֶעְקַר פָּלְחָנָא נֻכְרָאָה מֵאַרְעָא
וְלַאֲתָבָא פָּלְחָנָא דִשְׁמַיָּא לְאַתְרֵהּ
וְיַמְלִיךְ קֻדְשָׁא בְּרִיךְ הוּא בְּמַלְכוּתֵהּ וִיקָרֵהּ
(נוסח ספרד: וְיַצְמַח פּוּרְקָנֵהּ וִיקָרֵב מְשִׁיחֵהּ)
בְּחַיֵּיכוֹן וּבְיוֹמֵיכוֹן וּבְחַיֵּי דְכָל בֵּית יִשְׂרָאֵל
בַּעֲגָלָא וּבִזְמַן קָרִיב, וְאִמְרוּ אָמֵן.

יְהֵא שְׁמֵהּ רַבָּא מְבָרַךְ לְעָלַם וּלְעָלְמֵי עָלְמַיָּא.

יִתְבָּרַךְ וְיִשְׁתַּבַּח וְיִתְפָּאַר וְיִתְרוֹמַם וְיִתְנַשֵּׂא
וְיִתְהַדָּר וְיִתְעַלֶּה וְיִתְהַלָּל
שְׁמֵהּ דְּקֻדְשָׁא בְּרִיךְ הוּא
לְעֵלָּא מִן כָּל בִּרְכָתָא
/בעשרת ימי תשובה: לְעֵלָּא לְעֵלָּא מִכָּל בִּרְכָתָא/
וְשִׁירָתָא, תֻּשְׁבְּחָתָא וְנֶחֱמָתָא, דַּאֲמִירָן בְּעָלְמָא
וְאִמְרוּ אָמֵן. (קהל: אָמֵן)

עַל יִשְׂרָאֵל וְעַל רַבָּנָן
וְעַל תַּלְמִידֵיהוֹן וְעַל כָּל תַּלְמִידֵי תַלְמִידֵיהוֹן
וְעַל כָּל מָאן דְּעָסְקִין בְּאוֹרַיְתָא
דִּי בְּאַתְרָא (בארץ ישראל: קַדִּישָׁא) הָדֵין, וְדִי בְּכָל אֲתַר וַאֲתַר
יְהֵא לְהוֹן וּלְכוֹן שְׁלָמָא רַבָּא
חִנָּא וְחִסְדָּא, וְרַחֲמֵי, וְחַיֵּי אֲרִיכֵי, וּמְזוֹנֵי רְוִיחֵי
וּפֻרְקָנָא מִן קֳדָם אֲבוּהוֹן דִּי בִשְׁמַיָּא
וְאִמְרוּ אָמֵן.

יְהֵא שְׁלָמָא רַבָּא מִן שְׁמַיָּא
וְחַיִּים (טוֹבִים) עָלֵינוּ וְעַל כָּל יִשְׂרָאֵל
וְאִמְרוּ אָמֵן.

Bow, take three steps back, as if taking leave of the Divine Presence, then bow, first left, then right, then center, while saying:

עֹשֶׂה שָׁלוֹם/ בעשרת ימי תשובה: הַשָּׁלוֹם/ בִּמְרוֹמָיו
הוּא יַעֲשֶׂה בְרַחֲמָיו שָׁלוֹם, עָלֵינוּ וְעַל כָּל יִשְׂרָאֵל
וְאִמְרוּ אָמֵן.

The following Kaddish requires the presence of a minyan.

Magnified and sanctified may His great name be,
in the world that will in future be renewed,
reviving the dead and raising them up to eternal life.
He will rebuild the city of Jerusalem
and in it re-establish His Temple.
He will remove alien worship from the earth
and restore to its place the worship of Heaven.
Then the Holy One, blessed be He,
will reign in His sovereignty and splendor.
May it be in your lifetime and in your days,
(*Nusaḥ Sepharad:* make His salvation flourish,
and hasten His messiah,)
and in the lifetime of all the House of Israel,
swiftly and soon – and say: Amen.

May His great name be blessed for ever and all time.

Blessed and praised,
glorified and exalted,
raised and honored,
uplifted and lauded
be the name of the Holy One,
blessed be He,
beyond any blessing,
song, praise and consolation uttered in the world –
and say: Amen.

To Israel, to the teachers,
their disciples and their disciples' disciples,
and to all who engage in the study of Torah,
in this (*in Israel add:* holy) place or elsewhere,
may there come to them and you great peace,
grace, kindness and compassion,
long life, ample sustenance and deliverance,
from their Father in Heaven –
and say: Amen.

May there be great peace from heaven,
and (good) life for us and all Israel –
and say: Amen.

Bow, take three steps back, as if taking leave of the Divine Presence, then bow, first left, then right, then center, while saying:

May He who makes peace in His high places,
in His compassion make peace for us and all Israel –
and say: Amen.

תלמוד ירושלמי

הוצאת קורן ירושלים

— מהדורת נאה —

מסכת שקלים
דף יג. עד כב:

COMMENTARY BY

Rabbi Adin Even-Israel
Steinsaltz

EDITOR-IN-CHIEF

Rabbi Dr Tzvi Hersh Weinreb

EXECUTIVE EDITOR

Rabbi Joshua Schreier

•

STEINSALTZ CENTER
KOREN PUBLISHERS JERUSALEM

תלמוד בבלי

— מהדורת נאה —

שקלים חלק ב

Steinsaltz Center

KOREN